Tolley's Stamp Taxes

19th Edition

by

Patrick Cannon
LLB BCL CTA (Fellow) Barrister

AF744798

LexisNexis®

Members of the LexisNexis Group worldwide

United Kingdom	LexisNexis, a Division of Reed Elsevier (UK) Ltd, Halsbury House, 35 Chancery Lane, London, WC2A 1EL, and RSH, 1–3 Baxter's Place, Leith Walk Edinburgh EH1 3AF
Australia	LexisNexis Butterworths, Chatswood, New South Wales
Austria	LexisNexis Verlag ARD Orac GmbH & Co KG, Vienna
Benelux	LexisNexis Benelux, Amsterdam
Canada	LexisNexis Canada, Markham, Ontario
China	LexisNexis China, Beijing and Shanghai
France	LexisNexis SA, Paris
Germany	LexisNexis Deutschland GmbH, Munster
Hong Kong	LexisNexis Hong Kong, Hong Kong
India	LexisNexis India, New Delhi
Italy	Giuffrè Editore, Milan
Japan	LexisNexis Japan, Tokyo
Malaysia	Malayan Law Journal Sdn Bhd, Kuala Lumpur
New Zealand	LexisNexis NZ Ltd, Wellington
Poland	Wydawnictwo Prawnicze LexisNexis Sp, Warsaw
Singapore	LexisNexis Singapore, Singapore
South Africa	LexisNexis Butterworths, Durban
USA	LexisNexis, Dayton, Ohio

© Reed Elsevier (UK) Ltd 2011

Published by LexisNexis

All rights reserved. No part of this publication may be reproduced in any material form (including photocopying or storing it in any medium by electronic means and whether or not transiently or incidentally to some other use of this publication) without the written permission of the copyright owner except in accordance with the provisions of the Copyright, Designs and Patents Act 1988 or under the terms of a licence issued by the Copyright Licensing Agency Ltd, Saffron House, 6–10 Kirby Street, London EC1N 8TS. Applications for the copyright owner's written permission to reproduce any part of this publication should be addressed to the publisher.
Warning: The doing of an unauthorised act in relation to a copyright work may result in both a civil claim for damages and criminal prosecution.

Crown copyright material is reproduced with the permission of the Controller of HMSO and the Queen's Printer for Scotland. Parliamentary copyright material is reproduced with the permission of the Controller of Her Majesty's Stationery Office on behalf of Parliament. Any European material in this work which has been reproduced from EUR-lex, the official European Communities legislation website, is European Communities copyright.
A CIP Catalogue record for this book is available from the British Library.

ISBN 978 0 7545 3907 0

Printed and bound in Great Britain by Hobbs the Printers Ltd, Totton, Hampshire

Visit LexisNexis at www.lexisnexis.co.uk

About this Book

This book is written for practitioners seeking a concise guide to stamp duty land tax, stamp duties and stamp duty reserve tax. This edition is up to date as of 1 August 2011 and includes the relevant provisions of the *Finance Act 2011*.

This edition is divided into three parts. Part One relates to SDLT, Part Two to stamp duties and stamp duty reserve tax as they apply following the introduction of SDLT, and Part Three contains useful reference material arranged in appendices. The chapters in Part Two follow earlier editions of this book in being laid out in alphabetical order of subject as this allows for quick reference and is well suited to a tax on particular types of instrument. The chapters in Part One are however more conventionally arranged according to subject matter as befits a tax that applies across a wide range of transactions rather than to specific instruments. There is a detailed index, tables of cases, statutes and statutory instruments.

Patrick Cannon qualified originally as a slicitor, but was subsequently called to the Bar and practices in Tax Chambers, 15 Old Square, Lincoln's Inn. He is also the author of *Stamp Duty Tax Cases* and *Tolley's Disclosure of Tax and VAT Avoidance Schemes*. His SDLT newsletters and various other publications can be viewed online free at: www.patrickcannon.net. Comments on this book and suggestions for improvements are welcome.

Whilst care has been taken to ensure the accuracy of the contents of this book, no responsibility for loss occasioned to any person acting or refraining from action as a result of any statement in it can be accepted by the author or the publisher. Readers should take specialist professional advice before entering into any specific transaction.

Contents

Appendix B Statements of Practice

Appendix C Extra Statutory Concessions

Appendix D Inland Revenue Publications

Appendix E Stamp Taxes Bulletins

Appendix F IR Stamp Taxes Customer (sic) Newsletters

Appendix G Miscellaneous Stamp Office Publications

Abbreviations and references

Abbreviations

A-G	Attorney-General
CA	Court of Appeal
CCR	Court for Crown Cases Reserved (roughly equivalent in status to the Court of Appeal)
Cf	Compare
CH	Compliance Handbook (HMRC's)
Ch D	Chancery Division
CIR	Commissioners of Inland Revenue
CP	Common Pleas Division (now part of the Queen's Bench Division)
CP (I)	Common Pleas Division (Ireland)
CS	Court of Session (Scotland)
CTA	Corporation Tax Act 2010
Ex D	Exchequer Division (now part of the Chancery Division)
Ex (S)	Court of Exchequer (Scotland)
FA	Finance Act
F(No 2)A	Finance (No 2) Act 2005
FSMA	Financial Services and Markets Act 2000
HL	House of Lords
HMRC	HM Revenue and Customs
ICTA	Income and Corporation Taxes Act 1988
IHTA	Inheritance Tax Act 1984
KB	King's Bench Division
PC	Privy Council
PDA	Probate, Divorce and Admiralty Division (now Family Division)
QB	Queen's Bench Division

s	Section
SA	Stamp Act 1891
Sch	Schedule
SDMA	Stamp Duties Management Act 1891
SDLTM	Stamp Duties Land Tax Manual
SI	Statutory Instrument
SR & O	Statutory Rules and Orders
TCGA	Taxation of Chargeable Gains Act 1992

References (*denotes current series)

AC	*Law Reports, Appeal Cases, (Incorporated Council of Law Reporting for England and Wales, 3 Stone Buildings, Lincoln's Inn, London WC2A 3XN)
Ad & E	Adolphus & Ellis's Reports
All ER	*All England Law Reports, LexisNexis Butterworths, 35 Chancery Lane, London WC2A 1EL)
App Cas	Law Reports, Appeal Cases
ATC	Annotated Tax Cases, (Gee & Co (Publishers) Ltd, 7 Swallow Place, London W1R 8AB)
B & Ad	Barnewall & Adolphus's Reports
B & Ald	Barnewall & Alderson's Reports
B & C	Barnewall & Cresswall's Reports
B & S	Best & Smith's Reports
BCLC	*British Company Law Cases
BTC	*British Tax Cases
CB	Common Bench Reports
Ch	*Law Reports, Chancery Division
Ch App	Law Reports, Chancery Appeals
CM & R	Crompton, Meeson & Roscoe's Reports
E & B	Ellis & Blackburn's Reports
East	East's Reports
Ex D	Law Reports, Exchequer Division
Exch	Exchequer Reports

F(Ct of Sess)	Fraser, Court of Session Cases, 5th Series
HL Cas	Clark's House of Lords Cases
IR	*Irish Reports, (Law Reporting Council, Law Library, Four Courts, Dublin)
Ir LR	Irish Law Reports
KB	Law Reports, King's Bench Division
LR	Law Reports (followed by Court abbreviation)
LT	Law Times Reports
M & W	Meeson & Welsby's Reports
P	Law Reports, Probate, Divorce & Admiralty Division
QB/QBD	*Law Reports, Queen's Bench Division
QBR	Queen's Bench Reports
R (Ct of Sess)	Rettie, Court of Session Cases, 4th Series
SC	*Court of Session Cases (Scotland)
Sc LR	Scottish Law Reporter
SLT	Scots Law Times Reports
Sol Jo	Solicitors' Journal, Oyez Publishing Ltd, Norwich House, 11/13 Norwich St, London EC4A 1AB
STC	*Simon's Tax Cases, (LexisNexis Butterworths, as above)
Taunt	Taunton's Reports
TC	*Official Tax Cases, (The Stationery Office, 123 Kingsway, London WC2B 6PQ)
TLR	Times Law Reports
WLR	*Weekly Law Reports, (Incorporated Council of Law Reporting, as above)
WN	Weekly Notes, (Incorporated Council of Law Reporting, as above)

The first number in the citation refers to the volume, and the second to the page, so that [1978] 2 WLR 10 means that the report is to be found on page ten of the second volume of the Weekly Law Reports for 1978. Where no volume number is given, only one volume was produced in that year. Some series, such as the ATC, have continuous volume numbers. Where legal decisions are very recent and in the lower Courts, it must be remembered that they may be reversed on appeal. But references to the official Tax Cases ('TC') may be taken as final.

In English cases, Scottish and N. Irish decisions (unless there is a difference of law between the countries) are generally followed but are not binding, and

Republic of Ireland decisions are considered (and vice versa). Privy Council decisions are of persuasive, but not binding, authority.

Acts of Parliament and Statutory Instruments (SI) (formerly Statutory Rules and Orders) (SR & O) are obtainable from:

TSO Online Bookshop:
www.tsoshop.co.uk/parliament/bookstore.asp

Table of Statutes

Stamp Act 1891, Sch 1 which contained the heads of charge was repealed and replaced by *FA 1999, Sch 13* in relation to instruments executed on or after 1 October 1999.

Table of Statutory Instruments

Table of Cases

C

D

E

F

G

H

I

J

K

L

M

N

O

P

Q

R

S

T

U

V

W

Part One:

Stamp Duty Land Tax

Chapter 1

Introduction

[1.1] Stamp duty land tax or 'SDLT' replaced stamp duty on land in the UK from 1 December 2003. See **9.1 Transitional Provisions** for the transitional provisions which in some cases bring contracts entered into before this date within SDLT. Stamp duty has been retained for transactions in shares and securities including bearer instruments and acquisitions of certain partnership interests. [*FA 2003, s 125 and Sch 15*]. After more than 300 years stamp duty on land was perceived by HM Treasury as outdated, not suited to the development of e-conveyancing and relatively easy to avoid. The Inland Revenue (now known as HM Revenue and Customs ('HMRC')) initially concluded in 2001 that the existing stamp duty simply required surgical alteration in the manner of a provision deeming an electronic conveyance to be an 'instrument' for stamp duty purposes and triggering an obligation to pay the duty, to cope with the fact that under e-conveyancing there would not be a paper instrument on which to apply the stamp (Proceedings of the Tax Advisory Group set up by Inland Revenue Capital and Savings Division with the approval of a Treasury Minister (unpublished)). However, during the latter half of 2001 HM Treasury became aware of the scale of stamp duty avoidance in relation to land transactions caused by the quadrupling in rates since 1997, and instead of proposing further suitable amendments to stamp duty to counter the avoidance, chose the more complex task of replacing stamp duty on land with a new tax modelled along the lines of a compulsory self-assessed transaction tax (see 'A Consultative Document April 2002: Modernising Stamp Duty on land and buildings in the UK' issued by Inland Revenue). The desire on the part of Government to prevent avoidance of a tax which in some years has raised approximately £8bn annually became the driving force behind the new tax just as it became apparent that the original reason for replacing stamp duty, i.e. e-conveyancing, would not begin even on a voluntary trial basis for some time. The legislation in the Finance Act 2003 that followed the abrupt suspension of the consultation process on the new tax in January 2003 (see 'The Finance Bill 2003', Select Committee on Economic Affairs, 3rd report, session 2002–03, HL vol 1 paras. 4.4 and 4.9) created the impression of having been rushed out under pressure from Treasury Ministers anxious to abide by the statement in the foreword to the April 2002 Consultative Document that legislation would occur in 2003. The provisions themselves are in parts hard to follow, ill thought through and leave large gaps intended to be filled by copious amounts of regulations. Without sight of the briefs sent to Parliamentary Counsel it is not possible to determine the reason for this. During the debates in Parliament on these provisions MPs were given to protest that at the same time as they were scrutinising the provisions in committee under pressure of the guillotine, the Chief Secretary to the Treasury was continuing to consult widely outside Parliament with a view to introducing further amendments subsequently at the report stage (for example HC Official Report, Standing Committee Debates, Finance Bill, Tuesday 3 June 2003, col. 360). The unsatisfactory nature of the legislation was demonstrated by the need to issue detailed changes correcting mistakes, plugging gaps and in some cases recasting the charging provisions by way of statutory instrument prior to 1 December 2003 (for example, the *Stamp Duty and Stamp Duty Land Tax (Variation of the Finance Act 2003) (No 2) Regulations 2003 (SI 2003 No 2816)*). Further detailed changes have followed in subsequent Finance Acts and a problematic statutory general anti-avoidance rule for SDLT was introduced by statutory regulation in the Pre-Budget Report in December 2006 and enacted by *FA 2007* (see **11 General Statutory Anti-avoidance Rule**). Further guidance in the form of bulletins and 'customer' (sic) newsletters has also been issued. In practice, the unsatisfactory state of the legislation means that there are often alternative possible reasonable interpretations and applications of the relevant legislative provisions which require the professional adviser to take a view on how the transaction in question should be reported under the self-assessment system which operates for SDLT. The introduction of a wide ranging and problematic statutory general anti-avoidance rule has created even greater uncertainty. Some advisers are unwilling to back their own judgment and enter into detailed discussion with the Stamp Taxes Office in order to ascertain their views. This process is something of a lottery with individual advisers often rebuffed with the reminder that there is no adjudication process under SDLT, while other advisers who belong to favoured representative groups are in effect given access to internal HMRC views and shown drafts of primary and secondary legislation plus revisions to technical guidance on a confidential basis. The latter suits the Stamp Taxes Office because it amounts in effect to a free consulting service on the quality or otherwise of proposed legislation and technical guidance and suits those that belong to such groups because they get favoured access and notice of particular forthcoming changes. It must be asked whether such practices are fair to the majority of taxpayers and indeed may be questionable in terms of professional ethics because of the potential conflicts of interest they create. It is difficult to understand how a professional adviser can agree to receive information from HMRC under a condition of strict confidentiality and yet withhold such information from a client where such information is relevant to a proposed transaction. Either the adviser will breach his undertaking of confidentiality or he will not give his best advice to his client.

SDLT avoidance schemes involving commercial property worth £5m or more were brought within the scope of the rules relating to disclosure of tax avoidance schemes in *FA 2004, Pt 7* with effect from 1 August 2005 (see **10 Disclosure of SDLT Avoidance Schemes**). The rules were extended to residential property worth £1m or more in 2010 and now require identification of scheme users.

In addition to complex legislation, practitioners have also had to contend with a compliance system of enormous complexity and detail coupled with shortcomings in its administration. These difficulties during 2005 caused the Law Society of England and Wales to launch the 'Stamp Duty Strife' campaign, which led the responsible Minister Ivan Lewis MP to acknowledge that there were 'practical difficulties' with the administration of SDLT (see Law Society Press Release, 22 July 2005).

Chapter 2

Scope of the Charge

Introduction

[2.1] Stamp duty land tax is charged in accordance with *Part 4* of the *Finance Act 2003* on 'land transactions' (see **2.2** below). The tax is also charged on the consideration given for non-land transactions where the conditions for the operation of the statutory general anti-avoidance rule in *FA 2003, s 75A* are satisfied (see **11 General Statutory Anti-avoidance Rule**). The tax is under the care of the Commissioners for HMRC and is administered by HMRC Stamp Taxes. In contrast with the tax it replaces, SDLT is chargeable whether or not there is an instrument. It is also expressed to be chargeable whether or not any party to the transaction is present or resident in the UK although this was never a requirement for stamp duty to apply. [*FA 2003, s 42*]. The purchaser must deliver a land transaction return for every 'notifiable transaction' (see **7.1 Returns**) within 30 days of the 'effective date' of the transaction (see **2.3** below) containing a self-assessment of the tax chargeable. Payment of the SDLT chargeable is also due within 30 days of the 'effective date' of the transaction but need not accompany the return.

Land transactions

[2.2] A 'land transaction' is any acquisition of a 'chargeable interest', and stamp duty land tax applies however the acquisition is effected, whether by an act of the parties, an order of a court or other authority, by or under any statutory provision or by operation of law. [*FA 2003, s 43(1), (2)*]. A 'chargeable interest' is defined widely as:

(1) an estate, interest, right or power in or over land in the UK; or
(2) the benefit of an obligation, restriction or condition affecting the value of any such estate, interest, right or power;

other than an exempt interest. [*FA 2003, s 48(1)*].

The basis of the tax is therefore land in the UK. The common law definition of the UK applies in the absence of any statutory extension to the continental shelf. Hence the UK comprises England, Wales, Scotland and Northern Ireland (but not the Channel Islands or the Isle of Man) and ends at the low water mark without extending to the seabed under the territorial sea (*R v Keyn* (1876) 2 ExD 63).

Exempt interests are any security interest, a licence to use or occupy land and (in England, Wales or Northern Ireland) a tenancy at will, advowson, franchise or manor. [*FA 2003, s 48(2)*]. A 'security interest' means an interest or right (other than a rent charge) held for the purpose of securing the payment of money or the performance of any other obligation. An interest held by a financial institution as a result of the first transaction within an alternative finance property transaction within *FA 2003, s 71A, 72* or *72A* is also an 'exempt interest'. [*FA 2003, s 73B*]. Chargeable interests therefore include freeholds and leasehold interests and their Scottish and Northern Irish equivalents, rights over another's land and powers of appointment exercisable over trusts of land. Both legal and equitable interests are included and the exclusion of licences is for the avoidance of doubt because a licence, being a mere personal right, is not an estate, interest or right over land. An assignment of the right to receive rents is undoubtedly a transfer of an interest in land (see *IRC v John Lewis Properties plc* [2001] STC 1118 Ch D which considered the issue in detail and was confirmed by the Court of Appeal at *[2002] EWCA Civ 1869, [2003] STC 117*, and *Law of Property Act 1925, s 205*).

The 'purchaser' and 'vendor' in relation to a land transaction are defined as the person acquiring and the person disposing of the subject matter of the transaction (which will be the chargeable interest acquired together with any interest or right attached to it that is acquired with it). [*FA 2003, s 43(4), (6)*]. However, a person cannot be a 'purchaser' unless he has given consideration for or is a party to the transaction. [*FA 2003, s 43(5)*]. This is subject to the special tax charge arising on a contract under which A is to convey a chargeable interest at the direction or request of B to a person (C) who is not a party to the contract. B is deemed to have acquired a chargeable interest when the contract is substantially performed and SDLT will be payable accordingly. [*FA 2003, s 44A*].

The purchaser is the person who is required to file a land transaction return and pay any tax due. The following illustrates who will be regarded as the purchaser in a variety of transactions:

Transaction	***Purchaser***
Conveyance, assignment or assignation	Transferee or assignee
Grant of lease	Lessee
Grant of easement etc.	Person entitled to the right
Surrender of lease	Landlord
Certain variation of leases	Person whose estate interest or right is enlarged or benefits
Making or release of a covenant or condition	Person whose estate interest or right is enlarged or benefits

Having defined 'chargeable interest' in wide terms, the legislation then defines the concept of an 'acquisition' of such an interest in equally wide terms by providing that the creation, surrender, release or variation of a chargeable interest is an 'acquisition'. [*FA 2003, s 48(3)*]. The variation of a lease is treated as an acquisition and disposal of a chargeable interest where it is treated as the grant of a new lease or if there is a reduction in the rent or term or where the lessee give consideration for a lease variation other than a variation of the rent or the term of the lease. [*FA 2003, s 43(3)(d)* and *Sch 17A, para 15A* as amended by *F(No 2)A 2005, Sch 10, para 13*]. It is thought that the exercise of a break clause in a lease is not the acquisition of a chargeable interest because it does not cause a surrender or release of the interest (*Pennel v Payne* CA [1995] 2 All ER 592 as expressly approved in *Barrett v Morgan* HL [2000] 2 AC 264, [2000] 1 All ER 481 and also *FA 2003, Sch 17A, para 2(a)*).

Contracts, conveyances and 'effective date'

[2.3] A contract for a land transaction that contemplates completion by conveyance of the legal estate will have an 'effective date' for stamp duty land tax of the earlier of 'substantial performance' of the contract or the conveyance. The mere entry into such a contract itself is ignored and is not regarded as entering into a land transaction. [*FA 2003, s 44(1)–(3)*]. The occurrence of the 'effective date' triggers the duty to deliver the land tax return and pay the SDLT within 30 days of such date [*FA 2003, ss 76* and *119*], and is also the date on which the conditions for any available relief must be met, see for example **6.4 Group Relief**. It appears that in England contracts for equitable interests only (see *Peter Bone Ltd v IRC* [1995] STC 921 and **17.1** (*e*) **Agreement for Sale**) that will not be completed by conveyance are brought within the tax indirectly as being the acquisition of a chargeable interest [*FA 2003, ss 43 and 48*] that is a notifiable transaction [*FA 2003, s 77*] giving rise to the obligation to deliver a land tax return. [*FA 2003, s 76*]. 'Substantial performance' occurs when either:

(1) the purchaser (or a person connected with the purchaser) takes possession of the whole or substantially the whole of the chargeable interest (including receiving or becoming entitled to receive rents and profits whether under the contract or a separate licence or lease of a temporary character); or
(2) a substantial amount of the consideration is paid or provided (in the case of rent or both rent and other consideration this means the first payment of rent or in the case of other consideration substantially the whole of the other consideration). [*FA 2003, s 44(4)–(6)*].

A 'substantial amount' of the consideration is an amount that is equal to or greater than 90% of the consideration payable (see HC Official Report, Standing Committee Debate, Finance Bill, Tuesday 3 June 2003, col. 315). In the majority of cases substantial performance will occur at completion and therefore the effective date will arise on the date of the conveyance as it did with stamp duty. However, if substantial performance of the contract occurs earlier then so will the effective date, thus preventing the purchaser from deferring the SDLT indefinitely by 'resting on contract' and putting off taking a conveyance as could be done for contracts for a consideration of £10m or less under stamp duty (see **17.1** (*f*) **Agreement for Sale**).

This rule also affects how sub-sales are charged under SDLT, as to which see **8.4 Sub-Sales, Assignments and Novations**.

If the contract is substantially performed before completion and there is a subsequent conveyance both the contract and the conveyance are notifiable transactions [*FA 2003, s 77*] and additional SDLT is payable on the conveyance to the extent that the SDLT on the conveyance exceeds the SDLT on the contract. [*FA 2003, s 44(8)*]. The wording of *s 44(8)(b)* appears odd because one is required to compare the same amount with itself i.e. the tax chargeable on the conveyance, and pay the difference and logically there can be no difference. It is thought that a court would interpret the first 'chargeable' as meaning 'payable' to make sense of the sub-section. If the contract is rescinded or annulled or not carried into effect, any SDLT paid on the contract can be reclaimed by submitting an amended land transaction return. [*FA 2003, s 44(9)*].

Where the statutory general anti-avoidance rule in *FA 2003, s 75A* applies (see **11 General Statutory Anti-avoidance Rule**) the land transactions forming part of the scheme are disregarded for SDLT purposes and the notional land transaction which is deemed to replace those land transactions will have an effective date which is the last date of completion of the scheme transactions or if earlier, the last date on which a contract in respect of the scheme transactions is substantially performed. [*FA 2003, s 75A(4)* and *(6)*]. It follows that the disregarding of the real land transactions can occur before the occurrence of the effective date of the notional land transaction leaving the taxpayer 'resting on contract' within *s 75A* until the completion of the scheme transactions.

Confusing nomenclature

[2.4] The names given in the SDLT legislation to the various categories of interest are apt to confuse. The basic concept of the 'land transaction' is defined as an acquisition of a 'chargeable interest' which is in turn defined to exclude something called an 'exempt interest' (see **2.2** above). An 'exempt interest' is different from a 'chargeable interest' which benefits from either a general or a particular exemption or relief. An 'exempt interest' can never be the subject of a 'notifiable transaction' under *FA 2003, s 77* although the general rule is that a 'chargeable interest' that benefits from a particular exemption or relief will still be a 'notifiable transaction' and therefore require the filing of a land transaction return claiming the exemption or relief. A 'land transaction' is also defined as a 'chargeable transaction if it is not a transaction that is exempt from charge' and *FA 2003, Sch 3* currently contains six such exemptions which are not 'notifiable transactions'. [*FA 2003, ss 49* and *77A*]. Among the consequences of not being a 'chargeable transaction' is that HMRC's powers under *FA 2003, Sch 10* to charge various penalties, make enquiries, issue determinations of tax due and assessments do not apply (see **7.1 Returns, Liability and Compliance**). The basic approach amidst this confusing nomenclature should therefore be to ascertain whether one is dealing with a 'chargeable interest' and not an 'exempt interest'. If one has a 'chargeable interest' one then needs to ascertain if it benefits from a general exemption (such as that in *FA 2003, Sch 3 para 1* for transactions for no chargeable consideration) or a particular exemption or relief. One then needs to ascertain whether the transaction is a 'notifiable transaction' so that a land transaction return must be filed to report the transaction and also to claim any particular exemption or relief. [*FA 2003, ss 76–77A*].

Chapter 3

Chargeable Consideration

General

[3.1] Stamp duty land tax is charged as a percentage of the 'chargeable consideration' for the land transaction: see **2.2 Land Transactions**. [*FA 2003, s 55*]. The chargeable consideration is any consideration in money or money's worth given for the acquisition of the chargeable interest, whether given directly or indirectly by the purchaser or a person connected with him. [*FA 2003, s 50* and *Sch 4, para 1*]. The chargeable consideration may also include consideration given or received in respect of a non-land transaction where that transaction is 'involved in connection with' a land transaction and the conditions for the operation of the statutory general anti-avoidance rule in *FA 2003, s 75A* are satisfied (see **11 General Statutory Anti-avoidance Rule**).

The use of money or money's worth as the criterion means that a wider class of consideration is recognised for SDLT than for stamp duty on land where broadly only money, shares, the release or assumption of a debt and other property count as sale consideration: see **36 Consideration**. The expression money or money's worth is not defined for SDLT, although it must be something that is capable of being sold. This is the general principle and is reinforced by *FA 2003, Sch 4, para 7* which requires that the value of any chargeable consideration other than money or debt shall be taken to be its market value. In *Secretan v Hart* (1969) 45 TC 701 Buckley J thought that the expression included, 'services or other property, where the price or consideration which the acquirer gives for the property has got to be turned into money before it can be expressed in terms of money' (p 705). The main difference between SDLT and stamp duty is that the latter did not include the carrying out of building works or the provision of services as consideration, see for example Inland Revenue Tax Bulletin 43, October 1999, 'PFI projects—stamp duty': 'a contract to carry out works is not 'consideration [which] consists of property' for the purposes of *FA 1994, s 241*' (reproduced at **Appendix D**).

The carrying out of building works is however specifically excluded from constituting chargeable consideration to the extent that:

(1) the works are carried out after the effective date of the transaction;
(2) the works are carried out on land acquired or to be acquired under the transaction or on other land held by the purchaser or a person connected with him; and
(3) it is not a condition of the transaction that the works are carried out by the vendor or a person connected with him. [*FA 2003, Sch 4, para 10*].

In relation to the rule that where a contract is substantially performed before completion both the contract and the conveyance are notifiable transactions, the condition in (1) above is treated as met in relation to the conveyance if it is met in relation to the contract. [*FA 2003, Sch 4, para 10(2A)*]. In relation to (2) above, the references to land being acquired are to the acquisition of a 'major interest' in it which means freehold or leasehold either in law or in equity. [*FA 2003, Sch 4, para 10(3)(a) and s 117*]. Where land is being acquired wholly or partly in consideration of a purchaser developer carrying out building works on land to be retained by the vendor, it may be possible to avoid the value of the building works becoming chargeable to SDLT in certain cases through the use of a suitably drafted lease of the building land in favour of the purchaser developer.

However, where a purchaser developer agrees to grant a lease-back of the building land once the building has completed then there is the risk of an exchange transaction (see **8.5 Exchanges and Partitions**) by reference to the value of the interest in the land acquired and retained by the purchaser developer or the chargeable consideration given for the acquisition if greater. This problem may be avoided by the use of a surrender and re-grant of a lease where the SDLT exchange provisions are effectively disapplied: *FA 2003, Sch 17A, para 16*.

Where the value of building works is included in the chargeable consideration the value is taken to be the amount that would have to be paid in the open market for the carrying-out of the works in question. [*FA 2003, Sch 4, para 10(3)(b)*].

On 2 April 2004, HMRC Stamp Taxes issued a statement dealing with the sale of land by a vendor who also agrees to carry out building works on the land sold (reproduced at **Appendix G**). This situation should of course be distinguished from that above where the purchaser rather than the vendor is providing the building works. The statement concedes that the decision in *Prudential Assurance Co Ltd v IRC* [1992] STC 863 applies for SDLT as it did for stamp duty because the basis of the decision was the identification of the subject matter of the transaction and this is as relevant to SDLT as it was for stamp duty. It was also confirmed that SP 8/93 will be applied for SDLT. However, where the land contract and the building contract are 'in substance' one bargain then under SDLT there is a requirement to apportion the aggregate consideration on a just and reasonable basis, as to which see further below. (See also **Appendix B** for SP 8/93 and its now withdrawn predecessor SP 10/87, which in the author's view is a more useful and accurate statement of the legal position; for the stamp duty position; see **36.6 Covenants to Improve Property**.)

Where the consideration consists of the provision of services (other than the carrying out of works referred to above) the value of the consideration is taken to be the amount that would have to be paid in the open market for the works in question. [*FA 2003, Sch 4, para 11*].

HMRC regard the market value of an asset as not including VAT that may be chargeable on a transfer of the asset (see SDLTM 04140).

In determining the amount or value of the consideration no discount is allowed for postponement of the right to receive any of the consideration. [*FA 2003, Sch 4, para 3*]. Any value added tax chargeable is included in the consideration liable to SDLT, except any value added tax chargeable because of an option to tax made after the effective date of the transaction. [*FA 2003, Sch 4, para 2* and see *VATA 1994, Sch 10* for the option to tax, and **5.1 Leases and Agreements for Lease** for the position regarding leases]. Consideration attributable to two or more land transactions or in part to a land transaction and in part to another matter or in part to matters making it chargeable consideration and in part to other matters, is to be apportioned on a just and reasonable basis. [*FA 2003, Sch 4, para 4*]. It is provided that for these purposes any consideration given for:

> what is in substance one bargain shall be treated as attributable to all the elements of the bargain, even though:
>
> (a) separate consideration is, or purports to be, given for different elements of the bargain, or
>
> (b) there are, or purport to be, separate transactions in respect of different elements of the bargain.
>
> [*FA 2003, Sch 4, para 4(3)*].

It is difficult to understand how there can 'in substance be one bargain', even though in the words of the provision: 'there are separate transactions in respect of different elements of the bargain' given that SDLT is a tax on 'land transactions' and not on 'land bargains'; for example see *Kimbers v IRC* [1936] 1 KB 132 and **36 Consideration**. This provision may be yet a further attempt by HMRC Stamp Taxes to sidestep the consequences of there being in substance two or more legally separate transactions. It is also difficult to understand how a court faced with having to apply this provision can avoid being forced into rewriting the commercial bargain reached at arm's length by the parties and in effect substituting its own subjective opinion of how it would have apportioned if it were vendor and purchaser respectively. A court would normally take strenuous steps to avoid any such exercise precisely because it would be forced to substitute its own subjective views for those of the parties reached during actual commercial negotiations. This would be a tortuous exercise, particularly where it was clear that the parties had different priorities in terms of how the consideration was allocated as regards for example capital allowances and capital gains tax. (For the previous position under stamp duty where the parties were able to apportion consideration as they thought fit, provided they did not intend to defraud the Inland Revenue, see *Re Brown & Root McDermott Fabricators Ltd's Application* [1996] STC 483.)

The amount or value of consideration is measured in sterling and the sterling equivalent of an amount expressed in another currency is taken by reference to the London closing exchange rate on the effective date, unless the parties have used a different rate for the transaction. [*FA 2003, Sch 4, para 9*]. For exchanges of chargeable interests see **8.5**. In the case of a partition or division of a chargeable interest, the share held by the purchaser immediately before the partition or division does not count as chargeable consideration. [*FA 2003, Sch 4, para 6*].

Where the chargeable consideration consists wholly or partly of:

(1) the satisfaction or release of debt due to the purchaser or owed by the vendor; or

(2) the assumption of existing debt by the purchaser,

the amount of the debt is taken as chargeable consideration up to a maximum of the market value of the chargeable interest acquired. [*FA 2003, Sch 4, para 8*]. It will be observed in relation to (2) above that the equivalent provision in stamp duty, *SA 1891, s 57*, imposed a charge where the property was merely 'subject to' the debt whereas an SDLT charge requires the assumption of the debt by the purchaser. Under stamp duty, where property was transferred subject to a debt, the transferee did not assume any liability for it and there was no separate consideration given, it was necessary to rely on para 6 of SP 6/90 to avoid liability under *SA 1891, s 57*. Under SDLT it appears that it will be enough to avoid a charge if the transferee does not assume the liability even if he takes the property subject to a charge for the debt and so reliance on SP 6/90 will not be necessary. However, there will be a deemed assumption of debt by the purchaser constituting chargeable consideration where debt is secured on the property immediately before and immediately after the land transaction and the rights or liabilities in relation to that debt of any party are changed as a result if or in connection with the transaction. [*FA 2003, Sch 4 para 8(1A)*]. In such cases the amount of debt treated as assumed is intended to be restricted by reference to the vendor's share in the property (where the property is held jointly before the transaction) or the purchaser's share in the property (where the property is held jointly after the transaction). For example, if a property is transferred by A into the joint ownership of A and B in equal shares subject to mortgage, B will normally assume liability for the entire mortgage debt but for SDLT, B will be treated as assuming only half the debt corresponding to B's share in the property. If a property is owned by A and B as tenants in common in say, 60:40 shares subject to mortgage and it is transferred into the sole ownership of B, A will be released from the debt and B may also indemnify A against any continuing liability. The intention of the legislation is that B is treated as assuming debt equal to 60% of the amount of the debt: *FA 2003, Sch 4, para 8(1B)*. However, in this latter case *FA 2003, Sch 4, para 8(1)(a)* applies because there is a release of a liability and in such a case B is treated as giving chargeable consideration equal to the debt released which will normally be 100% of the debt given that A will have been liable for the entire debt. The restriction on B's liability only operates where there is an assumption (real or deemed) by B and here (although there may also be a deemed assumption of debt by B) the release means that there is a tax charge by reference to the entire debt. Nevertheless, it appears that this is not the intention of the legislature and the Stamp Taxes Office can be expected to accept that B's liability is restricted accordingly.

For these purposes, each beneficial joint tenant in equity is deemed to hold an equal undivided share in the property: *FA 2003, Sch 4, para 8(1C)*. However, in the case of joint owners who hold as tenants in common their shares in the property are taken to be their actual shares as tenants in common in equity. It is the ownership in equity which counts and not the undivided legal title.

It is thought that the 'debt' referred to in *FA 2003, Sch 4, para 8(1A)* must be the same debt both before and after the transaction. It may also be possible to structure a transfer subject to a mortgage in a way that treats an indemnity and any payment thereunder given by the purchaser to the vendor as outside the meaning of chargeable consideration by relying on the exemption for indemnity payments under *FA 2003, Sch 4, para 16* thereby achieving the transfer of land subject to mortgage without giving rise to SDLT.

Where accommodation is provided to an employee, the chargeable consideration for SDLT is the higher of a market value rent or the amount treated as employment income, unless the provision of the accommodation is treated as exempt from income tax. In that case there is no chargeable consideration for SDLT, except to the extent of any actual consideration given. In any other case the consideration is to be not less than market value of the chargeable interest at the effective date of the transaction. [*FA 2003, Sch 4, para 12*].

The following matters do not count as chargeable consideration in relation to both the grant of a lease and the assumption or release of such obligations on the assignment of a lease:

(1) tenant's repairing, maintaining or insuring obligations;
(2) service charges and similar items;
(3) other obligations not affecting the rent that a tenant would be prepared to pay;
(4) guarantees of payment or performance;
(5) penal rent payable for breach of tenants' obligations;
(6) costs borne by a tenant exercising a statutory right to be granted a new lease;
(7) any other obligation by a tenant to bear the landlord's reasonable costs incidental on the grant of a lease;
(8) an obligation under a lease, on its termination, to transfer to the landlord payment entitlements under the scheme of income support for farmers in respect of land subject to the scheme. [*FA 2003, Sch 17A, para 10* as amended by the *Stamp Duty Land Tax (Amendment to the Finance Act 2003) Regulations (SI 2006 No 875)*].

For surrenders of existing leases in return for new leases and reverse premiums see **5.3 Surrender and Regrant; Sale and Leaseback.**

Where the purchaser indemnifies the vendor in respect of a liability to a third party arising from a breach of an obligation owed by the vendor in relation to the land transferred, neither the agreement nor any payment pursuant to it counts as chargeable consideration. [*FA 2003, Sch 4, para 16*]. It may be possible to use such an indemnity as an alternative to an assumption of debt charged on land acquired and avoid the consequences of an assumption of debt under *FA 2003, Sch 4, para 8* (see above).

Where a purchaser becomes liable to pay, agrees to pay or does pay any inheritance tax due in respect of a land transaction that is a transfer of value or a disposition under a will or on intestacy of a chargeable interest, that does not count as chargeable consideration for SDLT. Where land is acquired otherwise than by way of a bargain made at arm's length or is treated as so acquired by *TCGA 1992, s 18* and the purchaser is or becomes liable to pay or does pay any capital gains tax due in respect of the corresponding disposal, his liability or payment does not count as chargeable consideration as long as there is no other chargeable consideration given. [*FA 2003, Sch 4, paras 16A and 16B*]. This ensures that where a trader incorporates his business and transfers his property under *TCGA 1992, s 165*, SDLT will not be charged in respect of the held-over capital gains tax liability.

There are also exemptions relating to arrangements involving public or educational bodies involved in so-called 'public/private finance initiative' transactions. [*FA 2003, Sch 4, para 7*].

In practice, HMRC Stamp Taxes accepts that no tax arises on the transfer of assets and liabilities between pension schemes where the only consideration is the assumption by the receiving scheme of the obligation to pay pension benefits. Any debts assumed or released by the transferee fund as part of the transfer are also ignored by HMRC. This practice appears to be concessionary. Any other consideration given will be chargeable consideration including any debt liabilities assumed to the extent that the consideration is apportioned to interests in land on a just and reasonable basis (see HMRC SDLT Manual at 31800 to 31812 and the previous Guidance Notes issued on 8 June 2005 which are reproduced for reference at **APPENDIX G**). The example given at SDLTM 31812 which treats a mortgage assumed by the transferee fund as chargeable consideration for SDLT purposes appears to contradict the statement in SDLTM 31810 that such an assumption of debt will not constitute chargeable consideration.

Contingent, uncertain or unascertained consideration and overage

[3.2] Stamp duty dealt with contingent consideration in a blunt manner. If the consideration was uncertain because the obligation to pay or the amount payable was linked to an event after execution, the contingency was ignored and stamp duty was charged by reference to any maximum, minimum or basic amount ascertainable at the date of execution. This resulted in stamp duty being payable by reference to an amount of consideration that might never be paid and there was no provision for a refund of the 'overpaid' stamp duty: see **36 CONSIDERATION**. In relation to land where the contingent consideration was truly unascertainable such that no maximum, minimum or basic sum could be ascertained the consideration was taken to be the market value of the estate or interest: see **37 CONTINGENCY PRINCIPLE.**

Stamp duty land tax adopts a more flexible approach to contingent consideration by not automatically requiring tax to be paid on any maximum ascertainable sum and by providing for the possibility of deferral of tax and the repayment of any tax paid on a greater amount of consideration than is eventually payable.

The relevant rules in relation to overage consideration are contained in *FA 2003, ss 51 (Contingent, uncertain or unascertained consideration)*, *80 (Adjustment where contingency ceases or consideration is ascertained)* and *90 (Application to defer payment in case of contingent or uncertain consideration)* plus *Part 4* of the *SDLT (Administration) Regulations 2003 (SI 2003 No 2837)*. One should also note that the amount or value of the chargeable consideration is to be determined without any discount for the postponement of the right to receive it: *FA 2003, Sch 4, para 3*.

FA 2003, s 51 assumes that the consideration will be either contingent, uncertain or unascertained although only 'contingent' and 'uncertain' are actually defined. It is worth noting that the outset that deferment of the tax is only available in relation to contingent or uncertain consideration and not in relation to unascertained consideration.

'Contingent' consideration is defined as consideration that is (a) to be paid or provided only if some uncertain future event occurs, or (b) that is to cease to be paid or provided if some uncertain future event occurs. This definition emphasises the future event giving rise to payment or non-payment and so it is usually taken to be referring to a fixed amount which may or may not become payable or by which a basic price is to be adjusted. This approach is supported by the rule that the SDLT is to be computed initially as if the contingent consideration will become payable or will not cease to be payable. It seems that under this definition there is no room for consideration which may vary depending upon the circumstances.

Example 1

Giles sells his freehold interest in Whiteacre to Mick's Developers Limited for £10m payable at legal completion plus a further £5m if planning permission for development is granted within 10 years. Mick's Developers Limited are treated for SDLT purposes as paying £15m chargeable consideration for the land (subject to any application to defer the tax on the £5m contingent sum — see below).

'Uncertain' consideration is defined as consideration whose amount or value depends upon uncertain future events. Thus variable consideration is taken to be 'uncertain' for SDLT purposes. Overage consideration falls within the definition because this type of consideration is dependent upon the grant of planning permission or possibly the onward sale of the land. Logically, it seems that overage consideration could be both 'contingent' and 'uncertain' because for example it is to be paid if an uncertain future event occurs, i.e., planning permission, where its amount or value depended upon that event. However, if one adopts the working interpretation suggested for 'contingent' consideration above so that this is limited to fixed amounts, then there will not, in practice, be an overlap. 'Uncertain' consideration is to be computed on the basis of a reasonable estimate made at the effective date of the transaction of its amount or value and SDLT paid initially on this amount. This gives rise to the issue of whether a discount (of up to 100%) can be assumed for the likelihood or unlikelihood that the payment will eventually be made — see further below.

'Unascertained' consideration is not defined. Taking the stamp duty treatment as a guide, this would appear to mean any consideration that is ascertainable at the effective date (because all the facts and matters necessary for its computation are in existence) but which has not yet been ascertained because the relevant work in ascertaining or collating the information has not been carried out or completed. Examples of this type of situation are where the land is sold at a price linked to a set of completion accounts that have yet to be drawn up or linked to market value or square meterage at completion where the necessary valuation or survey has not yet been carried out. Because overage consideration will not usually rely on such factors, 'unascertained' consideration will not normally feature in SDLT calculations on overage. As with 'uncertain' consideration, where there is 'unascertained' consideration it is to be determined on the basis of a reasonable estimate and SDLT is paid initially on this amount (plus any ascertained consideration). The possibility of deferring payment of the SDLT is not available for 'unascertained' consideration (see below).

Where the consideration includes contingent or uncertain consideration and that falls to be paid or provided on one or more future dates of which at least one falls or may fall more than six months after the effective date of the transaction, then the taxpayer may apply to defer the SDLT in respect of the contingent or uncertain element of the consideration — see *FA 2003, s 90* and *Part 4* of *SI 2003 No 2837* for the detailed regulations governing the application for deferral. Deferral is not available in respect of any rent forming part of the consideration. If the application is granted and the tax is eventually payable interest is not charged on the unpaid tax during the deferral period and begins to run only from 30 days after the deferred tax becomes payable. Overage consideration is a prime candidate for deferral of SDLT and the taxpayer should normally make application for it.

The application for deferral must be made within the same time period as the filing of the land transaction return i.e. normally 30 days. There is no express power for HMRC to grant an extension for late applications to be considered and they will normally reject late applications. It may be that such refusals are however susceptible to a judicial review.

In the case of all the three types of consideration mentioned above, an adjustment must be made by the taxpayer once the contingency occurs (or it becomes clear that it will not occur) or in the case of uncertain or unascertained consideration, whenever any relevant amount becomes ascertained — see *FA 2003, s 81*. If as a result, the original transaction becomes notifiable or tax or additional tax becomes payable, an SDLT return is required to be made within 30 days accompanied by the tax or additional tax now due. If any tax originally paid turns out to have been too much as a result of this new information the taxpayer may obtain a refund by either amending his original return (within 12 months of the filing date) or subsequently by making a claim to HMRC for repayment of the overpaid amount.

Two particular problems arise with the operation of the SDLT provisions in relation to overage. First, whether when initially computing the amount of any 'uncertain' consideration it is permissible to allow for the likelihood of the payment being made (as well as making a reasonable estimate of the amount that would be paid if the uncertain event occurred).

Example 2

Giles sells his freehold interest in Whiteacre to Mick's Developers Limited for £10m payable at legal completion plus a further variable sum depending upon the market value and acreage of the land over which planning permission is given and capped at £50m, but only in the event that planning permission for a casino is granted within 10 years. Mick's Developers Limited intend to apply for permission for residential development only and the planning officer has indicated that permission for a casino is unlikely ever to be granted. If planning permission for a casino was ever granted in the next 10 years it is estimated that a further £20m consideration would actually be payable to Giles. However, Mick's Developers Limited pay SDLT on the basic £10 million price only and estimate the value of the variable consideration as nil because of the unlikelihood of it ever becoming payable.

The Official SDLT Manual fails to address this issue and HMRC's view is not known by the author. For capital gains tax purposes it seems to be accepted by HMRC that one can take the likelihood of payment into account when valuing the chose in action representing the right to future payment. It may be, however, that for SDLT HMRC do not agree that the taxpayer is allowed to discount for the possibility of non-payment and that a return prepared on this basis could be at best negligent and at worst fraudulent. Where available the safest course of action may be to apply to defer the payment of SDLT on this amount.

The second problem with SDLT and overage is the continuing legal responsibility for adjustments to the tax once the contingency occurs or the consideration becomes ascertained. Legally, this responsibility (and the tax liability) stays with the original purchaser even though he may have disposed of the land because *FA 2003, s 80* refers to the purchaser and not a subsequent owner of the land (and so do the deferral regulations in *SI 2003 No 2837*), i.e. the responsibility and liability does not run with the land. Depending upon the precise terms of the over-age agreement, the original purchaser considering a disposal of land over which he has given an over-age agreement to the original seller should therefore consider extracting a positive covenant and/or charge from his purchaser and any subsequent transferees that either all the required information will be supplied to him or that they will assume such responsibility and liability (doubtless this will be reflected in the price). This also raises the issue of whether the passing down the chain of title in this way is the assumption of a liability and so falls to be treated as chargeable consideration for SDLT under *FA 2003, Sch 4, para 8*. Although HMRC Stamp Taxes regard such an assumption as chargeable consideration it may be possible to structure this as an indemnity arrangement so that there is no chargeable consideration under *FA 2003, Sch 4, para 16*. Novation of the original overage agreement may of course be possible and should be considered in the case of wishing to close the administration of a deceased purchaser's estate or the liquidation of a company where both are subject to outstanding overage liabilities. It seems that HMRC Stamp Taxes may be prepared to accept that a novation of the overage obligation does in practice pass the obligation to pay any deferred or additional SDLT on to the subsequent purchaser. It is accepted by HMRC Stamp Taxes Office that where instead of imposing an overage agreement the vendor has simply taken the benefit of a covenant against development on the land sold, this is not within the scope of *FA 2003, s 51* although if the purchaser or his successors pay the vendor to release the covenant then that will be a chargeable land transaction.

As noted above, an application to defer payment of tax may be made to HMRC Stamp Taxes where the amount of tax payable depends on the amount or value of chargeable consideration that at the effective date is contingent or uncertain and falls to be paid on one or more future dates, of which at least one falls or may fall more than six months after the effective date of the transaction (*FA 2003, s 90* and see *Stamp Duty Land Tax (Administration) Regulations 2003 (SI 2003 No 2837)* for the regulations governing deferred payment of

SDLT; see **7.3 Liability and Payment**). Where the tax is deferred interest will only run on any such tax after 30 days from the date the deferred payment is due. [*FA 2003, s 87(3)(b)*]. In respect of contingent or uncertain consideration on which tax is not deferred, interest runs on tax unpaid more than 30 days after the effective date of the transaction, although lodgement of the tax reduces interest accordingly: *FA 2003, s 87(5)* and *(6)*.

Consideration consisting of an annuity

[3.3] Where the chargeable consideration consists of annuity payments whether for life, in perpetuity, for an indefinite period or for a definite period exceeding 12 years, the consideration taken into account is limited to 12 years' annual payments. [*FA 2003, s 52(1), (2)*, and see **5.1 Leases and Agreements for Lease** for the application of this provision in relation to VAT payable under a lease that is not reserved as rent]. This contrasts with stamp duty which used a 20 year period for payments lasting more than 20 years or in perpetuity, and a 12 year period for payments lasting for life (see **36 Consideration**). Where the amount payable varies or may vary from year to year the twelve highest annual payments are taken. No account is taken of any provision in the annuity for adjustment of the amount payable in line with the retail price index and no discount is given for the fact that the amounts are payable in the future. [*FA 2003, s 52(3)*].

The rules relating to contingent and uncertain consideration discussed in **3.2** above apply to determine the value of any annuity payment where necessary and an 'annuity' means any consideration other than rent that falls to be paid or provided periodically. [*FA 2003, s 52(5) and (6)*]. No application can be made to defer the tax payable nor is there any facility to file a further land transaction return and make an adjusting tax payment or receive a repayment when a contingency or any uncertain consideration becomes known. [*FA 2003, s 52(7)* and see **3.2** above].

Connected companies

[3.4] When a company purchases a chargeable interest and the vendor is connected with the company or some or all of the consideration consists of the issue or transfer of shares in any company with which the vendor is connected, the chargeable consideration is to be taken to be not less than the market value of the interest acquired at the effective date of the transaction plus any rent if the acquisition is the grant of a lease. [*FA 2003, s 53(1)* and *(1A)*]. (*CTA 2010, s 1122* applies to determine whether the company and the vendor are connected. Instances where the vendor is not connected with the purchasing company and the consideration includes the issue of shares must surely be rare. For SDLT the 'market value' is determined as for capital gains tax: see *TCGA 1992, ss 272–274*; *FA 2003, s 118*.)

The fact that there may be no chargeable consideration actually given for the transfer does not affect the application of the market value rule. However, any other available exemption from SDLT overrides the market value rule. [*FA 2003, s 53(4)* disapplying *FA 2003, Sch 3, para 1* (no chargeable consideration)].

This provision means that tax is charged when a business is incorporated and land is transferred to the proprietors' company. Tax may also be chargeable on a surrender of leases to a flat management company owning the freehold where the tenant controls the company. Despite doubts about the equivalent market value rule in stamp duty, it has been confirmed that under SDLT the market value is based on the nature of the interest transferred and that if a legal but not a beneficial interest is transferred then the market value will be taken to be the nominal value of the legal interest and not the full value of the beneficial interest (HC Official Report, Standing Committee B, Thursday 5 June 2003, col. 389 reproduced in **APPENDIX A**). It may be that this transfer is any event ignored for SDLT under *FA 2003, Sch 16, para 3* which generally disregards transfers between a principal and his nominee or bare trustee. However, in the cases of a grant of a lease to a bare trustee and a grant of a lease by a bare trustee, tax is charged as if the whole of the interest in the lease was acquired or disposed of accordingly. [*FA 2003, Sch 16, para 2*, as amended by *F(No 2)A 2005, Sch 10, para 11*].

The market value rule does not apply in the following cases:

(1) Case 1 is where the company is to hold the property as trustee in the course of a business carried on by it that consists of or includes the management of trusts. [*FA 2003, s 54(2)*]. It is thought that this case relates to companies that carry on an actual business of managing trusts, and that a company that acts as nominee or bare trustee for a particular principal or beneficiary or partnership and has been incorporated or acquired simply to hold legal title for such persons cannot take advantage of this case.

(2) Case 2 is where the company is to hold the property as trustee and the vendor is connected with the company only because of *CTA 2010, s 1122(6)* (trustee connected with any individual who is a settlor in relation to the settlement etc.) and is not otherwise connected. [*FA 2003, s 54(3)*].

(3) Case 3 is where the vendor is a company and the transaction is, or is part of, a distribution of assets of that company (whether or not in connection with its winding up) and there has not been a claim for either stamp duty or SDLT group relief (see **6.4 GROUP RELIEF**) by the vendor in respect of the chargeable interest transferred in the previous three years. [*FA 2003, s 54(4)*]. It is not HMRC's intention that this Case should be prevented from operating where a group relief claim was made by the vendor but recovered under the claw-back rules in *FA 2003, Sch 7, para 3* either at the time or before the effective date of the transaction. [IR Tax Bulletin 71].

Although not provided for by statute, HMRC has accepted that the market value rule does not apply in the case of land which was distributed from a partnership to a company with which the partners were connected. HMRC regards the rules in *FA 2003, Sch 15 paras 18 and 20* which govern the SDLT charge on distributions of land from a partnership as taking precedence over the market value charge in *FA 2003, s 53*. This means for example that no SDLT charge would arise where the partners consist of individuals who own the company receiving the land.

The equivalent market value rule in stamp duty also had additional exemptions relating to transfers to and from nominees and bare trustees and transfers from one nominee or bare trustee to another. These exceptions are not required in stamp duty land tax because (except in relation to the grant of a lease) no SDLT arises on a transfer of a bare legal estate from a nominee to its principal and on a transfer to a nominee or bare trustee of bare legal title, the market value of such an interest will be nominal at most (HC Official Report, Standing Committee B, Thursday 5 June 2003, col. 390 reproduced in **APPENDIX A**, but see above for dealings in leases and bare trustees).

However, a further exception from the stamp duty market value rule relating to the transfer out of a settlement to a beneficiary who did not acquire his interest for money or money's worth being a distribution in accordance with the settlement, has not been carried over into SDLT. [*FA 2000, s 120(5)* and see HC Official Report, Standing Committee B, Thursday 5 June 2003, col. 390]. Under SDLT, HMRC appears to believe that there is a market value charge whenever the beneficiary who receives the land is a company, to avoid the possibility of land being passed through a settlement to avoid SDLT. However, it is by no means clear that this view can be supported given the relatively limited circumstances in which a company and a settlement will be 'connected' within *CTA 2010, s 1122*.

Chapter 4

Amount of Tax Chargeable

General

[4.1] Stamp duty land tax is charged as a percentage of the chargeable consideration for the transaction. Where the relevant land consists entirely of residential property, the percentages in Table A apply. [*FA 2003, s 55(1), (2)*, as amended by *FA 2006, s 162* for transactions after 22 March 2006]. For the definition of 'residential' and 'non-residential' property, see *FA 2003, s 116* and see **6.2 DISADVANTAGED AREAS RELIEF**.

TABLE A: RESIDENTIAL

Relevant consideration	*Percentage*
Not more than £125,000	0%
More than £125,000 but not more than £250,000	1%
More than £250,000 but not more than £500,000	3%
More than £500,000 but not more than £1m	4%
More than £1m	5%

Prior to 6 April 2011 the 4% rate was the top rate of SDLT. A 5% rate of SDLT applies to acquisitions of residential property where the 'relevant consideration' exceeds £1m and the effective date is on or after 6 April 2011. [*FA 2010, s 7* amending *FA 2003, s 55*]. It can be seen that where the relevant land does not consist entirely of residential property, the percentages in Table A do not apply and those in Table B apply instead and the top rate under Table B remains at 4% and has not been increased.

There is no apportionment of the relevant consideration between Tables A and B. 'Residential property' is defined in *FA 2003, s116* and means a building that is used or suitable for use as a dwelling or is in the process of being constructed or adapted for such use, land that is, or forms part of the garden or grounds of such a building and any interest or right over such building or land. 'Garden or grounds' in HMRC's view includes land required for the reasonable enjoyment of the dwelling having regard to its size and character, applying a similar test to that in *TCGA 1992, s222(3)* ie even if it is larger than 0.5 hectares.

A relief for first-time buyers was introduced for transactions with an effective date on or after 25 March 2010 and before 25 March 2012. The relief is an exemption from SDLT for purchasers of residential property only when the purchaser or all the purchasers are first-time buyers who intend to occupy the property as their only or main residence and the 'relevant consideration' is more than £125,000 but not more than £250,000. [*FA 2003, ss 57AA and 73CA and FA 2010, s 6(6)*].

Where the relevant land consists of or includes land that is not residential property, the percentages in Table B apply:

TABLE B: NON-RESIDENTIAL OR MIXED

Relevant consideration	*Percentage*
Not more than £150,000	0%
More than £150,000 but not more than £250,000	1%
More than £250,000 but not more than £500,000	3%
More than £500,000	4%

In the above tables the 'relevant consideration' is the chargeable consideration. When the amount of the chargeable consideration exceeds a rate threshold the higher rate applies to the total consideration and hence the system is known as the 'slab system'.

Linked transactions

[4.2] If the transaction forms part of a number of linked transactions the relevant consideration for the purpose of the tables above is the total of the chargeable consideration for all the linked transactions. [*FA 2003, s 55(4)*]. Transactions are 'linked' if they form part of a single scheme, arrangement or series of transactions between the same vendor and purchaser or persons connected with them. This means that it is not necessary for the transactions concerned to be part of the same legally binding contract or to be documented as one before they can be 'linked'. While it seems that the stamp duty cases on certificates of value will remain relevant in determining whether a transaction forms part of a series of transactions, it seems clear that the criteria for a 'linked' transaction are much wider than the criteria for certificates of value because they also refer to 'a single scheme' or 'arrangement', terms which did not feature in the 'larger transaction or series of transactions' criteria for certificates of value. [*FA 2003, s 108*]. (*CTA 2010, s 1122* is applied to determine whether persons are connected for these purposes. For the equivalent stamp duty position and cases see **30 Certificate of Value**). The current approach of the Stamp Taxes Office when asked for guidance on whether transactions are linked is generally to decline to give an opinion on the basis that there is no **Adjudication (12)** process under SDLT. However experience suggests that HMRC tends to accept that transactions are not 'linked' where the terms of a particular transaction are in all material respects identical to what they would have been had the other transaction(s) not occurred. Where a discount has been secured because of the other transaction(s) or one cannot complete without the other then the transactions are likely to be 'linked'. It is worth noting that the scheme, arrangement or series of transactions must be between the same vendor and purchaser (or persons connected with them). The Stamp Taxes Office sometimes erroneously assert that transactions are 'linked' when they form part of a scheme or arrangement but the scheme or arrangement is not between the vendor and purchaser (or person connected with them) but instead between one of the parties and an agent or other third party such as a property broker or agency.

There are exceptions from the linked transactions rule for transactions carried out in pursuance of a right of collective enfranchisement or of a crofting community right to buy where the tax is determined by reference to a fraction of the relevant consideration. [*FA 2003, ss 55(5), 74* and *75*].

Exchanges of land between connected persons are expressly excluded from the linked transactions rule (see *FA 2003, s 47* as amended by *FA 2007, s 76* and also **8.5 Exchanges and Partitions**).

Leases

[4.3] Where the whole or part of the chargeable consideration consists of rent, the tax on the rent is calculated separately under different rules: see **5.2 Leases and Agreements for Lease**. Although the tables above apply to compute the tax on any premium paid for the grant of the lease, for non-residential property, the nil rate band is not available if the average annual rent is £1,000 or more (where the relevant land is partly residential and party non-residential and the rent attributable to the non-resident property is at least £1,000, the transaction is taxed as two separate transactions for the purpose of tax on the non-rent considerations so that the nil rate band is not available in respect of the consideration for the non-residential property) [*FA 2003, s 56* and *Sch 5, para 9A* as added by *FA 2008, s 95*; see also **5.1 Leases and Agreements for Lease**] in order to prevent advantage being taken of the nil rate band twice in respect of the same lease.

Chapter 5

Leases and agreements for lease

General

[5.1] Stamp duty land tax is charged in respect of leases on any premium paid for the grant of a lease and also on any rent. Lease premiums are taxed in accordance with either Table A or Table B in **4.1 Amount of Tax Chargeable** and SDLT on the rent is calculated according to the special formula described in **5.2** below. As was the case with stamp duty, the distinction between a lease and a licence continues to be important because under SDLT a licence to use or occupy land and a tenancy at will are exempt interests and are not liable to the tax. [*FA 2003, s 48(2)*, and see **64.1 Leases**. See *FA 2003, Sch 17A, para 1* for the definition of a 'lease'].

Although there was no express charge in relation to agreements for lease in the original legislation, such agreements were in any event chargeable to SDLT by implication as contracts for a land transaction under which the transaction is to be completed by a 'conveyance', and the usual rules as to the timing of the tax charge applied according to whether or not substantial performance of the contract had occurred prior to completion in the form of the grant of the lease. [*FA 2003, s 44* and see **2.3 Contracts, Conveyances and 'Effective Date'**]. It seems that for SDLT a 'conveyance' includes the grant of a lease: *FA 2003, s 44(10)*]. Accordingly under an agreement for a lease where both a premium and rent were payable on the grant of the lease, the grant of the lease would be the effective date of the transaction giving rise to the obligation to file a land transaction return and pay the SDLT chargeable. [*FA 2003, s 44(3)*]. However, substantial performance of the agreement for lease was possible, giving rise to a tax charge for SDLT purposes in respect of the agreement for lease itself despite no lease having been granted, where substantially the whole of the premium was paid or the lessee had taken possession or been granted a licence to occupy in the meantime: *FA 2003, s 44(6)*. In such cases where the lease was granted following substantial performance of the agreement the term of the lease was taken to be the period from substantial performance of the agreement until the end of the lease period. [*FA 2003, Sch 5, para 6(3)*].

However, for transactions with an effective date after 17 March 2004, a new *para 12A* of *FA 2003, Sch 17A* specifically addresses the grant of an agreement for lease which is substantially performed prior to the grant of the actual lease. The agreement is treated as if it were the grant of a lease on the date of substantial performance. This notional lease is treated as if it were surrendered on the grant of the actual lease and the actual lease is treated as granted in consideration of the surrender of the notional lease. 'Overlap' relief will apply so that the rent payable under the actual lease for the same period as the notional lease will be reduced by the amount of rent that would have been payable for that period under the notional lease, in assessing SDLT on the rent under the actual lease. [*FA 2003, Sch 17A, paras 12A* and *9*.] However, the

5-year period during which any rent reviews will count towards computing the taxable rent (see further below) will begin to run again on the grant of the actual lease and so the tax on the actual lease may be higher than on the agreement for lease even if the rent provisions are the same. The notional lease and the actual lease are not treated as a single lease under *FA 2003, Sch 17A para 5* so that the rent under both is not aggregated: see **4.2~4.2UPDATED LINKED TRANSACTIONS**. There is also a provision dealing with the assignment of an agreement for lease prior to substantial performance: see **8.4 SUB-SALES, ASSIGNMENTS AND NOVATIONS**.

Leases granted to a company connected with the lessor or where some or all of the consideration consists of the issue or transfer of shares in a company with which the lessor is connected, fall within the scope of the market value rule for SDLT; see **3.4 CONNECTED COMPANIES**.

Any VAT chargeable in respect of the lease other than value added tax chargeable by virtue of an election to tax the property made after the effective date of the transaction is taken to be part of the chargeable consideration. [*FA 2003, Sch 4, para 2*]. It seems that any VAT payable in respect of the rent that is not reserved as rent under the lease will not be rent for SDLT purposes and as for stamp duty will be taxed as consideration other than rent. Accordingly, the total VAT payable over the term of the lease will be chargeable, except where the lease exceeds 12 years, when the amount chargeable will be limited to the total of the 12 highest annual payments; see also **3.3 CONSIDERATION CONSISTING OF AN ANNUITY**. *FA 2003, s 52*, and see *Blendett v IRC, Quietlece v IRC* [1984] STC 95. It is understood, however, that IR Stamp Taxes rarely, if ever, take this point.

None of the following counts as chargeable consideration on the grant of a lease:

(1) an undertaking by the tenant to repair, maintain or insure the let premises;
(2) a tenant's undertaking to pay in respect of services, repairs, maintenance, insurance or management costs;
(3) any other tenant's obligation that does not affect the open market rent;
(4) any rent or performance guarantee;
(5) penal rent;
(6) costs borne by a tenant exercising a statutory right to be granted a new lease;
(7) any other obligation by a tenant to bear the landlord's reasonable costs incidental on the grant of a lease;
(8) an obligation under a lease, on its termination, to transfer to the landlord payment entitlements under the scheme of income support for farmers in respect of land subject to the scheme.

A payment made under any of the above obligations is also ignored. The assumption or release of any obligation above on the assignment or surrender of the lease is also ignored. [*FA 2003, Sch 17A, para 10* as amended by the *Stamp Duty Land Tax (Amendment to the Finance Act 2003) Regulations 2006 (SI 2006 No 875)*].

Where on the grant or assignment of a lease the lessee or assignee makes a loan or pays a deposit to any person, and the repayment of the loan or deposit is contingent on anything done or omitted to be done by the lessee or assignee or on the death of the lessee or assignee, the amount is treated as chargeable consideration other than rent. This will not apply where the amount of the deposit does not exceed twice the rent determined under *FA 2003, Sch 17A, para 7(3)* (the 'relevant maximum rent'). In case of the grant of a lease, the relevant maximum rent is the highest amount of rent payable in respect of any consecutive 12-month period in the first five years of the term. In the case of a lease assignment, the relevant maximum rent is the highest amount of rent payable in respect of any consecutive 12-month period in the first five years of the term remaining outstanding as at the date of the assignment. [*FA 2003, Sch 17A, para 18A*]. No tax repayment claim may be made in respect of any such loan or deposit treated as chargeable consideration which is later repaid or in respect of the refund of any consideration given where the refund is made under arrangements made in connection with the transaction and is contingent on the determination or assignment of the lease or on the grant of a chargeable interest out of the lease. [*FA 2003, s 80(4A)*].

Where a break notice or notice to quit is withdrawn by agreement before it takes effect, a new implied lease will arise, see *Tayleur v Wildin* (1868) LR 3 Ex 303. Ordinarily, SDLT could become chargeable on the new lease, however HMRC treat the old lease as continuing unless perhaps the new lease contained significant changes compared to the old lease: see HMRC SDLTM 17030.

Rent

[5.2] Stamp duty land tax is charged on any chargeable consideration consisting of rent as a percentage of the net present value of the rent payable over the term of the lease. [*FA 2003, s 56* and *Sch 5, para 2*].

In other words, the total rent payable over the term of the lease is in principle charged to tax at a flat percentage (after discounting each annual rent by 3.5% per annum to arrive at its present value). This contrasts with stamp duty on rent that was charged on only one year's average rent at varying percentages according to the term of the lease. On average, the SDLT charge on rent represents an increase of four times the stamp duty charge on a ten-year lease.

The net present value (V) of the rent payable over the term of the lease is calculated by applying the formula in *FA 2003, Sch 5, para 3*:

$$V = \sum_{i=1}^{n} \frac{r_i}{(1+T)^i}$$

r_i is the rent payable in respect of year 'i'
i is the particular year for which the calculation is to be performed (a calculation being required for each year)
n is the term of the lease
T is the temporal discount rate (currently 3.5%)

Having calculated the net present value of the rent (referred to as the 'relevant rental value') the tax is charged as a percentage of so much of that value as falls within each rate band according to the following two tables. [*FA 2003, Sch 5, para 2(3)*]. Table A applies where the relevant land consists entirely of residential property and Table B applies where the relevant land consists of or includes land that is not residential property. Hence tax is chargeable on each 'slice' of the rental value at either the nil or 1% rate as appropriate, thus ensuring that a credit is given for the first £125,000 or £150,000 as appropriate where the rental value exceeds this figure.

TABLE A: RESIDENTIAL

Rate bands	*Percentage*
£0 to £125,000	0%
Over £125,000	1%

TABLE B: NON-RESIDENTIAL OR MIXED

Rate bands	*Percentage*
£0 to £150,000	0%
Over £150,000	1%

If the lease is one of a number of linked transactions for which the chargeable consideration includes rent then the net present values of the rents payable under all the linked leases are aggregated for the purpose of applying the percentages in the above tables. [*FA 2003, Sch 5, para 2(5)* and see **4.2~4.2UPDATED LINKED TRANSACTIONS** for 'linked transactions']. Where successive linked leases are granted or treated as granted (at the same time or different times) of substantially the same premises and the grants are linked transactions, then the series of leases is treated as a single lease granted at the time of the first lease for the aggregate term and rent of the series of leases, and a return is required under *FA 2003, s 81A* on the grant of each successive lease with the tax payable adjusted accordingly. [*FA 2003, Sch 17A, para 5*]. Note that where the latter provision applies, the total SDLT payable may be lower because of the effect of the discounting formula on the rent.

A single sum expressed to be payable in respect of rent or expressed to be payable in respect of rent and other matters such as a service charge, but not apportioned is treated as entirely rent. This is expressly without prejudice to a just and reasonable apportionment where separate sums are expressed to be payable in respect of rent and other matters. [*FA 2003, Sch 17A, para 6*].

Penal rent or increased rent in the nature of a penal rent payable in respect of the breach of any obligation of the tenant does not count as chargeable consideration. [*FA 2003, Sch 17A, para 10(1)(e)*].

'Rent' does not include any chargeable consideration for the grant of a lease that is payable in respect of a period before the grant of a lease: *FA 2003, Sch 5, para 1A*. For this purpose the date of the grant of a lease is when it is actually granted even if the term is expressed to commence at an earlier time: *Bradshaw v Pawley* [1979] 3 All ER 273, [1980] 1 WLR 10. Therefore rent payable in respect of the period between a prior commencement of the contractual term of a lease and the actual date of grant will be taxed as premium. This is however subject to the exception noted below where a new backdated lease is granted to a tenant who is holding over under an old lease.

Contingent, uncertain or unascertained rent is taken into account and dealt with under the usual rules for SDLT; see **3.2~3.2UPDATED CONTINGENT, UNCERTAIN OR UNASCERTAINED CONSIDERATION AND OVERAGE**, subject to the following modifications. No application may be made to defer payment of the tax on contingent or uncertain rent. [*FA 2003, s 90(7)*]. No account is taken of any provision for the rent to be adjusted in line with the retail price index and the starting rent is used for calculating to the tax. [*FA 2003, Sch 17A, para 7(5)*]. This apparently generous concession is counter-balanced by the relatively low temporal discount rate of 3.5% used for the purposes of discounting future rent payments in the formula above which does not take into account price inflation.

Where the lease provides for the rent to be reviewed or varied, or the rent is contingent, uncertain or unascertained, the actual rent payable in the first five years of the term is taken into account for the purposes of the tax computation. For this purpose, where the rent includes VAT and the effective date of the grant of the lease is on or after 27 July 2010 (the date on which *F(No2)A 2010, s 3* came into force increasing the standard rate of VAT from 17.5% to 20% from 4 January 2011) the VAT on the rent should be calculated at 17.5% from completion until the day preceding the first rent payment day on or after 4 January 2011 and at 20% on the rent payment from the first rent payment date on or after 4 January 2011. When the rent for the first 5 years becomes certain, the net present value of the actual rent can be reviewed and a return submitted if necessary to claim any overpayment (see HMRC Guidance Note 3 December 2008). However, the rent payable for any period after the end of the fifth year of the term is assumed to be at an annual amount equal to the highest amount of rent payable for any consecutive 12-month period in the first five years (including any contingent, uncertain or unascertained rent). [*FA 2003, Sch 17A, para 7*]. This rules favour leases with rent increases that occur after year five where the increases are not 'abnormal' and so not subject to the rule taxing 'abnormal' rent increase as if there had been the grant of a new lease for the excess rent (see below). However, this rule can also present a trap for leases where the rent is front-loaded and reduces to say a peppercorn after year five because the rent for year six and beyond is deemed to be the highest amount of rent in the first five years and the tax calculation is to be made accordingly.

Where the first rent review occurs in the final quarter of the fifth year the intention is that this is ignored for these purposes so that the rent is taken as fixed for the first 5 years. This rule is intended to deal with leases whose term commences on a quarter day but which are not actually granted until some time during the following quarter. If the first or only rent review occurs 5 years after a specified date and the specified date falls within 3 months before the beginning of the term of the lease, references in the SDLT rules to the first 5 years of the term of the lease are to be taken as referring to the period beginning with the start of the term and 'ending with the review date'. The wording in parenthesis will however bring the review into the first 5 years and so it is understood that HMRC accepts that the period should be taken as ending on the day before the rent review in order not to defeat the intention behind the rule. This rule is however, of no assistance when the lease term runs from 24 June but the lease is granted between 24 and 28 September given that the specified date is not within the permitted 3 months before the beginning of the lease. [*FA 2003, Sch 17A, para 7A*]. Where the end of the fifth year is reached or the amount of rent payable in the first five years ceases to be uncertain at an earlier date, the tenant must make a return to HMRC within 30 days and pay any tax due if as a result the transactions become notifiable or tax or additional tax becomes payable. If less tax turns out to be payable than has already been paid then a claim for repayment can be made. [*FA 2003 Sch 17A, para 8*].

Where a lease is varied so as to increase the rent as from a date before the end of the fifth year of the term, the variation is treated as if it were the grant of a lease for the additional rent payable and tax is chargeable. However, an increase in rent under the existing terms of a lease such as on a scheduled rent review is not chargeable unless it is an 'abnormal' rent increase after the fifth year of the term. [*FA 2003, Sch 17A, para 13*]. A variation of a lease to increase the rent from a date falling after the end of the fifth year of the term is only taxable if the rent increase is 'abnormal'.

If, after the end of the fifth year of the term, the amount of rent increases whether in accordance with the provisions of the lease or otherwise, and the increase is treated as 'abnormal' then the increase in the rent is treated as if it were the grant of a new lease in consideration of the excess rent and tax is payable accordingly. [*FA 2003, Sch 17A, paras 14 and 15*]. This rule applies only to lease granted on or after 1 December 2003. For rent increases on or after 19 July 2006 the previous criteria for an 'abnormal' rent increase of 5% plus RPI per annum compounded has been replaced by a less stringent criteria which permits a flat rate increase of 20% per annum. The rent increase will be regarded as 'abnormal' where the excess rent is greater than:

$$\frac{R \times Y}{5}$$

where R is the rent previously taxed, Y is the number of whole years between the start date and the date when the new rent becomes payable. There are a number of uncertainties in how the 'abnormal' rent income rule will operate but it is understood that HMRC will accept that the SDLT return reporting the increase can be filed within 30 days of the rent increase being agreed and not, if earlier, the date it becomes payable. HMRC will also not insist on the tenant having to reapportion the £150,000 nil rate band between the original and the new deemed lease.

In computing the tax payable on a lease for a fixed term no account is taken of any contingency which may cause the lease to end before the expiry of the fixed term or the existence of a break or renewal clause [*FA 2003, Sch 17A, para 2*]. When a lease continues after a fixed term it is treated as a single lease growing by one year at a time and tax is payable accordingly at each interval [*FA 2003, Sch 17A, para 3*]. A lease for an indefinite term is treated in the first instance as if it were a lease for a fixed term of one year and if it continues in existence it is treated as a single lease growing by one year at a time and tax is payable accordingly at each interval. [*FA 2003, Sch 17A, para 4*]. These rules do not apply to leases granted before 1 December 2003.

Where a tenant continues in occupation after the end of the contractual term and is subsequently granted a new lease of the premises with a term expressed to begin from the end of the old contractual term, the term of the new lease is treated for SDLT as beginning on the date it is expressed to begin. This is despite the rule in *Bradshaw v Pawley* [1979] 3 All ER 273, [1980] 1 WLR 10 that the lease term commences on the later of the contractual term start date and the actual date of grant. However, any rent payable under the new lease in respect of any period after the end of the old contractual term and before the actual date on which the new lease is granted is for SDLT purposes to be reduced by the amount of taxable rent that is payable in respect of that period otherwise than under the new lease. This means that a credit is given for SDLT payable in respect of that period under the notional lease which is treated as growing one year at a time following the end of the old lease. However, a credit will not be available to the extent that the actual date of grant of the new lease occurs before the next anniversary of the notional growing lease. Where possible therefore the new lease should not require rent to be payable in respect of any period from the date of grant of the new lease to the next anniversary of the notional growing lease. [*FA 2003 Sch 17A para 9A*].

The reduction in the rent payable for SDLT purposes under the new lease to reflect rent already paid in respect of the interim period is only available where the new lease is of *'the same or substantially the same premises'*: see *FA 2003, Sch 17A, para 9A*. If the tenant has previously sub-let part of its original holding then strictly the landlord can only be required to grant the new lease over that part of the premises actually occupied by the tenant for its business and not the whole premises originally let to the tenant: see *Landlord and Tenant Act 1954, ss 23(3) and 32(2)*. Where the landlord elects to so limit the new lease and the difference between the new and old holding is significant it may be that the availability of credit for the interim rent is put into doubt.

Surrender and regrant; sale and leaseback

[5.3] Where a lease is granted in consideration of the surrender of an existing lease between the same parties, the grant of the new lease does not count as chargeable consideration for the surrender and the surrender does not count as chargeable consideration for the grant of the new lease, so that *FA 2003, Sch 4, para 5* (exchanges: see **8.5~8.5UPDATED Exchanges and Partitions**) is disapplied. [*FA 2003, Sch 17A, para 16*]. In the case of the grant, assignment or surrender of a lease a reverse premium does not count as chargeable consideration. [*FA 2003, Sch 17A, para 18*].

The leaseback element of a sale and leaseback arrangement is exempt where the leaseback is granted out of the major interest in land transferred or granted if:

(1) the sale is entered into wholly or partly in consideration of the leaseback;
(2) the only other consideration for the sale is cash or debt;
(3) the sale is not by way of sub-sale; and
(4) the parties are not members of a group of companies for the purposes of group relief. [*FA 2003, s 57A*].

Lease variations

[5.4] The variation of a lease is an acquisition and disposal of a chargeable interest where (1) the variation takes effect in law, or is treated for SDLT as, the grant of a new lease, or (2) the lease is varied to reduce the rent. Where consideration in money or money's worth (other than an increase in rent — see above) is given by the lessee for any variation of a lease (other than a variation of the rent or the term of the lease), the variation is treated as an acquisition of a chargeable interest by the lessee. Where a lease is varied to reduce its term, the variation is treated for SDLT as an acquisition of a chargeable interest by the lessor. [*FA 2003, s 43(3)(d) and Sch 17A, para 15A*].

Chapter 6

Reliefs and Exemptions

General

[6.1] A number of reliefs are available from stamp duty land tax including the following:

(1) Disadvantaged areas relief — *FA 2003, s 57* (see **6.2** below).
(2) Sales and leasebacks — FA 2003, s 57A (see **5.3 SURRENDER AND REGRANT; SALE AND LEASEBACK**).
(3) Certain acquisitions of residential property — *FA 2003, s 58A* and *Sch 6A*.
(4) Acquisitions of multiple dwellings — *FA 2003, s58D* and *Sch 6B* (see **6.3 ACQUISITION OF MULTIPLE DWELLINGS**).
(5) First acquisitions of zero-carbon homes — *FA 2003, ss 58B, 58C*.
(6) Dwelling acquired from relocated employee — *FA 2003, s 58A*.
(7) Compulsory purchase facilitating development — *FA 2003, s 60*.
(8) Purchases by public authorities in connection with planning agreements — *FA 2003, s 61*.
(9) Group relief, reconstruction and acquisition reliefs — *FA 2003, s 62* and *Sch 7* (see **6.4–6.10** below).
(10) Demutualisation of insurance company — *FA 2003, s 63*.
(11) Demutualisation of building society — *FA 2003, s 64*.
(12) Initial transfer of land to a unit trust scheme — *FA 2003, s 64A* (withdrawn from 22 March 2006).
(13) Incorporation of limited liability partnership — *FA 2003, s 65*.
(14) Transfers between public bodies on a reorganisation — NHS Foundation Trusts have been prescribed as a public body for this relief (see *SI 2005 No 83*) — *FA 2003, s 66*.
(15) Transfers in consequence of reorganisation of parliamentary constituencies — *FA 2003, s 67*.
(16) Acquisitions by charities — *FA 2003, s 68* and *Sch 8* (see **6.11** below).
(17) Acquisitions by bodies established for national purposes — *FA 2003, s 69*.
(18) Right to buy and shared ownership transactions — *FA 2003, s 70* and *Sch 9* as amended by *FA 2009, s 81*.
(19) Acquisitions by registered social landlords — *FA 2003, s 71* as amended by *FA 2009, s 81*.
(20) Alternative property finance — *FA 2003, ss 71A, 72, 72A, 73, 73A, 73B, 73BA, 73AB, 73C, 73CA* and *FA 2009, s 123* and *Sch 61*.
(21) Collective enfranchisement by lease holders — *FA 2003, s 74* as amended by *FA 2009, s 80* removing the requirement that a 'Right to enfranchise' or RTE company be used.
(22) Crofting community right to buy — *FA 2003, s 75*.

(23) Restricted sub-sale relief — *FA 2003, s 45* (see **8.4 Sub-sales, Assignments and Novations**).

The following transactions are exempt from SDLT (and are therefore not chargeable transactions for SDLT: *FA 2003, s 49*):

(1) A transaction for no chargeable consideration — *FA 2003, Sch 3 para 1* (but this exemption is overridden by the market value rule for transfers to connected companies, see **3.4 Connected Companies**).
(2) Grant of leases by registered social landlords — *FA 2003, Sch 3, para 2*.
(3) Transfers between spouses on separation or divorce — *FA 2003, Sch 3, para 3*.
(4) Assents and appropriations by personal representatives — *FA 2003, Sch 3, para 3A*.
(5) Transfers in connection with the dissolution of civil partnerships — *FA 2003, Sch 3, para 3A*.
(6) Variation of testamentary dispositions — *FA 2003, Sch 3, para 4*.

Where the purchaser is a public office or department of the Crown no payment of SDLT is required if that would ultimately be borne by the Crown. This includes ministers of the Crown but not local authorities or similar bodies, and does not apply to the acquisition of private property for the Sovereign. [*FA 2003, s 107*].

Disadvantaged areas relief

[6.2] Relief for acquisitions of land in designated disadvantaged areas was introduced for stamp duty purposes with effect from 30 November 2001 and initially was available only for transfers on sale and lease premiums where the consideration did not exceed £150,000. [*FA 2001, s 92* and *Sch 30*, prior to its amendment by *FA 2002, s 110(1)* and see generally Statement of Practice 1/03 for stamp duty and Statement of Practice 1/04 for SDLT, both reproduced in **Appendix B**].

An area is disadvantaged for the purposes of the relief if it is designated as such in the *Stamp Duty (Disadvantaged Areas) Regulations 2001 (SI 2001 No 3747)* (made by the Treasury under *FA 2001, s 92(4)* and *(9)*). The designation is based on wards listed in the various indices of multiple deprivation maintained by central and regional government. The £150,000 cap was removed from non-residential property in disadvantaged areas after 9 April 2003 and transfers on sale and grants of leases for a premium or rent or both became absolutely exempt after this date and the £150,000 cap applied to residential property only. [*FA 2001, s 92A* and the *Stamp Duty (Disadvantaged Areas) (Application of Exemption) Regulations 2003 (SI 2003 No 1056)* made by the Treasury under *FA 2001, ss 92A, 92B* and *FA 2002, s 110(6)* following the grant of European Union state aid approval (due to expire in 2006) and revoking the *Variation of Stamp Duties Regulations 2001 (SI 2001 No 3746)*]. An equivalent relief for acquisitions of chargeable interests in designated disadvantaged areas has been carried over into stamp duty land tax and the regulations mentioned above designating areas as disadvantaged areas have continuous effect for SDLT. [*FA 2003, s 57* and *Sch 6, paras 1* and 2].

Disadvantaged areas relief for non-residential property was removed for transactions with an effective date after 16 March 2005. [*FA 2005, s 96* and *Sch 9*].

The term 'residential property' is defined and is used in the SDLT legislation for the purpose of distinguishing between residential and non-residential property in the application of the disadvantaged areas relief and also generally for determining which set of tables of rates apply to the chargeable consideration. [*FA 2003, s 116* and see **4.1 Amount of Tax Chargeable** and **5.2 Rent**]. Broadly, 'residential property' is a building or part of a building which is in use as a dwelling, or is suitable for use as a dwelling, or is in the process of being constructed or adapted as a dwelling, including any land forming part of the garden or grounds of such a building and any outbuilding on that land. A single transaction involving the acquisition of a major interest in or the grant of a lease over six or more separate dwellings is treated as relating to non-residential property. 'Non-residential' property is defined as any property that is not 'residential property'.

The relief operates according to whether the land in question is wholly or partly situated in a disadvantaged area. If the land is wholly situated in a disadvantaged area and all the land is non-residential property then since 16 March 2005 the transaction is no longer exempt from SDLT. If the land is wholly within a disadvantaged area but all the land is residential then the transaction is exempt from SDLT if either:

(1) the consideration does not include rent and the 'relevant consideration' does not exceed £150,000, or
(2) the consideration consists only of rent and the 'relevant rental value' does not exceed £150,000.

'Relevant consideration' is the consideration that would be taken into account in applying the relevant tables of rates in **4.1 Amount of Tax Chargeable** were it not for disadvantaged areas relief, and 'relevant rental value' is the amount that would be taken for the purpose of applying the relevant table of rates for the lease rentals in **5.2 Rent** were it not for the relief.

If the consideration includes rent and other consideration and the 'relevant rental value' does not exceed £150,000, the rent does not count as chargeable consideration. The other consideration is also ignored if it does not exceed £150,000. Where the land is partly non-residential and partly residential the consideration is to be apportioned on a just and reasonable basis. The consideration attributable to the non-residential property counts as chargeable consideration and the consideration attributable to the residential property is dealt with as above. [*FA 2003, Sch 6, Part 2*].

If the land is partly in a disadvantaged area and partly outside such an area, the consideration is to be apportioned on a just and reasonable basis.

Where the land situated in a disadvantaged area is, either all residential property, or partly residential and partly non-residential, the rules similar to those set out above relating to residential or mixed property wholly situated in a disadvantaged area apply to determine the extent to which the consideration including rent counts as chargeable consideration. [*FA 2003, Sch 6, Part 3*].

Acquisition of multiple dwellings

[6.3] A relief is available for the acquisition of two or more dwellings under *FA 2003, s58D* and *Sch 6B* (introduced by *FA 2011, s83* and *Sch 22* for transactions with an effective date on or after 19 July 2011). The relief is intended to lower the SDLT cost involved in bulk purchases of residential property to improve the supply of private rented housing. The relief operates by reducing the rate of SDLT charged on the acquisition of multiple dwellings which would normally be determined by the aggregate consideration so that it is related to the rate that would have been charged had the dwellings been acquired individually.

The relief must be claimed in the land transaction return. Where a transaction or a scheme, arrangement or series of linked transactions includes multiple dwellings, the rate of tax charged in respect of the dwellings is computed by reference to the mean consideration ie the total consideration attributable to the dwellings divided by the number of dwellings. However if the rate determined is nil, the rate is taken to be 1%.

Although *FA 2003, s58D* and *Sch 6B* refer to 'transfers' involving multiple dwellings it is understood that HMRC accept that the grant of new leases is included in the relief.

The normal rule that the acquisition of six or more dwellings is treated as not being an acquisition of residential property is disapplied for the purpose of the relief (*FA 2003, Sch 6B, para 5(6)(a)* disapplying *FA 2003, s116(7)*).

A building or part of a building counts as a dwelling if either (a) it is used or suitable for use as a single dwelling, or (b) it is in the process of being constructed or adapted for such use. Land that is, or is to be, occupied or enjoyed with a dwelling as a garden or grounds is included as is land that subsists, or is to subsist for the benefit of a dwelling (*FA 2003, Sch 6B para 7*). In HMRC's view 'garden or grounds' includes land required for the reasonable enjoyment of the dwelling having regard to its size and character, applying a similar test to that in *TCGA 1992, s222(3)* ie even if it is larger than 0.5 hectare. Acquisitions where construction or adoption of a single dwelling has not yet commenced at the time of substantial performance can also be included (*FA 2003, Sch 6B, para 7(5)*).

A further recomputation of the rate of tax and possible further return and payment of additional tax will be required where an event subsequently occurs which had it occurred immediately before the effective date of the transaction would have affected the relief. An example of this given by HMRC would be if the number of dwellings was reduced after the effective date of the transaction (*FA 2003, Sch 6B, para 6*).

The event to be caught must occur within the shorter of the period of three years beginning with the effective date of the transaction or the period between the effective date of the transaction and the date on which the purchaser disposes of the dwelling or dwellings to an unconnected purchaser. HMRC take the view that the onward sale of all the dwellings acquired in a single transaction to an unconnected purchaser will bring the period to an end. However, where the acquisition was one of a number of linked transactions, the onward sale of the dwellings acquired in the acquisition will bring the period to an end in respect of that acquisition but not in respect of the linked transactions. The onward sale of only some of the dwellings acquired in an acquisition will not bring the period to an end for that acquisition. The onward sales will not be an event in themselves which triggers a recomputation of the rate. However if the period continues to run and there is an event then a recomputation of the rate of tax will be necessary taking into account the whole of the original consideration and number of dwellings including those which have been sold on.

HMRC give the example of eight flats acquired for £1m on which multiple dwellings relief is claimed. The rate of tax is found by dividing £1m by eight giving £125,000. The nil rate is not available using the relief so the rate of tax is taken as 1%. If two flats are sold in the relevant period to an unconnected purchaser, this will not be an event requiring a recomputation of the rate. If the remaining six flats are converted into three dwellings within the relevant period, then this will be a relevant event and a recomputation of the rate will be required. Therefore the original consideration of £1m will be divided by five (the two sold plus the three converted dwellings) giving £200,000. The rate of tax will however remain unchanged at 1% and so no further return is required.

With regard to partnerships involved with multiple dwellings, HMRC regard the relief as applying to ordinary acquisitions by partnerships within *FA 2003, Sch 15, para 2*, the transfer of a chargeable interest to a partnership under *FA 2003, Sch 15, para 10*, the transfer of a chargeable interest out of a partnership under *FA 2003, Sch 15, para 18* and a transfer of a chargeable interest from one partnership to another under *FA 2003, Sch 15, para 23*. In each case the rate of tax is found by applying the relief to the chargeable consideration found by applying the relevant provisions of *FA 2003, Sch 15*.

However, HMRC do not regard the relief as available to deemed land transactions arising under *FA 2003, Sch 15, paras 14, 16* or *17* where there is a transfer of a partnership interest or under *para 17A* where there is a withdrawal of money, etc.

HMRC regard the relief as applicable were the deemed market value consideration rule in *FA 2003, s 53* for transfers to a connected company applies and also to where there is an exchange of chargeable interests where the chargeable consideration is found under *FA 2003, Sch 4, para 5*.

It should be noted that the relative brevity of the legislative provisions governing this relief mean the various interpretations applied by HMRC as discussed above are not necessarily mandatory and could be challenged where appropriate.

Group relief: Introduction

[6.4] A land transaction is exempt from stamp duty land tax if the vendor and purchaser are companies that at the effective date of the transaction are members of the same group. [*FA 2003, s 62* and *Sch 7, para 1(1)* and see **23 Associated Companies** et seq for the equivalent stamp duty group relief which differs in significant respects from the SDLT group relief as discussed below]. The equivalent stamp duty group relief concentrated on relieving specific instruments from stamp duty and therefore expressly required that the relevant instrument transferred a beneficial interest in the property and that the companies in question were members of the same group at the time the instrument (normally, the conveyance) was executed, even though the beneficial interest could pass on earlier exchange of contract and payment. Although in practice these factors will often be present they are not strict conditions for the SDLT group relief to be available. Accordingly, for SDLT group relief the acquisition of a chargeable interest will be exempt if at the 'effective date' the companies are grouped together. This will normally be the date of the conveyance but may be earlier when a substantial amount of the consideration is paid or provided before possession or a conveyance is taken: see **2.3 Contracts, Conveyances and 'Effective Date'**.

The relief must be claimed in the land transaction return and is subject to detailed anti-avoidance rules and to clawback if the acquiring company leaves the group pursuant to arrangements made within three years of the acquisition. [*FA 2003, s 62(3)* and *Sch 7, para 3*]; the equivalent stamp duty group relief clawback was restricted to where the acquiring company actually left the group within three years; see **23.3 Withdrawal of Group Relief**].

For the purposes of group relief a 'company' means any body corporate (wherever incorporated or resident) and companies are members of the same group if one is the 75% subsidiary of the other, or both are 75% subsidiaries of a third company. [*FA 2003, Sch 7, para 1(2)*]. A company ('A') is the 75% subsidiary of another company ('B') if B:

(1) is beneficial owner of not less than 75% of the ordinary share capital of A;
(2) is beneficially entitled to not less than 75% of any profits available for distribution to equity holders of A; and
(3) would be beneficially entitled to not less than 75% of any assets of A available for distribution to its equity holders on a winding-up. [*FA 2003, Sch 7, para 1(3)*].

The ownership referred to in (1) above is ownership either directly or through another company or companies and *CTA 2010, ss 1155–1157* applies to determine the amount of shares of A owned by B through another company or companies. [*FA 2003, Sch 7, para 1(4)*]. Indirect holdings are taken into account using a multiplication formula, so if P Ltd owns 80% of the shares in Q Ltd which owns 50% of the shares in R Ltd, P Ltd is taken to own 40% of the shares in R Ltd. [*CTA 1988, s 1156*]. 'Ordinary share capital' means all the issued share capital of the company other than capital the holders of which have a right to a dividend at a fixed rate but have no other right to share in the profits of the company. [*FA 2003, Sch 7, para 1(5)*]. The corporation tax group relief tests relating to equity holders and profits and assets available for distribution in *CTA 2010, Pt 5, Ch 6* apply for the purposes of 2 and 3 above save that *ss 121(1), (2)* and *(3)*, *173*, *174* and *176–178* are 'switched-off' for SDLT purposes in respect of both the transferor and the transferee (the equivalent stamp duty group relief switched these provisions off only in respect of the transferor). [*FA 2003, Sch 7, para 1(6) and (6A)*]. Given that corporation tax is an annual tax assessed retrospectively by reference to accounting periods, the tests in *TA 1988, Sch 18* (now *CTA 2010, Pt 5, Ch 6*) are applied over the accounting period current at the time in question and are only finally judged when the accounting period has ended. It is apparent therefore that the direct application of these provisions to a transaction tax such as SDLT gives rise to the question of how does one judge that the various tests for group relief to be available have been met at any point during the accounting period in which the land transaction occurs. It seems that logically this is not possible and one must wait for the end of the accounting period before deciding. Under the equivalent stamp duty provisions a pragmatic view of the position seems to have been adopted by taxpayers and HMRC Stamp Taxes, and applications for group relief that certified that the requirements of *TA 1988, Sch 18* were met at the date of the relevant instrument were not challenged on the basis that one strictly should 'wait and see' until the end of the accounting period. It may be, however, that because of the nature of SDLT as a mandatory transaction tax where in some circumstances the tax can be adjusted subsequently and corrective returns filed, the practice may change. It is unclear how this situation would be resolved under the existing SDLT provisions other than by initially paying the SDLT and then submitting a retrospective claim for the relief once the accounting period had ended.

With regard to partnerships and group relief, the 'look through' principle for SDLT in relation to land owning partnerships enshrined in *FA 2003, Sch 15 para 2* and considered in **8.1 Partnerships**, only goes so far. For the purposes of SDLT group relief, an LLP incorporated under the *Limited Liability Partnerships Act 2002* is regarded as a body corporate given that *section 1(2)* of that Act confers corporate status on LLPs incorporated under it. This means that an LLP can form its own SDLT group as the top body corporate in the group structure.

However, because an LLP does not have an issued ordinary share capital it cannot be a subsidiary of any other company nor can the LLP's subsidiary companies form a group with the company members of the LLP. The LLP cannot itself claim SDLT group relief because of the 'look through' principle in *FA 2003*, which requires the LLP's chargeable interests to be treated as held by its members. This had always been the correct position, however prior to 11th October 2010 HMRC did not accept that LLPs were bodies corporate for the purposes of SDLT group relief so that LLPs were 'looked through' in deciding whether an SDLT group existed between the members of the LLP and its subsidiaries. HMRC announced on 11th October 2010 that their view had changed and that an LLP was a body corporate for SDLT group relief purposes. SDLT group relief will in principle be available for transfers between members of the LLP's own group (excluding transfers to the LLP itself). However, a transfer by the LLP to a member of its own group will not attract group relief because the land is deemed to be owned by the members of the LLP and those members will not form a part of the same group of companies owned by the LLP. Therefore transfers between a member of the LLP and the subsidiary companies of the LLP cannot attract SDLT group relief. LLPs are therefore at a disadvantage to general or English limited partnerships because partners who control 75% or more of the latter types of partnerships can be treated as grouped with 75% subsidiary companies held by the partnership.

Transfers by companies to an LLP the members of which form part of an SDLT group with the company transferrer can attract group relief.

Group relief: Restriction on availability of relief

[6.5] There are four types of arrangements which can prevent group relief from applying. These relate to control of the purchasing company, the provision of consideration by someone outside the group, where the purchaser is to cease to be a member of the same group as the vendor, or where the transaction is not effected for bona fide commercial reasons or forms part of tax avoidance.

First, group relief is not available if at the effective date (see **2.3 Contracts, Conveyances and 'Effective Date'**) of the transaction there are arrangements in existence by virtue of which at that or some later time a person has or could obtain control of the purchaser but not of the vendor. [*FA 2003, Sch 7, para 2(1)*]. (This restriction does not apply to transfers in connection with the demutualisation of insurance companies: *FA 2003, Sch 7, para 2(3A)*).

'Arrangements' is defined to include any scheme, agreement or understanding, whether or not legally enforceable. [*FA 2003, Sch 7, para 2(5)*]. 'Control' for this purpose is the test contained in *CTA 2010, s 1124*. [*FA 2003, Sch 7, para 2(5)*]. In stamp duty, HMRC Stamp Taxes accepted that the equivalent anti-avoidance provision relating to arrangements for loss of control of the transferee [*FA 1930, s 42(2)*] was to be interpreted in the light of Statement of Practice 3/93 'Groups of companies—arrangements', which gives general guidance on how HMRC interprets 'arrangements' for corporation tax group relief purposes, and extra-statutory concession C10 which excludes certain types of arrangements including mortgages of shares. Although the stamp duty group relief provisions did not include a definition of arrangements and the SDLT provisions do include such a definition, it is submitted that Statement of Practice 3/93 and Extra-statutory Concession C10 should apply to the interpretation of 'arrangements' for SDLT purposes given that the corporation tax group relief provisions include a similar although truncated definition of arrangements [*CTA 2010, ss 155(3), 156(2) and 1176(2)*] and there can be no logical grounds for discriminating between the group relief provisions for corporation tax and those for SDLT by having a wider meaning of 'arrangements' for the latter tax (see Statement of Practice SP 3/93: Groups of companies—arrangements (13 January 1993) in **Appendix B** and **Appendix C** for ESC 10). Tax Bulletin No 70 (April 2004, see **Appendix D**) contains an article entitled 'Stamp Duty Land Tax: Group Relief' which in effect confirms that the principles and practice arising out of Statement of Practice 3/98 (see **23.2 Availability of Exemption** and **Appendix B**) which applied to stamp duty group relief will be applied to SDLT with the necessary adaptations.

One aspect of the group relief article in Tax Bulletin No 70 is highly misleading. Paragraphs 23 and 24 of the article are as follows:

> 23. The statements by the Economic Secretary during debate in Parliament on the equivalent stamp duty provision in Finance Act 2000 are still relevant. The Economic Secretary said:

> "I have received representations expressing concern about the blocking of relief for transfers from the company about to leave the group to another group member – in other words, when the company leaving the group is the transferor. I am persuaded that there are commercial situations in which an asset is transferred to another group company after arrangements are in place for the transferor company to leave the group. In a sense, therefore, the asset never leaves the original group. I am willing to make a concession for such cases, which will be useful to businesses, as their legal advisers have suggested.
>
> I have some worry that it might be possible to construct avoidance devices from the concession, so I have asked the Stamp Office to monitor carefully the use of the relief. If the concession is abused, the Government will not hesitate to act swiftly."

(See Hansard 18 July 2000, column 253.)

24. The Inland Revenue will not argue that paragraph 2(1) denies group relief in cases where the transferor is to leave the group having transferred the land to other group members.

Unfortunately the extract quoted above implies that the words of the Economic Secretary apply to the version of the wording of *s 42(2), FA 1930* as actually amended by *FA 2003, s 123* on which the equivalent SDLT provision is based. This wording focuses solely on the transferee leaving the group and not either the transferee or the transferor. In reality the words of the Economic Secretary were spoken in relation to the unamended version of the Finance Bill 2000 which was then before the house on 18 July 2000, (that is the bill as amended in Standing Committee H and printed on 29 June 2000). In that version of the bill, the proposed amendment to *FA 1930, s 42* was contained in cl 122, the relevant parts of which read (with author's emphasis):

122(1)Amend section 42 of the Finance Act 1930 as follows.

(2) In subsection (2B) (body to be parent of another if beneficial owner of 75% of ordinary share capital) after "if at that time the first body" insert "(a)" and at the end of the subsection add—

> "(b) is beneficially entitled to not less than 75 per cent of any profits available for distribution to equity holders of the second body; and
>
> (c) would be beneficially entitled to not less than 75 per cent of any assets of the second body available for distribution to its equity holders on a winding-up;
>
> but this subsection is subject to subsection (2C).".

(3) After subsection (2B) insert—

> "(2C) A body corporate shall not be regarded for the purposes of this section as the parent of another body corporate at a particular time if at that time arrangements are in existence by virtue of which at that or some later time any person has or could obtain, or any persons together have or could obtain, control of *one of the bodies but not of the other*.".

Under this proposed wording, arrangements for a change in control of either the purchaser or the vendor would have been caught. It was that version of the wording that the Economic Secretary was referring to when he uttered the words in Hansard 18 July Column 253 quoted above.

As a consequence of the 'concession' referred to by the Economic Secretary, the Government agreed amendments to the wording of cl 122 quoted above in which the wording in cl 122(3) was removed including new s 42(2C) and the result is the present wording in *s 42(2), FA 1930* (on which *FA 2003, Sch 7 para 2(1)* is based) which reads (author's emphasis):

> (2) This section applies to any instrument as respects which it is shown to the satisfaction of the Commissioners that—
>
> (a) the effect of the instrument is to convey or transfer a beneficial interest in property from one body corporate ("the transferor") to another ("the transferee"), and
>
> (b) the bodies in question are associated at the time the instrument is executed
>
> unless at the time the instrument is executed arrangements are in existence by virtue of which at that or some later time any person has or could obtain, or any persons together have or could obtain, control of *the transferee but not of the transferor*.

This is important because HMRC Stamp Taxes has been known to argue that when a company owning a target property has been sold by a vendor group to the purchaser group and the target property is transferred to another company in the purchaser group and the transferor company immediately transferred back to the vendor group, SDLT group relief is disallowed under *FA 2000, Sch 7, para 2(1)*. HMRC has based its argument on the words of the Economic Secretary quoted in para 23 of Tax Bulletin No 70 and argued that in the context of tax avoidance *FA 2000, Sch 7, para 2(1)* blocks SDLT group relief in this situation. However, once the legislative history of the relevant provision is examined it is apparent that HMRC's argument is based on an earlier version of the legislation that would have caught arrangements for a change of control of the transferor but which was expressly rejected by Parliament.

This first type of restriction on group relief does not apply to arrangements entered into with a view to an acquisition of shares to which exemption from stamp duty under *FA 1986, s 75* (see **34.2 Reconstructions**) will apply and as a result of which the purchaser will be a member of the same group as the acquiring company. [*FA 2003, Sch 7, para 2(1)*]. It is not clear how this exception will be policed in terms of what degree of likelihood is required at the time of the intra-group transfer so that the subsequent loss of control of the purchaser will indeed take the form of an acquisition of shares to which *FA 1986, s 75* applies (and what if anything will be done if exemption under that provision turns out not to be available). It is also unclear as to whether this exception will operate where the arrangements for subsequent loss of control of the purchaser could take the form of a *FA 1986, s 75* reconstruction but might alternatively take the form of some other transaction not qualifying for relief.

Second, group relief is not available if the transaction is effected in pursuance of, or in connection with, arrangements under which the consideration (or any part of it) is to be provided or received directly or indirectly by a person other than a group company. [*FA 2003, Sch 7, para 2(2)(a)*].

Third, group relief is not available if the transaction is effected in pursuance of, or in connection with, arrangements under which the vendor and the purchaser are to cease to be members of the same group by reason of the purchaser ceasing to be a 75% subsidiary of the vendor or a third company. [*FA 2003, Sch 7, para 2 (2)(b)*]. (This restriction does not apply to transfers in connection with the demutualisation of insurance companies: *FA 2003, Sch 7, para 2(3A)*.)

Fourth, SDLT group relief will be denied if the transaction is:

(a) not effected for bona fide commercial reasons; or
(b) forms part of arrangements of which the main purpose, or one of the main purposes, is the avoidance of liability to tax. [See *FA 2003, Sch 7, para 2(4A)* inserted by *F(No 2)A 2005, Sch 10, para 19*].

The thrust of judicial decisions based upon very similar anti-avoidance wording in *CTA 2010, s 731* and its predecessors in *TA 1988, s 703* ,*TA 1970, s 460* and *FA 1960, s 28*, suggest that this measure may not have a great impact on transactions that when looked at in the round are carried out for commercial reasons, but happen to have tax planning measures built into them. On the other hand, purely tax driven transactions will be at risk. The leading cases (see for example *IRC v Brebner* [1967] 43 TC 705) show that HMRC is not entitled to isolate particular steps in a transaction that were admittedly inserted to give tax efficiency and apply the above tests to that step only. Assuming that the courts follow precedent in this area, then a reading of the cases leads to the tentative conclusion that intra-group property transfers that are carried out as a preparatory step to a larger commercial restructuring or sale out of the group should continue to qualify for group relief (subject of course to the existing anti-avoidance rules) as long as the wider transaction is not tax driven. This view is reinforced by the helpful comments of the Economic Secretary to the Treasury in the debate on this measure:

> It is time to ensure that group relief is restricted to proper commercial transactions where tax avoidance is not the, or a, main purpose. I recognise that this measure has caused genuine concern among those who are not engaged in tax avoidance, on the grounds that it will stop legitimate commercial transactions. I can reassure the Committee that we do not accept that that will be the effect of the measure, which will only stop claims to group relief where tax avoidance is the, or a, main purpose. The fact that a transaction gives rise to a tax benefit does not mean that avoidance is the main purpose.
>
> I was asked earlier for the definition of the term "bona fide". Successive Governments have used that term and most Committee members, and practitioners, understand its meaning to be "genuine", which is a pretty straightforward understanding.
>
> The fact that a transaction gives rise to a tax benefit does not mean that avoidance is its main purpose.
>
> (Standing Committee B, 30 June 2005, Col 299).

It is noteworthy that the existing statutory provisions on which the wording of this provision is based have specific written clearance procedures, whereas the new SDLT provision has none. [See *CTA 2010, s 748* and *TCGA 1992, s 137*].

HMRC published guidance on 10 February 2006 setting out a list of examples where they accept that group relief is not denied by this measure (reproduced in **Appendix G**). The list is as follows:

(1) The transfer of a property to a group company having in mind the possibility that shares in that company might be sold more than three years after the date of transfer.

(2) The transfer of a property to a group company having in mind the possibility that shares in that company might be sold within three years of the date of transfer, with a consequent claw back of group relief, in order that any increase in value of the property after the intra-group transfer might be sheltered from SDLT.
(3) The transfer of property to a group company having in mind the possibility that either (1) or (2) might occur.
(4) The transfer of a property to a group company prior to the sale of shares in the transferor company, in order that the property should not pass to the purchaser of the shares.
(5) The transfer of property to a group company in order that commercially generated rental income may be matched with commercially generated losses from a Schedule A business.
(6) The transfer of property to a group company in order that commercially generated chargeable gains may be matched with commercially generated allowable losses.
(7) The transfer of property to a non-resident group company in the knowledge that future appreciation or depreciation in value will be outside the scope of corporation tax on chargeable gains.
(8) Transactions undertaken as part of a normal commercial securitisation.
(9) The transfer of the freehold reversion in a property to a group lessee in order to merge the freehold and the lease, and thus prevent the lease being subject to the wasting assets rules as respects corporation tax on chargeable gains.

A further example has since been added to this list in HMRC's SDLT Manual at 23040 — the transfer of property to a group company in order that the interest payable on borrowings from a commercial lender on ordinary commercial terms may be set against commercially generated rental income. It is thought that HMRC will also accept that intra-group loans can also be included if they are on commercial terms.

The thrust of this list suggests that that there will often be tax avoidance motives for a transfer without these necessarily preventing the availability of group relief. The rather surprising example at (7) above suggests that an obvious and overt UK tax avoidance motive does not rule out group relief and can be acceptable. It appears that this list lowers the bar for taxpayers in relation to this particular provision.

Group relief: Withdrawal and claw-back of relief

[6.6] Where a land transaction is exempt from SDLT because of group relief and the purchaser ceases to be a member of the same group of companies as the vendor within the three years beginning with the effective date (see **2.3 CONTRACTS, CONVEYANCES AND 'EFFECTIVE DATE'**) of the transaction (or at any time in pursuance of arrangements made before the end of that period), the group relief is withdrawn if at the time the purchaser leaves the group, it or a 'relevant associated company' holds the chargeable interest that was originally acquired (or is derived from it). [*FA 2003, Sch 7, para 3(1)*]. The relief is not withdrawn if the chargeable interest was subsequently reacquired at market value under a chargeable transaction for which group relief was available but was not claimed.

A 'relevant associated company' means a company that is a member of the same group as the purchaser immediately before the purchaser leaves the vendor's group and ceases to be a member of the vendor's group *in consequence of the purchaser so ceasing*. [*FA 2003, Sch 7, para 3(4)*].

The inclusion of relevant associated companies is to prevent the initial intra-group property transfer on which group relief was claimed escaping claw-back by the simple device of subsequently transferring the property to a third group company which would then leave the group with the purchaser (in a sub-group by themselves), a technique known as the 'double drop-down'. However, for the third company to be a 'relevant associated company' it must cease to be a member of the same group as the vendor *in consequence of the purchaser so ceasing*. It is arguable that in the following situations the third company (B Ltd) does not cease to be a member of the vendor's group *in consequence of the purchaser so ceasing* and so claw-back does not arise:

Example 1

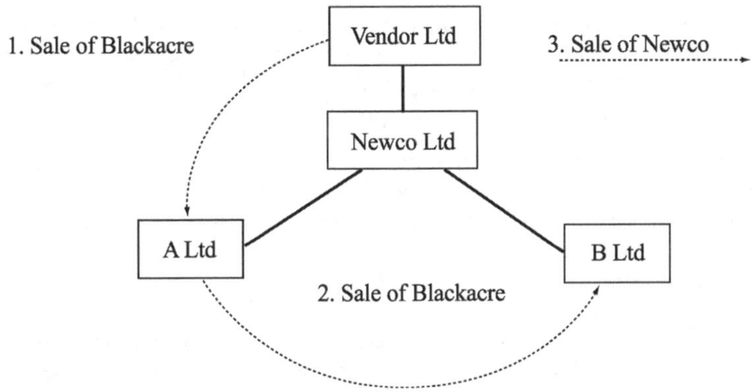

Example 2

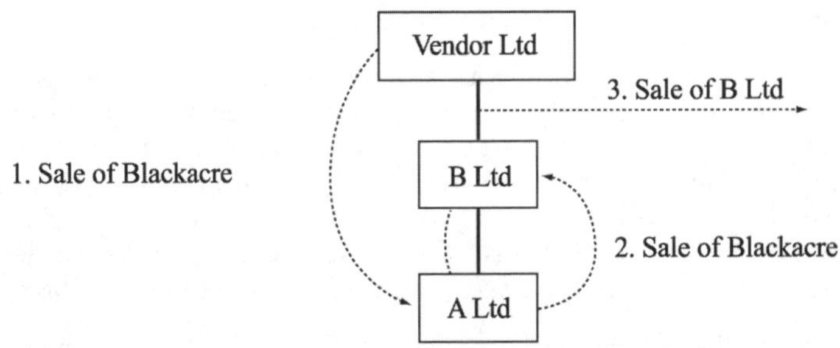

It is possible however that if a court were required to decide the matter policy considerations might dictate that the expression '*in consequence of*' was given a wide meaning equivalent to '*in concurrence with*' sufficient to bring the first and possibly the second examples above within the scope of the claw-back provisions. Although such an interpretation would stretch the language of the provision a court may be prepared to do so in order to achieve what it perceives to be the intention of Parliament in the face of what is pure tax avoidance and because there appears to be no compelling policy reason not to, other than the general concern about courts rewriting statutory wording.

However, rather than risk-testing the matter in the courts, HMRC has sought to reinforce the claw-back charge with a further anti-avoidance provision that concentrates on a change in control of the purchaser. [*FA 2003, Sch 7, para 4A*, inserted by *F(No 2)A 2005, Sch 10, para 6*]. This provision applies where:

(1) the purchaser claims group relief for a transaction ('the relevant transaction') and within three years beginning with the effective date of the relevant transaction (or at any time in pursuance of arrangements made before the end of that period);
(2) there is a change in control of the purchaser (within *CTA 2010, ss 450 and 451*); and
(3) group relief is not otherwise withdrawn.

In such a case, it is then necessary to identify the earliest 'previous transaction'. A previous transaction is one where:

(1) group relief, reconstruction relief or acquisition relief was claimed;
(2) the effective date of that transaction was within the last three years; and
(3) the chargeable interest acquired under the relevant transaction is essentially the same as that acquired under the previous transaction.

The claw-back provisions then have effect as if the vendor in the earliest previous transaction was also the vendor in the relevant transaction. In the two situations illustrated above and assuming that the events all occur within three years of each other, the change in control of B Ltd out of Vendor Ltd would result in the vendor in the sale of Blackacre to B Ltd being taken to have been Vendor Ltd rather than A Ltd, thus giving rise to the claw-back of group relief on the transfer of Blackacre to B Ltd. Unfortunately, this provision is capable of giving rise to multiple claw-back charges where there have been more than two successive transfers within three years. It appears that this possibility is unintended, but it is not yet known whether HMRC understands that this is the case and if so what its approach will be.

Group relief is not withdrawn in four situations. First, where the purchaser leaves the vendor's group because the vendor itself leaves the group. The vendor is regarded as leaving the group if the purchaser and the vendor cease to be members of the same group because of a transaction relating to shares in either the vendor or another company that is above the vendor in the group structure and as a result of the transaction ceases to be a member of the same group as the purchaser. [*FA 2003, Sch 7, para 4ZA* inserted by *FA 2008, s 96*].

The question of whether the purchaser could then be sold out of the original group within 3 years of the transaction free of claw-back once the vendor company had left the group had not been tested in the courts. However, for transactions on or after 13 March 2008, this question has been partly answered by *FA 2003, Sch 7 para 4ZA(4)* which provides that a change in control of the purchaser after the vendor leaves the group is deemed to be the purchaser leaving the same group as the vendor for the purposes of claw-back. There are detailed provisions defining what constitutes a change in the control of the purchaser for this purpose — see *FA 2003, Sch 7 para 4ZA(5)–(8)*. It should be noted that these change of control provisions are very wide and catch not only a sale of the purchaser itself out of the group but also a winding-up of the purchaser (subject to the second exception discussed below where the purchaser is above the vendor in the group), or a sale of the purchaser's parent company (indirect changes of control of the purchaser are included). The insertion of a new company above the purchaser in a group will not give rise to a change in control for claw-back purposes as long as there is no overall change in control.

Unfortunately, it is not entirely clear from the drafting of *FA 2003, Sch 7 para 4ZA* whether the winding-up of the vendor followed by a change in control of the purchaser results in claw-back. In principle, it seems that claw-back should not arise because of the exception from claw-back in *FA 2003, Sch 7 para 4(4)* discussed in the next paragraph. Indeed, HMRC has confirmed that 'paragraph 4ZA will not normally apply' in this situation in an article published on 26 November 2008 entitled 'Stamp Duty Land Tax: Group Relief – Paragraph 4ZA of Schedule 7 FA 2003' (see **APPENDIX G** for the full text of this article). Although the draftsman has failed to explicitly clarify the relationship between *FA 2003, Sch 7 paras 4(4)* (discussed below) and *4ZA(4)*, it seems fairly clear that because the list of claw-back provisions to which *FA 2003, Sch 7 para 4ZA(4)* expressly applies does not include *FA 2003, Sch 7 para 4*, then the latter provision is not subject to the former.

The second case is where the purchaser ceases to be a member of the same group as the vendor by reason of the winding up of the vendor or another company that is above the vendor in the group structure. [*FA 2003, Sch 7, para 4(4)*]. There seems to be nothing in the legislation that prevents the purchaser from being '*another company that is above the vendor in the group structure*' for this purpose and hence the winding up of the purchaser pursuant to a scheme under *Insolvency Act 1986, s 110* and the distribution of its assets qualifying for exemption under reconstruction relief in *FA 2003, Sch 7, para 7(1)* should not give rise to a withdrawal of group relief. It appears that HMRC may now agree with this interpretation because in the article of 26 November 2008 referred to above HMRC states that 'A company above the vendor in the group structure can be the purchaser'.

The third case is where there is an acquisition of shares by another company to which the exemption in *FA 1986, s 75* applies. [*FA 2003, Sch 7, para 4(5)* and see **34.2 RECONSTRUCTIONS**]. However, in such cases claw-back can still apply if the purchaser leaves the same group as the acquiring company within three years of the original land transaction (or at any time in pursuance of arrangements made before the end of that period) and it or a 'relevant associated company' own the chargeable interest. [*FA 2003, Sch 7, para 4(6), (7)*]. The fourth case is where the purchaser ceases to be a member of the vendor's group in connection with the demutualisation of insurance companies and the purchaser is immediately after the transfer of the vendor's business to another company, a member of the same group as the acquiring company: see *FA 1997, s 96* and *FA 2003, Sch 7 para 4(6A)*.

Where the tax is chargeable because group relief has been withdrawn as above and tax having been finally determined is not paid within six months after it became payable, it may be recovered from the vendor, any company that at any 'relevant time' was a member of the same group as the purchaser and above it in the group structure, or any person who at any 'relevant time' was a controlling director of the purchaser or of a company having control of the purchaser. [*FA 2003, Sch 7, para 5(1), (2)*]. 'Relevant time' means any time between the 'effective date' (see **2.3 CONTRACTS, CONVEYANCES AND 'EFFECTIVE DATE'**) of the land transaction and the purchaser ceasing to be a member of the same group as the vendor. [*FA 2003, Sch 7, para 5(3)(a)*]. In order to recover the tax HMRC must serve a notice on the relevant person stating the amount of tax to be paid and the notice must be served before the end of three years from the date of the final determination of the tax payable. [*FA 2003, Sch 7, para 6(1), (2)*]. The notice is treated as if it were a notice of assessment of SDLT (see **7.1 RETURNS**) and interest runs accordingly on any tax remaining unpaid following the issue of the notice. A person who has paid tax pursuant to such a notice has a statutory right to recovery from the purchaser although this is likely to be worth little in the circumstances of the purchaser having originally failed to pay. [*FA 2003, Sch 7, para 6(5)*].

Where the tax is chargeable the amount will be the tax that would have been originally chargeable if the chargeable consideration had been equal to the market value of the chargeable interest transferred, or if the acquisition was the grant of a lease at a rent, that rent. [*FA 2003, Sch 7, para 3(2)*].

Reconstruction relief

[6.7] An exemption from SDLT is available for land transactions entered into in connection with the acquisition by a company ('the acquiring company') of the whole or part of the undertaking of another company ('the target company') on a reconstruction of the target company. [*FA 2003, Sch 7, para 7(1)*].

In stamp duty, IR Stamp Taxes did not accept the wider interpretation of 'reconstruction' used for other taxes such as in Statement of Practice 5/85 which included a partition and its statutory enactment in *TCGA 1992, Sch 5AA*. It was, however, stated by the Government during the debates on the Finance Bill 2002 that this restrictive interpretation would be reconsidered for the new SDLT legislation (House of Commons Official Report, Standing Committee F, Tuesday 21 May 2002 (Morning) cols. 163 and 164). In the event this restrictive interpretation was confirmed in the November 2009 Stamp Taxes Bulletin by the addition of SDLTM 23210 to HMRC's SDLT Manual. Consequently a 'scheme for the reconstruction of the target company' requires that there is a transfer of an undertaking or part from an existing company to a new company with substantially the same membership as the old company and that undertaking continues substantially unaltered (see *Brooklands Selangor Holdings Ltd v IRC* [1970] 2 All ER 76; *Baytrust Holdings Ltd v IRC* [1971] 3 All ER 76; *IRC v Kent Process Control Ltd* [1989] STC 245; *Swithland Investments Ltd v IRC* [1990] STC 448). The liquidation of the target company is not essential. A scheme of amalgamation connotes the merging of two or more businesses with ownership through shareholdings remaining substantially the same and is therefore quite different from a scheme of reconstruction. Relief under *FA 2003, Sch 7, para 1* is limited to schemes of reconstruction (see *Crane Frueharf Ltd v IRC* [1975] 1 All ER 429; *Ufitec Group Ltd v IRC* [1977] STC 363).

It is noteworthy, however, that the requirement in the equivalent stamp duty reconstruction relief in *FA 1986, s 75(4)* that the registered office of the acquiring company is in the UK is not a requirement for the availability of the SDLT exemption. However, IR Stamp Taxes announced on 25 July 2005 that it will accept stamp duty claims under FA 1986, *ss 75–77* for acquisitions by a company anywhere in the European Economic Area.

The availability of the exemption is subject to meeting each of three conditions. The first condition is that the consideration for the acquisition consists wholly or partly of the issue of non-redeemable shares in the acquiring company to all the shareholders of the target company. The only other permitted consideration is the assumption or discharge by the acquiring company of the liabilities of the target company. [*FA 2003, Sch 7, para 7(2), (3)*].

The second condition is that after the acquisition has been made:

(1) each shareholder of each of the companies is a shareholder of the other; and
(2) the proportion of shares of one of the companies held by any shareholder is the same, or is nearly as may be the same, as the proportion of shares of the other company held by that shareholder. [*FA 2003, Sch 7, para 7(4)*].

If immediately before the acquisition either the target company or the acquiring company holds any of their own shares, such shares are treated as cancelled so that neither company is to be treated as a shareholder in itself. [*FA 2003, Sch 7, para 7(5A)*].

The third condition is that the acquisition is effected for bona fide commercial reasons and does not form part of a scheme or arrangement of which the main purpose, or one of the main purposes, is the avoidance of liability to stamp duty, income tax, corporation tax, capital gains tax or SDLT. [*FA 2003, Sch 7, para 5*].

The fact that a transaction has been structured in order to claim this exemption is not of itself evidence of such a scheme or arrangement since one is taking advantage of a statutory exemption from tax.

Acquisition relief

[6.8] There is also relief known as 'acquisition relief' for a land transaction entered into as part of the acquisition of an undertaking or part of an undertaking of another company in exchange for the issue of shares. [*FA 2003, Sch 7, para 8(1)*]. This relief reduces the rate of stamp duty land tax to 0.5%. The availability of this relief is subject to four conditions. First, the consideration for the acquisition must consist wholly or partly of the issue of non-redeemable shares in the acquiring company to the target company or to all or any of the target company's shareholders. Where the consideration does not consist wholly of the issue of shares as above, the rest of the consideration must consist wholly of either or both of cash not exceeding 10% of the nominal value of the shares issued or the assumption or discharge by the acquiring company of liabilities of the target company. [*FA 2003, Sch 7, para 8(2), (3)*]. The second condition is that the acquiring company is not 'associated' with another company that is party to 'arrangements' with the target company relating to the shares of the acquiring company issued in connection with the transfer of the undertaking or part. [*FA 2003, Sch 7, para 8(4)*]. (This is intended to prevent the parties setting up a new company which acquires the undertaking for shares which are issued to the target company (or its shareholders), which shares are then sold to the purchaser for cash and then claiming acquisition relief to reduce the SDLT from 4% to 0.5% on the transfer of the undertaking, with the subsequent sale of the issued shares to the purchaser giving rise to stamp duty (or stamp duty reserve tax) of 0.5% or nil if a non-UK incorporated company was used.)

For this purpose companies are 'associated' if one has control of the other or both are controlled by the same person or persons, with control construed in accordance with *CTA 2010, ss 450 and 451*. [*FA 2003, Sch 7, para 5(a)*]. 'Arrangements' includes any scheme, agreement or understanding, whether or not legally enforceable. [*FA 2003, Sch 7, para 5(b)*]. Unlike the equivalent stamp duty relief in *FA 1986, s 76* (see **34.2 RECONSTRUCTIONS**), it is not a requirement that the registered office of the acquiring company be in the UK.

The third condition is that the undertaking has as its main activity the carrying on of a trade that does not consist wholly or mainly of dealing in chargeable interests. [*FA 2003, Sch 7, para 8(5A)*].

The fourth condition is that the acquisition is effected for bona fide commercial reasons and does not form part of arrangements of which the main purpose or one of the main purposes is the avoidance of tax. [*FA 2003, Sch 7, para 8(5B)*].

Acquisition relief is subject to withdrawal as described in **6.9** below.

Withdrawal of reconstruction or acquisition relief

[6.9] Except in the cases mentioned in **6.10** below, where a land transaction is exempt because of reconstruction relief (see **6.7** above) or has taken advantage of the 0.5% rate of SDLT because of acquisition relief (see **6.8** above) but control of the acquiring company changes within three years of the effective date (see **2.3 CONTRACTS, CONVEYANCES AND 'EFFECTIVE DATE'**) of the transaction (or at any time if pursuant to arrangements made within that time), the reconstruction or acquisition relief is withdrawn and tax is chargeable if at the time control of the acquiring company changes, it or a 'relevant associated company' holds the chargeable interest that was acquired (or an interest that is derived from it). The amount chargeable is the tax that would have been chargeable if the consideration had been equal to the market value of the property concerned and, if the acquisition was the grant of a lease at a rent, that rent. [*FA 2003, Sch 7, para 9(2)*, as substituted by *F(No 2)A 2005, Sch 10. para 9*]. The relief is not withdrawn where the interest has been subsequently acquired at market value under a chargeable transaction for which reconstruction or acquisition relief was available but was not claimed. [*FA 2003, Sch 7, para 9(1)*]. A 'relevant associated company' means a company that is controlled by the acquiring company immediately before control of the acquiring company changes and of which control changes in consequence of the change of control of the acquiring company. [*FA 2003, Sch, 7, para 9(4)*]. 'Arrangements' includes any scheme, agreement or understanding whether or not legally enforceable and 'control' is construed in accordance with *CTA 2010, ss 450 and 451*. [*FA 2003, Sch 7, para 9(5)(a), (b)*].

References to control of the acquiring company changing are to the company becoming controlled:

(1) by a different person;
(2) by a different number of persons; or
(3) by two or more persons, at least one of whom is not a person, or one or more persons, by whom the company was previously controlled. [*FA 2003, Sch 7, para 9(5)(c)*].

It appears that a change of control of the acquiring company caused by the death of the owner of the acquiring company with the shares passing under his will may lead to a withdrawal of the relief even if the control of the target company also passes at the same time.

It also seems that where the acquiring company is not under the control of any person at the time of the land transactions qualifying for the relief and only becomes controlled by a person or persons after the transaction, there will not be a change of control for these purposes because a change of control implies that the company was previously controlled by a person or persons.

Where reconstruction or acquisition relief is withdrawn and the amount of tax chargeable has been finally determined and remains unpaid six months after the date it became payable, the following persons may be required to pay the unpaid tax:

(1) any company that at any 'relevant time' was a member of the same group as the acquiring company and was above it in the group structure;
(2) any person who at any 'relevant time' was a controlling director of the acquiring company or a company having control of the acquiring company. [*FA 2003, Sch 7, para 12(1), (2)*].

'Relevant time' means any time between the effective date (see **2.3 CONTRACTS, CONVEYANCES AND 'EFFECTIVE DATE'**) of the transaction and the change of control causing the tax to become chargeable. [*FA 2003, Sch 7, para 12(3)*].

HMRC must serve a notice on a person within (1) or (2) above requiring him to pay within 30 days of service, and such a notice must be served with three years of the final determination of the tax chargeable. [*FA 2003, Sch 7, para 3*].

Reconstruction and acquisition relief not withdrawn

[6.10] There are five cases in which reconstruction and acquisition relief is not withdrawn despite a change of control of the acquiring company [*FA 2003, Sch 7, para, 10*]. These are where control changes:

(1) as a result of transactions in connection with divorce [*FA 2003, Sch 3, para 3(a)–(d)*];
(2) as a result of the variation of a testamentary disposition [*FA 2003, Sch 3, para 4*];
(3) as a result of a transfer of shares that is exempt from stamp duty under stamp duty group relief (see **23 ASSOCIATED COMPANIES**) (but see below);
(4) as a result of a transfer of shares to another company that is exempt from stamp duty under *FA 1986, s 77* (see **34.5 ACQUISITION OF TARGET COMPANY**) (but see below); or
(5) as a result of a loan creditor becoming, or ceasing to be, treated as having control of the company and the other persons who were previously treated as controlling the company continue to be so treated (see *CTA 2010, s 453(1) and (2)* for the meaning of 'loan creditor').

Where (3) above applies, if a company holding the shares in the acquiring company that were subject to stamp duty group relief ceases to be a member of the same group of companies as the target company within three years of the relevant land transaction (or at any time if pursuant to arrangements made within that period) and the acquiring company or a 'relevant associated company' [see *FA 2003, Sch 7, para 11(5)*] holds the chargeable interest acquired, the reconstruction or acquisition relief is withdrawn and tax is chargeable. [*FA 2003, Sch 7, para 11(1)*].

Where (4) above applies, if control of the other company changes within three years of the relevant land transaction (or at any time if pursuant to arrangements made within that period) at a time when that other company holds any of the shares transferred to it and the acquiring company or a 'relevant associated company' [*FA 2003, Sch 7, para 11(5)*] holds the chargeable interest acquired, the reconstruction or acquisition relief is withdrawn and tax is chargeable. [*FA 2003, Sch 7, para 11(2)*].

In both cases the tax chargeable is the amount that would have been chargeable if the chargeable consideration for the relevant land transaction had been equal to the market value of the chargeable interest transferred. [*FA 2003, Sch 7, para 11(3)*].

Acquisitions by charities

[6.11] A land transaction is exempt from stamp duty land tax if the purchaser is a charity provided two conditions are met. [*FA 2003, s 68 and Sch 8, para 1(1)*]. First, the purchaser must intend to hold the subject matter of the transaction for qualifying charitable purposes which are defined as either:

(1) for use in furtherance of the charitable purposes of the purchaser or another charity; or

(2) as an investment from which the profits are applied to the charitable purposes of the purchaser. [*FA 2003, Sch 8, para 1(2)*].

Where the land transaction would not be exempt because the condition above is not met, exemption is still available if the charity intends to hold the greater part of the land for qualifying charitable purposes. [*FA 2003, Sch 8, para 3*].

The second condition is that the transaction must not have been entered into for the purpose of avoiding SDLT whether by the purchaser or any other person. [*FA 2003, Sch 8, para 1(3)*]. It has been confirmed by the Government that this condition does not relate to the claiming of the exemption from SDLT by the charity itself (HC Official Report, Standing Committee B, Tuesday 10 June 2003, col. 439).

'Charity' means any body or trust established for charitable purposes only. This definition has been extended to include 'charitable trusts', that is trusts of which all the beneficiaries are charities or unit trust schemes in which all the unit holders are charities. [*FA 2003, Sch 8, para 1(4)*]. This definition is to be replaced from a date yet to be appointed by the definition of 'charity' in *FA 2010, Sch 6, para 1* and the *Charities Act 2006, s 2*. Since 6 April 2010 the charity concerned must satisfy the jurisdiction, registration and management conditions in *FA 2010, Sch 6*. Previously it was thought that this exemption applied to charities formed or established under UK law only and not to non-UK charities (*Dreyfus (Camille and Henry) Foundation Inc v IRC* [1956] AC 39) and that this limitation was unlawful to the extent that it discriminated against charities established in other member states of the EU. However, as a result of *Persche v Finanzamt Ludenscheid C-318/08* [2009] All ER (EC) 673, [2009] STC 586, ECJ (GC), in 2009, the exemption has been extended to equivalent bodies in the EU with effect from 6 April 2009 and by regulation to Norway and Iceland with effect from 6 April 2009.

The exemption must be claimed in a land transaction return. [*FA 2003, Sch 8, para 1(2)*].

The exemption will be withdrawn and tax become chargeable if within three years of the land transaction (or at any time if pursuant to arrangements made within that time), the purchaser holds the land and ceases to be established for charitable purposes only or the land is used or held by the purchaser otherwise than for qualifying charitable purposes (as defined above). [*FA 2003, Sch 8, para 1(2)*]. Where the exemption was claimed because the charity intended to hold the greater part of the land for qualifying charitable purposes, the withdrawal of the relief will also occur on any transfer of a major interest in the whole or part of the land or any grant out of the land of a lease at a premium with a low rent within the same time frame, that is not made for charitable purposes. [*FA 2003, Sch 8, para 3*]. The tax that becomes chargeable is the tax that would have been chargeable in respect of the land transaction had the exemption not been claimed. The exemption is only withdrawn if the charity still holds the land at the time of the disqualifying event, and so the withdrawal of relief will not apply to a disposal of the land itself within the three year period or if the land falls vacant within such period. A disposal to a non-charity for less than market value consideration within that period might however raise the question of whether the charity originally intended to hold the land for qualifying charitable purposes and therefore satisfied the first condition above on the acquisition of the land by the charity.

When a charity is purchasing property jointly with a non-charity purchaser and the acquisition by the charity would otherwise meet the requirements for the exemption to apply, there is no reason in principle why the interest acquired by the charity should not be exempt. HMRC does not accept however that there can be a 'partial' claim to the exemption in these circumstances and therefore seeks to deny the exemption to the purchase by the charity. Although a single land transaction return will be made under *FA 2003, s 103(3)*, box 9 of the SDLT 1 return form allows for claims to relief on only part of the property acquired.

Chapter 7

Returns, Liability and Compliance

Returns

[7.1] A major difference between stamp duty on land and SDLT is the requirement in the latter tax to deliver a tax return to HMRC. Every 'notifiable transaction' must be reported by delivery of a land transaction return to HMRC before the end of 30 days after the 'effective date' (see **2.3 Contracts, Conveyances and 'Effective Date'**) of the transaction. [*FA 2003, s 76(1)*]. A land transaction return must include a self-assessment of the tax chargeable. However, the return need not be accompanied by payment of that amount of tax due, although the tax is payable before the end of 30 days after the 'effective date'. [*FA 2003, s 76(3)*]. The return must be signed by the purchaser (or each of them) or by someone holding a written power of attorney signed by an individual purchaser or by an authorised agent of an individual.

A 'notifiable transaction' is:

(1) an acquisition of a major interest in land that does not fall within one or more of the exceptions listed in (a)–(f) below;
(2) an acquisition of a chargeable interest other than a major interest in land where SDLT is chargeable at the rate of 1% or higher or would be so chargeable but for a relief;
(3) a land transaction that a person is deemed to have entered into under *FA 2003, s 44A(3)* see **2.2 Land Transactions**;
(4) a notional land transaction under *FA 2003, s 75A* see **11 General Statutory Anti-Avoidance Rule.**

[*FA 2003, s 77* as inserted by *FA 2008, s 94* for transactions with an effective date on or after 12 March 2008].

References to a 'relief' above do not include any exemption under *FA 2003, Sch 3*.

The exceptions referred to in (1) above are:

(a) an acquisition which is exempt under *FA 2003, Sch 3* other than an acquisition which is exempt by virtue of any regulations made under *para 5* of that Schedule;
(b) an acquisition (other than the grant, assignment or surrender of a lease) where the chargeable consideration for that acquisition, together with any linked transaction, is less than £40,000;
(c) the grant of a lease for a term of 7 years or more where any chargeable consideration other than rent is less than £40,000 and the relevant rent is less than £1,000;

(d) the assignment or surrender of a lease where the lease was originally granted for a term of 7 years or more and the chargeable consideration for the assignment or surrender is less than £40,000;
(e) the grant of a lease for a term of less than 7 years where the chargeable consideration does not exceed the 'zero-rate threshold'; and
(f) the assignment or surrender of a lease where the lease was originally granted for a term of less than 7 years and the chargeable consideration does not exceed the 'zero-rate threshold'.

[*FA 2003, s 77A* inserted by *FA 2008, s 94* and varied by *SI 2008/2338*].

Chargeable consideration does not exceed the 'zero-rate threshold' if it does not consist of or include any amount in respect of which tax is chargeable at a rate of 1% or higher or any amount in respect of which tax would be so chargeable but for a relief (excluding any exemption under *FA 2003, Sch 3*).

No account is to be taken for the purposes of the requirement to notify of the provisions of *FA 2003, Sch 6* to the effect that consideration is not 'chargeable consideration' in relation to acquisitions of land qualifying for disadvantaged areas relief.

In general, therefore, acquisitions of major interests in land including the grant of leases which are not exempt are notifiable where the chargeable consideration is £40,000 or more including acquisitions of residential property benefiting from the temporary increase in the SDLT threshold to £175,000 until 31 December 2009 (see **4.1 Amount of Tax Chargeable**). Interests other than major interests are notifiable only if the tax is charged at the 1% rate or higher or would be chargeable but for a relief.

A 'major interest' in land is defined as:

(1) (in England and Wales) an estate in fee simple absolute (freehold) or a term of years absolute (leasehold) whether in law or in equity;
(2) (in Scotland) the interest of an owner of land or the tenant's right over or interest in a property subject to a lease; and
(3) (in Northern Ireland) any freehold or leasehold estate whether in law or in equity. [*FA 2003, s 117*].

There are detailed rules relating to returns, enquiries, assessments and appeals in *FA 2003, Sch 10, FA 2007, Sch 24* and *FA 2008, Sch 36* and the following is a summary of the main provisions:

(1) A land transaction return must be in the prescribed form. Since 4 July 2011, the main land transaction return has required a range of unique identifiers for the main purchaser and not just an individual's national insurance number but also date of birth, VAT registration, company or partnership unique tax reference number or overseas equivalent: *SI 2011/455* amending the *Stamp Duty Land Tax (Administration) Regulations SI 2003/2837* [*FA 2003, Sch 10, paras 1, 2*].
(2) Failure to deliver a land transaction return by the filing date give rise to a flat rate penalty of £100 (if the return is delivered within three months after the filing date) and £200 in any other case plus (in the case of a 'chargeable transaction') where the return is not delivered within 12 months of the filing date, a tax-related penalty not exceeding the tax

chargeable (the filing date is the last day of the period within which the return must be delivered). [*FA 2003, Sch 10, paras 2, 3, 4*, and 'chargeable transaction' is a transaction that is not exempt from SDLT: *FA 2003, s 49*]. Under *FA 2003, s97(2)* reasonable excuse is a defence against the imposition of a penalty. In the absence of evidence that a return had been posted, it was not a reasonable excuse to argue that it must have been lost in the post or elsewhere:*Stephen Paviser* [2010] TC 00725; reliance by a lay client on her solicitor to file the return in time can be a reasonable excuse where the solicitor fails to file on time: *Carolyn Browne* [2010] TC00754 and [2011][SFTD 67; loss of a return in the post followed by prompt action when the SDLT 5 certificate was not received from HMRC and the filing of a new return can be a reasonable excuse: *Runham and Another* [2011] TC00933; receipt by HMRC of the covering letter enclosing a return and a cheque for the SDLT where HMRC say that they did not receive the actual return until 18 days later could give rise to a presumption that a valid return had been enclosed with the letter so that no penalty would be done: *A N Pericleous* [2011] TC00930; where a single return is filed by the purchaser of both the freehold and leasehold titles to property under a single contract showing the same vendor for both freehold and leasehold interests when in fact there were different vendors the fact that a correcting return is subsequently filed does not mean that the purchaser failed to deliver a return in respect of both titles by the due date: *Stuart William Broughall* [2011] TC01062. A lack of knowledge of the requirement to file an SDLT return is not a reasonable excuse within *FA 2003, s 97(2)* for failing to file a return and a penalty can be charged: *Ryan v Revenue & Customs Comrs* [2010] UKFTT 309 (TC) TC00596 (6 July 2010, unreported).

(3) A purchaser may amend a land transaction return given by him by notice to HMRC normally within 12 months of the filing date. [*FA 2003, Sch 10, para 6*].

(4) HMRC may by notice to the purchaser amend a land transaction return so as to correct obvious errors or omissions whether errors of principle, arithmetical mistakes or otherwise within nine months of the day the return was delivered or the amended return was made; the purchaser may reject the correction by amending the return or if after the period during which he may amend the return but within three months of the notice of correction, give notice rejecting the correction. [*FA 2003, Sch 10, para 7*].

(5) A penalty arises in the case of deliberate or careless inaccuracy in the SDLT return which leads to an understatement of the SDLT liability; the amount of the penalty varies from 30% of the additional tax due for carelessness through to 100% for deliberate and concealed action; there is also a penalty of 30% of the additional tax due where an assessment is issued that understates the SDLT liability and reasonable steps to notify HMRC of the underassessment are not taken within 30 days of the assessment. These penalties have applied from 1 April 2010 [*FA 2007, Sch 24, paras 1, 2, 3 and 4*]. If a return is inaccurate because of a mistake or failure to take reasonable care by the taxpayer's professional adviser, a penalty will not be chargeable if the taxpayer took

reasonable care such as appointing a competent adviser, supplying all relevant information or checking the return as far as they could: *FA 2007 Sch 24 para 18(3)* and HMRC's 'Briefing on new tax penalties — FAQs' issued on 14 December, 2010, Q20 (reproduced in **APPENDIX G**).

(6) A purchaser required to deliver a return must keep sufficient records preserved for six years after the effective date of the transaction or until any later date on which any enquiry into the return is completed, or HMRC no longer has power to enquire into the return. [*FA 2003, Sch 10, para 9*].

(7) There are detailed powers for HMRC to conduct an enquiry into a return generally within nine months of the filing date. [*FA 2003, Sch 10, Part 3*]. SDLT was brought within HMRC's new enquiry powers in *FA 2008, Sch 36* with effect from 1 April 2010. Under this new regime HMRC have very wide powers to issue an information notice which requires a taxpayer to provide information or documents 'if the information or document is reasonably required for the purpose of checking the taxpayers' tax position'. [*FA 2008, Sch 36, para 1*]; there are also powers to obtain information and documents from third parties and to inspect property and premises. There are few time limits within *Schedule 36* itself. For example, there is a general restriction which means that a person does not have to produce a document where the whole of it originates more than six years before the date of the notice requiring production, but this time limit can be overridden by an authorised officer of HMRC. [*FA 2008, Sch 36, para 20*]. Also, an information notice may not be given for the purpose of checking the tax position of a deceased person more than four years after the death. [*FA 2008, Sch 36, para 22*]. In the absence of any real time limits in the Schedule itself, the taxpayer will have to fall back on the general time limits (and restrictions) for raising assessments in relation to whichever tax may be relevant to an enquiry. In SDLT these will be the usual time limits under *FA 2003, Sch 10, para 31* (see (9) below). That is to say, four years generally and six years for carelessness and 20 years for deliberate error. The restrictions on issuing assessments in *FA 2003, Sch 10, para 30* have also been retained so that the making of a *Veltema* disclosure (see **7.3B** below) should in principle prevent the issuing of a 'discovery' assessment following the expiry of the nine-month enquiry window (except of course in cases of negligence or fraud). HMRC accept that where it is out of time to open an enquiry (or if relevant, issue a discovery assessment) so that requiring information could not affect a person's tax position then it would not be reasonable to require it: see CH21620.

(8) HMRC has the power to make a determination of the tax payable if no return is delivered by the filing date, within four years of the effective date of the transaction. [*FA 2003, Sch 10, Part 4*].

(9) HMRC has the power to issue a discovery assessment for any tax that ought to have been assessed, or for an assessment that is or has become insufficient, where a relief given is or has become excessive or where tax has been repaid that ought not to have been repaid; generally such an assessment may not be made more than four years after the effective date of the transaction, but this is increased to six years for carelessness

and 20 years in the case of a loss of tax: (a) brought about deliberately by the taxpayer; (b) attributable to a failure to deliver a return; or (c) attributable to a failure to comply with a with a requirement to notify a SDLT avoidance scheme which might be disclosed (see **10 DISCLOSURE OF SDLT AVOIDANCE SCHEMES**). [*FA 2003, Sch 10, Part 5* and see **7.3B 'DISCOVERY ASSESSMENTS' AND FINALITY**].

(10) A mistake in a return leading to excessive tax may be corrected by giving notice of such a claim to HMRC within four years of the effective date of the transaction, and such repayment will be made as is reasonable and just. No repayment shall be given however if the return was made on the basis of or in accordance with the practice generally prevailing at the time it was made or in respect of a mistake in a claim or election included in the return. [*FA 2003, Sch 10, Part 6*].

(11) There are detailed rules governing the right to bring an appeal relating to an assessment before the tribunal including a facility to apply for postponement of payment of tax and internal HMRC review of the matter. [*FA 2003, Sch 10*, as amended by the *Transfer of Tribunal Functions and Revenue and Customs Appeals Order 2009* (SI 2009/56)].

(12) Where a later transaction that is linked to an earlier transaction results in the earlier transaction becoming notifiable or liable to tax or additional tax, a return must be delivered within 30 days of the later transaction. Payment of the tax due must also be made within 30 days of the later transaction. A return must also be made in respect of the later transaction, and tax paid in respect of that. [*FA 2003, s 81A*].

(13) Detailed provision has been made for the making of claims that are not made in a return. [*FA 2003, s 82A and Sch 11A*].

Where the chargeable consideration for a land transaction was contingent, uncertain or unascertained and the contingency occurs (or it becomes clear that it will not occur) or any amount or instalment of uncertain or unascertained consideration becomes ascertained, a further return must be made within 30 days. Payment of the tax (or any further tax) payable is also due within 30 days. If the effect of the new information is that less tax is payable than has already been paid, a purchaser may claim repayment of the overpaid tax together with interest as from the date of payment of the tax by the purchaser. [*FA 2003, s 80* and see **3.2 CONTINGENT, UNCERTAIN OR UNASCERTAINED CONSIDERATION AND OVERAGE**].

Where either group relief, reconstruction or acquisition relief or charities relief is withdrawn the purchaser must deliver a further return within 30 days after the occurrence of the disqualifying event. Payment of the tax chargeable must also be made within the 30 days. [*FA 2003, s 81* and see **6.6 GROUP RELIEF: WITHDRAWAL AND CLAWBACK OF RELIEF**, **6.9 WITHDRAWAL OF RECONSTRUCTION OR ACQUISITION RELIEF** and **6.11 ACQUISITIONS BY CHARITIES**].

HMRC may treat a return as not having been delivered or a document as not having been provided where it has been lost or destroyed or been so defaced or destroyed as to be illegible or otherwise useless. In such cases HMRC may proceed as if the return or document had not been made or delivered, but any tax paid in respect of the transaction will reduce any further tax charged or give rise to a repayment as appropriate. [*FA 2003, s 82*].

Although any assessment, determination or notice must be in the prescribed form it will not be ineffective for want of form or by reason of any mistake, defect or omission in it if it substantially conforms with the specified requirements and its intended effect is reasonably ascertainable by the person to whom it is directed. Any mistake as to the name of the person liable or the amount of tax charged will not affect the validity of the assessment or determination, nor will any variance between the notice of assessment or determination and the assessment or determination itself. [*FA 2003, s 83*]. Delivery and service of documents is regulated by *FA 2003, s 84*. A notice of enquiry into a land transaction return that was accompanied by a covering letter from HMRC which wrongly stated that HMRC intended to make enquiries into 'your self-certificate' did not render the notice of enquiry ineffective, by virtue of *FA 2003, s83(2)*: *Coolatinney Developments Limited v Commissioners of Revenue and Customs* [2011] TC011/6.

Where the taxpayers did not receive the notice of enquiry but was made aware of it by way of copies sent to their agent who then informed them and sent copies to them within the enquiry period, the notice was valid: *Weber and Weber v Commissioners of Revenue and Customs* [2011] TC01290. In this case the judge Miss Blewitt remarked that it was for the taxpayer to prove that the notices were not received given that the *Interpretation Act 1978 s7* provides that service would be deemed effective 'unless the contrary is proved'. However the judge also said that it was difficult to envisage a situation in which independent or documentary evidence would be available to prove this negative unless the notices were sent by recorded delivery.

The return must be signed by the purchaser (or each of them or someone holding a written power of attorney signed by the individual purchaser or by an authorised agent of the individual). [*FA 2003, s 81B and Sch 10, paras 1(1)(c) and 1A*].

Since 13 July 2005, a land transaction return may be delivered using the internet, provided that the terms and conditions on the website of HM Revenue and Customs for the Stamp Taxes Online Land Transaction Return are observed (see the *Stamp Duty Land Tax (Electronic Communications) Regulations SI 2005 No 844*).

Registration of land transactions and certificates

[7.2] Except for sub-sales, assignments of agreements for lease, agreements for lease which are substantially performed prior to grant of the lease, certain lease variations and contracts caught by *FA 2003, s 44A* (see **2.2. LAND TRANSACTIONS**), a notifiable land transaction must not be registered at the Land Registry unless there is produced with the application to register a certificate of compliance. The certificate must be a certificate by HMRC that a land transaction return has been delivered in respect of the transaction (a Revenue certificate known as 'SDLT 5'). The certificate by the purchaser that no land transaction return was required in respect of the transaction (a 'self-certificate' known as 'SDLT 60') was abolished for transactions with an effective date on or after 12 March 2008. [*FA 2003, s 79* as amended by *FA 2008, s 94 and Sch 30*.]

A certificate is not required where the land registrar is obliged to act without receipt of an application such as under the commonhold regime, or where the entry relates to an interest or a right other than the chargeable interest acquired by the purchaser under the land transaction giving rise to the application. [*FA 2003, s 79*].

Liability and payment

[7.3] Except in the case of bearer instruments where the person issuing the instrument is specifically made liable to pay the duty chargeable, stamp duty has not specified the person who is liable to pay the duty ever since the changes introduced by FA 1999. [*FA 1999, s 109(1)* replaced the old *SA 1891, s 15* which had specified which person was liable to a penalty for late stamping and by implication who was principally liable to pay the stamp duty, normally the purchaser]. For SDLT however, *FA 2003, s 85* provides that the purchaser is liable to pay the SDLT in respect of a chargeable transaction. Joint purchasers are jointly and severally liable to pay the SDLT. [*FA 2003, s 103(2)(c)*]. Partners who are partners at the effective date of the transaction (but not any person who becomes a partner afterwards) are jointly and severally liable to pay the SDLT in respect of purchases of chargeable interests by the partnership. [*FA 2003, Sch 15, para 6(2)* and *7(1) and (1A)*]. SDLT may be recovered from any one or more of the trustees of a settlement who were trustees at the effective date of the transaction or who subsequently became a trustee. [*FA 2003, Sch 16, para 5(1), (3)*].

SDLT payable in respect of a land transaction must be paid no later than the filing date of the relevant return although it need not accompany the return. [*FA 2003, s 86(1)*]. Any tax payable as the result of the withdrawal of either group relief, reconstruction or acquisition relief and charities relief must be paid no later than the filing date of the return made in respect of the withdrawal. [*FA 2003, s 86(2)* and see **6.6 Group Relief: Withdrawal and Clawback of Relief, 6.9 Withdrawal of Reconstruction or Acquisition Relief** and **6.11 Acquisitions by Charities**].

These provisions are subject to any application to defer payment of tax in the case of contingent or uncertain consideration under *FA 2003, s 90* (see **3.2 Contingent, Uncertain or Unascertained Consideration and Overage**) or to postpone payment of tax pending an appeal under *FA 2003, Sch 10, paras 39, 40*.

Interest is payable on the amount of any unpaid SDLT after 30 days from the effective date (see **2.3 Contracts, Conveyances and 'Effective Date'**) of the transaction. However, interest on unpaid and late paid SDLT only runs from 26 September 2005 because HMRC overlooked the need to set the actual rate of interest to be charged. Belatedly, the *Taxes (Interest Rate) (Amendment) Regulations 2005* (SI 2005/2462) provide for the setting of rates of interest as from 26 September 2005. HMRC announced that it would not seek recovery of interest wrongly paid out in SDLT repayments. In the case of the withdrawal of group relief, reconstruction or acquisition relief or charities relief giving rise to tax, interest is charged after 30 days following the disqualifying event (see

6.5 Group Relief: Withdrawal and Clawback of Relief, **6.9 Withdrawal of Reconstruction or Acquisition Relief** and **6.11 Acquisitions by Charities**). In the case of tax deferred under *FA 2003, s 90* (see **3.2 Contingent, Uncertain or Unascertained Consideration and Overage**) interest is charged after 30 days from when the deferred payment is due. [*FA 2003, s 87*]. However, where contingent, uncertain or unascertained consideration is not deferred under *FA 2003, s 90*, interest on any tax that becomes payable under *FA 2003, s 80* (adjustment where the contingency ceases or consideration becomes ascertained) runs from the effective date of the transaction. [*FA 2003, s 87(5)* and see **2.3 Contracts, Conveyances and 'Effective Date'** for 'effective date']. An amount of tax lodged with HMRC in respect of the tax will reduce the interest payable accordingly. [*FA 2003, s 87(6)*].

Penalties carry interest from the date they are determined until payment. [*FA 2003, s 88*. Interest is charged at the rate applicable under *FA 1989, s 178*]. A repayment of SDLT (including an amount lodged under *FA 2003, s 87(6)*) carries interest at the rate applicable under *FA 1989, s 178* between the payment of the tax and the repayment (unless it is a payment made in consequence of a court order or judgment of a court having power to allow interest on the payment). Any such interest paid is not income for tax purposes. [*FA 2003, s 89*].

FA 2003, s 91 and *Sch 12* govern the collection and recovery of SDLT including any penalties and interest. Under *FA 2003, s 92* where payment to HMRC is made by cheque and the cheque is paid on its first presentation to the bank on which it is drawn, the payment is treated as made on the day the cheque was received by HMRC.

Contacting HMRC Stamp Taxes

[7.4] A Stamp Taxes 'Helpline' is available between 08.30 – 17.00 Monday to Friday on telephone 0845 603 0135.

Except as noted below, all postal correspondence concerning Stamp Taxes should be sent to:

Birmingham Stamp Office
9th Floor
City Centre House
30 Union Street
Birmingham
BS 4AR

Correspondence relating to Scotland should be sent to:

Edinburgh Stamp Office
68 Queen Street
Edinburgh
EH2 4NF

SDLT Returns unless filed electronically should be sent to:

Taxes/SDLT
Comben House
Farriers Way
Natherton
Merseyside
LS30 4RN

'Discovery assessments' and finality

[7.5] If HMRC 'discover' that tax that ought to have been assessed has not been assessed or an assessment is or has become insufficient or a relief has been given that is or has become excessive, they can make a 'discovery' assessment to make good the loss of tax. [*FA 2003, Sch 10, para 28(1)*]. If the purchaser has delivered a land transaction return for the transaction in question, a 'discovery' assessment can only be issued where there is either:

(a) fraudulent or negligent conduct by the purchaser or his agent; or
(b) HMRC could not reasonably have been expected, on the basis of the information made available to them before the end of the standard nine-month enquiry period, to be aware of the insufficiency of tax paid. [*FA 2003, Sch 10, para 30*].

The general time limit for making a 'discovery' assessment is six years after the effective date of the relevant land transaction although this is extended to 21 years in the case of negligence or fraud. [*FA 2003, Sch 10, para 31*]. From 1 April 2011 the general time limit of six years will be reduced to four years and the 21-year time limit will be reduced to six years for carelessness and 20 years for deliberate error [*FA 2009, s 99 and Sch 51*].

Assuming that there has been no negligence or fraud, finality and protection from the possibility of a 'discovery' assessment can therefore be achieved by making a disclosure to HMRC. The nature of the disclosure required for income tax purposes was considered in *Langham v Vellema* [2004] STC 544 and this gave rise to Statement of Practice SP 1/06 which sets out the extent of the disclosure required in order to gain finality. Where any kind of SDLT planning is involved, the disclosure should be drafted in the clearest possible terms in order to achieve finality: see *R (on the application of Pattullo) v Revenue and Customs Comrs* [2009] CSOH 137, [2010] STC 107, although strangely SP1/06 was not in that case argued before the court. A disclosure which on its facts made it obvious that a tax avoidance scheme had been entered into will normally be sufficient. This will be especially so where the scheme is a disclosed scheme and the DOTAS scheme reference number (see **10 DISCLOSURE OF SDLT AVOIDANCE SCHEMES**) has been disclosed: *Charlton & Others v Commissioners of Revenue and Customs* [2011] TC01317.

HMRC Stamp Taxes has confirmed that SP 1/06 applies to SDLT (see SDLT Technical News Issue 4, March 2007).

The text of SP 1/06 is reproduced in **APPENDIX B**. Any such disclosures should be sent to Birmingham Stamp Office at the address in **7.3A** above enclosing a copy of the relevant land transaction return.

Code of Practice 10

[7.6] HMRC guidance on the interpretation of the law relating to SDLT is available under Code of Practice 10. Although as a general rule, such guidance is only available for legislation passed in the last four Finance Acts, it is understood that for SDLT purposes this facility has been extended indefinitely. The extension of the facility was a response to demands from taxpayers and their agents for an advance clearance procedure, especially in the wake of the introduction of the general statutory anti-avoidance rule in *FA 2003, s 75A* (see **11 General Statutory Anti-Avoidance Rule**). A clearance procedure has been refused (most likely on ground of manpower and associated cost) and taxpayers are left with a guidance facility that is non-binding and which tends to produce legalistic and heavily caveated responses. Requests for Code of Practice 10 guidance should be sent to the Birmingham Stamp Office at the address in **7.3A** above.

A recurring theme at the moment is the apparent inability of HMRC to deal effectively with technical issues in the context of requests for guidance. A related problem is the discarding of detailed covering letters accompanying SDLT returns sent to Birmingham Stamp Office which explain why the SDLT returns have been completed in the way they were, resulting in that information being ignored when processing the return and necessitating further correspondence.

The problems experienced by taxpayers submitting requests for technical guidance (whether these be formal Code of Practice 10 requests for a non-statutory clearance or merely straightforward technical queries) seem to grow in direct proportion to the number of pronouncements from HMRC concerning its revamped clearance services. The latest announcement in SDLT Practitioners' News, Issue 21 of June 2008 (and now withdrawn due to technical errors relating to late filing penalties) is entitled 'Giving certainty to business through clearances' and seems to create a two-tier service with 'business customers' intended to get a better service than non-business customers. The issue of whether this is fair (surely private taxpayers are subject to the same legal obligations as business taxpayers and should get the same level of service? Has HMRC ever suggested that interest and tax penalties should be lower for private taxpayers?) is beyond the scope of this section, but what can business customers expect from the revamp? HMRC in its 'Mission Statement' say that its purpose will be 'to provide certainty for businesses operating in the UK, as a useful practical service at a level whereby speed of response from HMRC can be reasonably assured'. Leaving aside the rather ponderous wording of this statement, HMRC goes on to say that it aims to provide clearances within 28 days on areas of material uncertainty arising within four Finance Acts of the introduction of new legislation and on older legislation where there is material uncertainty 'around the tax outcome of a real issue of commercial significance to the business itself, determined by reference to the scale of the business and the impact of the issue upon it'.

Disregarding the in-built get-outs for HMRC to decline a clearance application in any particular case, it seems that taxpayers in SDLT would be well satisfied if HMRC would simply address the technical issues put to it and deal correctly with the application of the statutory provisions to the question put to it.

Some recent examples come to mind. First, a distribution of land from a partnership to a connected company where the partnership rules in *FA 2003, Sch 15* produced a nil SDLT charge but the connected company provisions of *FA 2003, s 53* arguably and inconsistently provide for a market value SDLT charge. The resulting COP 10 application requesting confirmation of a nil SDLT charge was refused despite the writer of the application being in possession of correspondence with the former head of policy at HMRC Stamp Taxes confirming that no charge arose.

Second, a number of complex transactions have had their SDLT returns sent to Birmingham for manual processing with detailed covering letters explaining how the SDLT charge in each case had been computed. Unfortunately, the covering letters were not even acknowledged and SDLT 12s were sent to the taxpayers demanding full SDLT on the consideration, resulting in further unnecessary correspondence. In one instance, no SDLT 12 was received. The taxpayer having received the SDLT 5 and registered the property acquisition at the Land Registry then received a letter from HMRC months later stating that their 'account' was now long overdue and asking why this was. Ironically, under the 'de-regulation' changes to the SDLT compliance rules announced in the *Finance Act 2008* (see **7.2 Registration of Land Transactions and Certificates**), a SDLT return for some of these types of transaction is no longer required and the transfer would go direct to the Land Registry, avoiding this situation.

A further example concerns COP 10 requests relating to the new *para 4ZA* added to the group relief provisions of *FA 2003, Sch 7* by the *Finance Act 2008* (see **6.6 Group Relief: Withdrawal and Claw-back of Relief**). This new provision is drafted in a way that leaves taxpayers unsure of whether group relief claw-back arises when after the transfer the vendor company is wound-up and the purchaser then leaves the group. Requests for guidance have been taking a lot longer than the target 28 days. It is rather trite to say that had the new provision been drafted properly in the first place this would not have arisen.

These examples suggest that if HMRC's resources were to be directed away from those parts of the organisation responsible for dreaming up initiatives and publicising them and instead towards those hard pressed parts which actually deal with taxpayer technical issues at the sharp end, there would be less of a need for such initiatives in the first place.

It is apparent that HMRC refuse to give clearances in relation to the general statutory anti-avoidance rule in *FA 2003, s 75A*. This appears to be in breach of the assurance given in Hansard by the Chief Secretary to the Treasury on 5 June 2007 in relation to the section that HMRC would be 'happy to advise those who have queries about complex transactions on a case-by-case basis', and see further **11.6** below.

HMRC enquiries

[7.7] A recent trend to emerge in HMRC Stamp Taxes enquiries is the informal attempt to move away from the extremely wide standard information and documentation request routinely issued when an enquiry is opened. What normally happens is that a letter is sent to the taxpayer's agent or adviser who submitted the return informing them of the opening of the enquiry. Attached to this letter is a schedule listing the categories of information and documentation which are required to be copied and sent to HMRC. The categories are very wide and, read literally, almost all documents associated with a transaction need to be copied and sent to HMRC. It appears that the numerous ongoing enquiries commenced by HMRC, particularly into sub-sale schemes have resulted in a harvest of ring-binders so copious that the relatively limited personnel resources at HMRC are finding it difficult to cope. The result appears to have been that when an enquiry is now opened by HMRC Stamp Taxes, the taxpayer is offered the choice of a full enquiry or a kind of informal 'fast-track' enquiry consisting of a meeting and a 'limited document request'. This appears to be an attempt by HMRC to identify those promising cases which may merit further examination without having to trawl through all the transaction documentation. As such, it is difficult to understand why a taxpayer selected for enquiry should opt for the 'fast track' procedure unless he is particularly anxious to avoid the cost of putting a full disclosure bible together. Certainly, the reaction of HMRC to those taxpayers who decline the 'fast-track' procedure appears to be one of slight disappointment.

One important point that requires detailed consideration under both the 'fast-track' and the standard enquiry routes is the extent to which legal professional privilege means that documents can either be withheld from disclosure to HMRC entirely or the key parts redacted. Clearly the disclosure of a counsel's opinion or other legal advice giving a frank assessment of any weaknesses in the taxpayer's case would be prejudicial and so a key task will be to identify those documents over which privilege can be asserted. An allied issue is the extent to which disclosure of privileged legal documents to third parties such as accountants, banks and the other parties involved in the transaction will have had the effect of waiving privilege. This often happens during a transaction particularly where banks are involved. However, recent judicial authority will often allow for privilege to be maintained where there has been limited disclosure to such persons.

This is an issue which should also be considered when, as sometimes happens, a legal opinion or an extract thereof is submitted with a COP 10 application or other correspondence with HMRC in order to seek to persuade HMRC to arrive at a sensible technical conclusion. Taxpayers should of course be made aware that the disclosure of such advice even in summary form could, if not controlled carefully, result in the waiver of legal privilege generally, thus requiring disclosure of all correspondence between the taxpayer and his legal advisers however prejudicial that might be.

Compliance and offences

[7.8] *FA 2003, s 93* and *Sch 13* (as amended) and *FA 2008, Sch 36* govern the powers of HMRC to call for documents and information for the purposes of stamp duty land tax.

FA 2003, s 95 creates the statutory criminal offence of a person being knowingly concerned in the fraudulent evasion of SDLT by him or any other person. If found guilty the person is liable on summary conviction to imprisonment for a term not exceeding six months or a fine not exceeding the statutory maximum (or both) and on conviction on indictment to imprisonment for a term not exceeding seven years or a fine (or both). This section is based on and largely copies *FA 2000, s 144* which was introduced to make prosecution of PAYE and NIC fraud involving payment of wages by cash in hand without deducting tax more effective. When that provision was introduced into the Finance Bill 2000 at a late stage unease was expressed about the imprecision inherent in the phrases 'knowingly concerned' and 'fraudulent evasion'. In response the Paymaster General explained the use of these phrases as follows:

> I will deal with the important point about the words "knowingly" and "fraudulent evasion" . . . My officials will smile when they hear this, but initially I said to them, "Surely evasion is fraud", and asked why it needed to be qualified as "fraudulent evasion". I have received assurances which I will pass on to the Committee. The juxtaposition of the words "knowingly" and "fraudulent evasion" reinforces exactly which offences the provision is aimed at.
>
> Let us take the question of someone who is knowingly concerned in the evasion of income tax. I want to make it clear that it is not enough for this purpose to show that a person should have suspected that someone was evading tax. The person must have knowledge and involvement in the fraud. For example, he could help someone evade tax by the helping to produce false business records.
>
> People may ask why we have put the words "fraudulent" and "evasion" together. I am reliably informed by people who know better than I do that, in English usage, "to evade" can mean to dodge, without any dishonest intent. Although "evasion" has come to imply dishonesty in the context of tax, the Bill needs to be drafted tightly. "Fraudulent" may not appear to add much to "evasion", but the expression "fraudulent evasion" is well precedented and subject to interpretation by the courts.
> (HC Official Report, Standing Committee H, 29 June 2000, col 1010.)

Therefore the phrase 'knowingly concerned' requires knowledge of (rather than mere suspicion) and involvement in the evasion of tax, and the phrase 'fraudulent evasion' requires proof of dishonest intent. In relation to tax planning, assurances were sought as to the meaning of 'evasion' and in particular whether those involved in tax avoidance schemes might be charged with the commission of this offence where the scheme was adjudged to have failed on technical grounds. In this respect the Paymaster General said:

> No one could be convicted as a matter of general law unless it was proved that he or she had a dishonest intention . . .
>
> The Right Hon. Member for Wells asked about tax advisers who gave advice on avoidance schemes that failed. A failed scheme whose details are not hidden from the Revenue amounts not to tax evasion, but to tax planning . . . The Government may not like some of that planning and may legislate against it, but, as it is not hidden, it does not fall within the remit of the measure . . .
>
> . . . avoidance is not evasion; there are separate laws to deal with the latter. The Right Hon. Gentleman asked when avoidance became evasion. Unless he can give an

example, I cannot think of such an eventuality.
(HC Official Report, Standing Committee H, 29 June 2000, cols 1012 and 1013.)

Further guidance has been issued in Inland Revenue Tax Bulletin, Issue 49 (October 2000) to the effect that those persons who advise on what turn out to be fiscally ineffective tax avoidance schemes are only likely to be charged with the offence where dishonesty is involved. In the opinion of HMRC such dishonesty may be evident where those involved in a scheme 'are not merely relying on the intrinsic technical soundness of the arrangements actually put in place to reduce their liability, but also on concealment of the true facts from the inspector'. HMRC would not expect a criminal offence to have been committed where there is no concealment of the facts and there is a 'respectable technical case'. Thus a critical question in determining whether a prosecution will occur is likely to be whether there has been 'concealment of the true facts'. However, this phrase gives rise to its own uncertainty given that 'concealment' can occur in different ways ranging from deliberate covering up of facts through partial disclosure of accurate information which conveys a misleading impression to failure to appreciate (and therefore disclose) that certain information would be considered relevant by HMRC. Given the guidance available, however, it seems that in any case where the technical merits of a tax mitigation structure involving SDLT are open to different interpretations the safest course of action will be to disclose all material facts to IR Stamp Taxes and argue the case on technical merit rather than risk an allegation that facts were concealed if a prosecution under *FA 2003, s 95* is to be safely ruled out. However, it is legitimate for a taxpayer who has complied with any requirement to file an SDLT return or who takes the view on reasonable grounds that a return is not required, to decide not to expose himself to the chance of a potentially lengthy and expensive enquiry by HMRC which could arise from a voluntary disclosure. As long as any necessary returns have been filed such a decision not to make a voluntary disclosure could not be 'concealment' even where avoidance was involved if there is a reasonable technical basis for the position adopted by the taxpayer and even if the avoidance ultimately fails to succeed.

A person who assists in or induces the preparation or delivery of any information, return or other document that he knows will be, or is likely to be used for any purpose of SDLT, and he knows to be incorrect is liable to a penalty not exceeding £3,000. [*FA 2003, s 96*].

FA 2003, Sch 14 (as amended by *FA 2009, Sch 51*) governs the determination of penalties and related appeals.

Chapter 8

Special Situations

Partnerships

[8.1] A 'partnership' for SDLT is defined as a partnership under any of the *Partnership Act 1890*, the *Limited Partnerships Act 1907*, the *Limited Liability Partnerships Act 2000*, or a firm or entity of a similar character to any of these formed under the law of a foreign jurisdiction. [*FA 2003, Sch 15, para 1*]. For SDLT purposes a chargeable interest held by or on behalf of a partnership is treated as held by or on behalf of the partners and a land transaction entered into for the purposes of a partnership is treated as entered into by or on behalf of the partners and not by the partnership as such despite the partnership being regarded as a legal person or body corporate by the law under which it was formed. [*FA 2003, Sch 15, para 2*]. For how this principle affects SDLT group relief claims involving partnerships see **6.4 Group Relief: Introduction**.

A partnership is treated as the same person despite a change in the partners as long as at least one person who was a partner before the change remains a partner after the change. [*FA 2003, Sch 15, para 3*]. A partnership is not treated for SDLT as a unit trust scheme or open-ended investment company. [*FA 2003, Sch 15, para 4*]. See **7.3 Liability and Payment** for the liability of partners for pay SDLT.

SDLT applies in the usual way to what are referred to as 'ordinary partnership transactions' which are transactions entered into as purchaser by or on behalf of the members of a partnership other than transactions subject to which the special partnership provisions apply. [*FA 2003, Sch 15, para 5*]. The special partnership provisions apply where:

(1) land is transferred to a partnership by a partner (or a person who becomes a partner in return for the land or the land is transferred by a person connected with either person);
(2) there is a transfer of an interest in a partnership; or
(3) land is transferred from a partnership to a partner (or a person who has been a partner or a person connected with either person). [*FA 2003, Sch 15 Part 3*].

Stamp duty continues to apply to any instrument by which the transfer of an interest in a partnership is effected. It was intended by the Government that a stamp duty charge would only apply to the extent that the partnership held shares. This would deal with concerns that partnerships might be used as a stamp duty free wrapper for share deals. The stamp duty charge was therefore supposed to be restricted to that which would arise on a direct sale of the shares themselves held by the partnership and if the partnership held no shares then no stamp duty would arise. *Paragraphs 31–33 of Sch 15*, as originally enacted, however did not achieve this. Rather, those provisions applied a full stamp duty charge at up to 4% on transfers of partnership interests even by reference to assets held such as free-standing goodwill and intellectual property which were exempt from stamp duty before. *Paragraph 33* was intended to restrict the overall stamp duty charge as mentioned above, but the drafting failed to achieve this and there was further error which resulted in the stamp duty charge relating to the share of the partnership that was not transferred. *Paragraph 33*, as amended by *F(No 2)A 2005, Sch 10, para 21*, now provides that there is no stamp duty charge unless the partnership property includes stock or marketable securities, in which case the stamp duty charge is on the amount of consideration equal to the net market value of the stock and marketable securities attributable to the interest of the incoming partner or increase in an existing partner's share. There is still a slightly redundant provision that where the partnership owns land the consideration liable to stamp duty is reduced by a proportion of the market value of the land less any loan secured solely on the land, representing the proportionate interest acquired by the purchaser of the interest in the partnership. The intention is to give a credit against the stamp duty charge for the SDLT payable in relation to the land under 2 above. [*FA 2003, Sch 15, paras 31–33*]. It is understood that HMRC intends to deal with this unsatisfactory situation by only charging stamp duty by reference to the shares held if any. It is interesting to note that the instrument will not be duly stamped unless it is adjudicated.

The transfer of an interest in land to a partnership by a partner or a person who becomes a partner (or someone connected with either) is a chargeable transaction. The chargeable consideration is normally taken to be the proportion of the market value of the land equal to the total of the other partners' shares immediately after the transfer. The shares of partners who are individuals and who are connected with the transferor are ignored for this purpose. [*FA 2003, Sch 15 para 10*]. However, an election may be made to disapply this treatment and instead pay tax by reference to the market value of the whole chargeable interest transferred. Where such an election is made the value of the chargeable interest is not taken into account on any subsequent 'Type B' transfer of an interest in the partnership (see below) nor on any subsequent distribution of the property out of the partnership and is disregarded under *FA 2003, Sch 15 para 17A* (see below). [*FA 2003, Sch 15 para 12A*].

Where there is such a transfer of land into a partnership and within three years of the transfer there is a withdrawal of money or money's worth other than income profit or a loan is repaid (in relation to the transferor or a person connected with him), the withdrawal or repayment is treated as a chargeable transaction and the chargeable consideration is taken to be the withdrawal or repayment up to the market value of the chargeable interest transferred, less any tax previously chargeable. [*FA 2003, Sch 15, para 17A*, inserted by *F(No 2)A 2005, Sch 10, para 10*]. This provision may lead to a double-charge to SDLT where one partner contributes land and the other partner contributes a cash equalisation payment which is then paid out to the partner contributing the land so that each partner going forward has made the same net contribution. This will occur because the contribution of the land will be taxed on the market value of the proportionate share of the land attributable to the other partner, and a further tax charge will then arise by reference to the money paid out to equalise their respective contributions. There are also special provisions for partnerships consisting of bodies corporate who are members of the same group of companies. [*FA 2003, Sch 15, para 13*].

The transfer of a partnership interest in a property investment partnership (a 'PIP') but not in any other form of partnership, is a chargeable transaction when the partnership property includes land whether any consideration is given. A PIP is a partnership whose sole or main activity is investing in or dealing in land whether that involves carrying out construction operations on land or not. The chargeable consideration is taken to be equal to a proportion of the market value of the 'relevant partnership property' where there is consideration. That proportion is equal to the partnership interest acquired. A transfer of a partnership interest occurs when a person acquires or increases a partnership share. Consideration for this purpose can take the form of either money or money's worth given for the interest acquired or under arrangements where a person becomes a partner and the interest of an existing partner reduces or ceases and money or money's worth is withdrawn by the existing partner other than out of resources available to the partnership prior to the transfer. Such transfers are referred to by the legislation as 'Type A' transfers. The 'relevant partnership property' in relation to a Type A transfer is every chargeable interest held by the partnership except that transferred to the partnership in connection with the transfer and market value leases.

Transfers occurring in any other circumstances are known as 'Type B' transfers. For Type B transfers the chargeable consideration is taken to be equal to a proportion of the market value of the 'relevant partnership property' equal to the partnership interest acquired. The 'relevant partnership property' for a Type B transfer is every chargeable interest held by the partnership but excluding a chargeable interest transferred to the partnership in connection with the transfer, market value leases, any chargeable interest not attributable economically to the partnership interest transferred, any chargeable interest transferred to the partnership before 23 July 2004, any chargeable interest in respect of whose transfer to the partnership an election has been made under *FA 2003, Sch 15 para 12A* to pay tax by reference to market value and any other chargeable interest whose transfer to the partnership did not attract SDLT under the market value rule in *FA 2003, Sch 15 para 10*. [*FA 2003, Sch 15 para 14* as amended by *FA 2008, s 97 and Sch 31* with effect from 19 July 2007]. The intention with a 'Type B' transfer is that any chargeable interest on which a full market-value SDLT charge arose on its acquisition by the partnership because it was acquired from an unconnected person or by virtue of an election under *FA 2003, Sch 15, para 12A* is excluded from an SDLT charge on certain increases in partnership share attributable to the 'carried interests' of investment managers in investment funds structured as partnerships.

The transfer of an interest in land from a partnership to a partner or former partner (or a person connected with either) is a chargeable transaction. The chargeable consideration is taken to be a proportion of the market value of the land equal to the shares of partners who are not the transferee of the land and who are not individuals connected with the transferee. [*FA 2003, Sch 15, para 18–22*].

It has been confirmed that where the acquisition of the underlying land would qualify for the disadvantaged areas relief, the transfer of the partnership interest will to that extent also be exempt. (See *FA 2003, Sch 15, para 26* and Hansard, Wednesday, 28 April 2004, Col 946 reproduced in **APPENDIX A**.) Other reliefs are also available [*FA 2003, Sch 15, paras 25, 27* and *28*].

Partnership property is any interest or right held by or on behalf of a partnership, or the members of a partnership, for the purposes of partnership business: *FA 2003, Sch 15, para 34(1)*. In the view of HMRC Stamp Taxes Office, it follows from this that property held by one of the partners and used for the purposes of the partnership business may be partnership property so that a charge to tax may arise on contribution, on its ceasing to be used and on a transfer of an interest in the partnership, as above. This view may be open to question.

Unit trusts and open-ended investment companies

[8.2] A unit trust scheme is treated generally for SDLT as if the trustees were a company and the units in it were shares, and each part of an umbrella unit trust scheme is treated as a separate unit trust. [*FA 2003, s 101(1), (2), (3)* and *(4)*; 'unit trust scheme' has the same meaning as in the *Financial Services and Markets Act 2000*]. However, a unit trust scheme is not treated as a company for the purposes of group relief, reconstruction relief or acquisition relief (see **6.4 GROUP RELIEF**). [*FA 2003, s 101(7) as amended by FA 2006, s 166*].

Open-ended investment companies are intended to be treated in a similar fashion to unit trusts for SDLT purposes and regulations have been made accordingly. [*FA 2003, s 102*; 'open-ended investment company' has the meaning in the *Financial Services and Markets Act 2000*].

Prior to 22 March 2006, the acquisition of an interest in land by the trustees of a unit trust scheme was exempt from tax if:

(1) immediately before the acquisition there were no assets held by the trustees and no units were in issue;
(2) the only consideration for the acquisition is the units; and
(3) immediately after the acquisition the vendor is the only unit holder of the scheme. [*FA 2003, s 64A* but withdrawn from 22 March 2006 by *FA 2006, s 166*].

Trusts

[8.3] Where a chargeable interest (or an interest in a partnership) is acquired by a bare trustee or a nominee, SDLT applies as if the interest had been acquired by the person for whom the bare trustee or nominee acts, except in relation to the grant of a lease, where the bare trustee is treated as the purchaser of the whole of the interest acquired. [*FA 2003, s 105* and *Sch 16, paras (1) and (3)*, as amended by *F(No 2)A 2005, Sch 10, para 11*]. Where the trustee or trustees of any other type of trust acquire a chargeable interest (or an interest in a partnership) as trustees they are treated for SDLT purposes as purchasers of the entire interest acquired including the beneficial interest. [*FA 2003, Sch 16, para 4*].

Beneficiaries of trusts formed under Scots or non-UK laws are treated for SDLT as having an equitable interest in trust property if that would be the case had the trust been formed under English law. The acquisition of the interest of such a beneficiary under the trust is treated expressly as the acquisition of an interest in the trust property for SDLT purposes. [*FA 2003, Sch 16, para 2*].

However, there is no equivalent provision for English trusts expressly providing that the acquisition of the equitable interest of a beneficiary under a trust formed under English law is to be treated as the acquisition of an interest in the trust property for SDLT purposes. Instead, the SDLT legislation assumes that under the principles of equity and trust law the interest of a beneficiary is an interest in the underlying trust property. Does the beneficiary merely have a right *in personam* against the trustee to see that the trust is administered properly or does he have a right *in rem* or a proprietary interest as owner of the beneficial interest? It seems that English law had not been capable of supplying a conclusive answer to this question and had been content to adopt a pragmatic approach to the issue, usually in tax cases where the language of the statute determined the answer (see Hanbury and Martin, *Modern Equity* 18th edn, at 1-019 which suggests that the interest of a beneficiary may actually be *sui generis*, and see *Baker v Archer-Shee* [1927] AC 844 and *Archer-Shee v Garland* [1931] AC 212). There was a series of cases in which the courts had to decide whether a beneficiary under a trust for sale of land had an interest in land for the purposes of a particular statute, and the courts have held that an interest in land existed (see Megarry & Wade, *The Law of Real Property* 7th edn at 10-032 and the cases referred to in footnote 143 at p 407). The *Trusts of Land and Appointment of Trustees Act 1996* however puts the matter beyond doubt by referring to a beneficiary who is 'beneficially entitled to an interest in possession in land subject to the trust': see for example *ss 9, 11* and *12*. In SDLT a 'chargeable interest' is defined in *FA 2003, s 48(1)(a)* to include an interest, right or power in or over land in the UK and therefore, it seems that for SDLT purposes the life tenant of a trust formed under English law has an equitable interest in the trust property. The purchase of a life interest in possession, or an interest in an accumulation and maintenance trust or a reversionary interest in a trust formed under English law whose assets include land in the UK will be a land transaction for SDLT purposes (as will be the purchase of an equivalent type of interest under a Scots or foreign trust [*FA 2003, Sch 16, para 2*]). However, a discretionary beneficiary does not have an equitable interest or any other interest in the assets of the trust under English law and so the interest of such a person is not a 'chargeable interest' for SDLT (see for example, Hanbury and Martin, *Modern Equity* 18th edn, at 8-015 and see *Baker v Arscher-Shee* [1927] AC 844 and *Archer-Shee v Garland* [1931] AC 212).

Where an equitable interest in a trust holding land in the UK is acquired by the exercise of a power of appointment or the exercise of a discretion vested in the trustees, any consideration given for the exercise is treated as chargeable consideration for SDLT purposes. [*FA 2003, Sch 16, para 7*]. During the debates on the Finance Bill 2003, the Chief Secretary to the Treasury declined to give an assurance that the exercise of a power of appointment or the surrender of a life interest to a remainderman for no consideration did not give rise to stamp duty or SDLT (HC Official Report, Standing Committee B,

Tuesday 3 June 2003, cols. 344 and 345). See **7.3 Liability and Payment** for the liability of trustees to pay SDLT and *FA 2003, s 106* for the rules governing persons acting in a representative capacity. See also **3.4 Connected Companies** for a market value charge if the beneficiary who receives land is a company.

It is specifically provided that where the trustees of a settlement reallocate trust property in such a way that a beneficiary acquires an interest in certain trust property and ceases to have an interest in other trust property and the beneficiary consents, the fact that he consents does not mean that there is chargeable consideration for his acquisition: *FA 2003, Sch 16, para 8 as added by FA 2006, s 165.*

HMRC treat the trustees' settlement as a single and continuing body of persons and do not regard a change of trustees as a land transaction. No SDLT return is therefore required and no tax arises even when the trust property is subject to a mortgage: see HMRC SDLT Manual at 31745.

Sub-sales, assignments and novations

[8.4] Stamp duty land tax does not contain any general equivalent of stamp duty sub-sale relief under *Stamp Act 1891, s 58(4)* (see **38.8 Sub-sales**). Instead, where there is an assignment, sub-sale or other transaction relating to a contract for a land transaction that is to be completed by a conveyance ('the original contract') the assignee or sub-purchaser is treated as the purchaser under a hypothetical contract (called the 'secondary contract') and the chargeable consideration for the secondary contract is that which remains to be paid by the assignee or sub-purchaser under the original contract (or by a person connected with him) if any, plus any consideration given to the original purchaser for the assignment or sub-sale.

It is vital to a correct understanding and application of SDLT and the various reliefs and exemptions to appreciate that the sub-sale provisions are not relieving or exempting provisions but actually substitute a notional land transaction for one or both of the actual land transactions which are taking place for all SDLT purposes. This is true regardless of whether or not what is often mistakenly referred to as the 'sub-sale relief' applies because the original actual land transaction has been substantially performed or completed at the same time as the subsequent actual transaction. This means for example that when one is required by other provisions of the SDLT code to compare the sub-sale transaction with a further notional transaction under *FA 2003, s 75A* (see **11.2 General Statutory Anti-avoidance Rule**) or to see whether a tax advantage has been obtained, it is the notional transaction arising under the sub-sale provisions that should be taken as the base transaction for comparison with the further notional transaction and not the actual land transactions. The reason for this should be apparent from the analysis below.

The application of the SDLT sub-sale rules to complex property transactions often requires the adviser to re-visit the basic rules of English law about how and when the beneficial and equitable interests in land pass under a sale transaction particularly where there are multiple parties in a chain. Perhaps surprisingly, experience shows that there is scope for disagreement between advisers about the operation and effect of these rules. This lack of certainty arises because the rules are largely judge-made and are often interpreted in difficult cases where policy reasons may influence with the judges' process of reasoning. The latest and most important judicial remarks on the issue were by Lord Walker in *Jerome v Kelly* [2004] STC 887 at 896 and suggest that the movement of the beneficial and equitable interests proceeds in stages and on the basis of certain assumptions as to the availability of specific performance (which is a discretionary remedy) and that the contract will eventually be completed. Scots lawyers do not need to address this issue because of the strict division in Scots law between personal and real rights and have a system under which ownership *in rem* only passes at registration: see *Burnett's Trustee v Grainger* [2004] UKHL 8, [2004] 11 ECGS 139.

Having reached agreement in principle with the other side (or agreed to disagree) on the legal effect of a particular proposed property sale structure the adviser then has to interpret and apply the SDLT rules relating to sub-sales in a way that will permit the client to take advantage of them. This is something of a challenge because the SDLT sub-sale rules are obscurely drafted and leave considerable scope for uncertainty about whether the anticipated tax effect which will be assumed by the self-assessment return will be denied should the Stamp Taxes Office choose to enquire into the return. This uncertainty affects funders' and credit-raters' view of the risks attached to the deal given that a single, or in some cases, multiple hits of up to 4.75% (calculated on the price plus VAT) of the sale price of each stage will usually ruin the economic rationale for the deal.

The particular areas of SDLT uncertainty at the moment relate to the identity of the seller (this may affect the availability of an associated tax relief that depends on a particular person being the seller or the impact of the connected company provisions), the amount of the chargeable consideration, the 'best practice' when filing the tax return to report the transaction and whether the statutory general anti-avoidance rule in *FA 2003, s 75A* can apply.

What is a sub-sale?

A sub-sale is where A contracts to sell land to B who then contracts to sell the land to C before completion of the A to B contract. There will be two separate sale contracts being that between A and B and that between B and C. Completion can occur by separate conveyances of the legal estate from A to B and B to C or by a single conveyance by A to C at the direction of B. In the latter case B will never be registered at the Land Registry. It is helpful if the A to B sale contract does not prohibit a sub-sale and permits B to direct A as to whom the conveyance is made. This ensures that the equitable interest (but not necessarily the beneficial interest) in the property passes to C during the contract period. It may be however, that the vendor, A, insists on the inclusion of Standard Condition 1.5 (4th edition) (or Standard Commercial Property Condition (2nd edition) 1.5) in his contract. Standard Condition 1.5 merely provides that: 'The buyer is not entitled to transfer the benefit of the contract'. It has been held that this provision does not prevent a purchaser from requiring the vendor to transfer the property on completion to a third party of his choosing because sub-sales are not excluded and so the general position at common law applies and this permits a sub-sale unless expressly excluded. [*Pittack v Naviede* [2010] EWHC 1509 (Ch), [2010] 26 EG 91 (CS), [2010] All ER (D) 206 (Jun)]. On the other hand, Standard Commercial Property Condition 1.5 in addition to providing that the buyer is not entitled to transfer the benefit of the contract also states expressly that the seller may not be required to transfer the property to any person other than the buyer, and so this provision does therefore prevent a conveyance from A to C.

In contrast with a sub-sale, an assignment occurs when B transfers the benefit of his contract with A to C. Under English law the assignment does not also transfer the burdens of the contract between A and B and thus the mutual obligations between A and B remain. The original sale contract remains in existence. The contract of assignment between B and C would itself normally amount to a 'chargeable interest' for SDLT purposes because it is a contract carrying the benefit of A's obligation to convey the land in accordance with the terms of the A to B contract. However the operation of the relevant SDLT rules explained below means that this contract is ignored and replaced by what the legislation calls the 'secondary contract'.

A novation is different from a sub-sale or an assignment and occurs when A, B and C agree that C should stand in the place of B with the result that the A to B contract is extinguished and replaced by a new contract between A and C. A novation does not assign a right or obligation but replaces one contract with another.

It can be a matter of some difficulty to chart the precise movement of the equitable and beneficial interests in the underlying land under each of the above arrangements. However, for SDLT purposes this will not normally be of direct relevance because of the concept of the 'effective date'. This concept determines when SDLT becomes chargeable and this will either be when there is 'substantial performance' if that occurs before completion or completion itself if there has been no prior substantial performance. Hence what matters for SDLT is not whether the equitable or beneficial interests have passed as a matter of land law but whether the statutory test that the buyer has taken possession or paid 90% or more of the price is satisfied.

The reason for looking at assignment and novation in addition to sub-sales is that the SDLT rules lump all these concepts together in a 'one size fits all' approach which in part is responsible for the confusion surrounding the operation of the SDLT rules. It is noteworthy that the equivalent stamp duty relief did not attempt such an ambitious feat and concentrated only on sub-sales, leaving assignments and novations to be dealt with under general stamp duty principles. This meant for instance that in stamp duty there was a double charge on the deposit element of the original contract (once when C reimbursed B and again when C took the conveyance for a consideration that included the amount of the deposit). Under SDLT this double charge on the deposit element of an assignment is removed. It is by no means clear that this difference in the tax treatment of the deposit was appreciated by the draftsman of the legislation or those instructing him.

SDLT and sub-sales

The SDLT rules relating to sub-sales (and assignments and novations) are contained in *FA 2003, ss 45 and 45A*. The SDLT sub-sale provisions are limited when compared with the old stamp duty relief because the SDLT version does not permit the original or intermediate buyer to 'substantially perform' their contracts prior to 'substantial performance' by the end buyer and still come within the rule disregarding the first sale. In other words, under SDLT there is a simple rule that if the 'substantial performance' or completion of the A to B contract is postponed until the 'substantial performance' or completion of the B to C contract and occurs at the same time, then the 'substantial performance' or completion of the A to B contract 'shall be disregarded'. The phrase '*at the same time*' is interpreted by the Stamp Taxes Office as meaning '*in the same completion meeting*' and they do not take the point that arguably there may be a *scintilla temporis* between the substantial performance or completion of the first contract and the second in order to deny the operation of the rule. It is not material whether one or two transfers are executed, ie A to C or A to B and B to C. The result is that SDLT is not chargeable in relation to the A to B contract and conveyance. Under stamp duty a buyer could 'rest on contract' indefinitely having paid the full price to the seller and never pay stamp duty whereas under SDLT this is not possible except perhaps perversely, and no doubt unintentionally, where the general statutory anti-avoidance rule in *FA 2003, s 75A* applies: see **11.4 General Statutory Anti-avoidance Rule**. A curious and surely unanticipated result of the SDLT version of the relief is that the property speculator buying 'off-plan' who flips the property onto an investor at a marked-up price will not pay SDLT but a developer who acquires a site, builds homes on it and sells the homes on to families will pay SDLT. It is noteworthy however that the SDLT relief does not contain a requirement present in the stamp duty relief that the price paid under the sub-sale contract that the chargeable consideration moving from the sub-purchaser (C) should not be less than the value of the property.

The drafting of *FA 2003, s 45* is unnecessarily complex and creates the appearance that those instructing the draftsman were unsure of the manner in which sub-sales, assignments and novations operate. However it is clear that the draftsman was hoping not to provide any scope for exploitation of the sub-sale rule by tax planners in the manner in which sub-sale relief in stamp duty had effectively made it a matter of choice as to whether one paid the duty or not.

Section 45(3)

The sub-sale rule is embodied principally in *FA 2003, s 45(3)*. In short the rule applies where:

- there is a contract between A and B for the sale of land which is to be completed by a conveyance;

- there is an assignment, sub-sale or 'other transaction' (referred to as a 'transfer of rights' in the legislation) as a result of which C becomes entitled to call for the conveyance of the land to him (other than when the assignment of an agreement for lease rule applies — as to which see below and *FA 2003, Sch 17A, para 12B*); and
- the substantial performance or completion of the A to B contract occurs at the same time as, and in connection with, the substantial performance or completion of the B to C contract.

In such cases the substantial performance or completion of the A to B contract is to be 'disregarded' for SDLT, ie B escapes a charge and is not required to file a return except where the secondary contract is itself exempt from tax under the exemptions for alternative property finance arrangements in *FA 2003, ss71A* to *73*.

HMRC's position on this is clearly stated in their at SDLT Manual:

> SDLTM01080 - Scope: What is chargeable
>
> Transfer of rights: Impact on original contract FA03/S45
>
> Where a purchaser (B) transfers his rights under a contract for a land transaction (the "original contract") to a third party (C) the charge on B depends on whether completion or substantial performance of the original contract takes place before completion or substantial performance of the secondary contract (SDLTM01070).
>
> Completion or substantial performance of the original contract at the same time as, and in connection with, completion or substantial performance of the secondary contract is disregarded. This means there is no charge on B, and no requirement for B to submit a land transaction return, if completion or substantial performance of the original contract takes place at the same time as, and in connection with, completion or substantial performance of the secondary contract. This is often referred to as "sub-sale relief". "At the same time as" should be interpreted in accordance with normal conveyancing practice, with no event intervening between completion of the original contract and completion of the secondary contract.
>
> This is illustrated by example 1 at SDLTM01090a.
>
> It is immaterial for stamp duty land tax purposes whether the transfer of the chargeable interest to C is effected by one document or two documents, provided that both documents take effect at the same time and there is no intervening event. Where both documents require registration a covering letter to the appropriate registry may be needed.
>
> Where, on the other hand, substantial performance of the original contract takes place in advance of completion or substantial performance of the secondary contract there will be a charge on B under FA03/S44(4).
>
> This is illustrated by example 2 at SDLTM01090a.

However, the above short description is an oversimplification of the technical position. *Section 45* actually requires that C (referred to as the 'transferee' in the legislation) is not to be regarded as having entered into a land transaction by reason of his contract with B. Instead there is to be a deemed contract (referred to as a 'secondary contract' in the legislation) under which:

- C is the buyer; and

- the consideration is (i) so much of the consideration under the original contract as is referable to the land transferred under the B to C contract and is to be given by C or someone with whom C is connected, and (ii) the consideration paid by C to B for the transfer of rights.

The same rules apply where there is more than one sub-sale so that successive intermediate buyers in a chain will all be entitled to the benefit of the rule if their contract also meets the conditions for the rule to apply.

To summarise at this point, the legislation requires that where a sub-sale, assignment or novation occurs, the B to C contract is in effect ignored and in its stead there is a deemed contract known as the 'secondary contract'. All we are told about the secondary contract is that C is the buyer and the consideration under this contract is to be computed as above. As far as the A to B contract is concerned this may or may not be chargeable with SDLT depending upon whether the substantial performance or completion of this contract occurs at the same time as that under the secondary contract.

Who is the seller under the secondary contract?

When *s 45* was initially drafted it was silent as to the identity of the seller under the secondary contract. In the author's view this was a deliberate omission by the draftsman because as a matter of logic if the substantial performance of the A to B contract fell to be disregarded, it followed that the secondary contract was between A and C. If on the other hand the substantial performance of the A to B contract occurred before that under the secondary contract so that B was liable to SDLT, then because the A to B contract was chargeable it made sense to treat the secondary contract as between B and C.

This reasoning is also consistent with the omission of a provision similar to *FA 1967, s 27(3)(b)* from the SDLT group relief provisions. This provision prevented a corporate buyer from sub-selling a property bought from a third party down to a subsidiary company and claiming stamp duty group relief on the conveyance from the third party to the subsidiary as in *Escoigne Properties Ltd v IRC* [1958] AC 549. The omission of this provision in SDLT is consistent with treating A as the seller when B escapes a charge under the sub-sale rule. If A is the seller then C has not acquired the property from a group company (B) under the secondary contract and so SDLT group relief is not available. On the other hand if B pays SDLT because the A to B contract is not disregarded and so B is regarded as the seller under the secondary contract then SDLT group relief should (subject to the normal conditions) be available. In other words if B paid SDLT then SDLT group relief was available on the B to C contract but if B took advantage of the sub-sale rule then SDLT group relief should be denied on the B to C contract. This interpretation of *s 45* leads to the conclusion that an equivalent of *FA 1967, s 27(3)(b)* was not needed in SDLT because of the modifications made to the sub-sale rule in SDLT.

During the early stages of SDLT however, some advisers spotted the omission of the equivalent of *FA 1967, s 27(3)(b)*. They started promoting *Escoigne* schemes thinking that the draftsman had made an error and forgotten to re-enact the necessary anti-avoidance rule. Arguably however no such rule was needed because on the above interpretation of *s 45* the *Escoigne* schemes did not work.

What then appears to have happened is that a 'helpful' adviser wrote to HMRC Stamp Taxes setting out how the scheme was intended to work and requesting confirmation that it did work.

By then the persons dealing with policy in HMRC Stamp Taxes had changed and it appears that they too did not appreciate the scheme of their own legislation. They also thought that it mattered a lot whether A conveyed to B who then conveyed to C instead of A conveying direct to C with the former suggesting that B was C's seller. The issue of whether A or B conveys the legal estate to C may actually tell us little about the identity of the seller because the conveyances deal only with the legal estate. The courts when faced with a tax scheme are likely to recall the words of Millett LJ (as he then was) in *Parinv (Hatfield) Ltd v IRC* [1998] STC 305 at 313:

> The provisions of the contract, which described the subject matter of the contract as the vendor's equitable and beneficial interest and prescribed the mode of completion, were matters of conveyance and not substance, and were dictated by stamp duty considerations.

Instead of informing advisers that such schemes did not work on a correct interpretation of the legislation, HMRC Stamp Taxes enacted blocking legislation as new *FA 2003, s 45(5A)(a)*. This provides that references to the seller in the SDLT group relief rules are to be taken as references to the seller under the original contract, ie to A. This of course is a bit of overkill because although it puts beyond doubt that SDLT group relief and the sub-sale rule are mutually incompatible, it also means that even if B pays SDLT, the seller is now always regarded as A and so even then SDLT group relief is not available. Unfortunately, new *s 45(5A)* went on in *para (b)* to say that in cases other than group relief, 'references . . . . to the vendor shall be read, where the context so permits, as referring to either the vendor under the original contract or the transferor'.

The effect of this amendment to the legislation is to create considerable uncertainty as to the identity of the seller under the secondary contract. One can speculate as to whether or not it will be clear in any particular context who out of A or B should be treated as the seller. For example it has been speculated that the effect of *s 45(5A)(a)* is that in other situations B must now be taken to be the seller because if it was otherwise the legislative amendment would have been unnecessary. Whether or not a court would follow this logic in the context of a tax scheme is a moot point especially following the decision of the House of Lords in *West v Trennery* [2005] UKHL 5, [2005] STC 214. It may even be the case that the draftsman was attempting to distinguish between sub-sales, assignments and novations. However what is clear is that HMRC Stamp Taxes have done themselves a disservice. Before the amendment, one could discern a general principle that the sub-sale rule and other reliefs were incompatible but following the amendment the uncertainty created casts doubt on this principle. This is an example of how the instinctive reaction of HMRC Stamp Taxes to legislate away tax avoidance is not always either necessary nor produces sensible results. A little time considering the decided cases can often pay dividends. It also now seems that in most cases it will be open to C to report either A or B as his seller on the SDLT 1 return and in either case be able to claim that he had adopted a reasonable filing position. Any suggestion that it is somehow improper (or as one adviser has written, 'fraudulent') to state that A is C's vendor on the SDLT 1 is, in the author's opinion, unsupported by the legislation. However, where there are a number of original sellers who sell plots to B who then sub-sells them all to C, the Stamp Taxes Office treat B as the vendor for the purposes of *FA 2003, s 108* so that the aggregate consideration paid by C is relevant for the purposes of determining the appropriate rate of SDLT payable by C under the linked transactions rule: see **4.2 LINKED TRANSACTION**. This view is questionable given the freedom to nominate the vendor in other contexts.

What is the chargeable consideration?

There is further uncertainty over the amount on which C will be chargeable to SDLT under the secondary contract. The way in which *FA 2003, s 45(3)(b)* is intended to work on a sub-sale is illustrated by the following example.

A exchanges contracts with B for 100 and B pays a deposit of 10. B then exchanges contracts with C for 120 and C pays B a deposit of 12. Completion occurs by A conveying the legal estate at B's direction to C. At completion C pays B the balance of 108 and out of this B simultaneously pays the balance of 90 to A. B has profited by 120 – 100 = 20. The substantial performance and completion of the A to B contract is disregarded for SDLT and so B pays no tax and does not file a return. The consideration under the secondary contract consists of (i) so much of the consideration under the A to B contract that is given by C – here, nil; and (ii) the consideration given by C to B – here, 120. C pays tax on 120.

If instead B had assigned the A to B contract to C, the SDLT consequences would have been as follows. B pays A a deposit of 10 and then assigns the A to B contract to C. C pays B 30 representing 20 profit and 10 reimbursement of B's deposit, and C pays A 90 to complete the contract. The substantial performance and completion of the A to B contract is disregarded for SDLT and so B pays no SDLT. The consideration under the secondary contract consists of (i) so much of the consideration under the A to B contract that is given by C – here, 90; and (ii) the consideration given by C to B – here, 30. C pays tax on 90 + 30 = 120.

It is noteworthy that the requirement under stamp duty sub-sale relief that the consideration moving from C be not less than the value of the property immediately before the B to C contract has not been carried over into SDLT. However there is a concern over the inclusion as chargeable consideration in *FA 2003, s 45(3)(b)(i)* of consideration under the A to B contract that is to be given not only by C but also by any person connected with C. What effect does this have when B and C are connected with each other? On the face of it the wording of the provision leads to double counting where the A to B contract is not disregarded (because substantial performance of that contract occurs prior to the B to C contract) so that B pays tax and then when C pays tax the consideration paid by B under the A to B contract is added to the consideration payable by C under the secondary contract because B is connected with C. This anomalous result alone suggests that such an effect is not within the scope of the wording. The purpose of the wording dealing with consideration provided by a connected person is to prevent the simple device of C arranging for a person connected with him to discharge the balance payable under the A to B contract so that in the absence of such wording that amount would not fall to be aggregated with any consideration paid by C to B and so escape tax. The example 3 at SDLTM 01090a of the SDLT Manual suggests that normally C would have had to have assumed B's liability to pay under the A to B contract before such payment could be treated as consideration for the secondary contract under *FA 2003, s 45(3)(b)(i)*. However the position is not free from doubt and specialist advice should be sought if this point is relevant particularly where any tax mitigation is involved.

'Best practice' when filing the returns

The SDLT compliance rules do not address specifically the position of the A to B contract when substantial performance or completion of it occurs at the same time as the B to C contract. It is clear that the substantial performance or completion of the secondary contract is a notifiable transaction (unless it falls within one of the exceptions in *FA 2003, s 77A* – see **7.1 RETURNS**) for which an SDLT 1 will be necessary. This will be filed and the buyer or his advisers will have to take a view on whether to state that A or B is the seller. The SDLT 5 certificate will be issued showing the seller as stated in the SDLT 1 although perhaps strangely an SDLT 5 is not required in order to register a sub-sale transaction – see *FA 2003, s 79(2)(a)(i)* and **7.2 LAND REGISTRATION AND CERTIFICATES**. Although the wording of this provision seems to be clear, Land Registry practice is not to follow it on the ground that this produces an 'absurd' result and to insist on at least one SDLT 5 certificate. If B is named as the seller but the conveyance is from A to C then if both documents are submitted to the Land Registry, they may request an explanation of the difference in the named sellers unless a covering letter is enclosed explaining the position. In cases where there are conveyances from A to B and B to C, the Land Registry may have a concern about the payment of the correct amount of SDLT when presented with both conveyances especially if notwithstanding that an SDLT 5 is not needed only one SDLT 5 for the B to C conveyance is available. In this situation the Land Registry may be reassured by an explanation in a covering letter although for a time a practice seemed to be emerging with the encouragement of the Stamp Taxes Office for B to file an SDLT 1 claiming relief for the A to B sale using the 'other' category in Box 28 in order to obtain an SDLT 5 which could then be presented to HM Land Registry together with the SDLT 5 for the B to C conveyance. The filing of an SDLT 1 for the A to B transaction when the substantial performance and completion of that contract is disregarded under *FA 2003, s 45(3)* raised a number of concerns. First, because the A to B transaction will never be a notifiable transaction it appears to be contrary to the scheme of the legislation (although it has to be said not clearly beyond the power of HMRC) for an SDLT 1 to be filed and an SDLT 5 to be issued. Second, and perhaps more importantly the filing of an SDLT 1 by B appears to bring B within the direct scope of the rules allowing for enquiry into SDLT returns and it must be asked whether this will normally be in the best interest of B unless the facilitation of the registration of C is of overriding importance to B. It would appear however, that the submission of a tax return by B may protect him from penalties, if it is later found that tax was due from him.

However, the above procedure seems no longer to be requested by the Stamp Taxes Office and the Land Registry had issued internal guidance to its staff stating that when dealing with the registration of a title acquired by way of sub-sale: ' . . . *you need not concern yourself with the intervening transaction.*' The guidance also made it clear that there may be one or two conveyances and there is only need for one SDLT 5 certificate, not two. This guidance is of course erroneous to the extent that it assumes incorrectly that an SDLT 5 is required when it is not (see **7.2 LAND REGISTRATION AND CERTIFICATES**). However, Land Registry practice seems to have changed again and where no SDLT 5 is produced the applicant may be asked to produce a letter from HMRC confirming that no SDLT is chargeable. This de facto procedure ignores the fact that the adjudication process under stamp duty which was used for certifying the correct charge was deliberately not carried over into SDLT, and also in cases where the general anti-avoidance rule in *FA 2003, s 75A* may be in point HMRC will refuse to give any clearance. The position is entirely ad hoc, unsatisfactory and without authority to support it.

Does FA 2003, s 75A apply to sub-sales?

In the view of the author (although it must be said not HMRC), the statutory general anti-avoidance rule will not apply in relation to sub-sales when the completion of the A to B contract falls to be disregarded under *FA 2003, s 45(3)*. This is because the completion of the A to B contract cannot then be a 'scheme transaction' for the purposes of *FA 2003, s 75A* nor can A and B be treated as V and P respectively for those purposes (see **11 GENERAL STATUTORY ANTI-AVOIDANCE RULE**). It is likely that the author's view will be tested in the tribunal and courts in due course.

Assignment of an agreement for lease

Where a person assigns his interest as lessee under an agreement for a lease after substantial performance, the sub-sale rule as such does not apply. If the assignment occurs before the agreement is substantially performed, the agreement is treated as if it were with the assignee and the consideration given included any given by the assignee for the assignment. If the assignment occurs after substantial performance the assignment is a separate land transaction. [*FA 2003, Sch 17A, para 12B*]. In the author's view the sub-sale rule may still apply to disregard the first transaction when the substantial performance of the agreement for lease occurs at the same time as the completion of it by the grant of the lease to an assignee.

Case law

HMRC have lost the first case involving an SDLT avoidance scheme to come before the tax tribunal. Although the result seems correct, the reasons given by the tribunal for its decision seem unrealistic and in some respects may be wrong. The case was also notable for the absence of any argument by HMRC that this was a tax avoidance scheme and should have been dealt with as such under case law principles of purposive interpretation derived from *Ramsay*. Instead HMRC adopted a relentlessly literal interpretation of the relevant SDLT rules and foundered on that approach.

The case, *DV3 RS Limited Partnership v the Commissioners for Her Majesty's Revenue and Customs* [2011] SFTD 531, involved the purchase of the Dickens and Jones store in Regent Street in 2006 for £65m. Calling the seller A and the purchaser B, B would normally have had to pay SDLT of £2.6m on its acquisition from A. However B used a sub-sale into partnership scheme to reduce the SDLT to nil. The scheme worked by B on completing its purchase from A, immediately selling the property into a partnership ('C') of which it and some associated companies were the partners. Under the relevant SDLT rules the sale from A to B would be disregarded if it completed at the same time as the completion of the B to C sub-sale. The sub-sale from B to C took advantage of the SDLT partnership rules which can reduce the SDLT to nil where the seller or persons connected with it are partners in the partnership buying the property. Result: no SDLT on either leg of the transaction.

Counsel for HMRC took an extremely literal approach and argued that the seller in this situation was A and not B. Hence C had acquired from a non-partner and full SDLT must be due. Counsel argued that if the legislation disregarded the sale from A to B then B did not have the property to sell to C. The tribunal commented that if B had never acquired the property then it could also be said that C had never received it which was going too far.

The taxpayer's counsel argued that the seller must have been B because it was the completion of the B to C contract under which C acquired the property.

In this and other types of A to B to C situation the SDLT legislation actually disregards both the real world A to B and B to C contracts and deems that a notional contract exists under which C is the purchaser. The SDLT legislation refers to this artificial contract as the 'secondary contract'. Unfortunately the legislation is intentionally vague on whether A or B is the seller. The identity of the seller matters of course where, as here, if it was B then C pays no SDLT.

The tribunal held that the 'secondary contract' was actually between A, B and C. Because B was a partner in C the tribunal said that there was nothing to prevent the partnership rules applying to C's acquisition from B and hence no SDLT arose on C's acquisition. This, said the tribunal, was unaffected by the fact that B had simultaneously acquired the property from A using another provision which removed the SDLT on that transaction.

Despite this being the correct result there are problems with the tribunal's reasoning. Ignoring the mistake at para 79 of the judgment which refers to a payment by B to C as escaping tax when the judge must have meant a payment by B to A, there are two fundamental concerns. (The original version of the judgment which appeared on the tribunal website contained various worrying mistakes about the identity of A, B and C but most of these were subsequently corrected apparently without any mention that an amended version of the judgment had replaced the original version).

The problems revolve around the tribunal's decision that the secondary contract was between A, B and C. First, this finding appears to have been unnecessary in order to arrive at a decision and to fly in the face of the statutory provision in *Finance Act 2003, section 45(5A) (b)* which provides that the seller under the 'secondary contract' shall be either A or B. In deciding that the 'secondary contract' with C has both A and B as parties to it the tribunal seems to have overlooked this even though the judgment quotes the statutory provision verbatim. In fact the tribunal said that they did not find the provision to have been of any help. At the very least one would have expected some attempt to explain the apparent inconsistency but there is none.

Second, treating A and B together as parties to the 'secondary contract' appears to have been unrealistic in this case. The tribunal said that in cases where there was an assignment by B to C of his contract with A or where C had agreed to pay the balance of what was owed under the A to B contract directly to A, it was intended that A be a party to the 'secondary contract'. This does not seem unreasonable. However in a single sentence without any reason being given the tribunal then goes on to say: 'That suggests that the same is the case in relation to a sub-sale of the type in this appeal'. No explanation for this conclusion was given and a moment's reflection will reveal how unrealistic it is. If this transaction followed the usual course then when A sold to B it had no knowledge of C and may well have inserted a special condition in its contract preventing a sub-sale in the sense that A could not be compelled to transfer the property to anyone but B. If this was the case then it seems strange to decide that A was a party to the 'secondary contract' with C given that A had no involvement or connection with C. Surely the sensible conclusion would have been to decide that in this type of sub-sale the parties to the 'secondary contract' are B and C. The tribunal could still have reached the same conclusion that C escaped tax without the unnecessary and difficult conclusion that both A and B were parties to the 'second contract' with C.

Despite the flaws in the judge's reasoning this case represents a strong win for the taxpayer. Reliance on a blatant tax avoidance scheme did not affect the literal operation of two different parts of the SDLT code when combined together to produce a nil tax result.

This transaction occurred just before the introduction of the general statutory anti-avoidance provision in *FA 2003 s75A* in December, 2006. What of similar transactions undertaken post-section 75A? These were effectively exempted from *section 75A* until the changes made by *FA 2010, section 55* from March, 2010 (see **11.4(8) General Statutory Anti-Avoidance Rule**). So transactions up until at least then are probably covered by this judgment. There are also flaws in the changes made by *FA 2010*. HMRC may well appeal the decision and if so it remains to be seen if they stay with the same approach on appeal.

Exchanges and partitions

[8.5] Where there is an exchange of chargeable interests each leg of the exchange is treated for stamp duty land tax as a separate land transaction. [*FA*

2003, s 47(1) and see **5.3 Surrender and Regrant; Sale and Leaseback** for surrenders and regrant of leases]. Each such transaction is charged to SDLT separately from the other and the 'single-sale' route previously available under stamp duty is not available in SDLT (see **36.7 Exchanges of Property**). If either leg of an exchange involves a 'major interest' in land then the chargeable consideration for each acquisition is:

(1) the market value of the interest acquired plus any rent payable if the acquisition is the grant of a lease; or if greater;
(2) the actual chargeable consideration given for the acquisition. (*FA 2003, Sch 4, para 5(3)* and *(3A)* and see *FA 2003, s 117* for the definition of a 'major interest' being broadly a freehold or leasehold interest).

Prior to 24 March 2011 the chargeable consideration was taken to be only the market value of the interest acquired (plus any rent payable if the acquisition was the grant of a lease). By charging SDLT on the actual chargeable consideration if greater than the market value of the interest acquired, the legislation has created a potentially harsh regime that would for example tax a grandparent who exchanges a £1m home with her grandson for his £300,000 flat, on the £1m of actual consideration she gives rather than on the £300,000 value of the interest she receives (with the grandson paying tax on the £1m market value of what he receives). It is understood that this type of consequence was not intended by HMRC. Consequently HMRC may be willing to ameliorate this harshness by arguably bending the just and reasonable apportionment rules in *FA 2003, Sch 4, para 4* by treating £700,000 of the £1m consideration given by the grandmother being the excess over the value of the £300,000 flat received by her as a gift from her and as such not taxable consideration. This treatment appears to be concessionary and not supported by the relevant legislative wording.

In a sale and leaseback the interest sold is treated as encumbered by the obligation to grant the leaseback. Hence the market value of the interest sold to the person granting the leaseback could be less than the value of the lease granted in return so that the tax charge should be on the higher value of the leaseback. However, HMRC do not seem to pursue this consequence particularly where the value of the interest sold is purely nominal after taking into account the value of the leaseback. For example where a developer sells the freehold interest in a block of flats worth £5m to a company subject to the company granting 999 year leases back to the developer at a nominal rent, the company should pay tax on the value of the leasebacks which will be approximate to the value of the freehold. However, HMRC are apparently willing to overlook this consequence of the exchange rule and treat the company as giving only nominal consideration for its freehold acquisition.

In an exchange where cash equality money is paid HMRC seem willing to allow the person who gives the higher value property and receives the lower value property plus a cash equality payment in exchange as having given only the value of the property acquired by him with the market value of the property given by him apportioned between the market value of the property acquired (taxable) and the cash equality sum (not taxable). For example, where A and B exchange their properties valued at £375,000 and £400,000 respectively so that A also gives B cash equality of £25,000, A pays tax on the

£400,000 value of the property he receives. However, HMRC appear to be open to B paying tax not on the £400,000 value of the consideration he has given to B (the correct result) but only on the £375,000 value of the property he receives with the £25,000 apportioned to the (non-taxable) cash equality sum. It appears that having imposed a change to the exchange rules in *FA 2011* which creates a harsher regime for exchanges, HMRC are concerned to ameliorate those consequences on a discretionary basis in situations where as sole arbiter they decide that no tax avoidance is involved. Arguably this concessionary treatment is unlawful under the decision in *R (on the application of Wilkinson) v. IRC* [2006] STC 270. However, despite the uncertainty that this creates, few if any taxpayers will challenge being untaxed by concession.

With regard to VAT the chargeable consideration actually given for the exchange will include any VAT actually chargeable under general principles. This is in contrast to HMRC's practice in SDLT of regarding the market value (as distinct from the chargeable consideration given) as not including any VAT chargeable even if VAT is chargeable on the transfer of the asset.

Where neither leg of an exchange involves a 'major interest' in land, SDLT is charged on each acquisition to the extent that any chargeable consideration is given for the acquisition separate from the interest given for the acquisition, ie only on the equality money or equivalent. [*FA 2003, s 47(4)*]. Where a house building company or a property trader acquires a dwelling from an individual in exchange for a new dwelling supplied to the individual, the acquisition by the company is treated as if it were for nil chargeable consideration if the conditions in *FA 2003, Sch 6A, para 1* are satisfied.

Although each leg of an exchange is a separate land transaction, in the view of HMRC Stamp Taxes they could nevertheless be linked transactions where the parties were connected with each other so that the value of each had to be aggregated in order to ascertain the appropriate rate of SDLT: see **4.2 Linked Transactions**. This view was questionable given that under *FA 2003, s 47* each leg of the exchange is to be treated '*as if each were separate and distinct from the other*.' It was therefore difficult to understand how they could at the same time form part of '*a single scheme, arrangement or series of transactions between the same vendor and purchaser or, in either case, persons connected with them*', as required for a linked transaction by *s 108*. However, for land transactions on or after 19 July 2007, exchanges between connected persons are now expressly excluded from the linked transactions rule. Where persons who are jointly entitled to land partition or divide their interest, the share of the interest held by each person immediately before the transaction does not count as chargeable consideration. [*FA 2003, Sch 4, para 6*]. This is intended to ensure that no SDLT will be chargeable on a partition or division of land where there is no other consideration passing in money or money's worth. Given that a partition or division involves an 'exchange' of land within the scope of *FA 2003, Sch 4, para 5(1)*, the SDLT charge applies (in the case of a major interest in land) to what is received rather than what is given up (ie the interest held immediately before the transaction will not be the same interest received by the other joint owner). Accordingly, in treating what is given up as not chargeable consideration, the provision strictly does not remove a charge under *FA 2003, Sch 4, para 5*. However, HMRC does not take this point and regards *FA 2003, Sch 4, para 6* as sufficient to remove an SDLT charge on a partition or division except to the extent that there is any other consideration in money or money's worth. Cash or other consideration may arise on a partition or division where the resulting partition results in a change in the value of the parties' respective interests and a balancing payment is made by the party whose interest has been enlarged at the expense of the other.

Options

[8.6] The acquisition of an option binding the grantor to enter into a land transaction and the acquisition of a right of pre-emption restricting or preventing the grantor from entering into a land transaction (i.e. a right of first refusal) are each land transactions in their own right for stamp duty land tax purposes. They are separate from any land transactions that result from the exercise of the option or right. [*FA 2003, s 46(1)*, but see **9.1 Transitional Provisions** for options and rights granted after 16 April 2003 and before 1 December 2003 which are excised on or after the latter date]. The effective date of the land transaction is when the option or right is acquired and not when it is exercisable. [*FA 2003, s 46(3)*]. In the author's view the grant of an option by the purchaser under a contract to acquire a chargeable interest which occurs at the same time as the substantial performance or completion of the purchase contract will be an 'other transaction' within the rules for sub-sales in *FA 2003, s45* (see **8.4 Sub-Sales, Assignments And Novations**)

Treatment of goodwill

[8.7] Taxpayers who check the box at the start of the SDLT 4 return to confirm that the land transaction is part of the sale of a business that includes goodwill can normally expect to receive an enquiry letter. That letter will ask whether SDLT was paid on the goodwill element of the amount of the total price identified in the SDLT 4 and refer the taxpayer to what is said about goodwill in the HMRC Capital Gains Tax Manual.

If the taxpayer has not paid SDLT on the goodwill, letters will usually be exchanged between the taxpayer's advisers and HMRC debating whether some or all of the price attributable to the goodwill should be included as part of the price of the land and additional SDLT paid accordingly. This debate may also consider whether there is any legal basis for charging SDLT on the goodwill at all. In the author's experience these debates will often be inconclusive and reach an impasse, with HMRC apparently unwilling to call the taxpayer's bluff by taking a case only to lose and the taxpayer feeling that the amounts involved do not justify funding an appeal. There are many of these unsettled cases and in aggregate a considerable amount of tax revenue is at stake.

Apportionment

[8.8] An apportionment of the total price paid for a business that includes land and buildings may be needed for various tax purposes, not just for SDLT. These include calculating the available capital allowances for loose plant and fixtures and for a claim by a company for a deduction for purchased goodwill under *Corporation Taxes Act 2009, Part 8*.

There may be a tension between maximising capital allowances (by arguing that there is little or no goodwill and that the price should be apportioned mainly to the fixtures and chattels but with a consequent increase in the SDLT charge in the case of the fixtures) and maximising the amount apportioned to goodwill for the purpose of a claim under *Corporation Taxes Act 2009, Part 8* (and also arguing that this goodwill is not part of the land and so does not attract SDLT).

These issues are particularly acute in the case of the sale of businesses as a going concern occupying land and buildings such as pubs and hotels, nursing and residential homes, restaurants, cinemas and petrol stations.

Just and reasonable and fair

[8.9] The business being acquired may include land and fixtures, moveable plant and equipment and other chattels, and intangible assets such as a brand name and goodwill. For capital gains, SDLT and capital allowance purposes any apportionment of the total price must be done on a 'just and reasonable' basis, even if this produces a different apportionment from that agreed in the sale and purchase agreement. In the case of capital allowances an election for an alternative apportionment of the price may also be available under *Capital Allowances Act 2001, s 198*. In relation to the cost of purchased goodwill this will be based on the difference between the total price paid and the 'fair' value of the identifiable assets and liabilities.

Of course this raises the question what is 'just and reasonable' and 'fair' and ultimately the answer will turn on a valuation. A fundamental question in arriving at a valuation will be whether the value of the land includes any goodwill in the true sense of the term 'goodwill'. It is here where the sands may be shifting and it appears that valuers and to some extent HMRC may now be taking a more realistic approach to goodwill and land as being separate things. Such an approach accords with case law.

HMRC's position

[8.10] In attempting to understand HMRC's position, the SDLT adviser's first port of call is likely to be the SDLT Manual. This currently states at SDLTM04005:

SDLTM04005 – Scope: How much is chargeable

Goodwill

Stamp duty land tax is a charge on transactions in "land".

> Thus the subject-matter of the charge includes anything forming part of the land as a matter of law, such as buildings and structures forming part of the land, and fixtures.
>
> This means that the subject-matter of the charge may or may not include what is described as goodwill.
>
> In some instances what is described as goodwill actually forms part of the land. This is often described as inherent goodwill because it is inherent in the land.
>
> In other cases goodwill, sometimes called free goodwill, is separate from the land.
>
> There is more guidance on the distinction between inherent goodwill and free goodwill in the Capital Gains Manual at pages CG0803–CG68046.
>
> Free goodwill will only be present on the sale of a business or part of a business, but not necessarily even then.
>
> Issues relating to the categorisation of goodwill, or the valuation of free goodwill where an apportionment is required, should be referred to the Valuation Office Agency.
>
> The exclusion of goodwill from the charge to stamp duty by FA02/S116 does not apply to stamp duty land tax.

HMRC's published guidance on how to fill in box 1 of the SDLT 4, as well as referring to SDLTM04005, also says 'It should be noted that "goodwill" is not often capable of separation from the land. A payment for goodwill that is part of the land is part of the chargeable consideration for Stamp Duty Land Tax purposes. The price paid for this goodwill should be included in the figure shown at question 10 of the SDLT 1 [ie the total consideration for the purchase]. Please see also the Valuation Office Agency guidance.' (see further below).

HMRC's published views on goodwill

[8.11] Goodwill is dealt with at CG68000 to CG68330 in a rewritten section but mainly only in relation to intellectual property.

However, anyone consulting the Valuation Office Agency guidance referred to above would find what in effect was a summary of the old guidance:

> 7.41 Forms of Goodwill
>
> The Inspector's instructions refer to three forms of goodwill:
>
> Inherent Goodwill
>
> (1) This is the goodwill generated by the location of the property rather than the carrying on of a particular business. It is perhaps wrongly described as goodwill at all because all it really represents is the locational advantages of the property. It may be attracted by the address (for example a hotel in Park Lane). It may occur because of its strategic position (for example the only hotel in town). It is impossible for such goodwill to be sold separately from the property and it will always be reflected in the property value.

Personal Goodwill

(2) This is any trade generated by the personality, special skills or reputation of the person conducting the business (for example a restaurant run by an internationally renowned chef). Such goodwill cannot be transferred to another person or occupier of the property and, therefore, cannot form part of the value of the property.

Free Goodwill

(3) This is goodwill created by a business conducted at the property and its value depends on how well that business has been carried on. It is the trade generated by the historical reputation of a business, the personality and skills of the staff and employees, the benefits of existing licences and contracts with suppliers, customers etc. In most types of property "free goodwill" is capable of being sold separately from the property and constitutes a separate asset. However, occasionally such as in some of the specialist types of property mentioned in 2.1. above, most or all of the "free goodwill" is often incapable of being transferred to another property. In such properties "free goodwill" can be sub-divided into two categories, namely:

(A) "Adherent goodwill" which, although not inherent in the locational advantages of the property, sticks with it (for example this may represent satisfied customers who were not attracted by the personality of the particular person running the business and will continue to patronise the property provided the business continues to be run in a competent manner). As any "adherent goodwill" cannot be sold separately from the property, it does not constitute a separate asset and should be included in the DV's valuation. In practice it may prove difficult to distinguish between "adherent" and "inherent" goodwill. However, DVs should not be too concerned with these definitions but should concentrate on arriving at a valuation reflecting all goodwill attaching to and inseparable from the property.

(B) "Transferable goodwill" is any "free goodwill" which is capable of being sold completely independently of the property (for example the benefit of a trade name or a contract to provide a certain number of hotel beds etc). It is capable [of] constituting a separate asset and should not normally be reflected in the DV's valuation of the property.

The reference in the extract above to 'The Inspector's instructions' is presumably to the old guidance in the Capital Gains Manual and that guidance has been deleted. This change appears to have happened in response to the criticism of the elaborate categorisation of goodwill made by the Special Commissioner in *Balloon Promotions Ltd v Wilson (Inspectors of Taxes)* [2006] STC (SCD) 167. HMRC's approach had been to argue that both inherent (or locational) and adherent (or adaptional) goodwill was part of the land and that SDLT should be paid in relation to that part of the total price apportioned to inherent and adherent goodwill as well as in relation to the price apportioned to the land. Although this case concerned capital gains rollover relief, the Special Commissioner preferred to look at goodwill as a whole which can be sold separately from the business premises and questioned whether the value of adherent goodwill would be included in the value of the land and buildings.

The revised guidance on goodwill in the Capital Gains Manual is as noted above given in the context of intellectual property rights, not land. This may be due to the tension between the need for a change of view post-*Balloon Promotions* and the large amounts of tax riding on the currently unsettled outstanding cases.

In summary, the updated guidance in the Capital Gains Manual is as follows.

Goodwill is an asset for the purposes of capital gains tax and it is defined in case law, with the leading definition given by Lord Macnaghten in the stamp duty case *IRC v Muller & Co's Margarine Ltd* [1901] AC 217:

> 'It is a thing very easy to describe, very difficult to define. It is the benefit and advantage of the good name, reputation and connection of a business. It is the attractive force which brings in custom. It is the one thing which distinguishes an old-established business from a new business at its first start.'

In the same case, Lord Lindley said at AC 235:

> 'Goodwill regarded as property has no meaning except in connection with some trade, business or calling. In that connection, I understand the term to include whatever adds value to a business by reason of situation, name and reputation, connection, introduction to old customers and agreed absence from completion'.

For capital gains purposes goodwill should be construed in accordance with legal rather than accountancy principles, following *Balloon Promotions*.

Goodwill is inseparable from the business in which it is generated and has its existence; the disposal of a business as a going concern must involve the transfer of goodwill.

Consequences of HMRC's approach

[8.12] It appears that HMRC is, at least for capital gains purposes, now prepared to accept that the traditional analysis of goodwill, as appeared in the Valuation Office Agency guidance, into three categories is no longer useful and may be misleading. It seems that HMRC now accepts that what has been described historically as 'inherent' and 'adherent' goodwill are not part of the goodwill at all but are simply attributes of the land and buildings concerned and should be reflected in the valuation of them. Goodwill, properly so-called, passes separately from the land with the business and is not part of the land.

Despite this, HMRC Stamp Taxes still regards 'inherent' and 'adherent' goodwill as forming part of the land. SDLT is, in its view, chargeable on a 'just and reasonable' apportionment of the total price to these items. Nevertheless in the author's view, it is likely that the 'clarification' of HMRC's view explained above will filter through to HMRC Stamp Taxes in due course and be accepted by it.

Will this approach make any difference?

[8.13] In principle this approach should make little difference, at least in relation to 'inherent' goodwill. This is because whether the locational advantage of the land is categorised as part of the goodwill and added to the price of the land (the old approach) or simply included in the valuation of the land for apportionment purposes (the new approach) should not alter the total amount of the price apportioned to the land for SDLT purposes. In practice however, the new approach, by making a clear distinction between goodwill and land as separate assets, may place more of an evidential burden on HMRC in attacking that part of the price expressly apportioned to goodwill in the sale agreement. In other words, in order to challenge an apportionment by the parties HMRC will now have to show that some or all of the price of the goodwill has unjustly and unreasonably been allocated by the parties to the goodwill and should be reallocated to the land. Under the old approach HMRC merely had to try to carry out a reallocation of the total goodwill in favour of the inherent and adherent category in order to secure additional SDLT. Under the new approach, HMRC will have to reallocate price from one asset (goodwill) to a separate asset (land). Although in principle independent valuations should resolve the issue, in practice very few such cases ever proceed to litigation and therefore in the cut and thrust of negotiations with HMRC this change of approach may favour the taxpayer.

A further issue concerns 'adherent' goodwill. HMRC Stamp Taxes treats this as part of the value of the land and so taxable but the authority for this is questionable. In the *Balloon Promotions* case the Special Commissioner questioned whether the value of what HMRC regarded as adherent free goodwill would as a matter of course be incorporated in the valuation of the business premises. It is possible that HMRC may not wish to risk a taxpayer challenge on this issue and so taxpayers should assert the doubts created by the Special Commissioners on this point when negotiating open cases with HMRC.

HMRC's Practice Note of 30 January 2009

[8.14] HMRC issued a 'Practice Note' on 30 January 2009 entitled: 'Apportioning the Price Paid for a Business Transferred as a Going Concern'. (reproduced at **APPENDIX J**). HMRC's general approach in relation to trade related properties for capital gains and SDLT purposes is that the value of goodwill and any other separately identifiable assets will usually be represented by the difference between the value of the business as a going concern and the value of the tangible assets such as property and chattels. Has the above position changed as a result of the Practice Note? The answer is that it is currently rather difficult to say because the note appears to have been the subject of some disagreement for the time being. This has come about because of the use made in the Practice Note of valuation material published by the Royal Institution of Chartered Surveyors which could be taken to suggest that the RICS tacitly support the approaches contained in the note. This is not the case and the RICS has in fact taken issue with various parts of the Practice Note.

Aside from this, what does the note reveal about HMRC's view in relation to goodwill and SDLT? The Practice Note is intended to explain how HMRC intends to apportion the price paid for a property related business as a going concern between goodwill and the other assets included in the sale.

For those completing SDLT returns in relation to the purchase of such businesses, the most important aspect of the Practice Note is in paragraph 10.10 where HMRC acknowledges that:

> . . . subdivisions of goodwill that were previously used are no longer considered helpful as they tend to cause confusion. The view now is that what used to be referred to as "inherent" and "adherent" goodwill are, in reality, attributes which add value to the property in which a business is carried on and that they do not represent goodwill at all.

This indicates that the sands have shifted and that clarity of language is helping to dispel the confusion over whether the locational advantages of a property (so-called inherent goodwill) were really goodwill or just an aspect of the property's value.

However, as suggested above, at least two aspects of this change deserve comment. First, tactically, this change may assist taxpayers in resisting an attempt by HMRC to assert that a portion of the price which the parties to a sale agreement have apportioned separately to goodwill should be reallocated to the property. Instead of reallocating price within the goodwill categories from say free goodwill to inherent goodwill, HMRC will now have to reallocate from one asset, ie goodwill, to another asset, ie the property, and allege that the arm's length apportionment by the parties is not just and reasonable. At the end of the day this will depend in large part on valuations but in practice, this shift in approach may be to the taxpayer's advantage.

Second, it is apparent that HMRC are still smarting from the doubts created by the Special Commissioner's decision in *Balloon Promotions Ltd v Wilson (Inspectors of Taxes)* [2006] STC (SCD) 167 over whether adherent (adaptional) goodwill should be included in the value of the business premises. It does not appear to be willing to accept this aspect of the decision and seeks to distinguish that case on its facts. One wonders however, whether HMRC would be willing to risk defeat on this point before the courts and taxpayers may well adopt a firm line in negotiations on this with HMRC.

HMRC's Current Approach in Practice

[8.15] Where a property-related business has been acquired and goodwill has been separately identified and a part of the purchase price apportioned to it, HMRC will in most cases seek to re-apportion that part of the price to the business premises for SDLT purposes. HMRC will typically cite the requirement in FRS 7 for 'fair value' to be used in the accounts for the assets acquired. Under FRS 7 'fair value' equates to 'market value' in the case of tangible fixed assets, and HMRC will say that FRS 15, para 53 requires 'existing use value' to be used and that this means that any goodwill with the exception of personal goodwill is really part of the trading potential of the premises and so forms a part of the value of that asset. It is apparent that HMRC rely heavily on the accounting-based approach to goodwill when the proper approach is to apply the legal definition for capital gains tax and SDLT purposes. The legal approach following *Balloon Promotions Ltd v Wilson (Inspectors of Taxes)* [2006] STC (SCD) 167 (see **8.14** above) is that the value of the goodwill as an assets is enhanced when all the asset are sold together and that the value of individual premises should not be affected by whether or not they are sold individually or as part of a business, and it is the goodwill as a separate asset whose value is affected. HMRC's approach should therefore be resisted and currently it seems that HMRC are unwilling to test their approach before the tribunal.

Chapter 9

Transitional Provisions

General

[9.1] The provisions of *FA 2003* governing the transition from stamp duty on land to stamp duty land tax are confusing and hard to follow. The relevant provisions are contained in *FA 2003, s 125* and *Schs 15, 19* and *20* and their effect can be summarised as follows.

A transaction is not an SDLT transaction unless:

(1) 'the effective date' of the transaction is on or after 1 December 2003 [*FA 2003, Sch 19, para 2(1)*]; and
(2) it is pursuant to a contract entered into after 10 July 2003 [*FA 2003, Sch 19, para 3(1)*] (or it is pursuant to a contract entered into on or before 10 July 2003 if subsequently that contract was varied or assigned, or an option, right of pre-emption or similar right has been exercised or where the purchaser is a person other than the purchaser under that contract because of an assignment, sub-sale or other transaction made after that date. [*FA 2003, Sch 19, para 3(3)*]).

The 'effective date' of the transaction is normally the date of completion by conveyance unless the contract is 'substantially performed' before completion, when the effective date is when the contract is substantially performed. [*FA 2003, s 44* and see **2.3 Contracts, Conveyances and 'Effective Date'**]. However, in the transitional provisions 'effective date' has an extended meaning. Where (2) above applies and the contract is substantially performed after 10 July 2003, but before 1 December 2003 and is not completed until on or after the latter date, the effective date of the transaction is the date of completion (regardless of the fact that substantial performance occurred before 1 December 2003). [*FA 2003, Sch 19, para 4*].

From 1 December 2003 ('the implementation date': to be appointed by Treasury order under *FA 2003, Sch 19, para (2)(2)*) stamp duty is chargeable only on:

(1) instruments relating to stock or marketable securities (this includes shares and non-exempt loan capital) [*FA 2003, s 125(1)*];
(2) bearer instruments; [*FA 1999, Sch 15* remains in full force and effect];
(3) acquisition of partnership interests [*FA 2003, s 125(8)* and *Sch 15, para 13(2)*]; and
(4) any dealing in land that is not an 'SDLT transaction' [*FA 2003, s 125(5)(b)*]. (This ensures that stamp duty continues to apply where a contract relating to land was entered into on or before 10 July 2003 (Royal Assent to *FA 2003*) but was not completed by instrument until

> on or after 1 December 2003. Under the original terms of clause 125 such instruments would not have been SDLT transactions and stamp duty would not have applied so the transaction would have escaped both SDLT and stamp duty.)

Therefore, contracts that are completed before 1 December 2003 will not be SDLT transactions, and contracts that were entered into on or before 10 July 2003 and have not been varied or novated, sub-sold etc. since that date but do not complete until on or after 1 December 2003 will give rise to stamp duty only and not SDLT. Where there is a sub-sale after 10 July 2003 that is not completed until on or after 1 December 2003 and the original contract was substantially performed on or before 10 July 2003 the sub-sale does not make the first contract an SDLT transaction given that the policy is to exclude from SDLT any contract substantially performed on or before 10 July 2003. It is understood that HMRC accepts this as the position. However, where the original contract was not substantially performed on or before 10 July 2003, a sub-sale occurring after that date will cause the original sale to be potentially chargeable with SDLT if it was substantially performed on or after 17 March 2004 because it will be an SDLT transaction as a result of the substitution of *FA 2003, Sch 19 para 3(3)(c)* by *FA 2004, Sch 29 para 12*.

Where a transaction chargeable to SDLT is effected pursuant to a contract entered into before 1 December 2003, any ad valorem stamp duty paid on the contract is available as a credit against the SDLT payable (but no refund is available should the stamp duty exceed the SDLT). [*FA 2003, Sch 19, para 5(1)*].

In relation to the stamping of agreements for lease entered into before 1 December 2003 where the lease is granted on or after that date and the transaction is an SDLT transaction, the protection against interest and penalties under *FA 1994, s 240* (see **16 Agreement for Lease** on the presentation of the agreement for stamping is continued by *FA 2003, Sch 19, para 8*. If the agreement is presented for stamping together with a Revenue certificate in relation to the grant of the lease then the payment of SDLT (or the fact that no SDLT was payable) on the grant of the lease is to be denoted on the agreement and the agreement shall be deemed to be duly stamped. The lease must be either in conformity with the agreement or relate to substantially the same property and term as the agreement.

Where an option to enter into a land transaction or a right of pre-emption relating to a land transaction was acquired after 16 April 2003 but before 1 December 2003 and exercised on or after the latter date, any consideration given for the grant of the option or right is treated as part of the chargeable consideration for the land transaction resulting from the exercise of the option or right. [*FA 2003, Sch 19, para 9(1), (2)*].

Unwinding split title structures

[9.2] Prior to the introduction of SDLT, many properties were acquired and held within what were known as split title structures in order to take advantage of resting on contract and stamp duty sub-sale relief in order to defer the payment of stamp duty indefinitely. Such properties would be registered in the names of two corporate nominees for the beneficial owner. The effect of acquiring the beneficial ownership within such a structure was that any subsequent transfer of the legal title was vulnerable to *ad valorem* stamp duty on the purchase consideration paid under the purchase contract unless the property was sub-sold within the terms of *SA 1891, s 58(4)* with the sub-purchaser paying *ad valorem* duty on his acquisition (unless some relief applied). Following the introduction of SDLT it is often asked whether such structures can be rolled-up and the legal and beneficial ownership reunited in one person or entity without giving rise to a stamp duty charge. What seems clear is that to successfully avoid giving rise to an *ad valorem* stamp duty charge on the all the intermediate uncompleted sale contracts, the transaction under which the legal and the beneficial interests are reunited should be by way of a transaction which satisfies the conditions for sub-sale relief under *SA 1891, s 58(4)* – see **39.8 Sub-sales**. It may be that some exemption or relief from SDLT on the final sub-sale transaction is available. However it should be noted that SDLT group relief will not be available in such cases because of *FA 2003, s 45(5A)* which treats the vendor in a sub-sale as the original vendor and not the immediate vendor so that the conditions for group relief to apply will not be met.

Chapter 10

Disclosure of SDLT Avoidance Schemes

General

[10.1] Since 1 August 2005, disclosure has been required of certain stamp duty land tax ('SDLT') schemes. The rules have been built onto and incorporate most of the direct tax scheme disclosure rules that were already in existence on 1 August 2005, referred to here as 'the basic rules'. The basic rules contain the definitions and other matters relating to tax scheme disclosure generally.

Detailed guidance on the basic rules, including the definitions of key terms, is published by LexisNexis in *Simon's Direct Tax Service* (Division A3.19). The relevant statutory instruments are:

(a) the *Stamp Duty Land Tax Avoidance Schemes (Prescribed Descriptions of Arrangements) Regulations 2005 (SI 2005 No 1868)*; and
(b) the *Tax Avoidance Schemes (Information) (Amendment) Regulations 2010 (SI 2010 No 410)*.

[10.2] The scope of the SDLT disclosure rules was significantly extended from 1 April 2010 so that they now apply to arrangements relating to any of the following:

(a) wholly non-residential property whose market value is at least £5m;
(b) wholly residential property whose market value is at least £1m; or
(c) mixed non-residential and residential property where either the residential property is worth at least £1m or the value of all the property is at least £5m.

In addition, since 1 April 2010 HMRC will allocate a scheme reference number to notifiable SDLT schemes notified to them and the promoter is required to notify that reference number to scheme users on form AAG 6 (SDLT). The user (purchaser) of a notifiable scheme must then supply details of the transaction and the scheme reference number to HMRC on form AAG 4 (SDLT).

However, even if the scheme otherwise meets the requirements for disclosure, it may still be excepted from disclosure if either of the exemptions in *reg 2(3B)* of *SI 2005 No 1868* apply, namely:

(a) the arrangements are of a type excluded from disclosure under the provisions in the Schedule to *SI 2005 No 1868*; or
(b) the arrangements are of the same, or substantially the same, description as arrangements which were first made available for implementation by any person before 1 April 2010.

Decision chart

[10.3] Before describing the detailed requirements it may be helpful to see a decision tree in order to fix the main points in the reader's mind.

Figure 1: SDLT Disclosure Decision chart

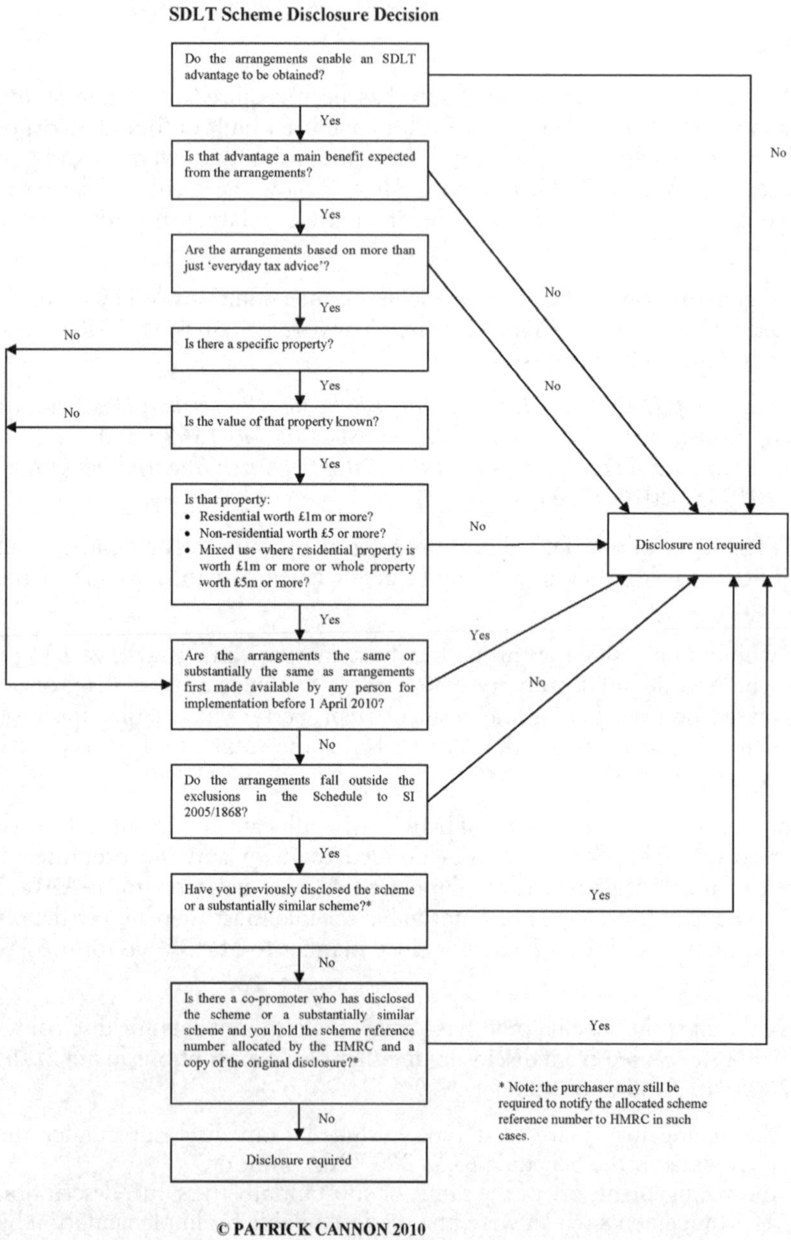

What has to be disclosed?

[10.4] Disclosure is required of SDLT arrangements and proposals:

(a) where an SDLT advantage might be expected to be a main benefit;
(b) the arrangements relate to any of the following:
- wholly non-residential property whose market value is at least £5m;
- wholly residential property whose market value is at least £1m;
- mixed non-residential and residential property where either the residential property is worth at least £1m or the value of all the property is at least £5m; or
- the *market value* or the type of the property is not known; and

(c) none of the exceptions from disclosure apply.

Residential property is defined in *FA 2003, s 116* as being a building used or suitable for use as a dwelling or in the process of being constructed or adapted for such use, plus the garden or grounds. Non-residential property is any other property. A single transaction involving six or more dwellings is treated as involving non-residential property and may therefore be disclosable even though it involves only dwellings which are worth less than £1m individually but at least £5m collectively.

Market value is ascertained in the same way as it is for capital gains tax and it would seem that any mortgage secured on the property is ignored for this purpose. [see *TCGA 1992, s 26(3)*]. All chargeable interests held by all connected persons in the same property are added together. The market value is taken for this purpose at the time the requirement to disclose arises.

When to disclose?

[10.5] For marketed SDLT schemes the obligation to disclose arises when the proposal is made available for implementation by any person. If a promoter does not know the market value or type of property or makes a proposal available 'generally', it is to be assumed that the criteria listed in **10.4**(b) above are satisfied. There is no clear guidance on the meaning of 'generally' and it appears that HMRC's Anti-Avoidance Group (Intelligence) ('AAG') takes the view that this includes making a scheme available through a distributor at a time when no specific users have been identified.

By 'marketed schemes' HMRC mean 'schemes planned with no specific client in mind or possibly marketed to a class of user, for example wealthy individuals, large companies or employers' (see HMRC guidance on Disclosure of Tax Avoidance Schemes dated February 2010 with effect from 1 April 2010 ('HMRC Guidance') at **10.3.2**). Essentially, the way in which the SDLT advantage is expected to be achieved remains as originally planned or pre-packaged and can be applied with minor changes to all expected users.

According to the HMRC Guidance, a marketed scheme will be treated as having been made available for implementation when the promoter:

- communicates (whether orally or in writing) what is essentially a fully formed proposal to existing or potential clients; or

- provides an existing proposal to a client in respect of arrangements that would otherwise be a bespoke scheme (see further below).

By 'bespoke scheme' HMRC means 'a tax arrangement designed in response to a client's specific tax management issue' (HMRC Guidance at 10.3.3).

For bespoke SDLT schemes, HMRC practice (which appears to be concessionary) is that the obligation to disclose only arises when the promoter becomes aware that a transaction forming part of the arrangements has occurred.

In each case the disclosure by the promoter must be made within five days of the disclosure obligation arising. This contrasts with the 30 days in which to disclose given to users when there is no promoter involved. If the user has used a lawyer promoter but has not waived legal professional privilege then the user must disclose within five days of entering into the first transaction forming part of the arrangements.

Who has to disclose?

Promoters

[10.6] The primary obligation to disclose falls on the promoter of the SDLT scheme. Barristers and solicitors (unless covered by legal professional privilege which their client has not waived), accountants, chartered tax advisers, estate agents, chartered surveyors and other advisers whose work includes an element of tax advice can all be a promoter (as can banks and securities houses regardless of whether they supply tax services or not). Disclosure is required within five days.

A promoter is someone who is to any extent responsible for the design of a scheme, makes a scheme available for implementation to other persons or who organises or manages the implementation of a scheme. However, certain persons are not to be treated as promoters. These are persons who either:

(a) in the course of providing tax advice do not contribute to the design of the scheme; or
(b) although involved in the design of the scheme do not give any tax advice in relation to the scheme (banks or securities houses cannot take advantage of this exception); or
(c) persons who are not responsible for the design of all the elements of the scheme and could not reasonably be expected to know whether the scheme was notifiable or how to comply with disclosure if it was required.

Examples of these exceptions are (a) a lawyer who advises on compliance only; (b) a lawyer who advises on the company law aspects; and (c) a chartered surveyor who markets the property subject to the scheme.

Barristers and solicitors who suggest bespoke SDLT schemes to their clients, and who are therefore prevented from disclosing by legal professional privilege, are excluded from being a promoter and the disclosure obligation is in principle transferred to the user, who is treated as if there were no promoter (although the exemption from disclosure for legally privileged information continues to apply in full to such information in the user's hands).

Persons dealing with non-UK promoters

[10.7] The disclosure obligation falls on the user and disclosure is required within five days of entering into the transaction.

When there is no promoter

[10.8] When there is no promoter, any person who enters into a transaction forming part of the arrangements must disclose within 30 days.

When the promoter is covered by legal professional privilege

[10.9] The disclosure obligation in principle falls on the user unless he chooses to waive his right to privilege (but subject to the same exemption in the user's hands for information that is the subject of a claim to legal professional privilege). Disclosure of any information that is not subject to legal professional privilege is required to be made by the user within five days of entering into the first transaction forming part of the scheme.

Exclusions from disclosure

[10.10] These are two sets of exclusions from disclosure in SDLT. These are first, where the arrangements are excluded because they meet the tests for exclusion involving the steps designated in the Schedule to *SI 2005/1868*; or second, if the arrangements are the same, or substantially the same, as arrangements which were first made available by any person for implementation before 1 April 2010.

The Schedule

[10.11] The Schedule to *SI 2005 No 1868* contains a list of six excluded steps designated by the capital letters A to F. The Schedule also contains two rules (Rule 1 and Rule 2) which relate to certain combinations of steps A to F which are not excluded.

The purpose of those exclusions is to avoid the need to disclose certain basic SDLT avoidance measures which are in common use and known to HMRC. Disclosure is not required of SDLT schemes which consist of either a single step from the list or a combination of steps, unless the combination of steps is prevented from being excluded by Rules 1 and 2.

It is important to note that the inclusion of an unlisted step necessary to obtain the SDLT advantage in an otherwise excluded scheme will make the scheme disclosable where all the other requirements for disclosure are met.

The listed steps A to F are as follows.

Step A: Acquisition of a chargeable interest by special purpose vehicle

The acquisition of a chargeable interest in land by a company created for that purpose (a special purpose vehicle).

It would appear that the use of an 'off-the-shelf' company created for general purposes, but which is then used to acquire land, may not be an excluded step. It is not clear whether 'company' includes a unit trust scheme, which generally is treated as a company for SDLT purposes. The wording of the relevant regulations (*SI 2005 No 1868*) expressly imports the SDLT definitions for selected terms only, such as 'chargeable interest'. Because the regulations do not define 'company' and use the term 'unit trust' separately elsewhere (in step B), by implication unit trusts are therefore not to be included in the meaning of 'company'. The AAG has informed the author that it is of the same view in relation to unit trusts.

Step B: Claims to relief

Making:

(a) **a single claim to relief under any of the following provisions of the *FA 2003*:**
  - (i) ***s 57A* (sale and leaseback arrangements);**
  - (ii) ***s 60* (compulsory purchase facilitating development);**
  - (iii) ***s 61* (compliance with planning obligation);**
  - (iv) ***s 64* (demutualisation of building society);**
  - (v) **[*s 64A* (initial transfer of assets to trustees of unit trust scheme);]**
  - (vi) ***s 65* (incorporation of limited liability partnership);**
  - (vii) ***s 66* (transfers involving public bodies);**
  - (viii) ***s 67* (transfer in consequence of reorganisation of parliamentary constituencies);**
  - (ix) ***s 69* (acquisition by bodies established for national purposes);**
  - (x) ***s 71* (certain acquisitions by registered social landlords);**
  - (xi) ***s 74* (collective enfranchisement by leaseholders);**
  - (xii) ***s 75* (crofting community right to buy);**
  - (xiii) ***Sch 6* (disadvantaged areas relief);**
  - (xiv) ***Sch 6A* (relief for certain acquisitions of residential property);**
  - (xv) ***Sch 7* (group relief, reconstruction and acquisition reliefs);**
  - (xvi) ***Sch 8* (charities relief); or**
  - (xvii) ***Sch 9* (right to buy, shared ownership leases etc);**

(b) **one or more claims to relief under any one of the following provisions of the *FA 2003*:**
  - (i) ***s 71A* (alternative property finance: land sold to financial institution and leased to individual);**
  - (ii) ***s 72* (alternative property finance in Scotland: land sold to financial institution and leased to individual);**

(iii) **_s 72A_ (alternative property finance in Scotland: land sold to financial institution and leased to individual in common); or**

(iv) **_s 73_ (alternative property finance: land sold to financial institution and resold to individual).**

HMRC accepts that steps taken to avoid a clawback of group, reconstruction or acquisition relief by ensuring that the purchaser ceases to be a member of the vendor's group, or control of the purchaser changes only at the end of the three-year clawback period, can be included within Step B.

Step C: Sale of shares in special purpose vehicle

The sale of shares in a special purpose vehicle, which holds a chargeable interest in land, to a person with whom neither the special purpose vehicle, nor the vendor, is connected.

It is not clear whether a sale of units in a unit trust is included in this step, although it probably is not – see the note at Step A above for the reasoning. It is also unclear whether an issue of shares, as distinct from a transfer of existing shares to a purchaser, is included within step C, although on a purposive interpretation an issue of shares for money or money's worth may be a 'sale'.

Step D: Not exercising election to waive exemption from VAT

No election is made to waive exemption from value added tax (VAT) contained in the _Value Added Tax Act 1994, Sch 10, para 2_ (treatment of buildings and land for VAT purposes).

Normally a decision not to waive exemption will be done for VAT and commercial reasons and so it is difficult to see how a main benefit can be said to be the relatively small saving of SDLT on the VAT that would otherwise be charged.

Step E: Transfer of a business as a going concern

Arranging the transfer of a business, connected with the land which is the subject of the arrangements, in such a way that it is treated for the purposes of VAT as the transfer of a going concern.

In most cases the matter is simply one of fact – that is, the transfer by its very nature is or is not a transfer of a going concern and it is rare for a client to 'arrange' for the transfer to be of a going concern as distinct from it already being one. The explanation for steps D and E may simply be that someone got a little over-excited about the interaction of SDLT and VAT.

Step F: Undertaking a joint venture

The creation of a partnership (within the meaning of the _VATA 2003, Sch 15, para 1_) to which the property which subject to a land transaction is to be transferred.

The rather cumbersome wording involving the phrase 'subject to a land transaction' may have been devised to ensure that any ingenious transfer to a partnership that did not constitute a 'land transaction' would not qualify for exclusion.

Combination of steps

Arrangements which involve Steps B (Claims to relief), D (Not waiving exemption from VAT), E (Transfer of going concern for VAT purposes) or F (Creation of a partnership) are excluded unless rule 2 applies.

Rule 1

Arrangements which involve Steps B (Claims to relief), D (Not waiving exemption from VAT), E (Transfer of going concern for VAT purposes) or F (Creation of a partnership) are excluded unless Rule 2 applies.

Rule 2

Arrangements are not excluded arrangements if they:

(a) **include all, or at least two of, Steps A (Acquisition by special purpose vehicle), C (Sale of shares in special purpose vehicle) and D (Not waiving exemption from VAT); or**

(b) **involve more than one instance of Step A (Acquisition by special purpose vehicle), C (Sale of shares in special purpose vehicle) or D (Not waiving exemption from VAT).**

It is difficult to understand what function Rule 1 performs, given that arrangements involving a combination of steps B, D, E and F are as a matter of logic already excluded in any event by the general rule that any combination of steps A to F is in principle excluded. The AAG has informed the author that the purpose of rule 1 is to make it clear that combinations of certain steps are excluded unless Rule 2 applies.

Rule 2 is therefore the important rule and this prevents any combination of steps A to F from being excluded if the combination involves at least two of steps A, C or D, or more than one instance of any one of steps A, C or D. The reference in Rule 2(a) to including all of Steps A, C and D would seem to be unnecessary given that any two of these steps is all that is required to prevent the arrangements from being excluded.

Rule 2(b) prevents more than one instance of any one of steps A, C or D from being excluded from disclosure. By clear implication, more than one instance of steps B, E or F will not therefore prevent exclusion from disclosure and indeed the opening words of the Schedule expressly provide at (a) that one or more of steps A to F are excluded subject to Rules 1 and 2. However, in the HMRC Guidance at para 9.9.1 it is said that arrangements which comprise more than one claim to the same listed relief within group (a) of Step B do not qualify for exclusion and are not within step B at all. Examples given by HMRC are two claims to group relief or a claim to group relief and a claim to reconstruction relief (both being within group (a)(xv) 'Schedule 7'). Although this view may be arguable on the basis that more than one claim to the same listed relief is merely making multiple uses of step B which is permitted, it seems probable that HMRC's view would be upheld by a tribunal on the basis that there would be no point in the wording of Step B group (a) referring to a single claim to a listed relief if one could make multiple claims under that heading.

HMRC do accept however that multiple single claims to the same listed relief can be made under group (a) of Step B so long as they each relate to separate properties. The use of two or more separate listed reliefs within group (a) of Step B for the same transaction is also accepted by HMRC as qualifying for exclusion from disclosure.

Exemption for schemes made available before 1 April 2010

[10.12] **Arrangements are not discloseable** if they are the same or substantially the same as arrangements which were first made available for implementation before 1 April 2010. [*reg 2(3B), SI 2005 No 1868*]. The HMRC Guidance interprets this as meaning that arrangements which were made available by any person before 1 April 2010 are excluded from disclosure or 'grandfathered'.

The problem of how one promoter or user can know whether a separate promoter has previously made a scheme available is only partially addressed by the 'list' of two schemes published at para 9.7.1 of the HMRC Guidance which HMRC regard as having been 'grandfathered', namely:

(a) arrangements which rely on the completion of the original contract being disregarded under *FA 2003, s 45* i.e. sub-sale arrangements; and
(b) arrangements which rely on the interaction between the definition of a connected person at *CTA 2010, s 1122* and the computational rules for partnerships in *FA 2003, Sch 15*.

It is somewhat surprising that the 'grandfathering' test was not set in terms of schemes that had actually been disclosed to HMRC prior to 1 April 2010. The failure to do so means that arrangements made available before this date which were used for residential property of any value or for commercial property of less than £5m may not be known to HMRC but became exempt from disclosure on 1 April 2010 even if the arrangements are used on or after that date for property above the disclosure thresholds. The stated aim of the 'grandfathering' rule is to ensure that only new or innovative schemes and which HMRC do not know about are discloseable, but this objective has only been partially achieved by the fairly crude 'grandfathering' rule.

Making the disclosure

[10.13] There are two parts to the disclosure process. The first part concerns disclosure of the detailed description of the arrangements by the promoter or the user to HMRC (on forms AAG 1–3 as appropriate). HMRC will then allocate an 8-digit reference number for the disclosed scheme and give that to the promoter or user. The promoter must the notify the scheme reference number (on form AAG 6 (SDLT)) to users of the scheme. The second part of the disclosure process requires the user to enter detailed information about the land transaction using the scheme on form AAG 4 (SDLT) including the scheme reference number, and send that to HMRC within the specified period.

Disclosure by the promoter or user

[10.14] The information required to be disclosed (subject to legal professional privilege) when a scheme is disclosable consists of:

(a) the name and address of the promoter or user;
(b) that the arrangements are notifiable under the SDLT regulations;
(c) a summary of the proposal and the name (if any) by which it is known;
(d) information explaining each element of the proposed or actual arrangements from which the expected SDLT advantage arises; and
(e) the statutory provisions on which that SDLT advantage is based.

Once a promoter has disclosed an SDLT scheme, he is not required to make a further disclosure of the same scheme or a scheme that is substantially the same.

If there is a co-promoter of the same or substantially the same scheme, he is in principle also required to make a disclosure. However, a co-promoter is excused from making his own disclosure if the promoter who has disclosed has:

(a) supplied the identity and address of the co-promoter to HMRC or the co-promoter holds the relevant scheme reference number; and
(b) the co-promoter holds a copy of the disclosure made by the disclosing promoter.

Disclosure by user

[10.15] The user of a disclosed SDLT scheme should receive the scheme reference number allocated by HMRC from the promoter (or from HMRC direct where the user disclosed the scheme). The promoter must disclose the scheme reference number to the user on form AAG 6 (SDLT) within 30 days of the later of being provided with the scheme reference number by HMRC or becoming aware of any transaction forming part of the scheme. [*FA 2004, s 312*]. In practice, it may be easier if the scheme reference number (if known) is supplied to the user at completion of the land transaction concerned.

When a user has been provided with a scheme reference number by a promoter, he is required to supply the scheme reference number using form AAG 6 (SDLT) to any other person who is or is likely to be a party to the arrangements concerned and might reasonably be expected to gain a tax advantage. [*FA 2004, s 312A*]. This notification of other parties must be done within 30 days of the user becoming aware of any transaction forming part of the scheme or if later, the day on which the scheme reference number is notified to the user by the promoter. [*reg 7A, SI 2004 No 1864*]. This requirement to notify co-users of a scheme may be particularly relevant in SDLT planning where a scheme may involve more than one land transaction and more than one purchaser.

When a purchaser is using a notifiable SDLT scheme, he must no later than 30 days following the later of the effective date of the first land transaction which forms part of the arrangements or the receipt of the scheme reference number, provide the following information to HMRC using form AAG4 (SDLT):

- name and address of purchaser;
- the scheme reference number;
- address and title number of property concerned;

- unique transaction reference number of any relevant land transaction return i.e. either the electronic SDLT submission receipt or, for a paper return, the number in the reference box on the payslip;
- market value of property taking into account all chargeable interests in it held by the same person or persons connected with him;
- effective date of first land transaction forming part of the arrangements;
- name of person making the declaration of accuracy and completeness of the notification; and
- the capacity in which that person is acting.

[*regs 8(5A), (14A), (14B) and (15)(e), SI 2004 No 1864*].

A purchaser is required to make a separate notification to HMRC using form AAG 4 (SDLT) each time he enters into a land transaction using the disclosed scheme, but only of course where the arrangements are notifiable. This means that land transactions that are not within the prescribed description of arrangements in relation to SDLT will not require a notification, so that only land transactions which meet the threshold criteria set out in **10.4**(b) above need to be notified.

Penalties

[10.16] A failure to make the required disclosure of a SDLT scheme, whilst not a criminal offence, renders the offender liable to an initial penalty of up to £1m and is determined by the First-tier Tribunal. If the failure to make disclosure continues after the initial penalty is imposed by the First-tier Tribunal, an Officer of the Board of HMRC may impose a further penalty of up to £600 per day.

Chapter 11

General Statutory Anti-Avoidance Rule

Introduction

[11.1] A statutory general anti-avoidance rule for SDLT was introduced with effect from 6 December 2006 by regulations in the form of the *Stamp Duty Land Tax (Variation of the Finance Act 2003) Regulations 2006 (SI 2006/3237)*. This provision was replaced retrospectively by *FA 2003*, new *ss 75A*, *75B* and *75C* with effect from the same date by *FA 2007, s 71*. The rule is intended to block both existing and new SDLT avoidance schemes as they emerge without the need for HMRC to continually enact targeted anti-avoidance provisions. The need for it reflects the poor quality of the drafting of the SDLT provisions (although this may not be the fault of the parliamentary draughtsman). Unfortunately the drafting of the rule is itself problematic and leaves open many important questions about the scope and effect of the rule. It is therefore likely to be some time, if at all, before those questions are answered conclusively and the meaning of some of the phrases included in the rule refined sufficiently to avoid ambiguity and uncertainty (see **11.7 Some Problems with ss 75A–75C**).

The rule formula

[11.2] It is important to note that the provision is a rule and not a principle which means that individual transactions must be judged objectively as either within the terms of the rule or not rather than asking whether they fall within the spirit but not the letter of the provision.

Essentially, the rule is intended to operate whenever there are a number of transactions involved in connection with the disposal and acquisition of a chargeable interest and the total SDLT chargeable is less than HMRC would normally have intended. The rule applies where—

(1) one person (called 'V') disposes of a chargeable interest and another person (called 'P') acquires the interest or an interest deriving from it;
(2) a number of transactions (which we are told includes the actual disposal and acquisition) are *involved in connection with* the disposal and acquisition (those are collectively referred to as 'the scheme transactions'); and
(3) the sum of the amounts of SDLT payable in respect of the scheme transactions is less than the amount that would be payable on a notional land transaction effecting the acquisition of V's chargeable interest by P on its disposal by V.

When the rule applies the scheme transactions which are land transactions are disregarded for SDLT purposes and in their place is a notional land transaction. The chargeable consideration for the notional land transaction is the largest amount (or aggregate amount) either:

(a) given by or on behalf of any one person by way of consideration for the scheme transactions, or
(b) received by or on behalf of V (or someone connected with V) by way of consideration for the scheme transactions. [*FA 2003, s 75A*].

Any consideration for transactions which are merely 'incidental' to the transfer of the chargeable interest from V to P is ignored. [*FA 2003, s 75B*]: see **11.3 Incidental Transactions**. A number of exclusions also apply. [*FA 2003, s 75C*]: see **11.4 Supplementary Provisions**.

The 'scheme transactions' can include a non-land transaction, an agreement, offer or undertaking not to take a specified action, any kind of arrangement and a transaction taking place after the acquisition of the chargeable interest. Therefore, consideration paid for a non-land transaction can be taxed as if it were consideration for a notional land transaction.

'Incidental transactions'

[11.3] The original version of the rule when introduced on 6 December 2006 contained a serious flaw in that it automatically took into account any consideration paid for any non-land transaction that was 'involved in connection with' the disposal and acquisition of an interest in land. This meant that a simple sale of a business for say £10m which included an interest in land from which the business operated (market value, say nil if it was a lease at market rent) and which would normally attract no SDLT would be chargeable with SDLT on £10m (the highest amount paid or received by any person). This was an absurd result and reflected the general quality of the drafting of the rule. HMRC has attempted to resolve this issue by excluding from the rule consideration given for a transaction if or insofar as, the transaction is 'merely incidental' to the transfer of the interest in land: *FA 2003, s 75B(1)*. Examples are given of transactions that 'may' be incidental, namely:

- the construction of a building on property to which the chargeable interest relates;
- the sale or supply of anything other than land; or
- a loan to P to enable him or another person to pay for the chargeable interest: *FA 2003, s 75B(2)*.

However, a transaction cannot be treated as incidental to the transfer of a chargeable interest from V to P:

(a) if, as insofar as, it forms part of a process, or series of transactions, by which the transfer is effected;
(b) if the transfer of the chargeable interest is conditional on the completion of the transaction; or
(c) it is of a kind specified in *FA 2003, s 75A(3)* — a list of 'scheme transactions'.

It is unclear how the sale of a business which includes land can be 'merely incidental' to the transfer of the land given that it will form part of the process or series of transactions by which the transfer of land is effected (being part of the same bargain) and that the transfer of the land will inherently be conditional on the completion of the transaction. The same can be said for loan funding given to P which will almost always be conditional on the completion of the transaction. In practice, the drafting of this provision illustrates the de facto discretionary nature of the rule which hints at an exclusion for things which may be inoffensive to HMRC but then removes the exclusion leaving taxpayers at the mercy of HMRC should they subsequently decide that the 'proper' amount of tax was not paid on the transaction.

Supplementary provisions

[11.4] A series of supplementary provisions which attempt to finesse the application of the rule are contained in *FA 2003, s 75C*. These are:

(1) a transfer of shares or securities shall be ignored if it would be the first of a series of transactions, so that preparatory share transfers in say a special purpose vehicle are permitted;

(2) the notional land transaction created by the rule will attract any available SDLT relief, but this will depend upon the identities of V and P;

(3) if any of the scheme transactions is entered into for the purposes of or in connection with the transfer of an undertaking (or part) for the purposes of *FA 2003, Sch 7, para 7 or 8* (reconstruction or acquisition relief) then the notional land transaction is also deemed to have been entered into for the same purposes or connection, so that the notional land transaction can qualify for the relief;

(4) any consideration which would qualify for various specified statutory reliefs is ignored in computing the consideration for the notional transaction;

(5) if the notional transaction involves a deemed transfer to a connected company then the market value rule in *FA 2003, s 53* applies to substitute market value for any lesser consideration;

(6) the exchange rules which determine the chargeable consideration also apply to the notional transaction where an exchange of interests is involved (see **8.5 EXCHANGES AND PARTITIONS**);

(7) an interest in a property investment partnership is treated as if it were a chargeable interest to the extent that it concerns land owned by the partnership. Where V or P is a partnership the provisions of *FA 2003 Sch 15 Pt 3* apply as they would to the transfer of a chargeable interest into or out of the partnership;

(8) previously where V or P was a partnership, the provisions of *FA 2003, Sch 15, Pt 3* applied to the notional transaction as they would to the transfer of a chargeable interest into or out of the partnership; this situation arose because *FA 2003, s 75C(8)(b)* overrode the normal rule that the partners are treated as the purchasers and not the partnership and provided for V or P to be the partnership and then applied the special partnership provisions to the notional transaction; however, this gave rise to avoidance schemes which relied on the special

partnership provisions to substitute the often nil or nominal SDLT charge arising under them for the full SDLT charge which would otherwise arise on the notional transaction under *s 75A*, and so this rule was omitted from 24 March 2010 by *FA 2010, s 55*; the intention is to deny the notional transaction the benefit of any reduction in SDLT which could otherwise have been available under the special partnership provisions; unfortunately, this change has also meant that many 'innocent' partnership transactions which previously would rely on the special partnership rules for transactions between connected persons and the partners to reduce the SDLT chargeable are now caught necessarily but unintentionally by *s 75A* because of the wide definition of 'scheme transaction', and considerable confusion has thereby been caused; this confusion has however been partly allayed by the latest official guidance from HMRC on *s 75A* published on 28 February 2011 which provided examples of partnership transactions which HMRC regard as innocuous and also states that "'Section 75A is an anti-avoidance provision. HM Revenue & Customs (HMRC) therefore takes the view that it applies only where there is avoidance of tax. On this basis, HMRC will not seek to apply s75A where it considers transactions have already been taxed appropriately.' (see below and the guidance reproduced in **Appendix G**); it also seems that not all of the partnership schemes that were the intended target of this change have been blocked;

(9) any SDLT paid in respect of a land transaction disregarded under the rule is taken to have been paid in respect of the notional land transaction — the rule is silent about any right of restitution which the real purchaser may then have against the deemed purchaser, P, in the notional land transaction or indeed whether the real or the notional purchaser can claim a deduction for income tax or capital gains tax purposes as appropriate, for the SDLT paid.

A notional land transaction arising under *FA 2003, s 75A* is in principle a notifiable transaction and so will require a SDLT 1 return to be filed: see *FA 2003, s 77(1)(d)* as is substituted by *FA 2008, s 94(2)*.

Where the statutory general anti-avoidance rule applies the land transactions forming part of the scheme are disregarded for SDLT purposes and the notional land transaction which is deemed to replace those land transactions will have an effective date which is the last date of completion of the scheme transactions, or if earlier, the last date on which a contract in respect of the scheme transactions is substantially performed. [*FA 2003, s 75A(4)* and *(6)*]. It follows that the disregarding of the real land transactions can occur before the occurrence of the effective date of the notional land transaction leaving the taxpayer 'resting on contract' within *s 75A* until the completion of the scheme transactions. This is a surprising result but appears to follow from the plain meaning of the words used in the provision.

Targetted schemes

[11.5] There were five main SDLT mitigation schemes in use at the time the rule was introduced and an earlier version of HMRC's official guidance contained in SDLT Technical News Issue 5 of 15 August 2007 illustrated how the rule is intended to operate in the context of these schemes. It is by no means clear that the rule does operate successfully to block these schemes particularly in the case of Examples 4 and 5 below (see **11.7 Some Problems with ss 75A–75C**).

Example 1

V grants a 999-year lease to N for no premium and a peppercorn rent. V assigns the freehold reversion to P for a nominal sum. P pays N £X in consideration of N's agreement to vary the lease by the insertion of a provision giving the landlord the right to terminate the lease for no payment. P exercises the right to terminate.

The notional consideration is £X, the amount given by P and received by N.

Example 2

V grants a 999-year lease to N for no premium and a peppercorn rent. The lease includes a right for the landlord to terminate the lease on payment of £X to the tenant. V assigns the freehold reversion to P for a nominal sum. P exercises the right to terminate and pays N £X.

The notional consideration is £X, the amount paid by P and received by N.

Example 3

V grants a 999-year lease to P for no premium and a peppercorn rent. The lease gives the landlord a right to terminate it within 14 days of the date of grant. P offers to pay V £X if V allows the 14 days to elapse without exercising the right to terminate. V does so (an example of a scheme transaction which occurs after the acquisition of the chargeable interest by P).

The notional consideration is £X, the amount paid by P and received by V.

Example 4

V agrees to sell property to N for £10m. N agrees to sub-sell the property to P for £5. Both transactions are completed at the same time.

The notional consideration is £10m, the amount received by V.

Example 5

V agrees to sell property to N Ltd for £10m. N Ltd declares a dividend in favour of P, its sole shareholder, the dividend to consist of the property and to be paid at the same time as completion of the V to N Ltd contract. The contract is completed and the property transferred to P.

The notional consideration is £10m, the amount received by V.

HMRC official guidance

[11.6] The latest official guidance issued by HMRC on the interpretation and application of *FA 2003, s 75A* on 28th February 2011 and the August 2007 version are reproduced in **APPENDIX G**. One significant difference between the latest guidance and earlier versions is the statement in the latest guidance that: '*Section 75A* is an anti-avoidance provision. HM Revenue & Customs (HMRC) therefore takes the view that it applies only where there is avoidance of tax. On this basis, HMRC will not seek to apply *s75A* where it considers transactions have already been taxed appropriately.'. The official guidance contains various simple examples of transactions and arrangements which in the view of HMRC are outside the anti-avoidance rule. An extract from the parliamentary debates on the anti-avoidance rule during the passage of the *Finance Bill 2007* is also reproduced at **APPENDIX A**. Both the official guidance and the statements by the Minister during the parliamentary debates suggest implicitly that the anti-avoidance rule introduces what in effect is a form of discretionary taxation under which HMRC expects to decide the identity of V and P for the purposes of the rule (although HMRC denies this) where there are multiple transactions and various permutations as to who is V and P. Indeed in the debates in the Public Bill Committee on the Finance Bill on 5 June 2007, the Chief Secretary to the Treasury Stephen Timms said about the application of the rule:

> if there are any uncertainties, [HMRC] is happy to advise those who have queries about complex transactions on a case-by-case basis.
>
> (column 410);

and in response to a question about what will happen if there are multiple parties that could be treated as P, the Minister said:

> There may well be some quite complex arrangements where sensible questions could be raised. My advice would be that those questions should be raised directly with HMRC in the light of what is already on the website. I think that appropriate clarification could then be provided.
>
> (column 410).

The Minister also said in relation to lack of certainty in the application of the legislation that:

> The answer, therefore, is that certainty can be secured through clear guidance from HMRC.
>
> (column 419).

In effect, these remarks by the Minister, taken together, suggest that the Minister and HMRC are aware that the application of the statutory rule to complex transactions may be unclear and that in such cases HMRC will in effect decide on the application of the rule on the hoof and therefore whether or not tax is chargeable. Indeed the last statement quoted above reveals that the responsible Minister accepts that the wording of the rule is unclear and that he did not know the answer to the question and was content to leave it to HMRC to decide. HMRC has in practice reneged on the assurances given to Parliament by refusing to give specific guidance on *s 75A*.

It has long been established as a matter of constitutional principle that the courts will be reluctant to enforce discretionary taxation in the absence of the clearest possible statutory wording: see for example Lord Wilberforce's speech in *Vestey v IRC (Nos 1 and 2)* [1980] AC 1148 at 1172.

HMRC's approach in applying the rule so far, appears to be at odds with the manner in which a court is likely to apply the rule. Two instances are worth mentioning here although there may be others also. First, HMRC's approach in practice is to say that the first step in applying the rule is to identify a disposal and the relevant V; the second steps is to identify an acquisition and the relevant P; and the third steps is to consider whether a number of transactions are 'involved in connection with' the disposal and acquisition. Taken in this order, the provision enables HMRC to select V and P for the purposes of the rule (in some cases virtually at random) and then argue that any transaction in between is of necessity 'involved in connection with' the disposal by V and its acquisition by P. This is the current position adopted by HMRC at operational level when challenging transactions under the rule. It is thought that this approach is misconceived and that a court would apply the third step as the intermediate step, ie step two, in relation to any potential V because that test is the logical link between V and any potential P and limits who may be P in relation to V. Second, HMRC stated in the earlier versions of its official guidance that except in a sub-sale situation it is 'unlikely' that the rule can apply where (1) neither P nor his associates nor his advisers have had any involvement in or any connection with transactions other than the one by which P acquired the property; and (2) neither P nor his associates obtains any SDLT benefit from the way in which the acquisition is effected. It is not clear in principle why an exception is made for sub-sale transactions other than the fact that HMRC is aware that such transaction can be utilised to save tax. HMRC goes on to state that despite this, the rule will apply to sub-sales regardless of whether or not P or his associates or his advisers had any involvement in or connection with the contract between V and the intermediate purchaser. Again, this seems to be at odds with the wording of the rule which requires the intermediate contract to be 'involved in connection with' the disposal and acquisition.

The application of *FA 2003, s 75A* to sub-sale transactions was also thrown into doubt by earlier versions of the official guidance. At para 14 of the guidance of August 2007 some examples were given of where *s 75A* did not apply and the fifth example was as follows:

> V agrees to sell land to P. P agrees to sell on to C. The transactions are completed at the same time. Section 75A does not apply as regards the disposal by V and the acquisition by P (although section 75A will apply as regards the disposal by V and the acquisition by C). The sale on to C is not "involved in connection with" the disposal by V and the acquisition by P because it does not in any way affect the nature of the interest acquired by P.

Taken at face value, this example said that the sale on to C will not be 'involved in connection with' the disposal by V and the acquisition by P when the nature of the interest acquired is not affected, as will usually be the case. This suggests that *s 75A* cannot apply to a sub-sale because the test of being 'involved in connection with' is not satisfied. This example has however not reappeared in the latest version of the guidance.

Although this last example is surprising, the approach taken in the official guidance appears to be an attempt by HMRC to finesse the statutory wording of the rule to bring within it those transactions it finds offensive while allowing 'inoffensive' transactions to remain unaffected by wording that could affect them also. The status of guidance of this nature was considered by the House of Lords in *R (Westminster City Council) v NASS* [2002] 4 All ER 654 where Lord Steyn at 658 said that the plain meaning of the statutory language used is likely to prevail where this differs from the official guidance to its interpretation. More recently the High Court in *Chief Constable of Cumbria v Wright* [2006] EWHC 3574 (Admin), [2007] 1 WLR 1407, [2006] All ER (D) 265 (Nov) has said the following in relation to official Home Office guidance on the meaning of particular legislation:

> In any given case, it may be helpful for a court to refer to the guidance on the interpretation of the legislation. It may be of some persuasive authority. However, to my mind that is the limit of its influence. It does not differ in that regard from a statement by an academic author in a textbook or an article. It does not enjoy any particular legal status. There seems to me to be no satisfactory basis for the submission that it gives rise to a presumption that the views it contains are correct and should be rejected only for good reason.

Some problems with ss 75A–75C

[11.7] There are many issues surrounding the interpretation and application of the new rule including the following.

What does 'involved in connection with' mean?

This is the key phase in the rule and appears in *FA 2003, s 75A(1)(b)*. It is intended to draw a line between transactions that are caught and those that are not caught by the rule. While HMRC have indicated that mere linkage of transactions through conveyancing succession is not sufficient to fall within the rule, one suspects that the phrase has been chosen because it is vague and therefore flexible in its application. The case law authorities on the meaning of the phrase 'in connection with' suggest the following possible meanings:

(a) 'having to do with': Somerville LJ in *Johnson v Johnson* [1952] 1 All ER 250 at 251–252;
(b) 'a less definite causal link' (when contrasted with the causal link required by 'whereby'), per Nourse LJ in *Emery v IRC* [1981] STC 150 at 171;
(c) the phrase could describe a wide range of links and the court must look closely at the surrounding words and the context of the legislative scheme: per Arden LJ in *Barclays Bank plc v CIR* [2007] EWCA Civ 442, [2008] STC 476; and
(d) 'One of the very generally accepted meanings of "connexion" is "relation between things one of which is bound up with or involved in another"; or again, "having to do with". The words include matters occurring prior to as well as subsequent to or consequent upon so long as they are related to the principal thing. The phrase "having to do

with" perhaps gives as good a suggestion of the meaning as could be had': per McFarlane J in *Re Nanaimo Community Hotel Ltd* [1944] 4 DLR 638 at 639 (cited with approval by Sommerville LJ in (a) and by Nourse J in (b) above).

It is interesting to note that in the decision of the Court of Appeal referred to in (c) above, Arden LJ also held that in an appeal from the Commissioners, the question of the meaning of the expression and whether the facts as found by the Commissioners were capable of satisfying the meaning were questions of law not fact and were thus appealable: see [2007] EWCA Civ 332, [2008] STC 476 at [31].

In a sub-sale has FA 2003, s 45 been 'switched-off'?

If on a sub-sale one takes the secondary contract postulated by *FA 2003, s 45(3)* and disregards the completion of the original contract as required where the original and secondary contract complete at the same time, there will only be a single deemed land transaction with the consideration specified by *FA 2003, s 45(3)(b)*. Accordingly *s 75A* appears to have limited application to sub-sales (see Example 5 at para 14 of HMRC's Official Guidance of August 2007 set out above, and **8.4 Sub-sales, Assignments and Novations**). Although this interpretation is contrary to HMRC's stated intention in Spotlight 10 issued on 7 June 2010 (and a document headed 'Version 1: Stamp Duty Land Tax Schemes' issued on 11 January 2011 to professional bodies) to attack schemes involving sub-sales, where official guidance as to the interpretation of a statutory provision differs from the plain meaning of the words enacted, the plain meaning is likely to prevail: see Lord Steyn's speech in *R (Westminster City Council) v National Asylum Support Service* [2002] UKHL 38, [2002] 4 All ER 654 at 658. In any event the first case involving SDLT avoidance to come before the First-tier Tribunal involved the sale of property by way of a sub-sale into a partnership and relied on both *FA 2003, 45(3)* and the special partnership rules in *FA 2003, Sch 15, Part 3*. This was a case involving a transaction that was carried out before *s75A* came into being and so *s75A* was not tested but the case was won by the taxpayer: *DV3 RS Limited Partnership v. Revenue and Customs Commissioners* [2011] SFTD 531. An appeal to the Upper Tribunal (Tax and Chancery) is awaited. It is thought that the interaction of *FA 2003, ss 45(3)* and *75A* will be tested in the tribunal and the courts in due course.

How will FA 2003, s 75A operate if there is more than one notional land transaction? Which transaction will be chosen as the relevant one for the purpose of the rule?

Another way of looking at this is to ask where there is more than one potential P due to multiple purchasers how will P be chosen? Even in a simple sub-sale of one property from A to B to C, it appears that both B and C can be P leaving each party liable for tax on the highest consideration paid. There appears to be no solution to this dilemma on the wording of the rule and that HMRC will simply ignore any inconvenient result while applying the wording in any case where they decide that the 'proper' amount of SDLT has not been paid.

Do V and P have to be dealing directly with each other?

HMRC says no to this proposition but in the absence of express wording in the rule permitting V and P to be separated by an intermediate sale, the natural assumption on reading *FA 2003, s 75A(1)(a)* suggests that V must dispose of a chargeable interest to P directly. Indeed both *s75B(1)* and *s75B(2)* refer expressly to 'the transfer of the chargeable interest from V to P'. Also, *s75C(10)* provides that any SDLT paid in respect of a land transaction which is disregarded under *s75A* is to be treated as having been paid in relation to the notional land transaction by P. In other words the SDLT paid by the actual purchaser is available as a credit against any SDLT payable by P. This suggests that the actual purchaser and P must be the same person otherwise the tax paid by the real purchaser would unfairly it seems be available to fund another person identified as P who may have relied on an avoidance scheme.

No requirement that to be caught a transaction must be motivated by tax avoidance

Although the statutory wording does not contain an motive test, in practice and out of necessity HMRC have in their latest guidance stated that *s75A* will be applied only where there is avoidance of tax and will not seek to apply it where HMRC considers that the transactions have already been taxed 'appropriately'. Unfortunately in many cases this only creates further confusion as to the meaning of 'appropriately' particularly in commercial transactions which are bona fide and commercially driven but into which as is normal some tax planning has been inserted. In effect, this leaves taxpayers at the mercy of HMRC discretion.

Code of Practice 10 Procedure ('COP 10')

A related issue to the point above is that although HMRC intends to extend the availability of the COP 10 procedure indefinitely to businesses, all that COP 10 offers is non-binding guidance. COP 10 is not a proper clearance procedure offering certainty that a transaction cannot subsequently be attacked by HMRC (assuming full disclosure has been given to them). In addition COP 10 applications tend to be dealt with by HMRC in a legalistic and heavily caveated manner often leaving the taxpayer with less comfort than he was seeking. COP 10 cannot effectively disapply the rule and leaves the taxpayer open to subsequent HMRC enquiry and a possible reassessment by HMRC of the 'guidance' given at the time of the transaction concerned. As noted above, HMRC has in practice reneged on the assurances given to Parliament by refusing to give specific guidance on *s 75A*.

Absence of a time limit between disposal by V and acquisition by P

The absence of such a time limit suggests that once the test of a transaction being 'involved in connection with' the disposal by V is met, the actual time between the disposal and the acquisition by the person alleged by HMRC to be P is irrelevant and in principle, unlimited.

Conclusion

[11.8] The statutory general anti-avoidance rule for SDLT represents a departure from the principle that tax legislation should be clearly drafted and capable of objective interpretation and application. It creates a *de facto* power of discretionary taxation through the deliberate use vague and imprecise wording and is intended to exist *in terrorem* ie in order to frighten, taxpayers. It creates the possibility of a subsequent re-assessment of the SDLT liability of someone whose transaction was 'involved in connection with' a disposal and acquisition of land together with interest and penalties. The purpose of the rule is to deter anyone from utilising the SDLT provisions in a way in which HMRC could decide gives them an unfair tax advantage. It will be interesting to see how the tax tribunal and the courts interpret and apply the rule. It will also be interesting to see which cases HMRC decides to take to appeal and which ones it decides not to fight.

Part Two:

Stamp Duties and Stamp Duty Reserve Tax

Chapter 12

Introduction

Note: *FA 2003* abolished stamp duty on land and buildings and in its place created stamp duty land tax ('SDLT') for transactions (broadly) from 1 December 2003: see Part One of this book. Stamp duties continue to apply to instruments relating to shares and securities (including non-exempt loan capital), bearer instruments and transfers of partnership interests. The following chapters remain relevant to instruments that remain within the charge to stamp duty. Stamp duty reserve tax remains in effect including the charge in relation to unit trusts. For the provisions dealing with the transition from stamp duty on land to SDLT see **9 TRANSITIONAL PROVISIONS**.

[12.1] Stamp duties have been charged since the *Stamp Act 1694*. The last consolidating Acts were the *Stamp Act 1891 (SA 1891)* and the *Stamp Duties Management Act 1891 (SDMA 1891)*. The *Stamp Act 1891* has been amended annually by subsequent Finance Acts to the point where a fresh consolidation has long been overdue. There was an attempt in the words of the Inland Revenue (now known as HM Revenue and Customs ('HMRC')) to 'streamline' and 'modernise' the stamp duty legislation in *FA 1999*. However, in the author's view this attempt in practice only succeeded in complicating the structure of the stamp duty legislation. This is because there are now two principal sources of legislation, whereas before there was only one i.e. the *Stamp Act 1891*, important parts of which have been retained or amended in situ and *FA 1999*, containing as it does, fifteen sections and eight schedules relating to stamp duty; some of which insert new sections into the *Stamp Act 1891* and some of which replace or add to provisions of the 1891 Act. Any practitioner wishing to acquire a working knowledge of the stamp duty legislation faces an even harder task then before. The addition of a series of complex anti-avoidance measures in *FA 2000* and *FA 2002* further complicated matters.

Ten years ago there was talk of the abolition of stamp duties and in the wake of the abolition of **CAPITAL DUTY (29)** and unit trust instrument duty by *FA 1988*, the prospective abolition of stamp duty on transfers of shares and securities, bearer instrument duty and **STAMP DUTY RESERVE TAX (84)** was announced by *FA 1990*. The 1990 Budget Press Release stated that abolition would occur late in 1991/92 to coincide so far as possible with the introduction of paperless share dealing under the Stock Exchange's new share transfer system (TAURUS). Also linked to the introduction of TAURUS was the prospective abolition of stamp duty on property other than land and buildings provided for by *FA 1991*. However, on 11 March 1993, the Stock Exchange announced the indefinite suspension of development of TAURUS because of the complexity of the computer software. The project was taken over by a task force backed by the Bank of England, which announced in July 1993 the adoption of a slimmed-down electronic system known as 'CREST' to speed up the settlement of equity share trading in the London Stock Market. The new system became operational in 1996 and provides a settlement mechanism for equity trades allowing those holding stock within the system to electronically receive stock and make payment. It is doubtful whether the abolition of stamp duty and **Stamp Duty Reserve Tax (84)** on shares and securities as announced by *FA 1990* will now occur and indeed the re-elected Labour Government announced in July 2001 that there was no firm evidence to suggest that stamp duty was causing UK companies involved in mergers to incorporate outside the UK. This is reinforced by the fact that stamp duties and stamp duty reserve tax are by far the cheapest of the different taxes to administer and collect and yet each year yield more tax revenue than capital gains tax, inheritance tax and petroleum revenue tax combined.

As regards the abolition of stamp duty on property other than land and buildings, *FA 2002* abolished stamp duty on instruments relating to goodwill and the Government announced its intention to take trade debts and receivables out of the charge to duty in *FA 2003*. In addition, the Government issued a consultative document in April 2002 entitled 'Modernising Stamp Duty on land and buildings in the UK' and announced its intention to legislate in *FA 2003* to 'modernise' stamp duty with three objectives in mind—

(1) to attack the increasing use of stamp duty avoidance schemes caused by the recent quadrupling in the top rate of stamp duty;
(2) to adapt the tax to operate effectively following the introduction of paperless electronic conveyancing expected to commence on a voluntary basis not earlier than 2007; and
(3) to change the basis of charge from a tax on documents to a tax on transactions and thereby create a modern tax based on the substance of a transaction rather than on the legal documents used to effect the transaction.

Accordingly, *FA 2003* abolished stamp duty on land and buildings and in its place created stamp duty land tax ('SDLT') from 1 December 2003—see Part One.

In addition, the Government proposed to bring within the scope of the new tax transfers of substantial interests in entities (30%) such as companies owning mainly UK land (70% or more of total gross assets) and charge tax at the full property rates. Such provisions were conspicuously absent from the SDLT provisions in *FA 2003*. It is understood that HM Treasury may have concluded that such provisions are too difficult to draft in a way that distinguishes between 'genuine' property companies and special purpose vehicles created to take advantage of the difference between the property and the share rates of stamp duty. Although the consultative document referred to 'modernising' stamp duty, the legislative provisions in fact amount to the creation of a new property transfer tax based on concepts of self-assessment backed up by post-transaction audits of selected transactions by HMRC.

Stamp duties continue to apply to transactions in shares and securities (including non-exempt loan capital), bearer instruments and acquisitions of an interest in a partnership. The following chapters remain relevant to such transactions as well as to pre 1 December 2003 land transactions, and also provide guidance on the application of the SDLT provisions where certain legal concepts have been carried over into the SDLT.

During the recent past there have been some significant changes. First the trend towards simplification of stamp duties was reversed by *FA 1994*. In particular, ad valorem conveyance on sale duty was extended to the transfer of an interest in land or the grant of a lease in exchange for any property with the government issuing official guidance on how to avoid an unintended double charge to sale duty: see **36.7 Exchanges of Property**. Also in relation to transactions involving land, where the consideration cannot be ascertained it is to be taken to be the market value of the land concerned and stamp duty charged accordingly instead of the fixed 50p (now £5) duty which previously applied: see **36.8 Unascertained and Contingent Consideration**. These changes fundamentally altered the structure of stamp duties in relation to land and unfortunately were not properly thought through before implementation and are still causing some uncertainty as to their scope and relationship with pre-existing stamp duty principles.

Second, the rates of ad valorem duty on sales (other than stock and marketable securities) were trebled over a period of nine months in 1997/98 from 1% to 3% and were increased to 3.5% by *FA 1999* and to 4% by *FA 2000*. Third, the fundamental changes to **Stamp Duty Reserve Tax (84)** introduced by *FA 1996* and amendments to the Regulations governing the administration and payment of the tax have now made this the principal tax on share transfers with stamp duty beginning to assume the role of a 'reserve' tax.

On the judicial front, the Court of Appeal decisions in *Parinv (Hatfield) Ltd v IRC* CA [1998] STC 305 and *LM Tenancies 1 plc v IRC* CA [1998] STC 326 have undermined some established stamp duty principles and widened the scope of stamp duty in relation to execution of documents offshore, the **Contingency Principle (37)** and the construction of documents, and in so doing have made it more difficult for practitioners to advise with confidence as to how a document will be construed for stamp duty purposes where an element of tax mitigation has been incorporated into the transaction. A surprising and potentially far reaching change occurred from the beginning of August 2001 with the Bar Council announcing in a low-key manner the revocation of the barristers' rule of etiquette that it was unprofessional generally to take a stamp duty objection. See **47.1 Evidence**. The High Court undermined the indirect enforcement of stamp duties by permitting evidence of equitable ownership to be adduced in evidence despite the existence of an unstamped bill of sale in *BMBF (No 24) v IRC* [2002] EWHC 2466 (Ch), [2002] STC 1450. In *Stamp Comr v Carreras Group Ltd* [2004] UKPC 16, [2004] SWTI 990 a long-standing stamp duty avoidance scheme was held by the Privy Council in the circumstances of the case to be ineffective in saving stamp duty: see **19 Anti-avoidance** for a discussion of this and subsequent decisions.

Significant changes were made as mentioned above by *FA 1999*. These changes to both the fabric and the rubric of the stamp duties can be summarised as follows:

- the old heads of charge in *SA 1891, Sch 1* were replaced by a restatement of the instruments chargeable with duty in *FA 1999, Sch 13*;
- a stricter compliance regime was introduced from 1 October 1999 particularly with regard to the charging of interest on duty paid later than thirty days after execution (whether overseas or not);

- the way ad valorem rates are calculated was changed from an amount per £100 to a percentage of the relevant chargeable amount;
- the fixed duties were increased from (generally) 50p to £5;
- the penalties other than for late stamping, e.g. registration of an instrument not duly stamped, were substantially increased;
- the charge on bearer instruments was restated in *FA 1999*, *Sch 15*;
- a new stamp duty reserve tax regime was introduced for transfers of units in unit trusts from 6 February 2000;
- there were some excruciatingly complex amendments to the stamp duty reserve tax provisions relating to the use of non-sterling bearer instruments in a merger or takeover with one particular sub-section having four different versions over a period of ten months from January to October 1999; and
- there was the usual annual crop of routine tidying-up amendments to the stamp duty reserve tax provisions.

More recently, *FA 2000*:

- increased the top rate of ad valorem duty for transfers for more than £500,000 from 3.5% to 4.0% and the rate for transfers for between £250,000 and £500,000 from 2.5% to 3.0%;
- created something close to a mini-general anti-avoidance rule for stamp duty;
- attacked the structuring of exchanges of land or marketable securities carried out in such a way as to avoid a sale for stamp duty purposes;
- attacked the transfer of land to connected companies for a consideration less than market value;
- tightened up considerably the exemption for transfers of assets within a group of companies by aligning the stamp duty group relief provisions with those for corporation tax;
- attacked the use of redeemable shares in the context of the company reorganisation reliefs to disguise an intended change of ownership;
- made the right to receive a future issue of securities part of the stampable consideration;
- made a further attempt to charge stamp duty when a lease is surrendered by operation of law (the last attempt was in *FA 1994*); and
- abolished stamp duty on transfers of intellectual property.

FA 2001 has:

- provided an exemption for land in disadvantaged areas: see **APPENDIX F** Stamp Taxes: Customer Newsletter—Disadvantaged Areas Stamp Duty Exemption;
- removed the stamp duty reserve tax charge from surrenders of units in unit trust schemes and shares in open-ended investment companies held within individual pension accounts; and
- abolished stamp duty and stamp duty reserve tax in relation to transfers of shares to employees by the trustees of approved employee share ownership plans.

FA 2002 has:

- introduced a distinction between residential and non-residential property and (subject to European Commission state aid approval due to run until 2006 only) provides an unlimited exemption for non-residential property in disadvantaged areas while limiting the exemption for residential property to £150,000: see **APPENDIX F** Stamp Taxes: Customer Newsletter—Disadvantaged Areas Stamp Duty Exemption — the exemption for non-residential property was removed for instruments executed after 16 March 2005 by *FA 2005, s 96* and *Sch 9*;
- imposed a two-year clawback period (now extended to three years by *FA 2003*) for transfers of UK land that have been stamped on the basis that either group relief or relief under *FA 1986, s 76* applies, under which the relevant relief is withdrawn if within two years the transferee company leaves the group or control of the acquiring company changes;
- attacked the use of schemes intended to exploit the relief under *FA 1986, s 76*;
- imposed a penalty on instruments relating to UK land that are executed outside the UK but not presenting for stamping within 30 days of execution;
- introduced an ad valorem charge to stamp duty on contracts for the sale of UK land where the consideration relating to the land exceeds £10m and the contract is not followed by the presentation for stamping of the conveyance within 90 days (or such longer period as the Commissioners think is reasonable); and
- abolished stamp duty on instruments relating to goodwill.

FA 2003 has:

- introduced SDLT and abolished stamp duty on land transactions from 1 December 2003;
- restricted stamp duty to transactions in shares and securities (including non-exempt loan capital), bearer instruments, transfers of land into and out of partnerships by partners and acquisitions of an interest in a partnership from 1 December 2003;
- lengthened the period of the clawback of group and acquisition relief from two to three years and widened its scope to certain associated companies;
- provided an exemption for leases of temporary accommodation by registered social landlords;
- amended the provisions dealing with the purchase by a company of its own shares consequent upon the introduction of Treasury Shares.

FA 2004 has:

- abolished stamp duty on transfers of land into and out of partnerships by partners (and made such transfers subject to SDLT along with acquisitions of partnership interests); but
- also retained stamp duty on acquisition of partnership interests.

FA 2005 raised the £60,000 threshold for residential property to £120,000, and removed the relief for non-residential property in disadvantaged areas.

F(No 2)A 2005 provided power to extend the exceptions relating to recognised exchanges.

FA 2006 has raised the £120,000 residential property threshold to £125,000 and relaxed some of the formal conditions for relief in relation to company restructuring.

FA 2008 has allowed for share transfers to be exempt from ad valorem duty where the consideration is £1,000 or less and the instrument is certified at £1,000. It has also abolished the fixed £5 duty on most instruments which previously attracted a fixed duty.

The following paragraphs summarise the structure of stamp duty law.

Stamp duties are in general charged on instruments and specifically those instruments referred to in *FA 1999*, *Schs 13* and *15*. See **INSTRUMENTS (60)** and **CHARGEABILITY (31)**. Transactions which are carried out orally do not attract stamp duty but note that in relation to chargeable securities **STAMP DUTY RESERVE TAX (84)** can still arise on an oral agreement to sell such securities; see **ORAL TRANSACTIONS (71)** for examples of transactions which may be carried out so as to avoid stamp duty. The enforcement of stamp duties is ensured by the consequences of **FAILURE TO STAMP (52)**, which are the incidence of interest and **PENALTIES (75)** and inadmissibility of the instruments in **EVIDENCE (47)**. These consequences apply where an instrument has been insufficiently or incorrectly stamped. There is a presumption in favour of the taxpayer that an instrument is properly stamped in the absence of contrary evidence. In relation to sales of securities **STAMP DUTY RESERVE TAX (84)** imposes a directly enforceable charge equivalent to the rate of stamp duty in relation to an agreement to sell securities which is automatically cancelled by the creation of a duly stamped instrument of transfer, transferring the securities to the purchaser.

For an instrument to be chargeable it must fall within one of the categories mentioned in *FA 1999*, *Schs 13* and *15*. The head of charge is determined by the substance of the transaction recorded in an instrument rather than its form and the wording used by the parties is not conclusive. The tide of judicial opinion appears to be running against the tone of the judgment of Rowlatt J in *Cape Brandy Syndicate v IRC* [1921] 1 KB 64: 'In a taxing Act one has to look merely at what is clearly said. There is no room for an intendment. There is no equity about a tax. There is no presumption about a tax. Nothing is to be read in, nothing is to be implied. One can only look fairly at the language used.' Compare that with the situation in *Fitch Lovell Ltd v CIR Ch D*, [1962] 3 All ER 685 which concerned 'a scheme for the avoidance of, or at any rate a substantial reduction of, the stamp duty payable on a take-over bid into which, to use the words of the appellant company's solicitors, a little ingenuity has been put' per Wilberforce J. The appellant's case was dismissed. Part of Wilberforce's judgment reads, 'It seems to me that an analysis of this transaction which seeks to produce the result that the property re-sold is the same property as that first sold, if it can be made at all, involves a degree of formalism which the law in the application of *s 58(4)* should not indorse.' Vinelott J went further in his judgment in *Ingram v CIR* Ch D, [1985] STC 835 where after stating that the transactions involved were highly artificial and considering the observations of Lord Atkin in *IRC v Duke of Westminster*, [1936] AC 1 stated, 'Stamp Duty is a tax on instruments. But (in the language of the older cases) to determine whether an instrument falls within a chargeable category and the duty payable the court must ascertain the substance of the transaction effected by it.'

In *Parinv (Hatfield) Ltd v IRC* CA [1998] STC 305 the Court of Appeal held that the method by which the contract of sale had prescribed the mode of completion, i.e. declaration of trust executed offshore, was in the words of the Court 'a matter of conveyance and not substance' and was dictated by stamp duty considerations. Accordingly and because the offshore declaration of trust and the onshore land transfer had been executed on the same day, there was not a sale of the equitable interest but a sale of the land and both the declaration and the transfer were conveyances on sale with the result that the onshore transfer was stampable with ad valorem duty.

However, a narrowing of this approach towards stamp duty could be detected in the judgment of the House of Lords in *MacNiven v Westmoreland Investments Ltd* [2001] UKHL 6, [2001] STC 237 where Lord Hoffman suggested that stamp duty planning was less vulnerable to attack than other taxes that are based on concepts to which Parliament intended to give a 'commercial meaning'. Of course this narrowing of approach was not relevant to SDLT, which is a transaction based tax similar in principle to capital gains tax and PAYE (see **12.1** above). However, Lord Hoffmann altered his approach in *Stamp Comr v Carreras Group Ltd* [2004] UKPC 16, [2004] SWTI 990 where he gave the only speech (with which the other members of the Privy Council agreed) holding that a simple stamp duty avoidance scheme failed and by implication holding that the *Ramsay/Furniss v Dawson* principle applied fully to stamp duty: see further **19 ANTI-AVOIDANCE**.

If an instrument falls within two heads of charge, the Crown can only levy one duty, but may choose the higher (*Speyer Bros v CIR* HL, [1908] AC 92).

The principles of construction of a taxing statute apply, inter alia, as follows:

(a) the onus of proof is on the Crown to show that an instrument is within a stamp duty charge;
(b) the wording of a charge to stamp duty must be clear and unambiguous and if the language is clear, the court must give effect to it;
(c) in a case of real ambiguity, the construction most favourable to the taxpayer should be given.

There are numerous exemptions from specific heads of charge or from stamp duties generally (see **50 EXEMPT INSTRUMENTS**). Here the onus is on the taxpayer to show that the instrument qualifies for exemption.

Rates of duty are prescribed for type of instrument and fall into two categories:

(a) **fixed duty of £5** which is payable on certain instruments; and
(b) **ad valorem duties** calculated by reference to value, usually the value of the consideration recorded in the instrument.

For summaries of the rates of duties see **15 AD VALOREM DUTIES** and **54 FIXED DUTIES**.

Payment of duty is generally to be made before or shortly after **EXECUTION (49)** of the instrument charged and there are penalties for late stamping. See **74 PAYMENT OF DUTY OR TAX** and **75 PENALTIES**. There is no general rule as to the incidence of duty but see **74 Payment of Duty or Tax** for persons who have an obligation to ensure correct stamping.

Although stamp duty is charged on a world-wide basis (see **72 Overseas Matters**) the stamp duty legislation applies to GB (England, Wales and Scotland), though there are some special provisions for the purposes of Scots law—see **81 Scotland.** Separate charging provisions apply to Northern Ireland (which together with GB comprises the UK)—see **62 Ireland.** The stamp duty legislation does not apply in the Channel Islands or the Isle of Man.

Administration of stamp duties is carried out by the Commissioners for HMRC, also referred to as 'the Board'. See **14 Administration.**

Chapter 13

Adjudication

[13.1] Adjudication is the process whereby the Commissioners formally assess the amount of duty, if any, chargeable on an instrument. It is also a necessary step in the appeal procedure (see **20 Appeals**). Adjudication is normally conclusive of the liability of an instrument to stamp duty (see **13.3** below).

Adjudication may be:

(a) voluntary (see **13.2** below) so as to ensure the correctness of stamp or to initiate an appeal to the Special Commissioners (in relation to a penalty for late stamping) or to the High Court; or
(b) compulsory (see **13.3** below) where legislation or practice requires an assurance that the correct amount of duty has been paid, where an exemption has been claimed or where the correct basis of charging duty may not be clear.

Voluntary [SA 1891, s 12; FA 1999, Sch 12, para 1]

[13.2] Any person may request the Commissioners to adjudicate (or in the language of the old *SA 1891, s 12* 'express their opinion'—it is not clear to the author why this phrase needed to be replaced) with reference to any executed instrument on:

(a) whether it is chargeable to duty;
(b) the amount of duty chargeable;
(c) whether any penalty is payable (see **75 Penalties**); and
(d) what penalty is appropriate.

The procedure is straightforward. The instrument and a copy of it are sent to one of the offices listed in **13.1 Administration**. In addition to the instrument and copy, there must be a full disclosure of all the facts and circumstances affecting liability to duty. Failure to do so renders the offender liable to a fine of up to £3,000, although it does not render the document a nullity being a mere irregularity. (*Re Brown & Root McDermott Fabricators Ltd's* Ch D [1996] STC 483). [*SA 1891, s 5*] – see **75 Penalties**. Representations about liability and the amount of the duty may be included.

The Commissioners will not consider draft or partly executed instruments.

If no duty is chargeable, the instrument will be stamped 'Adjudged not chargeable with any stamp duty'.

If duty is chargeable, the Commissioners assess the duty and when the instrument is stamped in accordance with the assessment it is also stamped 'Adjudged duly stamped'.

For instruments executed on or after 1 October 1999 it is necessary to 'lodge' an amount representing the stamp duty payable with the Commissioners within 30 days of execution in order to avoid a charge to interest on the stamp duty ultimately assessed as due (see **74.1**(*b*) **DATE OF STAMPING AND PAYMENT**).

The Commissioners may call for whatever information they think necessary to make an assessment (*R v IRC ex p Evill KB*, [1951] 2 TLR 857).

An instrument which has been adjudicated must only be stamped in accordance with the Commissioners' decision on the adjudication and not otherwise. If an adjudicated instrument is not duly stamped within 30 days of notice of the Commissioners' decision the person requiring the adjudication is liable to a penalty not exceeding £300. [*SA 1891, s 12A*].

Compulsory

[13.3] The following are the principal cases where legislation provides that an adjudication stamp is obligatory:

(a) Where exemption is claimed from stamp duty on **COMPANY REORGANISATIONS (34)** under *FA 1986, ss 75, 76, 77*.
(b) Where exemption is claimed on transactions between **ASSOCIATED COMPANIES (23)** under *FA 1930, s 42*.
(c) Where exemption is claimed on conveyances, transfers or lettings to **CHARITIES (32)** under *FA 1982, s 129*.
(d) Conveyances in contemplation of sale chargeable under *FA 1965, s 90* (see **39 CONVEYANCE OR TRANSFER**).
(e) Where exemption is claimed in respect of maintenance funds for historic buildings under *FA 1980, s 98* (see **86 TRUSTS AND TRUSTEES**).
(f) Where the consideration for sale as calculated under *SA 1891, s 57* is reduced to the value of the property conveyed under *FA 1980, s 102* (see **36 CONSIDERATION**).
(g) Orders made by the court under the *Companies Act 1985, s 427* or *Companies Act 2006, s 900*. In these cases the solicitors are required to give an undertaking to the court that the order will be submitted for adjudication.
(h) Where exemption from stamp duty is claimed on the transfer of property to a limited liability partnership within one year of its incorporation under the *Limited Liability Partnerships Act 2000, s 12* (see **73 PARTNERSHIPS**).

These documents are not duly stamped unless they have been adjudicated and bear a stamp denoting that no duty is chargeable or that they are adjudged duly stamped.

Adjudication is not conclusive in the following cases:

(a) On a conveyance on sale of freehold land or a lease or agreement for lease for seven years or more—a **PRODUCED STAMP (77)** is also required. In practice, adjudication and production may be effected at the same time. [*FA 1931, s 28*].
(b) Where an instrument is liable to more than one stamp [*SA 1891, s 4*] adjudication of one stamp is not conclusive of the other. (See *Fitch Lovell Ltd v CIR* Ch D [1962] 3 All ER 685.)

(c) **BEARER INSTRUMENTS (24)** on which duty is payable on issue must also bear the **DENOTING STAMP (44)** required by *FA 1999, Sch 15, para 21.*
(d) Where an adjudication stamp was obtained by misrepresentation or non-disclosure of the relevant facts.
(e) In the case of a contract for the sale of UK land where the consideration exceeds £10m, any adjudication to the effect that stamp duty is not chargeable on the contract does not prevent a charge arising under *FA 2002, s 115* where a conveyance is not presented for stamping within 90 days of the contract. [*FA 2002, s 115(4)*].

An applicant for adjudication is entitled to withdraw from the procedure at any time and to have his document returned to him subject to a penalty not exceeding £300 if the instrument is without reasonable excuse not duly stamped within 30 days of notice of the Commissioners' decision on the adjudication under *SA 1891, s 12A(2)*. See also **69 NEGOTIATING WITH THE STAMP OFFICE.**

Chapter 14

Administration

[14.1] The care and management of stamp duties is with the Commissioners for HMRC. [*SDMA 1891, s 1*]. The technical, policy and operational areas of work have been combined within one unit now known as HMRC Stamp Taxes. The unit is headed by a Business Director within the Capital and Savings Division of HMRC based at Somerset House, London.

Following a reorganisation in 2007, stamp duties are dealt with generally at:

Birmingham Stamp Office
9th Floor
City Centre House
30 Union Street
Birmingham B2 4AR
DX: 15001 Birmingham 1
Tel: 0845 603 0135
Fax: 0121 643 8381

A 'same day' stamping of share transfers is available by telephoning 0121 616 4513.

Stamp duty reserve tax is dealt with by the SDRT Team at Birmingham Stamp Office.

Applications relating to land in Scotland are dealt with at:

Edinburgh Stamp Office
68 Queen Street
Edinburgh EH2 4NF
Tel: 0131 528 3833
Fax: 0131 528 3846

Chapter 15

Ad Valorem Duties

[15.1] Certain stamp duties are ad valorem, that is they are calculated by reference to the value of the transaction. For duties which are not ad valorem, see **54 Fixed Duties**.

The value on which the ad valorem duty is charged is sometimes the stated **Consideration (36)** and sometimes the market value.

The following are the ad valorem duties described in detail under the headings listed.

Heading		*Rate of duty*
Bearer Instruments (24)	—Inland	1.5%
	—Overseas	1.5%
	—Deposit certificate for overseas stock etc.	0.2%
Clearance Services (33)		1–1.5%
Conveyance or Transfer (39) on sale	—Generally	4.0%
	—Stock and marketable securities	0.5%
Depositary Receipts (45)		1–1.5%
Exchange or Partition (48)		4.0%
Leases (64)	—Rent	1–24.0%
	—Premium	4.0%

These rates are approximate because the amount of stamp duty chargeable ad valorem is rounded up where necessary to the nearest multiple of £5. In the case of a **Conveyance or Transfer (39)** on sale there is an exemption for sales of £125,000 or less and a sliding scale of between 1% and 3.0% for sales of between £125,000 and £500,000 when the instrument bears a **Certificate of Value (30)**. The £125,000 exemption and sliding scale are not available for sales of stock and marketable securities, although stamp duty is not chargeable on a transfer of stock and marketable securities where the consideration is not more than £1,000 and the instrument bears a **Certificate of Value (30)**.

Chapter 16

Agreement for Lease

[16.1] An agreement for a lease for any term is charged to duty as if it were an actual lease made for the same term and consideration mentioned in the agreement. [*FA 1999, Sch 13, para 14(1)*]. A lease subsequently granted which conforms with the agreement or is related to substantially the same property and term as the agreement is chargeable to duty; however credit is given for the duty paid on the agreement. [*FA 1999, Sch 13, para 14(2)*].

Duty paid on an agreement for a lease is not repayable if the lease is not subsequently granted or if the duty on the agreement turns out to be more than the duty on the subsequent lease due to the operation of the **CONTINGENCY PRINCIPLE (36)**. Although duty paid on an agreement for lease is available as a credit against duty on the lease the credit does not operate the other way round. That is to say duty on the lease cannot be transferred to the agreement.

Leases executed on or after 6 May 1994 must either contain a certificate (in the form suggested by the Stamp Office—see below) to the effect that there was no prior agreement or be stamped with a stamp denoting either that the agreement is not chargeable with duty or the duty paid on the agreement. [*FA 1994, s 240A*].

Agreements for lease executed on or after 6 May 1994 can be submitted with the lease without interest and a penalty for late stamping, provided that they are submitted within 30 days of the date of execution of the lease. Where both lease and agreement are submitted more than 30 days after execution of the lease, the interest and penalty provisions will be applied to both documents. However, the interest and penalty on the agreement will be calculated from the date of execution of the lease, not the date the agreement was executed. [*FA 1994, s 240*].

The certificate included in a lease to which there was no agreement should be along the following lines:

> I/We certify that there is no agreement for lease to which this lease gives effect.

In the absence of a certificate the Stamp Office will decline to stamp the lease unless it is accompanied by the agreement for lease.

Where an agreement for lease is entered into before 1 December 2003 (the implementation date for SDLT) and a lease giving effect to the agreement is executed on or after that date and the transaction is an SDLT transaction, then if the Revenue certificate is produced when the agreement is presented for stamping the payment of the SDLT in respect of the lease is to be denoted on the agreement and the agreement is deemed to be duly stamped. [*FA 2003, Sch 19, para 8*]. And see **9 TRANSITIONAL PROVISIONS**.

Where a freehold or leasehold interest in land is conveyed subject to an agreement for a lease for a term exceeding 35 years, the conveyance must bear a **DENOTING STAMP (43)** denoting the duty paid on the agreement for lease.

This does not apply when the agreement for lease is directly enforceable against another interest in the land. [*FA 1984, s 111(2)(3)*].

An agreement for a lease for a term of seven years or more must be produced to the Commissioners and stamped with a **PRODUCED STAMP (76)**. [*FA 1931, s 28*].

Until *FA 1984, s 111* an agreement for a lease for a term exceeding 35 years was exempt from duty and this exemption was exploited in an attempt to mitigate duty on sales of houses. *FA 1984, s 111*, by bringing agreements for leases for more than 35 years within the charge to duty, put an end to the avoidance schemes as did the decision in *Ingram v CIR* Ch D, [1985] STC 835. See **19 ANTI-AVOIDANCE.**

Under *FA 1995, s 151* an agreement for lease between **ASSOCIATED COMPANIES (22)** is exempt from duty subject to the requirements of that section. See **23.5 STAMP DUTY RESERVE TAX.**

Chapter 17

Agreement for Sale

[17.1] With the abolition of stamp duty on land and buildings from 1 December 2003, stamp duty is restricted to transactions in shares and securities, bearer instruments and acquisitions of partnership interests. Accordingly, the few remaining assets vulnerable to stamp duty on the sale of a business such as tenant's fixtures, the benefit of contracts and trade debts, ceased to be liable to stamp duty from 1 December 2003. Sales and certain other transfers of land and buildings will be liable to stamp duty land tax and stamp duty will apply only to the extent that the consideration is apportioned to shares and securities, bearer instruments and partnership interests. See Part One.

The following explains the position regarding sale agreements entered into before 1 December 2003.

Certain agreements or contracts for sale are charged to ad valorem duty as if they were a **CONVEYANCE OR TRANSFER (38)** on sale. A contract or agreement for sale operates to transfer beneficial ownership but is not a **CONVEYANCE OR TRANSFER (38)** because it looks forward to subsequent specific performance (*CIR v Angus & Co* CA, (1889) 23 QBD 579).

But a contract or agreement for sale of:

(a) any equitable interest in any property; or
(b) any estate or interest in any property except:
  (i) land;
  (ii) property locally situate outside the UK;
  (iii) goods, wares or merchandise;
  (iv) stock or marketable securities;
  (v) ships, vessels or part interest therein;

is charged with ad valorem duty to be paid by the purchaser, as if it were an actual conveyance on sale. [*FA 1999, Sch 13, para 7(1)*]. See *Farmer & Co v CIR* QB, [1898] 2 QB 141, *Peter Bone Ltd v CIR* Ch D, [1995] STC 921. See **16.7**(*e*) below. For calculations of the duty see **39 CONVEYANCE OR TRANSFER.**

Because of these widely drawn exclusions relatively few types of sale agreement attract duty under *FA 1999, Sch 13, para 7(1)*. An agreement for the sale of **GOODWILL (58)** (e.g. *West London Syndicate v CIR* CA, [1898] 2 QB 507) is now exempt from duty. [*FA 2002, s 116*]. If the goodwill related to a business carried on entirely outside the UK, the agreement was exempt in any event under (*b*)(ii) above (*CIR v Muller & Co's Margarine Ltd* HL, [1901] AC 217; cf *Benjamin Brooke & Co v CIR* QB, [1896] 2 QB 356). Where goodwill and other property are sold together the consideration is required to be apportioned on a 'just and reasonable' basis. [*FA 2002, Sch 36*].

However, the following agreements are still liable to duty:

(a) An agreement to exchange shares in one company in return for an issue of shares in another company where the shares in the first company were to be held on trust for the second company was either a conveyance on sale of an equitable interest or an agreement to sell it (*Chesterfield Brewery Co v CIR* QB, [1899] 2 QB 7).

(b) An acknowledgement of receipt given by a reversioner for money in respect of his reversionary interest was an agreement for sale of the reversionary interest (*Fleetwood-Hesketh v CIR* CA, [1936] 1 KB 351).

(c) An agreement for the sale of tenant's fixtures (see *Lee v Gaskell* QB, 1876 1 QBD 700).

(d) An agreement for the sale of trade receivables. The Government has, however, announced its intention to exclude sales of trade debts from the introduction of the modernised property transfer tax intended to occur in late 2003. See Budget 2002 Press Release REV4: Stamp Duty on UK Land and Buildings.

(e) An agreement for the sale of the benefit of a contract.

(f) An agreement for the sale of an estate or interest in UK land where the amount or value of the consideration exceeds £10m (approximately £8.5m plus VAT where VAT could be charged) becomes chargeable with ad valorem duty payable by the purchaser unless a conveyance conforming to the agreement is presented to IR Stamp Taxes within 90 days of the execution of the contract (or such longer period as IR Stamp Taxes thinks is reasonable in the circumstances). The rules as to inadmissibility of an unstamped instrument and interest and penalties for late stamping do not bite until after the end of the 90-day period (or longer period if allowed). If the agreement is later rescinded or not substantially performed any duty paid is repayable. [*FA 2002, s 115*]. A subsequent conveyance to the purchaser is only chargeable with duty to the extent (if any) that the ad valorem duty that would be chargeable on it exceeds the duty paid on the agreement. If the ad valorem duty on the conveyance turns out to be less than on the agreement, the difference is repayable to the person who paid the duty on the agreement the difference is repayable to the person by whom the duty was paid on the original sale. [*FA 2002, Sch 36 paras 5* and *6*]. It seems that while duty paid on the agreement is available as a credit against duty on the conveyance the reverse is not true. For the position regarding sub-sales see **39.8 SUB-SALES** and the Customer Newsletter (sic) issued by IR Stamp Taxes in July 2002 reproduced at **APPENDIX D**.

An agreement creating an option to purchase is not liable under *FA 1999, Sch 13, para 7(1)*, but may be liable to duty as a **CONVEYANCE OR TRANSFER (38)** on sale. But an agreement for the sale of a subsisting option may attract duty under *FA 1999, Sch 13, para 7(1)*. (*George Wimpey & Co Ltd v CIR* CA, [1975] 2 All ER 45). See **70 OPTIONS AND WARRANTS**.

'Property locally situate outside the UK' includes the benefit of a contract enforceable against a non-resident. An agreement for the sale of debts owing by a non-resident debtor is therefore exempt. (*English, Scottish and Australian Bank Ltd v CIR* HL, [1932] AC 238).

The following points arise in connection with **agreements for the sale of businesses.**

(a) Where a number of assets (some of which do not attract duty under *FA 1999, Sch 13, para 7(1)*) are acquired for one consideration, a bona fide apportionment must be made of the consideration. Stamps form no 22 is used to apportion the consideration: see **APPENDIX H** for a copy of the form. *Section 58(1)* confers a broad entitlement on the parties where many assets are acquired for a single consideration to apportion the consideration 'as they think fit' (*Re Brown & Root McDermott Fabricators Ltd's and another's application* Ch D [1996] STC 483). But see **30.1 CERTIFICATE OF VALUE** and Stamp Taxes Bulletin, August 2001 p 3 reproduced at **APPENDIX D**.

(b) Although cash at bank is a debt from a banker and liable to ad valorem duty if agreed to be sold, duty is not in practice claimed on current accounts.

(c) An agreement to sell debts as at a prior date attracts ad valorem duty on the amount of the debts at that date and not the amount outstanding at the date of the agreement (*Measures Brothers v CIR* QB, (1900) 82 LT 689). Duty may be avoided by arranging for the book debts to be collected on behalf of the vendor and used to discharge his liabilities, providing that any surplus belongs to the vendor and there is no undertaking by the purchaser to make good any deficiency.

(d) A written contract of sale to a limited company in consideration of the issue of shares was required to be filed, duly stamped, with the Registrar of Companies within one month. [*Companies Act 1985, s 88(2)*]. Where the transaction was concluded by an oral contract, written particulars had to be filed instead. [*Companies Act 1985, s 88(3)*]. The requirement for the written particulars to be stamped was removed upon the introduction of SDLT. [The *Stamp Duty and Stamp Duty Land Tax (Consequential Amendment of Enactments) Regulations (SI 2003 No 2868)*]. This could be avoided by contracting orally to sell the business for cash and using that consideration to pay for the shares by way of set-off (*Re Harmony and Montague Tin & Copper Mining Co, Spargo's Case* CA, (1873) 8 Ch App 407). There is now no requirement to produce a duly stamped contract or particulars of the contract under the *Companies Act 2006, s 555* which replaced the *Companies Act 1985, s 88* on 1 October 2009. Details of any non-cash consideration must, however, be entered on form SH01.

(e) An agreement for the sale of a business including land to a company under which the sale and purchase was expressed to be completed upon exchange of the agreement, the vendors were to be nominees of the purchaser but the vendors did not have the right (which the vendor under an uncompleted contract has) to require the purchaser to take a conveyance of the legal title to the land was held to attract ad valorem duty. Strictly, this was because the agreement operated as a transfer of the equitable estate in the land under *FA 1999, Sch 13, para 1(2)*, rather than as an agreement for the sale of the equitable estate under *FA 1999, Sch 13, para 7(1)*. However, it made no practical difference under which provision the liability arose. The parties' intention had been to avoid a 'double' stamp duty charge on the transfer of the land to the company for onward sale to developers. They had intended that stamp duty would be payable only once on the conveyance direct from the vendors to the developers at the direction of the company. Had the agreement included provision for a conveyance of the legal estate to the company at the insistence of the vendors then the company could have then claimed sub-sale relief and duty would then only have been payable once. [*SA 1891, s 58(5)*]. See **39.8 Sub-sales**. (*Peter Bone Ltd v CIR* Ch D, [1995] STC 921).

Where an agreement for sale falls within one of the exclusions ((*b*)(i)–(v) above), it may be possible to complete the transaction without attracting ad valorem duty as a **Conveyance or Transfer (38)** on sale. See **71 Oral Transactions.**

A subsequent conveyance or transfer made to a purchaser or another person on his behalf does not attract further duty if the agreement is duly stamped ad valorem. The Commissioners will stamp the conveyance with a stamp denoting that ad valorem duty has been paid or transfer the ad valorem duty from the agreement to the conveyance or transfer. [*FA 1999, Sch 13, para 7(3), (4)*]. See **44 Denoting Stamp.**

An agreement need not be stamped under *FA 1999, Sch 13, para 7(1)* if a conveyance or transfer in conformity with the agreement is presented for stamping within six months of the execution of the agreement (or a longer time at the discretion of the Commissioners) and the agreement would not be chargeable with duty apart from *FA 1999, Sch 13, para 7(1)*. The conveyance or transfer then bears the ad valorem duty and the agreement is deemed duly stamped. [*FA 1999, Sch 13, para 8*].

Where ad valorem duty is paid on an agreement which is later rescinded or not carried into effect so as to operate or be followed by a conveyance or transfer, the duty will be refunded. [*FA 1999, Sch 13, para 9*].

Agreement for sub-sale

[17.2] Where the purchaser has paid ad valorem duty on an agreement for sale and before obtaining a conveyance or transfer of the property enters into an agreement for sale of the same, duty on the second agreement is payable as follows:

(a) where the sub-sale consideration is greater than the original consideration—ad valorem duty on the difference;
(b) in any other case—no duty. [*FA 1999, Sch 13, para 7(2)*].

A subsequent conveyance or transfer to the sub-purchaser or another person on his behalf attracts no further duty as in **17.1** above.

If exemption from duty on an agreement under one of the exclusions (**17.1** (*b*)(i)–(v) above) is claimed, **Adjudication (12)** may be necessary in order to ensure that the correct amount of duty has been paid.

Certain agreements for the lease of land are charged with lease duty as actual leases. [*FA 1999, Sch 13, para 14*]. See **16 Agreement for Lease.**

Chapter 18

Annuities

[18.1] Annuities are not charged to duty under a separate head and the charges are found as follows:

(a) The creation and sale of annuities other than purchased life and superannuation annuities are charged under the head **CONVEYANCE OR TRANSFER (39)** on sale.

(b) The conveyance or transfer of property in consideration of annuities. For the valuation of consideration consisting of an annuity see **36.4 PERIODICAL PAYMENTS**.

Purchased life and superannuation annuities

[18.2] These are now exempt from duty.

Other annuities

[18.3] The creation and sale of an annuity effected by actual grant or conveyance prior to 1 December 2003 is charged to ad valorem duty as a **CONVEYANCE OR TRANSFER (39)** on sale. If the annuity is merely secured by a bond or similar instrument, that document is deemed to be a conveyance on sale. See generally **39 CONVEYANCE OR TRANSFER**. [*SA 1891, s 60*].

It has been held that *s 60* does not apply to a term annuity (*Commercial Union Assurance Co v CIR* KB 1937, [1938] 2 KB 551). It does apply to the purchase of a perpetual annuity described as a borrowing (*Mersey Docks and Harbour Board v CIR* CA, [1897] 2 QB 316) and to a deed of covenant to make annual payments out of income in exchange for the issue of shares (*Faber v CIR* KB, (1936) 155 LT 228).

Sale in consideration of an annuity

[18.4] There are special rules for valuing sale consideration consisting of periodic sums, including annuities. See **36.4 PERIODICAL PAYMENTS**.

The sale of an annuity and a sale in consideration of an annuity must be distinguished. An instrument securing an annuity in consideration for the transfer of property is treated as a sale in consideration of an annuity (*Blandy v Herbert* KB, (1829) 9 B & C 396; *Mestayer v Biggs Ex*, (1834) 1 Cr M & R 110; cf *Faber v CIR*, above).

Chapter 19

Anti-avoidance

[19.1] In *Ingram v CIR* Ch D, [1985] STC 835 it was held that the new approach to tax avoidance as developed by the House of Lords in *W T Ramsay Ltd v CIR* [1982] AC 300 and *Furniss v Dawson*, [1984] STC 153, applied to stamp duty.

In *Ingram* the taxpayer agreed to buy a freehold house for £145,500. In an attempt to reduce the stamp duty payable on this purchase the taxpayer and the vendor entered into an artificial scheme which relied on the fact that an **AGREEMENT FOR LEASE (16)** for more than 35 years did not attract stamp duty. [*SA 1891, ss 59(1), 75(1)* (now repealed and restated by *FA 1999, Sch 13, para 14*)]. This scheme was subsequently stopped by *FA 1984, s 111*. Under the scheme:

(a) the vendor and the taxpayer entered into an agreement for the lease of the house for 999 years for a premium of £145,000 and an annual rent of £25;
(b) a company owned by the taxpayer's solicitors then agreed to buy the freehold of the house from the vendor for £500;
(c) the company then agreed to sub-sell the freehold to the taxpayer for £600;
(d) the vendor then conveyed, and the company confirmed, the freehold to the taxpayer.

The taxpayer presented the conveyance for **ADJUDICATION (13)** contending that stamp duty was chargeable only on the sub-sale consideration of £600, the agreement for the lease being exempt from duty. [*SA 1891, ss 3, 58(4), 59(1), 75(1)*]. The duty was assessed instead on £145,600, i.e. £1,456. The taxpayer appealed to the Chancery Division which held that although stamp duty was a tax on instruments rather than transactions, it was the substance of the transaction that determined the charge to duty. The new approach to tax avoidance applied and the agreement for the lease would be ignored and the two agreements for the sale of the freehold would be treated as an agreement for the sale of the unencumbered freehold to the taxpayer for £145,600, giving rise to stamp duty of £1,456.

Despite the decision in *Ingram* the application of the new approach to stamp duty was not easy. For example, whatever the substance of the transaction there must be in existence an instrument for the Commissioners to stamp and that instrument must fall under one of the heads of charge in the legislation. Moreover, the three cases *Craven v White, CIR v Bowater Property Development Ltd* and *Bayliss v Gregory* HL, [1988] STC 476 held that the new approach could not apply where it was not known at the outset that all the transactions in a series of transactions would actually occur.

There was then a further refining of the new approach with the courts emphasising that it was really concerned with ascertaining the true legal nature of the transaction and then correctly applying the relevant statutory taxing provisions to it instead of rewriting the transaction (*Ensign Tankers (Leasing) Ltd v Stokes* [1991] STC 136). The statutory provisions are to be applied to the substance of the transaction, disregarding artificial steps in a composite transaction or series of transactions inserted only for the purpose of seeking to obtain a tax advantage (*IRC v McGuckian* HL [1997] STC 908). In *MacNiven v Westmoreland Investments Ltd* [2001] UKHL 6 [2001] STC 237, the House of Lords held that the Ramsay principle involved construing the language of a statute and determining whether it referred to a concept which Parliament intended to give a commercial meaning, transcending the individual steps in a pre-planned series of transactions. If a commercial meaning was intended then artificial steps which had no commercial purpose were to be ignored when applying the relevant tax concept. However, purely legal concepts which had no broader commercial meaning could not be construed in that way and in relation to these if the transaction fell within the legal description then it did not matter that it had no business purpose. Even if the statutory expression referred to a business concept, one could not disregard a transaction which came within the language simply because it was entered into solely for tax reasons. In relation to purely legal concepts, Lord Hoffman gave as an example stamp duty payable on a document which constitutes a conveyance on sale and he confirmed that the court could not tax a transaction which uses no document on the ground that it achieves the same economic effect. On this basis it was thought that stamp duty planning was less susceptible to the Ramsay approach than taxes that are based on concepts to which Parliament intended to give a commercial meaning. In order to distinguish between a purely legal concept and a commercial concept, Lord Hoffman suggested that if a commercial man asking what a concept meant, was given the reply 'you had better ask a lawyer', then that concept would be a legal concept. In *DTE Financial Services v Wilson* [2001] EWCA Civ 455, [2001] STC 777, the Court of Appeal adopted this approach and held that in the context of the PAYE system the concept of 'payment' was a practical, commercial concept and thus applied the Ramsay principle to a composite transaction.

However there were certain difficulties with the approach of Lord Hoffman in *MacNiven*. In framing his distinction between 'legal' and 'commercial' concepts Lord Hoffman had proceeded on the basis that the distinction between income and capital in *McGuckian* and the question of whether there had not been a disposal under the statutory share exchange provisions in *Furniss* were commercial rather than legal concepts. However these are normally regarded as questions of law (see for example *Beauchamp v FW Woolworth plc* [1990] 1 AC 478 at 491A) and it is unlikely that a businessman or woman would approach such an issue without seeking a lawyer's advice. Indeed it can be said that the stamp duty payable on a conveyance on sale (which Lord Hoffman gave as an example of a 'legal' concept) is something that most businessmen and women would feel reasonably comfortable in deciding—after all a transfer of property is in normal circumstances something that most people would recognise and understand without the assistance of a lawyer, and 1 to 4% of the price payable for a typical transfer of land is not such a challenging intellectual problem. For further on this see the judgment of Carnwath LJ in *Barclays Mercantile Business Finance Ltd v Mawson* [2002] EWCA Civ 1853

[2003] STC 66. Lord Hoffmann, however, effectively recanted from the approach he used in *MacNiven v Westmoreland Investments Ltd* [2001] STC 237 when delivering the only speech in the unanimous decision of the Privy Council in *Stamp Comr v Carreras Group Ltd* [2004] UKPC 16, [2004] SWTI 990. The decision confirmed that the *Ramsay* doctrine is a rule of construction and that while many statutory provisions are in such terms as to require transactions having a 'commercial unity' to be taken as a whole, other provisions are of a very particular, prescriptive nature requiring a 'step by step' analysis. This approach does not deny the existence or legality of the individual steps but may deprive them of significance for the purposes of the characterisation required by statute; Lord Hoffmann avoided expressly criticising his earlier approach in *MacNiven* by continuing: 'This has been said so often that citation of authority since *Ramsay*'s case is unnecessary'. The question in *Carreras* was whether the issue of a debenture in exchange for shares fell within provisions relating to the reorganisation of share capital which had the effect (if they applied) of treating the acquisition of the shares as not liable to stamp duty. If the relevant transaction was confined to the share for debenture exchange there was no doubt that the exemption applied. However, if as their Lordships held, one took a wider view and treated the issue of the debenture and its redemption for cash two weeks later as part of the relevant transaction then the matter looked very different. From this perspective there was a sale of the shares for cash and the issue of the debenture was only a formal step having no apparent commercial purpose of significance. On this basis the reorganisation exemption did not apply and stamp duty was chargeable.

The subsequent decisions of the House of Lords in *Barclays Mercantile Business Finance Ltd v Mawson* [2005] STC 1 and *IRC v Scottish Provident Institution* [2005] STC 15 were an attempt in a sense to draw a line under the earlier decisions and formulate a consistent interpretation of the *Ramsay* principle and achieve clarity. Unfortunately, there was no attempt by their Lordships to reconcile the two decisions (IR Stamp Taxes won in *Scottish Provident* and the taxpayer won in *Barclays*). *Barclays* tells us that the essence of the *Ramsay* approach is to give the statutory provision a purposive construction in order to determine the nature of the transaction to which it was intended to apply and then to decide whether the actual transaction (looked at as a whole if necessary) answered to the statutory description. *Scottish Provident* tell us that the language of a statute would often have to be given a wide practical meaning which required the court to have regard to the whole of a series of transactions which were intended to have a commercial unity. The deliberate insertion of a commercially irrelevant contingency creating a risk that the scheme might not work as planned in order to invoke *Craven v White* (see above) should in effect be ignored and the scheme should be considered as it was intended to operate, i.e. 'anti-*Ramsay*' devices may be inoperative. These decisions appear initially at least to have liberated the courts to pursue an aggressive style of purposive statutory interpretation and the House of Lords decision in *West v Trennery* [2005] STC 214 illustrates just how far their Lordships were prepared to go in construing what was arguably a defective anti-avoidance provision in a manner that achieved what their Lordships took to be Parliament's intention.

Rather strangely, however, from a practical perspective IR Stamp Taxes appears to have been reluctant to invoke *Ramsay* in the context of stamp taxes. Instead, IR Stamp Taxes seems content to enact statutory anti-avoidance whenever it encounters 'unacceptable' stamp tax avoidance.

Even this refined approach may prove embarrassing for the Stamp Office given the issue of the Press Release of 18 April 1994 which in relation to the new ad valorem charge on exchanges of interests in land contained in *FA 1994, s 241* (see **36.7 Exchanges of Property**), contains official guidance on how to draft the documentation so as to avoid the multiple charges to duty which were originally intended to be levied.

The relevance of motive or intention in relation to stamp duty avoidance is currently uncertain. On traditional stamp duty principles the presence of a stamp duty avoidance motive was not taken into account when construing a document, e.g. *IRC v Littlewoods Mail Order Stores Ltd* [1963] AC 135. In both *Combined Technologies Corpn plc v IRC* Ch D [1985] STC 348 and *Peter Bone Ltd v CIR* Ch D [1995] STC 921 Vinelott J. held that 'purpose' meant the effect of the instrument and not what the parties intended to achieve and that extrinsic evidence was inadmissible in construing the instrument. However, the decision of the Court of Appeal in *Parinv (Hatfield) Ltd v IRC* CA [1998] STC 305 undermines this line of authority because the Court without referring to these cases drew inferences as to the parties' intentions and without requiring a finding of fact in the case stated.

Statutory anti-avoidance

[19.2] Regarding statutory anti-avoidance—

(a) Every instrument must be written in such a way that the stamp may appear on the face of the instrument and cannot be used for any other instrument written on the same piece of material. [*SA 1891, s 3(1)*].

(b) More than one instrument may be written on the same piece of material but each instrument must be separately stamped with its own duty. [*SA 1891, s 3(2)*; but see *FA 1988, s 143(7)*]. A memorandum endorsed on an assurance policy to rectify a mistake in the instrument was a separate instrument liable to duty (*Prudential Assurance Co Ltd v CIR* KB, [1935] 1 KB 101).

(c) All the facts and circumstances affecting the liability to duty must be set out in the instrument. [*SA 1891, s 5*]. In practice any facts and circumstances not set out in the instrument can be disclosed in a covering letter to the Commissioners. A breach of *s 5* is a mere irregularity and does not render the instrument a nullity (*Re Brown & Root McDermott Fabricators Ltd's* Ch D [1996] STC 483).

(d) Three statutory changes referred to by the Chancellor as anti-avoidance measures were introduced by *FA 1994* for documents executed on or after 8 December 1993 (see **35.7 Exchanges of property**; **48 Exchange or Partition**; **37 Contingency Principle**; and **64.4**(*b*) **Surrenders and Variations**). [*FA 1994, ss 241, 242* and *243*].

(e) A number of specific anti-avoidance measures were introduced by *FA 2000* aimed at particular stamp duty avoidance schemes. The schemes attacked included exchanges of land or marketable securities in a manner that avoided ad valorem duty, transfers of land to connected companies or for shares for a nominal consideration and the use of artificial stamp duty groups of companies. These statutory measures are explained in detail in each relevant chapter. However, *FA 2000, s 117* and *Sch 33* also introduced a power of the Treasury to vary stamp duties by regulation. This power was taken because of the limitations of the power to introduce amending legislation under the procedure in *FA 1973, s 50*. (See **74.6 CHANGES IN RATES OF DUTY**). Any regulations made require a subsequent affirmative resolution by the House of Commons broadly within 28 days and even when confirmed cease to apply after 18 months in order to allow time for such provisions to have been incorporated in a subsequent finance bill. The intention is to allow the Treasury flexibility in attacking immediately any stamp duty avoidance schemes that come to light during the course of the tax year instead of waiting for the next finance bill. To this extent the power merely places the stamp duties on the same footing as stamp duty reserve tax and the other assessed taxes. However, the power is wider than this and includes a power to alter the descriptions of documents on which stamp duty (or an existing rate or amount of duty) is chargeable. Given that stamp duty is a tax on documents the scope of this power is therefore very wide indeed. For instance, it would be possible to make contracts for the sale of land which are currently not stampable come within the scope of ad valorem duty and thus effectively repeal the exemption in *FA 1999, Sch 13, para 7(1)(b)(I)*. There are, however, some restrictions in the scope of the power. The power can only be used for documents that to any extent relate to land, stock or marketable securities. Also, the power cannot be used to vary rates or thresholds (except to the extent of altering the descriptions of documents in respect of which stamp duty is chargeable).

(f) Further specific anti-avoidance measures were introduced by *FA 2002* with the intention of shoring-up the stamp duty regime and protecting stamp duty revenue pending the 'modernisation' of the tax proposed by the consultative document issued in April 2002 entitled: 'Modernising Stamp Duty on land and buildings in the UK'. These statutory measures are explained in detail in each relevant chapter but in summary:

  (i) clawback group relief where UK land has been transferred from one company to another and within three (originally two) years the transferee company leaves the group (see **23.3 WITHDRAWAL OF GROUP RELIEF**);

  (ii) clawback group relief under FA 1986, s 76 where a company acquires the undertaking of another company in exchange for the issue of shares and within three (originally two) years control of the acquiring company changes (see **34.3 UNDERTAKINGS: REDUCED RATE**);

(iii) extend the penalty for late stamping of documents to documents relating to UK land executed outside the UK that are not presented for stamping within 30 days of execution; and

(iv) make contracts for the sale of UK land for a consideration exceeding £10m liable to stamp duty unless a conveyance is presented for stamping within 90 days or such longer period as the Commissioners may think is reasonable.

Inland revenue practice

[19.3] Following their victory in *Parinv (Hatfield) Ltd v IRC* CA [1998] STC 305 the Inland Revenue announced their practice in the Tax Bulletin of August 1997 page 460 as follows:

(a) not to accept in support of a claim to relief or as evidence in relation to any liability to tax, any unstamped original or conformed unstamped copies of documents.

(b) to treat any failure by the parties or their advisers to disclose the fact that the parties are attempting to rely on an unstamped document in executing a transfer which purports to convey the bare legal estate as a breach of *SA 1891, s 5* and tantamount to fraud and 'appropriate action' will be taken.

(c) to treat any attempt by the parties to an instrument containing a certificate under the exempt instrument regulations to rely on another instrument executed overseas which was not duly stamped as a breach of *SA 1891, s 5.*

See **Appendix D** where the article is reproduced in full.

Chapter 20

Appeals

[20.1] The system of stamp duty appeals was changed by *FA 1999* which replaced the old *SA 1891, s 13* with three new sections *13*, *13A* and *13B* which provided for appeals in relation to penalties to go to the Special Commissioners rather than the High Court. Since 1 April 2009, appeals in relation to penalties go to the First-Tier Tribunal rather than to the Special Commissioners. [The *Transfer of Tribunal Functions and Revenue and Customs Appeals Order 2009* (SI 2009/56)].

Any person who is dissatisfied with an **ADJUDICATION (13)** by the Commissioners may, within 30 days of the date of notice of the Commissioners' decision being given and after paying the duty assessed plus any penalty and interest, appeal. [*SA 1891, s 13* as substituted by *FA 1999, Sch 12, para 2*]. The Stamp Office in practice nearly always issues a provisional adjudication decision first and will only issue a (final) notice of decision once it is clear that agreement on the amount of duty payable is not possible. It is the issue of the (final) notice of decision which gives rise to the right of appeal and starts the 30-day period during which an appeal must be commenced within *SA 1891, s 13(2)*. A notice of decision is made as part of the **ADJUDICATION (13)** procedure. Note, however, that there is no provision under which the Commissioners can be required to issue a notice of decision on a timely basis short of a successful application to the Court for a judicial review.

An appeal relating only to the penalty payable on late stamping is brought to the First-Tier Tribunal in accordance with *SA 1891, s 13A* as amended by *SI 2009/56*. The taxpayer must within 30 days of notice of the adjudication decision, give written notice of appeal to the Commissioners specifying the grounds of appeal. On the appeal the First-Tier Tribunal may set the penalty aside, confirm it, reduce it or increase it as it considers appropriate. An appeal lies against the decision of the First-Tier Tribunal in relation to the amount of a penalty to the Upper Tribunal.

Any other appeal is brought to the High Court in accordance with *SA 1891, s 13B*. The appeal commences with the taxpayer requiring the Commissioners to state and sign a case setting out the questions upon which they were required to adjudicate and their decisions upon them and deliver it to the appellant. In practice the case is normally agreed in draft beforehand. The appellant may then set the appeal down for a hearing within 30 days. [*SA 1891, s 13A(2), (3)*]. The High Court then decides the question and assesses the duty. The case is heard in the Chancery Division. Appeals from the High Court lie to the Court of Appeal and then, with leave, to the Supreme Court.

The court may order the repayment of any excess duty paid together with any penalty paid. [*SA 1891, s 13A(4)*]. For instruments executed before 1 October 1999 the court may also order interest to be paid to the appellant on any sum repaid. [*FA 1965, s 91*]. Interest has been awarded to run from the date of overpayment (*Crane Fruehauf Ltd v CIR* Ch D, [1974] 1 All ER 811). For instruments executed on or after 1 October 1999, the general right to a payment of interest on a repayment of stamp duty and penalties applies from the later of 30 days after the instrument was executed or the date on which the duty or penalty was paid. [*FA 1999, s 110*].

There is no provision under which the appellant can be required to pay the excess if the court assesses an amount of duty higher than that assessed by the Commissioners.

Appeals in relation to **STAMP DUTY RESERVE TAX (84)** are referred to the First-Tier Tribunal and the High Court. [*Stamp Duty Reserve Tax Regulations 1986 (SI 1986 No 1711) reg 8*].

Chapter 21

Appointments

[21.1] The head of charge 'Appointment of a new trustee, and appointment in execution of a power of any property' in *SA 1891, Sch 1* (now restated in *FA 1999, Sch 13*) was abolished by *FA 1985, s 85(1), Sch 24(b)*.

An instrument of appointment of a new trustee did, however, attract a maximum duty of £5 if it contained an express declaration vesting the trust property in the new trustee. See *Hadgett v CIR Ex D*, (1877) 3 Ex D 46. This fixed duty could have been avoided by including the appropriate certificate in the instrument (see **50 Exempt Instruments**). Where the instrument of appointment did not expressly vest the trust property in the trustee but relied instead on an implied vesting under the *Trustee Act 1925, s 40*, it did not in practice attract the £5 duty. However, this fixed duty was abolished for instruments executed on or after 13 March 2008, except for instruments effecting a land transaction. [*FA 1999, Sch 13 para 16* repealed by *FA 2008, Sch 32*].

An appointment under a general power of appointment may be liable to ad valorem duty as a conveyance on sale (see **39 Conveyance or Transfer**).

Chapter 22

Assents

[22.1] There is no specific head of charge for assents. However, an assent to vest property agreed to be sold by the deceased is liable to ad valorem duty as a conveyance on sale (see **39 Conveyance or Transfer**) (*GHR Co Ltd v CIR KB*, [1943] KB 303).

Formerly, ad valorem duty was charged on assents where a pecuniary legacy was satisfied by the transfer of property with the consent of the legatee (see *Dawson v CIR KB(I)*, [1905] 2 IR 69; *Jopling v CIR KB*, [1940] 2 KB 282). The transfer was treated as a conveyance on sale because the legatee was entitled to money from the estate. Ad valorem duty could also arise on the appropriation of property by the personal representatives in satisfaction of the surviving spouse's interest in an intestate's estate. Where ad valorem duty was not charged an assent could attract a fixed 50p (now increased to £5) duty (see second paragraph below).

An assent which vests property appropriated in satisfaction of a general legacy of money or in satisfaction of any interest of a surviving spouse in an intestate's estate is no longer subject to ad valorem duty as a conveyance on sale. [*Finance Act 1985, s 84(4)–(7)* and see also *Administration of Estates Act 1925, s 36(10)*]. It was, however, necessary to pay a fixed duty of 50p (subsequently increased to £5) and have the assent adjudicated. This fixed duty has been abolished for instruments executed on or after 13 March 2008 except in relation to instruments effecting a land transaction: *FA 2008, Sch 32* (see below and **50 Exempt Instruments**).

An assent which gives effect to any of the following transactions and which includes the appropriate certificate is exempt from the fixed duty of £5 and does not have to be adjudicated:

(a) the conveyance or transfer of property the subject of a specific devise or legacy to the beneficiary named in the will (or his nominee);

(b) the conveyance or transfer of property which forms part of an intestate's estate to the person entitled on intestacy (or his nominee);

(c) the appropriation of property within *Finance Act 1985, s 84(4)* or *(5)* or *(7)* (see above);

(d) the conveyance or transfer of property which forms part of the residuary estate of a testator to a beneficiary (or his nominee) entitled solely by virtue of his entitlement under the will. [*Stamp Duty (Exempt Instruments) Regulations 1987 (SI 1987 No 516)*].

See **50 Exempt Instruments.**

Chapter 23

Associated Companies

Note. This exemption was altered significantly by *FA 2002, s 111* and *Sch 34* for instruments relating to UK land executed on or after 24 April 2002 by the introduction of a clawback of the relief in certain circumstances (see **23.3** below). For transactions that are SDLT transactions see the equivalent relief in **6 Reliefs and Exemptions**.

Exemption

[23.1] Stamp duty is not charged under the head **Conveyance or Transfer (39)** on sale of an instrument provided that:

(a) the effect of the instrument is to convey or transfer a beneficial interest in property from one body corporate to another; and
(b) the bodies in question are associated at the time the instrument is executed,

unless at the time the instrument is executed arrangements are in existence by virtue of which at that or some later time any person has or could obtain control of the transferee but not of the transferor. 'Control' for this purpose is the test contained in *CTA 2010, s 1124*.

To be duly stamped, it is necessary for the instrument of transfer to be stamped either with a stamp denoting that no duty is chargeable or with the duty which is otherwise chargeable under the head **Conveyance or Transfer (39)** on sale. [*FA 1930, s 42*, amended by *FA 1995, s 149* and *FA 2000, s 123*]. The exemption has been extended to **Leases (64), Agreement for Lease (16)** and an 'agreement with respect to a letting'. [*FA 1995, s 151*, amended by *FA 2000, s 125*]. (See **23.5** below).

Bodies corporate, wherever incorporated or resident, are associated at a particular time if at that time one is the parent of the other or another body corporate is the parent of each. One body corporate is regarded for this purpose as the parent of another at a particular time if at that time the first body:

(a) is the beneficial owner of not less than 75% of the ordinary share capital of the second body;
(b) is beneficially entitled to not less than 75% of any profits available for distribution to equity holders of the second body; and
(c) would be beneficially entitled to not less than 75% of any assets of the second body available for distribution to its equity holders on a winding-up.

The corporation tax group relief provisions in *CTA 2010, Part 5, Chapter 6* apply in order to determine whether the tests in (b) and (c) above are satisfied except that *CTA 2010, ss 177(1)(b) and (3), 173, 174 and 176–178* have been 'switched-off' as regards transferor (but not transferee) companies and do not apply.

'Ordinary share capital' means all the issued share capital of a body corporate except shares having the right to a dividend at a fixed rate but no other right to share in profits.

In determining whether 75% of the ordinary share capital is held, indirect holdings are counted. Fractional elements through a chain of companies are determined by multiplying the fractions in the chain. [*FA 1938, Sch 4*].

In relation to beneficial ownership it has been held that:

(a) an unconditional contract to sell shares in a company will deprive the transferor of beneficial ownership on execution, notwithstanding that conditions remain to be fulfilled prior to completion (*CIR v Ufitec Group Ltd* QB, [1977] 3 All ER 924; *Parway Estates Ltd v CIR* CA, (1958) 45 TC 135);
(b) a conditional contract will pass beneficial ownership where the purchaser can waive the conditions (see at first instance *Wood Preservation Ltd v Prior* Ch D, [1968] 2 All ER 849) or where the vendor is otherwise unable to sell (*Brooklands Selangor Holdings Ltd v CIR* Ch D, [1970] 2 All ER 76);
(c) a company loses beneficial ownership of its assets when it is placed in liquidation (e.g. *CIR v Olive Mill Spinners Ltd* Ch D, [1963] 2 All ER 130; *Ayerst v C & K (Construction) Ltd* HL, [1976] AC 167);
(d) arrangements to which a company is or is not a party may deprive the company of beneficial ownership (*Holmleigh (Holdings) Ltd v CIR*, above);
(e) the overall effect of a scheme is considered in determining whether and when beneficial ownership passes (e.g. *Leigh Spinners Ltd v CIR* Ch D, (1956) 35 ATC 58).

For the exemption to apply, the effect of the instrument must be to convey or transfer a beneficial interest in the property from the transferor to the transferee. It often happens that a sale agreement is entered into prior to the formal conveyance and the beneficial interest passes not by the conveyance but by implication on the sale agreement being entered into. In such cases it has been held that the conveyance or transfer attracts the relief because it is to be stamped according to the value of the beneficial interest which passed from the seller to the buyer under the sale agreement. See *Escoigne Properties Ltd v CIR* HL, [1958] AC 549 at 563, 564.

Availability of exemption

[23.2] The exemption is not available unless it is shown to the Commissioners' satisfaction that the instrument was not executed as part of any of the types of arrangement set out below. On 13 October 1998 the Inland Revenue published statement of practice SP 3/98 which explains its interpretation of the anti-avoidance rules in *FA 1967, s 27*. See below for commentary and **APPENDIX B** where the statement of practice is reproduced in full.

(a) The consideration or part of the consideration for the transfer was to be provided or received, directly or indirectly, by a person other than a company itself associated with either the transferor or transferee. In particular, this extends to arrangements whereby the transferor or transferee company or another associated company was enabled to provide any of the consideration or was to part with any of it by carrying out a transaction involving a payment or other disposition by a person other than an associated company. Bank borrowing on normal commercial terms with no obligation in the loan agreement to apply the loan in a particular way or to repay the loan out of sales proceeds of the property purchased, is not regarded as an 'arrangement'. In the Standing Committee debates on the 1995 Finance Bill the Minister of State at the Treasury stated that the exemption would not be available if a loan was taken out specifically for the purpose of financing the transfer and was secured on the assets transferred. A general purpose loan which the borrower could apply in any way it chose would not jeopardise the exemption (Hansard Committee D, 20th Sitting, 7 March 1995, cols 620–621). However, the Stamp Office has since relaxed its approach in this area and issued statement of practice SP 3/98 on 13 October 1998. The relevant parts of the statement read as follows.

8. Section 27(3)(a) denies relief where the instrument was executed in pursuance of or in connection with an arrangement under which any of the consideration is to be provided or received, directly or indirectly, by a person outside the group. It also denies relief if the arrangement is one under which the transferor or transferee (or a member of the same group as either of them) is to be enabled to provide any of the consideration, or is to part with it, in consequence of a transaction involving a payment or other disposition by a person outside the group. Section 151 lays down similar rules for leases.

9. In some cases, the question arises whether loan finance for the purchase or lease will disqualify an intra-group transaction from relief. It is necessary to look at all the facts of the individual case, but the Stamp Office will interpret the provisions in the light of their general purpose of denying relief where the intra-group transaction is a means of saving stamp duty when the property, or an interest in it, moves out of the group. Accordingly, the Stamp Office are likely to be satisfied that relief is due if the intra-group transaction is not to be followed by a sale of the property transferred, or an underlease, to a person outside the group. If the intra-group transaction is to be followed by a sale or underlease to a person outside the group, but the claimant can demonstrate that stamp duty will be paid in respect of that transaction in approximately the same amount as would have been payable if the intra-group transferor or lessor had itself sold the property or granted the underlease, the Stamp Office are likely to be satisfied that the intra-group transaction and the transfer or lease out are independent for stamp duty purposes and grant the relief sought.

10. A transaction is not disqualified merely because the transferee within the group obtains a specific loan for the purchase of the asset; or the loan is secured on the asset; or arrangements are made to replace or novate an existing charge on the property transferred. It will be necessary to consider the facts as a whole, especially if the loan finance is not straightforward finance on ordinary commercial terms.

11. Intra-group transactions will be very carefully scrutinised, and relief may be refused, where, for example, the intra-group transaction involves or is to be followed by:
    — the creation or transfer of loan stock or equity capital;
    — a capital reorganisation of the transferee;
    — a creation of a new charge or financial arrangement whereby title to the property is, or may be, vested in the lender otherwise than in satisfaction of all or part of the debt; or
    — the assignment of the freehold reversion or the intra-group lease to a person outside the group.
12. Similarly transactions will be very carefully scrutinised where:
    — all or part of the consideration for the transaction is to remain outstanding or is represented by intra-group debt, (as the aim and effect may be to reduce the value of the transferee company on a possible future sale outside the group); or
    — the existing shareholders of the transferee include shareholders outside the group and the transaction is to be followed by the declaration of a dividend in specie, or by the liquidation of the transferee.
13. Further assurances by way of statutory declaration—the document in which the claim is made to the Stamp Office—will be required in any case in which the property transferred or vested intra-group is the only, or only substantial, asset of the transferee. Information to that effect should be provided in the statutory declaration submitted with the documents.
14. Where group member A has granted a lease to a person outside the group, and subsequently grants an underlease to its fellow group member B, so that the rent already payable by the lessee becomes payable to B rather than A, relief is likely to be given for the intra-group underlease, provided, there are no other factors which suggest that relief should be denied.

For examples of arrangements which would now be caught by this provision see *Shop and Store Developments Ltd v CIR* HL, [1967] 1 AC 472; *Curzon Offices Ltd v CIR* CA, [1944] 1 All ER 606.

(b) The beneficial interest was previously conveyed or transferred, directly or indirectly, by a person other than an associated company. 'Conveyed or transferred' has been widely construed to include the passing of the beneficial interest in property to a purchaser where the property was sub-sold and the conveyance taken direct to the sub-purchaser (*Escoigne Properties Ltd v CIR* HL, [1958] AC 549), and the transfer of the beneficial interest in property by a lease (*CIR v Littlewoods Mail Order Stores Ltd* HL, [1963] AC 135).

(c) The transferor and transferee were to cease to be associated by reason of the transferor or third body corporate ceasing to be the transferee's parent (within the meaning of **23.1** above). For an example of an arrangement now caught by this provision, see *Times Newspapers Ltd v CIR* Ch D, [1971] 3 All ER 98. This provision can apply where there are arrangements for the transferee to leave the 75% group but it will not normally apply where the transferor is leaving the 75% group. The fact that the property is being sold within the group in preparation for a possible sale of the shares in the transferee company outside the group ought not to prevent the exemption being available unless there are arrangements in existence for the sale of the transferee or a change in control. In its statement of practice SP 3/98 the Stamp Office states that it will apply these provisions so as to preclude the exemption if there is evidence of a plan or scheme to dispose of the transferee company and there is 'no practical likelihood' that the scheme will not be followed through. This requires the taxpayer to show that there is some practical likelihood of the transaction not proceeding (ignoring a mere theoretical or unforeseen difficulty or event).

In *Times Newspapers Ltd v CIR* Ch D, [1971] 3 All ER 98 it was said by Plowman J:

> The words quoted must, in my judgment, mean that the arrangement contemplated is one necessarily involving the provision of the consideration or some part of it by the person in question, and it is not enough for the Crown to say that it may or probably will do so.

Although as Plowman J held, the test should be framed in the positive so that to be caught the arrangement must be one that will necessarily occur, it appears that the test as formulated in SP3/98 amounts to the same thing, because if there is no practical likelihood that the scheme will not be followed through, then it will be one necessarily involving the offensive result. IR Stamp Taxes appears to have acknowledged this by the enactment of the group relief clawback charge in relation to UK land transfer by *FA 2002, s 111* explained in **23.6** below. This clawback charge is intended to recover stamp duty in cases involving UK land where HMRC Stamp Taxes would have sought to apply (*c*) above but has found that the legislation does not operate as widely as it would have wished. [*FA 1967, s 27*].

Withdrawal of group relief

[23.3] In relation to instruments transferring, granting or surrendering an interest in UK land that have been executed on or after 24 April 2002 and stamped on the basis that the exemption applies the exemption is withdrawn if within two years of the execution of the instrument the transferee company ceases to be a member of the same group as the transferor, and at that time the transferee company holds the land or an estate or interest derived from it. In such a case the stamp duty that would have been payable on the instrument but for the exemption had the UK land been transferred at market value, is payable by the transferee company within 30 days after that company ceases to be a member of the group. [*FA 2002, s 111*].

For instruments executed after 14 April 2003 the two year period has been extended to three years and the exemption will be withdrawn if within three years the transferee company ceases to be a member of the same group as the transferor company and at that time the transferee company or a relevant associated company holds the land or an estate or interest derived from it. [*FA 2002, s 111* as amended by *FA 2003, s 126*].

A 'relevant associated company' in relation to the transferee company means a company that:

(a) is a member of the same group as the transferee company immediately before that company ceases to be a member of the same group as the transferor; and
(b) ceases to be a member of the same group as the transferor company in consequence of the transferee company so ceasing. [*FA 2002, s 111(4A)*].

See also **6 Reliefs and Exemptions.**

Where the instrument deals with UK land together with other property, the withdrawal of the exemption operates as if there were two separate instruments, one relating to the UK land and the other relating to the other property. If when the transferee company leaves the group it, or a relevant associated company owns only a portion of what was originally transferred to the transferee company, only the appropriate proportion of the exemption is withdrawn. [*FA 2002, s 111*].

The exemption is not withdrawn if the transferor company leaves the group. [*FA 2002, Sch 34, para 2*]. This provision prevents the withdrawal of the exemption operating when the transferor leaves the group and thus technically causes the transferee to cease to be a member of the same group as the transferor.

The exemption is also not withdrawn in the case of the transferor company or another company above it in the group being wound-up or if the transferee company leaves the group as a result of the acquisition of its shares by another company where relief under *FA 1986, s 75* applies: see **34.2 Reconstructions.** [*FA 2002, Sch 34 paras 3* and *4*]. There appears to be nothing in the legislation that prevents the transferee company from being 'another company above [the transferor] in the group' and so the winding up of the transferee company in an *Insolvency Act 1986, s 110* hive-up scheme should not cause a withdrawal of group relief in respect of earlier transfers to the transferee company.

In the case of a withdrawal of the exemption, the transferee company is required to notify the Commissioners within 30 days of ceasing to be a member of the group and pay the appropriate stamp duty. [*FA 2002, s 111 (2)(b)* and *Sch 34, para 6*]. Interest is payable on any duty remaining unpaid from the end of the 30 days within which payment should have been made. [*FA 2002, Sch 34, para 5*]. The Commissioners have full powers of collection and recovery against not only the transferee company but also against the transferor company any other company that at the 'relevant time' was a fellow group company above the transferee in the group structure and any person who at any 'relevant time' was a controlling director of the transferee or of a company having control of it. [*FA 2002, Sch 34, paras 7, 8, 9* and *10*].

'Relevant time' means any time between the execution of the instrument and the transferee ceasing to be a member of the same group the transferor.

Procedure

[23.4] **ADJUDICATION (13)** is required for any instrument for which exemption is claimed. It is also necessary to submit a written claim (normally by letter rather than statutory declaration) setting out the facts justifying the claim for relief. HMRC publish a helpful information guide on how to apply for the relief and this is reproduced in **APPENDIX G**. A specimen claim letter used by the author is included at **APPENDIX I**.

Stamp duty reserve tax

[23.5] There is no equivalent exemption from **STAMP DUTY RESERVE TAX (84)** for transfers of shares between associated companies. However, if the stock transfer form is adjudicated and exemption from stamp duty is given under *FA 1930, s 42* the charge to stamp duty reserve tax will be cancelled. If stamp duty reserve tax has been paid within the previous six years it can be reclaimed. Where a stock transfer form is not executed and subsequently adjudicated and the intra-group share transfer effected merely on the basis of a board minute or a declaration of trust, stamp duty reserve tax is payable. It is therefore necessary to have each intra-group share transfer completed by a transfer which is adjudicated if a charge to stamp duty reserve tax is to be avoided. See **84 STAMP DUTY RESERVE TAX**.

Leases etc.

[23.6] The associated company exemption was extended to **LEASES (64)**, **AGREEMENT FOR LEASE (16)** and 'agreements with respect to a letting' in relation to instruments executed on or after 1 May 1995. By *FA 1995, s 151* and was significantly altered by *FA 2000, s 125*.

Stamp duty is not charged under the head Lease charge in *FA 1999, Sch 13, Part II* provided that:

(a) the lessor is a body corporate and the lessee is another body corporate;
(b) those bodies are associated at the time the instrument is executed;
(c) in the case of an agreement, the agreement is for the lease to be granted to the lessee or to a body corporate associated with the lessee at the time the instrument is executed;
(d) at the time the instrument is executed there are no arrangements in existence by virtue of which, at that time or some later time, any person has or could obtain control of the lessee but not of the lessor; and
(e) the instrument is not executed in pursuance of or in connection with an arrangement of the sort described in **23.2**(*a*) and (*c*) above (for 'transferor' and 'transferee' read 'lessor' and 'lessee'). 'Lessor' means the person granting the lease or agreeing to grant the lease. 'Lessee' means the person granted the lease or agreeing for the lease to be granted to him or another. [*FA 1995, s 151(6)*].

'Control' for the purpose of (*d*) above is the test contained in *ICTA 1988, s 840*.

To be duly stamped it is necessary for the instrument of transfer to be stamped either with a stamp denoting that no duty is chargeable or with the duty which is otherwise chargeable under the charge in *FA 1999, Sch 13, Part II*. [*FA 1995, s 151(5)*].

Whether bodies corporate are associated is decided according to the same criteria as set out in **23.1** above.

It will be noted that in contrast with the exemption under *FA 1930, s 42* (see **23.1** above) there is no requirement that the lease should be beneficially owned by the lessor or any other associated company and this is due to the fact that nominee arrangements occur frequently in relation to leases. However, it is thought that the Stamp Office would resist granting the exemption where this was exploited by the use of a nominee lessor acting for a non-associated person.

The withdrawal of group relief under *FA 2002, s 111* and as explained in **23.3** above applies also to instruments granting leases and agreements for lease that have been stamped on the basis that the exemption in *FA 1995, s 151* applied. Reference should be made to these provisions in the case of a lessee ceasing to be a member of the same group as the lessor company within two years of the relevant lease or agreement for lease.

Non-UK bodies corporate — Delaware LLCS — Delaware partnerships

[23.7] Issue 51 of the *Inland Revenue Tax Bulletin* of February 2001 confirmed that it is possible for a US limited liability company ('LLC'), and a Delaware LLC ('DLLC') in particular, to be a member of a capital gains group, a group relief group and be party to share exchanges for UK tax purposes provided the LLC has an issued ordinary share capital. The Tax Bulletin did not, however, mention stamp duty groups where this issue has long been relevant due to stamp duty group relief operating on a worldwide basis.

When considering the presence of an LLC in a worldwide stamp duty group it is not sufficient just to confirm that the LLC is a body corporate. Unless the LLC is the parent company of the relevant group or sub-group, it is also necessary to ensure that the LLC has an issued ordinary share capital if it is to be treated as a subsidiary member of the stamp duty group. This is because the statutory tests for a company to be a subsidiary member of a stamp duty group operate on the basis of the company having an issued ordinary share capital (*FA 1930, s 42 (2B)*).

However, in the past Stamp Office practice has not always been consistent and in at least one instance stamp duty group relief has been obtained merely on the basis that the LLC concerned was a body corporate, and the absence of an issued ordinary share capital was not addressed by the Stamp Office. This was a technical oversight and should not be relied upon without specific written confirmation from the Stamp Office that it is prepared to overlook the absence of an issued share capital.

In the light of Tax Bulletin 51 it is thought that such confirmation would be unlikely to be given.

The importance of this issue is highlighted with US/UK group restructuring exercises commonly intended to de-group a sub-group for UK capital gains planning with the insertion of a DLLC without issued ordinary share capital. It is sometimes initially assumed that stamp duty group relief will be available on the transfer of assets to the de-grouped sub-group because the DLLC is a body corporate. Unfortunately, the fact that the DLCC has no issued ordinary share capital means that as for capital gains purposes, the sub-group cannot form part of the parent company's stamp duty group and so stamp duty group relief will not be available.

And see also *Memec plc v IRC* [1998] STC 754 at 764–765, 71 TC 77, CA and *Swift v Revenue and Customs Comrs* [2010] UKFTT 88 (TC), [2010] SFTD 553 at 572.

Limited partnerships

[23.8] Correspondence with the Stamp Office indicates that it will accept that a Delaware Limited Partnership ('DLP') can be a body corporate because it has perpetual succession and a legal personality separate from its members. However, because a DLP will not have an issued share capital it can only ever be the parent body corporate of a stamp duty group and never a subsidiary member of such a group.

It is understood that both Scottish limited partnerships and general partnerships are not regarded as bodies corporate because although they have separate legal personality they do not have perpetual succession because their separate existence depends upon the existence of the partners. Because of their separate legal personality HMRC do not regard them as a 'look through' when establishing corporate bodies that form a group of companies.

English limited partnerships do not have separate legal personality and are therefore 'looked through' when establishing bodies corporate that form a group. Companies that are partners in an English limited partnership can in principle therefore form a group with companies below the limited partnership in the structure.

General partnerships

[23.9] It is understood that in practice IR Stamp Taxes is normally prepared to grant the exemption for instruments transferring property or granting leases between a general partnership formed under English law between associated companies and another associated company. This practice appears to be viewed by IR Stamp Taxes as concessionary and appears to be based on the concept of the partners having a proprietary interest in the property of the partnership. However it is arguable that such transfers qualify for relief as of right under the statutory provisions. Foreign partnerships similar to English partnerships can also benefit from the concession but as noted above Scottish partnerships cannot, due to their nature as separate legal persons. Where the exemption has been granted in the case of a partnership the withdrawal of the relief in relation to instruments relating to UK land (as explained in **23.3** above) does not arise in the case of a mere change in the identity of the partnership within three (previously two) years.

LLPs

[23.10] A limited liability partnership incorporated under the *Limited Liability Partnerships Act 2002* is a body corporate and can be the parent of a group but as it cannot have an issued share capital it cannot be the subsidiary of another company. Therefore transfers of shares attracting group relief can be made between the LLP and its subsidiaries in the same group but group relief is not available on transfers between the LLP and a parent body corporate or between the parent and a subsidiary beneath the LLP.

See also generally HMRC Notice dated 12 October 2011 entitled 'Group relief for Stamp Duty Land Tax and Stamp Duty – Partnerships'.

Chapter 24

Bearer Instruments

[24.1] The head 'Bearer Instrument' was inserted into *SA 1891, Sch 1* by *FA 1963, s 59* and the stamp duty charge on bearer instruments was restated in *FA 1999, Sch 15* in relation to bearer instruments issued on or after 1 October 1999. As bearer instruments can be transferred by delivery, the charge to stamp duty is on issue or in certain cases on first transfer in the UK. The charge applies only to bearer instruments expressed in sterling. Bearer instrument duty is not chargeable on bearer instruments expressed in a foreign currency or in units of account relating to more than one currency. [*FA 1999, Sch 15, para 17*]. See **24.7**(*a*) below and **24.8** for when a **STAMP DUTY RESERVE TAX (84)** charge can arise on the transfer of a UK bearer instrument despite this exemption from stamp duty.

Instruments charged and rates of duty

[24.2] **Note.** The terms Inland and Overseas bearer instrument are no longer used by *FA 1999, Sch 15*, however it is considered that this classification provides a useful method of understanding the rules.

(a) **Inland bearer instrument** (other than a deposit certificate for overseas stock) — 1.5%.
(b) **Overseas bearer instrument** (other than a deposit certificate for overseas stock or bearer instrument by usage) — 1.5%.
(c) **Inland or overseas deposit certificate for overseas stock or bearer instrument by usage** — 0.2%.
(d) **Inland or overseas bearer instrument given in substitution for a like instrument duly stamped ad valorem** — the fixed duty of £5 was abolished for instruments executed on or after 13 March 2008. However, the substitute instrument is not treated as duly stamped unless it bears a stamp confirming that full and proper duty was paid on the original instrument. [*FA 2008, Sch 32 para 11*].

The duty is charged (except in the case of (*d*) above) as a percentage of the market value of the stock constituted by or transferable by the bearer instrument. (See **24.6** below).

Definitions

[24.3] For the purposes of **24.2** above:

(a) An *inland bearer instrument* is an instrument issued by or on behalf of a company or body of persons formed or established in the UK, which is:
    (i) a marketable security transferable by delivery;

- (ii) a share warrant or stock certificate to bearer or similar instrument;
- (iii) a deposit certificate to bearer; or
- (iv) any other bearer instrument by which stock can be transferred.

(b) An *overseas bearer instrument* is an instrument as in (*a*) issued by a company or body of persons not formed or established in the UK, or a bearer instrument by usage issued by such persons.

(c) A *deposit certificate* is an instrument acknowledging the deposit of stock and entitling the bearer to rights in that or equivalent stock.

(d) A *deposit certificate for overseas stock* is a deposit certificate as in (*c*) in respect of stock of one company or body of persons formed or established outside the UK.

(e) A *bearer instrument by usage* is an instrument not otherwise treated as a bearer instrument, delivery of which is treated by usage as sufficient for sale on the market, whether or not delivery constitutes a legal transfer.

(f) *Stock* is widely defined as including securities, rights and interests in stock (including fractions) and rights to an allotment of or subscription to stock. [*FA 1999, Sch 15, paras 3, 9, 10, 11, 12*].

A Societas Europaea ('SE'), which has its registered office in the UK following a transfer, is within (*a*) above, but an SE which has transferred its registered office out of the UK, is not within (*a*). (See *F(No 2)A 2005, s 58(3)(a)*).

Occasions of charge

[24.4] A charge will arise on the following occasions—

(a) **On issue**

The following bearer instruments attract duty on *issue*:

- (i) any instrument *issued* in the UK;
- (ii) any instrument *issued* by or on behalf of a company or body of persons formed or established in the UK, other than a *foreign loan security* i.e. a security *issued* outside the UK in respect of a loan expressed in a currency other than sterling and which is neither offered for subscription in the UK nor offered with a view to an offer for sale in the UK. [*FA 1999, Sch 15, paras 1, 13* and note the other exemptions in *Sch 15, Part II*].

Issue in this context occurs when and where the instrument gets into the hands of a person who can avail himself of it (*Baring v CIR* CA, [1898] 1 QB 78).

(b) **On transfer**

Instruments not chargeable under (*a*) above are chargeable on first (but not subsequent) transfer (including negotiation) in the UK, but only if the transfer would be chargeable with conveyance on sale duty if the transfer were by an instrument other than a bearer instrument or the stock constituted or transferable by the bearer instrument consists of units under a unit trust scheme. [*FA 1999, Sch 15, para 2*].

Stamping procedure

[24.5] Different procedures apply to instruments chargeable on issue and on transfer. [*FA 1999, Sch 15, Part III*].

(a) **Instruments chargeable on issue** must be delivered to the Commissioners before issue for the instrument to be stamped with a **DENOTING STAMP (44)** denoting that it has been produced. The instrument is not duly stamped unless it bears this denoting stamp, but the duty is not payable until six weeks after issue, when a statement must be delivered to the Commissioners.

(b) **Instruments chargeable on transfer** must be presented to the Commissioners for stamping before transfer and they will then be deemed to be duly stamped.

(c) **Substituted bearer instruments** should be presented to the Commissioners either on issue or on transfer as appropriate together with the original instruments. In order to be duly stamped the substituted instrument must be stamped with a **DENOTING STAMP (44)** as in (*a*) above if it is chargeable on issue or with a stamp denoting 'original security duly stamped' if it is chargeable on transfer.

There are penalties for failure to comply with these requirements. See **75 PENALTIES**.

Valuation

[24.6] Ad valorem duty on a bearer instrument is calculated on its market value. [*FA 1999, Sch 15, paras 7, 8*]. Market value is ascertained as follows.

(a) **Instrument chargeable on issue**
  - (i) Where the underlying stock was offered for public subscription (whether in registered or bearer form) within twelve months before the issue of the bearer instrument—the amount subscribed.
  - (ii) If the underlying stock was not so offered for public subscription but is dealt in on a stock exchange in the UK within one month of the issue of the instrument—its value on the first day of dealing.
  - (iii) In any other case—its value immediately after issue.

(b) **Instrument chargeable on transfer**
  - (i) Transfer pursuant to a contract of sale—its value on the date of the contract. The contract price under an arm's length contract will normally be used.
  - (ii) In any other case—the value on the day preceding presentation to the Commissioners for stamping; if it is not so presented—the value on the date of transfer.

Exemptions

[24.7] The following are exempt from duty—

(a) **Non-sterling currency stock.** Duty is not charged on bearer instruments relating to stock expressed in a foreign currency or in units of account relating to more than one currency. If the instrument relates to a loan and repayment could, at the option of the holder only, be made in a foreign currency, it qualifies for exemption. Instruments relating to the capital stock of companies or bodies which is not expressed in any currency (e.g. shares of no par value) are treated as if they were expressed in the currency of the territory under the law of which the company or body is formed or established. Units in a unit trust scheme or a share in a foreign mutual fund are treated as if they were capital stock of a company or body formed or established in the country whose law governs the scheme or fund. [*FA 1999, Sch 15, paras 17, 18, 19*]. This exemption and the equivalent exemption from **STAMP DUTY RESERVE TAX (84)** in *FA 1986, s 90(3)(b)* had been used successfully to avoid ad valorem duty on sales of the shares of UK companies under the scheme described in **83.4**(*a*) **TRANSFERS OF SHARES GENERALLY** prior to the widening of the scope of **STAMP DUTY RESERVE TAX (84)** in relation to inland bearer instruments by *FA 1997, s 105* as described in **24.8** below.

(b) **Renounceable letters of allotment**, letters of rights and similar instruments, e.g. renounceable letters of acceptance, where the rights are renounceable not later than six months after issue, are exempt. [*FA 1999, Sch 15, para 16*]. Such a document is also exempt from duty as a **CONVEYANCE OR TRANSFER (39)** on sale, except in relation to arrangements where rights to company shares under an instrument are renounced in favour of someone, who together with persons connected with him, has or will have control of the company as a result of the arrangements. [*FA 1999, Sch 13, para 24(d); FA 1985, s 81*]. The exception to the conveyance on sale exemption was directed at a version of the 'pref-trick' which practitioners had developed to counter the decision in *Furniss v Dawson*, [1984] STC 153. (See **19 ANTI-AVOIDANCE.**) It is considered, however, that a letter of allotment may not attract duty as a **CONVEYANCE OR TRANSFER (39)** on sale because it is not a transfer. It is the delivery of the letter that effects a transfer and not the letter itself.

    Dealings in renounceable letters of allotment etc. do, however, attract **STAMP DUTY RESERVE TAX (84)**, except in relation to overseas bearer instruments. [*FA 1986, ss 87, 90(3)(a)*]. See also **65 LETTERS OF ALLOTMENT AND ACCEPTANCE.**

(c) **Government stocks etc.** Bearer instruments relating to government stocks and other stocks exempt from all stamp duties are themselves exempt. For details of stocks covered by exemptions, see **50 EXEMPT INSTRUMENTS.** [*FA 1999, Sch 13, para 24(a)* and *Sch 15, para 14*].

(d) **LOAN CAPITAL AND DEBENTURES (66).** Duty is not charged on the issue or transfer of all forms of bearer loan capital. [*FA 1986, s 79(2)*].

(e) **Variations of overseas bearer instruments** in respect of a loan expressed in sterling do not bear duty provided that the original has been duly stamped. [*FA 1999, Sch 15, para 20*].

(f) **DEPOSITARY RECEIPTS (45)** and **CLEARANCE SERVICES (33).** The transfer, issue or appropriation of an inland bearer instrument into a depositary scheme or a clearance service is exempt from **STAMP DUTY RESERVE TAX (84)** unless either (i) the instrument is a renounceable letter of allotment or (ii) it is within the exemption for non-sterling stock in (*a*) above and does not raise new capital and is not issued in exchange for an instrument raising new capital. The tax charge under (ii) does not apply to an instrument giving effect to an agreement for a company merger or takeover entered into in writing by the companies involved before 30 January 1999. [*FA 1986, ss 95(2), 97(3)* as substituted by *FA 1999, s 117* and amended by *FA 1999, Sch 16, paras* 7 and 8, and see also the relief for replacement securities in *FA 1986*, new *ss 95A* and *97AA*].

(g) **Paired shares.** Exemption from duty is available on the issue of units and warrants to acquire units of the type issued by Eurotunnel. [*FA 1988, s 143*].

Stamp duty reserve tax

[24.8] Note. From 1 October 1999, the **STAMP DUTY RESERVE TAX (84)** legislation refers to inland bearer instruments as 'UK bearer instruments'.

Prior to *FA 1997, s 105* inland bearer instruments were generally exempt from the tax except for dealings in renounceable letters of allotment, renounceable no later than six months after issue. As a result of the increasing use of the scheme described in **83.4**(*a*) **TRANSFERS OF SHARES GENERALLY** to avoid ad valorem duty on sales of shares in UK companies which relied on the exemption for bearer instruments relating to stock expressed in a foreign currency in *FA 1999, Sch 15, para 17*, the general exemption from the tax for agreements to transfer inland bearer instruments was repealed in relation to securities issued after 25 November 1996. With effect from that date a new exemption from the tax for agreements to transfer inland bearer instruments is introduced by *FA 1986, s 90(3A)* except where any of *FA 1986, s 90(3B), (3C)* or *(3E)* apply. These new sub-sections apply as follows.

(a) **Renounceable letters of allotment.** Agreements to transfer renounceable letters of allotment which are renounceable no later than six months after issue remain chargeable to tax as before (*FA 1986, s 90(3B)*).

(b) **Foreign currency bearer instruments.** Agreements to transfer bearer instruments denominated in a foreign currency and issued by a body incorporated in the UK are chargeable to tax unless the chargeable securities constituted by the instrument (or a depository receipt for them) are listed on a recognised stock exchange and the agreement is not made in contemplation of, or as part of an arrangement for, a takeover of the body corporate which issued the bearer instrument (*FA 1986, s 90(3C)* and *(3D)*).

(c) **Bearer instruments relating to loan capital.** Agreements to transfer bearer instruments issued by a body incorporated in the UK which are exempt from bearer instrument duty because of the exemption for loan capital bearer instruments in *FA 1986, s 79(2)* or because of that exemption and the fact that the instrument is denominated in a foreign currency and (in either case) where stamp duty would have been charged on an instrument transferring the loan capital to which the instrument relates because it is convertible or carries special rights (*FA 1986, s 79(5)* and *(6)*), are chargeable to tax. However, tax is not chargeable if the chargeable securities in question (or a depository receipt for them) are listed on a recognised stock exchange, the agreement is not made in contemplation of, or as part of an arrangement for, a takeover of the body corporate issuing the instrument and those securities do not carry conversion or acquisition rights over shares not listed on a recognised stock exchange (*FA 1986, s 90(3E) and (3F)*).

From the above it will be noted that an agreement to transfer an inland bearer instrument denominated in sterling (which is not convertible or carries special rights) is still exempt from tax. Although the Finance Bill 1997 contained a new draft *s 97C* for insertion into *FA 1986* which would have charged tax at 1.5% on any increase in value of such an instrument caused by a change in the rights attaching to the instrument, this new clause was not enacted. It may therefore be possible for a company incorporated in the UK to issue sterling denominated share warrants to bearer with restricted rights and with bearer instrument duty payable on their correspondingly low value. Subsequently, the rights attaching to the bearer share warrants could be adjusted at the expense of the existing registered shares so that the value of the issuing company flows into the bearer share warrants which are then sold to a purchaser with title passing on delivery free of stamp duty and stamp duty reserve tax. Whilst the general taxation and commercial consequences of such an arrangement would need to be considered carefully, it is thought that this arrangement may offer a degree of tax mitigation on the sale of shares in a UK incorporated company, although the outcome cannot be guaranteed.

Chapter 25

Bills of Exchange

[25.1] The head of charge 'Bill of Exchange or Promissory Note' in *SA 1891, Sch 1* was abolished by *FA 1970, Sch 2, para 7*. This head formerly covered bills of exchange, cheques and promissory notes. Such documents are now unlikely to attract any stamp duty.

Chapter 26

Bills of Sale

[26.1] An absolute bill of sale executed before 1 December 2003 is liable to duty as a **Conveyance or Transfer (39)** on sale. This was the position under *SA 1891, Sch 1* and is thought to remain so upon the repeal of *Sch 1* and its restatement in *FA 1999, Sch 13* despite the fact that the head Bill of Sale in *Sch 1* appears to have no direct equivalent in *FA 1999, Sch 13*. For bills of sale executed on or after 1 December 2003 stamp duty is no longer charged in relation to sales of goods and other items not affixed to land.

A bill of sale cannot be registered unless a duly stamped original is produced to the proper officer. [*SA 1891, s 41*].

In *Delta Finance Newco v IRC SpC 316* [2002] STC (SCD) 274 the Special Commissioners held that a purchaser was unable to claim capital allowances in respect of equipment due to its failure to produce a duly stamped bill of sale with the result that it could not establish that the equipment belonged to it. However on appeal in *BMBF (No 24) Ltd v IRC* [2002] EWHC 2466 (Ch), [2002] STC 1450 it was held that a claimant for capital allowances who is unable to prove that he has legal title to equipment due to the inadmissibility of an unstamped bill for sale could nevertheless prove the necessary ownership in equity by showing that it became the beneficial owner of the equipment under the terms of the relevant acquisition agreement, and by reference to the conduct and intention of the parties. It is considered that this decision is questionable in that the court did not appear to consider the best evidence rule under which the claimant should have been required to produce the best evidence, namely the bill of sale proving legal title in order to prove ownership. Although it is the case that the strict rules of evidence do not apply to hearings before the Special Commissioners, nevertheless, had the court taken notice of this rule of evidence, the claimant would not have been allowed to rely on lesser evidence in the form of the non-stampable agreement and the parties' conduct to prove ownership. In failing to apply this rule the Court undermined the statutory policy enshrined in *SA 1891, s 14(4)* which is the principal means by which the payment of stamp duty is enforced.

Chapter 27

Bonds

[27.1] Nearly all the 'Bond' headings in *SA 1891, Sch 1* no longer existed at the time *SA 1891, Sch 1* was repealed and restated by *FA 1999, Sch 13*. [*FA 1971, s 64; FA 1973, Sch 22; FA 1989, s 173*]. Bonds and covenants in relation to an annuity on the original creation and sale of the annuity were charged as a **CONVEYANCE OR TRANSFER (39)** on sale (see **18 ANNUITIES**). [*SA 1891, s 60*].

The head 'Bond, Covenant' formerly charged bonds, covenants and similar instruments and extended to:

(a) a principal or primary security for an annuity (other than a superannuation annuity or on original creation by sale or security) or for periodic sums of money (other than interest on principal secured by a duly stamped agreement or rent reserved by a lease), e.g. a seven-year deed of covenant; and

(b) a collateral or substituted security for annuities or periodic sums as in (*a*).

These duties were abolished *except* as regards documents increasing rent [*FA 1971, s 64(1)(a)*] which were charged under the head 'Bond, Covenant' but attracted lease duty. [*SA 1891, s 77(5)*]. Documents increasing rent or which confirm or record any oral agreement to this effect were charged to stamp duty under *FA 1999, Sch 13, para 20*. See **64 LEASES**.

The duty charged on superannuation annuities and purchased life annuities under paragraph (3) of the head 'Bond, Covenant' was abolished by *FA 1989, s 173*.

The miscellaneous head 'Bond of any kind whatsoever not specifically charged with any duty' has also been abolished. [*FA 1971, s 64(1)(b)*].

Exemption from other duties. The documents formerly charged under the heads described above do not now attract duty under any other head unless an instrument contains several distinct matters (see **63 LEADING AND PRINCIPAL OBJECT**), when it will only be exempt to the extent that it falls within the former head of charge. [*FA 1971, s 64(2); FA 1989, s 173(2)*].

Bonds for securing the payment of money or the transfer or retransfer of stock were formerly charged under the head 'Marketable Security', but that head of charge has been abolished. [*FA 1973, Sch 22*].

Chapter 28

Building Societies

[28.1] The following instruments are exempt from all stamp duties:

(a) any copy of the rules of a building society;
(b) any transfer of a share in a building society;
(c) any bond or other security given to, or on account of a building society;
(d) any instrument appointing an agent of a building society or revoking such an appointment; and
(e) any other instrument whatsoever which is required or authorised to be given, issued, signed, made or produced pursuant to the Building Societies Act 1986 or the rules of a building society. [*Building Societies Act 1986, s 109(1)*].

Conversion to a public limited company

[28.2] No stamp duty liability can arise on the transfer of the business of a building society to a successor company effected under the *Building Societies Act 1986, s 97(6)* or *(7)*. [*Building Societies Act 1986, s 109(2); FA 1988, s 145, Sch 12, para 8*].

Chapter 29

Capital Duty

[29.1] Capital duty was abolished with effect from 16 March 1988. [*FA 1988, s 141*].

The duty was charged at the rate of 1% on the documents relating to increases in the capital of certain types of company and to various other transactions involving such companies.

Chapter 30

Certificate of Value

[30.1] A certificate of value is required where either nil duty or the reduced rates are claimed in respect of an instrument otherwise attracting the full rate of ad valorem duty as a **CONVEYANCE OR TRANSFER (39)** on sale. This includes:

(a) conveyances or transfers on sale;
(b) equality money paid on an **EXCHANGE OR PARTITION (48)**;
(c) premiums paid under **LEASES (64)**. [*FA 1999, Sch 13, para 6*].

An instrument containing a certificate of value where the nil rate of duty applies does not need to be presented for stamping.

A certificate of value can be given for transfers of stock or marketable securities where the consideration does not exceed £1,000. [*FA 1999, Sch 13 paras 1(3A) and 6* for instruments executed on or after 13 March 2008].

An instrument is 'certified' at a particular amount if it contains a statement that the transaction effected by the instrument does not form part of a larger transaction or series of transactions in which the total amount or value of the consideration exceeds the certified amount. [*FA 1999, Sch 13, para 6(1)*]. The value of goods, wares, merchandise exempt intellectual property and goodwill can generally be left out of account for these purposes. [*FA 1999, Sch 13, para 6(2), FA 2000 Sch 34, para 4* and *FA 2002, Sch 37, para 3*]. For instruments executed after 22 March 2006 (other than transfers of shares or securities where a £1,000 limit applies – see above) the reduced rates are as follows:

(a) where the amount or value of the consideration is £125,000 or under—nil;
(b) where the amount or value of the consideration does not exceed £250,000—1% of the consideration;
(c) where the amount or value of the consideration does not exceed £500,000—3% of the consideration.

Where the consideration exceeds £500,000 (or is less but the instrument is not certified as above) the rate of ad valorem duty is 4% of the consideration.

In relation to ad valorem duty chargeable on a premium paid on the grant of a lease where the average rent exceeds £600 per year the nil rate of duty is not available.

However the reduced rates of duty are available as mentioned in (*b*) and (*c*) above and lease premiums exceeding £500,000 are chargeable to duty at the rate of 4% of the premium.

Where the value cannot be determined at the time of the certificate, a truncated certificate can be given certifying that the transaction does not form part of a larger transaction or series of transactions and that the correct amount of duty will be applied when the amount or value of the consideration is determined.

Although the certificate should appear in the instrument, the Commissioners may permit the addition of a certificate at a later stage if it is signed by the parties who executed the instrument. See the Stamp Office Manual (March 2002) para 4.14.

Whether a transaction forms part of a **larger transaction or series of transactions** depends on the circumstances of each transaction.

The following need not necessarily be so treated:

(a) the purchase of more than one lot at an auction (*A-G v Cohen* CA, [1937] 1 KB 478);
(b) a related transaction which is not a sale (*Kimbers & Co v CIR* KB, [1936] 1 KB 132);
(c) a purchase and sub-sale of property;
(d) a number of acquisitions from different vendors even if each is conditional on completion of the others;
(e) the Stamp Office has stated that the £120,000 threshold can be applied separately to each side of an exchange of properties. However, where there is a multiple exchange of properties, e.g. properties A and B are exchanged for property C—the transfers of A and B are regarded as parts of a larger transaction, and the threshold would not apply to either of them if the total consideration for both was more than £120,000. The threshold would be applied separately however to the transfer of C. (Inland Revenue Press Release, 18 April 1994 and see **36.7 Exchanges of Property**).

However, where there is more than one transaction negotiated at the same time between two parties, it may be more difficult to show that they do not form part of a larger transaction or series of transactions whether or not they are included in separate contracts (see *A-G v Cohen* KB, [1936] 2 KB 246 and CA, [1937] 1 KB 478).

In relation to the use of certificates of value, it was stated in *Saunders v Edwards* CA, [1987] 1 WLR 1116 at 1125 that a solicitor involved in an apportionment between the value of the property and that of the chattels, which he knows not to be in accordance with the facts must be guilty of professional misconduct and apart from possible criminal offences, the consequence for the buyers may well be that their contract becomes unenforceable. (And see Stamp Taxes Bulletin, Issue 1, page 3 'When is a Fixture not a Fixture?' and Stamp Taxes Bulletin, Issue 3, page 3 'Options – a response to press articles' [both reproduced at **Appendix D**].) A client who jointly engages with his solicitor in the fraud is not however precluded from suing his solicitor for negligent conveyancing (see *Sweetman v Nathan*, The Times, 1 September 2003).

In relation to the use of certificates of value in conveyances or leases of building plots see **36.6 Covenants to Improve Property**.

A separate certification procedure is available for instruments that would otherwise attract a £5 fixed duty (see **50 Exempt Instruments**).

Chapter 31

Chargeability

[31.1] Stamp duties are generally charged on the **INSTRUMENTS (60)** referred to in *FA 1999, Sch 13* and *15* (*SA 1891, s 1* has been repealed) and not on transactions that are carried out orally (see **71 ORAL TRANSACTIONS**) or on persons as such (see for instance Lord Hoffmann's speech in *MacNiven v Westmoreland Investments Ltd* [2001] UKHL 6, [2001] STC 237). It should be noted, however, that there are exceptions to this principle in relation to the charge on **BEARER INSTRUMENTS (24)** where a failure to account for the duty chargeable will lead to the person issuing the instrument and his agent becoming personally liable for the unpaid duty. Exceptions also occur in relation to the withdrawal of relief for transfer of assets within a group of companies and for company acquisitions, where the transferee or acquiring company becomes liable to pay the duty arising and if they fail to pay, certain other group companies and the controlling directors can become liable to pay (see **23 ASSOCIATED COMPANIES** and **34 COMPANY REORGANISATIONS**). **STAMP DUTY RESERVE TAX (84)** is charged on transactions and not instruments.

Instruments are chargeable to stamp duty if they are:

(a) executed in the UK; or
(b) executed anywhere, relating to property situate or any matter or thing to be done in the UK. [*SA 1891, s 14(4)*].

Thus only instruments executed abroad and relating to non-UK matters will be outside the stamp duty charge (but see **50 EXEMPT INSTRUMENTS**). It has been held, inter alia, that:

(i) a transfer executed in France of French property by an English company to another English company in consideration of shares in that company related to property situate in England (the shares) and was dutiable as a conveyance on sale (see **39 CONVEYANCE OR TRANSFER**) (*Maple & Co (Paris) Ltd* HL, [1908] AC 22);
(ii) a covenant executed in Canada whereby, in consideration for a Canadian company issuing shares and debentures, an individual covenanted to pay the company a proportion of his professional income, related to the carrying on of his profession in the UK and was liable to duty (*Faber v CIR* KB, (1936) 155 LT 228).

Duty is not, however, payable on a chargeable instrument executed outside the UK until it is received in the UK although interest will be charged on duty paid more than 30 days after the execution of any instrument on or after 1 October 1999 wherever the instrument is executed. In relation to instruments executed on or after 24 July 2002 that to any extent relate to UK land a penalty will also arise if the instrument is not presented for stamping within 30 days of execution even if the instrument is executed outside the UK. [*FA 2002, s 114*]. The Government has confirmed in a letter to the Opposition during the debates on the Finance Bill 2002 that on a sale of a business including UK land where the assets excluding the UK land are transferred by means of a separate document executed outside the UK, that document is not considered to relate to UK land for the purposes of the amended penalty provision with the result that a penalty will only begin to run 30 days after the document is received in the UK. (See **74.1**(*c*) **DATE OF STAMPING AND PAYMENT**.)

STAMP DUTY RESERVE TAX (84) is chargeable whether the transaction is made in the UK or elsewhere and whether or not any party is resident or situate in the UK. [*FA 1986, s 86(4), FA 1996, s 187.*]

Chapter 32

Charities

[32.1] Stamp duty is not charged on any conveyance, transfer or lease made or agreed to be made to a charity which meets the jurisdiction, registration and management conditions in *FA 2010, Sch 6*, the Trustees of the National Heritage Memorial Fund, or the Historic Buildings and Monuments Commission for England. [*FA 1982, s 129(1); FA 1983, s 46(3)(c); FA 1999, Sch 14, para 7*]. The definition of a charity contained in these provisions is to be replaced by 'a charitable company or the trustees of a charitable trust' as further defined in *FA 2010, Sch 6, para 1* and the *Charities Act 2006* from a date to be appointed. Similar exemption is not available for conveyances etc. made by a charity.

For the above exemption to apply it is necessary to have the conveyance etc adjudicated. [*FA 1982, s 129(2)*]. See **13 ADJUDICATION**. It is thought that this exemption applies to charities formed or established under the laws of EU member states only and not to non-EU charities. See *Dreyfus (Camille and Henry) Foundation Inc v IRC* [1956] AC 39 and *Persche v Finanzamt Ludenscheid* C-318/08 [2009] All ER (EC) 673, [2009] STC 586, ECJ (GC), where as a result HMRC have confirmed that the exemption extends to equivalent bodies in the EU and (by regulation) to Norway and Iceland.

Chapter 32

Chloride

Chapter 33

Clearance Services

Note: On 18 March 2009 the Advocate General in *HSBC Holdings plc and Vidacos Nominees Ltd v HMRC* Case C–569/07 opined that the 1.5% stamp duty reserve tax charge on the issue of new securities, or on the transfer of existing securities, into clearance services, contravenes EU law because it is in breach of the Capital Duty Directive 69/335 and the free movement of capital under Art 56 of the EU Treaty (see also *HSBC Holdings plc v Revenue and Customs Comrs* [2008] STC (SCD) 502, [2008] SWTI 190). The decision of the ECJ on 1 October 2009 confirmed that this was the position and as a consequence HMRC no longer apply the 1.5% SDRT charge on the issue of new shares into an EU depositary receipt or clearance service. However, the existing exemptions from SDRT for transfers from one clearance service to another or between the two types of system as explained in **33.3**(a) and (e) below are not available where there is an arrangement for chargeable securities to be issued into an EU service (now free of the 1.5% entry charge) and then subsequently transferred from the EU service to a non-EU service. [*FA 1986, s 97C*].

[33.1] Clearance services allow the shares and securities of UK incorporated companies registered in the name of a nominee to be bought and sold free of stamp duty. A special charge is therefore imposed on the entry of shares or securities into a clearance service to compensate for the non-payment of stamp duty on subsequent purchases and sales of the shares or securities within the service. Generally, the charge is at 1.5%, three times the normal rate of ad valorem duty on the **CONVEYANCE OR TRANSFER (39)** on sale of **SHARES AND SECURITIES (83)**. The special charge can be either stamp duty (see **33.2** below) or **STAMP DUTY RESERVE TAX (84)** (see **33.3** below) depending on the circumstances.

The term 'clearance services' is not defined in the relevant legislation. There must be many arrangements relating to the transfer of shares and involving nominee ownership which are potentially within the scope of the special charge. It is thought that the special charge was originally intended to apply only to the widely used commercial clearance services such as Euroclear; however, the potential scope of the special charge is wide.

Stamp duty

[33.2] Subject to the alternative arrangements described in **33.4** below, stamp duty at the special rate is charged on an instrument which *transfers* 'relevant securities' of a UK incorporated company to a person:

(a) whose business consists exclusively of holding shares, stock or marketable securities as nominee or agent for a person whose business is or includes providing a clearance service for the purchase and sale of 'relevant securities'; or

(b) who is specified by a statutory instrument and whose business is or includes providing a clearance service; or
(c) who is specified by a statutory instrument and whose business does not consist exclusively of holding 'relevant securities' as nominee or agent for a clearer.

In relation to paired shares the foreign company is treated as a company incorporated in the UK for 'relevant securities' which consist of units representing paired shares of the type issued by Eurotunnel. [*FA 1986, s 70(1)(6)–(8); FA 1988, s 143(6)*].

'Relevant securities' are shares or stock or marketable securities of any company wherever incorporated. [*FA 1986, s 72(1)*].

Where the instrument of transfer attracts duty as a **CONVEYANCE OR TRANSFER (39)** on sale, duty is charged at the special rate of 1.5% of the amount or value of the sale consideration. [*FA 1986, s 70(2)*]. If the transfer is otherwise than on sale, duty is charged at 1.5% of the value of the securities on the date of transfer. Bearer instruments are exempt from the special rate. A transfer of 'relevant securities' of a UK incorporated company between corporate nominees resident in the UK attracted a fixed £5 duty for transfers executed before 13 March 2008 but is no longer chargeable with duty. [*FA 1986, s 70(9)* as amended by *FA 2008, Sch 32 para 7*].

Before 20 October 1997 transfers by qualified dealers attracted a reduced rate of £1 per £100 or part of £100 when transferring securities otherwise than on sale into a clearance system but this relief has been withdrawn. [*FA 1986, s 70(4), FA 1997, s 99(3)*].

A provider of clearance services relating to 'relevant securities' of UK incorporated companies and a person whose business includes (albeit not exclusively) holding such securities as a nominee or agent for a clearer is required to notify the Commissioners of that fact within one month of providing such services. [*FA 1986, s 71(1)(2)*]. A penalty of up to £1,000 can be imposed for failing to do so. [*FA 1986, s 71(4)*]. A UK incorporated company which becomes aware that its shares are held by a clearer or his agent or nominee is also required to notify the Commissioners of that fact within one month of becoming so aware. A penalty of up to £100 can be imposed for failing to do so. [*FA 1986, s 71(3)(5)*].

Stamp Duty Reserve Tax

[33.3] Subject to the alternative arrangements described in **33.4** below, **STAMP DUTY RESERVE TAX (84)** is charged where 'chargeable securities' are *issued* or *transferred* to a person whose business is or includes providing a clearance service for the purchase and sale of 'chargeable securities' or to his nominee. [*FA 1986, s 96(1)*]. **Note:** HMRC no longer apply SDRT to the issue of securities into an EU clearance service – see **Note** above.

For the definition of 'chargeable securities' see **84 STAMP DUTY RESERVE TAX**.

In relation to the *transfer* of 'chargeable securities' any ad valorem stamp duty chargeable on the instrument of transfer (see **33.2** above) cancels the equivalent amount of stamp duty reserve tax chargeable up to the full amount of the reserve tax. [*FA 1986, s 96(5)*].

In the case of the securities being *issued* to a clearer or his nominee, stamp duty reserve tax is charged at 1.5% of the issue price. In the case of securities being *transferred* for money or money's worth, the rate is 1.5% of the amount or value of the consideration. In any other case the rate is 1.5% of the *value* of the securities. [*FA 1986, s 96(2); FA 1996, s 194*].

Before 20 October 1997 transfers by qualified dealers attracted a reduced rate of 1% when transferring chargeable securities otherwise than on sale into a clearance system but this relief has been withdrawn. [*FA 1986, s 96(3), FA 1997, s 104(3)*].

There are the following exceptions to the tax charge:

(a) a transfer of securities between corporate nominees whose businesses are exclusively that of holding securities as nominees for a clearer, but this exception is disapplied if the securities are issued to an EU clearance service where there are arrangements for the securities to be subsequently transferred to a non-EU service [*FA 1986, ss 97(1) and 97C*];

(b) the transfer or issue of an inland bearer instrument except in the case of:
   (i) a renounceable letter of allotment where the rights are renounceable no later than six months after issue; or
   (ii) an instrument within the exemption from stamp duty on bearer instruments for non-sterling stock (see **24.7**(*a*) above) which does not raise new capital and is not issued in exchange for an instrument raising new capital (the tax charge arising does not apply to an instrument giving effect to an agreement for a company merger or takeover entered into in writing by the companies involved before 30 January 1999) [*FA 1986, s 97(3), (3A)–(3D)* and amended by *FA 1999, Sch 16, para 8* and see also the relief for replacement securities in new *FA 1986, s 97AA* inserted by *FA 1999, s 118*];

(c) the *issue* by one company of securities in exchange for shares in another company where the first company has control of the second (or will have control as a result of the exchange) and the shares in the second company are held within a clearance service. Shares issued under a scheme of arrangement where the shares of the target company are cancelled are still treated for these purposes as having been issued in exchange for shares in the target. [*FA 1986, s 97(4); FA 1998, s 151*]; and

(d) the transfer or issue of replacement securities in place of existing securities held in a clearance service to the extent that the value of the new securities does not exceed the value of the old securities. [*FA 1986, s 97AA; FA 1999, s 118*].

(e) the transfer of securities between a clearance system and a **DEPOSITARY RECEIPT (44)** system and vice versa, but this exception is disapplied if the securities are issued into an EU system where there are arrangements for the securities to be subsequently transferred to a non-EU system. [*FA 1986, ss 97B and 97C*].

Clearance service option

[33.4] The operator of a clearance service is able to elect that the above special stamp duty and **STAMP DUTY RESERVE TAX (84)** charges shall not apply and instead give a written undertaking to the Commissioners for HMRC to collect and account for **STAMP DUTY RESERVE TAX (84)** at the normal rate of 0.5% on dealing within the system. The normal rate of stamp duty of 0.5% on shares and marketable securities will apply on transfers on sale into the system and the normal rate of 0.5 per cent **STAMP DUTY RESERVE TAX (84)** will apply to the issue of shares into the system. The approval of Commissioners to these alternative arrangements is required. Where an election is terminated either by the Commissioners or the clearance service operator, there is an 'exit charge' of **STAMP DUTY RESERVE TAX (84)** at 1.5% of the value of the chargeable securities held by the clearance service operator or his nominee, immediately before the election was terminated. [*FA 1986, s 97A; FA 1996, s 196*]. The exemptions in *FA 1986, ss 72A* and *97B* for transfers of securities from a clearance system to a **DEPOSITARY RECEIPT (44)** system do not apply if such an election is in force. [*FA 1986, ss 72A(3)* and *97B(3)*].

Chapter 34

Company Reorganisations

[34.1] There are four main exemptions and reliefs from stamp duty on a **CONVEYANCE OR TRANSFER (39)** on sale for company reorganisations, as follows:

(a) exemption where one company acquires the whole or part of an undertaking of another company under a scheme of reconstruction of that other company (see **34.2** below);
(b) a relief in the form of a reduced rate of 0.5% on certain other acquisitions by one company of the undertaking of another company (see **34.3** below);
(c) exemption for the placing of a new holding company above an existing company (see **34.5** below);
(d) exemption for internal reorganisations involving the transfer of property within a 75% owned group of companies (see **23 ASSOCIATED COMPANIES**).

Also relevant in the context of company reorganisations are the exemptions for transfers in connection with divorce [*FA 1985, s 83*] and deeds of variation [*FA 1985, s 84*] where shares in family companies are concerned (see **53 FAMILY ARRANGEMENTS AND DIVORCE**).

Reconstructions [*FA 1986, S 75*]

[34.2] Exemption from stamp duty on a **CONVEYANCE OR TRANSFER (39)** on sale is available where one company ('the acquiring company') acquires the whole or part of an undertaking of another company ('the target company') under a *scheme of reconstruction* of the target company.

A '*scheme of reconstruction*' requires that there is a transfer of the undertaking or part of the undertaking from an existing company to a new company with substantially the same membership as the old company and that the undertaking continues substantially unaltered (*Brooklands Selangor Holdings Ltd v CIR* Ch D, [1970] 2 All ER 76; *Baytrust Holdings Ltd v CIR* Ch D, [1971] 3 All ER 76; see also *CIR v Kent Process Control Ltd* Ch D, [1989] STC 245 and *Swithland Investments Ltd v CIR* [1990] STC 448).

A *partition* is not a *reconstruction* and so the division of an existing company business or businesses resulting in different parts going to separate companies with each company owned by different sets of shareholders, will not qualify for exemption as a *scheme of reconstruction*. (*Fallon v Fellows* ChD [2001] STC (SCD) 45 and see also The Stamp Office Manual (March 2002) section 6.200). This was in contrast with the position relating to the taxation of chargeable gains on company reconstructions where the case law definition of reconstruction was expanded by SP 5/85 to include a partition.

Although the rules for the taxation of capital gains relating to company reconstructions have been restated to confirm that partitions are included and widened in scope by *TCGA 1992, Sch 5AA* (Meaning of 'Scheme of Reconstruction'), the Financial Secretary to the Treasury, Ruth Kelly, stated during the debates on the Finance Bill 2002 that in relation to the introduction of a statutory definition of a 'scheme of reconstruction' for the purposes of the taxation of chargeable gains:

> The hon. Member for Arundel and South Downs asked about the interaction of [these] provisions with the stamp duty regime. CGT and stamp duty are entirely different taxes, with different aims and separate rules. I can assure him, however, that modernisation of the statutory regime, to which we shall come in due course and which was announced in the Budget, provides an opportunity to reconsider the stamp duty rules for schemes of reconstruction. Consideration of the reconstruction reliefs is included in the modernising stamp duty consultation process, which is intended to produce new legislation in next year's Finance Bill. If any anomalies arise, we shall have an opportunity to take them into account.
>
> [Hansard Standing Committee F, Tuesday 21 May 2002 (Morning) Columns 163 and 164.]

The restrictive interpretation of 'scheme of reconstruction' for stamp duty (and SDLT) purposes was confirmed in the November 2009 Stamp Taxes Bulletin by the addition of SDLTM 23210 to HMRC's SDLT Manual and so the wider meaning of 'scheme of reconstruction' that applies for the taxation of chargeable gains does not apply to stamp taxes.

Under the now repealed *FA 1927, s 55* relief was available for *schemes of reconstruction* and also for *schemes of amalgamation* of companies. A '*scheme of amalgamation*' connotes the *merging* of two or more businesses with ownership through shareholdings remaining substantially the same (*Crane Fruehauf Ltd v CIR* CA, [1975] 1 All ER 429; *Ufitec Group Ltd v CIR* QB, [1977] STC 363). A *scheme of amalgamation* is therefore quite different from a *scheme of reconstruction* and the omission of the former from *FA 1986, s 75* indicates that relief is limited to *schemes of reconstruction.*

The relief is subject to the following requirements:

(a) Prior to 22 July 2005 the registered office of the acquiring company had to be in the UK. Following the decision of the European Court of Justice in *Halliburton Services BV v Staatssecretaris van Financiën* [1994] STC 655, this requirement was incompatible with European Union law where the registered office of the acquiring company is in another member state of the European Union. IR Stamp Taxes accepted that this requirement was defective in law and from 22 July 2005 accepted claims to relief by companies with a registered office in any European Economic Area state: IR Statement, 22 July 2005. The requirement for a UK registered office has been removed completely since 19 July 2006 by *FA 2006, s 169*.

(b) The *consideration for the acquisition* must consist of the *issue of non-redeemable shares* in the acquiring company to all the shareholders of the target company and nothing else except the assumption or discharge of the liabilities of the target company by the acquiring company. For the relief to be available it will be necessary therefore for each shareholder in the target to receive a share in the acquiring company and for there to be no cash element in the consideration paid by the acquiring company.

(c) The acquisition must be effected for bona fide commercial reasons and should not form part of a tax avoidance scheme. If clearance has been granted by HMRC under the *Taxation of Chargeable Gains Act 1992, ss 138–139,* it is likely that the Commissioners will regard this requirement as satisfied.

(d) After the acquisition each shareholder of each of the companies is a shareholder of the other and the proportion of shares of one of the companies held by any shareholder is the same or as nearly as may be the same, as the proportion of shares of the other company held by that shareholder. It is necessary therefore that the new shares in the acquiring company are allotted to the shareholders in the acquired company in exactly the same proportions as their holdings in the acquired company. For this purpose, any shares held by the acquiring or the acquired company in itself are ignored.

The Stamp Office may be prepared to accept that this exemption can apply where the reorganisation involves the transfer of a trading subsidiary of the target company to the acquiring company on the basis that the trading subsidiary is the whole or part of the target company's undertaking. Note, however, that the acquiring company must issue shares to the shareholders of the target company and not to the target company itself.

In this situation the target company may be the holding company of a group of companies and the acquiring company will have been formed by the target company for the purpose of acquiring a trading subsidiary of the target company in return for the issue of shares in the acquiring company to the shareholders of the target company. Due to the existence of the subscribers' shares issued by the acquiring company to the target company, a precise mirror image of the target company's share structure cannot be achieved in the acquiring company. Technically, therefore, the exemption from stamp duty will not be available due to the failure of the acquiring company to satisfy (*d*) above. In the past the Stamp Office was sometimes co-operative in this matter and when the acquiring company was a private company with say, two subscribers' shares, it was sometimes prepared to ignore the existence of these shares on the de minimis ground. If the acquiring company is a public limited company it will be required to have an allotted share capital of a nominal value of at least £50,000 of which at least one quarter must be paid-up. [*CA 1985, s 117* and *CA 2006, ss 761 and 763*]. In these cases the Stamp Office was in the past prepared to ignore those shares provided they were cancelled very soon after the transaction so as to create a precise mirror image of the target company's share structure.

In this connection it may also happen that the acquiring company offers to acquire all the shares of the other company in exchange for the issue of shares in the acquiring company to the shareholders of the target company. The offer will be conditional on the acquiring company acquiring all the shares in the other company, either by all the shareholders accepting the acquiring company's offer, or by reason of the acquiring company exercising the statutory right to acquire minority shareholdings. [*CA 1985, ss 428–430F* and now *CA 2006, ss 974, 979*]. In the event that it becomes necessary to acquire the minority shareholdings under *CA 2006, ss 974, 979* the acquisition of the shares would take place in stages over a period of time. In such cases the Stamp Office has normally been reluctant to fail a claim for exemption on this ground. Care should be taken, however, to ensure that at some point in time the share structure of the acquiring company is a precise mirror image of that of the target company, e.g. if trading in the acquiring company's shares occurred before the minority shareholdings were acquired, the claim for exemption would probably fail.

However, evidence suggests that the Stamp Office has become stricter in their approach and the Stamp Office Manual (March 2002) states at section 6.196: 'The relief provided by each of the three sections [i.e. *75, 76* and *77* of *FA 1986*] is subject to a number of conditions, all of which are **strictly enforced**'. Accordingly the position should always be confirmed with the Stamp Office prior to entering into a transaction in reliance on Stamp Office goodwill where the strict requirements will not be met.

Undertakings: reduced rate [*FA 1986, S 76* As amended by *FA 2002, S 112* and *113*]

[34.3] A reduced rate of ad valorem duty on a **Conveyance or Transfer (39)** on sale can be claimed where one company ('the acquiring company') acquires the whole or part of the undertaking of another ('the target company'). The reduced rate is 0.5% of the amount or value of the consideration attributable to chargeable assets. [*FA 1986, s 76(4)*]. Unlike *FA 1986, s 75* where exemption from duty is available (see **34.2** above) it is not necessary under *FA 1986, s 76* for there to be a *scheme of reconstruction* of the target company.

The reduced rate of duty is available on an instrument executed for the purposes of or in connection with the transfer of an undertaking or part of an undertaking, or the assignment to the acquiring company by a creditor of any 'relevant debts' owed by the target company. A 'relevant debt' is any debt where the assignor is a bank or trade creditor and any other debt which is not less than two years old at the date of the instrument.

The relief is subject to the following requirements:

(a) Prior to 22 July 2005 the registered office of the acquiring company had to be in the UK. Following the decision of the European Court of Justice in *Halliburton Services BV v Staatssecretaris van Financiën* [1994] STC 655, this requirement was incompatible with European Union law where the registered office of the acquiring company is in another member state of the European Union; IR Stamp Taxes now accepts that this requirement is defective in law and from 22 July 2005 accepted claims to relief by companies with a registered office in any European Economic Area state: IR Statement, 22 July 2005. The requirement for a UK registered office has been removed completely since 19 July 2006 by *FA 2006, s 169*.

(b) The *consideration for the acquisition* must consist of or include the *issue of non-redeemable shares* in the acquiring company to the target company or to all or any of its shareholders and nothing else except cash not exceeding 10% of the nominal value of those shares, or the assumption or discharge of the liabilities of the target company by the acquiring company. Unlike *FA 1986, s 75*, there is no requirement that each shareholder in the target receive a share in the acquiring company and there is no bar on including a cash element in the consideration, paid by the acquiring company. In relation to the cash element of the consideration the offer will normally be looked at as a whole; and

(c) In the case only of instruments transferring land in the UK and executed on or after 24 April 2002, a further condition applies. The acquiring company must not be 'associated' with another company that is party to 'arrangements' with the target company relating to shares of the acquiring company issued in connection with the acquisition of the undertaking. This condition was introduced to attack schemes that had successfully exploited the relief in the context of what in reality were arm's length sales of an undertaking for cash. These schemes relied on an intermediate step involving the incorporation of a new company by the purchaser that would issue the consideration shares for the undertaking to the target company followed by a sale of the consideration shares to the purchaser for cash. The transfer of the undertaking would attract the reduced rate of duty and the sale of the shares a further 0.5% duty or nil duty if the acquiring company was an unlimited company that repurchased its shares for cash. Where the instrument transfers land in the UK together with other property, this further condition operates as if there were two separate instruments, one relating to UK land and the other relating to the other property. For the purposes of this condition companies are 'associated' if one has control of the other or both are controlled by the same person or persons and 'control' is construed in accordance with *ICTA 1988, s 416,* and the term 'arrangements' include any scheme, agreement or understanding whether or not legally enforceable. [*FA 1986, s 76(3)(3A)(3B) and (6A)*].

Withdrawal of relief

[34.4] In relation to instruments transferring an interest in UK land, that have been executed on or after 24 April 2002 and been stamped on the basis that the relief applies, the relief is withdrawn if within two years of the execution of the instrument control of the acquiring company changes and at that time the acquiring company holds the land or an estate or interest derived from it. In such a case the additional stamp duty that would have been payable on the instrument but for the relief had the land been transferred at market value, is payable by the acquiring company within 30 days after control of that company changes. [*FA 2002, s 113*].

For instruments executed after 14 April 2003 the two-year period has been extended to three years. The relief is withdrawn if control of the acquiring company changes within three years and at that time the acquiring company or a relevant associated company holds the land or an estate or interest derived from it. [*FA 2002, s 113* as amended by *FA 2003, s 127*].

A 'relevant associated company' in relation to the acquiring company means a company that:

(a) is controlled by the acquiring company immediately before the control of that company changes; and
(b) of which control changes in consequence of the change of control of that company. [*FA 2002, s 113(3A)*].

Where the instrument deals with UK land together with other property the withdrawal of the relief operates as if there were two separate instruments, one relating to the UK land and the other relating to the other property. If, when control changes, the acquiring company (or a relevant associated company) only owns a portion of what was originally transferred to the acquiring company, only the appropriate proportion of the exemption is withdrawn. [*FA 2002, s 113*].

The relief is not withdrawn if the control of the acquiring company changes:

(i) as a result of any transaction listed in the Schedule to the *Stamp Duty (Exempt Instruments) Regulations 1987* (see **50 Exempt Instruments**);
(ii) as a result of a transfer of shares in relation to which group relief applies (see **23 Associated Companies**); but if before the end of the two years beginning with the execution of the instrument a company holding shares in the acquiring company ceases to be a member of the same group as the 'target company', i.e. the company whose undertaking was originally acquired, and the acquiring company where undertaking was originally acquired and the company or a relevant associated company holds the land or an estate or interest derived from it, then the relief is withdrawn;
(iii) by reason of control of the acquiring company changing as a result of a transfer of shares to another company to which relief under *FA 1986, s 77* (see **34.5** below) applies; but if before the end of the two years beginning with the execution of the instrument control of the parent company changes at a time when that company holds shares transferred to it by the exempt transfer and the acquiring company or a relevant associated company holds the land or an estate or interest derived from it, then the relief is withdrawn; and
(iv) by reason of a loan creditor (within *ICTA 1988, s 417(7)* to *(9)*) becoming or ceasing to be treated as having control of the acquiring company if the other persons who were previously treated as controlling the company continue to be so treated. [*FA 2002, Sch 35, paras 2 to 5* as amended by *FA 2003, s 127*].

In the case of a withdrawal of the relief, the acquiring company is required to notify the Commissioners within 30 days of the event causing the withdrawal of relief and pay the additional stamp duty. [*FA 2002, s 113 (2)(b)* and *Sch 35, para 7*]. Interest is payable on any additional duty remaining unpaid from the end of the 30 days within which payment should have been made. [*FA 2002,*

Sch 35, para 6]. The Commissioners have full powers of collection and recovery against not only the acquiring company but also against any company that at any 'relevant time' was a fellow group company above the acquiring company in the group structure and any person who at any 'relevant time' was a controlling director of the acquiring company, or of a company having control of it. 'Relevant time' means any time between the execution of the instrument and the change of control. In contrast to the withdrawal of group relief under *FA 2002, s 111* and *Sch 34*, a company that is 'above' the acquiring company in the group structure includes any company having control of that company or another company above that company, i.e. a 51% test applies rather than the 75% test for group relief. [*FA 2002, Sch 35, para 9*].

Acquisition of target company [*FA 1986, S 77*]

[34.5] Exemption from stamp duty on a **CONVEYANCE OR TRANSFER (39)** on sale is available where a new holding company is placed above an existing company. The exemption applies to an instrument transferring shares in one company (the 'target company') to another company (the 'acquiring company') but is so restricted that it is frequently of limited use.

The following requirements have to be met:

(a) Prior to 22 July 2005 the registered office of the acquiring company had to be in the UK. Following the decision of the European Court of Justice in *Halliburton Services BV v Staatssecretaris van Financiën* [1994] STC 655, this requirement was incompatible with European Union law where the registered office of the acquiring company is in another member state of the European Union. HMRC Stamp Taxes accepted that this requirement was defective in law and from 22 July 2005 has accepted claims to relief by companies with a registered office in any European Economic Area state: IR Statement, 22 July 2005. The requirement for a UK registered office has been removed completely by *FA 2006, s 169*.

(b) The transfer of shares must be part of an arrangement under which the acquiring company acquires all the issued shares of the target company. The relief is unlikely to be available, therefore, where the acquiring company already holds shares in the target.

(c) The acquisition must be effected for bona fide commercial reasons and should not form part of a tax avoidance scheme. If clearance has been granted by HMRC under the *Taxation of Chargeable Gains Act 1992, ss 138–139* it is likely that the Commissioners will regard this requirement as satisfied.

(d) The *consideration for the acquisition* must consist only of the *issue of shares* in the acquiring company to the shareholders of the target company. Unlike *FA 1986, ss 75, 76* liabilities undertaken or discharged by the acquiring company are not ignored. Unlike *FA 1986, s 76* there can be no cash element in the consideration paid by the acquiring company.

(e) After the acquisition each person who immediately before it was a shareholder of the target is a shareholder of the acquiring company.
(f) After the acquisition the shares in the acquiring company are of the same classes as were shares in the target immediately before the acquisition. It is understood that a change in the coupon attaching to preference shares or a change in the nominal value of shares of the same class is not regarded by the Commissioners as a reason to refuse the exemption under this requirement or the following two requirements.
(g) After the acquisition the number of shares of any particular class in the acquiring company bears to all the shares in the acquiring company the same or, as nearly as may be the same, proportion as the number of shares of that class in the target company bore to all the shares in the target company immediately before the acquisition.
(h) After the acquisition, the proportion of shares of any particular class in the acquiring company held by any particular shareholder is the same or, as nearly as may be the same, as the proportion of shares of that class in the target company held by him immediately before the acquisition.
(i) Any shares held by either the acquiring company or the target company in itself are ignored for the above purposes.

It will be apparent from the above requirements that for the exemption to be available at all it will be necessary for the acquiring company following the acquisition to have a share capital which is virtually identical to that of the target.

It is understood that the inclusion of 'stock' in the meaning of 'shares' and 'share capital' by *FA 1986, s 77(4)* was not intended to make debentures and other forms of funded debt subject to the above requirements as strictly required by *FA 1986, s 114(4)* and *SA 1891, s 122(1)*, and that in practice the Commissioners may ignore this unintended result.

General interpretation

[34.6] As follows—

(a) '*Consideration for the acquisition*' includes consideration warranted by the transferee company, even if it does not move from that company (*Central and District Properties v CIR* HL, [1966] 2 All ER 433). The consideration for the acquisition does not consist of not less than 90% in shares if those shares are subject to a contract to sell or an option to sell or an option to purchase imposed by the transferee company (*Crane Fruehauf Ltd v CIR* CA, [1975] 1 All ER 429). However, the fact that the consideration shares are issued to the target company which then immediately sells the shares for cash to its holding company does not mean that the acquiring company has in reality provided cash consideration. Accordingly, the acquiring company will not be deprived of the exemption on the ground that the consideration for the acquisition failed to consist as to 90% of the issue of shares by the acquiring company (*CIR v Kent Process Control Ltd* [1989] STC 245). These cases were decided under the now repealed *FA 1927, s 55* but are relevant to the legislation contained in *FA 1986, ss 75–77* in appropriate cases.

(b) *'Issue of shares'* means allotment *and* registration (*Oswald Tillotson Ltd v CIR* CA, [1933] 1 KB 134; *National Westminster Bank plc v CIR* HL, [1994] 3 All ER 1). A renounceable letter of allotment is not sufficient. Shares must be issued to the registered holders of shares in an existing company or to the existing company; issue to new nominees or to beneficial owners where nominees are the registered holders is unacceptable (*Brotex Cellulose Fibre Ltd v CIR* KB, [1933] 1 KB 158; *Murex Ltd v CIR* KB, [1933] 1 KB 173). Where consideration shares are issued to a target company which then immediately sells the shares for cash to its holding company, it is not correct for the Stamp Office to argue that the consideration shares are not in reality issued to the target company because the holding company could compel the transfer by virtue of its control of the target company in the absence of a formal agreement to that effect. Accordingly, relief will not be refused on this ground unless a requirement to transfer the consideration shares to the holding company is imposed on the target company by the acquiring company (*CIR v Kent Process Control Ltd* [1989] STC 245).

Adjudication (12)

[34.7] This is required where exemption or relief is claimed under *FA 1986, ss 75–77*. The claim is made by a letter. The Commissioners previously issued specimen letters of claim and notes for guidance which appear no longer to be available but which are reproduced in **APPENDIX H** for reference.

Chapter 35

Compulsory Purchase

General

[35.1] Where by virtue of any Act of Parliament either:

(a) property is vested by way of sale in any person, or
(b) any person is authorised to purchase property,

the person must produce to the Commissioners, duly stamped with ad valorem duty as a conveyance on sale (see **39 Conveyance or Transfer**), a Queen's Printer's copy of the Act or an instrument relating to the vesting in the case of (*a*), or an instrument of conveyance in the case of (*b*). Production must be made within three months of the passing of the Act or the date of vesting, whichever is the later, in the case of (*a*) and completion of the purchase in the case of (*b*). [*FA 1895, s 12*]. A certificate that *FA 1895, s 12* has been complied with is then given on each instrument. For the application of the section to nationalisation schemes, see **35.4** below.

This provision does not require that a conveyance be taken of goods, wares or merchandise forming part of the property. If the acquisition relates exclusively to goods etc. no instrument need be produced to the Commissioners. [*FA 1949, s 36(4)*]. If the conveyance does include goods etc., ad valorem duty will be payable on the attributable compensation moneys.

Consideration/compensation moneys

[35.2] Ad valorem duty will be paid on the consideration for the transaction and reference should be made generally to **36 Consideration**. See **35.3** below for consideration for the compulsory purchase of land. See **35.1** above for consideration attributable to goods etc.

Compulsory purchase of land

[35.3] The following applies in the compulsory purchase of land—

(a) A general vesting declaration under *Compulsory Purchase (Vesting Declarations) Act 1981*, under which a local authority acquires land compulsorily, may cover more than one property but will nevertheless be regarded as a separate transaction for each property with the consequence that a **Certificate of Value (30)** can be given in respect of each transaction where appropriate. However, if there is more than one acquisition from a single owner it is the aggregate of the chargeable sums due to that owner which must be used for the certificate and not the individual amounts.

(b) A compulsory purchase effected by deed poll bears duty as a conveyance on sale to the acquiring authority. [*Compulsory Purchase Act 1965, s 28(2)*]. See also *Lands Clauses Consolidation Act 1845, s 77* (as amended by *Administration of Justice Act 1965, ss 17, 18* and *Compulsory Purchase Act 1965, s 39*); *Acquisition of Land Act 1981*.

(c) Duty is charged on the total compensation moneys payable in respect of the sale of land including any part representing compensation for severance relating to land not transferred (*Law Society's Gazette 1953 p 206*). Compensation for loss of business may be included as consideration for the sale of land (*Glasgow and South-Western Rly Co v CIR* HL, (1887) 12 App Cas 315).

(d) Compensation moneys may be undetermined at the date of acquisition and the following is the practice relating to the charging of stamp duty:
   (i) wholly determined—ad valorem duty on the compensation moneys; a **CERTIFICATE OF VALUE (30)** may be given;
   (ii) partly determined—ad valorem duty on the market value of the property in accordance with *FA 1994, s 242(1)*—see **36.8 UNASCERTAINED AND CONTINGENT CONSIDERATION**; a **CERTIFICATE OF VALUE (30)** may be given;
   (iii) wholly undetermined—ad valorem duty on the market value of the property in accordance with *FA 1994, s 242(1)*—see **36.8 UNASCERTAINED AND CONTINGENT CONSIDERATION**; a **CERTIFICATE OF VALUE (30)** may be given.

   The open market valuation required under (ii) and (iii) above must be on the basis of the price which the property might reasonably be expected to fetch on a sale in the open market at the date of the general vesting declaration and must be on the basis that no compulsory purchase order was in place nor contemplated, i.e. unblighted.

(e) A declaration is a conveyance on sale and so must be produced under *FA 1931, s 28* (see **77 PRODUCED STAMP**).

Nationalisation

[35.4] The rules set out in **35.1** above are modified in the case of nationalisation schemes so that:

(a) in computing duty under *FA 1895, s 12* (see **35.1** above) the consideration is left out of account; and

(b) no stamp duty is payable on any conveyance, agreement or assignment or other instrument made solely for the purpose of effecting a transfer.

A nationalisation scheme to which this exemption applies is one effected by an Act embodying a scheme for the carrying on of the whole or part of an industry or an undertaking under national ownership or control. The exemption extends to transfers made to the Crown or a specially constituted body as part of the initial putting into force of the scheme. [*FA 1946, s 52*].

Generally the Acts enabling the creation, dissolution or reorganisation of a nationalised industry or other government organisation contain special provisions relating to exemption from stamp duty; nationalised industries etc. are not exempt without special provision. Most commonly the Acts provide that *FA 1895, s 12* (see **35.1** above) shall not apply, but other provisions exempting certain instruments are sometimes included (e.g. exemption for shares in nationalised companies—*FA 1948, s 74*).

Chapter 36

Consideration

[36.1] Ad valorem duty on a **CONVEYANCE OR TRANSFER (39)** on sale is normally charged by reference to the amount or value of the consideration. However, for instruments relating to interests in land, the market value of the property conveyed or transferred is used to calculate the stamp duty charge when the consideration cannot be ascertained at the time of sale or where an interest in land is transferred to a connected company (see **36.8** and **36.9** below).

Exemption and reduced rates are available if the instrument contains a **CERTIFICATE OF VALUE (30)** that the amount or value of the consideration does not exceed £125,000, £250,000 or £500,000 (or £1,000 in the case of a transfer of shares or securities) as appropriate. The following paragraphs explain the way in which the amount or value of the consideration is calculated or the stamp duty charge is otherwise calculated.

Cash

[36.2] Where sterling constitutes the consideration for sale no problem generally arises (but see **36.4** below).

If the consideration is expressed in a foreign currency, the currency is converted at the rate of exchange at the date of the instrument. If the instrument contains a statement of the rate of exchange, the instrument will be deemed duly stamped in accordance with that statement unless and until it is shown that the statement is untrue and the instrument is insufficiently stamped. [*SA 1891, s 6*]. *FA 1985, s 88* ended the system of converting various specified currencies at fixed rates published from time to time in the London Gazette.

Stock (including shares) and securities

[36.3] There are two main categories of stock and securities.

(a) **Stock and marketable securities as consideration**
The value of stock or marketable securities is taken into account regardless of whether or not the stock or marketable securities have been issued at the time of execution and whether or not their issue is certain or contingent. [*SA 1891, s 55(1)* and *(1A)* inserted by *FA 2000, s 126*]. This value is calculated according to the average price of the stock or security; an instrument containing a statement of the average price and stamped in accordance with that statement is deemed duly stamped unless and until it is shown that the statement is untrue and the instrument is insufficiently stamped. [*SA 1891, s 6*].

(i) **Quoted stock or securities** are in practice valued at the value used for capital gains tax purposes which is usually the lower of:

(A) the lower of the two prices shown in The Stock Exchange Daily Official List plus one-quarter of the difference between the two prices; and

(B) halfway between the highest and lowest prices at which bargains were recorded on that day (ignoring special bargains). [*Taxation of Chargeable Gains Act 1992, s 272(3)*].

(ii) **Unlisted shares or marketable securities** will be valued on a net assets, earnings or yield basis as appropriate. They may be valued by reference to the value of the property for which they form the consideration (e.g. *Foster (John) & Sons Ltd v CIR* CA, [1894] 1 QB 516; *Carlyon Estate Ltd v CIR* KB, (1937) 46 TC 41n).

For instruments executed on or after 28 March 2000, an anti avoidance measure applies to charge ad valorem duty on a transfer of marketable securities as part of a swap for exempt securities where due to the way the transaction is legally structured there would be a sale of the exempt securities with the marketable securities being transferred otherwise than on sale. This measure applies where the consideration for the marketable securities is or includes debt, stock or securities that are not 'chargeable securities' for **STAMP DUTY RESERVE TAX (84)**. The transfer of the marketable securities which would otherwise have escaped ad valorem duty is treated as a sale and ad valorem duty is charged by reference to the value of the consideration up to the market value of the marketable securities. [*FA 2000, s 122*].

(b) **Unmarketable securities**, e.g. some debentures in private companies, are valued at the principal amount outstanding plus accrued interest at the date of the conveyance. [*SA 1891, s 55(2)*].

Periodical payments

[36.4] Where the consideration consists of periodical payments (e.g. an annuity, payments by instalments etc.), amounts are charged to ad valorem duty as follows:

(a) payable periodically for a definite period not exceeding 20 years—the total of the payments;

(b) payable periodically for a definite period exceeding 20 years or in perpetuity or for an indefinite period (not terminable with life)—the total amount which will or may, according to the terms of sale, be payable during 20 years from the date of the instrument;

(c) payable periodically for a life or lives—the total amount which will or may, according to the terms of sale, be payable during twelve years from the date of the instrument. [*SA 1891, s 56; FA 1971, s 69, Sch 14, Part VI*].

The periodic payments charged are those which form a part of the sale transaction and not those which are an inherent part of the property. Thus, rent payments under a leasehold would not be chargeable, but the reservation of a rent charge would. Contingent payments are chargeable, for example, on a company achieving a certain level of profits (*Underground Electric Railways Co of London Ltd v CIR* HL, [1906] AC 21); and see **37 CONTINGENCY PRINCIPLE**. Sums which can only become payable on breach of the sale contract are not taken into account (*Western United Investment Co Ltd v CIR* Ch D, [1958] Ch 392). The Court of Appeal considered the application of (*b*) above in *Blendett v CIR* and *Quietlece v CIR* CA, [1984] STC 95 (heard together). In the *Blendett* case a company was granted a lease for a premium of £240,500 payable as to £50,000 on execution and as to the balance on the 23rd anniversary of the lease. In the *Quietlece* case a company was granted a lease for a premium of £370,900 payable as to £50,000 on execution and as to the balance in three equal yearly instalments commencing on the 23rd anniversary of the lease. Ad valorem duty was paid in both cases only on the initial payments of £50,000 and the companies argued that the premiums were payable periodically for a period exceeding 20 years within (*b*) above and therefore duty was payable only on the consideration paid in the first 20 years. The Court held in the *Blendett* case that two payments only, made more than 20 years apart, were not periodical payments. In the *Quietlece* case it was held that the instalments were not 'payable periodically for a definite period' because there was only one payment during the first 20 years.

In both cases the Court held that (*b*) above did not apply and accordingly ad valorem duty was payable on the total premium paid by each company.

Debts and liabilities

[36.5] Where property is conveyed:

(a) for consideration consisting wholly or in part of a debt due to the transferee, or
(b) subject to the payment or transfer of money or stock, whether or not charged on the property and whether or not contingent,

the debt, money or stock is deemed to be the consideration. [*SA 1891, s 57*].

The amount of the debt is to be taken into account notwithstanding that the debt may be considered to be bad or doubtful and therefore worth less commercially. However, in relation to (*a*) above (but not (*b*)) if the application of *SA 1891, s 57* results in a consideration which would exceed the value of the property conveyed, the consideration is limited to that value provided that the instrument is adjudicated (see **13 ADJUDICATION**). [*FA 1980, s 102*].

Foreclosure orders are subject to special rules (see **56 FORECLOSURE**). For the ascertainment of an amount contingently payable see **37 CONTINGENCY PRINCIPLE.**

The conveyance of property subject to a mortgage will be charged to ad valorem duty on the consideration including the amount outstanding on the mortgage (e.g. *CIR v City of Glasgow Bank (Liquidators)* CS, (1881) 8 R (Ct of Sess) 389).

The Commissioners have published a Statement of Practice (SP 6/90) on conveyances and transfers of property subject to a debt. The text of this Statement and the accompanying press release is reproduced in **APPENDIX B**.

Paragraph 4 of the text of the Statement of Practice recognises the existence of transactions that are not sales *per se* for these purposes and therefore are not turned into sales for the purposes of *SA 1891, s 57*.

A transfer of property subject to a mortgage where the transferee does not assume any liability for it can be certified exempt under Category L of the *Stamp Duty (Exempt Instruments) Regulations 1987* as long as there is no actual consideration, e.g. a transfer of mortgaged property from subsidiary company to parent by way of dividend in specie.

An agreement to settle trade or other liabilities as part of the consideration for the sale of a business will cause the amount of those liabilities to be added to the consideration (*E Gomme Ltd v CIR* Ch D, [1964] 3 All ER 497); but it is possible to provide for the settlement of liabilities by the vendor out of the realisation of the monetary assets without the purchaser's undertaking to find any deficiency, in which case duty may be saved.

Liabilities inherent in the property (e.g. future calls on partly-paid shares, rent under a lease) are not treated as part of the consideration (*Swayne v CIR* CA, [1900] 1 QB 172).

Covenants to improve property

[36.6] A conveyance on sale made for any consideration chargeable to ad valorem duty is not liable to duty in respect of any further consideration consisting of a covenant by the purchaser to make substantial improvements or additions to the property conveyed (or in consideration of his having done so) or a covenant relating to the subject matter of the conveyance. [*FA 1900, s 10*]. This section was held to apply to a contract for the sale of land and a separate contract (conditional on the first) for the vendor to build a house for the purchaser so that ad valorem duty was charged only on the consideration for the first contract (*Kimbers & Co v Inland Revenue* KB, [1936] 1 KB 132; *Paul v CIR* CS 1936, SC 443; cf *McInnes v Inland Revenue* CS 1934, SC 424).

Following its defeat in the case of *Prudential Assurance Co Ltd v CIR* [1992] STC 863 the Inland Revenue (now known as 'HMRC') has issued a new Statement of Practice (SP8/93) to supersede those issued in 1957 and 1987 (SP10/87). The text of SP8/93 is reproduced in **APPENDIX B**.

The facts of the case were that Prudential agreed to purchase freehold land including unfinished buildings from developers. Three documents were executed simultaneously. The first document was a sale agreement by which Prudential agreed to purchase the property for £2.5m. The second document was a development agreement by which the developers were to execute existing building contracts and Prudential were to provide the required moneys up to an agreed maximum on a monthly basis after taking into account the £2.5m payable under the sale agreement. The third document was a transfer of the land to Prudential. The question was whether the transfer was stampable on the £2.5m sale price plus the cost of building work already completed (total £6m) or on the total amount payable for the land and the cost of all building work (total £10.7m). It was held that although all three documents were part of one transaction, the sale agreement was, as the parties had intended, completed independently of the carrying out of the remaining building works under the development agreement. The transfer was therefore properly stampable on £6m and not £10.7m.

SP 8/93 applies where:

(a) there is a contract for the sale or lease of a building plot and the builder or developer is to construct buildings on the site for the purchaser; and
(b) at the date of the contract, building work on the plot has either not been started or is incomplete; and
(c) at the time of the conveyance or execution of the lease, building work on the plot has begun (or has been completed).

Whilst each case will depend on its own facts, in broad terms the treatment will be as follows:

(i) Where there is a contract for a conveyance or lease of land, and, as a separate transaction, a further contract for building works to be carried out, stamp duty on the conveyance or lease will be calculated without regard to the further contract.
(ii) Where, within a single transaction, there are separate contracts for the sale or lease of land, and for building works on the land, the stamp duty charge depends on whether the contracts are genuinely independent. If the contracts are independent, duty is charged on the price paid or payable for both the land itself and for any building that is on the land at the time the instrument is executed, including partly completed buildings. If the contracts are not genuinely independent, stamp duty will be charged on the total price for the land and completed buildings.

The statement will not apply where there is evidence of a sham or artificial transaction.

The Statement of Practice does not affect the common situation where a contract for the sale of a new house on a plot of land is subsequently given effect by a conveyance of the whole property, in the same way as most ordinary sales of new houses.

If stamp duty is offered on the total price paid for the building plot and the completed buildings, the documents should be submitted to the Stamp Office in the usual way. If the total price does not exceed the £125,000 threshold (see **30 CERTIFICATE OF VALUE**), the documents can be sent direct to the Land Registry under the *Stamp Duty (Exempt Instruments) Regulations 1985 (SI 1985 No 1688)*. Where the total price paid exceeds the threshold and the purchaser contends that the duty is payable on a lesser sum than the total price, the Board have requested that the documents should be sent to the Stamp Office together with a full explanation.

Exchanges of property

[36.7] Prior to *FA 1994, s 241* duty on a **CONVEYANCE OR TRANSFER (39)** on sale was only charged where there was a 'sale' for stamp duty purposes. This meant that there had to be a transfer of property in consideration of stock, marketable securities or debt.

An exchange of property is not a 'sale' for stamp duty purposes and therefore sale duty was not charged except in the case of an exchange of one freehold property for another and even then sale duty was only charged by reference to any equality money, under *SA 1891, s 73*. On any other exchange of property including freehold for leasehold property, *SA 1891, s 73* did not apply and the Inland Revenue seemed to accept that the payment of equality money did not make the exchange a 'sale' for stamp duty purposes.

As a result of the exploitation of this rule involving the transfer of a freehold property in exchange for a lease of low value plus equality money equal to the balance of the price the position was altered by *FA 1994, s 241*.

As a consequence, where the consideration for the transfer or vesting of any estate or interest in land or the grant of **LEASES (64)** consists of or includes any property (which would not previously have been taken into account), then the market value of that property is to be taken as the consideration (or part thereof) for the purposes of charging sale duty.

However, there are some difficulties with the drafting and operation of *FA 1994, s 241*. By far the most serious difficulty relates to the amount of sale duty to be charged on an exchange. In the November 1993 Budget the Inland Revenue at first maintained that an exchange of properties of unequal value with equality money would have to be stamped on both legs of the exchange on the full value of the most expensive property, e.g. on an exchange of property A worth £150,000 for property B worth £100,000 plus £50,000 cash, duty would be charged on both transfers by reference to £150,000 on the basis that the consideration for property B was property A.

However, in its Press Release of 18 April 1994, the Inland Revenue revised this to state that, 'where it is clear from the contract that the intention of the parties to the transaction is that the cheaper property should be transferred for the more expensive property *less* the equality money, the Stamp Office will limit the charge to duty accordingly'. Therefore in the above example duty would be charged on the transfer of property B by reference to £100,000 and not £150,000.

In the same Press Release the Inland Revenue somewhat surprisingly went on at paragraph 12 to explain how *FA 1994, s 241* could be avoided and sale duty saved on one leg of the exchange. In many cases, transactions which could normally be structured and documented as exchanges can equally well be carried out as sales for a price which is partly satisfied in kind. To achieve this result, a single contract should provide for a sale of the more expensive property (A) in consideration of the transfer of the cheaper property (B) plus the cash. To assist the calculation of duty, the single contract should state the values which the parties place on A and B. The parties should be referred to as Seller and Buyer and should agree in advance who will pay the duty. The single contract should be completed by two transfers. The transfer of A, being on the sale of A, attracts ad valorem duty on the consideration, i.e. the value of B plus the cash. The transfer of B attracts only the fixed £5 duty because this transfer is not on sale but is merely the means whereby part of the consideration for the sale of A is vested in the seller. The transfer of A should be expressed as 'being in consideration of the transfer of B and the payment of £. . . . . . . '. The transfer of B should be expressed as being 'pursuant to the terms of the Agreement for Sale dated . . . . '.

One of the solicitors should submit both transfers for adjudication plus a copy of the contract, although this is not compulsory. The transfer of A will need to be produced under *FA 1931, s 28* (see **77 PRODUCED STAMP**).

ADJUDICATION (13) is recommended to protect against the possibility of a third party or a defendant in future legal proceedings raising a stamp objection by arguing that the transfer of B is insufficiently stamped. The August 1995 issue of the Inland Revenue publication Tax Bulletin confirms the above approach. However, the Inland Revenue takes the view that the exchange of two properties of equal value results in a double charge to duty under *FA 1994, s 241* even if the contract is drafted as a sale rather than an exchange.

See **39.8 CONVEYANCE OR TRANSFER (SUB-SALES)** in relation to sub-sales.

And see **APPENDIX D** where the relevant section of the Tax Bulletin is reproduced in full.

The ability to limit the ad valorem duty to the more expensive property was exploited to avoid ad valorem duty completely by structuring what would otherwise have been a cash sale of property as a sale of exempt property such as a government gilt security (easily liquidated) with the price satisfied largely in kind by a house or other cheaper property. In this way it was in effect possible to sell a house or other property free of ad valorem stamp duty.

For instruments executed on or after 28 March 2000, the transfer of the cheaper property will be treated as on sale for stamp duty purposes and ad valorem duty charged by reference to the value of the consideration up to the market value of the cheaper property, but reduced to the extent that ad valorem duty is chargeable on the transfer of the other property. [*FA 2000, s 118*].

Unascertained and contingent consideration

[36.8] See also **37 CONTINGENCY PRINCIPLE**, including *LM Tenancies 1 plc v CIR*.

In addition to the matters described in **36.7** above, *FA 1994* also changed another basic stamp duty principle. That principle was that if the consideration for a sale was unascertainable at the date of the instrument, no ad valorem duty could be charged. This was always subject to the **CONTINGENCY PRINCIPLE (37)** which holds that where the consideration payable under an instrument is uncertain and dependent on a contingency, but a maximum, minimum or basic figure can be ascertained then ad valorem duty is payable by reference to that figure regardless of the fact that such figure may not ultimately be paid.

FA 1994, s 242 altered this basic principle in relation to interests in land by charging ad valorem duty on the market value of the property transferred where all or part of the consideration is unascertainable and the **CONTINGENCY PRINCIPLE (37)** does not apply (because there is no prima facie figure).

As with *FA 1994, s 241* (see **36.7** above) there are some difficulties with the drafting and operation of *s 242*. It is clear that *s 242* is intended to introduce an ad valorem charge in situations where the consideration takes the form of a right to a future payment which is unascertainable at the date of the instrument and there is no maximum, minimum or prima facie sum for the **CONTINGENCY PRINCIPLE (37)** to operate on. However, it is also clear from the decision in *Marren v Ingles* HL, [1980] STC 500 that a right to a future payment is a form of property, being a chose in action. On the basis that that right is property for the purposes of *s 241*, does *s 241* override *s 242* and charge ad valorem duty on the market value of that right on the basis that the value of that right (property) has been ascertained? Indeed, it is arguable that *s 242* has no effect because it is either overridden by *s 241* or the **CONTINGENCY PRINCIPLE (37)**. However, it is thought that a court would be reluctant to hold that *s 242* has no function and would probably conclude that a right to a future payment is not property for the purpose of *s 241* thereby allowing *s 242* to operate.

Also, it is unclear as to whether the intention that *FA 1994, s 242* should not apply where the **CONTINGENCY PRINCIPLE (37)** operates has been achieved. *FA 1994, s 242(3)(a)* excludes from the effect of *s 242* cases where the consideration or rent could be ascertained on the assumption that a future event mentioned in the instrument were or were not to occur. However, the **CONTINGENCY PRINCIPLE (37)** is wider than this and operates even when there is no express mention of an event in the instrument. For example, on the grant of a lease where the rent could later increase by reason of the exercise of the option to tax the rent for VAT purposes, the Stamp Office charges duty on the rent on the basis that the option to tax has been exercised (see **89 VAT AND STAMP DUTY**). Clearly, there will be leases which contain no reference to the option to tax for VAT purposes. Does this result in *s 242* applying to the exclusion of the **CONTINGENCY PRINCIPLE (37)** on the basis that no relevant event is mentioned in the instrument and so stamp duty must be charged on the market rent, i.e. the actual rent and not the rent as increased by the notional VAT charge?

FA 1994, s 242 applies where the consideration, or any part of the consideration, for the transfer or vesting of any estate or interest in land or the grant of any lease or tack cannot be ascertained at the time the instrument is executed and the **CONTINGENCY PRINCIPLE (37)** does not apply. The consideration is then taken to be the market value of the estate or interest or lease or tack immediately before the instrument is executed and ad valorem duty is charged on such value. In relation to duty chargeable on rent under the Lease heading in *FA 1999, Sch 13, Part II*, if the rent or any part of the rent cannot be ascertained, the rent is taken to be the market rent at the time the lease is executed.

Where *FA 1994, s 242* applies it will be necessary to carry out a valuation of the property concerned.

And see paras 18–24 of the article in the August 1995 Tax Bulletin reproduced in **APPENDIX D**.

Transfer of land to connected company

[36.9] Where an interest in land is transferred to or vested in a body corporate and either:

(a) the transferor is connected with the body corporate (regardless of whether there is any consideration); or
(b) where there is consideration it includes the issue or transfer of shares in a company connected to the transferor,

then the transfer or vesting is deemed to be on sale and ad valorem duty is charged by reference to the market value of the interest in land, but reduced by any actual consideration not consisting of property [*FA 2000, s 119*].

This provision is an anti-avoidance measure that is essentially aimed at 'value swamping' schemes where as a result of the abolition of voluntary disposition duty by *FA 1985*, it became possible to transfer an interest in land or other property to a company which had been pre-capitalised with a large number of issued shares of low denomination. If the transferee company issued a very low number of further shares as consideration, the ad valorem duty on the transfer of the interest in land was calculated by reference to the very low market value of the consideration shares issued and not by reference to the actual value of the interest transferred. The stamp duty is charged by reference to the market value of the interest in land as reduced by any consideration not consisting of property. For this purpose the Stamp Office regards an obligation to carry out building works on the land or an obligation to pay benefits under a pension scheme as examples of consideration not consisting of property.

For the purposes of this provision, whether any person is connected with another is determined in accordance with *CTA 2010, s 1122*. [*FA 2000, s 119(9)*].

There are some important exceptions for transfers or vestings that would otherwise be caught by (*a*) above, where:

(1) the transferor holds the interest as nominee or bare trustee for the body corporate;
(2) the body corporate is to hold the interest as nominee or bare trustee for the transferor;
(3) the transferor holds the interest as nominee or bare trustee for some other person and the body corporate is to hold as nominee or bare trustee for that other person;

(4) in a case outside 1 or 3 above, the transfer or vesting is out of a settlement to a beneficiary who did not acquire his beneficiary's interest for money's worth and the distribution is under the terms of the settlement;

(5) in a case outside 2 above, the body corporate is a trust manager and is to hold the interest in the course of that business;

(6) in a case outside 2 above, the body corporate will hold the interest as a trustee and apart from *CTA 2010, 1122(6)* (trustees as connected persons) would not be connected with the transferor;

(7) the transferor is a company, the transfer or vesting is, or is part of, a distribution of assets (on a winding-up or otherwise) and the interest was acquired by the transferor company using a duly stamped instrument. [*FA 2000, s 120*].

Note. *FA 2000, s 119* which charges ad valorem duty as mentioned above applies to instruments executed on or after 28 March 2000 however the exceptions noted above apply by virtue of *FA 2000, s 120* which only applies to instruments executed after 28 July 2000. For instruments caught by *FA 2000, s 119* that were executed between 28 March and 28 July 2000 but would have been exempted had *FA 2000, s 120* been in force, a claim for repayment of the duty may be made before 1 April 2001 (IR 24/00 issued on 14 July 2000 and *FA 2000, s 131*).

In relation to the grant of leases to connected companies, a similar provision applies except that none of the exceptions listed above are available. [*FA 2000, s 121*].

Miscellaneous

[36.10] Additionally—

(a) Interest on the purchase price is not included in the amount of the consideration on which duty is charged (*Hotung v Collector of Stamp Revenue* PC, [1965] AC 766).

(b) If the purchaser undertakes to bear the vendor's legal costs, this will normally form part of the consideration. In practice this does not generally extend to a lessee's undertaking to bear the lessor's costs.

Value added tax

[36.11] For the calculation of stamp duty where the consideration includes or may include value added tax see **36.8** above and **89 VAT AND STAMP DUTIES**.

Chapter 37

Contingency Principle

[37.1] The amount of consideration chargeable to ad valorem duty is the amount ascertainable at the date of the execution of the instrument (see e.g. *Underground Electric Railways Co of London Ltd v CIR* HL, [1906] AC 21). While the instrument should contain all the facts and circumstances affecting the liability to duty and the amount of the duty [*SA 1891, s 5*], there may often be circumstances where the amount of the consideration itself cannot be stated in the instrument.

Where the consideration payable under an instrument is uncertain and dependent on the happening of a contingency, the contingency principle applies as follows:

(a) Where the maximum amount which will be payable on the happening of the contingency can be ascertained, duty is payable on the maximum (*Underground Electric Railways Co of London Ltd v CIR* CA, [1916] 1 KB 306; *Coventry City Council v CIR* Ch D, [1978] 1 All ER 1107).

(b) Where, although the maximum amount which will be payable on the happening of a contingency cannot be ascertained, there is an ascertainable minimum amount, duty is payable on that minimum (*Underground Electric Railways Co of London Ltd v CIR* HL, [1906] AC 21).

(c) Where no maximum or minimum can be ascertained because it is a basic figure subject to increase or reduction by reference to unknown factors, duty is payable by reference to the basic figure (*Independent Television Authority v CIR* HL, [1961] AC 427).

See also **36.8 UNASCERTAINED AND CONTINGENT CONSIDERATION**.

If the consideration is undetermined, but ascertainable at the date of the instrument (e.g. where the consideration is agreed to be ascertained by reference to a valuation or a set of accounts which are not yet available), the duty will be assessed on the amount of the consideration as subsequently ascertained.

In a case where the consideration is undetermined and unascertainable at the date of the instrument the general rule was that no ad valorem duty was chargeable. For example, where there is no maximum, minimum or basic figure and the consideration is to be determined by a formula which is dependent on some future event taking place. However, in relation to the transfer or vesting of any estate or interest in land or the grant of any lease the position has been changed by *FA 1994, s 242*. In such cases ad valorem duty is charged on instruments executed after 7 December 1993 and the consideration is for this purpose taken to be the market value of estate or interest or lease. See also **36.8 UNASCERTAINED AND CONTINGENT CONSIDERATION**. Moreover, in relation to both land and non-land transactions the number of situations in which the consideration will be regarded as unascertainable has been considerably reduced following the decision in *LM Tenancies 1 plc v CIR* CA [1998] STC 326—see below.

LM Tenancies 1 plc v CIR CA [1998] STC 326. This decision considerably widened the scope of the contingency principle and in so doing has reduced the situations in which the consideration will be regarded as unascertainable where as a result the market value charge in *FA 1994, s 242* could have been expected to apply. The case was concerned with the disposal of land for a consideration which was linked to the market value of a gilt some time after the date of the execution of the relevant instrument. It was argued by the taxpayer that on general principles because the market value of the gilt in the future could not be known the consideration was not ascertainable. This argument was rejected by both the High Court and the Court of Appeal who stated that a reference to, for example, the market value at a date in the future is to be taken as a reference to the market value of the property at the date when the instrument is executed. This is of course a novel principle of construction and a considerable extension of the powers of the Stamp Office.

This principle had already been considerably enlarged and applied by the Stamp Office from early in 1995 in relation to property leased for a rent where there was in the rental formula a provision that the rent shall be increased, if appropriate, in line with the increase, if any, in the RPI over successive periods of 20 years. The Stamp Office initially sought to charge stamp duty by reference to the rate of increase in RPI over the 20 years preceding the execution of the instrument, or (if this produced a better result) by reference to the increase in RPI over the 12 months preceding the instrument multiplied by 20. This practice was subsequently modified to exclude the effect of compounding although, in cases where the review period was short the compounding effect began to reinstate itself inevitably. By using this decision in relation to index-linking arrangements the Stamp Office was seeking to increase the stampable consideration to the maximum amount that could become payable on its application of the index formula and any implicit compounding effect. However, in relation to leases with index-linked rents a change of practice was announced by the Inland Revenue in Press Release 98/99 issued on 14 May 1999 and this represents a major change in favour of the taxpayer. See **64.2** (*d*) **DUTY ON RENT**.

Chapter 38

Contract Notes

[38.1] Contract note duty was abolished by *FA 1985, s 86*. This duty was payable on notes sent by brokers to their clients in respect of the purchase and sale of shares and securities.

The obligation under *F(1909–10)A 1910* to issue contract notes has also been cancelled. [*FA 1987, s 49*].

Chapter 39

Conveyance or Transfer

Note: With the abolition of stamp duty on land and buildings from 1 December 2003, stamp duty is restricted to transactions in shares and securities, bearer instruments and acquisitions of partnership interests. Sales and certain other transfers of land and buildings are liable to stamp duty land tax and stamp duty applies only to the extent that the consideration is apportioned to shares and securities, bearer instruments and partnership interests.

[39.1] The two heads of charge in relation to Conveyances or Transfers in *SA 1891, Sch 1* relating to sales and to other transfers not on sale were repealed and restated in *FA 1999, Sch 13, Parts I and III* for instruments executed on or after 1 October 1999. As did their predecessors, the two restated charges cover the following conveyances or transfers:

(a) On sale of any property—ad valorem duty (for rates, see **39.3** below). See **39.2** to **39.10** below. [*FA 1999, Sch 13, Part I*].
(b) Any other kind—fixed duty £5 (**Note:** The fixed duties have been largely abolished for instruments executed on or after 13 March 2008 except for instruments effecting a land transaction [*FA 2008, Sch 32*]). See **39.11** below. [*FA 1999, Sch 13, Part III*].

For non-land transactions on or after 1 December 2003 the phrase 'conveyance or transfer' has been changed to 'transfer' and 'conveyance on sale' to 'transfer on sale'. [*FA 2003, Sch 20*].

Conveyance or transfer on sale

[39.2] In addition to being charged on instruments directly operating as conveyances or transfers on sale, ad valorem duty is charged on the following:

(a) certain agreements and contracts for sale—see **17.1 Agreement for Sale.**
(b) instruments creating and selling **Annuities (18).**
(c) absolute **Bills of Sale (26).**
(d) instruments charged under *FA 1895, s 12* (see **35 Compulsory Purchase**).
(e) **Foreclosure (56)** orders.
(f) **Release and Renunciation (80)** of property on sale.
(g) certain transfers of land and the grant of leases to connected companies and exchanges of land and shares that would otherwise not be on sale, are treated as transfers on sale attracting ad valorem duty (see **36 Consideration**).
(h) lease premiums—see **64 Leases.**

For exemptions available in respect of company transactions see **23 Associated Companies, 34 Company Reorganisations.**

Rates of ad valorem duty

[39.3] The rates are as follows. [*FA 1999, Sch 13, paras 1(3A), 3 and 4*].

Property conveyed	*Amount or value of consideration*	*Rate*
Stock or marketable securities	£1,000 or less	Nil, if certificate of value given
	Any other sum	0.5%
Other property	£125,000 or less	Nil, if certificate of value given
	£125,001–£250,000	1.0% if certificate of value given
	£250,001–£500,000	3.0% if certificate of value given
	£500,001 and above	4.0%

Where no certificate of value is given the standard rate of 4.0% applies (except in relation to sales of stock and marketable securities which are charged at 0.5%) even if the consideration is £500,000 or less. See **CERTIFICATE OF VALUE (30)**. The £125,000 exemption and the sliding scale are not available for transfers of stock, marketable securities or unit trust units, and the rate is 0.5% of the consideration; however, where the consideration is not more than £1,000 and the instrument contains a **CERTIFICATE OF VALUE (30)**, no stamp duty is chargeable.

A special rate of ad valorem duty of 1.5% is charged in connection with **DEPOSITARY RECEIPTS (45)** and **CLEARANCE SERVICES (33)**.

Conveyance on sale

[39.4] This includes every instrument or decree or order of any court or commissioners whereby any property (or estate or interest therein) on sale is transferred to or vested in a purchaser, or any person on his behalf or on his direction. [*FA 1999, Sch 13, para 1(2)*].

The following have been held to be conveyances on sale:

(a) A deed executed pursuant to an agreement for the dissolution of a partnership (*Garnett v CIR* QB, (1899) 81 LT 633; cf. *MacLeod v CIR* Ex (S) (1885), 22 SLR 674); and see **73 PARTNERSHIPS**.

(b) A lease (see *CIR v Littlewoods Mail Order Stores Ltd* HL 1962, [1963] AC 135).

(c) An agreement creating an option to purchase land (*George Wimpey & Co Ltd v CIR* CA, [1975] 2 All ER 45). See **70 OPTIONS AND WARRANTS**.

(d) A declaration of trust in favour of a purchaser (*Chesterfield Brewery Co v CIR* QB, [1899] 2 QB 7).

(e) An incomplete transfer of shares where the transferee and the consideration were not shown (*Fitch Lovell Ltd v CIR* Ch D, [1962] 3 All ER 685).

(f) A receipt for the sale consideration (*Fleetwood-Hesketh v CIR* CA, [1936] 1 KB 351). See **79 Receipts**.
(g) An agreement for the sale of inter alia land under which the vendors were nominees of the purchaser and did not have the right, which the vendor under an uncompleted contract has, to require the purchaser to take a conveyance of the legal title. (*Peter Bone Ltd v CIR* Ch D, [1995] STC 921). See **17.1**(second (*e*)) **Agreement for Sale**.

The property conveyed need not be the same property as that which was the subject of the sale bargain if the property conveyed represents it but not if its conveyance is merely a consequence of the sale (*Henty and Constable (Brewers) Ltd v CIR* CA, [1961] 3 All ER 1146). A conveyance or transfer will be chargeable as a conveyance or transfer on sale notwithstanding that at the time of execution of the instrument of conveyance or transfer the beneficial interest in the property contracted to be sold has already passed or passes at some time other than that of contract. Examples are conveyances where the purchaser is already the beneficial owner of the property under a prior contract (*Parway Estates Ltd v CIR*, (1958) 45 TC 135) and a transfer pursuant to what was at the time a conditional sale agreement (*Ridge Nominees Ltd v CIR* CA, [1961] 3 All ER 1108).

A transfer of property in the UK from trustee to beneficiary, which would normally have attracted only the fixed £5 miscellaneous conveyance duty, was held liable to ad valorem duty as a conveyance on sale because it was made consequent upon the sale of the property and in implementation of it and only the transfer was legally effective for that purpose because the unstamped declaration of trust executed and held offshore was not available for any purpose (*Parinv (Hatfield) Ltd v IRC* CA [1998] STC 305). (See **47.1 Evidence**.)

For conveyances in contemplation of sale see **39.10** below.

Sale

[39.5] 'Sale' is not defined in the legislation but will require a vendor, a purchaser, something sold and a price.

Reference should be made to the following sections of this book for transactions which may be treated as sales:

(a) **Assents (22)**.
(b) **Consideration (36)**.
(c) **Exchange or Partition (48)**.
(d) **Family Arrangements and Divorce (53)**.
(e) **Partnerships (73)**.
(f) **Receipts (79)**.
(g) **Release and Renunciation (80)**.

See also *Ridge Nominees Ltd v CIR* CA, [1961] 3 All ER 1108 (compulsory acquisition of shares from dissentients under *Companies Act 1985, ss 428–430* (now *CA 2006, ss 974, 979*) liable as a conveyance on sale); *Great Western Rly Co v CIR* CA, [1894] 1 QB 507 (amalgamation of two railway companies by transfer of undertakings to a new company and dissolution of transferor companies liable as a sale); *Belch v CIR* Ex(S) 1877, 14 SLR 389 and *Gibb v CIR* Ex(S) 1880, 18 SLR 389 (exercise of right of repurchase or extinction of an interest which was created by the document giving the right not liable as a sale).

Property

[39.6] For a conveyance or transfer to be liable it must relate to property. 'Property' is not defined in the legislation, but includes anything which belongs to one person exclusive of others and which can be made the subject-matter of bargain and sale to another (*Potter v CIR* Ex, (1854) 10 Exch 147). A right which a company did not in law possess (the exclusive right to use the company's asphalt in certain areas) was not property and could not, therefore, be conveyed or transferred (*Limmer Asphalte Paving Co Ltd v CIR* Exch, (1872) LR 7 Ex 211).

The following, inter alia, are property:

- land;
- personalty—many forms of personal property may be transferred by delivery and need not attract ad valorem duty unless incorporated in an instrument of transfer;
- stock and marketable securities—instruments of transfer are required for transfers of shares and debentures [*Companies Act 1985, s 183(1)*];
- **GOODWILL (59)**;
- copyrights and trademarks (*Leather Cloth Co Ltd v American Leather Cloth Co Ltd* HL, (1865) 11 HL Cas 523);
- patents;
- the benefit of a contract (*Western Abyssinian Mining Syndicate Ltd v CIR* KB, (1935) 14 ATC 286);
- debts (*Measures Bros Ltd v CIR* QB, (1900) 82 LT 689—debts sold as at a date prior to the instrument dutiable even though collected and, therefore, not in existence at the date of the contract);
- cash at bank is a debt due by the bank (*Foley v Hill* HL, (1848) 2 HL Cas 28), see above; cash in hand may transfer by delivery and will only be dutiable if included in an instrument of conveyance or transfer.

The following, inter alia, have been held not to be property:

- a policy of insurance under which no loss has occurred (*Blandy v Herbert* KB, (1829) 9 B & C 396); the principle is doubtful, cf *Western Abyssinian Mining Syndicate Ltd v CIR*, above;
- know-how (see *Handley Page v Butterworth* HL 1935, 19 TC 328; cf *Re Keene* CA, [1922] 2 Ch 475);
- licence to construct and retain a jetty (*Thames Conservators v CIR* QB, (1886) 18 QBD 279).

Property includes any estate or interest in property and so conveyances or transfers of equitable or limited interests are chargeable.

Consideration for sale

[39.7] In the case of a conveyance or transfer on sale or an agreement or contract for sale, ad valorem duty is calculated on the 'amount or value of the consideration'. A sale normally implies money consideration but the following are also treated as sale consideration for stamp duty purposes:

(a) stock or marketable securities [*SA 1891, s 55*];
(b) debts and other liabilities [*SA 1891, s 57*].

In relation to the transfer or vesting of an estate or interest in land or the grant of a lease where the consideration is property other than cash, stock or debts, ad valorem duty is charged on the market value of the property given as consideration. [*FA 1994, s 241*]. See **36.7 Exchanges of Property**.

For further details on the amount on which ad valorem duty is calculated see **36 Consideration** generally.

If the consideration does not comprise money or one of the specified considerations, the transaction will not be treated as a sale for stamp duty purposes unless *FA 1994, s 241* applies but see also **36 Consideration**.

Sub-sales

[39.8] With respect to sub-sales—

(a) **General.** Where a person has contracted to purchase any property and, before he has obtained a conveyance, contracts to sell that property to a sub-purchaser ad valorem duty is charged only on the consideration for the sub-purchase and not on the two transactions. The property must be conveyed directly to the sub-purchaser for the relief to operate. For the relief to operate the chargeable consideration moving from the sub-purchaser must be equal to or greater than the value of the property immediately before the contract of sale to him. [*SA 1891, s 58(4)(7); FA 1984, s 112; FA 1985, s 82*]. In *Keston v IRC* [2004] EWHC 59 (Ch), [2004] STC 902 it was held that a conveyance by a vendor to a sub-purchaser is, in the absence of sub-sale relief, chargeable to stamp duty by reference to both the consideration moving from purchaser to vendor and from sub-purchaser to purchaser. It was also held that because in that case the sub-sale consideration had been structured so that only £10,000 of the sub-sale consideration moving from the purchaser was chargeable with stamp duty and this was less than the £1.3m value of the property at the date of the sub-sale, sub-sale relief did not apply. The relief also applies to cases where the property contracted to be purchased is contracted to be sub-sold in parts to more than one sub-purchaser. The property must be conveyed in parts to the sub-purchasers by the original seller. Ad valorem duty on each conveyance is only charged on the sub-purchase price for that conveyance and the original consideration is ignored. For this relief to apply, the aggregate of the sale consideration for the separate parts must be equal to or greater than the value of the whole of the property immediately before the contract for their sale, or the first contract for the sale of any of the parts where there are separate contracts. [*SA 1891, s 58(5)(7); FA 1984, s 112; FA 1985, s 82*].

It is understood that the Stamp Office accepts that sub-sale relief is available where the original purchase is an exchange of interests in land to which *FA 1994, s 241* applies and the property is conveyed direct to the sub-purchaser. See **36.7 Exchanges of Property**.

Relief is also given where the sub-purchaser takes an actual conveyance of the interest of the person immediately selling to him and a later conveyance of the same property from the original seller. If the first conveyance is chargeable with ad valorem duty on the sub-purchase consideration and is duly stamped, the second conveyance will only attract the miscellaneous conveyance or transfer duty of £5 (see **39.11** below). [*SA 1891, s 58(6)*].

If the sub-purchases do not cover the whole of the property originally contracted to be purchased, duty is payable as follows:

(i) on the conveyances to sub-purchasers;—duty on those considerations described above;

(ii) on the conveyance of the remainder of the property to the original purchaser—duty on a proportion of the original purchase price based on the relative values of the part or parts retained and the part or parts sub-sold.

(*Maples v CIR* KB, [1914] 3 KB 303).

For the above reliefs to apply the property sub-sold must be the same as the property originally purchased. See e.g. *Fitch Lovell Ltd v CIR* Ch D, [1962] 3 All ER 685 (shares contracted to be sub-sold were different from those originally purchased because of the intervening issue of new shares with prior rights). There is some evidence that IR Stamp Taxes has begun to take this point to deny the relief, for example in relation to the sale of a freehold interest where long leaseholds are granted out of the freehold and the reversion is then sub-sold.

(b) **Contracts for the sale of UK land where the consideration exceeds £10m.** The scheme of sub-sale relief described above is effectively reversed in the case of a conveyance where there is a prior contract for the sale of UK land where the consideration exceeds £10m (approximately £8.5m plus VAT where VAT could be chargeable) and ad valorem duty is paid on the contract under *FA 2002, s 115* (see **17.1**(*f*) **Agreement for Sale**). In such a case duty on a sub-sale contract or subsequent sub-sale contract is chargeable only in respect of the amount (if any) by which the chargeable consideration for the sub-sale exceeds that on the earlier sale or if there has been more than one sale, on the highest amount of chargeable consideration on which duty has been paid. Where there are sub-sales of part an appropriate proportion determined on a just and reasonable basis is taken for this purpose. [*FA 2002, Sch 36, para 3*]. In relation to the sale contract this follows the existing treatment of sale contracts where duty is paid on the original contract and before taking a conveyance the property is sold on and duty is payable only in respect of the excess consideration. [*FA 1999, Sch 13, para 7(2)*].

However, the sub-sale treatment of the actual conveyance is reversed in the sense that with duty now having been paid on the original sale contract (and in respect of any additional consideration, on any intermediate sub-sale contracts), the conveyance from the original seller to a sub-purchaser will be chargeable with duty only to the extent that the duty that would have been chargeable on it exceeds the duty already paid on the original sale contract and on any intervening sub-sale contracts. [*FA 2002, Sch 36 para 5*]. There is a provision for a repayment of duty to the extent that the duty that would have been chargeable on the conveyance would be less than the duty paid in the original sale and any intervening sub-sale. [*FA 2002, Sch 36 para 6*]. And see IR Stamp Taxes Customer Newsletter issued in July 2002 entitled 'Contracts for the sale of an estate or interest in UK land–Section 115 and Schedule 36 Finance Act 2002' reproduced at **APPENDIX D**.

Several conveyances

[39.9] These include—

(a) **Conveyances of separate parts of property.** Where property is contracted to be sold for one consideration, but the property is conveyed to the purchaser in separate parts, the parties must apportion the whole consideration as they think fit to the separate parts. A distinct consideration must be shown in each conveyance and ad valorem duty is charged on this consideration. [*SA 1891, s 58(1)*].

(b) **Conveyances of separate parts to several persons.** Property may be conveyed in separate parts because, although the purchase contract relates to the whole property for the one consideration, it has been purchased by persons jointly or by a person wholly or partly on behalf of others. In these cases, each instrument of conveyance to the persons by or for whom the property was purchased for distinct parts of the consideration must specify the relevant part of the consideration and ad valorem duty is calculated on that part. [*SA 1891, s 58(2)*].

(c) **Several conveyances to complete title.** Where there are several instruments of conveyance to complete the purchaser's title, ad valorem duty is charged only on the principal instrument. The other instruments bear the £5 miscellaneous conveyance stamp (see **39.11** below). [*SA 1891, s 58(3)*]. The parties may determine between them which of several instruments is the principal instrument. [*SA 1891, s 61*].

Conveyance in contemplation of sale [FA 1965, s 90]

[39.10] This legislation was introduced to nullify the decision in *William Cory & Son Ltd v CIR* HL, [1965] AC 1088, where a conveyance prior to a sale avoided ad valorem duty as a conveyance or transfer on sale.

Any instrument whereby property is conveyed or transferred in contemplation of a sale is treated as a conveyance or transfer on sale for a consideration equal to the **value** of the property.

If the instrument conveys property to which *s 90* applies together with other property, *s 90* does not affect the amount of duty chargeable in respect of that other property.

ADJUDICATION (13) is required before the instrument is deemed duly stamped.

Provision is made for the repayment of duty paid under *s 90* in the following cases:

(a) Where the contemplated sale did not take place and the property has been reconveyed or retransferred to the person who conveyed or transferred it (or a person to whom his rights have been transmitted on death or bankruptcy), the duty repaid is the amount paid less any duty which would have been payable on the first conveyance (e.g. miscella neous conveyance duty of £5—see **39.11** below).

(b) Where the sale has taken place for a consideration which is less than the value on which duty was paid, the amount repaid is the difference between the duty paid and ad valorem duty on the actual consideration.

In each case the claim must be made within two years of the execution of the instrument of conveyance or transfer charged under *s 90*.

Although *s 90* does not define the phrase in 'contemplation of a sale', HMRC Stamp Taxes issued a Customer Newsletter (sic) in July 2002 entitled 'Split Title Schemes and Section 90 FA 1965' which is reproduced at **APPENDIX D**. In this publication HMRC Stamp Taxes states that it equates an intention to sell the property with 'in contemplation of a sale' in the sense that a transfer of the legal interest at a time when such an intention exists will be regarded as liable to duty under *s 90*. Not only is the relevance of 'intention' in stamp duty currently a matter of some uncertainty (see **19.1 ANTI-AVOIDANCE**), but it also seems that HMRC Stamp Taxes' statement that an intention to sell is enough to trigger the 'in contemplation of a sale' itself simply begs a further question about what sort of intention to sell is required. For example, it is now a trite point within property companies that everything is for sale 'at the right price'. It is not clear whether this means that there is the requisite intention to sell or not. However, the publication goes on to state that the presence of the following factors will be taken as indicating that a sale was in contemplation at the relevant time:

- the property is being marketed;
- negotiations for a sale have commenced;
- an offer to purchase the property has been received;
- the property is owned by a company and the company's Board of Directors has resolved to sell it.

HMRC Stamp Taxes also goes on to state that it will seek duty under *s 90* on nominee transfers, unless when presented for stamping such transfers are accompanied by a letter confirming that no sale is in contemplation.

Miscellaneous conveyance or transfer

[39.11] The fixed duty of £5 applied to conveyances or transfers which are not either sales of property or otherwise caught under *FA 1994, ss 241 and 242* and *FA 2000, ss 118–122* (see **36 Consideration**). However, this duty was abolished for instruments executed on or after 13 March 2008 except for instruments effecting a land transaction. [*FA 1999, Sch 13 para 16* as omitted by *FA 2008, Sch 32 para 10(3)(a)* subject to *para 22(1)(b)*].

It is provided that every instrument and decree or order of a court or commissioners whereby any property, on an occasion other than a sale is transferred or vested in any person is charged with duty as a conveyance or transfer of property.

Examples of instruments which attracted the £5 fixed duty are:

(a) conveyances or transfers where no beneficial interest passes;
(b) conveyances or transfers by way of security;
(c) conveyances or transfers for a consideration not taken into account for ad valorem duty (see **39.7** above);
(d) distribution of assets by a liquidator to shareholders in satisfaction of their rights in a winding-up (*Henty and Constable (Brewers) Ltd v CIR* CA, [1961] 3 All ER 1146).

However, where permitted, instruments certified in accordance with the *Stamp Duty (Exempt Instruments) Regulations 1987* (*SI 1987 No 516*) were in any event exempted from the fixed £5 duty and did not have to be presented to the Commissioners either for duty or **Adjudication (13)**. Thus, for example, the inclusion of the appropriate certificate in an instrument within (*d*) above exempted the instrument from the £5 duty and the need to present it to the Commissioners for duty or adjudication. See **50 Exempt Instruments**. Not all instruments liable to the fixed £5 duty could have been so certified under these regulations. Examples of instruments which could not have been certified are:

- conveyances or transfers from a beneficial owner to his nominee and vice versa;
- conveyances or transfers from one nominee to another nominee for the same beneficial owner; and
- conveyances or transfers by way of security.

Chapter 40

Court Orders

[40.1] A decree or order of a court or Commissioners whereby property (or any estate or interest in property) on the sale thereof is transferred to or vested in a purchaser is treated as a conveyance on sale liable to ad valorem duty as a **CONVEYANCE OR TRANSFER (39)** on sale. [*FA 1999, Sch 13, para 1(2)*]. This includes foreclosure decrees. [*FA 1898, s 6*]. See **56 FORECLOSURE.**

A decree or order which vests or transfers property otherwise than by sale or mortgage was chargeable with the fixed *£5* duty applicable to a miscellaneous **CONVEYANCE OR TRANSFER (38).** [*FA 1999, Sch 13, para 16*]. This included vesting orders. See **38.11 MISCELLANEOUS CONVEYANCE OR TRANSFER.**

The date of execution of an order is the date when it is drawn and dated (*Sun Alliance Insurance Ltd v CIR* Ch D 1971, [1972] Ch 133).

ADJUDICATION (13) is required in practice for orders made under the *Variation of Trusts Act 1958* and *Companies Act 1985, s 427* and *Companies Act 2006, s 900* (reconstruction or amalgamation of companies) and the solicitors involved are required to give an appropriate undertaking to the court.

Chapter 41

Covenants

[41.1] For the treatment of covenants relating to annuities and other periodic sums, see **27 BONDS** and **18 ANNUITIES**. Covenants on the creation and sale of annuities are dealt with as conveyances on sale.

The former head of charge 'Covenant' which charged duty at 50p or the amount of the ad valorem duty on the consideration if less, was repealed by *FA 1985, s 85, Sch 24(d)*.

Chapter 42

Declaration of Trust

[42.1] Declarations of trust in writing concerning any property were formerly liable to a fixed duty of £5 unless the declaration related to a life insurance policy and was certified under the *Stamp Duty (Exempt Instruments) Regulations 1987 (SI 1987 No 516)*. See **50.2 Exempt Instruments Regulations.** [*Stamp Duty (Exempt Instruments) (Amendment) Regulations 1999 (SI 1999 No 2539)*]. This charge did not apply to trusts created by wills. [*FA 1999, Sch 13, para 17*].

The fixed duty of £5 was abolished generally for instruments executed on or after 13 March 2008 but it is retained for instruments effecting a pre-SDLT transaction. [*FA 2008, Sch 32 paras 10(3)(b) and 22(1)(b)*].

The charge only applied to written declarations and did not affect oral declarations concerning personalty. A declaration of trust could have attracted ad valorem duty as a **Conveyance or Transfer (39)** on sale. See **39.4**(*d*) **Conveyance on Sale.**

See generally **86 Trusts and Trustees.**

Chapter 43

Deeds

[43.1] The fixed duty of 50p charged on miscellaneous deeds, being deeds of any kind not otherwise described in *SA 1891, Sch 1* was abolished by *FA 1985, s 85, Sch 24(e)*.

Chapter 44

Denoting Stamp

Duty paid denoting stamp

[44.1] A denoting stamp is used where the duty with which an instrument is chargeable depends upon the duty paid on another document. The payment of duty on that other document is denoted on the instrument by the Commissioners. [*SA 1891, s 11*].

A denoting stamp is required in the following cases:

(a) A **DUPLICATE OR COUNTERPART (46)** of an instrument liable to duty attracts £5 if it bears a denoting stamp 'Duplicate or counterpart—original fully and properly stamped'. A denoting stamp is not required for a counterpart of a lease if the counterpart is not executed by the lessor or grantor. [*FA 1999, Sch 13, para 19*].

(b) A **CONVEYANCE OR TRANSFER (39)** to a purchaser or sub-purchaser under a contract or agreement which has attracted ad valorem duty is not liable to ad valorem duty if the earlier payment of duty is denoted by a 'duty paid, ad valorem' stamp. [*FA 1999, Sch 13, para 7(4)*]. See **17.1 AGREEMENT FOR SALE, 17.2 AGREEMENT FOR SUB-SALE.**

(c) A conveyance, transfer, or lease requires a 'duty paid, ad valorem' stamp where the conveyance or transfer of an interest in land is subject to an agreement for a lease for a term exceeding 35 years or where a lease is granted for a term exceeding 35 years. The duty paid on the **AGREEMENT FOR LEASE (16)** is denoted on the conveyance, transfer, or lease. [*FA 1984, s 111(2), (3)*].

(d) A lease which does not contain a certificate that there is no agreement to which it gives effect. To be duly stamped such a lease must be stamped with a stamp denoting either that there is an agreement to which it gives effect which is not chargeable with duty or the duty paid on the agreement.

The Commissioners usually require production of the original stamped instrument (duty on which is to be denoted on the later instrument) but will accept copies issued by the Land Registry of documents registered there if the duty is clearly shown.

A denoting stamp does not indicate that the original document has been duly stamped; this is only possible if the original instrument has been adjudicated. See **13 ADJUDICATION.**

Other denoting stamps

[44.2] In the following cases denoting stamps are required but do not indicate duty being paid on any other instrument:

(a) A bearer instrument chargeable on issue must be produced to the Commissioners before issue and stamped with a denoting stamp. This stamp precedes the payment of duty (which is within six weeks of issue) but the instrument is deemed to be duly stamped. [*FA 1999, Sch 15, para 21(2)(b)*]. See **24.5**(*a*) **STAMPING PROCEDURE**.

(b) A bearer instrument given in substitution for a like instrument stamped ad valorem is not treated as duly stamped unless it bears a stamp denoting that full and proper duty has been paid on the original instrument. [*FA 1999 Sch 15, para 12A*].

(c) The transfer of stock on sale to an intermediary or as part of repurchase and stock lending arrangements on an EEA exchange or recognised foreign exchange does not attract any duty if it bears a stamp denoting that it is not chargeable with any duty. [*FA 1986, s 80A(7), 80C(5)*]. See **83.5 TRANSFERS OF SHARES TO INTERMEDIARIES ETC.**

Chapter 45

Depositary Receipts

[45.1] Note: On 18 March 2009 the Advocate General in *HSBC Holdings plc and Vidacos Nominees Ltd v HMRC* Case C–569/07 opined that the 1.5% SDRT charge on the issue of new securities, or on the transfer of existing securities, into clearance services, contravened EU law because it was in breach of the Capital Duty Directive 69/335/EEC and the free movement of capital under art 56 of the EU Treaty (see also *HSBC Holdings plc v Revenue and Customs Comrs* [2008] STC (SCD) 502, [2008] SWTI 190). The decision of the ECJ on 1 October 2009 confirmed that this was the position and as a consequence HMRC no longer apply the 1.5% SDRT charge on the issue of new shares into an EU depositary receipt or clearance service. However, the existing exemptions from SDRT for transfers from one system to another or between the clearance services and depositary systems as explained in **45.4**(a) and (f) below are not available where there is an arrangement for chargeable securities to be issued into an EU system (now free of the 1.5% entry charge) and then subsequently transferred from the EU system to a non-EU system. [*FA 1986, s 97C*].

[45.2] A depositary receipt scheme involves the issue by a bank of depositary receipts which are backed by shares held by the bank's nominee. The depositary receipts can be in registered or bearer form and will acknowledge the right of the holder of the receipt to the underlying shares and to any dividends and rights issues. In practice the depositary receipts will be bought and sold in overseas stock markets without attracting ad valorem stamp duty. The bank's nominee will remain the registered holder of the underlying shares or securities in the share register of the company whose shares have been 'converted' into depositary receipts. The increasing use of depositary receipts, particularly American Depositary Receipts or 'ADRs' representing shares in UK companies, led to an erosion of the yield of ad valorem stamp duty from share purchases. A special 'entry' charge of three times the normal rate of ad valorem duty on a **CONVEYANCE OR TRANSFER (39)** on sale was therefore imposed by *FA 1986* on the issue, transfer or appropriation of shares and securities in connection with the issue of depositary receipts. The special 'entry' charge of three times the normal duty is designed to compensate for the fact that the depositary receipts will be traded subsequently free of ad valorem duty.

The special charge can be either stamp duty (see **45.3** below) or **STAMP DUTY RESERVE TAX (84)** (see **45.4** below) depending on the circumstances.

Stamp duty

[45.3] Stamp duty at the special rate is charged on an instrument which *transfers* 'relevant securities' of a UK incorporated company to a person:

(a) whose business consists exclusively of holding 'relevant securities' as nominee or agent for a person whose business is or includes issuing depositary receipts for 'relevant securities'; or
(b) who is specified by a statutory instrument and whose business is or includes issuing depositary receipts for 'relevant securities'; or
(c) who is specified by a statutory instrument and whose business does not consist exclusively of holding 'relevant securities' as nominee or agent for an issuer of depositary receipts.

In relation to 'relevant securities' consisting of units representing paired shares of the type issued by Eurotunnel, the foreign company is treated as a company incorporated in the UK. [*FA 1986, s 67(1)(6)–(8); FA 1988, s 143(6)*].

'Relevant securities' are shares or stock or marketable securities of any company wherever incorporated. [*FA 1986, s 69(3)*].

A 'depositary receipt for relevant securities' is an instrument acknowledging that a person holds relevant securities or evidence of the right to receive them and that another person is entitled to rights, whether expressed as units or otherwise, in or in relation to relevant securities of the same kind, including the right to receive such securities (or evidence of the right to receive them) from the first person. [*FA 1986, s 69(1)*].

Where the instrument of transfer (other than a bearer instrument) attracts duty as a **CONVEYANCE OR TRANSFER (39)** on sale, duty is charged at the special rate of 1.5% of the amount or value of the sale consideration. In any other case duty is also charged at the special rate (except for bearer instruments) [*FA 1986, s 67(2), (3)* as amended by *FA 2008, Sch 32 para 14*]. A transfer of 'relevant securities' of a UK incorporated company between corporate nominees resident in the UK is not chargeable with duty [*FA 1986, s 67(9)* as amended by *FA 2008, Sch 32 para 6*].

Before 20 October 1997 transfers by qualified dealers attracted a reduced rate of £1 per £100 or part of £100 when transferring securities otherwise than on sale into depository receipts but this relief has been withdrawn. [*FA 1986, s 67(4); FA 1997, s 99(1)*].

An issuer of depositary receipts for 'relevant securities' of UK incorporated companies and a person whose business includes (but is not exclusively) holding such securities as nominee or agent for an issuer is required to notify the Commissioners of that fact within one month of the issuing of the receipts or holding the relevant securities. A penalty of up to £1,000 is imposed for failing to do so. [*FA 1986, s 68(1)(2)(4)*]. A UK incorporated company which becomes aware that its shares are held by an issuer of depositary receipts or his nominee or agent is also required to notify the Commissioners of that fact within one month of becoming so aware. A penalty of up to £100 can be imposed for failing to do so. [*FA 1986, s 68(3)(5)*].

Stamp Duty Reserve Tax

[45.4] **STAMP DUTY RESERVE TAX (84)** at the special rate is charged where 'chargeable securities' are *issued, transferred* to or *appropriated* by a person whose business is or includes issuing depository receipts for chargeable securities or to a person who holds such securities as nominee or agent for an issuer of depositary receipts as part of an arrangement for the issuer to issue depositary receipts. [*FA 1986, s 93(1); FA 1996, s 193*]. **Note:** HMRC no longer apply SDRT to the issue of securities into an EU depositary receipt system – see **Note** above.

For the definition of 'chargeable securities' see **84 Stamp Duty Reserve Tax.**

In relation to the *transfer* of 'chargeable securities' any ad valorem stamp duty chargeable on the instrument of transfer (see **45.3** above) cancels the equivalent amount of the reserve tax chargeable up to the full amount of the reserve tax. [*FA 1986, s 93(7)*].

The special rate is 1.5%:

(a) of the issue price, where securities are *issued*;
(b) of the amount or value of the consideration where the securities are *transferred*; or
(c) of the *value* of the securities, in any other case. [*FA 1986, s 93(4); FA 1996, s 194*].

Before 20 October 1997 transfers by qualified dealers attracted a reduced rate of 1% when transferring chargeable securities otherwise than on sale into depository receipts but this relief has been withdrawn. [*FA 1986, s 93(5); FA 1997 s 104*].

The person liable to pay the reserve tax is the issuer of the depositary receipts except where securities are *transferred* and the issuer is not resident in the UK and has no UK branch or agency in which case the transferee is liable for the tax. [*FA 1986, s 93(8)(9)*].

There is no charge to tax under *s 93* in the following circumstances:

(a) a transfer of securities between corporate nominees whose businesses are exclusively that of holding 'relevant securities' as nominees for an issuer of depositary receipts, but this exception is disapplied if the securities are issued to an EU system where there are arrangements for the securities to be subsequently transferred to a non-EU system [*FA 1986, ss 95(1) and 97C*];
(b) the *issue, transfer*, or *appropriation* of an inland bearer instrument except in the case of:
    (i) a renounceable letter of allotment where the rights are renounceable no later than six months after issue; or
    (ii) an instrument within the exemption from stamp duty on bearer instruments for non-sterling stock (see **24.7**(*a*) **Exemptions**) which does not raise new capital and is not issued in exchange for an instrument raising new capital (the tax charge arising does not apply to an instrument giving effect to an agreement for a company merger or takeover entered into in writing by the companies involved before 30 January 1999). [*FA 1986, s 95(2), (2A)–(2D)* and amended by *FA 1999, Sch 16, para 7* and see also the relief for replacement securities in new *FA 1986, s 95A* inserted by *FA 1999, s 118*];

(c) the *issue* by one company of securities in exchange for shares in another company where the first company has control of the second (or will have control as a result of the share for share exchange) and the shares in the second company are held within a depositary receipt scheme. Shares issued under a scheme of arrangement where the shares of the target company are cancelled are still treated for these purposes as having been issued in exchange for shares in the target. [*FA 1986, s 95(3); FA 1998, s 151*]; and

(d) the transfer, issue or appropriation of replacement securities in place of existing securities held under a depositary receipt scheme to the extent that the value of the new securities does not exceed the value of the old securities. [*FA 1986, s 95A; FA 1999, s 118*].

(e) UK depositary interests in foreign securities. [*FA 1999, s 119* and the *Stamp Duty Reserve Tax (UK Depositary Interests in Foreign Securities Regulations 1999 (SI 1999 No 2383* and amending regulations *SI 2000 No 1871)*]. See **84 Stamp Duty Reserve Tax.**

(f) the transfer of securities between a **Clearance Services (33)** system and a depositary receipt scheme and vice versa, but this exception is disapplied if the securities are issued into an EU system where there are arrangements for the securities to be subsequently transferred to a non-EU system. [*FA 1986, ss 97B and 97C*].

Chapter 46

Duplicate or Counterpart

Note: Stamp duty on duplicates and counterparts has been abolished to the same extent as on principal instruments. [*FA 2003, s 125(5)* as amended].

[46.1] Duplicates or counterparts of any instrument chargeable to duty were liable for a fixed duty of £5. However this fixed duty has been abolished for instruments executed on or after 13 March 2008 except for instruments effecting a land transaction. [*FA 1999, Sch 13 para 19(1) and FA 2008, Sch 32 paras 10(3)(d) and 22*].

A duplicate or counterpart (other than the counterpart of a lease not executed by or on behalf of the lessor or grantor) is not deemed duly stamped unless it is stamped as an original instrument or bears a stamp denoting that the correct duty has been paid on the original document. [*FA 1999, Sch 13 para 19(2)*]. See **44.1 Duty Paid Denoting Stamp**.

Chapter 47

Evidence

[47.1] An unstamped or insufficiently-stamped document will not be admitted as evidence in any civil proceedings, even for a collateral purpose (*Fengl v Fengl* PDA, [1914] P 274), nor will secondary evidence thereof (*Rippiner v Wright* KB, (1819) 2 B & Ald 478). Because *SA 1891, s 14(4)* provides that an instrument should not be available for any purpose whatever unless duly stamped, an unstamped copy of a declaration of trust executed and retained outside the UK, or an abstract or the recitals were also inadmissible in civil proceedings, and the rule prohibiting the admission of secondary evidence had a similar effect. (*Parinv (Hatfield) Ltd v IRC* CA [1998] STC 305). If an instrument is within *s 14* it does not matter why and there is no sub-rule that the instrument may be used against the party who ought to have got it stamped but did not (*Re Brown & Root McDermott Fabricators Ltd's and another's application* Ch D [1996] STC 483). It has been held that a claimant for capital allowances who is unable to prove that he has legal title to equipment due to the inadmissibility of an unstamped bill for sale could nevertheless prove the necessary ownership in equity by showing that he became the beneficial owner of the equipment under the terms of the relevant acquisition agreement and by reference to the conduct and intention of the parties. [*BMBF (No 24) Ltd v IRC* [2002] EWHC 2466 (Ch), [2002] STC 1450]. It is considered that this decision is questionable in that the court did not appear to consider the best evidence rule under which the claimant should have been required to produce the best evidence, namely the bill of sale proving legal title in order to prove ownership. Although the strict rules of evidence do not apply in proceedings before the Special Commissioners, had the court taken notice of this rule of evidence the claimant would not have been allowed to rely on lesser evidence in the form of the non-stampable agreement and the parties' conduct to prove ownership. In failing to apply this rule the Court undermined the statutory policy enshrined in *SA 1891, s 14(4)* which is the principal means by which the payment of stamp duty is enforced.

Where the wrong stamp has been used, the instrument is not duly stamped and will not be admitted in evidence (*Ashling v Boon* Ch D, [1891] 1 Ch 568 where an adhesive postage stamp appropriate to a receipt had been used on an instrument which should have been stamped with an appropriated 'bill or note' stamp). However, if the instrument may be stamped after execution (see **74.1 Date of Stamping and Payment**), it may be received in evidence on payment to the Court of the duty and any interest or penalty plus £1. [*SA 1891, s 14(1), FA 1999, Sch 12, para 3(2)*].

Notwithstanding the statutory provisions, it has been the practice of the court to allow an unstamped document to be used on the personal undertaking by the solicitors to stamp it (see e.g. *Re Coolgardie Goldfields Ltd* Ch D, [1900] 1 Ch 475) though doubt has been cast on this practice where deliberate disregard of the stamp duty legislation is involved (*Lloyds and Scottish Finance Ltd v Prentice* CA (1977), 121 Sol Jo 847). Prior to August 2001 the General Council of the Bar regarded a stamp duty objection as unprofessional except in a revenue case or where the stamping defect went to the root of the validity of the document. It appears from the August 2001 edition of the Bar Council's in-house magazine that this rule has been revoked as obsolete after consulting the Chancery judges and indeed, it is now arguably the duty of counsel to advise his client of the fact that a stamping objection is open for him to make or that the other side may be able to do so.

An unstamped or insufficiently-stamped document is admissible in evidence in criminal cases. (See *Saunders v Edwards* CA, [1987] 2 All ER 651.)

Chapter 48

Exchange or Partition

[48.1] For instruments executed after 7 December 1993, stamp duty under the head 'Exchange or excambion' and *SA 1891, s 73* has ceased to apply to the exchange of freehold property. Instead, *FA 1994, s 241* now treats exchanges of freehold property and other interests in land as liable to ad valorem duty as a **CONVEYANCE OR TRANSFER (39)** on sale. For an explanation of this change and how in practice the Inland Revenue will permit a double charge of duty to be avoided see **36.7 EXCHANGES OF PROPERTY**.

For the position regarding instruments executed before 8 December 1993 see the third edition of this work.

In the case of a partition or division of any estate or interest in land where consideration exceeding £100 is paid or given, ad valorem duty is charged on the consideration at the rate applicable to a **CONVEYANCE OR TRANSFER (39)** on sale. The nil rate and reduced rates of duty are available if a **CERTIFICATE OF VALUE (30)** is given in respect of the consideration. Where a sum in respect of value added tax is paid on a partition, the Stamp Office treats this payment as equality money. [*FA 1999, Sch 13, para 21(1)*].

In any other case a partition was charged with a fixed duty of £5. However, this fixed duty has been abolished generally for instruments executed on or after 13 March 2008 although the charge has been retained for instruments effecting a land transaction. [*FA 1999, Sch 13 para 21(3) and FA 2008, Sch 32 paras 10(a) and 22*]. Although a partition is not a sale (*Henniker v Henniker* QB (1852), 1 E & B 54) it is important that following *FA 1994, s 241*, a partition of land is not drafted as an exchange of beneficial interests in jointly owned property because this may be treated by the Stamp Office as series of sales and liable to ad valorem duty on each leg. (See **36.7 EXCHANGES OF PROPERTY**).

The partition of any property other than an estate or interest in land is no longer liable to a fixed duty of £5 even if there is equality money. [*FA 1999, Sch 13, para 21(2) and FA 2008, Sch 32 para 10(c)*].

Chapter 49

Execution

[49.1] In the case of instruments not under seal, execution means signing. [*SA 1891, s 122(1)*]. However, if execution is truly conditional, as with a document executed and delivered in escrow, the execution is not operative until the condition has been fulfilled (*Terrapin International Ltd v CIR* Ch D, [1976] 2 All ER 461; *Crane Fruehauf Ltd v CIR* Ch D, [1974] 1 All ER 811). This has been confirmed by *SA 1891, s 122(1A)* which treats a deed as executed when it is delivered, or if delivered subject to conditions, when the conditions are fulfilled. [*FA 1994, s 239*]. This is to be distinguished from the case where execution is operative immediately so that the contract becomes legally effective but performance of the contract is subject to a condition. In such cases the stamp duty liability arises upon execution notwithstanding that performance has not yet occurred due to the non-fulfilment of the condition. If the contract is not substantially performed or is rescinded there is provision for repayment of the duty. [*FA 1999, Sch 13, para 9*]. The Stamp Office normally accepts as the date of execution of an instrument the date appearing on its face; and see **40 Court Orders**.

The date of execution is relevant, inter alia, to the time of payment of duty (see **74.1 Date of Stamping and Payment**); for the importance of place of execution see **31 Chargeability**.

Chapter 50

Exempt Instruments

[50.1] Numerous heads of charge in *SA 1891, Sch 1* were abolished by subsequent Finance Acts prior to the restatement of *Sch 1* in *FA 1999*, *Sch 13*. In addition to outright repeals of heads of charge there are exemptions contained within the existing charges, e.g. the exemptions from bearer instrument duty in *FA 1999*, *Sch 15*, *Part II*. There are also some general exemptions from all stamp duties, e.g. the instruments mentioned in *FA 1999*, *Sch 13*, *Part IV*. There are also the various exemptions and reliefs such as those relating to **ASSOCIATED COMPANIES (23)**, **COMPANY REORGANISATIONS (34)** and **LOAN CAPITAL AND DEBENTURES (66)** for example. There is also a general exemption for conveyances, transfers or leases to a Minister of the Crown or to the Treasury Solicitor. [*FA 1987, s 55*].

Exempt Instruments Regulations

[50.2] [*Stamp Duty (Exempt Instruments) Regulations 1987 (SI 1987 No 516)*].

In addition to the above exemptions, the Treasury has made regulations under *FA 1985, s 87* which apply to certain instruments executed on or after 1 May 1987 which would normally attract a fixed £5 duty. Instruments which have been correctly certified under the regulations are exempt from the fixed £5 duty and do not have to be presented to the Commissioners either for payment of duty or for **ADJUDICATION (13)**. They can be sent direct to registrars for recording and registration. Although a registrar is always entitled to require an **ADJUDICATION (13)** it is understood that the Land Registry for example will accept a certified instrument for registration without requiring **ADJUDICATION (13)**, so long as it appears to fall within one of the categories specified in the schedule to the regulations and the certificate has been given properly (see below).

Not all instruments attracting a fixed £5 duty can be dealt with by certification. Only the instruments of a kind specified in the schedule to the regulations are exempt and those are instruments effecting any one or more of the following transactions only:

(a) The vesting of property subject to a trust in the trustees of the trust on the appointment of a new trustee, or in the continuing trustees on the retirement of a trustee.
(b) The conveyance or transfer of property the subject of a specific devise or legacy to the beneficiary named in the will (or his nominee).
(c) The conveyance or transfer of property which forms part of an intestate's estate to the person entitled on intestacy (or his nominee).

(d) The appropriation of property within *s 84(4)* of the *Finance Act 1985* (death: appropriation in satisfaction of a general legacy of money) or *s 84(5)* or *(7)* of that Act (death: appropriation in satisfaction of any interest of surviving spouse and in Scotland also of any interest of issue).

(e) The conveyance or transfer of property which forms part of the residuary estate of a testator to a beneficiary (or his nominee) entitled solely by virtue of his entitlement under the will.

(f) The conveyance or transfer of property out of a settlement in, or towards satisfaction of, a beneficiary's interest, not being an interest acquired for money or money's worth, being a conveyance or transfer constituting a distribution of property in accordance with the provisions of the settlement.

(g) The conveyance or transfer of property on and in consideration only of marriage to a party to the marriage (or his nominee) or to trustees to be held on the terms of a settlement made in consideration only of the marriage.

(h) The conveyance or transfer of property within *s 83(1)* of the *Finance Act 1985* (transfers in connection with divorce etc).

(i) The conveyance or transfer by the liquidator of property which formed part of the assets of the company in liquidation to a shareholder of that company (or his nominee) in or towards satisfaction of the share holder's rights on a winding-up.

(j) The grant in fee simple of an easement in or over land for no consideration in money or money's worth.

(k) The grant of a servitude for no consideration in money or money's worth.

(l) The conveyance or transfer of property operating as a voluntary disposition inter vivos for no consideration in money or money's worth nor any consideration referred to in *s 57* of the *Stamp Act 1891* (conveyance in consideration of a debt etc.).

(m) The conveyance or transfer of property by an instrument within *s 84(1)* of the *Finance Act 1985* (death: varying disposition).

Note. Declarations of trust within life insurance policies have been brought within the exemption as a new Category N from 1 October 1999 by *SI 1999 No 2539* and thereby avoid the fixed £5 duty which would have otherwise arisen as announced by IR Press Release 112/99.

The form of wording of the certificate suggested by the Commissioners is: 'I/We hereby certify that this instrument falls within category . . . in the *Schedule* to the *Stamp Duty (Exempt Instruments) Regulations 1987*'.

This certificate should be included in, endorsed on, or attached to the instrument. Where the certificate is endorsed after the instrument is executed the certificate must also contain a description of the instrument, e.g. title, date, parties and property passing. In the case of a **CONVEYANCE OR TRANSFER (39)** of land the Commissioners prefer the certificate to be included in or endorsed on the instrument and not attached to it. Endorsement on the reverse of a share transfer is acceptable to the Commissioners. The certificate should be signed by the transferor or grantor or his solicitor or duly authorised agent such as a licensed conveyancer, accountant etc. Where the certificate is not signed by the transferor, grantor or his solicitor, it should contain a statement of the capacity in which the signatory signs, that he is authorised to sign and that he gives the certificate from his own knowledge of the facts stated in it.

Various instruments which transfer property otherwise than on sale and which attract the fixed £5 duty are not covered by the regulations and remain liable to duty. Examples include:

- transfers from a beneficial owner to his nominee and vice versa and transfers between nominees for the same beneficial owner;
- transfers by way of security for a loan or retransfer on repayment of the loan; and
- transfers from the trustees of a Profit Sharing Scheme to a participant.

See also **19.3**(*c*) **INLAND REVENUE PRACTICE**.

Disadvantaged areas

[50.3] For the exemptions relating to land in designated disadvantaged areas see **6 RELIEFS AND EXEMPTIONS** and **APPENDIX D**. [*FA 2001, s. 92, 92A and 92B* and *Sch. 30* and also the *Stamp Duty (Disadvantaged Areas) (Application of Exemptions) Regulations 2003, SI 2003 No 1056* effective from 10 April 2003]. The exemption for non-residential land was withdrawn in relation to instruments executed after 16 March 2005. [*F(No 2)A 2005, s 96* and *Sch 9*].

Chapter 51

Extra-Statutory Concessions

Note: From 29 April 1996 the concessions in **51.1** and **51.2** were enacted in *SDMA 1891, s 12A*, inserted by *FA 1996, Sch 39, para 10(1), (3)*. (See **73.3 Allowance for Spoiled Stamps and Lost or Spoiled Instruments**.) [Extra-Statutory Concessions—Revenue booklet IR 1 as at 10 August 2009].

Stamp allowance on lost documents

[51.1] Allowance of the stamp duty on lost documents is made either by repayment, where replicas have been stamped, or by free stamping of the replicas.

Stamping of replicas of documents which have been spoilt or lost

[51.2] Where the stamp duty is allowed on a document because it has been spoilt or lost and replaced by a replica but the duty has been increased so that the amount to be impressed on the replica is more than the amount allowable on the original, the additional duty is impressed free of charge.

Transfer of stock from persons to themselves operating as an executors' assent

[51.3] Stamp duty is not claimed on a transfer of stock in a company registered in England, Wales or Northern Ireland from a person to himself (or from two or more persons to themselves) which operates as an executors' assent. The point does not arise in relation to companies registered in Scotland. See **22 Assents**.

Transfer of assets between non-profit making bodies with similar objects

[51.4] When the reconstruction of a non-profit making body with objects in a field of public interest such as education, community work or scientific research, or the amalgamation of two or more such bodies involves a transfer to the successor body of assets for which there passes no consideration in money or money's worth, the instruments of transfer are treated as exempt from ad valorem stamp duty and charged 50p [£5] fixed duty only. There must be sufficient identity between the members of the transferor and transferee bodies. The rules of both must prohibit the distribution of assets to members and provide that on a winding-up the assets can only be transferred to a similar body subject to like restrictions.

Chapter 52

Failure to Stamp

[52.1] In general, stamp duties, which are chargeable on instruments, are not recoverable by the Commissioners by direct recovery procedures. Exemptions to this rule are dealt with at **74.2 Liability for Duty and Penalties**.

Enforcement of the duties is achieved by providing that an instrument is not to be given in **Evidence (46)** or to be available for any purpose whatever unless it is duly stamped in accordance with the law in force at the time when it was executed. [*SA 1891, s 14(4)*]. An unstamped instrument which was chargeable to duty could not be used in civil proceedings even during the 30-day period of grace permitted by *SA 1891, s 15(3)(a)* (see **74.1**(*c*) **Date of Stamping and Payment**). (*Parinv (Hatfield) Ltd v IRC* Ch D CA [1998] STC 305). In addition, the enrolment or registration of an instrument not duly stamped gives rise to a penalty not exceeding £300, but the enrolment is not a nullity and provided that the registrar acts in good faith, the Commissioners may not wish to enforce recovery of the penalty (*Re Brown & Root McDermott Fabricators Ltd's application* Ch D [1996] STC 483). [*SA 1891, s 17*; *FA 1999, Sch 17, para 3(5)*]. It has been held that a claimant for capital allowances who is unable to prove that he has legal title to equipment due to the inadmissibility of an unstamped bill for sale could nevertheless prove the necessary ownership in equity by showing that it became the beneficial owner of the equipment under the terms of the relevant acquisition agreement and by reference to the conduct and intention of the parties. [*BMBF (No 24) Ltd v IRC* [2002] EWHC 2466 (Ch), [2002] STC 1450]. It is considered that this decision is questionable in that the court did not appear to consider the best evidence rule under which the claimant should have been required to produce the best evidence, namely the bill of sale proving legal title in order to prove ownership. Had the court taken notice of this rule of evidence the claimant would not have been allowed to rely on lesser evidence in the form of the non-stampable agreement and the parties' conduct to prove ownership. In failing to apply this rule the court undermined the statutory policy enshrined in *SA 1891, s 14(4)* which is the principal means by which the payment of stamp duty is enforced.

Conditions precluding stamp duty objections or agreements for undertaking liability in the event of absence or insufficiency of stamp are void. [*SA 1891, s 117*].

Instruments (60) may generally be stamped late on payment of general penalties and interest (see **74.1 Payment of Duty or Tax (Date of Stamping and Payment)**) and specific **Penalties (75)** may arise.

In relation to agreements for the sale of shares or securities **Stamp Duty Reserve Tax (84)** arises and is only cancelled when an instrument transferring the shares or securities to the purchaser or his nominee is executed and duly stamped. In practice, the Stamp Office will not seek interest if a duly stamped instrument is produced within 60 days of the transaction and no notice of liability to the tax needs to be given in the meantime. However, interest and penalties may be charged from 7 days after the end of the month in which the transaction occurred if the 60-day concessionary period is exceeded and it appears that a transfer instrument will not be produced for stamping. This treatment is explained in the Inland Revenue Tax Bulletin October 1998 reproduced in **APPENDIX D**. See the Stamp Taxes Manual (March 2002) para 13.18 and **84.6–84.8 STAMP DUTY RESERVE TAX**.

Chapter 53

Family Arrangements and Divorce

Family Arrangements

[53.1] Ad valorem duty on a **CONVEYANCE OR TRANSFER (39)** on sale is not chargeable on an instrument which varies a disposition of property effected by a will or under the law of intestacy or otherwise within two years after a person's death. The instrument can be executed by all or any of the persons who benefit or would benefit under the dispositions. The exemption does not apply where the variation is made for any consideration in money or money's worth other than consideration consisting of the variation of another of the dispositions. The exemption applies whether or not the administration of the estate is complete or the property distributed according to the original dispositions. [*FA 1985, s 84(1)–(3)*].

Where property is appropriated by a personal representative in or towards satisfaction of a general legacy of money, no ad valorem duty is chargeable. Also, ad valorem duty is not charged in an intestacy on the appropriation of property by a personal representative for clearing any interest of the surviving spouse in the intestate's estate. This includes the capital value of a life interest elected to be redeemed under the *Intestates' Estates Act 1952*. [*FA 1985, s 84(4)–(6)*]. See **22 ASSENTS**.

In order for the instrument to be exempt from ad valorem duty it used to be necessary to have it adjudicated and stamped with a fixed £5 duty. [*FA 1985, s 84(8)(9)*]. Now, under the *Stamp Duty (Exempt Instruments) Regulations 1987 (SI 1987 No 516)* such instruments do not have to be produced to the Stamp Office for stamping or **ADJUDICATION (13)** provided they are properly certified in accordance with the regulations. See **50 EXEMPT INSTRUMENTS.**

The above requirement of either fixed duty plus adjudication or certification has been abolished for instruments executed on or after 13 March 2008 but has been retained for instruments effecting a land transaction [*FA 2008, Sch 32 paras 3 and 22*].

Divorce

[53.2] Ad valorem duty on a **CONVEYANCE OR TRANSFER (39)** on sale is not chargeable on an instrument by which property is conveyed or transferred from one party to a marriage to the other. This is provided that the instrument is executed for one or more of the following reasons:

(a) a court order made on granting a divorce, annulment of marriage or judicial separation;

(b) a court order made in connection with the dissolution or annulment of a marriage or a judicial separation and the court order is made at any time after the dissolution, annulment or separation;

(c) a court order made under *ss 22A, 23A* or *24A* of the *Matrimonial Causes Act 1973*;

(d) an agreement made between the parties in contemplation of or otherwise in connection with the dissolution or annulment of their marriage or judicial separation. [*FA 1985, s 83(1); Family Law Act 1996, s 66(1)*].

Similar exceptions are also available in respect of civil partnerships. [*FA 1985, s 85(1A)*].

The instrument was formerly liable to a fixed £5 duty unless certified. [*FA 1985, s 83(2)*]. See **50 Exempt Instruments**. However this fixed duty was abolished generally for instruments executed on or after 13 March 2008 but has been retained for instruments effecting a land transaction. [*FA 2008, Sch 32 paras 2 and 22*].

Chapter 54

Fixed Duties

[54.1] Fixed duties are those charged without regard to the value of the transaction. For duties calculated by reference to value, see **15 Ad Valorem Duties**. Many obsolete fixed duties were abolished by *FA 1985, s 85, Sch 24*, including the 50p duties on the appointment of a new trustee, deeds of covenant, deeds and powers of attorney. For instruments executed on or after 1 October 1999 the amount of every fixed duty is £5. [*FA 1999, s 112(2)*].

The fixed duty most commonly met was the miscellaneous **Conveyance or Transfer (39)** duty of £5. The practical importance of this duty was greatly diminished by the *Stamp Duty (Exempt Instruments) Regulations 1987 (SI 1987 No 516)*. See **50 Exempt Instruments**. This fixed duty together with most other fixed duties were abolished for instruments executed on or after 13 March 2008, although these have been retained for instruments effecting a pre-SDLT land transaction. [*FA 2008, Sch 32*].

Other fixed duties dealt with in this book are:

Heading	*Duty on instruments liable to fixed duty executed before 1 October 1999*	*Duty on instruments liable to fixed duty executed on or after 1 October 1999 but before 13 March 2008*
Clearance Services (33)	50p	
Declaration of Trust (42)	50p	
Depositary Receipts (45)	50p	
Duplicate or Counterpart (46)	50p	
Exchange or Partition (48)	50p	£5
Family Arrangements and Divorce (53)	50p	
Leases (64)—small furnished lettings	£1	
Leases (64)—miscellaneous	£2	
Release and Renunciation (80)	50p	
Surrenders (85)	50p	

Chapter 55

Flotations, etc.

[55.1] The abolition of **CAPITAL DUTY (29)** by *FA 1988, s 141* removed not only a potential charge to capital duty on the raising of share capital but also the need to structure the arrangements in particular ways in order to attract exemption from capital duty where available. For example, it was often necessary to avoid the use of renounceable letters of allotment and to ensure that the consideration shares allotted were actually issued and registered in the names of the vendors (see *Tillotson v CIR* CA, [1933] 1 KB 134). It is still necessary to consider the impact of **STAMP DUTY RESERVE TAX (84)** in connection with agreements to transfer renounceable letters of allotment and acceptance. Such agreements are a feature of flotations etc. and careful attention must be paid to each step in a particular transaction in order to ascertain whether a tax charge can arise and if so whether it is possible to alter the arrangements to avoid the charge. What follows examines some of the types of transactions commonly met.

Offers for sale

[55.2] An offer for sale of new shares for cash involves the issue by the company raising share capital of a nil paid renounceable letter of allotment to the issuing house. The nil paid renounceable letter of allotment will be deemed to become fully paid as soon as the admission of the company's shares to the Official List of the Stock Exchange comes into effect. The issuing house issues fully paid renounceable letters of acceptance to the applicants and dealings in these letters then occur. Once the renunciation period has ended the issuing house renounces its letter of allotment in favour of the ultimate holders of the renounceable letters of acceptance who will become the registered shareholders. Stamp duty reserve tax is charged on each sale of the renounceable letters of acceptance during the renunciation period. Stamp duty reserve tax is not charged on the issue of the renounceable letters of acceptance by the issuing house provided the conditions of *FA 1986, s 89A(2)* are met (see **55.6** below). No other stamp duty or stamp duty reserve tax charges should arise.

An offer for sale by the existing shareholders may involve the allotment of bonus shares to the existing shareholders represented by fully paid renounceable letters of allotment. The issuing house will purchase the renounceable letters of allotment and issue renounceable letters of acceptance to the applicants and dealings in these letters may then occur. Once the renunciation period has ended the ultimate holders of the renounceable letters of acceptance will become the registered shareholders. Stamp duty reserve tax is not charged on the purchase by the issuing house of the renounceable letters of allotment provided the conditions of *FA 1986, s 89A(1)* are met (see **55.6** below). Nor is stamp duty reserve tax charged on the issue of the renounceable letters of acceptance provided the conditions of *FA 1986, s 89A(2)* are met. The tax is charged on each sale of the renounceable letters of acceptance during the renunciation period. No other stamp duty or stamp duty reserve tax charges should arise.

An offer for sale by the existing shareholders may involve the sale of their existing shares in addition to or instead of the sale of newly allotted bonus shares (see above). The issuing house agrees to purchase the existing shares from the shareholders who grant powers of attorney to enable the issuing house to transfer the shares to whoever the issuing house nominates. The issuing house issues renounceable letters of acceptance to the applicants and dealings in those letters may then occur. Once the renunciation period has ended, the ultimate holders of the renounceable letters of acceptance will become the new registered shareholders. Stamp duty reserve tax is not charged on the purchase of the shares by the issuing house provided the conditions of *FA 1986, s 89A(1)* are met (see **55.6** below). Nor is there a stamp duty reserve tax charge on the issue of the renounceable letters of acceptance by the issuing house so long as the conditions of *FA 1986, s 89A(3)* are met (see **55.6** below). The tax is charged on each sale of the renounceable letters of allotment during the renunciation period. Stamp duty will be charged on the transfer of the shares themselves from the existing shareholders to the original applicants or where the letters of acceptance have been renounced, to the ultimate renouncees of the letters of acceptance. Where a renounceable letter of acceptance has been retained by the applicant for the shares, and in due course the shares are transferred to him, there will have been no stamp duty reserve tax charge and the only charge will be a stamp duty charge on the share transfer calculated according to the average market price of the shares during the renunciation period. However, where the renounceable letters of acceptance have been sold, stamp duty reserve tax will have been charged on each sale, including the sale to the ultimate renouncee, but stamp duty will also be charged on the transfer of the shares themselves to the ultimate renouncee. This problem is sometimes referred to as 'the double hit' and occurs because *FA 1986, s 88(2)(3)* does not permit the stamp duty on the share transfer to cancel the stamp duty reserve tax charge on the sale of the letter of acceptance to the ultimate renouncee (see **84 Stamp Duty Reserve Tax**). In particular cases the vendor may agree to bear the stamp duty charge and this will be stated in the relevant prospectus.

Rights issues

[55.3] A rights issue will involve the issue by the company concerned of fully paid renounceable letters of allotment or nil paid provisional renounceable letters of allotment to the existing shareholders. Once the renunciation period has ended the ultimate holders of the renounceable letters of allotment will become the registered holders of the new shares. Stamp duty reserve tax is charged on each sale of the renounceable letters of allotment during the renunciation period according to the price paid by each renouncee. No stamp duty reserve tax or stamp duty is charged on the issue of the renounceable letters of allotment or on the issue of the shares themselves at the end of the renunciation period.

Vendor placings

[55.4] A vendor placing occurs when an acquiring company acquires the shares (or undertaking) of an unlisted company from the vendors in consideration of the allotment to the vendors of shares in the acquiring company. The vendors will then sell these shares in the market with the assistance of an issuing house. Following the abolition of capital duty there is normally no need to issue consideration shares to the vendors which was a necessary condition for obtaining capital duty exemption; it is sufficient to allot the consideration shares on renounceable letters of allotment. No stamp duty arises on the issue of the renounceable letters of allotment to the vendors. Stamp duty reserve tax may not be charged on the purchase of the renounceable letters of allotment by the issuing house for sale to the placees provided the conditions of *FA 1986, s 89A(1)* are met. In particular it appears that the Revenue have not yet reached a firm view on whether a vendor placing can be regarded as an 'offer to the public' (see **55.6** below). Stamp duty reserve tax is charged on any sale of the renounceable letters of allotment during the renunciation period. No stamp duty or stamp duty reserve tax charges arise on the registration of the holders as members of the company at the end of the renunciation period. Stamp duty will normally be charged on the transfer of the shares or assets of the target company to the acquiring company.

Underwriting

[55.5] The underwriting of shares can give rise to stamp duty and stamp duty reserve tax charges. See **87 UNDERWRITING**.

Exceptions for public issues

[55.6] An unintended effect of the introduction of stamp duty reserve tax was to impose additional tax charges in connection with flotations and new issues where an issuing house, acting traditionally as principal, bought and sold shares or renounceable letters of allotment or acceptance as part of the arrangements. This quickly led to issuing houses acting as 'agents to procure' purchasers and subscribers rather than as principals in order to avoid the stamp duty reserve tax charges that would apply if they acted as principals. HMRC treats only the principals and not their agents in a transaction as being A or B for the purpose of *FA 1986, s 87*. However, when an issuing house acts as agent rather than as principal, members of the public are not offered a common root of title i.e. the issuing house, and instead face the risk of the vendors having a bad title or going bankrupt or dying. In an attempt to solve the problem *FA 1986, s 89A* (inserted by *F(No 2)A 1987, s 100*) provides that stamp duty reserve tax shall not apply where the issuing house acts as principal as regards the following:

(a) an agreement to transfer securities other than units under a unit trust scheme to B or B's nominee if:

- (i) the agreement is part of an arrangement entered into by B in the ordinary course of B's business as an issuing house under which B is to offer the securities for sale to the public;
- (ii) the agreement is conditional upon the admission of the securities to the Official List of the Stock Exchange;
- (iii) the consideration under the agreement for each security is the same as the price at which B is to offer the security for sale; and
- (iv) B sells the securities in accordance with the arrangement referred to in (i) above.

This is intended to except from stamp duty reserve tax the purchase by the issuing house of existing registered shares or fully paid renounceable letters of allotment representing bonus shares held by existing shareholders as part of an offer for sale (see **55.2** above).

(b) an agreement if the securities to which the agreement relates are newly subscribed securities other than units in a unit trust scheme and:
- (i) the agreement is made in pursuance of an offer to the public made by A under an arrangement entered into in the ordinary course of A's business as an issuing house;
- (ii) a right of allotment in respect of, or to subscribe for, the securities has been acquired by A under an agreement which is part of the arrangement;
- (iii) both those agreements are conditional upon the admission of the securities to the Official List of the Stock Exchange; and
- (iv) the consideration for each security is the same under both agreements;

and for these purposes 'newly subscribed securities' are securities which in pursuance of the arrangement referred to in (i) above, are issued wholly for new consideration.

This is intended to except from the stamp duty reserve tax the issue of renounceable letters of acceptance by an issuing house to applicants for shares in an offer for sale of new shares (see **55.2** above).

(c) An agreement if the securities to which the agreement relates are registered securities other than units under a unit trust scheme and:
- (i) the agreement is made in pursuance of an offer to the public made by A;
- (ii) the agreement is conditional upon the admission of the securities to the Official List of the Stock Exchange, and
- (iii) under the agreement A issues to B or his nominee a renounceable letter of acceptance, or similar instrument, in respect of the securities.

This is intended to except from the stamp duty reserve tax the issue of renounceable letters of acceptance (by anyone, not just an issuing house) to applicants for shares in an offer for sale of existing registered shares (see **55.2** above).

Where it is sought to rely on one or more of the exceptions provided by *FA 1986, s 89A*, care should be exercised to ensure that all the relevant conditions are met. For example, there is some doubt as to whether *FA 1986, s 89A(1)* can apply in a vendor placing due to uncertainty as to whether a vendor placing involves an 'offer to the public'.

Chapter 56

Foreclosure

[56.1] A foreclosure order is charged to ad valorem duty as a **CONVEYANCE OR TRANSFER (39)** on sale. [*FA 1999, Sch 13, para 1(2); FA 1898, s 6*].

Ad valorem duty is not to be charged on a higher amount than the value of the property and if the value is stated in the order, that statement is conclusive for the calculation of ad valorem duty. The conveyance following the order is not liable to ad valorem duty if ad valorem duty has been paid on the order. [*FA 1898, s 6*].

Chapter 57

Furnished Lettings

[57.1] Duty is charged on furnished lettings under the **LEASES (64)** charge in *FA 1999*, *Sch 13*, *Part II*. It is charged as follows:

(a) Definite term of less than one year:
  (i) rent not exceeding £5,000—Nil;
  (ii) rent exceeding £5,000—fixed duty £5.

(b) Term exceeding one year or indefinite—ad valorem duty on rent and premium. For details of rates of duty and what constitutes rent and length of term, see **64 LEASES**.

An agreement for a furnished letting is liable as if it were an actual letting. [*FA 1999*, *Sch 13*, *para 14(1)*]. See **16 AGREEMENT FOR LEASE**.

Chapter 58

Gifts

[58.1] Ad valorem duty was charged by *F(1909–10)A 1910, s 74* on a **Conveyance or Transfer (39)** operating as a voluntary disposition inter vivos and calculated according to the value of the property conveyed; this charge was abolished by *FA 1985, s 82(1)*. However it was necessary to have the instrument stamped with a fixed 50p (now £5) duty as a **Conveyance or Transfer (39)** 'of any kind not hereinbefore described' and to submit it for **Adjudication (13)**. [*FA 1985, s 82(5)*].

The *Stamp Duty (Exempt Instruments) Regulations 1987 (SI 1987 No 516)* provided that a gift inter vivos which had been certified in accordance with the regulations was exempt from the fixed £5 duty and the requirement to submit it for **Adjudication (13)**. See **50 Exempt Instruments**. However, the requirement for either the payment of fixed duty and adjudication or certification was abolished generally for instruments executed on or after 13 March 2008 but has been retained for instruments effecting a land transaction. [*FA 2008, s 100*].

The exemption does not apply to a sale at an undervalue nor to a gift of property subject to a debt. See **39 Conveyance or Transfer**.

Chapter 59

Goodwill

[59.1] No stamp duty is chargeable on an instrument for the sale, transfer or other disposition of goodwill executed on or after 23 April 2002. [*FA 2002, s 116*]. In the case of an instrument that relates partly to goodwill and partly to other property, the consideration is apportioned on a just and reasonable basis and the instrument is chargeable only in respect of the consideration attributed to the other property. [*FA 2002, Sch 37, para 1*]. The amount attributed to goodwill is also disregarded for the purpose of deciding whether a **CERTIFICATE OF VALUE (30)** can be given. [*FA 2002, Sch 37, para 3*].

For instruments executed prior to 23 April 2002 the position was as follows.

Goodwill is property for the purposes of stamp duty (e.g. *Potter v CIR* Ex (1854), 10 Exch 147; *CIR v Muller & Co's Margarine Ltd* HL, [1901] AC 217). Liability on a transfer of goodwill would be attracted:

(a) on sale (see **39 CONVEYANCE OR TRANSFER**); or
(b) on an **AGREEMENT FOR SALE (17)** under *FA 1999, Sch 13, para 7*.

The following have been held liable to ad valorem duty:

(a) an agreement for the sale of goodwill, existing independently of the property to which it relates (*West London Syndicate v CIR* CA, [1898] 2 QB 507); and
(b) an agreement by a former proprietor not to operate a business in a specified area was held dutiable because it was equivalent to an agreement for the sale of goodwill (*Eastern National Omnibus Co v CIR* KB 1938, [1939] 1 KB 161).

Goodwill situated outside the UK did not attract duty if included in a sale agreement [*FA 1999, Sch 13, para 7(1)*] (see **16.1 AGREEMENT FOR SALE**), or in a **CONVEYANCE OR TRANSFER (39)** executed outside the UK [*SA 1891, s 14(4)*] (see **31 CHARGEABILITY**). For goodwill to be located outside the UK, both the business and the customers must be abroad (see *Benjamin Brooke & Co v CIR* QB, [1896] 2 QB 356; *CIR v Muller & Co's Margarine Ltd* HL, [1901] AC 217).

As a consequence of the abolition of stamp duty on instruments relating to intellectual property, the Revenue indicated, prior to the abolition of stamp duty on goodwill generally, that any goodwill inherent in such intellectual property was also to be regarded as exempt. [*FA 2000, s 129* and *Sch 34*].

Despite the abolition of stamp duty on goodwill and intellectual property stamp duty remains chargeable in respect of the sale of the benefit of contracts, trade debts and tenant's fixtures on instruments executed before 1 December 2003. [*FA 2003, s 125*].

For an analysis of the different types of goodwill and when goodwill may be treated as part of a sale of land, see **8 SPECIAL SITUATIONS**.

Chapter 60

Instruments

[60.1] Stamp duty is charged generally on instruments and not on individuals or transactions as such. [*FA 1999, Sch 13*] and see also Lord Hoffman's speech in *MacNiven v Westmoreland Investments Ltd* [2001] UKHL 6 [2001] STC 237. But see **31.1 CHARGEABILITY** for some exceptions to this principle where the tax can be assessed directly against persons.

'Instrument' is not fully defined, but includes every written document. [*SA 1891, s 122(1)*]. The following provisions apply to instruments:

(a) They must be written in such a way that the stamp may appear on the face of the instrument and cannot be used for any other instrument written on the same piece of material. [*SA 1891, s 3(1)*].

(b) More than one instrument may be written on the same piece of material but each instrument must be separately stamped with its own duty. [*SA 1891, s 3(2)*]. A memorandum endorsed on an assurance policy to rectify a mistake in the original was a separate instrument liable to duty (*Prudential Assurance Co Ltd v CIR* KB, [1935] 1 KB 101).

(c) All the facts and circumstances affecting the liability to duty must be set out in the instrument but a failure to do so is a mere irregularity and does not render the instrument a nullity (*Re Brown & Root McDermott Fabricators Ltd's application* Ch D [1996] STC 483). [*SA 1891, s 5*].

STAMP DUTY RESERVE TAX (84) is charged not on instruments but on oral and written agreements to transfer chargeable securities (as defined) for a consideration in money or money's worth. The tax is cancelled if an instrument transferring the securities to the purchaser is executed and duly stamped. [*FA 1986, ss 87, 92*].

For transactions that can be carried out without an instrument so as to avoid duty see **71 ORAL TRANSACTIONS**.

Chapter 61

Insurance Policies

[61.1] Insurance and reinsurance policies are no longer liable to stamp duty. Since *FA 1970* only policies of life insurance or assurance had been liable to duty and this remaining charge was abolished for instruments made after 31 December 1989 by *FA 1989, s 173*.

Assignments. The assignment of an insurance policy before 1 December 2003 may attract ad valorem duty as a **CONVEYANCE OR TRANSFER (39)** on sale (but see *Blandy v Herbert* KB, (1829) 9 B & C 396 where no duty was payable on the assignment of a policy of marine insurance under which no loss had occurred; cf. *Western Abyssinian Mining Syndicate Ltd v CIR* KB, (1935) 14 ATC 286). Alternatively, a £5 duty may have been attracted as a miscellaneous **CONVEYANCE OR TRANSFER (39)**. However, this fixed duty has been abolished for instruments executed on or after 13 March 2008. [*FA 2008, Sch 32 para 10(3)(a)*].

Declarations of trust of policy moneys executed before 1 December 2003, whether incorporated in any policy or executed separately, bear the £5 duty as a **DECLARATION OF TRUST (42)**, unless certified in accordance with the *Stamp Duty (Exempt Instruments) Regulations 1987 (SI 1987 No 516)* as amended by *SI 1999 No 2539* for documents relating to life policies executed on or after 1 October 1999. See **50.2 EXEMPT INSTRUMENTS REGULATIONS**.

Chapter 62

Ireland

Northern Ireland

[62.1] Until 1974, stamp duties in Northern Ireland were charged by separate legislation and administered by the Minister of Finance for Northern Ireland. From 1 January 1974 (inclusive) the responsibility for administering stamp duties rests with the Commissioners for HMRC. (See the *Northern Ireland Constitution Act 1973*, *Northern Ireland Act 1974* and *SI 1973 No 2163*, and **14 ADMINISTRATION**.)

Stamp duties prior to 1974 are found in Northern Ireland legislation. The duties charged are broadly the same as those described in this book but reference should be made to *SR & O 1922 No 80* (which applied *SA 1891* and *SDMA 1891*, as amended, to Northern Ireland) and subsequent *Finance (Northern Ireland) Acts*.

CAPITAL DUTY (29) was introduced for Northern Ireland in the same form as *FA 1973* and was abolished by *FA 1988, s 141*.

Republic of Ireland

[62.2] The Republic has its own stamp duties and UK stamp duties do not extend to that country. See **62.3** below.

Relief from double stamp duty

[62.3] Instruments chargeable with stamp duty in Great Britain, Northern Ireland and the Republic of Ireland are relieved from a double charge as follows:

(a) an instrument duly stamped in one country is deemed to be duly stamped to the extent of the duty it bears in the other country;
(b) but if a higher duty is charged in the other country the extra duty must be paid and denoted in the other country before it is duly stamped;
(c) where duty is paid by way of composition in one country, an instrument is treated in the other country as duly stamped with the amount of duty which would have been chargeable but for the composition. [*Government of Ireland Act 1920, s 29*; *SR & O 1923 No 406*; *Irish Free State (Consequential Provisions) Act 1922*; *Ireland Act 1949 and FA 1998, s 150*].

Chapter 63

Leading and Principal Object

[63.1] It is a basic principle of stamp duty law that an instrument is stamped for its leading and principal object and this stamp covers incidental and accessory matters (see e.g. *Limmer Asphalte Paving Co Ltd v CIR* Ex, (1872) LR 7 Exch 211). Accordingly, an exemption attaching to the leading and principal object should extend to any accessory matter.

If the instrument relates to *several distinct matters*, however, it is to be separately stamped for each matter. [*SA 1891, s 4(a)*].

Separate stamps have been required, inter alia, in the following cases:

(a) a lease with a contract for sale of fixtures (*Corder v Drakeford* CP, (1811) 3 Taunt 382);
(b) an instrument providing for both the sale and sub-sale of shares (*Fitch Lovell Ltd v CIR* Ch D, [1962] 3 All ER 685);
(c) an order which appointed new trustees to a charity and also vested the property in them (*Hadgett v CIR* Ex D, (1877) 3 Ex D 46);
(d) an instrument whereby separate properties were leased to different lessees (*Doe d Copley v Day* KB, (1811) 13 East 241);
(e) an instrument executed once as a lease and once as a conveyance on sale (*Brightman v CIR* Ex, (1868) 18 LT 412);
(f) a lease containing an option to purchase separate property (*Lovelock v Franklyn* QB, (1847) 8 QB 371);
(g) an instrument comprising both a lease and a distinct agreement by another to pay penalties in case of the lessee's breach of an exclusive purchase covenant (*Wharton v Walton* QB, (1845) 7 QB 474).

Separate stamps have not been required, inter alia, in the following cases:

(a) an instrument executed by more than one person where there is some common object or interest (e.g. *Baker v Jardine* QB, (1784) 13 East 235n);
(b) a surrender of a lease and grant of new leases (*Doe d Phillipps v Phillipps* QB, (1840) 11 Ad & E 796);
(c) a transfer by trustees to a life tenant following purchase of remainder-man's interest stamped as a conveyance on sale of the interest but not as a transfer of the bare legal estate (*Oughtred v CIR* HL, [1960] AC 206);
(d) a lease to joint tenants (*Cooper v Flynn* CP(1), (1841) 3 ILR 472);
(e) a lease containing an option to the tenant to purchase the leased property (*Worthington v Warrington* CP, (1848) 5 CB 635; cf. *Lovelock v Franklyn* above);
(f) a lease containing a guarantee of the payment of rent (*Price v Thomas* KB, (1831) 2 B & Ad 218; cf. *Wharton v Walton* above).

An instrument made for any consideration which is chargeable to ad valorem duty is separately charged in respect of any other valuable consideration. [*SA*

1891, s 4(b)]. For examples of the application of this see **64.1 LEASES**; **35.3**(*d*) **COMPULSORY PURCHASE OF LAND**.

SA 1891, s 4(b) can be excluded by express provisions, for example in relation to covenants to improve property (*FA 1900, s 10*, see **36.6 COVENANTS TO IMPROVE PROPERTY** and *SA 1891, s 77(2)*, see **64.3**(*b*) **DUTY ON PREMIUMS** and penal rents (*SA 1891, s 77(1)*, see **64.2**(*c*) **DUTY ON RENT**).

Chapter 64

Leases

Note: *FA 2003* abolished stamp duty on land and buildings including leases from (broadly) 1 December 2003 and in its place created stamp duty land tax—see Part One.

[64.1] Stamp duty on leases is charged under the heading 'Lease' in *FA 1999, Sch 13, Part II*. The charge applies only to land, tenements or heritable subjects and does not extend to leases of personalty.

A licence does not attract stamp duty and must be distinguished from a lease. A licence does not give exclusive possession of the property (e.g. *Taylor v Caldwell* QB, (1863) 3 B & S 826). See *Jones v CIR* QB, [1895] 1 QB 484 (agreement licensing installation of automatic washing machines not a lease); *Thames Conservators v CIR* QB, (1886) 18 QBD 279 (licence to construct and retain a jetty not a lease); *Shell-Mex and BP v Manchester Garages* CA, [1971] 1 All ER 841 (agreement in respect of a petrol station not a lease). See generally *Winter Garden Theatre (London) Ltd v Millennium Productions Ltd* HL 1947, [1948] AC 173, *Street v Mountford* HL, [1985] AC 809, and *National Car Parks Ltd v Trinity Development Co (Banbury) Ltd* CA [2001] EWCA Civ 1686 [2002] I P & CR D37.

An **AGREEMENT FOR LEASE (16)** is charged to duty as a lease for the term and consideration provided in the agreement. [*FA 1999, Sch 13, para 14*]. Leases executed on or after 6 May 1994 must either contain a certificate to the effect that there was no prior agreement, or be stamped with a stamp denoting either that the agreement is not chargeable with duty or the duty paid on the agreement. [*FA 1994, s 240A*]. See also **16 AGREEMENT FOR LEASE.**

Stamp duty is charged on both the rent and premium reserved in a lease (see **64.2** and **64.3** below). Where the instrument contains matters additional to the grant of a lease, it is necessary to consider whether additional duties are payable. See **63 LEADING AND PRINCIPAL OBJECT.**

A lease for no rent or premium and not in a form which attracts ad valorem duty under *FA 1994, ss 241* and *242* (see **64.2**(*c*) and **64.3**(*e*), (*f*) below), attracts a fixed duty of £5. [*FA 1999, Sch 13, para 13*].

Duty on rent

[64.2] [*FA 1999, Sch 13, Part II*].

(a) **FURNISHED LETTINGS (57)** for a definite term of less than one year bear no duty if the rent for the term does not exceed £5,000. Where the rent exceeds £5,000, duty of £5 is charged.
(b) Any other lease for a definite term or any indefinite term bears duty as follows.

Term	*Rate of Duty*
(1) Term less than 7 years or indefinite—	
(a) if the rent is £5,000 or less	Nil
(b) if the rent is more than £5,000	1%
(2) Term more than 7 years but not more than 35 years	2%
(3) Term more than 35 years but not more than 100 years	12%
(4) Term more than 100 years	24%

[*FA 1999*, *Sch 13*, *para 12(3)*].

A lease for a definite term of less than a year bears duty as a lease for a year at the rent reserved for the term.

Note. Due to a drafting error in *FA 1999, Sch 13*, leases of exactly 7 years were not subject to stamp duty on the rental element of the lease. Press Release 159/99 issued on 17 September 1999 announced that retrospective legislation charging stamp duty in such cases would be included in the Finance Bill 2000. For such leases executed on or after 1 October 1999, the taxpayer has the alternative of leaving the rental element unstamped until the new measures take effect in 2000 after the Budget resolutions and then stamping it without interest or penalty within 30 days of the Budget resolution; or of stamping the document immediately with the 1% duty to avoid any need to present the lease for stamping if and when the relevant Budget resolution is passed. This was confirmed by *FA 2000, s 116* and *Sch 32* which also corrected the drafting error.

(c) **Rent**

'Rent' is not defined, but is generally a payment reserved out of the land (*Hill v Booth* CA, [1930] 1 KB 381) as recompense paid by the tenant to the landlord for exclusive possession. The wording used by the parties is not conclusive (*Donellan v Read* KB, (1832) 3 B & Ad 899; *Duke of Westminster v Store Properties Ltd* Ch D, [1944] Ch 129; *Samuel v Salmon and Gluckstein Ltd* Ch D 1945, [1946] Ch 8).

Where a service charge is reserved as rent, it will bear duty as such (*Cox v Harper* Ch D, [1910] 1 Ch 480).

Where the amount of the rent reserved is unascertained, but the lease specifies a maximum rent, that amount will attract duty under the **CONTINGENCY PRINCIPLE (37)** (*Coventry City Council v CIR* Ch D, [1978] 1 All ER 1107). Under the contingency principle, unascertained rent would also be subject to duty if only a minimum rent or basic rent subject to adjustment is stated in the lease. Where no maximum, minimum or basic rent is stated and the rent is otherwise unascertainable then the contingency principle does not apply and the rent is taken to be the market rent at that time and duty is charged accordingly. [FA 1994, s 242(2)]. Note however, the effect of the decision of the Court of Appeal in *LM Tenancies 1 plc v CIR* [1998] STC 326 which has considerably widened the scope of the contingency principle and has thus reduced the situations in which the rent will be regarded as unascertainable where as a result the market value charge in FA 1994, s 242 could have been expected to apply. See **37 CONTINGENCY PRINCIPLE** for an explanation of this decision. See also **36.8 UNASCERTAINED AND CONTINGENT CONSIDERATION** and **64.2**(*e*)(vi) below.

Duty is not charged on penal rents reserved in a lease (additional rent payable in the case of the lessee's breach of covenant). [*SA 1891, s 77(1)*].

See **89 VAT AND STAMP DUTY** for the application of stamp duty where value added tax may be chargeable in relation to rent.

(d) **Stamp duty on leases with index-linked rents**

The Stamp Office's approach to the calculation of stamp duty on new leases where future rent levels are linked to an index was changed as from 14 May 1999. This change of practice was announced by Inland Revenue Press Release 98/99 and represents a major change in favour of the taxpayer. The Inland Revenue also announced that repayments of excessive amounts of stamp duty paid under their previous practice would be made to those taxpayers who submit a claim, not only within the normal two-year period from execution of the relevant lease, but also to taxpayers outside this period where the relevant lease was executed on or after 25 February 1995 (this is apparently the date when the first Parliamentary question was raised regarding the Revenue's previous practice).

(i) *Background.* The decision in *LM Tenancies 1 plc v CIR* [1998] STC 326 was concerned with the disposal of land for a consideration which was linked to the market value of a gilt some time after the date of the execution of the relevant instrument. It was argued by the taxpayer that on general principles, because the market value of the gilt in the future could not be known, the consideration was not ascertainable. The argument was rejected by both the High Court and the Court of Appeal who stated that a reference to, for example, the market value at a date in the future is to be taken as a reference to the market value of the property at the date when the instrument was executed. This was of course a novel principle of construction and a considerable extension of the powers of the Stamp Office. It was used by the Stamp Office, based on legal advice, to expand the application of the contingency principle to cases where the price or rent was linked to an index of prices such as the RPI in order to increase the amount of stamp duty payable.

The Stamp Office's initial approach where the property was leased for a rent and there was in the rental formula a provision that the rent should be increased, if appropriate, in line with the increase, if any, in the RPI for example, over successive periods of 20 years, was to charge stamp duty by reference to the rate of increase in RPI over the 20 years preceding the execution of the instrument, or (if this produced a better result) by reference to the increase in RPI over the 12 months preceding the instrument multiplied by 20.

As announced in a Parliamentary written answer on 6 November 1996, and also in the Stamp Office's November 1997 Newsletter, this approach was subsequently modified to take into account only the change in RPI over the 12 months ending with the date the document was executed. The previous approach had produced some bizarre results including a case involving a lease of sheltered accommodation for a premium of £68,000 and a ground rent of £300, to be reviewed every 21 years by reference to RPI, where the Stamp Office originally claimed approximately £65,000 stamp duty on the lease.

This new approach seemed in practice to be confined to leases, but in theory was wider-ranging and could have been applied in any situation where the consideration for the transfer of property consisted of the issue of some form of corporate bond or debt, the capital of which was linked to an index, and also to earn-outs where the previous profits of the business being sold could have been used to produce a figure for the earn-out element of the consideration formula. It was also apparent that the Stamp Office's practice appeared to vary between offices and in one part of the UK, colleagues have informed the author that this local office rarely, if ever, took the index-linking point when stamping leases.

(ii) *Change of Practice.* The Stamp Office has, however, taken fresh legal advice and Press Release 98/99 is the result. This states that:

> In future, where there is a formula expressed in the lease for rent reviews based on the RPI, only any change in the RPI up to the date of its execution will be taken into account for Stamp Duty purposes. This is expected to result, in most cases, in the average rent being little more than the initial rent.

Although this represents a welcome change of practice, the Press Release itself does not make it clear what will be the date from which changes in RPI will be taken into account before the date of execution of the lease in question. It seems obvious, however, that changes in RPI before the date of execution will now only be taken into account for the purposes of the stamp duty calculation where the lease in question specifies a period of time during which any RPI change is to be used in calculating the first rent review and that period of time commences before the date of execution of the lease. The Stamp Office has subsequently confirmed that this is the case and they have provided the following examples:

(A) 'A lease is executed on 1 January 1999. The term is specified as 99 years from 1 January 1998. There is no prior agreement for lease and the rent reviews are upward only. The first rent review is on 1 January 2000 by reference to the increase in RPI between the date of execution of the lease and the rent review date. In a document such as this, where the base date for the RPI calculation is on or after the date of execution of the lease, we would not apply any RPI increase. Since the rent review is upwards only, we would calculate the average annual rent for the period from 1 January 1999 to the end of the term, 31 December 2096 and apply the appropriate rate of stamp duty to that rent. The calculation would not include any RPI element.'

(B) 'Let us say now that the same lease had a rent review clause which specified the base date for the RPI calculation as 1 January 1998. It follows that the increase in RPI between 1 January 1998 and 1 January 1999 is known as at the date of execution of the lease. We will therefore apply the stamp duty contingency principle to the rent and assume that at the first review date the initial rent as at 1 January 1999 will increase on 1 January 2000 by the percentage change in RPI between 1 January 1998 and 1 January 1999. We will, of course, apply that increase by reference to the rent review formula used in the lease but if it was a straightforward increase in line with RPI, and RPI had increased, say, 3% in the period 1 January 1998 to 1 January 1999, we would say the contingency is that the rent at the first review will be the rent at 1 January 1999 increased by 3%. We will not apply any subsequent contingent increase in such a case.'

In simple terms, the change announced on 14 May 1999 means that no longer will RPI changes over the 12 months prior to execution automatically be taken into account as a guide to future rent increases. Only where there is RPI linkage (and the RPI base date occurs before execution) will the RPI changes be taken into account and then only up to the date of execution. This charge will be applied once only at the first rent review. Thus, the compounding effect of the previous practice where the RPI increase was applied at each rent review date will be eliminated.

(iii) *Agreements for lease.* Although the Press Release does not mention agreements for lease in this context, it seems that each document will be treated separately for these purposes. This means that where there is an agreement for lease followed by a lease in conformity with it, the stamp duty calculations for each may differ. This could arise where, at the date of execution of the agreement for lease, the relevant RPI period had not yet commenced (or only commenced upon execution), but when the lease came to be executed the RPI period had already begun, resulting in a higher amount of stamp duty on the lease.

(iv) *Stamp duty planning.* The simple message following this change of practice is that, where commercially possible, the base date for calculating RPI changes should be on or after the date of execution of the lease so that no RPI changes will then be taken into account for the purposes of calculating stamp duty. Of course, should the UK enter a period of RPI deflation, then this advice should be revisited.

(e) **Term of lease**

(i) A lease for a specified period but terminable on an earlier event is treated as a lease for the specified period and not for an indefinite period (*Earl of Mount-Edgcumbe v CIR* KB, [1911] 2 KB 24; cf *Kushner v Law Society* KB, [1952] 1 KB 264). Thus a lease for life or lives or for a term of years determinable on the marriage of the lessee treated as a lease for 90 years determinable on the death or marriage of the lessee under *Law of Property Act 1925, s 149(6)* is so treated for the purposes of stamp duty.

(ii) A lease or agreement granted for a fixed term and thereafter until determined is treated as a lease for a definite term equal to the fixed term plus any further period which must elapse before the earliest date at which the lease can be determined. [*FA 1999, Sch 13, para 15*].

(iii) A lease for a term of years with an option to renew for a further specified period is charged to duty only on the original term (*Hand v Hall* CA, (1877) 2 Ex D 355).

(iv) Weekly or other periodic tenancies are probably the only examples of indefinite terms.

(v) The length of the lease is determined from the date of execution and any part of the term (and rent) in respect of the period prior to execution is ignored (see *Colton v Becollda Property Investments Ltd* CA, [1950] 1 KB 216).

(vi) Where on the grant of a lease the amount of the rent was ascertainable for part of the term and unascertainable for the remainder, the practice of the Stamp Office prior to *FA 1994, s 242* was that the lease was treated as a lease for a term equal to the period for which the rent was ascertainable and duty was charged accordingly, and the (then) fixed duty of £2 was charged in respect of the remaining period for which the rent was unascertainable. No further duty was charged when the rent for the remainder of the lease was finally ascertained, for example by rent review or according to an agreed formula. See Inland Revenue Statement (1963) *The Law Society's Gazette pp 175–6*. Following this statement the Commissioners charged duty, for example, on a lease for a term of 101 years at a fixed rent for seven years with the rent for the remainder of the term to be agreed subsequently, as if the lease were a lease at the rate or average rate of rent for a seven-year term. The fixed duty of £2 was charged in respect of the remainder of the lease. However, if there was a ground or peppercorn rent of a known amount for the entire term, ad valorem duty was charged on the average ascertainable annual rent payable throughout the term and the fixed duty of £2 was charged in respect of the unascertainable rent.

Following *FA 1994, s 242(2)* the previous practice of the Stamp Office has changed as confirmed by the August 1995 edition of the Inland Revenue publication, Tax Bulletin. The Stamp Office takes the market rent for the entire term of the lease (but not the market rent plus the ascertainable consideration) in order to calculate the average annual rent. See **APPENDIX D**.

FA 1994, s 242(3)(a) excludes from the effect of *s 242(2)* cases where the rent could be ascertained on the assumption that a future event mentioned in the lease were or were not to occur. (See **64.2**(*c*) above.) Accordingly, it is thought that attempts by the Stamp Office to use the market rent in the following situations should be resisted.

First, when the rent is ascertainable for part of the term of a lease after which the rent is subject to an upwards only rent review. Because a contingent rent is ascertainable for the entire term of the lease duty should be calculated on the assumption that the rent which is ascertainable continues for the entire term.

Second, where the rent consists of a basic ascertainable amount plus a further amount which is unascertainable when the lease is granted, there is still arguably a prima facie rent payable and duty should be charged accordingly.

Third, the inclusion in a lease of a minimum rent should prevent the application of *FA 1994, s 242*, although the Stamp Office resists this application of the **CONTINGENCY PRINCIPLE (37)** where the minimum rent is merely nominal and appears to have been included to avoid *s 242*, whilst continuing to apply the principle when there is a maximum rent stated in the lease.

Duty on premiums

[64.3] [*FA 1999, Sch 13, para 12(2); FA 1994, s 241(1)*].

(a) Where part or all of the consideration for a lease for a definite term of more than one year or for an indefinite term consists of any money, stock, security or other property, duty is charged at the same rates as on a **CONVEYANCE OR TRANSFER (39)** on sale. The nil and reduced rates of duty apply if a **CERTIFICATE OF VALUE (30)** is included in the lease unless a part of the consideration includes rent exceeding £600 p.a. when the nil rate of duty is not available. [*FA 1999, Sch 13, para 12(2)*]. For valuation of the amount chargeable see **36 CONSIDERATION** and (*e*) below.

(b) A lease granted for any consideration chargeable to ad valorem duty is not liable to duty in respect of any further consideration consisting of a covenant by the tenant to make a substantial improvement or addition to the leased property or a covenant relating to the matter of the lease. [*SA 1891, s 77(2)*]. This exemption does not apply if the covenant would be chargeable with ad valorem duty if contained in a separate deed and the consideration is charged as a separate matter. [*Revenue Act 1909, s 8*].

(c) A premium is chargeable to duty if it consists of consideration moving either to the lessor or to any other person. This covers the case where a lease is granted to a builder's nominee and a premium is paid to the builder. (See also **36.6 COVENANTS TO IMPROVE PROPERTY**.)

(d) Sums paid to a lessor before the granting of a lease in respect of the costs of works to meet the lessee's particular needs are dutiable as a premium.

(e) For leases executed after 7 December 1993, duty is charged not only when the premium consists of money, stock or securities but also when it consists of any other property. [*FA 1994, s 241(1)*]. This means that on a sale and leaseback transaction consisting of the sale of the freehold in consideration of the grant of a new lease back, stamp duty should strictly be charged as follows:

(i) on the freehold sale with reference to the market value of the lease back; and

(ii) on the leaseback with reference to the market value of the freehold.

However, see paras 16 and 17 of the article in the August 1995 Tax Bulletin reproduced in **Appendix D**.

(f) Where the premium in whole or in part cannot be ascertained when the lease is granted, it is taken to be the market value of the lease on a sale in the open market at that time and duty is charged accordingly. [*FA 1994, s 242(1)*]. The **Contingency Principle (37)** will however take precedence where there is a maximum, minimum or basic figure. See **36.8 Unascertained and Contingent Consideration** and **37 Contingency Principle**.

Surrenders and variations

[64.4] Regarding surrenders and variations—

(a) No duty is charged on a lease or agreement made in consideration for the surrender or abandonment of an existing lease relating to the same property (although duty is charged on any premium and rent payable for the new lease). [*SA 1891, s 77(1)*]. It is understood that the Stamp Office accepts that this continues to be the position notwithstanding *FA 1994, s 241*, which arguably would impose an ad valorem charge to duty on the market value of the property immediately before the grant of the lease.

(b) Where a lease is surrendered, duty is payable on any consideration paid by the landlord (but not on any consideration paid by the tenant to the landlord) as a **Conveyance or Transfer (39)** on sale. Where the consideration for the surrender consists of the grant of a new lease of a different property, the surrender used to attract only a fixed 50p duty under the head **Surrender (85)**. However, *FA 1994, s 241* creates an ad valorem charge to duty on the surrender of a lease in consideration of the grant of a new lease of the same or a different property. The duty is charged with reference to the market value of the new lease (if any). The new lease will itself attract stamp duty on any premium and rent and the value of the surrendered lease unless the new lease is of the same property when the value of the surrendered lease will be ignored under *SA 1891, s 77(1)* (and see **64.4**(*a*) above). Previously no duty was charged where there was no stampable instrument such as a deed of surrender, memorandum or receipt. Surrender by operation of law, where the landlord pays the tenant and in exchange receives the keys and the lease, avoided duty because there was nothing to stamp. However, a written agreement to surrender a lease made after 7 December 1993 where there is no deed of surrender, is treated as a deed of surrender and is chargeable to duty accordingly. [*FA 1994, s 243*]. See paras 13, 14 and 15 of the article in the August 1995 Tax Bulletin reproduced in **APPENDIX D**. And for surrenders after 28 July 2000, any document evidencing the surrender or renunciation is treated as it if were a deed executed at that time effecting the surrender or renunciation and is stampable accordingly. For this purpose a statutory declaration filed at HM Land Registry evidencing the surrender is made specifically stampable notwithstanding *r 316(1)* of the *Land Registration Rules 1925*. [*FA 2000, s 128*].

(c) Where the terms of a lease can only be varied by a surrender and regrant (e.g. the lengthening of the term), the regranted lease bears the appropriate duty but no extra duty is paid on the surrendered lease. It is understood that the Stamp Office does not seek to charge duty on the surrender with reference to the market value of the new lease under *FA 1994, s 241*. However, where there is a written agreement to surrender *FA 1994, s 243* may apply to charge ad valorem duty on any cash consideration paid by the landlord.

(d) The withdrawal by mutual agreement of a notice to determine a tenancy constitutes a new tenancy liable to ad valorem duty (*Tayleur v Wildin* Ex, (1868) L R 3 Exch 303; *Freeman v Evans* CA, [1922] 1 Ch 36).

(e) A variation which does not operate as a surrender and regrant is not charged under the heading 'Lease' but may attract duty under some other head.

(f) An instrument increasing the rent under a lease, not being a surrender and regrant and liable to duty as in **64.4**(*c*) above, attracts duty calculated as lease duty on the additional rent. (*Gable Construction Co Ltd v CIR* Ch D, [1968] 2 All ER 968) [*FA 1999, Sch 13, para 20*]. An instrument agreeing an increased rent by reference to a formula in a lease is not, however, chargeable with ad valorem duty unless it operates as a regrant (**64.4**(*c*) above).

(g) The grant of an option to extend the term of a lease may cause a surrender and re-grant of the lease by operation of law (*Baker v Merckel* CA, [1960] 1 All ER 668). However, the exercise of a break clause does not cause a surrender of the lease in question (*Pennell v Payne* CA [1995] 2 All ER 592 as expressly approved in *Barrett v Morgan* HL [2000] 2 AC 264, [2000] 1 All ER 481).

(h) The grant of an underlease which expires on the same day as the headlease operates as an assignment of the headlease (*Allied Dunbar Pension Services Ltd v Baker* Ch D [2001] All ER (D) 46 (Aug)).

Shared ownership leases

[64.5] The usual rules for calculating duty on leases are varied for certain types of lease granted by a local housing authority, registered or unregistered housing association, housing action trust, development corporation, the Commission for the New Towns and some similar bodies. [*FA 1980, s 97; FA 1981, s 108; FA 1987, s 54; FA 1988, s 142*]. In a shared ownership scheme the tenant purchases part of his council house, pays rent for the remainder and is given an option to acquire the reversion. The tenant is permitted to pay ad valorem duty once under the **Conveyance or Transfer (39)** on sale head on the market value of the house instead of paying duty first under the lease head and second, when he acquires the reversion. A private sector landlord who has acquired a council housing estate is also included in these provisions so that a tenant may insist on a shared ownership lease even though his council estate has been bought by a private landlord. *Section 97* applies:

(a) where the lease is of a dwelling for the exclusive use of the lessee (or joint lessees);
(b) where the lease is granted partly in consideration of a premium calculated by reference to the market value of the dwelling or a sum calculated by reference to that value and partly in consideration of rent;
(c) where the lease provides for the lessee to acquire the reversion; and in addition states the market value or the sum referred to in (*b*) above and a statement that the parties intend duty to be charged in accordance with *s 97* by reference to that sum.

The stamp duty consequences are then as follows:

(i) when the lease is granted duty is payable under the **Conveyance or Transfer (39)** on sale head as if it were a conveyance in consideration of the amount mentioned in the lease as in (*b*) above and no duty is payable under the lease head;
(ii) an instrument executed in pursuance of the lease on which duty has been paid as in (i) (and containing a statement to that effect), whereby the reversion is transferred to the lessee, bears no duty.

Charities

[64.6] Leases granted to charities are not chargeable with duty, although it is necessary to have the lease adjudicated. [*FA 1982, s 129*]. See **Adjudication (13)**.

Crown exemption

[64.7] Leases granted to a Government Minister or to the Treasury Solicitor are not chargeable with duty. [*FA 1987, s 55*].

Produced stamp

[64.8] A lease or **Agreement for Lease (16)** for a term of seven years or more must be not only stamped but also 'produced' to the Commissioners and stamped with a **Produced Stamp (77)**. A lease granted pursuant to and consistent with a produced agreement for a lease need not itself be produced. [*FA 1931, s 28(2)*].

Leases between associated companies

[64.9] Because stamp duty on leases is charged under the head 'Lease', the exemption for transfers between **ASSOCIATED COMPANIES (23)** under *FA 1930, s 42* does not apply. However, for instruments executed on or after 1 May 1995, *FA 1995, s 151* exempts leases, agreements for leases and 'agreements with respect to a letting' between associated companies from duty subject to the requirements of that section. The scope of this exemption was tightened up significantly by *FA 2000, s 125*. See **23.5 STAMP DUTY RESERVE TAX**.

Leases to connected companies

[64.10] Where a lease is granted to a company and either:

(a) the person granting the lease is connected with the company (regardless of whether there is any consideration); or
(b) where there is consideration it includes the issue or transfer of shares in a company connected to the grantor,

then the lease is liable to sale duty on the market value of the lease, but reduced by any actual consideration not consisting of property. [*FA 2000, s 121*]. Note that none of the exceptions that apply to the similar charge on transfers of land to connected companies apply to this charge. See **36.9 TRANSFER OF LAND TO CONNECTED COMPANY**.

Registered social landlords

[64.11] No duty is charged on transfers or leases of land to registered social landlords. [*FA 2000, s 130*]. No duty is charged on certain leases of dwellings by registered social landlords to individuals under arrangements with a housing authority for the provision of temporary accommodation. [*FA 2003, ss 128–130*]. The instrument must be adjudicated.

Chapter 65

Letters of Allotment and Acceptance

Stamp duty

[65.1] The head of charge Letters of Allotment or Renunciation, Scrip Certificates or Scrip in *SA 1891, Sch 1* was abolished by *FA 1949*. The instruments formerly charged were:

(a) letter of allotment and letter of renunciation of shares in or of loans raised by a company, municipal body or corporation (including overseas bodies and governments where issued in the UK);

(b) scrip certificates or scrip entitling any person to become the proprietor of any share in or denoting the right of any person as a subscriber in respect of any loan raised by a company, municipal body or corporation (including overseas bodies and governments where issued or delivered in the UK). See **82 SCRIP DIVIDENDS**.

Renounceable letters of allotment and acceptance where the rights are renounceable not later than six months after issue are also exempt from duty under the **BEARER INSTRUMENTS (24)** charge. [*FA 1999, Sch 15, para 16*]. There is also a general exemption for such letters from duty under the **CONVEYANCE OR TRANSFER (39)** on sale head although this exemption is no longer available in relation to company take-overs where the 'Pref-trick' could otherwise be used to avoid stamp duty on the transfer of the company. [*FA 1999, Sch 13, para 24(d); FA 1985, s 81*]. See **24.7**(*b*) **EXEMPTIONS**.

The previous exemption from duty under the **BEARER INSTRUMENTS (23)** head for bearer letters of allotment, bearer letters of rights, scrip and scrip certificates to bearer required to be surrendered not later than six months after issue, has been withdrawn. [*FA 1986, s 80*].

STAMP DUTY RESERVE TAX (84). The exemptions from stamp duty for renounceable letters of allotment and acceptance, and similar instruments where the rights are renounceable not later than six months after issue, do not protect such instruments from the **STAMP DUTY RESERVE TAX (84)** charge on agreements to transfer such instruments for money or money's worth. The structure of the tax is such that the exemption from bearer instrument duty results automatically in a tax charge on short-term renounceable letters of allotment and acceptance. [*FA 1986, ss 87(1), (2), 90(3A), (3B)*]. See **24.8**(*a*) **STAMP DUTY RESERVE TAX**.

For a more detailed description of the tax charge on agreements to transfer short-term renounceable letters of allotment and acceptance see **84 STAMP DUTY RESERVE TAX**. For an explanation of the situations in which the tax will normally arise see **55 FLOTATIONS, ETC**.

Chapter 66

Loan Capital and Debentures

[66.1] As a result of the exemptions from duty for both bearer and registered loan capital under *FA 1986, s 79*, and the abolition of the duty on the transfer of debentures by *FA 1971, s 64* most types of loan capital are exempt from stamp duty.

Loan capital is defined as:

(a) any debenture stock, corporation stock or funded debt, by whatever name known, issued by a body corporate or other body of persons (which here includes a local authority and any body whether formed or established in the UK or elsewhere);
(b) any capital raised by such a body if the capital is borrowed or has the character of borrowed money, and whether it is in the form of stock or any other form;
(c) stock or marketable securities issued by the government of any country or territory outside the United Kingdom.

[*FA 1986, ss 78(7), 79(12)*].

This definition is similar to that used for the former head of charge 'Loan capital' (abolished by *FA 1973*) and cases decided under that head are therefore relevant to the current definition. In *Reed International Ltd v CIR* HL, [1975] 3 All ER 218 it was held that 'funded debt' requires the characteristics of long-term borrowing but does not have to be created out of existing debt; in *A-G v South Wales Electrical Power Distribution Co* CA, [1920] 1 KB 552 it was held that interest-bearing deferred warrants issued by a company in respect of the unpaid interest due on its debenture stock was not 'loan capital' or 'funded debt' and not 'borrowed money' because it was not of a capital nature; in *A-G v Regents Canal and Dock Co* CA, [1904] 1 KB 263 it was held that new debenture stock issued following the extinction of existing debenture stock was 'loan capital'—new money is not required.

It is thought that short-term debt of a capital nature is within the definition of loan capital and will therefore also qualify for the following exemptions.

Bearer loan capital is exempt from duty under the **BEARER INSTRUMENTS (24)** charge on issue and on transfer. [*FA 1986, s 79(2)*]. But see **66.3** below.

Registered loan capital. Transfers of most types of registered loan capital are exempt from duty as a **CONVEYANCE OR TRANSFER (39)** on sale. [*FA 1986, s 79(3)(4)*]. The exemption does not apply to:

(a) an instrument transferring loan capital which, at the time it is executed, carries a right, exercisable then or later, of conversion into shares or other securities, or to the acquisition of shares or other securities including loan capital of the same description; or
(b) an instrument transferring loan capital which at the time it is executed or any earlier time carries or has carried:
    (i) a right to interest exceeding a reasonable commercial return on the nominal amount of capital;

(ii) a right to interest the amount of which is determined by reference to the results of a business or the value of property; or

(iii) a right on repayment to an amount which exceeds the nominal amount of the capital and is not reasonably comparable with what is generally repay able on loan capital listed on the Stock Exchange.

The fact that the interest or the amount repayable is index-linked does not prevent the exemption from applying. [*FA 1986, s 79(7)*]. Paragraph (b)(ii) above does not prevent the exemption from applying by reason only that the loan capital carries a right to interest which:

(A) reduces in the event of the results of a business improving or the value of any property increasing; or

(B) increases in the event of the results of a business deteriorating, or the value of any property diminishing [*FA 1986, s 79(7A)* inserted by *FA 2000, s 133*].

Also, para (b)(ii) above does not prevent the exemption from applying to a capital market instrument by reason only that the capital market investment concerned carries or has carried a right to interest which ceases or reduces if, to the extent that the issuer after meeting or providing for other obligations in the capital market arrangement concerned, has insufficient funds available from that arrangement to pay all or part of the interest otherwise due. Capital market instrument means an instrument transferring a capital market investment, issued as part of a capital market arrangement and these latter two terms have the meaning given to them by *Insolvency Act 1986, s 72B*. [*FA 1986, s 79(7B) and (13)* inserted by *FA 2008, s 101*].

In relation to (a) above, loan capital is not excluded from the exemption because it carries an unexpired right of conversion into or acquisition of loan capital which itself comes within the terms of the exemption (statement of practice 3/84 which originally applied to *FA 1976, s 126*, but continues to apply to the exemption now contained in *FA 1986, s 79*).

Where the transfer of registered loan capital is not exempt duty is charged at the rate of 0.5% of the amount or value of the consideration for the transfer as a **CONVEYANCE OR TRANSFER (39)** on sale. [*FA 1986, s 79(8)*].

Debentures

[66.2] Debentures are normally exempt from duty under the abovementioned provisions. A further exemption is available by reason of the abolition of the Mortgage, Bond, Debenture, Covenant head of charge including the charge on the transfer of debentures other than marketable securities. [*FA 1971, s 64(1)*]. It follows from this that the transfer of debentures which are not marketable securities will be exempt from duty [*FA 1971, s 64(2)*; *FA 1999, Sch 13, para 25(a)*] (see **68 MORTGAGES**). A debenture has been defined as a written instrument creating, acknowledging or evidencing indebtedness (*Levy v Abercorris Slate Slab Co* Ch D, (1888) 37 Ch D 260) and there is judicial support for the view that a bank facility letter can be a debenture even though no money has been drawn down at the time (*NV Slavenburg's Bank v Intercontinental Natural Resources Ltd* Ch D, [1980] 1 WLR 1076).

Stamp duty reserve tax

[66.3] See **24.8**(*c*) **STAMP DUTY RESERVE TAX** for the charge to the tax on agreements to transfer certain bearer instruments relating to loan capital. [*FA 1986, s 90(3B)*].

Chapter 67

Manner of Stamping

Denoting of duty

[67.1] Stamp duties are generally denoted on the instruments to which they relate by an impressed stamp. [*SA 1891, s 2*].

See **60 Instruments** for how stamps should appear on instruments.

See **74 Payment of Duty or Tax** for details of dates of stamping and liability for duty and penalties.

FA 1993, s 204 has given the Treasury wide powers to make regulations as to the manner by which stamp duty is denoted. The regulations may for example provide for duty to be denoted by the traditional impressed stamp, by adhesive stamp or by computer record.

Chapter 68

Mortgages

[68.1] Stamp duty formerly charged by *SA 1891, Sch 1* on mortgages was abolished by *FA 1971, s 64(1)(c), Sch 14*.

The documents formerly charged were mortgages and similar documents of the following descriptions:

(a) the principal or primary security under a legal mortgage for the payment or repayment of money;
(b) a collateral or substituted security under a legal mortgage;
(c) an equitable mortgage;
(d) a transfer or assignment of a mortgage or any money or stock secured by a mortgage;
(e) a reconveyance or release or similar instrument of a mortgage or the money secured thereby.

Instruments formerly charged under the head 'Mortgage' will not attract duty under any other head. For example, that head of charge included a charge on the transfer of debentures other than marketable securities and the abolition of that charge does not permit duty to be charged under the head **CONVEYANCE OR TRANSFER (39)** on sale. [*FA 1971, s 64(2)* and *FA 1999, Sch 13, para 25(a)*]. (See **66 LOAN CAPITAL AND DEBENTURES**.) However, an instrument containing several distinct matters (see **63 LEADING AND PRINCIPAL OBJECT**) will only be exempt to the extent that a matter falls within the former head of charge.

Transfer of property subject to a mortgage. See **36 CONSIDERATION**.

Chapter 69

Negotiating with the Stamp Office

[69.1] Stampable documents are stamped at one of the offices listed in **14 Administration** following a cursory examination of the document by one of the marking clerks. Documents stamped in this way are not guaranteed to be correctly stamped. Consequently, a registrar may properly refuse to register such a document stamped in this way if it appears that it does not bear the correct stamp. It is open to the registrar or the person wishing to stamp the document to request that the document be adjudicated. **Adjudication (13)** is the process whereby the Stamp Office formally assesses the amount of duty, if any, chargeable on the document. Except in the cases mentioned in **13.3 Compulsory**, adjudication is conclusive of the liability of the document to stamp duty. [*SA 1891, s 12(6)*]. In addition to disputes about the liability of a document to stamp duty, adjudication is used where it is not possible to determine the liability of a document to stamp duty without detailed consideration. This occurs most commonly with sales when a set of accounts or a property valuation is required or the consideration clause in a sale document contains complicated financial formulae or legal wording. In these cases the usual practice is to submit the document for adjudication. When a valuation is required, the Stamp Office may refer to specialist valuers in other departments. Adjudication is also used in order to decide whether a document qualifies for a specific exemption or relief from stamp duty, such as those available for **Company Reorganisations (34)**.

Following the submission of the document for adjudication the Stamp Office practice, prior to 1 October 1999, was to examine it and issue stamps form ADJ 407 to the applicant. This form contains a statement of the amount of stamp duty payable based on the information supplied to the Stamp Office. Following the issue of form ADJ 407, the stamp duty will either be paid or the applicant for adjudication will normally write back explaining that, in his opinion, the duty payable is wrong and discussions will then ensue leading, usually, to agreement of the amount of duty payable. Stamps form ADJ 407 was not the 'formal assessment' for the purposes of both penalties and whether the 21-day period for appealing had begun to run under old *SA 1891, s 13*. What was referred to as the 'formal assessment' was in practice only issued once an appeal to the High Court was in prospect. For documents executed on or after 1 October 1999 Stamp Office practice remains broadly similar and a formal notice of decision under new *SA 1891, s 12(3)* will only be issued once it becomes clear that an appeal is in prospect. In this way the 30-day period for commencing an appeal under new *SA 1891, s 13(2)* and also the 30-day period for payment of duty subject to a £300 penalty under *SA 1891, s 12A(2)*, will not begin to run until the formal notice of decision has been issued. (See **20.1 Appeals**.)

Prior to 1 October 1999, the effect of the old *SA 1891, s 15* was that as long as the document to be adjudicated was lodged within 30 days there was in practice never any question of penalties (unless the document was returned to the applicant and later resubmitted). This was because an 'assessment' was never actually issued except where there was an appeal to the High Court. This meant that actual payment of the stamp duty liability could be deferred often for a considerable time without risk of interest and penalty pending agreement of the stamp duty liability.

However, for documents executed on or after 1 October 1999 new *SA 1891, ss 15, 15A* and *15B* provide for interest and penalties to arise automatically on duty unpaid and instruments not presented respectively, within 30 days of execution. In the case of penalties these will not arise in the case of a document executed outside the UK until 30 days after the document is first received in the UK, unless the document relates to UK land.

To avoid an interest charge therefore it is necessary to either pay the stamp duty within 30 days of execution (whether execution occurs in the UK or overseas) or lodge with the Stamp Office a payment equal to the stamp duty liability that will eventually be assessed (and see **74.1**(*b*) **DATE OF STAMPING AND PAYMENT**).

The discussions with the Stamp Office which often occur following the issue of stamps form ADJ 407 are a very important practical stage in settling the liability of the document to stamp duty. Such discussions may extend over a considerable time—a year or more is not unusual. In relation to agreements to transfer chargeable securities however, the requirement to account for and pay any **STAMP DUTY RESERVE TAX (84)** in the interim should not be overlooked.

In practice, the Stamp Office usually tries to be helpful during negotiations and is usually prepared to exchange correspondence several times with the applicant or his advisers where an important legal point is involved, so long as the applicant is arguing in good faith. If the adjudication officer and the applicant cannot agree the liability on the basis of arguments put forward by the officer on his own, it is usual for the officer to seek the views of a specialist in the solicitor's department of HMRC or in rare cases, consult outside counsel. If the solicitor's department confirm the adjudication officer's view of the stamp duty liability, the applicant for adjudication will normally be faced with the issue of a formal 'notice of decision' under *SA 1891, s 12(3)* which triggers the 30-day period during which an appeal must be commenced under *SA 1891, s 13(2)* and he must decide whether to commence a formal appeal to the High Court or Special Commissioners under *SA 1891, s 13* (see **20 APPEALS**) or withdraw his document from the adjudication (subject to payment of a penalty not exceeding £300 for non-payment of the duty assessed in the document under *SA 1891, s 12A(2)*).

The Stamp Office Manual containing technical instructions and guidance for Stamp Office staff was published in March 2000 just ahead of the Finance Bill and so deals with the law prior to *FA 2000*. It is nevertheless a useful guide to the approach of the Stamp Office to various technical and procedural issues. A copy of the Manual is available to download at http://www.inlandrevenue.gov.uk/so/manual.htm. It was reissued as the Stamp Taxes Manual in March 2002 with some updated information.

Chapter 70

Options and Warrants

Stamp duty

[70.1] There is no head of charge specifically for options. Options may be chargeable as a **CONVEYANCE OR TRANSFER (39)** on sale, as a miscellaneous conveyance or transfer, or under the **BEARER INSTRUMENTS (24)** charge, unless any of the exemptions listed in **70.6** below applies.

Conveyance or transfer (39)

[70.2] An agreement creating an option to purchase land has been held to attract ad valorem duty as a conveyance on sale on the grounds that (i) the option was property or an interest in property, (ii) the instrument creating the option vested property or an interest in property (namely the option) in the purchaser and (iii) the agreement was therefore a conveyance on sale as defined in *FA 1999*, *Sch 13*, *para 1* (see **39.4 CONVEYANCE ON SALE**). (*George Wimpey & Co Ltd v CIR* CA, [1975] 2 All ER 45). Instruments granting put or call or put and call options may therefore attract ad valorem duty at 4% of the consideration, unless the option is a marketable security in which case the reduced rate of 0.5% applies. A **CERTIFICATE OF VALUE (30)** may be given where appropriate but such a certificate is not available where the option is a marketable security.

Leases (64)

[70.3] A lease of land containing an option to purchase the freehold does not require to be stamped in relation to the option unless the option relates to separate property. (*Worthington v Warrington*, (1848) 5 CB 635; *Lovelock v Franklyn*, (1846) 8 QB 371).

Agreement for sale (17)

[70.4] An agreement for the sale of a subsisting option to purchase a legal interest is thought to be liable under *FA 1999*, *Sch 13*, *para 7*, as either an agreement for the sale of an equitable interest, or an agreement for the sale of an estate or interest in property not falling within one of the specified exemptions (see **17 AGREEMENT FOR SALE**). (See *George Wimpey & Co Ltd v CIR* above; *Muller & Co's Margarine Ltd v CIR* CA, [1900] 1 QB 310 explained in *Danubian Sugar Factories Ltd v CIR* CA, [1901] 1 KB 245.) However, an agreement for the sale of a legal interest in land with an option to take a declaration of trust is not an agreement for the sale of an equitable interest in land (*West London Syndicate v CIR* CA, [1898] 2 QB 507) and an agreement granting an option to purchase coupled with an immediate transfer of shares, no beneficial interest passing, was not liable under *FA 1999, Sch 13, para 7* (*Wm Cory & Son Ltd v CIR* HL, [1965] AC 1088).

Bearer options

[70.5] If the instrument granting the option is a bearer instrument it may attract duty on issue or on first transfer in the UK under the **BEARER INSTRUMENTS (24)** head of charge. [*FA 1999, Sch 15, paras 1 and 2*]. The transfer by delivery of an existing bearer option will not attract duty.

Exemptions

[70.6] A put or call option is exempt from stamp duty under the heads mentioned above if it relates to:

(a) gilt-edged securities;
(b) exempt loan capital (see **66 LOAN CAPITAL AND DEBENTURES**);
(c) debentures which are not marketable securities;
(d) bearer securities relating to stock expressed in any currency except sterling or in units of account defined by reference to more than one currency (see **24 BEARER INSTRUMENTS**). [*FA 1987, s 50*].

Equity warrants

[70.7] Instead of issuing convertible loan stock a borrower may issue loan stock with warrants to subscribe for shares in the borrower or another company. These equity warrants may be detached from the loan stock and traded separately in the market. When detached from the loan stock the equity warrant will attract stamp duty in the manner described above in relation to options.

Transfers of loan stock with equity warrants attached may not qualify for the general exemption from stamp duty for transfers of registered loan capital, by reason of the loan stock carrying the right of conversion into shares. [*FA 1986, s 79(4)(5)*]. See **66 LOAN CAPITAL AND DEBENTURES**.

Stamp duty reserve tax (84)

[70.8] An option to acquire stocks or shares which are not themselves exempt from stamp duty on transfer is a 'chargeable security' for the purposes of the tax. The same applies to an option to acquire loan capital. [*FA 1986, s 99(3)(c); FA 1988, s 144(2)*]. See **84.7 CHARGEABLE SECURITIES**. Therefore, an agreement to transfer an existing call option or equity warrant in registered form relating to stocks or shares or loan capital which are not themselves exempt from stamp duty will attract tax unless a duly stamped instrument of transfer is produced to cancel the tax charge.

The issue of such a call option or equity warrant may also attract tax under the principle established in *George Wimpey & Co Ltd v CIR* CA, [1975] 2 All ER 45 (see **70.2** above). However, it has been argued that the grant of an option although constituting a conveyance of the option is not actually an 'agreement' to transfer as required by the *FA 1986, s 87(1)* and the Stamp Office apparently accepts this. A put option is not a 'chargeable security' for the purposes of the tax because it is an option enabling the holder to sell rather than to acquire stocks or shares or loan capital.

Options in bearer form are generally exempt from the tax except for agreements to transfer instruments of the types listed in **24.8**(*a*) (*b*) and (*c*) **STAMP DUTY RESERVE TAX**.

Chapter 71

Oral Transactions

[71.1] Stamp duty is charged on **INSTRUMENTS (60)**. Transactions which are done by word of mouth or physical delivery are not liable to duty. Duty may thus be avoided when a transaction is carried out orally instead of being reduced to writing (see Lord Hoffmann's speech in *MacNiven v Westmoreland Investments Ltd* [2001] UKHL 6 [2001] STC 237). However, in relation to oral agreements to transfer 'chargeable securities' for money or money's worth **STAMP DUTY RESERVE TAX (84)** will arise and will only be cancelled if an instrument transferring the securities to the purchaser is executed and duly stamped.

Transactions that can be effected orally include the following:

(a) The transfer of various types of personalty by delivery such as stock in trade, jewellery, furniture, plant and machinery and fixtures (after severance).

(b) A written agreement for the sale of 'goods, wares and merchandise' does not attract duty under *FA 1999, Sch 13, para 7* (see **17 AGREEMENT FOR SALE**) and subsequent completion of the transaction by delivery as in (*a*) above will avoid duty. This means that the consideration for the goods etc. is left out of account in deciding whether a **CERTIFICATE OF VALUE (30)** is appropriate.

(c) **BEARER INSTRUMENTS (24)** can pass by delivery and so do not attract duty on transfer.

(d) Oral declarations of trust of personalty (see **86 TRUSTS AND TRUSTEES**).

It will often be desirable to have a written record of a transaction that has been carried out orally. The written record may be treated as one with the oral transaction and stampable as an instrument effecting the transaction (*Cohen and Moore v CIR* KB, [1933] 2 KB 126). However, a written record of the transaction which is brought into existence not for the purpose of recording the transaction but to fulfil a legal requirement such as a board minute prepared pursuant to *Companies Act 2006, s 248* is not vulnerable under the rule in *Cohen and Moore* and is not therefore stampable. Moreover, a memorandum prepared before the transaction occurs cannot be liable to duty because liability depends on the facts and circumstances which exist at the date of the document.

The following transactions, inter alia, require a written instrument:

(a) the conveyance of land [*Law of Property Act 1925, s 52*];

(b) the disposition of an equitable interest [*Law of Property Act 1925, s 53*];

(c) the transfer of shares in a company subject to regulations made under *Companies Act 2006* which enable title to securities to be evidenced and transferred without a written instrument and also to shares passing by operation of law [*Companies Act 2006, s 770(1), (2)*].

See **83 SHARES AND SECURITIES**.

An attempted oral disposition of an equitable interest has been held ineffective with the result that a subsequent declaration of trust was stampable as a **CONVEYANCE OR TRANSFER (39)** (*Grey v CIR* HL 1959, [1960] AC 1). See **86 TRUSTS AND TRUSTEES.**

Chapter 72

Overseas Matters

Charge to stamp duty

[72.1] Stamp duty applies to:

(a) any instrument executed in the UK even if it relates to property outside the UK; and

(b) any instrument executed outside the UK that relates to any property in the UK, or to any matter or thing done or to be done in the UK. For the consequences of failing to stamp see *SA 1891, s 14(4)* and **31 CHARGEABILITY.**

For stamp duty the UK comprises England, Scotland, Wales and Northern Ireland but not the Channel Islands or the Isle of Man. The territorial extension of the UK to the continental shelf by *ICTA 1988, s 830* for the purposes of income tax and corporation tax does not apply to stamp duty, instead the position at common law applies and the UK ends at the low water mark and does not extend to the seabed under the territorial sea (*R v Keyn* (1876) 2 Ex D 63).

Instruments executed abroad

[72.2] The payment of duty on an instrument executed abroad and relating to UK matters is deferred until the instrument is received in the UK. However, for documents executed on or after 1 October 1999, interest on unpaid duty runs from 30 days after the date of execution whether the document is executed in the UK or elsewhere and for instruments relating to UK land and executed on or after 24 July 2002 a penalty also arises unless the instrument is presented for stamping within 30 days after execution. [*SA 1891, ss 15A* and *15B*, as amended by *FA 2002, s 114*]. See **74 PAYMENT OF DUTY OR TAX.**

Foreign currency

[72.3] Where the consideration is expressed in a foreign currency it is converted at the rate current at the date of the instrument. See **36 CONSIDERATION.**

Overseas company

[72.4] An overseas company may be an associated company for the purpose of the **ASSOCIATED COMPANIES (23)** relief. The reliefs for **COMPANY REORGANISATIONS (34)** are not available unless the registered office of the acquiring company is in the UK.

Overseas branch registers

[72.5] The transfer of a share registered in an overseas branch register (other than a register in Northern Ireland) is deemed to be a transfer of non-UK property and unless executed in the UK the transfer is exempt from stamp duty. [*Companies Act 2006, s 133*]. See also **78.1** below.

Bearer instruments

[72.6] **BEARER INSTRUMENTS (24)** relating to stock expressed in any currency other than sterling or in any units of account defined by reference to more than one currency are exempt from duty under the charge relating to **BEARER INSTRUMENTS (24)**. But see **24.7**(*f*) and **24.8**(*b*) **BEARER INSTRUMENTS** for details of a potential **STAMP DUTY RESERVE TAX (84)** charge.

Stamp duty reserve tax

[72.7] In relation to agreements to transfer chargeable securities which are made after 30 June 1996, or if made before 1 July 1996 become unconditional on or after that date, and to all transfers (and in the case of depositary receipt or clearance systems, issues or appropriations) on or after 1 July 1996, the territorial scope of the tax has been extended. [*FA 1996, s 187*]. Prior to this change the tax was not charged in relation to agreements to transfer chargeable securities made between persons not resident in the UK where the transaction was carried out abroad. However, with the introduction of electronic share transfers under CREST there could have been a loss of revenue if agreements to transfer dematerialised securities between non-UK persons did not attract the tax because there will not be a subsequent transfer of the shares attracting stamp duty. Accordingly, a new *FA 1986 s 86(4)* has been created which charges the tax whether the transfer etc. is effected in the UK or elsewhere, and whether or not any party is resident or situate in the UK. The Commissioners are empowered to assess non-resident purchasers in the name of a branch or agent and the 'accountable person' rather than the purchaser can be required to pay the tax. [*Stamp Duty Reserve Tax Regulations 1986 (SI 1986 No 1711)*].

Chapter 73

Partnerships

Stamp duty or Stamp Duty Land Tax?

[73.1] Partnerships are seen by HMRC Stamp Taxes as difficult creatures and this was reflected in the fact that transfers of land into and out of partnerships by a partner and the sale of interests in partnerships were excluded from SDLT until Royal Assent to *FA 2004* when such transactions become chargeable with SDLT: see **8.1 PARTNERSHIPS**. [*FA 2003, Sch 15, Part 3*]. Stamp duty continued to apply to such transactions, which were treated as though they were not land transactions for SDLT. [*FA 2003, Sch 15, para 13(1), (2)*]. What are called 'ordinary partnership transactions' were nevertheless within the new SDLT regime from the beginning, that is to say land transactions entered into by the partnership as purchaser. [*FA 2003, Sch 15, para 5* and see Part One]. Stamp duty continues to apply to acquisitions of partnership interests despite the imposition of SDLT. [*FA 2004, Sch 41, para 31* and see **8.1 PARTNERSHIPS**]. The rest of this chapter should be read on this basis.

Nature of partnership interest

[73.2] As a matter of partnership law it is considered that it is not correct to regard a particular partner as the beneficial owner of all or a part of any partnership asset. It is correct that collectively the partners own the assets beneficially. However, the question of the ownership of partnership assets by individual partners can only be determined by reference to a partner's net entitlement upon a dissolution: see Lindley & Banks on Partnership at paragraphs 19-05 et seq. Therefore what an individual partner has is more accurately described as a collection of equitable rights of account for the net assets on a dissolution of the firm plus other elements such as the right to participate in profits and in the case of the general partner, a right to manage the business of the firm.

In stamp duty this analysis is supported by the Stamp Office Manual (2nd edn) at paragraph 4.442: 'A partner cannot claim to be the owner of any particular asset or, indeed, any specific share in an asset. A partner's interest is a peculiar form of property known as an interest in *a unum quid* or, in other words, in an indivisible whole. This is not a share in any goods, money or other assets. It is merely a right as a partner, with others, to control the partnership assets and affairs so long as the partnership exists and, upon dissolution, a right to have the assets liquidated, the liabilities discharged and a division of any surplus.'

Stamp Office practice also supports this analysis. For example, in the case of the sale of a partnership interest where the sole asset of the firm consists of UK equities, the Stamp Office robustly asserts that the 4% rate of duty applies to the instrument of transfer as a transfer of a chose in action, i.e. a partnership interest, and not the 0.5% rate of stamp duty applicable to a sale of the underlying marketable securities.

SA 1891 s 57 and incoming partners

[73.3] *SA 1891 s 57* provides that the transfer of property subject to the assumption of liabilities is chargeable with stamp duty in respect of the liabilities assumed. (See **36.5 Debts and Liabilities**). This section applies where the incoming partner is purchasing an existing interest in the partnership by paying cash to an existing or retiring partner to the extent that he assumes a proportionate share in the liabilities of the firm. In the case of a limited partnership the incoming partner's share of the liabilities assumed will be limited by the nature of the partnership to the amount of his capital.

Where an incoming partner is not purchasing an existing partnership interest but is merely contributing cash or property to the capital of the firm and there is no related withdrawal of capital by an existing partner, and no monies are paid direct to existing partners, then there will be no sale. The correct analysis is that there has been the creation of a partnership interest *de novo* on which no *ad valorem* duty is chargeable under *s 57* or otherwise. *Section 57* will not apply because no property is conveyed.

This is supported by the Stamp Office Manual (2nd edn) at paragraph 4.444: 'Similarly, any document executed wholly to introduce a new partner to an existing partnership is generally not chargeable with *ad valorem* duty, provided any price for membership consists of assets contributed to the partnership and not paid directly or indirectly to the existing partner.'

The two practical examples given at paragraph 4.451 of the Stamp Office Manual showing how stamp duty should be calculated in the case of an incoming partner show *s 57* as relevant. However this is because both examples are based on a *sale* of existing partners' interests, because both examples feature cash paid direct to the existing partners. These examples are therefore not applicable to the introduction of a partner who is merely contributing capital and loans to the firm without making payments to existing partners. Where cash is not paid to existing or retiring partners paragraph 4.444 of the Manual quoted above correctly describes the position. It would however be prudent in a case where the incoming partner or investor is introducing 'loan' capital and the existing partners wish to reduce their existing 'loan' capital in the firm for the existing 'loans' to be reduced first using bank or other borrowing by the firm which can subsequently be repaid when the incoming partner joins. So-called partner 'loans' in the sense of loans made by partners to their partnership may simply represent a bundle of equitable rights of account held by each partner. A 'loan' by a partner to a partnership in which he is a partner is a 'loan' to himself, and thus raises awkward conceptual issues. Because the sale of such a bundle of rights would be stampable rather than exempt it will be prudent not to sell a partner's interest in 'loan' capital to an incoming investor, but to consider alternative means of admitting a new investor and extracting existing partner capital such as that described above. See *Green v Hertzog* [1954] 1 WLR 1309.

Corporate nominees and partnerships

[73.4] Another issue was the connected company charge in *FA 2000, s 119* which could give rise to a stamp duty charge on market value when the legal title to land contributed to a partnership is typically transferred from contributing partner to nominee companies held by the general partner to be held for the partnership. HMRC Stamp Taxes appears not to take the point in relation to transfers of land to connected corporate nominees to hold for the corporate partners. The exemption for transfers to nominees in *FA 2000, s 120* will usually not apply because there will be a change in the beneficial ownership upon the transfer of the property because it will be held for all the partners and not just the contributing partner. HMRC Stamp Taxes' practice could change, as it has not been published, so it may be prudent when contributing property to ensure that the nominees are not connected with the contributing partner at the time of the transfer (because the charge does not arise if the parties become connected only as a result of the transaction), or where the other partners are members of the same group it may be possible to fall within the conditions for relief under *FA 1930, s 42*.

Formation of partnerships

[73.5] A partnership deed or agreement as such does not attract any stamp duty. Before the repeal of the 'Deeds' head of charge an instrument under seal attracted a fixed duty of 50p. [*FA 1985, s 85, Sch 24(e)*]. A limited partnership was a 'capital company' for the purposes of **CAPITAL DUTY (29)** and as such was within the charge to duty. This duty has been abolished. [*FA 1988, s 141*]. Limited partnerships remain liable to stamp duty as before.

Incoming partners

[73.6] If a new partner pays money direct to existing partners in return for an interest in the partnership property, any document transferring the interest to the new partner will attract ad valorem duty as a **CONVEYANCE OR TRANSFER (39)** on sale of the interest in the partnership property purchased by the new partner. However, if the new partner contributes cash equal to the amount credited to his capital account, no ad valorem duty is chargeable unless there is a simultaneous withdrawal of capital by an existing or retiring partner, in which case the document effecting the transaction is treated as a **CONVEYANCE OR TRANSFER (39)** on sale and is chargeable to duty as such. And see **73.3** above where an incoming partner purports to acquire a 'loan' to the partnership from an existing or outgoing partner.

Dissolution of partnership

[73.7] The division of assets on a dissolution of partnership in accordance with the terms of the partnership will not normally attract *ad valorem* duty (*Macleod v CIR* Ex(S) (1885), 22 SLR 674). The instrument effecting a dissolution will, however, attract a fixed £5 duty under the 'Partition or division' charge in *FA 1999*, *Sch 13*, *para 21(3)* to the extent that it effects a land transaction. (See **48 Exchange or Partition**.) If there is an element of sale in the dissolution, *ad valorem* duty may be charged on the dissolution instrument as a **Conveyance or Transfer (39)** on sale (*Christie v CIR* Ex, (1866) LR 2 Exch 46; *Garnett v CIR* QB (1899), 81 LT 633).

Conversion to a company

[73.8] Where the business of a partnership is transferred to a company, the transfers of assets to the company are charged to *ad valorem* duty as a **Conveyance or Transfer (39)** on sale, notwithstanding that the partners are the same persons as the owners of shares in the company (*Foster (John) & Sons v CIR* CA, [1894] 1 QB 516).

Incorporation of limited liability partnerships

[73.9] Stamp duty is not charged on an instrument conveying or transferring property to a limited liability partnership formed under the *Limited Liability Partnerships Act 2000* where the transfer is in connection with the incorporation of the partnership and occurs within one year beginning with the date of the incorporation. The relief is subject to two conditions:

(a) the transferor is a partner in a partnership comprised of all the persons who are to be members of the limited liability partnership and no-one else, or holds the property transferred as nominee or bare trustee for one or more partners in such a partnership; and

(b) the proportions of entitlement to the property amongst the partners remain the same before and after the transfer or any difference arising is not part of a tax or stamp duty avoidance scheme.

Adjudication (13) is required in order to obtain the relief. [*Limited Liability Partnerships Act 2000, s 12*].

The requirement in (*b*) above that the partners' entitlement to the property transferred remains the same is not enforced by HMRC Stamp Taxes (at least in relation to such partnerships carrying on a trade or profession) given that the contributors' interests in the property will as a matter of property law be replaced by their interests in the partnership. See the article entitled 'Limited Liability Partnerships' in Tax Bulletin 50, December 2000 reproduced at **Appendix D**.

Transfer of interests in limited liability partnerships

[73.10] Although incorrect as a matter of law, HMRC Stamp Taxes treat the transfer of an interest in a limited liability partnership as liable to stamp duty at the rates applicable to property i.e. from 1 to 4% and certificate of value where appropriate, rather than the 0.5% rate applicable to the transfer of stock or marketable securities. (See the article in Tax Bulletin 50 referred to in **73.9** above.)

Liquidation of limited liability partnerships

[73.11] There are no particular provisions dealing with stamp duty on a liquidation of a limited liability partnership. It is therefore a matter of debate whether to apply the principles relating to the winding up of a company (strictly correct given that the partnership is in law a body corporate) or the principles applicable to the winding up of a partnership formed under the *Partnership Act 1890* or the *Limited Partnerships Act 1907* (consistently with the 'transparent' treatment set out in HMRC Tax Bulletin 50 (see **73.9** above)). HMRC Tax Bulletin 50 itself treats the liquidation of a limited liability partnership for capital gains purposes as on a non-transparent basis where the partnership has ceased trading, but applies the 'transparent' basis where the partnership is being wound up 'informally'. Whether Parliament intended that the *Limited Liability Partnerships Act 2000* be applied in such a selective manner is open to doubt, but in appropriate cases it will be possible to distribute assets on a winding up whether on the strict corporate basis or the 'transparent' basis without attracting any stamp duty liability.

Chapter 74

Payment of Duty or Tax

Date of stamping and payment

[74.1] Regarding date of stamping and payment—

(a) *General.* The position regarding interest and penalties for late stamping has been changed by *FA 1999* for documents executed on or after 1 October 1999 and by *FA 2002* for documents executed on or after 24 July 2002. For the position regarding documents executed before this date please refer to earlier editions of this book. Old *SA 1891, s 15*, which governed the penalty position previously, has been replaced by a new *SA 1891, s 15* and two brand new sections, *15A* and *15B*, relating to interest and penalties respectively. [*FA 1999, s 109*]. In addition, new *SA 1891, s 12A* introduces for the first time a penalty of up to £300 for failure to stamp within 30 days after the Commissioners have given formal notice of their decision on an **ADJUDICATION (13)** (and see **69 NEGOTIATING WITH THE STAMP OFFICE**). Under the new penalty provisions, the old theory of the Stamp Acts that instruments should be stamped before execution has been notionally preserved by the wording of new *SA 1891, s 15(1)*, but the reality is of course that almost all documents are now stamped after execution. In general, the new rules simplify the position and for the first time impose an interest charge on a document executed outside the UK from 30 days after execution if it is later brought to the UK and stamped with ad valorem duty. For documents relating to UK land and executed on or after 24 July 2002, a penalty arises regardless of where the document is executed unless it is presented for stamping within 30 days of execution.

(b) *Interest.* Interest is charged on the stamping of any instrument liable to ad valorem duty and which has not been duly stamped within 30 days of execution, whether executed in the UK or elsewhere. Interest is payable on the amount of the unpaid duty from the end of 30 days after execution until the duty is paid. The interest charged is calculated at the rate applicable under *FA 1989, s 178* and set from time to time by statutory instrument. The amount of interest is rounded down to the nearest multiple of £5 and is not payable if less than £25. Interest is paid without deduction of income tax and is not an allowable deduction for tax purposes. Under the old *SA 1891, s 15*, interest and penalties were not payable if the document was first submitted for **ADJUDICATION (13)** within 30 days of execution (or if executed outside the UK, within 30 days of entering the UK), and in due course duly stamped. This of course meant that payment of duty could be deferred either indefinitely (in the case of documents executed outside the UK) or for a considerable period in the case of documents executed in the UK and submitted for adjudication without payment of interest or penalty. The new rules alter this position by imposing an automatic interest charge on any ad valorem duty remaining unpaid after the end of the period of 30 days following execution, whether in the UK or elsewhere. This interest is payable if and when the document is presented for stamping. The new rules recognise that in relation to documents submitted for **ADJUDICATION (13)**, even within the 30 days following execution, it will often be impossible to calculate the precise amount of stamp duty payable because, for example, a set of accounts has to be prepared and agreed or a valuation needs to be performed in order to settle the sale price. They do this by providing for the taxpayer to 'lodge' an amount in respect of the duty payable with the Commissioners and then the amount on which interest is payable is reduced by the amount lodged [*SA 1891, s 15A(2)*].

(c) *Penalties.* For instruments executed on or after 24 July 2002 a penalty is payable on the stamping of an instrument which is not presented for stamping within 30 days after:
   (i) if the instrument was executed in the UK, or relates to land in the UK—the date of execution;
   (ii) if the instrument is executed outside the UK and does not relate to land in the UK—the date it is first received in the UK.

   If the instrument is presented for stamping within one year of the end of the 30-day periods mentioned in (i) and (ii) above, the maximum penalty is the lesser of £300 and the amount of the unpaid duty. If the instrument is presented later than this the maximum penalty is the greater of £300 or the amount of the unpaid duty. The Commissioners can mitigate or remit these penalties and no penalty is payable if there is a reasonable excuse for the delay in presenting the instrument for stamping. It is understood that in the case of documents liable only to a fixed £5 duty, the Commissioners will not charge the £5 penalty on documents presented up to one year late and will consider on an individual basis mitigation of the £300 penalty that will otherwise apply to such documents presented more than one year late. [*SA 1891, s 15B* as amended by *FA 2002, s 114*]. (See Stamp Taxes Customer Newsletter February 2001, reproduced at **APPENDIX D**, for details of penalty mitigation where the duty exceeds £5,000 and is over one year late, and see also Stamp Office Manual section 3.32 for cases under one year late, and also cases of one year late or more where the duty is under £5,000, reproduced at **APPENDIX D**.

(d) *Payment.* Payment of ad valorem stamp duty is normally made by cheque and for cheques received by the Commissioners on or after 1 October 1999 which are paid on first presentation to the bank on which it is drawn, payment is deemed to have been made on the day the cheque was received by the Commissioners. [*FA 1999, Sch 18, para 2*].

(e) *Interest on repayment of overpaid duty.* From 1 October 1999, the power of a court to award interest on any duty ordered to be repaid by the Commissioners following a successful appeal has been replaced by an automatic right generally whether in an appeal or otherwise, to interest on a repayment by the Commissioners of duty or any penalty. [*FA 1965, s 91* repealed by *FA 1999, Sch 20*; *FA 1999, s 110*].

Liability for duty and penalties

[74.2] See generally **75 Penalties**.

The legislation does not lay down general rules for the liability for duty and penalties. In some cases there is a power of recovery of duty and penalties from persons connected with, but not parties to, the transaction charged. In most cases the duty and penalties are in practice recoverable only when the instrument is presented for stamping. However, since 1 October 1999 new rules provide for the determination of penalties (except for those on late stamping) by an authorised officer of the Commissioners and for penalty proceedings in the High Court in the case of fraud. In addition, the Treasury has been given power to make regulations applying the provisions of the *Taxes Management Act 1970* relating to collection and recovery, to the enforcement of such penalties. [*FA 1999*, *Sch 17*, *para 17*]. The regulations are contained in the *Stamp Duty (Collection and Recovery of Penalties) Regulations 1999 (SI 1999 No 2537)*, as amended by the *Transfer of Tribunal Functions and Revenue and Customs Appeals Order (SI 2009/56)* from 1 April 2009, which came into force on 1 October 1999 and provide for the collection and recovery of penalties by distraint including the power for a collector 'to break open in the daytime, any house or premises, calling to his assistance any constable'. The provision in *FA 1999*, *Sch 13*, *para 7(1)* requiring the duty to be paid by the purchaser is not regarded as placing an enforceable obligation on the purchaser to pay the duty.

The following paragraphs set out the specific rules which apply to the payment of certain stamp duties and penalties:

(a) **Bearer Instruments (24)**:
   - (i) chargeable on issue—liability for duty, interest and penalties is on the person making the issue or his agent. [*FA 1999*, *Sch 15*, *para 22*].
   - (ii) chargeable on transfer—liability for duty, interest and penalties is on the person making the transfer or a broker or agent concerned in the transfer. [*FA 1999*, *Sch 15*, *para 23*].

(b) **Clearance Services (33)**. The transferee is liable for any penalty for late stamping. [*FA 1986, s 69(5)*].

(c) **Compulsory Purchase (35)**. The person in whom property is vested or who is authorised to purchase property must produce a duly-stamped document to the Commissioners and in default is liable for duty and interest recoverable as a debt due to the Crown. [*FA 1895, s 12*].

(d) **Depositary Receipts (45)**. The transferee is liable for any penalty for late stamping. [*FA 1986, s 72(3)*].

(e) **Associated Companies (23)**. On a withdrawal of group relief under *FA 2002, s 111*, the transferee company is liable for payment and if it fails to pay the transferor, certain other group companies and controlling directors can be forced to pay.

(f) **Company Reorganisations (34)**. On a withdrawal of relief under *FA 1986, s 76* (undertaking in return for shares) under *FA 2002, s 113*, the acquiring company is liable for payment and if it fails to pay, certain other group companies and controlling directors can be required to pay.

In addition to the above provisions, any person who receives money in respect of duty but does not apply the money to payment of duty and improperly withholds or detains it is accountable for the duty which is a debt due to the Crown. [*SDMA 1891, s 2(1)*]. This section has been held to apply to a solicitor who withheld from a client a sum for duty (*Lord Advocate v Gordon* (1901), 8 SLT 439).

Allowance for spoiled stamps and lost or spoiled instruments

[*SDMA, ss 9–12A; Revenue Act 1898, s 13*].

[74.3] Allowances may be made for spoiled stamps if an application is made within two years after the stamp is spoiled, or, in the case of an executed instrument, the date of the instrument or, if undated, the date of first or only execution. These allowances apply in the following cases:

(a) A stamp on any material inadvertently obliterated before the material is signed or the instrument is executed by any party.

(b) A stamp which has been used on any instrument which:
- (i) is later found to be void from the beginning;
- (ii) is later found to be unfit for the original purpose by reason of any error or mistake therein;
- (iii) is not used at all and is incomplete or insufficient because of non-signature or non-completion by some party;
- (iv) fails the intended purpose or becomes void due to refusal by some person to act thereunder or want of enrolment within a time required by law;
- (v) becomes useless because the intended transaction was in fact effected by some other duly stamped instrument.

Allowance may also be made if a stamp of a higher value than necessary has been used inadvertently or if a stamp has been used inadvertently on an instrument not liable to duty.

In the case of an executed instrument, the instrument must be handed in for cancellation, but allowance cannot be given if any legal proceeding has commenced where the instrument could be used in evidence.

The allowance is made by giving new stamps to the applicant or by way of refund.

See **51 EXTRA-STATUTORY CONCESSIONS** for treatment of lost or spoilt documents before 29 April 1996. Relief from duty on lost or spoiled documents is provided by statutory enactment from 29 April 1996 instead of by extra-statutory concession. The replacement instrument is not chargeable with any duty but is to be stamped with the duty which it would otherwise have been chargeable. A lost instrument must be delivered to the Commissioners if it is later found. An application for relief must be made to the Commissioners and certain conditions satisfied before the relief will be granted. [*SDMA 1891, s 12A*].

Repayment for unused stamps

[74.4] Since 1 October 1999 it has no longer been possible to obtain repayment for an unused stamp. [*SDMA 1891*, *s 12* repealed by *FA 1999*, *Sch 20*, *Part V(4)*].

Repayment of duty in other cases

[74.5] With respect to the repayment of duty in other cases—

(a) **Agreements charged as conveyances on sale.** Certain agreements and contracts for sale are chargeable as actual conveyances on sale under *FA 1999*, *Sch 13*, *para 7*. (See **17 Agreement for Sale.**)
Ad valorem duty paid on an agreement is refunded if it is rescinded or annulled or for any reason not substantially performed or carried into effect so as to operate or be followed by a conveyance or transfer. [*FA 1999*, *Sch 13*, *para 9*].

(b) **Conveyance in contemplation of sale.** Certain conveyances in contemplation of sale are liable to duty as a conveyance or transfer on the value of the property. (See **39.10 Conveyance in Contemplation of Sale.**)
If a claim is made within two years of the conveyance or transfer on the grounds that:
   (i) the contemplated sale did not take place and the property has been reconveyed to the transferor; or
   (ii) the sale took place at a consideration less than the value on which duty was paid;
   the excess duty is repaid. [*FA 1965, s 90(2)*].

(c) **Conveyance following sale contract for UK land for a consideration exceeding £10m.** Where duty is paid on a contract to which *FA 2002, s 115* applies and the duty that would have been chargeable on the subsequent conveyance is less than that paid on the contract, the difference is refunded to the person by whom the duty was paid in the original contract. [*FA 2002, Sch 36, para 6*]. (See **17.1**(*f*) **Agreement for Sale**).

Changes in rates of duty

[74.6] Changes in rates of duty could formerly be implemented only when a Finance Act received Royal Assent. *FA 1973, s 50* (as amended by *FA 1993, s 207*) gives power to vary or abolish stamp duties by House of Commons resolution for limited periods pending enactment. The resolution has statutory effect from the date stated in the resolution; the date of cessation must also be stated but cannot end later than up to 31 days from the earliest of the following:

(a) the 30th day on which the House of Commons sits after the passing of the resolution without a Bill containing the resolution provisions being read a second time and without a Bill being amended to include the provisions;

(b) the rejection of a Bill containing the provisions;
(c) the dissolution or prorogation of Parliament;
(d) the expiration of six months from the day on which the resolution takes effect.

A resolution also ceases to have effect when the Act varying or abolishing the stamp duty comes into effect.

Instruments stamped in accordance with a resolution which has statutory effect under *s 50* are validly stamped notwithstanding that the provisions are not ultimately enacted.

For an example of this see *FA 1986, s 78(1)* (since repealed by *FA 1999, Sch 20)* which reproduces the effect of a 1986 Budget resolution withdrawing the exemption for transfers of loan capital. The resolution was subsequently withdrawn by the government and the exemption reinstated so a statutory provision was enacted to give effect to the withdrawal of the exemption for the period from 25 March 1986 to 6 July 1986 during which time a charge on transfers of loan capital therefore arose.

The power to vary stamp duties by regulation does not include the power to vary rates or thresholds. [*FA 2000, Sch 33, para 3*]. (See **19.2**(*e*) **STATUTORY ANTI-AVOIDANCE.**)

Stamp duty reserve tax

[74.7] See **84.6 LIABILITY AND ACCOUNTABILITY** and **84.8 ADMINISTRATION AND INTEREST ON OVERDUE TAX; 14 ADMINISTRATION** and **52 FAILURE TO STAMP.**

Chapter 75

Penalties

[75.1] The majority of the penalties are specific to a particular charge or type of instrument, but reference should be made to **75.8** below which deals with penalties applicable to stamp duties generally.

Fines and penalties

[75.2] Prior to 1 October 1999 there was a distinction between fines and penalties imposed for various offences as follows:

Fines—recoverable by High Court proceedings.
Penalties—paid on stamping of the instrument, the sanction being refusal by the Commissioners to stamp.

Since 1 October 1999 fines no longer exist and the system of penalties has been updated to include: powers for the determination of penalties by an authorised officer of the Commissioners; power to bring penalty proceedings in the High Court for fraud and power by regulations to enforce the collection and recovery of penalties (other than on late stamping) under the *Taxes Management Act 1970*.

Bearer instruments (24)

[75.3]

Heading and Offence	Penalty	Legislation
(*a*) Chargeable on issue—non-compliance with *FA 1999, Sch 15, para 21*(*see* **24.5**(*a*) STAMPING PROCEDURE).	Maximum fine £300 plus amount equal to duty. Also the duty due with interest from the date of default.	*FA 1999, Sch 15, para 22*
(*b*) Chargeable on transfer—transfer by instrument not duly stamped.	As above.	*FA 1999, Sch 15, para 23*
(*c*) Furnishing false particulars of instruments wilfully or negligently.	Maximum fine £300 plus twice difference between duty actually paid and duty chargeable.	*FA 1999, Sch 15, para 25*

Clearance services (33)

[75.4]

Failure to notify Commissioners of relevant facts.	Maximum fines £1,000 or £100.	*FA 1986, s 71(2)–(5)*

Compulsory purchase (35)

[75.5]

Non-production of Act or vesting instrument.	Interest on duty of 5% p.a. from date of Act or vesting.	*FA 1895, s 12*

Depositary receipts (45)

[75.6]

Failure to notify Commissioners of relevant facts.	Maximum fines £1,000 or £100.	*FA 1986, s 68(1), (2), (4), (5)*

Instruments (60)

[75.7]

Not setting out facts fully and truly with intent to defraud.	Maximum fine £3,000	*SA 1891, s 5*

Payment of duty or tax (74)

[75.8]

(*a*) Stamping after execution.	Within one year—lesser of £300 and duty payable	*SA 1891, s 15B*
(but see details of mitigation available set out at **APPENDIX F**)	After one year—greater of £300 and duty payable	
(*b*) Failure to give written notice of each charge to stamp duty reserve tax.	Penalty of £100 plus tax geared penalty not exceeding tax due where failure continues for 12 months or more.	*TMA 1970, s 93(5) (as applied by SI 1986/1711)*

Produced stamps (77)

[75.9]

Failure to produce instrument or comply with *FA 1931, Sch 2.*	Maximum fine—Level 3 on standard scale	*FA 1931, s 28(1)*

Shares and securities (83)

[75.10]

(*a*) Transfer etc. of foreign or Commonwealth government security not duly stamped.	Maximum fine £300	*SA 1891, s 83*
(*b*) Blank transfers. Parting with possession or removing from GB a blank transfer not duly completed.	Maximum fine £300 plus twice duty chargeable on original transfer in blank.	*FA 1963, s 67(1)*

Offences relating to stamps

[75.11]

(*a*) Fraudulent acts in connection with stamps on summary conviction; 14 years on indictment	Maximum sentence six months' imprisonment	*SDMA 1891, s 13; Forgery Act 1913*
(*b*) Fraud generally.	Maximum fine £3,000	*SDMA 1891, s 21*
(*c*) Fraudulent removal and reuse or sale.	Maximum penalty £3,000	*SA 1891, s 9*

Miscellaneous

[75.12]

(*a*) Refusal by public officer to permit inspection of rolls, books etc. by Commissioners.	Maximum fine £300	*SA 1891, s 16*
(*b*) Registration of an instrument not duly stamped.	Maximum fine £300	*SA 1891, s 17*

Chapter 76

Powers of Attorney

[76.1] The head of charge 'Letter or powers of attorney etc.' was abolished by *FA 1985, s 85, Sch 24(g)*.

Chapter 77

Produced Stamp

[*FA 1931, s 28, Sch 2*].

[77.1] The following instruments must be produced to the Commissioners in relation to pre-SDLT land transactions:

(a) the transfer on sale of fee simple of land;
(b) the grant or lease of land for a term of seven years or more;
(c) transfer on sale of a lease as in (*b*).

An **AGREEMENT FOR LEASE (16)** for a term of more than seven years must also be produced, but a lease granted in pursuance of the agreement and consistent with it need not be produced.

Production must be made within 30 days of execution (or 30 days from being received in GB if executed abroad) and the obligation to produce is on the transferee or lessee.

The Commissioners will stamp the instrument with a stamp denoting that it has been produced. The produced stamp is required in addition to any stamp denoting duty and any adjudication stamp; the instrument is not duly stamped unless it bears a produced stamp.

The particulars required to be given to the Commissioners in respect of a produced instrument are found in *FA 1931, Sch 2* as amended and are set out in the 'Particulars delivered' form (form L(A) 451) used for this purpose. (See **APPENDIX E** where the form is reproduced.)

An instrument relating solely to incorporeal heriditaments or a grave or right of burial need not be produced.

The purpose of these requirements is to give district valuers information on land values.

Since 1 January 1986 a new procedure has applied in relation to transfers of registered freehold or leasehold land which contain a **CERTIFICATE OF VALUE (30)** i.e. on which no stamp duty is payable. The new procedure does not apply to the grant of a lease or to transfers which require **ADJUDICATION (13)**. Where it applies, the new procedure requires the 'Particulars delivered' form to be sent direct to the appropriate District Land Registry (together with the transfer and application for registration), and not to the Stamp Office. [*FA 1985, s 89; Stamp Duty* (*Exempt Instruments*) *Regulations 1985* (*SI 1985 No 1688*)].

Chapter 78

Purchase of Own Shares

[78.1] When a company purchases its own shares under *Companies Act 2006, s 690*, the shares can be delivered to the company and surrendered by the shareholder without the need for an instrument of transfer. A company is required to file a return on form SH03 with the Registrar of Companies whenever it purchases its own shares, whether for cancellation or for those shares to be held in treasury under *Companies Act 2006, s 707*. Each return is chargeable with stamp duty at the 0.5% rate. [*FA 1986, s 66* as amended by *FA 2003, Sch 40, paras 2–5*]. If once held in treasury, i.e. registered in the name of the company, the shares are subsequently cancelled or disposed of to an employee share scheme then a further return must be filed with the Registrar of Companies under *Companies Act 2006, ss 728, 730*. This return is no longer liable to a stamp duty of £5. [*FA 1986, s 66(2A)* omitted by *FA 2008, Sch 32 para 5*].

Where treasury shares are subsequently sold or transferred, the sale or transfer instrument is no longer liable to a fixed £5 duty as a transfer otherwise than on sale. [*FA 1999, Sch 13 para 1(5)* as amended by *FA 2008, Sch 32 para 10(2)*]. However, if the transfer is to a person whose business is issuing depositary receipts or who provides clearance services, then the 1.5% rate will apply. [*FA 1999, Sch 13, paras 1(3)–(6) added by FA 2003, Sch 40, para 5*].

In appropriate cases exemption under *FA 1930, s 42* is available. (See **23 Associated Companies**.)

No duty arises on the redemption of redeemable shares under *Companies Act 2006, s 687*.

If the shares are held in an overseas branch register, the transfer is exempt from stamp duty unless the return (form SH03) which relates to the shares is executed in the UK. [*Companies Act 2006, s 133*, and see HMRC's announcement on 7 September 2009 confirming its acceptance of this position].

Chapter 79

Receipts

[79.1] The former head of charge applying to receipts in *SA 1891, Sch 1* was abolished by *FA 1970, Sch 8.*

Duty may be charged under some other head. An acknowledgement of receipt of the purchase price of a reversionary interest was held to be liable to ad valorem duty as an **AGREEMENT FOR SALE (17)** or as a **CONVEYANCE OR TRANSFER (39)** on sale of an equitable interest (*Fleetwood-Hesketh v* CIR CA, [1936] 1 KB 351).

Chapter 80

Release and Renunciation

[80.1] A release or renunciation of any property or right or interest in property is charged to duty as follows:

(a) on a sale—ad valorem duty as a conveyance on sale (see **39 CONVEYANCE OR TRANSFER**);
(b) any other case—formerly a fixed duty of £5 applied. However, this has been abolished generally for instruments executed on or after 13 March 2008 but has been retained for instruments effecting a land transaction. [*FA 1999, Sch 13 para 22* and *FA 2008, Sch 32 para 10(1)(f)*].

For a release or renunciation to be chargeable it must relate to property and amount to a transfer or assignment. The following have been held, inter alia, not to be chargeable as releases:

(a) an undertaking not to work coal (*Great Northern Rly v CIR* CA, [1901] 1 KB 416);
(b) a release of a widow's claim to *jus relictae* under Scottish law (*Cormack's Trustees v CIR* CS, 1924 SC 819).

Disclaimers. A release or renunciation entails acquisition of proprietary rights and subsequent disposition. A disclaimer on the other hand operates as a refusal to accept proprietary rights and cannot therefore be charged as a release or renunciation or as a **CONVEYANCE OR TRANSFER (39)** on sale. (*Re Stratton's Deed of Disclaimer* CA 1957, [1958] Ch 42; *Re Paradise Motor Co* CA, [1968] 2 All ER 625).

Renounceable letters of allotment and acceptance are not chargeable under this head. These documents will normally attract **STAMP DUTY RESERVE TAX (84)** on sale.

Chapter 81

Scotland

[81.1] The stamp duty legislation in this book applies to Scotland but its application requires some adaption to Scots law. There are also a few charges dealt with in the following paragraphs which relate only to instruments which have effect under Scots law.

Missives of let in Scotland that constitute an actual lease are charged to duty as leases and not as agreements for lease. [*FA 1999*, *Sch 13*, *para 14(3)*].

Dispositions

[81.2]

(*a*) of heritable property to singular successors or purchasers;	See **CONVEYANCE OR TRANSFER (39)**	*FA 1999*, *Sch 13*, *para 18(1)*
(*b*) of heritable property to a purchaser containing a clause declaring the purchase money a real burden on or affecting that property;	See **CONVEYANCE OR TRANSFER (39)**	*FA 1999*, *Sch 13*, *para 18(1)*
(*c*) containing constitution of feu or ground annual right;	See **CONVEYANCE OR TRANSFER (39)**	*FA 1999*, *Sch 13*, *para 18(1)*
(*d*) of any property or right or interest therein not elsewhere described.	£5	*FA 1999*, *Sch 13*, *para 18(2)*

The fixed duty of £5 under (d) above has been abolished generally for instruments executed on or after 13 March 2008 but has been retained for instruments effecting a land transaction. [*FA 2008, Sch 32 para 10(3)(c)*].

Produced stamp (76)

[81.3] Since 1 September 1974 the grant or transfer on sale of a lease of land in Scotland does not need to be produced to the Commissioners under *FA 1931, s 28* if the term of the lease exceeds 20 years. [*Land Tenure Reform (Scotland) Act 1974*].

Chapter 82

Scrip Dividends

[82.1] A scrip dividend is a dividend in the form of additional shares rather than in cash. The shares are allotted fully paid-up out of the company's distributable reserves. No stamp duty arises on the making of a scrip dividend. The old head of charge 'Scrip certificate, scrip or other document' was abolished by *FA 1949, s 35, Sch 8* (repealed by *FA 1999, s 139, Sch 20, Pt V(2)*).

Chapter 83

Shares and Securities

Note: Despite the abolition of stamp duty on land and buildings from 1 December 2003, stamp duties continue to apply to transactions in shares and securities, and this chapter remains relevant to such transactions. For instruments executed on or after 1 December 2003 that relate partly to shares and securities and partly to other property, the consideration is to be apportioned on a just and reasonable basis, as between the shares and securities and the other property, and the instrument is to be charged with stamp duty only in respect of the consideration attributed to the shares and securities. [*FA 2003, Sch 20 para 1*].

See also **STAMP DUTY RESERVE TAX (84)**.

[83.1] The following paragraphs summarise the stamp duty implications of transactions in shares and securities:

(a) on issue (**83.2–83.3**);
(b) on transfer—generally (**83.4**);
(c) on transfer to intermediaries (**83.5**);
(d) on transfer in connection with **DEPOSITARY RECEIPTS (44)** or **CLEARANCE SERVICES (32)** (**83.6**);
(e) special categories of stock (**83.7**);
(f) repurchases and stock lending (**83.8**).

Issue of shares

[83.2] *FA 1988, s 141* abolished the **CAPITAL DUTY (29)** chargeable on the issue of shares by a capital company. Shares may be issued as the consideration for a sale and therefore ad valorem duty under the head **CONVEYANCE OR TRANSFER (39)** on sale may be payable on the transfer of the property sold calculated according to the value of the shares issued. But see the exemptions and relief from stamp duty for **COMPANY REORGANISATIONS (34)**. The issue of bearer shares may attract duty under the **BEARER INSTRUMENTS (24)** charge. There is no requirement to produce a duly stamped contract or particulars of the contract under *Companies Act 2006, s 555*, although any non-cash consideration must be entered on form SH01.

Issue of other securities

[83.3] Since the abolition of the heads 'Marketable security' and 'Loan capital' [*FA 1973, Sch 22*], duty is not generally charged on the issue of securities. Certain bearer securities are, however, chargeable on issue.

Transfers of shares generally

[83.4] Regarding transfers of shares generally—

(a) **On sale.** The transfer of shares etc on sale is liable to duty generally at the rate of 0.5% as a **Conveyance or Transfer (39)** on sale. The nil rate of duty for consideration of £1,000 or less is available where a **Certificate of Value (30)** is given in respect of transfers of stocks, shares, and marketable securities. [*FA 1999, Sch 13 para 1(3A)* for instruments executed on or after 13 March 2008]. The creation of a duly stamped transfer instrument within 6 years of the sale agreement cancels the **Stamp Duty Reserve Tax (84)** charge at the equivalent rate. A limited number of bearer instruments are chargeable on transfer and a transfer on sale will be liable under the **Bearer Instruments (24)** charge. Prior to *FA 1997, s 105* there was a scheme which appears to have been successful in avoiding ad valorem stamp duty on the sale of shares in UK companies. The scheme relied on the exemptions from stamp duty and **Stamp Duty Reserve Tax (84)** for bearer instruments expressed in a foreign currency. See **24.7**(*a*) **Exemptions** and **84.4**(*b*) **Repos and Stock Lending.** The scheme involved the following steps:

   (i) the existing ordinary shares of the target company were converted into deferred shares worth very little and share warrants to bearer denominated in a foreign currency were issued to the shareholders of the target by way of bonus issue capitalised from the target's reserves;

   (ii) the share warrants to bearer were sold by delivery for most of the agreed sale price of the target and the deferred shares were transferred for the balance of the sale price in the normal way with stamp duty being paid only in respect of the latter transfer.

   Several detailed company law and capital gains tax points had to be considered by the vendor when using this scheme and it was appropriate to seek an indemnity from the purchaser for the risks and costs involved. However, the transfer of the share warrants to bearer would now give rise to **Stamp Duty Reserve Tax (83)** as explained in **24.8**(*b*) **Stamp Duty Reserve Tax.** See **24.8 Stamp Duty Reserve Tax** for an alternative structure involving the use of share warrants denominated in sterling.

(b) **By gift.** A transfer of shares etc by way of gift no longer attracts duty following the abolition of the charge on **Gifts (58)** by *FA 1985, s 82* and the requirement for adjudication by *FA 2008, s 100*.

(c) **By exchange.** A transaction of exchange involving shares is not liable under the head **Exchange or Partition (48)** (*Coates (J & P) Ltd v CIR* CA, [1897] 2 QB 423), but is liable to ad valorem duty as a **Conveyance or Transfer (38)** on sale (although see **34 Company Reorganisations** for relief from duty and **36.3 Stock (Including Shares) and Securities** for anti-avoidance).

(d) **CREST.** Transfers of securities to the electronic share transfer system known as CREST on or after 1 July 1996 are exempt from stamp duty so long as the transferee is a member of CREST and the transfer is in a form which will ensure that the securities become held in an uncertificated form within CREST. [*FA 1996, s 186*].

Subject to regulations made under *Companies Act 2006, ss 783, 784(3), 785 and 788* it is unlawful for a company to register a transfer of shares in the company or debentures of the company unless a proper instrument of transfer has been delivered to it (unless the transfer arises by operation of law). [*Companies Act 2006, s 770*]. A registrar who registers a transfer of shares or debentures which has not been duly stamped is liable to a fine of £300, however, neither the enrolment nor the transfer is thereby rendered a nullity (*Re Brown & Root McDermott Fabricators Ltd's application* Ch D [1996] STC 483, *Nisbet v Shepherd* [1994] 1 BCLC 300). [*SA 1891, s 17*]. *Companies Act 2006, s 785* provides for regulations to be made to enable title to securities to be evidenced and transferred without a written instrument.

The *Stock Transfer Act 1963*, as amended, provides for standard forms to be used for the transfer of the registered securities of:

(i) companies limited by shares;
(ii) certain other bodies incorporated in Great Britain;
(iii) the Government, other than Post Office securities and national savings certificates;
(iv) local authorities;
(v) unit trusts.

Blank transfers may be used to effect the transfer by sale of registered stock. A transfer in blank is one where the name of the transferee has not been inserted. It is an offence (see **75 Penalties**) to part with possession of the blank transfer or remove it from Great Britain before it is duly completed (which means the insertion of the names of the purchaser, his agent or nominee or a person entitled to a charge on the stock for money lent to the purchaser or donee). [*FA 1963, s 67*]. The purpose of this provision is to ensure that duty is charged on transfers on sale of registered stock.

Stock Exchange transactions. In order to enable the implementation of the Stock Exchange's computerised transfer and settlement system ('Talisman'), special rules were introduced by *FA 1976, s 127* concerning transfers involving stock exchange nominees (persons designated for the purposes of *FA 1976, s 127* by the Secretary of State). Under *s 127* transfers to the nominee company of the International Stock Exchange, SEPON Ltd, executed for the purposes of a stock exchange transaction are exempt from duty. (See also **83.3**(*d*) above.)

Transfers of shares to intermediaries etc.

[83.5] For instruments executed before 20 October 1997, *FA 1986, s 81* provided an exemption from stamp duty for purchases of shares, etc by market makers. For instruments executed on or after that date, this exemption was replaced by an exemption for such purchases by intermediaries. The exemption was contained in *FA 1986, s 80A*. A number of supplementary definitions are contained in *FA 1986, s 80B*.

The scope of this exemption was widened significantly for instruments executed on or after 1 November 2007 following the implementation of the

Markets in Financial Instruments Directive (2004/39/EC) on that date by *FA 2007, s 73* and *Sch 21*. A detailed explanation of the relief is contained in a note entitled 'Intermediary and Stock Lending Reliefs – FA 2007 Changes' published by HMRC and reproduced in **APPENDIX G**.

An instrument qualifying for this exemption must be stamped with a stamp denoting that the instrument is not chargeable with any duty.

Transfers in connection with depositary receipts (44) and clearance services (32)

[83.6] A special charge arises on transfers of certain shares and securities in connection with such schemes. See the chapters referred to above.

Special categories of stock

[83.7] There are special considerations for the following special categories of stock—

(a) Government stocks are exempt from all stamp duties. [*FA 1999, Sch 13, para 24(a)*].
(b) Treasury guaranteed stocks are transferable free of all stamp duties. [*FA 1947, s 57*].
(c) No stamp duty is charged on the issue or transfer of the stock of a designated international organisation. [*FA 1984, s 126*].
(d) **LOAN CAPITAL AND DEBENTURES (66)**. Most forms of loan capital and debenture are now exempt from all stamp duties.
(e) Warrants to purchase government stock are themselves exempt from all stamp duties. [*FA 1987, s 50; F(No 2)A 1987, s 99*]. See **70 OPTIONS AND WARRANTS**.
(f) Paired shares. Units comprising paired shares of the type issued by Eurotunnel are treated as single shares for both stamp duty and **STAMP DUTY RESERVE TAX (84)**. [*FA 1988, ss 143, 144*].
(g) Employee share ownership plans. Stamp duty is not charged on the transfer of partnership or dividend shares by the trustees to an employee. [*FA 2001, s 95*].

Repurchases and stock lending

[83.8] Repurchases ('repos') and stock lending arrangements are arrangements for the sale and return or lending and return, of securities. Under *FA 1986, s 80C* these transactions are exempt from stamp duty (and from stamp duty reserve tax under *FA 1986, s 89AA*) provided that securities of the same kind and amount are returned to the seller or lender under the terms of the arrangement. The instruments of transfer must be stamped with a stamp denoting that the instrument is not chargeable with any duty. At least one of the parties must be authorised under the law of the state of the European

Economic Area to provide investment services or execution of orders, etc in stock of the kind concerned and stock of that kind must be regularly traded on a regulated market. There are also other conditions stipulated in *FA 1986, s 80C*. With effect from 1 September 2008, new *s 80D* (inserted by *FA 2009, s 82* and *Sch 37*) has provided that where the securities are not returned to the seller or lender because one of the parties has become insolvent, stamp duty is not chargeable on any instrument transferring to the solvent party replacement stock or any further replacement stock.

Chapter 84

Stamp Duty Reserve Tax

General

[84.1] A chain of agreements for the sale of shares or securities followed by an instrument of transfer from the first seller direct to the last purchaser normally results in stamp duty being charged only once on the instrument of transfer according to the price paid by the last purchaser. All the intermediate sale agreements escape stamp duty. This is because agreements for the sale of a legal interest in stock or marketable securities escape stamp duty under *FA 1999*, *Sch 13*, *para 7(1)* (see **17.1 Agreement for Sale**) and the instrument of transfer is only charged with duty in respect of the price paid by the last purchaser under *SA 1891, s 58(4)* (see **17.2 Agreement for Sub-sale**). This meant that it was possible to deal in shares or securities during a Stock Exchange period of account without paying stamp duty. Only the transfer to the ultimate purchaser at the end of the account would attract stamp duty.

Stamp duty reserve tax was introduced to impose an ad valorem charge on the intermediate sale agreements. However, since its introduction by *FA 1986* the tax has assumed a much greater role and is now the primary tax, liability for which is cancelled by the payment of stamp duty. The tax is charged at the rate of one half per cent of the amount or value of the consideration for the sale rounded to the nearest penny. Unlike stamp duty, the tax applies to the agreement to transfer (whether oral or written) and does not depend upon the execution of a written instrument of transfer for a charge to arise. The tax charge arises on the date the agreement is made or becomes unconditional and the tax is payable seven days after the end of the month in which the charge arises, except where the tax is accounted for by special arrangement between the Stamp Office and operators of electronic transfer systems and exchanges. Interest is charged on tax paid late but in its 'Notes for Guidance' (February 1998) the Stamp Office stated that it would not seek interest in relation to transfers of securities held outside CREST if a duly stamped instrument or transfer was produced by the later of seven days after the end of the month in which the charge arose or 30 days after the agreement. This was extended to 60 days from the date the charge arises by concession as explained in the Inland Revenue Tax Bulletin of October 1998—see **Appendix D**. However, with the introduction of interest on late paid stamp duty this practice has ceased and the Stamp Office Manual states at para 13.17 that cases will only be pursued if 'difficulty is experienced in securing the stamping of the document'.

Stamp duty reserve tax is not a stamp duty but a separate tax with its own rules, procedure and collection machinery. It applies to agreements to transfer *chargeable securities* for consideration in money or money's worth and hence is wider in scope than conveyance on sale duty which arises only when the consideration is money, shares or securities or debts. However, when the consideration is not money, shares or securities or debts there will not normally be a sale for stamp duty purposes and the share transfer will not attract any duty. Although most of the exemptions and reliefs from stamp duty have no equivalents in stamp duty reserve tax, a share transfer which is submitted for **ADJUDICATION (12)** and stamped exempt from stamp duty counts as a duly stamped instrument and as such cancels any stamp duty reserve tax charge.

There are five types of stamp duty reserve tax charge: the principal charge (see **84.2–84.5** below), the charges in relation to **CLEARANCE SERVICES (33)** and **DEPOSITARY RECEIPTS (45)**, the optional regime for **CLEARANCE SERVICES (33)** introduced by *FA 1996*, and the new regime for dealings in units in **UNIT TRUSTS (87)** effective from 6 February 2000.

The principal charge [*FA 1986, s 87*]

[84.2] The principal charge applies where a person (A) agrees with another person (B) to transfer *chargeable securities* for consideration in money or money's worth. The charge is at the rate of one half per cent of the amount or value of the consideration. The open market value of the consideration is taken when the consideration is not money. When B agrees to buy chargeable securities from A and resells some of those securities to C, the tax has effect as if there were two separate agreements between A and B. The first agreement relates to the securities which B retains and in respect of which an instrument transferring the securities to him is executed and stamped. The tax charge is cancelled if the stamp duty is paid on the instrument, or is repaid if the instrument is duly stamped after the tax has been paid, in each case within six years of the sale agreement. The second agreement between A and B relates to the securities which B has resold to C and in respect of which there will be a duly stamped instrument transferring the securities direct from A to C. Stamp duty reserve tax is charged on this second agreement between A and B according to the price paid by B because there will be no instrument transferring those securities to B. The following example illustrates this:

B buys 10,000 shares from A for £10,000

B resells 7,500 of the shares to C

A transfers 2,500 shares to B and 7,500 shares direct to C

B is treated as if he had made two agreements. The first relates to the 2,500 shares transferred to him by A on which B will pay stamp duty on £2,500. The second agreement relates to the 7,500 shares which B has sub-sold to C and on which B will pay stamp duty reserve tax on £7,500. C will pay stamp duty on the transfer of the 7,500 shares direct from A. Where *chargeable securities* are transferred not to B but to a bank or other person as security for a loan made to B (but not to secure a guarantee given by B in relation to another's debt) the lender is treated as if he were B's nominee. Therefore, a duly stamped instrument transferring the securities to the lender instead of B will nevertheless cancel a stamp duty reserve tax charge [*FA 1986, s 92(1)*]. The stamp duty reserve tax legislation fails to identify clearly who A and B are when buyer and/or seller act through agents, as for example when an investor buys securities on an exchange through a broker. In their revised edition of 'Stamp Duty Reserve Tax—Notes for Guidance' published in February 1998 the Stamp Office states:

> 7.3 . . . Where securities are bought on an exchange via a broker acting as agent, the buying broker will normally be the person responsible for accounting for SDRT to the Inland Revenue though his client will be liable. The contractual arrangement between the member and his client does not constitute a separate chargeable agreement (i.e. because he is an agent). Where an investor buys securities direct from an exchange member firm (i.e. where the firm is selling as a principal) the person ultimately liable in law for the tax will be the investor; but under the Regulations the member will be responsible for notifying the Revenue of the charge and accounting for the tax.

The 1993 and 1998 editions of the Notes reflect a change of view by the Stamp Office from the previous October 1986 edition in which it was clear that in Stock Exchange transactions the Stamp Office was treating the agents and not their client principals as A and B. One problem with this old approach was that there would be no duly stamped instrument transferring the securities to the person treated as B, i.e. the buying broker-dealer. The transfer would of course be direct to the client principal and could not therefore forestall a stamp duty reserve tax charge on the broker-dealer. A double charge should therefore arise consisting of stamp duty reserve tax on the broker-dealer and stamp duty on the client principal. To avoid this the Stamp Office also stated in its 'Notes for Guidance':

> 2.4. To allow time for an instrument of transfer to be produced Section 87 provides for the charge to arise two months after the date of the agreement, unless in the meantime a duly stamped instrument of transfer has been executed (normally this would be a stock transfer form or, in the case of most Stock Exchange transactions, a TALISMAN bought transfer) transferring the securities either to the person described in paragraph 2.1 above as B or B's nominee. Where in the case of a transaction carried out on The Stock Exchange the agreement is concluded between a member firm selling as a principal and a broker-dealing acting as an agent, this condition is regarded as satisfied if within the two-month period a duly stamped instrument of transfer is executed transferring the securities to which the agreement relates to the broker-dealer's principal.

The old approach by the Stamp Office seemed to be limited to Stock Exchange transactions and it did not seek to make agents liable in other situations, e.g. offers for sale and placings where the sponsoring bank acts not as a purchaser and seller but as 'agent to procure' purchasers to avoid a charge to stamp duty reserve tax on the sponsor.

Renounceable letters of allotment and acceptance are *chargeable securities* and dealings in renounceable letters, where the rights under the letter are renounceable, not later than six months after the issue of the letter attract stamp duty reserve tax. The tax charge arises automatically on the date of each agreement to transfer a renounceable letter. [*FA 1986, 90(3B)*]. See **65 LETTERS OF ALLOTMENT AND ACCEPTANCE, 55 FLOTATIONS, ETC.** and **24 BEARER INSTRUMENTS.**

Stamp duty reserve tax is the liability of the purchaser, i.e. the person referred to as B above. [*FA 1986, s 91; F(No 2)A 1987, s 100(2)*]. However, where the shares or securities are bought on an exchange through a broker, the broker is normally responsible for paying the tax even though the liability rests with the broker's client.

Where a tax charge has arisen and within six years of the date of the agreement an instrument transferring the chargeable securities to B or his nominee is executed and duly stamped, the tax, if paid, is repayable, and if not paid, is no longer payable although a liability to interest and possibly penalties can arise. Repayments of £25 or more carry tax-free interest from the date the tax was paid until the repayment order is issued. The interest is calculated at the rate applicable under *FA 1989, s 178*. [*FA 1986, s 92, FA 1989, ss 179, 180* and *FA 1996, s 192(4), (5), (6)*].

There is also provision for repayment or cancellation of the tax in relation to agreements to transfer shares in a company to that company where, within six years of the tax charge arising, a return required under *Companies Act 1985, s 169(1)* or *(1B)* has been duly stamped under *FA 1986, s 66*. [*FA 1986, s 92(1C), (1D), inserted by FA 2003, Sch 40, para 4*]. And see **78.1 PURCHASE OF OWN SHARES**.

Intermediaries, etc.

[84.3] The charge to stamp duty reserve tax in respect of agreements executed or becoming unconditional before 20 October 1997 between A and B to transfer chargeable securities did not apply in certain circumstances if B was a broker and dealer or a market maker. [*FA 1986, s 89*]. In respect of the agreements executed on or after that date, the charge to stamp duty reserve tax does not apply where B is an intermediary. [*FA 1986, ss 88A, 88B* inserted by *FA 1997, s 102(1)* which was brought into force on 20 October 1997 by the *Finance Act 1997 (Stamp Duty and Stamp Duty Reserve Tax) (Appointed Day) Order 1997* (SI 1997/2428). *FA 1997, s 102(2)* repealed *FA 1986, s 89* with effect from the same date]. The details of the relief, in particular the conditions for exemption, were similar to those for the corresponding relief from stamp duty in the case of transfers of stock to intermediaries. The scope of this exemption was widened significantly from 1 November 2007 following the implementation of the Markets in Financial Instruments Directive (2004/39/E) on that date by *FA 2007, s 73* and *Sch 21*. A detailed explanation of the relief is contained in a note entitled 'Intermediary and Stock Lending reliefs – FA 2007 Changes' published by HMRC reproduced at **APPENDIX G**.

Repos and stock lending

[84.4] Repurchases ('repos') and stock lending arrangements are arrangements for the sale and return or lending and return, of securities. Under *FA 1986, s 89AA* these transactions are exempt from stamp duty reserve tax (and from stamp duty under *FA 1986, s 80C*) provided that securities of the same kind and amount are returned to the seller or lender under the terms of the arrangement. At least one of the parties must be authorised under the law of a state of the European Economic Area to provide investment services or execution of orders, etc in stock of the kind concerned and stock of that kind must be regularly traded on a regulated market. There are also other conditions stipulated in *FA 1986, s 89AA*. With effect from 1 September 2008, *FA 1986, s 89AB* (inserted by *FA 2009, s 82* and *Sch 37*) has provided that where the securities were not returned to the seller or lender because one of the parties has become insolvent, no stamp duty reserve tax will be charged on the purchaser or borrower nor will stamp duty reserve tax be charged on an insolvent lender who fails to return collateral securities to a borrower. Stamp duty reserve tax will also not be charged where a party acquires replacement securities because of the insolvency of the borrower or the lender.

Other exemptions

[84.5] See **55 FLOTATIONS, ETC.** for the exemption for public offerings of listed securities [*FA 1986, s 89A*].

The following exemptions from the principal charge to stamp duty reserve tax are also available:

(a) certain transfers of units in a unit trust scheme, see **88 UNIT TRUSTS;**
(b) bearer instruments, except those to which *FA 1997, s 105* apply, certain renounceable letters of allotment and certain transfers of bearer instruments within the exemption for non-sterling stock into a depositary scheme or clearance service, see **24 BEARER INSTRUMENTS** and **65 LETTERS OF ALLOTMENT AND ACCEPTANCE;**
(c) transfers which are caught by the special charges in relation to **CLEARANCE SERVICES (33)** and **DEPOSITARY RECEIPTS (45)**;
(d) transfers of securities to **CHARITIES (32)** and similar bodies [*FA 1986, s 90*];
(e) government securities [*FA 1986, s 99(5)*];
(f) foreign securities unless registered in a UK register [*FA 1986, s 90(4)*];
(g) the grant, but not the subsequent transfer, of an option, see **70 OPTIONS AND WARRANTS;**
(h) the issue of new securities except for issues to a depositary receipt issuer or clearance service operator or nominee;
(i) surrenders of units in unit trust schemes and shares in open-ended investment companies held within individual pension accounts [*FA 2001, ss 93, 94*];
(j) transfers of shares to employees by the trustees of approved employee share ownership plans [*FA 2001, s 95*]; and
(k) Transfers of equity securities or agreements to transfer equity securities to the London Clearing House (or its nominee) as a provider of clearance services in connection with deals on the London Stock Exchange. [*Stamp Duty Reserve Tax (Investment Exchanges and Clearing Houses) (The London Stock Exchange) Regulations 2001* (*SI 2001 No 255*)]. Similar arrangements exist for virt-x, LIFFE, Jiway and the OM London Exchange.

Liability and accountability

[84.6] The person liable to pay the stamp duty reserve tax is the purchaser, i.e. the person referred to as B in **84.2** above [*FA 1986, s 91(1)*]. The tax must be notified and paid by the *accountable date* which means the seventh day of the month following the month in which the charge arises, i.e. the day on which agreement to transfer is made or becomes unconditional, unless the transfer is on CREST or a similar electronic system when the *accountable date* means the date agreed between the operator and Commissioners or if no such date is agreed, 14 days after the transfer. [*Stamp Duty Tax Regulations 1986 (SI 1986 No 1711) regs 2 and 3*, as amended].

Therefore unless the transfer is on an electronic system, where B agrees to buy chargeable securities from A on 9 May a charge to tax will arise on 9 May unless the agreement is concluded by a duly stamped transfer, and the tax must be paid by 7 June. Note however, that in its 'Notes for Guidance' (February 1998) the Stamp Office stated that it would not seek interest in relation to securities held outside CREST if a duly stamped instrument or transfer was produced by the later of the *accountable date* or 30 days after the agreement to transfer securities. This was extended to 60 days after the tax charge has arisen by concession as explained in the Inland Revenue Tax Bulletin of October 1998—see **APPENDIX D**. However, with the introduction of an automatic interest charge for late paid stamp duty the Stamp Office Manual states at para 13.17 that cases will only be pursued if there is difficulty in securing the stamping of the document.

The *accountable person* (or the operator of the exchange where appropriate) is required under regulations to give notice that a stamp duty reserve tax charge has arisen and to pay the tax due. [*Stamp Duty Reserve Regulations 1986 (SI 1986 No 1711) regs 4* and *4A*, as amended].

With effect from 20 October 1997 the *accountable person* is defined in the regulations as:

(a) the buying exchange member including an exchange member acting for his client who is not an exchange member; and failing that;
(b) the selling exchange member including an exchange member acting for his client who is not an exchange member; and failing that;
(c) the buying qualified dealer including a dealer acting for his client who is not a qualified dealer; and failing that;
(d) the selling qualified dealer including a dealer acting for his client who is not a qualified dealer; and failing that;
(e) B, i.e. the purchaser, where no exchange member or qualified dealer is involved in the transaction.

Normally, however, it will be the operator of the exchange who accounts for the tax. Under the regulations, operators of electronic transfer systems and recognised investment exchanges are accountable for stamp duty reserve tax, although different arrangements may be entered into with the Commissioners. Thus, arrangements have been made for the central collection of stamp duty reserve tax from participants in the CREST system. Under such arrangements the operator or exchange collects and accounts for the stamp duty reserve tax on behalf of those persons who would otherwise be liable.

The intention is that the collection and payment of the tax is carried out by the exchange operators and market professionals and not individual investors. Vendors in public offers of shares may enter into arrangements with the Commissioners to meet the stamp duty reserve tax liability arising and if so individual investors will not be required to pay it and where this is the case the relevant prospectus will mention this.

The definitions of 'exchange', 'operator' and 'qualified dealer' can be found in the Regulations. [*Stamp Duty Reserve Tax Regulations 1986 (SI 1986 No 1711)* as amended].

Chargeable securities

[84.7] **Chargeable securities** are:

(a) stocks, shares or loan capital;
(b) interests in, or in dividends or other rights arising out of stocks, shares or loan capital;
(c) rights to allotments of or to subscribe for, or options to acquire, stocks, shares or loan capital; and
(d) units under a unit trust scheme.

With the exception of units under a unit trust scheme, securities issued or raised by a company not incorporated in the UK are not *chargeable securities* unless:

(i) they are registered in a register kept in the UK by or on behalf of the company; or
(ii) the shares are paired with shares issued by a company incorporated in the UK; or
(iii) in the case of securities falling within (*b*) and (*c*) above, the underlying securities are registered in a UK register or are paired with shares issued by a company incorporated in the UK; or
(iv) they are issued or raised by a Societas Europaea with its registered office in the UK.

Securities falling within (*a*), (*b*) and (*c*) above are not chargeable securities if they are issued or raised by a Societas Europaea with its registered office outside the UK.

The reference in (ii) and (iii) above to shares being paired with shares of a UK incorporated company means that each unit representing paired shares of the type issued by Eurotunnel is treated as a single *chargeable security*.

Securities which are exempt from stamp duty on transfer, e.g. gilts, and securities falling within (*b*) and (*c*) above where the underlying securities are exempt from stamp duty on transfer, are not *chargeable securities*. Also excluded from the meaning of *chargeable securities* are interests in **DEPOSITARY RECEIPTS (44)** for stocks or shares and units under a unit trust scheme if all the trustees are non-UK resident and the units are kept in a non-UK register or the trust property can under the terms of the scheme only be invested in exempt investments (as defined). [*FA 1986, s 99(3)–(6a); FA 1988, s 144(1)(2); F(No 2)A 2005, s 57(1)*].

In relation to the special charges on **Depositary Receipts (45)** and **Clearance Services (33)** the definition of *chargeable securities* in **84.7** above applies except that (i) is ignored so that securities issued or raised by a company not incorporated in the UK but registered in a register kept in the UK are not *chargeable securities*. In the case of newly-subscribed shares or securities within (*b*) and (*c*) representing such shares, (ii) is ignored so that such securities issued by a company not incorporated in the UK but paired with shares issued by a company incorporated in the UK are not *chargeable securities* when issued in pursuance of arrangements for clearance services or depositary receipts. Also, shares registered in an overseas branch register which are exempt from stamp duty on transfer by *Companies Act 1985, Sch 14, para 8* are still *chargeable securities* despite this exemption. [*FA 1986, s 99(10)–(12); FA 1988, s 144(4), (5)*].

The Treasury also has the power by regulation to exclude from the definition of chargeable securities in **84.7** above, exempt UK depositary interests in foreign securities. [*FA 1999, s 119*]. This allows an operator of an electronic settlement system to provide a settlement service for transactions in foreign shares without the purchaser incurring a liability to stamp duty reserve tax. Regulations have been made specifying a number of classes of security as available to be in UK depositary interest form. [*Stamp Duty Reserve Tax (UK Depository Interests in Foreign Securities) Regulations 1999 SI 1999 No 1871* as amended by *SI 2001/3779*].

Administration and interest on overdue tax

[84.8] As mentioned above, regulations have been made under *FA 1986, s 98* governing the administration, assessment, collection and recovery of stamp duty reserve tax. These regulations are the *Stamp Duty Reserve Tax Regulations 1986 (SI 1986 No 1711)* as amended, and they also provide for the application of provisions of the *Taxes Management Act 1970* with the modifications specified in the Schedule to the regulations. Although some of the relevant provisions of the *Taxes Management Act 1970* have been substantially amended since 1986 (principally by *FA 1989*), it is thought that the correct view is that these subsequent amendments to the *Taxes Management Act 1970* itself are not to be taken into account for the purposes of the regulations (*Willows v Lewis* Ch D [1982] STC 141). It has subsequently been confirmed that the Treasury has power under *FA 1986, s 98* to make provision by regulation for penalties and interest on overdue tax and to require information to be provided etc. and to impose a penalty for failure to do so. [*FA 1999, s 121*]. The regulations may include provisions specifying the form or manner in which notices and information must be given to the Commissioners. [*FA 1989, s 177*]. Interest on overdue stamp duty reserve tax is charged at the rate applicable under *FA 1989, s 178* to overdue income tax and capital gains tax. [*Taxes Management Act 1970, s 86* and *Stamp Duty Reserve Tax (Amendment) Regulations 1989 (SI 1989 No 1301)* as amended by *SI 1999/2536*].

SDRT collection practice

[84.9] Given that, as explained above, stamp duty reserve tax is now the primary tax, liability for which is cancelled by the payment of stamp duty, problems can arise if there is any delay in stamping the document before the *accountable date*. However, with the introduction of automatic interest on late paid stamp duty the Stamp Taxes Manual (March 2002) states at para 13.17 that cases will only be pursued if there is difficulty in securing the stamping of the document.

Further treatment

[84.10] Further mention of stamp duty reserve tax will be found in the following chapters:

- **14 ADMINISTRATION;**
- **24 BEARER INSTRUMENTS;**
- **33 CLEARANCE SERVICES;**
- **45 DEPOSITARY RECEIPTS;**
- **55 FLOTATIONS, ETC.;**
- **60 INSTRUMENTS;**
- **65 LETTERS OF ALLOTMENT AND ACCEPTANCE;**
- **70 OPTIONS AND WARRANTS;**
- **72 OVERSEAS MATTERS;**
- **83 SHARES AND SECURITIES;**
- **86 TRUSTS AND TRUSTEES;**
- **87 UNDERWRITING;**
- **88 UNIT TRUSTS.**

Chapter 85

Surrenders

[85.1] A fixed duty of £5 was formerly payable on a surrender but this duty was abolished generally for instruments executed on or after 13 March 2008 except for instruments effecting a pre-SDLT land transaction. Where the surrender is for a consideration, it may be dutiable as a **CONVEYANCE OR TRANSFER (398)** on sale. [*FA 1999, Sch 13 para 23 and FA 2008, Sch 32 para 10(3)(g)*].

For surrenders of leases see **64.4 SURRENDERS AND VARIATIONS**.

Chapter 86

Trusts and Trustees

Note: *FA 2003* abolished stamp duty on land and buildings and in its place created stamp duty land tax from 1 December 2003 (see Part One). Stamp duties continue to apply to transactions in shares and securities, bearer instruments and acquisitions of an interest in a partnership, and this chapter remains relevant to such transactions. A written declaration of trust or vesting of property executed on or after 1 December 2003 will remain liable to stamp duty to the extent that it relates to property that remains within the charge to stamp duty on or after that date.

Creation of a trust

[86.1] Any inter vivos trust which is recorded by a written declaration of trust and is executed before 1 December 2003 formerly attracted a fixed duty of £5 as a **DECLARATION OF TRUST (42).** While this fixed duty has been abolished generally, it has been retained for instruments effecting a pre-SDLT land transaction [*FA 2008, Sch 32 paras 10 and 22*]. A written declaration of trust in favour of a purchaser of property may attract ad valorem duty as a **CONVEYANCE OR TRANSFER (39)** on sale (*Chesterfield Brewery Co v CIR* QB, [1899] 2 QB 7). The vesting by **CONVEYANCE OR TRANSFER (39)** of property by way of gift to trustees following a declaration of trust no longer attracts any duty and is not required to be adjudicated. [*FA 2008, s 100 and Sch 32 para 10*].

Appointment and retirement of trustees

[86.2] The fixed 50p duty formerly charged on the appointment of new trustees has been abolished. [*SA 1891, Sch 1; FA 1985, Sch 24(b)*]. The vesting by **CONVEYANCE OR TRANSFER (39)** of trust property in new trustees previously bore duty of a maximum of £5 [*FA 1999, Sch 13, para 16*] unless the instrument was certified in accordance with regulations, in which case it would have been exempt from duty. [*Stamp Duty (Exempt Instruments) Regulations 1987 (SI 1987 No 516)* Category A]. (See **50 EXEMPT INSTRUMENTS.**) If vesting was not express but merely took effect by virtue of *Trustee Act 1925, s 40*, the additional duty was not in practice claimed. The fixed duty no longer applies generally though it has been retained for instruments effecting a pre-SDLT land transaction. [*FA 2008, Sch 32 paras 10 and 22*].

Duty was also limited to £5 [*FA 1999, Sch 13, para 16*] on a **CONVEYANCE OR TRANSFER (39)** to give effect to the retirement of a trustee even though no new trustee is appointed unless the instrument is certified in accordance with regulations in which case it is exempt from duty (see the regulations referred to above).

Transfers of trust property or interests

[86.3] The **Conveyance or Transfer (39)** of trust property by trustees to a beneficiary will attract a fixed £5 duty under the head 'conveyance or transfer otherwise than on sale' to the extent that it effects a land transaction, unless the instrument is certified in accordance with regulations, in which case it is exempt from duty. [*Stamp Duty (Exempt Instruments) Regulations 1987 (SI 1987 No 516)* Category F]. (See **50 Exempt Instruments**.)

A transaction in trust interests by beneficiaries may attract ad valorem duty as a **Conveyance or Transfer (39)** on sale (see e.g. *Oughtred v CIR* HL, [1960] AC 206—release of reversionary interest). If the trust property includes *chargeable securities* a **Stamp Duty Reserve Tax (84)** charge may arise if a duly stamped instrument is not created to cancel the tax charge, depending upon the nature of the beneficiary's interest in the trust.

Variation of trusts

[86.4] As mentioned in **86.3** above the variation of an interest under a trust may involve a liability to ad valorem duty. However, an undertaking by solicitors with regard to stamping is no longer required to be included in an order made under the *Variation of Trusts Act 1958*. *Practice Note* [1966] 1 All ER 672 was withdrawn on 31 July 1989. Orders confined to the lifting of protective trusts are not liable to duty and need not be presented to the Stamp Office. Orders effecting a voluntary disposition inter vivos will attract a fixed £5 duty under the head 'conveyance or transfer otherwise than on sale' to the extent that the order effects a land transaction, unless the order is certified in accordance with the regulations mentioned above (Category L). Orders which contain declarations of trust but effect no disposition of the trust property are no longer liable to the £5 fixed duty under the head **Declaration of Trust (42)**. [*Practice Direction (Chancery: Stamp Duty on Orders under the Variation of Trusts Act 1958) (3/89)*].

Revocation of trust

[86.5] The head of charge 'Revocation of any trust etc.' has been abolished. [*SA 1891, Sch 1; FA 1985, Sch 24*].

Constructive trusts

[86.6] Under an agreement for sale, a constructive trust arises for the purchaser, but this does not amount to a **Conveyance or Transfer (39)** of the property liable to stamp duty (*G Angus & Co* CA, (1889) 23 QBD 579). Agreements for sale may be liable by virtue of *FA 1999, Sch 13, para 7* (see **17 Agreement for Sale**).

Maintenance funds for historic buildings

[86.7] No stamp duty is charged on an instrument whereby property leaves a settlement, if as a result of the property (or part of it) entering another settlement exemption from inheritance tax under *IHTA 1984, Sch 4, paras 9(1), 17(1)* is available, or only a reduced inheritance tax charge arises under *IHTA 1984, Sch 4, paras 9(4), 17(4)*. This does not apply where property leaves one settlement for another settlement by virtue of the instrument itself. Where only part of the property becomes comprised in the other settlement then stamp duty may be chargeable on the instrument in respect of the other part. The total or partial exemption is available only if the instrument is adjudicated (see **13 ADJUDICATION**). [*FA 1980, s 98*].

Chapter 87

Underwriting

[87.1] An underwriting agreement is capable of attracting **STAMP DUTY RESERVE TAX (84)** as an agreement to transfer *chargeable securities* depending upon how it is worded. To avoid this problem the agreement should provide for the lead underwriter to procure purchasers, or failing this to purchase for himself only those shares not otherwise taken up by the public or the existing shareholders. Such a provision avoids any suggestion that the underwriting agreement is an agreement to transfer *chargeable securities* because at the date of the agreement it is not known whether the underwriter will be required to take-up any shares and if so, how many shares he will be required to take. Sub-underwriting agreements are in a similar position.

STAMP DUTY RESERVE TAX (84) should therefore only arise in relation to existing shares which the underwriter has to take-up and for which a duly stamped instrument of transfer is not produced within two months.

Chapter 88

Unit Trusts and Open Ended Investment Companies ('OEICS')

Note: Dealings in units of authorised and unauthorised unit trusts and open ended investment companies ('OEICs') are no longer chargeable to stamp duty and have been subject to **STAMP DUTY RESERVE TAX (84)** from 6 February 2000. For details of the previous stamp duty regime please refer to earlier editions of this book.

The author would like to thank Stephen Lynam, Head of Tax at the Investment Management Association (IMA), for his kindness in reviewing this chapter and for permission to draw extensively from guidance issued to members of the IMA in the writing of this chapter.

The Revenue has issued guidance which can be found in Chapter 15 of the Stamp Taxes Manual ('STM') which is available at: www.hmrc.gov.uk/so/manual.pdf.

General

[88.1] Stamp duty on transfers of units in unit trusts is not chargeable in relation to transfers executed on or after 6 February 2000. From that date dealings in units of authorised and unauthorised unit trusts have been chargeable to **STAMP DUTY RESERVE TAX (84)** ('tax') and the trustees of the unit trust are liable for the tax. SDRT is charged on both authorised and unauthorised unit trust schemes since a 'unit trust scheme' for these purposes has the same meaning as in the *Financial Services and Markets Act 2000, ss 236, 237*), subject to the detailed exceptions for common investment schemes of charitable bodies etc listed or referred to in *FA 1999, Sch 19, paras 15–17*. An employee share ownership plan approved under the *Income Tax (Earnings and Pensions) Act 2003, Pt 7, Ch 6* is not a 'unit trust scheme'. [*Stamp Duty and Stamp Duty Reserve Tax (Definitions of Unit Trust Scheme) (Amendment) Regulations 2000 (SI 2000 No 2549)*].

Where the shares of an open-ended investment company are repurchased by its authorised corporate director, these rules mirror the stamp duty and SDRT rules for repurchases of units in authorised unit trusts. [*SI 1997 No 1156, reg 4*].

Umbrella funds

[88.2] Each sub-fund of an umbrella fund is treated as a separate entity for the purposes of tax. [*FA 1999, Sch 19, para 18*]. An umbrella scheme is defined at *FA 1999, Sch 19, para 18(2)* as a unit trust scheme which provides

' . . . arrangements for separate pooling of the contributions of participants and of the profits or income out of which profits are to be made to them'. In addition, participants must be entitled to exchange rights in one pool for rights in another. Each sub-fund of an OEIC is treated as a separate OEIC for these purposes.

Exclusions

[88.3] Certain types of unit trust are carved out of the regime. These are:

- common investment schemes and common deposit schemes under the Charities Acts;
- unit trust schemes under the terms of which units may only be held by charities;
- court common investment funds;
- common investment arrangements by the trustees of exempt approved pension schemes;
- unit trust schemes under the terms of which units may be held only within Individual Pension Accounts;
- pension funds pooling schemes;
- limited partnerships.

Schedule 19: Basic structure

[88.4] SDRT is charged in respect of transactions in unit trust units and OEICs, and under the provisions of *FA 1999, Sch 19* the charge arises on the value of surrenders of units/shares to the managers or trustees. *FA 1999, Sch 19* is a 'fund specific' regime which applies solely to such surrenders. It is understood that the policy underlying *FA 1999, Sch 19* was a concern that absent *FA 1999, Sch 19*, SDRT could be avoided by holding chargeable securities indirectly through collective investment vehicles. The UK fund management industry has lobbied for many years for the abolition of the Schedule on the grounds that it is uncompetitive in a UCITS environment, but so far without success.

The principal aspects of these rules are:

(a) tax is charged on redemptions on a two-week rolling basis at 0.5%;
(b) other transfers of units/shares are charged at 0.5% unless exempt;
(c) the level of the tax depends on the relative levels of issues and redemptions during the two-week rolling period, and not on whether units/shares are cancelled or recycled;
(d) investment funds which are wholly and directly invested in assets which do not attract stamp duty or tax on transfer are exempt from tax on dealings in units/shares;
(e) investment funds which are partially invested in assets which do not attract stamp duty or tax on transfer have a *pro rata* exemption from tax on dealings in units/shares;
(f) *pro rata in specie* redemptions do not attract tax at the unit/share level.

Although *FA 1999, Sch 19, para 4* states that tax must be calculated by reference to each 'class' of unit, STM Chapter 15 at paras 15.18 & 15.9 makes it clear that in practice one should not do this. Although the drafting of this section of the STM could be clearer, the cumulative effect of the analysis is to suggest that one should find a method to restate the various classes into one base class and then carry out the calculation for the entire fund or sub-fund. *Regulation 4A* of the OEIC Regulations (*SI 1997/1156*) makes clear that an OEIC with multiple share classes is to be treated as a single entity for the purposes of the tax. Income and accumulation units are to be treated as the same class of units as income units. HMRC suggest that the most convenient way for managers to do this is to restate accumulation units in terms of notional accumulation units.

Switches between classes of units are not to be treated as surrenders under paragraph 2 and such switches should be excluded from the I/S fraction. [STM at 15.24.]

Basic method of calculation

[88.5] The tax is charged on a two-week rolling basis. The charging period is one week: the level of tax ultimately payable will depend on the number of issues and surrenders of units dealt during the charging week and the following week.

If the number of issues during the charging week and the following week exceed the number of surrenders in the same period, the tax is payable at a rate of 0.5% of the value of redemptions dealt in the charging week.

If, as in the example below, the number of issues in the charging week and the following week is less than the number of surrenders in the same period, the tax liability is calculated as follows by applying the 'reduction fraction'.

Tax liability

$$= \text{Surrenders in week 1 @ 0.5\%} \times \frac{\text{No of units issued in weeks 1–2}}{\text{No of units surrendered in weeks 1–2}}$$

This is illustrated in the following example:

	Value of surren-ders	*SDRT @ 0.5% surren-dered*	*No of units sur-rendered*	*No of units issued*
Week 1	£	£		
Monday	100,000	500	10,000	
Wednesday	200,000	1,000	19,500	5,000
Friday	150,000	750	14,700	5,000
Total for charging week	450,000	2,250		

	Value of surrenders	*SDRT @ 0.5% surrendered*	*No of units surrendered*	*No of units issued*
Week 2				
Monday			10,000	15,000
Tuesday			7,000	20,000
Thursday			5,000	5,000
Friday			10,000	
Total issues and surrenders in period			76,200	50,000
			= S	= I

SDRT liability for week 1 = £2,250 × I/S = £1,476

[*FA 1999, Sch 19, paras 3 and 4*].

Full and partial exemptions from SDRT on dealings: the N/(N+E) reduction fraction

[88.6] The amount of tax payable is reduced by the application of a further reduction fraction where a fund holds investments in what the legislation refers to as 'exempt assets' ie those assets that are not routinely subject to stamp duty and tax. This means that funds investing directly in overseas equities and bonds are wholly or mostly exempt from tax on dealings in units. Funds such as UK balanced funds, and other funds that are partly invested in a mixture of chargeable and non-chargeable assets, are partially exempt from tax on dealings.

Where a fund is partially exempt, the initial tax liability is first calculated as set out in the example above. That liability can then be reduced further if the fund invests in exempt investments. This is done by applying the following fraction:

$$\frac{\text{Average market value of non-exempt investments}}{\text{Average market value of non-exempt investments + Exempt investments}}$$

HMRC has stated (at para 15.33 of the STM) that it does not intend to lay down a single rule for the purposes of measuring these average values. HMRC does, however, suggest that one of the following methods might be appropriate:

- averages of the values of N and E over all the valuation points falling within the relevant two-week period (including values where there is only one such point);
- averages of the values from valuation points at an equivalent time in each of the two weeks concerned – for example, an average of each Friday's valuation point;
- averages of the values on the last business day of month 1 and the last business day of month 2 to be used to calculate a ratio N/(N+E) which would be applied to all of the calculations relating to the two-week periods ending in month 2.

Definition of 'exempt investments'

[88.7] Exempt investments, for the purposes of the second reduction fraction, are:

(a) investments that would not give rise to an ad valorem stamp duty charge on transfer;
(b) investments which are not 'chargeable securities' as defined by *FA 1986, s 99*;
(c) units/shares in an authorised investment fund investing in bonds which meets the criteria of *FA 1986, s 99(5B)(b)*;
(d) derivative instruments that relate wholly to other exempt investments.

Funds held for the purposes of day-to-day management are not treated as investments. Items such as uninvested cash and short-term deposits would therefore be excluded from the calculation.

Derivatives which partly relate to non-exempt investments are themselves treated as non-exempt.

There is an anomaly in the drafting of this provision, in that while overseas equities are not chargeable securities, they are subject to *ad valorem* stamp duty if transferred within the UK. This does not reflect the stated intention of the legislation, which is that the tax treatment of surrendered units should mirror the stamp duty treatment of the underlying assets. The Stamp Office has indicated that in applying the rules it will ensure that this result is achieved and that shares in a non-UK company will be treated as exempt instruments unless the shares are registered in a UK register.

Funds of funds

[88.8] The *FA 1999, Sch 19* regime operated extremely harshly in the case of funds of funds (or indeed where any fund holds an investment in another fund). This was because of the definition of exempt investments and in particular because of the very narrow terms of *FA 1986, s 99(5B)(b)*, which provided that an interest in a collective investment scheme was an exempt investment if and only if the scheme was an authorised unit trust scheme or an open-ended investment company and under the terms of the scheme the property under the scheme must be exempt and must be taxable under Case III of Schedule D.

However *FA 2011, s84* amended the definition so that an interest in a collective investment scheme is exempt unless more than 20% of the market value of the investments in which the property subject to the scheme is invested is attributable to investments which are not exempt: *FA 1999 s99(5C)*.

In specie redemptions

[88.9] The transfer of investments from the trustee/OEIC to the investor is exempt from SDRT in accordance with *FA 1986, s 90(1B)* as amended by *FA*

1999, Sch 19, para 11(4). This is the case whether or not the investor receives a proportionate share in each asset; see STM para 15.48.

Pro rata in specie redemptions of units are not subject to tax at the unit level (*FA 1999, Sch 19, para 7*) and the redemption is excluded from the number of surrenders for the purposes of the I/S reduction fraction. HMRC say at 15.47 of the STM that to qualify for this exemption the unitholder must get a share of each asset that is proportionate to, or as nearly as practicable proportionate to, the unit holder's share.

However, the extension of the scope of exemption to funds investing in exempt investments means that all *in specie* redemptions of units of say, a Japanese equity fund, do not attract tax at the unit level.

Similarly, a redemption of units of a fund partly invested in exempt investments which is *in specie* but not *pro rata* should qualify for a reduction of tax, reflecting the proportion of exempt and non-exempt assets in the fund, if the underlying principle of the legislation is applied. Although this is not clear in the legislation as drafted, HMRC have confirmed that such a reduction will apply.

In specie redemptions of UK equity funds which are not *pro rata* will be charged to tax at 0.5%. This cannot be reduced, because the legislation stipulates that any issue or surrender of units which is not entirely for money may not be included in the first reduction fraction.

Third party transfers

[88.10] For the purposes of the *FA 1999, Sch 19* rules, there are two types of third party transfer. The first occurs when an investor completes a stock transfer form and asks the investment fund manager to register the change of ownership. This is treated in the same way as all other surrenders and is included in the manager's fortnightly SDRT calculation. Unlike shares, the tax liability on unit transfers cannot be discharged by paying stamp duty, and when registering third party transfers the manager as the accountable person should satisfy himself that either there is evidence of an exemption or pay over the tax.

A fund may, provided it has reserved the right in its prospectus, require the parties to a transfer of units/shares to pay a *FA 1999, Sch 19* provision against the liability which would otherwise fall on the fund (see the COLL rulebook 6.3.7–6.3.8 which can be found at: http://fsahandbook.info/FSA/html/handbook/COLL/6/3).

To minimise any discrepancy between this provision and the actual SDRT due, for *FA 1999, Sch 19* purposes, HMRC will accept the redemption price at the time the holder sends the transfer instructions, provided they are acted on promptly.

Third party transfers for value of partially exempt funds do benefit from a *pro rata* reduction; and the manager has the power to refuse to register the transfer if he is not satisfied either that the transfer is exempt, or if the investors involved have not paid him an amount in respect of any SDRT that may be payable on the transfer.

There are specific exceptions from the *FA 1999, Sch 19* charge for third party transfers set out in *FA 1999, Sch 19, para 6.*

FA 1999, Sch 19, para 6(6) excludes both the surrender and issue from the I/S fraction where:

- there is no consideration in money or moneys worth; or
- the transferee is a charity; or
- the transfer, were there to be a written instrument, is one to which the exempt instruments regulations or the Stamp Duty group relief provisions would apply.

HMRC at para 15.51 of the STM refer to a second type of third party transfer, which they describe as being rare, where units or shares are transferred between accounts operated by the same nominee. In this case, there may be a change of beneficial ownership, but there will be no alteration to the register of the relevant unit trust or OEIC. The current draft of the STM states that this type of transfer will attract a 0.5% charge to tax under *FA 1986, s 87*, read together with *s 90(1)*. It is understood that this section is being rewritten as the Stamp Office confirmed that this analysis is incorrect in SDRT Newsletter issue number 10 of July 2009 headed 'net dealing by intermediaries'.

The relevant section is as follows:

> 'Investors in collective investment schemes often make their investment through an intermediary. Intermediaries may deal with underlying fund managers by sending aggregated sell and aggregated buy instructions separately (known as "gross dealing"); or, intermediaries may net off buy and sell instructions for each fund and thus send only one net buy or sell instruction to each underlying fund manager (known as "net dealing").
>
> HM Revenue & Customs (HMRC) has historically taken the view that where net dealing occurs, the underlying fund managers should obtain gross transaction information from the intermediary and include that information in calculating their SDRT liability under Schedule 19 Finance Act 1999 ("Schedule 19").
>
> Following representations, HMRC has taken legal advice and, as a result, announces a change of view with effect from 14 July 2009. In future, underlying fund managers should only include in their Schedule 19 calculations transactions for which they have received instructions.
>
> Furthermore, HMRC previously took the view that net dealing would not generally give rise to any principal SDRT charges under section 87 Finance Act 1986. HMRC also announce a change in this position. HMRC advice is that net dealing will generally, depending on the facts of each case, give rise to two principal SDRT charges in respect of the transactions which have been netted off – one on the intermediary and one on the ultimate purchaser of the investment. HMRC will not pursue any such charges that arose on or before the date of this announcement.'

There are a number of exemptions from the *FA 1999, Sch 19* charge for transfers on the register, and in these cases issues and surrenders are excluded from I/S reduction fraction.

These are:

- gifts and transfers to a nominee without consideration in money or money's worth;

- transfers to charities and to trusts established for charitable purposes only;
- transfers to the National Heritage Memorial fund or the Historic Buildings and Monuments commission for England;
- where stamp duty group relief under *FA 1930, s 42* would apply if there were a transfer document; and
- transfers which would be exempt from fixed rate stamp duty.

None of these exemptions require adjudication, but the onus is on the manager/ACD to ensure that the relevant conditions have been met.

Liability

[88.11] In the case of unit trusts, the trustee is liable for the tax in accordance with *FA 1999, Sch 19, para 2(3)* although the regulations define the manager as the 'accountable person'. In most cases the manager or third party administrator will collect and administer the tax.

In the case of OEICS, the OEIC itself will be liable although the authorised corporate director is the 'accountable person'. Again, in most cases it will be they or the third party administrator who will collect and administer the tax.

Returns

[88.12] Where there is a charge to SDRT, a return is necessary (but not otherwise). The return is for a monthly period which is required on or before the prescribed 'accountable date'. The return for each month relates to surrenders occurring in the weeks for which the relevant two-week periods end during that month. The 'accountable date' is the 14th day of the following month and the SDRT is due and payable on or before that date.

A late return is subject to a fixed penalty of £100.

A monthly return covers a 4 or 5-week period of surrenders and comprises four or five subsidiary calculations.

Amalgamations and reconstructions of unit trusts and OEICs

[88.13] HMRC accept that no SDRT arises on the cancellation of the units/shares in the original fund where funds amalgamate. The rationale is discussed in the Stamp Taxes Customer Newsletter Stamp Duty Reserve Tax Issue 7 in May 2004 ('Newsletter 7'). This Newsletter also dealt more widely with the issue of amalgamations, mergers and other transactions relating to unit trusts and OEICs, outlining the circumstances in which HMRC accept that stamp duty and SDRT will not apply. See **APPENDIX F** where Newsletter 7 is reproduced.

On conversion, HMRC accept that no SDRT arises on the cancellation of the units/shares in the original fund for the reasons set out in Newsletter 7. There is a specific exemption from stamp duty where an AUT converts to an OEIC in *reg 7* of the *Stamp Duty and Stamp Duty Reserve Tax (Open-ended Investment Companies) Regulations 1997 (SI 1997 No 1156)*, and an equivalent exemption from SDRT in *reg 8*. There are equivalent provisions for stamp duty and SDRT relief in *regs 9* and *10* respectively that apply where an AUT is converted into an existing OEIC. Originally temporary, these exemptions have been made permanent.

See also the relief from SDLT where land is transferred from an authorised unit trust to an OEIC as part of an arrangement for the conversion of the trust to a company or the amalgamation of the trust with an existing company in the *Stamp Duty Land Tax (Open-ended Investment Companies) Regulations 2008 (SI 2008 No 710)* and HMRC's Guidance Note issued on 25 June 2008.

Chapter 89

VAT and Stamp Duty

[89.1] Stamp duty is charged on the consideration or rent including any value added tax for pre-SDLT land transactions (*Glenrothes Development Corpn v IRC* [1994] STC 74). This has always been the position although before the major extension of the standard rate of value added tax to transactions involving buildings and land by *FA 1989, s 18* and *Sch 3,* the point rarely arose due to land and share transactions being generally exempt from value added tax.

However, the application of the **CONTINGENCY PRINCIPLE (37)** to a transaction which is capable of being a standard-rated supply for value added tax purposes is not so straightforward. It is clear that on a standard-rated sale of freehold land stamp duty will be charged on the conveyance according to the value added tax inclusive consideration. Where the consideration is uncertain and depends on the happening of a contingency, but a maximum, minimum or basic price can be ascertained, stamp duty is charged by the Stamp Office on that ascertainable amount plus the hypothetical value added tax that would have been chargeable on that amount under the **CONTINGENCY PRINCIPLE (37)**. In other words, the Stamp Office takes the view that the potential value added tax arising as a result of the possible exercise of the election to waive exemption is within the scope of the **CONTINGENCY PRINCIPLE (37)**.

The major change in the value added tax chargeable on supplies relating to buildings and land made by *FA 1989, s 18* and *Sch 3* was the introduction of a mandatory value added tax charge on the sale of new commercial property. In addition, owners were given the option of charging value added tax on sales of old commercial property, and on leases of commercial property. The Revenue published a statement of practice (SP 11/91) on 12 September 1991 dealing with the interaction between stamp duty and value added tax. This revised and replaced the earlier statement of practice of 22 July 1991 (SP 6/91). Although SP 11/91 contains the official view, it should not be assumed that it is correct in all respects and in appropriate cases it may be open to challenge. SP 11/91 may be summarised as follows:

(a) For stamp duty purposes, the amount or value of the consideration for sale is the gross amount inclusive of value added tax. Therefore, where value added tax is chargeable on the sale of new non-residential property, stamp duty will be charged on the value added tax inclusive consideration.

(b) Sales of non-residential property, other than new buildings are generally exempt from value added tax. These include sales of old buildings, the assignment of existing leases and the creation of new leases in old or new property. However, the vendor can elect to waive the exemption. Where the election has been exercised at the time of the transaction, stamp duty is chargeable on the price, premium or rent inclusive of value added tax. Where the election has not been exercised at that time, value added tax should similarly be included in any payments to which an election could still apply for the purpose of calculating stamp duty unless there is a covenant or undertaking binding the vendor or lessor not to waive the exemption.

(c) For documents executed before 1 August 1991, the Stamp Office did not seek to include the value added tax element in the stamp duty charge in cases where an election to waive the exemption from value added tax had not yet been exercised. This practice has now altered for documents executed on or after 1 August 1991.

(d) Where value added tax is charged on the rent under a lease, and is treated as rent by the lease, stamp duty is charged on the value added tax inclusive figure. If the lease provides for payment of value added tax on the rent otherwise than as rent, stamp duty is charged on the value added tax element as consideration payable periodically. [*SA 1891, s 56*]. In both cases the rate of value added tax in force at the date of execution of the lease is used. Because *SA 1891, s 56* charges duty on a notional sum equivalent to the value added tax payable over the shorter of 20 years or the term of the lease, this can increase the stamp duty charge significantly and means it will nearly always be cheaper to reserve value added tax as part of the rent rather than as a separate sum.

(e) Where there is a formal deed of variation or similar document varying the terms of the original lease so as to provide for payment of value added tax by way of additional rent, further stamp duty may be payable. [*FA 1999*, *Sch 13*, *para 20*].

(f) Paragraphs (*b*) to (*e*) above also apply to an **AGREEMENT FOR LEASE (16)** if that is to be stamped.

In response to the difficulties which SP 11/91 caused some practitioners, the Institute of Chartered Accountants in England and Wales issued a guidance note based on questions submitted by the Tax Faculty to the Stamp Office (Tax 19/92 Guidance Note). The Guidance Note may be summarised as follows:

(a) **VAT groups.** A lease granted between companies in the same value added tax group [*Value Added Tax Act 1994, s 43*] is assessed by reference to the premium (if any) and rents reserved by reference to the value added tax exclusive sums, whether or not an election to waive exemption is in place on the property at the date of the grant.

(b) **VAT not recoverable as rent.** Where a lease is either silent as to the ability of the landlord to charge value added tax or states that value added tax is not recoverable by the landlord, the Stamp Office regards the **CONTINGENCY PRINCIPLE (37)** to be in point because the landlord, by virtue of *Value Added Tax Act 1994, Sch 10, para 2*, could still elect to waive exemption from value added tax at any time during the term granted. As such, value added tax on rent would still form part of the consideration for the enjoyment of the premises in the same way that the payment of value added tax on a sale forms part of the consideration for the thing sold. The stamp duty chargeable on a document, and accordingly the **CONTINGENCY PRINCIPLE (37)**, must be applied at the time the lease is executed. It is immaterial that the lease specifically states that value added tax is not recoverable by the landlord.

(c) **Property exchanges.** Where equality money is given or received on an exchange and neither property is subject to value added tax, stamp duty is payable on the equality money. [*SA 1891, s 73* (now repealed—see **36.7 CONSIDERATION**)]. Value added tax is however capable of forming part of the stampable consideration paid or agreed to be paid for equality where both or either freehold properties are subject to a value added tax charge. [Note: *SA 1891, s 73* was amended by *FA 1994, s 241* (repealed by *FA 1999, s 139, Sch 20*)].

(d) **Split-purpose buildings.** Where a landlord has the right to waive exemption on part only of the rent, stamp duty is charged only on the value added tax on that part of the rent. Examples include a shop with a flat above and a building where a certificate of qualifying use has been issued in relation to part of the building.

(e) **Sub-sales.** In a sub-sale, A sells to B who sells to C and the transfer of title is completed by a single conveyance from A to C. Stamp duty is charged only on the price paid by C. If that price is subject to value added tax, stamp duty is charged on the value added tax inclusive amount. Any value added tax element in the price paid by B to A is ignored unless that initial transaction is also stampable.

(f) **Transfer of going concern.** Where a lease is transferred as one of the assets of a business transferred as a going concern, it falls outside the scope of value added tax provided the conditions set out in *article 5* of the *Value Added Tax (Special Provisions) Order 1995 (SI 1995 No 1268)* are satisfied. In such a case the charge to ad valorem duty will be confined to the value added tax exclusive amounts, the transaction being a non-supply for the purposes of value added tax. But see the paragraph below, and the article in Stamp Office Customer (sic) Newsletter reproduced in **APPENDIX F**.

(g) **Binding agreement not to waive exemption.** Where there is a binding agreement between the parties not to exercise the option to waive exemption at the date of the grant of a lease, ad valorem duty will be assessed on the value added tax exclusive rents reserved in the lease.

(h) **Agreement for leases.** Where an **AGREEMENT FOR LEASE (16)** is stamped under the **CONTINGENCY PRINCIPLE (37)** on the basis that an election to waive exemption might subsequently be made, but between the date of the agreement and the grant of the lease a binding agreement is made not to waive the exemption, the lease is denoted with the duty paid on the agreement. There is no provision for a refund of duty even though the lease would have been stamped on the (lesser) value added tax exclusive basis.

(i) **Bare land.** The Statement of Practice relates not only to buildings but also to bare land.

On the transfer of a business as a going concern it will not be known for certain whether it (the transfer) will fall outside the scope of value added tax until afterwards. The practice of the Stamp Office when presented with a business sale agreement for stamping where transfer of going concern treatment is likely to apply is not to add the value added tax that could be charged to the stampable consideration, provided the applicant for stamping states in writing that:

(a) transfer of going concern treatment should apply and no value added tax has been included in the consideration;
(b) they will inform the Stamp Office if the position changes; and
(c) they undertake to arrange for the document to be resubmitted for additional stamping if value added tax becomes payable. (See section 4.473 of the Stamp Office Manual).

In practice, on the presentation of a business sale agreement which should qualify for transfer of going concern treatment, the Stamp Office does not always insist on the above written confirmation and will often just stamp on the value added tax exclusive amounts.

Part Three:

Appendices

Appendix A

Parliamentary Material

EXTRACTS FROM HANSARD DEBATES—FINANCE BILL 2003

5 June 2003

Column 387

CLAUSE 53

Deemed market value where transaction involves connected company

Question proposed, that the clause stand part of the Bill.

Mr. Prisk: The clause provides for a new land tax to be charged on market value when a company purchases land from a person with whom the company is connected. That principle is already established in the existing Taxes Act. However, it would be helpful if the Chief Secretary would confirm one aspect. I am grateful to a number of outside legal experts, particularly the Law Society, for the following point.

It is assumed that where the legal interest in property, but not the beneficial interest, is transferred in circumstances where clause 53(1) applies, the subject matter of the transaction will be the legal interest alone, which will have a nil or

Column 388

nominal value, and accordingly no charge would arise. I would be grateful if the Chief Secretary would confirm that.

Mr. Burnett: That is the point that I was going to make. It is important in relation to a situation where, to give one example of many, a new company has not been formed, but the land is purchased in Mr. or Mrs. Bloggs's name in his or her capacity as trustee, and in due course the legal estate is transferred to the company, which was always the intention. There is usually an underlying declaration of trust in such circumstances. Notwithstanding the absence of such a declaration of trust, when the legal estate and the land is eventually transferred to a limited liability company, or perhaps a limited liability partnership, will the Chief Secretary confirm that, as the hon. Member for Hertford and Stortford said, no liability to Stamp Duty land tax will arise?

Mr. Baron: I seek clarification from the Chief Secretary on a similar issue. The clause appears to create yet another stealth tax, which will hit small businesses, especially those entrepreneurs who wish to incorporate land and buildings to transfer. The Chief Secretary will correct me if I am wrong, but because one can rest on contract, one could defer a charge on incorporation. Once deferred, for example, a company could sub-sell the property and only the end purchaser would pay the Stamp Duty. As a result of the Bill, however, resting on contract is no longer with us, and there is no way in which one can defer the SDLT on incorporation. In other words, it will have to be paid, whereas previously it could have been deferred and perhaps not paid at all for legitimate reasons.

[**Mr. Mark Hendrick in the Chair**] I put it to the Chief Secretary that the change hurts small business entrepreneurs in particular. It appears that they will be hit by yet another stealth tax. On top of all the regulations that they have to endure, they will be given yet another burden at a particularly difficult point in the cycle. A number of entrepreneurs have raised that concern with me. Will the Chief Secretary clarify the point? It appears that there is an extra charge. The legitimate way of dealing with that and deferring it no longer exists; hence, a stealth tax is being created.

Mr. Boateng: There is no merit in the hon. Gentleman seriously proposing that we should return to permitting the technique known as resting on contract. The whole point of the legislation is to remove such opportunities for avoidance. There is no new charge. There is no Stamp Duty relief for incorporation at present. A measure to ensure that Stamp Duty was charged on the market value of land transferred to a connected company was introduced in the Finance Act 2000.

[**Mr. John McWilliam in the Chair**] This is an anti-avoidance measure. We could be talking about resting on contract, which it would be wrong to allow to return by the back door, or, in relation to the clause, a scheme commonly known as value shifting. That is the mischief that the clause was designed to prevent. We must ensure that the scheme

Column 389

does not return in any shape or form. I reject completely the notion that the clause is designed to introduce a stealth tax. Nor do I accept that it unfairly catches small businesses, such as corner shops, that want to incorporate.

Mr. Baron: Does the Chief Secretary accept that prior to the Bill there were perfectly legitimate reasons for deferring a charge on incorporation and that because of the Bill, and this clause in particular, those have been removed and SDLT will have to be paid on incorporation, come what may? In a small number of cases, that might be considered unfair.

Mr. Boateng: I would be interested if the hon. Gentleman could give me some practical examples drawn from the world of small businesses and corner shops. That world recognises and welcomes the new £150,000 threshold for commercial property. It recognises that many businesses will be taken out of SDLT entirely when they incorporate. We estimate that that will apply to some two thirds of businesses that hold property. In addition, many small businesses do not hold property at all. Taking that into account, we estimate that more than 90 per cent. of businesses will be completely unaffected by the change when they incorporate.

It is not necessary to over-egg the pudding. Hon. Members will find a ready ear when they raise genuine concerns about small and medium-sized enterprises, however they seek to raise their concerns. Many do, from all parties, and I am grateful to them, particularly those who, for reasons that are well understood, are obliged to remain silent in the course of our deliberations.

Mr. Prisk: Obliged?

Mr. Boateng: By usual form and practice.

I say to Opposition Members, please do not lecture us on small and medium-sized enterprises. All members of the Committee have their interests at heart, and I suggest that the clause in no way imposes an unfair burden on them.

In response to the questions raised by the hon. Members for Torridge and West Devon and for Hertford and Stortford about the market value if a legal but not a beneficial interest is transferred, the market value is based on the nature of the interest transferred. If nominal, the market value will be nominal, and that is the end of the matter. I hope that that allays the concerns of the hon. Gentlemen.

Question put and agreed to.

Clause 53 ordered to stand part of the Bill.

CLAUSE 54

Exceptions from deemed market value rule

Question proposed, that the clause stand part of the Bill.

Mr. Prisk: The clause is about providing exemptions to clause 53. I have received several representations, predominantly from the legal profession, but I shall highlight just three. I am grateful to Charles Elphick of Reed Smith, the British

Column 390

Property Federation and the Law Society for giving me background on the matter.

Could the Chief Secretary explain why bare trustees or nominee companies are absent from the exemptions? That is an important change in established law for such organisations. Could he define "immediately" in subSections (2) and (3)? I am not trying to engage in word play, but immediately is stretchable. Perhaps he could set some limit on it or explain why he has no wish to set a limit.

Lastly, subSection (4) states:

> Case 3 is where—
>
> (a) the vendor is a company and the transaction is, or is part of, a distribution of the assets of that company (whether or not in connection with its winding up).

Could the Chief Secretary identify the circumstances in which the distribution of assets is not exempt?

Mr. Boateng: Essentially, I am asked why case 4 has not been brought into SDLT. It is suggested that this would mean that the distribution out of a settlement would be charged SDLT at market value. My response is that there would be a charge based on market value only if the beneficiary who receives land is a company. The exception previously contained in case 4 could, and might well be, used to avoid the correct level of SDLT. If it was possible to transfer land into a settlement in favour of a corporate beneficiary, no SDLT would be charged on the transfer and settlement, and, if there was no consideration for the transfer, the exception could be used to transfer the land out of the settlement to a corporate beneficiary without SDLT being paid. That clear abuse of the rules would enable land to be passed through a settlement to a company without a charge to SDLT.

By removing the exception, the SDLT rules close the loophole. It does not affect the transfer of land to a company acting as a nominee or a bare trustee for an individual. In that case, it would be the individual who is the purchaser, so the market value would not apply. I hope that that reassures those who raised the matter.

The exceptions in relation to nominees have been removed, because the exception in case 1 of the old Stamp Duty is no longer required as there is no charge to SDLT when a nominee transfers title to the person for whom they act. Cases 2 and 3 are also no longer required, because they were introduced to ensure that there was no market value charge when title was transferred to a nominee by a person they act for or between nominees. In such cases, the market value of a title will be minimal, and that goes back to a point made by the hon. Member for Torridge and West Devon. In all normal cases the market value will be below the SDLT threshold. When beneficial ownership and not just title is transferred to the nominee by the person they act for, it will be the same as any other transfer of interest in land, and there is no reason why the market value should not apply.

On the distribution of assets on a winding up, if the land was subject to a group relief claim in the three years preceding the distribution, it would not be exempt. That is one example but others may have

Column 391

occurred to right hon. and hon. Members. With those explanations, I hope that we can now move on.

Question put and agreed to.

Clause 54 ordered to stand part of the Bill.

EXTRACTS FROM HANSARD DEBATES—FINANCE BILL 2004

28 April 2004

Column 946

Mr. Prisk: I am grateful to my right hon. Friend for helping me and, indeed, the Committee to identify weaknesses not only in the Bill but in the amendments

Column 946

tabled to it. It is always important that more recent arrivals in the House should listen with due care to their elders and betters. I am certainly happy to do so on this occasion.

There is a danger that a corner of an office block, for example, could be caught within the Government's definition of a disadvantaged area and be appropriate for relief. However, I understand that it is the whole address rather than any part of the hereditament that counts. I am therefore reasonably convinced that the concerns expressed by my right hon. Friend are needless. I am, of course, grateful to him for his contribution.

Will the Financial Secretary confirm that disadvantaged relief would be available in respect of a transfer of a partnership interest to the same extent as it would be if there were a transfer of the underlying property by the partnership? This is a probing amendment, with all the strengths and weaknesses rightly identified by the Committee, and I hope that the Financial Secretary will be able to provide sufficient clarification.

Column 947

Ruth Kelly: However, the hon. Gentleman asked a specific question about transfers of an interest within a partnership. I can assure him, and the Committee, that disadvantaged area relief will apply to such transfers.

EXTRACTS FROM HANSARD DEBATES—FINANCE BILL 2007

5 June 2007

Column 407

CLAUSE 70 [SECTIONS 75A–C, FA 2003]

Anti-avoidance

Question proposed, That the clause stand part of the Bill.

The Chairman: With this, it will be convenient to take the following: Amendment No. 213, in clause 70, page 44, line 7, leave out from 'a' to 'the' in line 9 and insert pre-ordained series of transactions is carried out in connection with the disposal and acquisition, and it is undertaken in pursuance of a scheme or arrangement the only or main purpose of which is the avoidance or reduction of Stamp Duty Land Tax payable on the acquisition by P or to secure or increase a repayment of Stamp Duty Land Tax in relation to that acquisition.'.

Amendment No. 234, in clause 70, page 44, line 13, leave out "its disposal by V" and insert

the disposal referred to in subsection (a) above.

Amendment No. 214, in clause 70, page 44, line 13, at end insert—

(1A) Transactions taking place more than three years before the acquisition of a property by P shall be disregarded for the purposes of subsection (1).'.

Amendment No. 235, in clause 70, page 44, line 40, leave out

the largest amount (or aggregate amount).

Amendment No. 236, in clause 70, page 44, line 42, after "(a)", insert 'the largest amount'.

Amendment No. 237, in clause 70, page 44, line 44, after "(b)", insert 'the aggregate amount'.

Amendment No. 238, in clause 70, page 45, line 7, at end insert—

(c) the exercise of a statutory right of enfranchisement, extension or enlargement of a leasehold interest.'.

Government amendments Nos. 184 to 186.

Amendment No. 239, in clause 70, page 46, line 1, leave out "and 75" and insert

75, and schedule 7, Part 1

Government amendments Nos. 187 to 192.

Column 408

As this group of amendments contains Government amendments, I shall ask the Chief Secretary if he wishes to speak first, and then I shall come to the hon. Member for Chipping Barnet. That will not preclude the Chief Secretary from responding to anything else that is raised in the course of the debate.

Mr. Timms: Thank you, Mr. Gale, for clarifying how you intend to deal with the clause, which is the first of two that tackle stamp duty land tax avoidance schemes. It amends the Finance Act 2003 to counter two types of scheme—those that use leaseholds and those that use sub-sales that have been developed specifically to avoid payment of the tax. Clause 71 is designed to counter schemes that use partnerships as a way of avoiding tax.

The two schemes that the clause tackles seek to avoid payment of stamp duty land tax by adding extra stages into the sale of property by one party to another in such a way as to remove the need to pay tax on the transaction. We have always said that we will deal robustly with any avoidance effort along those lines. We were first made aware of the schemes late last year. We initially took action at the pre-Budget report by introducing time-limited regulations that prevented those schemes. We acted quickly because we took the view that it was unfair for those using such schemes to benefit, while most taxpayers who paid stamp duty and land tax could not use such complex avoidance arrangements. The regulations have worked well, and the industry has, on the whole, been happy with that. The clause replaces those regulations, which were introduced at the end of last year, debated in Committee and approved by the House on 15 January.

Hon. Members might ask why we have included the clauses. First, we hope that they will prove to be more finely tuned instruments than the regulations that they replace. Not only do they target more effectively those schemes that we want to stop but, in response to representations about the regulations, they do more to protect those who are involved in innocent transactions whom the regulations might have caught inadvertently. Of course the clauses, unlike the regulations, will have permanent effect. In introducing the regulations, we explained that they would have effect for only 18 months from the date on which they were made. That has given us a chance to consult the sector and I am grateful to all those who took the time to discuss the regulations with HMRC. We have tried to accommodate their comments, and that has made for clearer legislation.

Throughout the process, we have been open to changes that will make it clear that legitimate transactions will not be caught. For example, the Government amendments are the result of further representations from the property sector. Dealing with the avoidance of stamp duty land taxes is, in many ways, different from dealing with avoidance in other areas of taxation. For example, it is much harder to establish whether the main driver in a developed scheme is avoidance of tax or not. It is also sometimes difficult to establish who benefits from schemes, as they can be arranged to benefit both the buyer and the purchaser. Therefore, where we have deviated from what we have done in other areas of taxation to prevent

Column 409

avoidance, we have done so simply because we have not been able to use the same types of legislation to prevent avoidance in this area.

We have been happy to listen to what groups such as the Law Society have had to say about how the clause is drafted and, where possible, we have agreed to changes that will protect those involved in legitimate land transactions.

Mrs. Theresa Villiers (Chipping Barnet) (Con): Does the Chief Secretary agree that a transaction caught by proposed section 75A would include the purchase of a long leasehold where the right to enfranchise is later taken up, because that involves a series of steps?

Mr. Timms: I am not sure quite how the measure would apply in the particular circumstance that the hon. Lady describes. Perhaps she would like to give a little more detail about the precise type of transaction that she envisages. The intention is to ensure that stamp duty is paid on the full value of the transaction. Artificial arrangements have been devised to try to avoid that; I do not imagine that her example is one of those arrangements. However, that is certainly the intention and I think that the effect of the clause, with the amendments that have been tabled, will be that, in whatever circumstances, the full value of the transaction will be captured for stamp duty land tax purposes.

On the Government amendments, we have made it clear that HMRC will only be allowed to use the retrospective taxation powers if it favours the taxpayer. We have clarified that only property investment partnerships are covered by the clause and that, where separate parcels of land are sold on as part of a transaction, we will use apportionment to reduce the amount of tax that purchasers might have to pay.

Making good anti-avoidance legislation involves dealing with two opposing requirements. First, we must ensure that the legislation is strong enough to stop the avoidance.

Secondly, however, we do not want to entangle law-abiding businesses in its scope or make the overall tax structure any more complex. That is a fine line to walk. In tabling the amendments, we have shown that we will listen to concerns about the unexpected effects of legitimate traders and that we will act on those. I will be happy to give more details about each amendment, but I hope that, in these few words, I have explained the intention behind them.

Mrs. Villiers: I want to take the Chief Secretary up on his reference to complexity. A concern that has been expressed to me is the complexity and lack of clarityin the provisions. In particular, how will proposed section 75A operate if more than one transaction could count as the notional transaction? How will the notional transaction be selected? Will it be the highest transaction, or the first transaction?

Mr. Timms: Let me come back to the hon. Lady's original question about the purchase of a long lease with a right to enfranchise. That kind of arrangement

Column 410

will not be caught unless there is some connection between the transactions—for example, if they are all carried out in a very short time scale. The aim and effect of the changes is to ensure that the full value of the transaction is caught for stamp duty land tax purposes and that the full tax payable will be required. I think that intention is being delivered by the changes.

The hon. Lady makes a fair point about complexity. The clause has to be quite complex. Its aim is to counter schemes that involve the creation of complex networks to avoid paying stamp duty land tax. HMRC has already published detailed guidance on its website explaining what is and is not affected by the clause, giving examples of how it will work. If there are any uncertainties, it is happy to advise those who have queries about complex transactions on a case-by-case basis.

Mrs. Villiers: If the Chief Secretary cannot answer the specific question about the possibility of multiple transactions that could qualify as a notional transaction, can he tell the Committee what will happen where there are multiple parties that could fall into the category P as defined by proposed section 75A(1)?

Mr. Timms: There may well be some quite complex arrangements where sensible questions could be raised. My advice would be that those questions should be raised directly with HMRC in the light of what is already on the website. I think that the appropriate clarification could then be provided.

The Chairman: Before we debate the other group of amendments, may I make the point that the debate is being conducted on a clause stand part basis, so I am not putting any amendments formally at this stage? If the Opposition Front Bench or, indeed, any other hon. Member wishes to move any of the other remaining amendments formally, they will need to indicate that to me at the appropriate time.

Mrs. Villiers: Thank you, Mr. Gale. I join others in welcoming you back to the Chair.

My understanding of the reaction that the provisions have provoked among those affected by them is very much at variance with the Chief Secretary's account of how they have been received. As ever, the Opposition would support attempts to shut down abusive and artificial tax avoidance schemes that would prevent stamp duty from being charged on transactions. However, we are concerned about the very wide scope of proposed section 75A. Although initially its provisions did not attract a huge amount of attention, considerable concern has since been expressed about their breadth.

The Chartered Institute of Taxation states:

> It is disappointing to note that despite a wide-ranging discussion of this legislation in January 2007 which identified various practical problems with its implementa-

> tion, nothing has been done to tackle the major defects in the legislation . . . In our view the drafting of section 75A is fundamentally deficient in a number of respects . . . Most seriously . . . the section is drafted in such wide and general terms as to be almost unworkable in practice. Its general application means that it may apply to many common commercial transactions, and it appears to cut across many areas where existing SDLT legislation provides reliefs including, for example, charities and reconstruction reliefs.

Column 411

The Institute of Indirect Taxation, the Law Society and the Stamp Taxes Practitioners Group all seem to share the CIOT's concern that innocent transactions could be caught by proposed section 75A. The Law Society points out:

> The uncertainty which this is generating is not simply the perception of a number of anxious professionals who cannot interpret the legislation and want a hand from HMRC.
>
> Seasoned conveyancing and tax professionals have pored over this legislation and want a hand from HMRC, not with a view to picking holes in it, but with a view to understanding it so that they can give advice to clients as to the consequences of undertaking real estate transactions.
>
> The fact that these professionals are still unclear as to the ambit of the legislation is testament to the fact that the legislation is unclear.

Similarly, in a letter to Crispin Taylor at HMRC, the Stamp Taxes Practitioners Group stated:

> As a matter of principle, anti-avoidance legislation should be proportionate to the problem . . . The Stamp Taxes Practitioners Group consider that s75A goes far beyond what is necessary to deal with the type of schemes mentioned in the Technical Note issued by HMRC . . . and cannot on any reasonable basis be allowed to be enacted without, at the very least, major revision.

The Government amendments to which the Chief Secretary referred help to deal with one or two problems and drafting errors, but serious issues remain unaddressed and unresolved. A key concern is that many high-street conveyancers and property lawyers who do not have access to specialist and sophisticated tax advice are unlikely to be aware of the risk that the transactions with which they are dealing could be hit by the provisions of proposed section 75A. There is a risk of widespread but unwitting non-compliance. At the heart of the problem is the fact that the mere linkage of transactions through conveyancing succession might trigger those provisions.

A number of examples of innocent transactions that might be caught by proposed section 75A have been canvassed with HMRC. In its briefing notes for the Committee, the Institute of Indirect Taxation set out the following case. In it, V owns a warehouse, which it sells to A for £250,000, the market value reflecting the hope that planning consent for redevelopment will be granted. However, consent is refused. As a result, A resells the building a year later to P for its then market value of £200,000. Proposed section 75A could bite in that situation because a series of transactions has taken place in relation to the property, ending in its purchase by P, and P could be liable for stamp duty on the higher original price of £250,000 rather than the price that he paid.

HMRC has indicated that proposed section 75A would not apply in that situation. However, the section requires that only one person, V, disposes of property, and that another person, P, acquires it, and that a number of transactions have taken place in connection with the disposal and acquisition of the property. The amount of SDLT payable in respect of those transactions is less than would have been due on a notional direct transfer between V and P. All those conditions would seem to be satisfied in the example given by the IIT, so P might be landed with an unexpected bill for extra stamp duty even though he had nothing to do with the earlier transaction. It seems that virtually all sub-sales could be caught in which A sells to B who then sells on immediately to C at a lower price.

Column 412

Another example of the innocent transaction that might be at risk is one that I gave to the Chief Secretary—a long lease that is enfranchiseable when the right is exercised after the purchase of the lease. There is a sufficient connection even if the purchase takes place some years later, as there is no temporal restriction on the operation of proposed section 75A. There is a connection between the original purchase of the lease and the enfranchisement because if one had not purchased the original lease one would not be able to enfranchise. That has the potential to be caught by proposed section 75A. It is difficult to see how it could qualify as an artificial avoidance scheme of the sort supposedly targeted by the legislation.

Proposed section 75A does not require the direct disposal from P to V, nor does it require that V should have disposal to P in mind when entering the transaction chain. All that is required is that P should end up with the interest originally held by V, even if it arose because something else had happened in a series of other transactions. As the Law Society points out, wholly unrelated Vs and Ps could find themselves party to notional transactions and thus to the application of the provisions of section 75A. There is no requirement that the transactions should constitute an artificial scheme or that they should be motivated by a wish to avoid tax. The mere fact that transactions occur one after the other could turn them into a scheme under proposed section 75A. The danger is that wholly innocent transactions could be caught simply because they involve a series of steps.

The concern becomes even greater when one realises that those steps could take place over several years and still trigger the operation of proposed section 75A. The wide scope of the provisions is reinforced when one notes that proposed subsection (2) makes it clear that not all of the relevant transactions need to relate to land.

I am told that HMRC asserts—this is in line with the response that the Chief Secretary made to the example that I put to him—that the words "involved in connection with", contained in proposed subsection (1)(b), mean that the provisions will bite only where V and P are party to the same arrangement. However, that is not what the Bill says. The words "in connection with" give a very limited and uncertain protection to those carrying out day-to-day real estate transactions. Both the Institute of Indirect Taxation and the Stamp Taxes Practitioners Group have expressed serious concern about the lack of clarity surrounding the phrase on which HMRC seeks to rely to ensure that its legislation does not have an impact on innocent transactions.

Leaving aside the infelicitous nature of the term "involved in connection with", considerable ambiguity is attached to the phrase. The question that is difficult to answer is how substantial a link is needed for HMRC to be able to show that proposed paragraph (b) is satisfied and the required connection is established between the transactions and the acquisition by P.

The words "in connection with" have been interpreted in different ways by the courts. Mr. Justice Nourse in Emery *v.* IRC thought that it meant a "definite causal link". In Johnson and Johnson, Lord Justice Somerville thought it meant merely "having to

COLUMN 413

do with". In one of the more recent cases, in HMRC *v.* Barclays Bank, Lady Justice Arden took a wide interpretation of the term and also emphasised that it could mean different things in different contexts, and that it had to be read in context.

The phrase "in connection with" provides an inadequate safeguard because it does not require the deliberate and consequential link between the transactions, which groups such as the Institute for Indirect Taxation believe is vital if proposed section 75A is not to hit a range of innocent transactions. The Stamp Taxes Practitioners Group points out that the term

> is seemingly capable of including . . . a merely causal or historic interpretation—without a time limit, motive connection or even knowledge of the other parts of the 'scheme'.

The inclusion of "involved in" seems to offer no effective additional protection.

We need something stronger than just the words "involved in connection with" to separate artificial avoidance schemes that should be restricted from normal, everyday transactions, which should not. That is why I tabled amendment No. 213. As well as introducing a purpose test, it would require a much closer link between the transactions in issue than is required by the original drafting of proposed section 75A. The purpose test that the amendment would introduce is similar to those that we have already discussed. They are not without their problems, but they have become a regular feature of our tax law. The Government propose to use purpose tests twice in the Bill in other contexts in relation to their targeted anti-avoidance rule on capital losses and in relation to sideways loss relief in schedule 4.

The amendment takes on board the discussion that we had in relation to capital losses and the TAAR rule, and proposes to cover not just those schemes motivated by a wish to avoid or reduce tax, but those aimed at securing or increasing a tax repayment. I am seeking to insert not only a requirement of a real connection between the different transactions, but an element of deliberation in carrying out a sequence of transactions.

The amendment would remove the risk that the mere fact of a number of transactions taking place sequentially in relation to the property would trigger the operation of proposed section 75A, even where such transactions were years apart and had nothing to do with stamp duty, stamp duty land tax, or a holding tax. The amendment would introduce a concept of a pre-ordained series of transactions that amount to a scheme or an arrangement. Both those ideas draw on case law. The concept of a pre-ordained series of transactions was considered in a line of cases running from *Ramsey v IRC* and *Furniss v Dawson*. It requires such a clear and well established link between the transactions that they are, in effect, a single composite transaction. That type of close link is missing in proposed section 75A.

Adam Afriyie: It occurs to me that if a scheme were designed to avoid stamp duty land tax and for whatever reason it fell apart halfway through, the individual who ended up buying the property but who had no connection whatever with the scheme would also be caught by the provisions.

Mrs. Villiers: There is a risk that that might happen. I understand that there have been troubling examples of artificial avoidance schemes that have fallen outside

Column 414

the scope of proposed section 75A. Not only has it the potential to hit innocent transactions, but it is not effective in catching all the non-innocent ones.

The term "scheme or arrangement", which is also utilised in the amendment, is familiar from case law. It echoes the wording used in a number of contexts in our tax law, such as sections 137, 139 and 140B of the Taxation of Capital Gains Act 1992.

In the view of the IIT, introducing the term "scheme or arrangement"—a phrase that it describes as commonly used and well understood—creates the consequential link that is needed and remedies the problems that occur when reliance is placed solely on the "in connection with" test. Confining the operation of proposed section 75A to instances in which that type of scheme or arrangement is entered into with the main purpose of avoiding tax, rather than for a bona fide commercial reason, would be a much more effective way to tackle the avoidance that concerns HMRC without imposing collateral damage on a range of transactions that have nothing to do with avoiding tax, and, critically, without imposing significant uncertainty and cost on those buying and selling property. The general approach taken in the amendment is broadly in line with representations made by the Institute of Indirect Taxation, the Law Society, the CIOT and the Stamp Taxes Practitioners Group.

Amendment No. 214 would also help to deal with the problems that I have outlined, in particular the issues connected with the absence of any time limit for the operation of the provision. It would provide that transactions taking place more than three years before the acquisition by P should be disregarded for the purposes of proposed section 75A. That would put a temporal limit on the scope of the operation of proposed subsection (1) which would significantly clarify the legislation, otherwise HMRC could in theory look back many years at transactions that happen to have been carried out in relation to a particular item of property. Like amendment No. 213, it would answer the very serious concerns raised by the representative groups to which I have referred.

In responding to calls for the scope of proposed section 75A to be tightened and for a motive test to be inserted, HMRC have responded that that is not necessary because uncertainties can be ironed out using the code of practice 10 clearance procedure. It is welcome that HMRC has indicated that access to the procedure will be extended indefinitely instead of being restricted to the early years of new legislation, as would normally be the case.

However, access to the procedure does not provide all the answers to the problems that I have outlined. For a start, it does not amount to the full clearance procedure for which organisations such as the CIOT and the IIT have called. The Law Society points out that if the Government want to introduce a mini-general anti-avoidance rule for SDLT in proposed section 75A, they need to have HMRC officials able and willing to provide the necessary clearances within a commercially acceptable timetable. An adjudicator under the COP10 procedure can give guidance only on what transactions are caught by proposed section 75A. He cannot disapply it to a transaction—even a wholly innocent one—if the law says that it applies.

Column 415

The Law Society put the position best in relation to the limitations of the COP10 procedure. It said that

> HMRC will have to take a view as to the "innocence" or otherwise of a transaction in deciding whether the legislation should apply. COP10 rulings are not given on what the legislation intends to hit; they are an interpretative provision, where a matter of tax law is unclear, allowing the taxpayer to receive clarity as to how the legislation, as it is laid down, should be applied to a particular set of facts. Our experience is that the complex transactions unit takes a very legalistic view towards legislation, and we have no doubt that transactions which are innocent will get negative COP10 rulings because on the face of the legislation, it applies to them when it was never intended to.

The Law Society went on to highlight a further problem with the procedure by saying:

> Taxpayers are reliant on HMRC's executive view as to what is an 'innocent' transaction such that two taxpayers in very similar circumstances could be taxed differently at the whim of the HMRC officer to whom a COP10 clearance request is made.

Moreover, application for such rulings takes time and generates costs, which is a problem. I have received representations about transactions that fell through because it was impossible to get a COP10 ruling quickly enough. Switching from the idea of precise and targeted legislation to a system more similar to US-style rulings has constitutional implications that should be properly debated. The implications for HMRC resources also have to be considered in light of the need for the prompt turnaround of applications.

Another argument put forward by HMRC, which echoes some of the points made by the Chief Secretary, is that we do not need to amend proposed section 75A because interpretive problems can be resolved using guidance. To that end, it has published a so-called white list of transactions that it does not believe should be covered by proposed section 75A. I am not keen on that phrase; I prefer cleared list. However, leaving aside what one should call it, its publication does not solve the problems with proposed section 75A. The Stamp Taxes Practitioners Group points out, with justification, that the white list approach is not an effective substitute for significant revision of the legislation. It identifies particular problems with the white list approach in this context because of the fact that the proposed section needs to be considered in relation to virtually all conveyancing transactions. Relying on non-statutory guidance is difficult enough in narrow specialist areas such as group relief and real estate investment trusts. However, it is much more difficult in relation to legislation that might have an impact on all conveyances and home purchases.

Many solicitors do not have in-house expertise or research staff who can regularly monitor HMRC's website for guidance. Certainly, an average high-street solicitor is highly unlikely to have access to such resources or expertise. It will also be very difficult to come up with anything like a comprehensive white list. There are even more fundamental constitutional concerns at issue, however.

Richard Stratton, chairman of the Law Society's tax law committee, wrote to the Paymaster General in March referring to the principles articulated by the House of Lords in R *v.* HMRC ex parte Wilkinson. He pointed out that

> however willing HMRC is to confirm that a transaction was not caught, Wilkinson makes it clear that a tax collecting authority cannot ignore legislation and cannot have significant discretion in tax collection.

Column 416

As Lord Upjohn once famously commented:

> A taxpayer should be taxed by law not untaxed by concession,

and as the IIT rightly points out:

> HMRC guidance is no substitute for introducing a fair law.

The Stamp Taxes Practitioners Group has called for a non-exhaustive white list to be inserted into the legislation to give certainty to practitioners and reassurance about how to comply with the law. I welcome proposed section 75C(10), which allows the Treasury to do that and to disapply proposed section 75A in certain cases. However, as the CIOT has commented, that

> does not obviate the need for proper drafting of primary legislation.

Amendment No. 234 seeks to amend paragraph (c) of proposed section 75A(1). That would deal with a problem that has been raised in a number of representations, which is that, as the clause is drafted, there is no need for the three paragraphs in proposed subsection (1) to be read in conjunction with one another. The amendment would clearly tie together proposed paragraphs (a) and (c) and ensure that they are read together rather than separately. Without that change, there would be an ambiguity about the chargeable interest to which the word "its" in the last line of proposed paragraph (c) refers. The amendment would ensure that the interest referred to in proposed paragraph (c) is that which is transferred to P and not the whole of V's original interest.

The concern is about the situation in which V transfers only part of his interest. For example, if A agreed to sell land to B for £3 million and then B agreed to sell, via a sub-sale, one third of the land to three purchasers, C, D and E, for £1 million each, there is a danger, as the section is currently drafted, that proposed section 75A could operate to impose an SDLT charge on each of the three purchasers for the full £3 million rather than the £1 million that each of them actually paid.

On amendments Nos. 235 to 237, the CIOT views proposed section 75A(5) as being too wide. The Stamp Taxes Practitioners Group feels that it should be more focused so that it catches only the chargeable consideration that would have been payable for the land but for the insertion of the phrase "scheme transactions". It would be useful if the Minister could confirm that no double counting will be allowed under proposed subsection (5)—in other words, that it should not be permissible to add up receipts and payments by the same party to arrive at the figure for the notional consideration.

Amendments Nos. 235 to 237 are aimed at reducing the risk of double counting. Subsection (5) refers to

> the largest amount (or aggregate amount).

That does not give rise to a problem so long as "or" is interpreted in the normal way; in other words, disjunctively, so that the tax is payable on either the largest amount or the aggregate amount. However in some legal contexts "or" has been interpreted conjunctively to mean "and".

My three amendments would help to remove the problem by moving the reference to the amount to match the relevant paragraphs. The term "largest amount" seems focused on paragraph (a) whereas the only relevant

Column 417

context for the application of "the aggregate amount" is the situation set out in paragraph (b). The amendments make it plain that either (a) or (b) applies and not both.

Amendment No. 238 is a simple amendment to resolve the problem that I drew to the Chief Secretary's attention. It makes it clear that exercising a statutory right of enfranchisement, extension or enlargement of a leasehold interest cannot trigger the operation of proposed section 75A. Without this change, there is a real danger that someone who buys a lease and later exercises a statutory right to extend it could be hit by proposed section 75A.

Turning to amendment No. 239 and section 75C, the Law Society expresses the concern that the statutory carve-out for reliefs in subsection (2) of proposed section 75C will be restrictively applied. The question here is whether the reliefs and disregards that would be available in relation to the actual transaction will still be available in relation to the notional one. A key problem here is that subsection (2) applies only to reliefs.

Many important SDLT rules that reduce the liability of the taxpayer are not reliefs in a technical sense. They are simply computational rules, exemptions or disregards. If they cannot be applied to the notional transaction under proposed section 75A, this will involve a significant increase in the SDLT bill faced by taxpayers. It would turn section 75A from an anti-avoidance provision into a simple tax increase.

The Stamp Taxes Practitioners Group is also concerned that there is no clear mechanism provided for crediting SDLT that has been paid in relation to transactions earlier in the chain against the SDLT charged on the notional transaction. Considerable uncertainty surrounds this point and any clarification that the Chief Secretary could give would provide significant reassurance to people who are potentially affected by these provisions.

Amendment No. 239 to subsection (4) of proposed section 75C would deal with the specific problem of group relief. It is a concern that the SDLT group relief rules have been excluded from the list carried over into section 75C and thus available to relieve liability under proposed section 75A. Group relief plays an important function in this context and its loss would disrupt many significant commercial transactions. Again, unless this problem is dealt with, section 75A looks much more like a straight tax increase than an anti-avoidance provision. If the Chief Secretary will not accept the amendment, I hope he will at least explain why group relief provisions on SDLT contained in part 1 of schedule 7 of the Finance Act 2003 should not apply to notional transactions under section 75A.

Before concluding, I would like to flag up two general concerns about proposed section 75A. As I said to the Chief Secretary, there could be a number of instances where there could be more than one transaction in the same case that could fall within the definition of a notional transaction for the purposes of these provisions. It is not clear how section 75A is supposed to operate in this situation. It does not surprise me that the Chief Secretary was unable to give me an answer on that point. I should be delighted to take him up on his invitation to address the query to HMRC, but it is a concern that we do not have a clear

Column 418

answer on that yet. In particular, how will a decision be made as to which transaction to select as the notional one?

Another concern is that it might not always be possible to ascertain who is P for the purposes of new section 75A(1). In a recent article for *Taxation Magazine*, Jeremy de Souza, a lawyer for Blake Lapthorn Tarlo Lyons, pointed out that in many cases there may be a number of potential Ps in the conveyancing chain. He concluded by stating of these provisions that

> warning flags should be flying over many property transactions from now on.

In conclusion, new section 75A as drafted is simply too wide-ranging. It will have to be considered in virtually all conveyancing transactions. Thousands of high street legal and conveyancing practices across the country will have to grapple with these highly complex provisions. It is highly likely that many will be unaware of the application of the new section and hence of the need to make an SDLT return. Even if they are aware of the rules, it may be difficult in practice to get hold of the information needed to ascertain whether linked transactions have occurred, sufficient to trigger section 75A. This provision could add a significant conveyancing headache for thousands who just want to buy a new home. I hope that the Chief Secretary will reassure me that those fears are unfounded.

It is particularly harsh to impose complex, unclear and hard-to-understand tax provisions in a self-assessment system, where taxpayers themselves have to determine whether the provisions apply. One expert told me that these rules could leave transactions open to re-examination by Her Majesty's Revenue and Customs, potentially backdating 21 years. The provisions are so unclear and uncertain that it will be difficult for HMRC to apply them consistently. The upshot is that significant extra costs will be imposed on the property market and on home buyers.

To return to Richard Stratton's letter to the Paymaster General on behalf of the Law Society, he wrote that

> uncertainty engenders costs, whether this is due to lenders increasing the cost of borrowing . . . or delay pending seeking clarification from HMRC either informally or under Code of Practice 10 procedure.

The Stamp Tax Practitioners Group said:

> This uncertainty is causing delays in major commercial—and indeed some everyday—transactions because, although clients acquiring high value properties are willing to take risks based on a professional analysis, the banks and institutions that are providing finance for such transactions are generally not. STPG members have reported experience, in relation to transactions in the pipeline at the time when the Regulations were introduced, of funding offers either being withdrawn or the funders being prepared to proceed only on the basis of increased interest rates.

The Chancellor has significantly increased the burden of stamp duty during his term of office at No. 11. Only a few weeks ago, we had the home information packs disaster, and I urge the Chief Secretary to think again before he imposes further costs and uncertainties on the property market, as a result of legislation which, I believe, contains some serious defects.

Mr. Timms: I hope that I can persuade the hon. Lady that her amendments are unnecessary. We have seen the text of them before, because they have been suggested

Column 419

by some of those involved in the property sector. As she knows, we have accepted quite a number of her proposals—they were in the Government amendments that we discussed a few minutes ago. We have rejected this particular group for good reason. Some of the amendments would reopen the avoidance opportunities that the clause is designed to shut down.

Understandably, the hon. Lady spent most time discussing amendment No. 213, which would, as she said, replace the clause's objective test with a different set of tests. First, there would have to be a "pre-ordained series of transactions". The problem is that it is often easy for the parties to arrange things so that the steps are not "pre-ordained" because they might or might not happen, so it is quite easy to avoid that test. A test of purpose is difficult to apply to a transaction tax such as stamp duty land tax, because the main purpose of the transaction is likely to be the commercial one of transferring economic ownership of the property from vendor to purchaser, so I do not think that the approach in this amendment works. It would not give greater certainty to those not engaged in tax avoidance either.

In most cases where a transaction is financed by borrowing, the lender is most concerned to have certainty about the tax consequences, but it is unlikely that lenders could satisfy themselves as to the purposes of the parties to the transaction. The answer, therefore, is that certainty can be secured through clear guidance from HMRC, both generally and in relation to specific transactions. As I have said, there is a firm commitment to giving that guidance.

I also hope that members of the Committee will be reassured to note that the Government have already responded constructively to representations made both during the original drafting of the Bill and in relation to the Government amendments that we discussed this morning, and we will continue to listen carefully to representations in the future. If it still proves to be the case that transactions that are not tax avoidance transactions are likely to be caught, we can and will help innocent taxpayers who are inadvertently caught. We can do that by using the power that the hon. Member for Chipping Barnet referred to, in new section 75C(10), which can disapply the application of new section 75A in specific circumstances.

Mrs. Villiers: Is HMRC contemplating using new section 75C(10) on an individual basis for individual taxpayers? It seems most peculiar to draft wide-ranging legislation and then implement secondary legislation to exempt specific individuals.

Mr. Timms: I refer the hon. Lady to what new section 75C(10) says:

> The Treasury may by order provide for section 75A not to apply in specified circumstances.

I do not think that it would be usual for the "specified circumstances" to apply to just one individual transaction, but the wording does not make that impossible.

Amendment No. 214 would assist those avoiding payment of stamp duty land tax by restricting the application of clause 70. It would disregard transactions occurring more than three years before the ultimate acquisition of the property by the purchaser. The intention

Column 420

there is understandable, but there is no reason why purchasers should have to make the inquiries that the amendment would spare them. As long as they are planning to pay stamp duty land tax on their purchase in the normal way or they qualify for a relief such as charities relief, the anti-avoidance provisions in the clause will not apply to them. Incidentally, the hon. Member for Chipping Barnet queried whether charities relief and reconstruction relief would be affected. Those reliefs are expressly preserved and are not affected.

Mrs. Villiers: I am grateful to the Chief Secretary for his clarification, which I accept entirely and very much welcome. I would like to ask him about the three-year time limit in amendment No. 214. His answer to my concern about enfranchisement of the leasehold interest was that there had to be sufficient connection between the transactions so that they happened very close together. He therefore seems to envisage that new section 75A should apply only when transactions are relatively close together. If that is the case, why does he not accept the amendment, have the three-year cap and reassure people who are very worried about this legislation?

Mr. Timms: Because it is not needed. As I have said, as long as the parties involved are planning to pay stamp duty land tax in the normal way on their purchase or they qualify for a relief, they will not be affected. It is only where their involvement results in a reduction of the tax that would normally be payable that the clause will be likely to affect them.

Mrs. Villiers: The issue is that people may not know that transactions way back in history are affecting their SDLT liability, so they may be planning to pay the SDLT that they think is due—I am sure that they would be. The concern is that, if HMRC can look back on a string of transactions in previous years, the party concerned will simply not know that that affects their current liability.

Mr. Timms: It may be of some reassurance to the Committee to know that transactions that occurred before 6 December 2006, when the regulations that preceded this clause were laid, would be disregarded in any event, and a provision such as that set out in the amendment would not have any effect until 2009 at the earliest. I do not think that there is a problem that needs to be fixed here.

I understand the purpose of amendment No. 234, but, again, I think it is unnecessary, because it is clear from the context that the interest referred to in subsection (4)(b) is the same as the interest disposed of by V in subsection (1)(a). Amendments Nos. 235, 236 and 237 do not add anything, and would in fact reduce the effectiveness of the anti-avoidance provisions by changing the circumstances in which the section could be applied. They would lead to the clause not being applied fully in circumstances where any one person gave consideration in the form of more than one transaction, and that would allow tax to be avoided by breaking the consideration into a series of transactions, only the largest amount of which would be liable to stamp duty land tax—which is precisely what we want to prevent.

Column 421

Amendment No. 238 would mean that newsection 75A would not apply to the exercise of a statutory right of enfranchisement—the point raised with me by the hon. Lady earlier on. That would create an opportunity for avoidance, however, because it is not possible to rule out the exercise of such a right as a step in new types of avoidance schemes. I want to reassure those involved in legitimate transactions that, in most cases, the exercise of such a right would not be one of a number of transactions involved in connection with a disposal and acquisition, so it would not be affected by new section 75A.

Rob Marris: I may have misunderstood, but would not much of the discussion be academic, as stamp duty land tax would never be payable anyway? If we talk about leasehold enfranchisement for many houses in the west midlands, for example, we may note that they were sold originally on a 99-year lease, and the usual multiple was 11 times the annual ground rent, which as I understand it would not get anywhere near stamp duty land tax. I am not saying that no transactions would be caught, but many of the average transactions of our constituents, using the Leasehold Reform Act 1967, would not be caught at all anyway, as they are below the stamp duty land tax threshold.

Mr. Timms: My hon. Friend is absolutely right, and the increases that we have made in the stamp duty land tax threshold have helped in this context.

Mrs. Villiers: The problem is that the enfranchisement cost is unlikely to be above the SDLT threshold in many cases, but if new section 75A bites, the cost of the original lease would have to be taken into account, which could well take the combined cost above the threshold, so it is relevant even where the enfranchisement cost is below the threshold.

Mr. Timms: Finally, amendment No. 239 would exclude from the application of new section 75A any consideration paid under a transaction that qualified for group relief.

We have, I am afraid, seen a number of avoidance schemes in the past that made use of group relief as part of a series of transactions, so I would not at this stage want to exclude considerations paid under a transaction that qualifies for group relief. Again, I can reassure the Committee that if there are specific categories of legitimate transactions involving group relief where it is appropriate to disapply newsection 75A, we would be prepared to consider exercising our powers under new section 75C(10). I hope that that is helpful to the hon. Lady.

My concern is that the Opposition amendments would allow, inadvertently I am sure, some of the very schemes that the clause aims to end, to carry on unchecked. Therefore, I hope that the Committee will not accept them.

I will pick up one or two further points made by the hon. Lady. The schemes that this clause is designed to prevent are wholly artificial, and those using them must expect that we will act to prevent their use, as they pose

COLUMN 412

a significant threat to Exchequer revenue. For example, before the pre-Budget Report, Revenue and Customs was aware of two transactions using these schemes, which alone were worth a combined total of £850 million. We had no option other than to act as quickly as we could to counter those schemes, hence the laying of the regulations at the time, and the clause.

The hon. Lady suggested that, if those involved in the transaction did not intend to save any stamp duty land tax through the transaction, the provision should not be applied. However, it is often difficult to establish what the motivation in any transaction was, and there is a real danger of leaving a gate wide open to those wishing to avoid tax.

The hon. Lady was concerned that mere linkage through conveyancing succession would be caught by proposed new section 75A. I assure her that that will not be the case. There must be more connection than mere succession, as is implied by the phrase "involved in connection with" in proposed new section 75A that she referred to. The acquisition involvement means more than mere temporal succession. When drafting the measure, we looked at the phrase "involved in connection with". Our legal advice was that the terms are not too vague, as she suggested, and that they will not create any difficulties of interpretation. In any case, as I have said, we will be issuing guidance to ensure that the meaning and intent of the legislation are clear.

The hon. Lady made the point that code of practice 10 rulings cannot disapply legislation. Of course that is true, but a code of practice 10 application might result in the Government exercising their disapplication power under proposed new section 75C(10), potentially with retrospective application. She was concerned about the speed of those rulings. HMRC aims to turn them around within 28 days.

Adam Afriyie: I thank the Chief Secretary for his generosity in giving way. Will he make it absolutely clear why there is no exemption for long-term leaseholders who may choose to enfranchise and buy the freehold, in cases in which that purchase exceeds the limit? Why is that not very clearly spelled out somewhere? I sensed a slight hesitancy in his response, even to the hon. Member for Wolverhampton, South-West.

Mr. Timms: I accept that there are some good intentions behind these amendments, and no doubt behind others, but in drafting the legislation we must avoid opening a new opportunity, or leaving open an opportunity, for avoidance because, sadly, there will be plenty of people piling in to take advantage of such openings if they are provided. That certainly applies to a number of the amendments tabled by Opposition Members, and one can envisage other blanket exclusions that could have the same effect. That is why we are being very cautious about the wording we have adopted.

The hon. Lady was concerned about double counting under proposed new section 75A(5). Subsection (5) will add up the amount paid by any one person or received by the vendor. It is aimed at identifying the true purchase price, which might be artificially split up, and ensuring that the full amount

COLUMN *423*

of tax is payable. She was also concerned that there was no clear mechanism to credit to the notional transaction stamp duty land tax paid earlier in the chain. Proposed new section 75C(9) contains precisely such a mechanism, so that issue is addressed.

Finally, in contrast with the concerns expressed by Opposition Members, let me refer to some of the comments made when the regulations that precede the clause, which I think have worked well, were made. Sue Taylor, head of real estate tax at Eversheds, said that this

> will catch most of the planning in current use....It is a serious bit of legislation.

Craig Leslie, head of stamp taxes at PricewaterhouseCoopers said:

> HMRC are making very good use of all the planning information they receive.

Patrick Cannon, a leading barrister in the area, said that

> this is a well aimed measure,

as indeed it is. I hope, on that basis, that the Committee will support my amendments, but not accept those tabled by Opposition Members.

Mrs. Villiers: The Chief Secretary may believe that the provision is designed to target a few wholly artificial schemes, but the reality is that the Government have not succeeded in focusing in on that target, and they are going to hit other innocent transactions as well.

I am grateful to the Chief Secretary for confirming on the record that mere linkage through conveyancing succession does not satisfy proposed new section 75A. That is very welcome. I am not sure whether it is consistent with what the statute states, but at least we have it on the record for the purposes of interpretation by the courts.

I continue to be concerned by the approach that the Chief Secretary seems to have confirmed today, which is that the intention is to create a broadly worded provision that can, if necessary, be disapplied in certain circumstances if it operates in an unintended way and applies to innocent transactions. That raises some constitutional concerns about the legislation.

I am also grateful for the Chief Secretary's reassurance on the operation of proposed newsection 75C(9) and credit for earlier stamp duty land tax paid. Given that relevant transactions can also include share transactions, it would be useful to clarify whether previous tax paid in relation to stamp duty on shares can also be taken into account, but proposed new section 75C(9) provides useful reassurance on the point that I made.

I have listened to the Chief Secretary's concerns about the purpose test that I have proposed. I will not press that issue to a vote because I wish to reflect further on the appropriate wording and approach of that measure in the light of what he said. There is no excuse, however, for turning down the three-year restriction proposed in amendment No. 214. I would like to press that amendment to the vote.

Amendment proposed: No. 214, in clause 70, page 44, line 13, at end insert—

> (1A) Transactions taking place more than three years before the acquisition of a property by P shall be disregarded for the purposes of subsection (1).'.—*[Mrs. Villiers.]*

COLUMN *424*

Question put, That the amendment be made:—

The Committee divided: Ayes 9, Noes 15.

Division No. 9]

AYES

Afriyie, Adam
Cable, Dr. Vincent
Dunne, Mr. Philip
Evennett, Mr. David
Francois, Mr. Mark
Goodman, Mr. Paul
Hosie, Stewart
Newmark, Mr. Brooks
Villiers, Mrs. Theresa

NOES

Brennan, Kevin
Brown, Lyn
Cunningham, Mr. Jim
David, Mr. Wayne
Healey, John
Hesford, Stephen
Johnson, Ms Diana R.
Keeble, Ms Sally
McCarthy-Fry, Sarah
McGovern, Mr. Jim
Marris, Rob
Reed, Mr. Andy
Timms, rh Mr. Stephen
Ussher, Kitty
Wright, Mr. Iain

Question accordingly negatived.

Amendments made: No. 184, in clause 70, page 45, line 20, leave out "(but subject to subsection (2))".

No. 185, in clause 70, page 45, line 29, at end insert—

(3A) In subsection (3)—

(a) paragraph (a) is subject to subsection (2)(a) to (c),
(b) paragraph (b) is subject to subsection (2)(a) and (c), and
(c) paragraph (c) is subject to subsection (2)(a) to (c).'.

No. 186, in clause 70, page 45, line 31, at end insert—

(5) In this section a reference to the transfer of a chargeable interest from V to P includes a reference to a disposal by V of an interest acquired by P..

No. 187, in clause 70, page 46, line 2, at end insert—

(4A) In the application of section 75A(5) an amount given or received partly in respect of the chargeable interest acquired by P and partly in respect of another chargeable interest shall be subjected to just and reasonable apportionment.'.

No. 188, in clause 70, page 46, line 7, after first "a" insert "property-investment".

No. 189, in clause 70, page 46, line 7, after "partnership" insert (within the meaning of paragraph 14 of Schedule 15).

No. 190, in clause 70, page 46, line 21, at end insert

and may make provision with retrospective effect.".

No. 191, in clause 70, page 46, line 25, after 'But' insert—

(a).

No. 192, in clause 70, page 46, line 28, at end insert—

, and

(b) a provision of new section 75C (inserted by subsection (1) above) shall not have effect where the disposal mentioned in new section 75A(1)(a) took place before the day on which this Act is passed, if or in so far as the provision would make a person liable for a higher amount of tax than would have been charged in accordance with those regulations.'.—*[Mr. Timms.]*

Question pu t and agreed to.

Clause 70, as amended, ordered to stand part of the Bill.

Column 425

CLAUSE 71

Partnerships

Mr. Timms: I beg to move amendment No. 106, in clause 71, page 47, line 9, leave out "sub-paragraph (1)(b)," and insert "sub-paragraphs (1)(b) and (4),".

The Chairman: With this it will be convenient to discuss Government amendment No. 107.

Mr. Timms: As I indicated earlier, clause 71 amends the Finance Act 2003 to counter known schemes that attempt to avoid stamp duty land tax by moving property tax-free into a partnership—that is, by the ceding of partnerships. The clause will prevent tax avoidance schemes that we initially dealt with by regulations in the pre-Budget report 2006. The two amendments that I am tabling are directly in response to representations from the property sector.

The first amendment is merely to rectify an omission from the clause; it is a minor omission, but if it was not rectified we would run the risk of confusing those trying to interpret the law. The second amendment follows some late representations suggesting that the clause could have an adverse effect on investment structures that use partnerships but are not engaged in avoidance. We have been lobbied to include a transitional provision, so that the provisions that will create the change do not apply where all the property in a partnership was acquired before Royal Assent and stamp duty land tax was paid in full on the gross market value of the property, and that is what the amendment does.

We have taken on all the suggestions we could that will facilitate those involved in legitimate, innocent transactions without creating further opportunity for those seeking to avoid tax. Of course, those developing avoidance schemes will keep on looking for new ways to avoid stamp duty land tax and we will respond by closing avoidance schemes quickly. We have a duty to the majority of taxpayers to maintain a level playing field for everybody, and of course we will keep this area under review.

I commend the amendments to the Committee.

Mrs. Villiers: I would like to address some of the issues surrounding the clause at the same time as addressing the amendments, to obviate the need for a separate clause stand part debate.

I appreciate that there are avoidance risks in relation to partnerships, which have not always proved easy to tackle in the past. However, there seems to me a significant risk that clause 71, like the clause that we have just discussed, could have some unintended consequences in relation to innocent transactions.

Again, some general concerns about the operation of the clause have been expressed to me by the Institute of Indirect Taxation. It believes that transactions that a taxpayer might contemplate without professional advice, such as gifts, could be affected by clause 71. It states:

> We are surprised that a Labour Government should take the view that a family that cannot afford professional advice should not expect to be able to make straightforward gifts without triggering tax consequences.

Column 426

I would like to raise two points in relation to the scope of clause 71, and I do not think that they are addressed by the Government amendments. One of them is partially addressed, but some remain and it would be excellent if the Chief Secretary could help to answer them.

The first issue concerns the deletion of the requirement of consideration. Under the old law, the relevant partnership anti-avoidance provisions did not bite on gifts, so they did not apply to a transaction where no consideration was given. The Law Society has expressed concern about the removal of the requirement of consideration by clause 71, pointing out that the consequence is that a gift of a partnership interest from individual to individual is now subject to a market value charge based on the value owned by the partnership. It should also be noted that that is a charge on the gross value of the land owned by the partnership rather than the real value of the gift, which could be considerably less where the partnership has borrowed to invest in the land. So the SDLT charge here could be quite a high one. The Law Society expressed concern that a gift of a partnership interest attracts a charge when a gift of the underlying property would not. It would be useful if the Minister could provide greater clarification on that point and explain the reasons behind the proposed deletion of the consideration requirement.

The second point is rather more worrying. It concerns one of the effects that are partially caused by the deletion of the requirement of consideration, but it also interacts with other changes made in clause 71, and it involves property investment partnerships. The point is best explained by looking at the example given by the Law Society in its briefing to the Committee. It concerns a relatively simple case, where A, B and C are in partnership, sharing income and profits equally, with partnership property of £450,000. Each partner is deemed to own £150,000-worth of property. Further property is purchased by the partnership, using its assets. If another person then joins as a new partner, providing £150,000 in cash, the value of everyone's interest will have stayed the same, at £150,000. I am told that before section 75A, it was accepted that the addition of a new partner did not trigger an SDLT charge.

The amendments to paragraphs 14(1)(b) and 36 contained in clause 71 would throw that into doubt. Will the Minister confirm whether the enactment of clause 71 will result in SDLT being payable in that situation? It seems that it would be. If so, it could have a significant impact on property investment partnerships.

The practice of second closing—bringing a second wave of investors into a partnership some months after it is first set up—is common. The changes proposed in clause 71 would result in SDLT being payable if the partnership had acquired land between the first and second closing, even though it was bought with money put up by the original investors. If second closings are now to trigger an SDLT charge, it could severely restrict the use of open-ended property investment partnerships. Similar problems occur when partners redeem their partnership interests. Coupled with a further concern, such problems could render partnerships almost unusable in the property investment field. I hope that I am wrong, and that the Chief Secretary will reassure me.

Column 427

My other concern is about changes in the profit sharing ratio in a partnership. The old law made it plain that, if a partner sold his interest for a consideration to another person, it would give rise to an SDLT liability. However, clause 71 would significantly expand the scope of SDLT by applying it not only in that situation but whenever the profit sharing ratio in a partnership changed.

That could give rise to significant problems, as profit sharing ratios can change automatically under the original partnership agreement. A common example might be an agreement that entitled the operator of a partnership to an increased profit share if the partnership reached a particular level of return. When that relevant level of profits was reached, the partnership shares would change. Under the old paragraph 36, there was no SDLT problem because no consideration had been given to changes in profit shares, and a partnership interest, as it was previously understood, had not been transferred. It now seems that SDLT will have to be paid in every case when a profit sharing ratio changes, even if it was provided for in the original partnership agreement, because of the new definition of what amounts to an interest in a partnership and the removal of the need for consideration.

Similarly, development funds using partnerships will typically include a provision to call for more money from investors: it is a well-known fact that developments frequently run over budget. Such calls are not compulsory; some investors may take them up and others not. However, in such cases, we again see that changes in the partnership ratios that to date would not have triggered an SDLT would now do so. Again, the Minister's guidance on whether that is the case would be useful. The same problem occurs where an investor defaults or goes bankrupt—another occupational hazard in the property development business. Until now, the resulting change in partnership ratios did not trigger SDLT. It now seems that it would.

I have received representations that, if my analysis is correct and SDLT is payable, partnerships will no longer be used for property funds. That is significant, as such partnerships have played an important role in property investment. A solicitor who contacted one of my colleagues about the problem described the change as lunacy, although I would not go that far. I am willing to hear the Chief Secretary's justification, but I want to know whether that effect was intended by the Government when drafting clause 71. If so, what was their justification for making such a significant change?

What avoidance problem was caused by property investment partnerships that justified penalising them in the way that clause 71 seems to do? What assessments have the Government carried out on the impact that the change will have on the property investment market? I would be interested to hear whether the Chief Secretary is prepared to publish the Department's research on the impact of the change. To what extent will the amendments assist in solving the problem? They are helpful in some contexts. In particular, they help to tackle the unfairness that the change in the law creates for people who are committed to partnerships on the basis of the existing law. However, they seem to cover only partnerships that bought land between December 2003, when the SDLT regime was introduced, and commencement of clause 71.

Column 428

While it is useful to give assistance in relation to those transactions, the Government amendments provide a very limited lifeline. In particular, they do not seem to solve any of the problems in relation to partnerships that want to carry on business in future, nor do they permit new partnerships to set up start-up arrangements in the property investment businesses. As the Chief Secretary has confirmed, they are merely transitional arrangements to ease the change that is being introduced.

A way should be found to address concerns about avoidance in this area without such radical restrictions on the use of property investment partnerships. In the debate on REITs, the Government have repeatedly stated that they wish to encourage collective investment in property. If that is the case, why are they effectively shutting down an important vehicle for doing so—the property investment partnership? The Committee should consider the likely consequences of that shutting down. The onshore alternative structures that might substitute for property investment partnerships are limited. Not all enterprises are suited to REIT status; as we debated at length in this Committee last year, REITs are usable only in certain circumstances. In particular, many property enterprises may not be large enough to justify the cost of the listing that is required for REIT status. I am concerned lest the net result of the changes is simply a shift of property investment into offshore unit trusts. I cannot believe that that is really what the Government want.

The Chief Secretary referred to Patrick Cannon's comments on section 75A. I, too, would like to draw to the Committee's attention to some comments by Mr. Cannon, who is a barrister. They appeared in *Property Week* a few days ago in an article helpfully entitled, "Latest tax clampdown is shoddy and rushed". Let me close with a quote from the article, which states:

> The SDLT partnership provisions are an unfortunate example of just how bad tax legislation can get when you have layer on layer of anti-avoidance amendments built on to basic provisions. The provisions seem to have been worked on at different times by different draftsmen, some of whom do not seem to have a full grasp of how property partnerships function.

I have to say, Mr. Chairman, that I am inclined to agree.

The Chairman: Before we progress, the hon. Lady has, perfectly reasonably, broadened this into a stand part debate. As the Committee knows, I have no problem with that so long as we do not try to cover the ground twice. However, I listened fairly attentively to what she has been saying and it strikes me that she might have placed the Chief Secretary in a slightly difficult position, because she has commented on one or two things that would otherwise have been raised under the next pair of amendments. If the

Chief Secretary wishes to respond now, he might find it necessary to curtail his remarks on the next pair of amendments.

Rob Marris: I had anticipated that you might turn this into a broader debate, Mr. Gale. The hon. Lady has got me totally confused—perhaps my right hon. Friend can help me. I had thought that stamp duty

COLUMN 429

land tax bit on land, but the hon. Lady has talked about changing profit shares in a partnership. I did not think that stamp duty land tax had anything to do with that, so I should appreciate some clarification.

Mrs. Villiers: That would be the impact of clause 31. If a partnership holds land and one of the situations that I have outlined, such as a new partner joining, occurs it will be subject to an SDLT charge on that land. That is the connection between the land and a partnership.

Rob Marris: I understood that part of the argument. I am not sure that I agreed with it, but I understood it. However, I did not understand at all what the hon. Lady said about changing profit share. I hope that my right hon. Friend can clarify that.

The second point that I should like to make to my right hon. Friend is that it is often, understandably, prayed in aid in this Committee that the Chartered Institute of Taxation says at paragraph 29.1 of its submission that the proposed changes to the Finance Act 2003, schedule 15, are welcome in that they eliminate some of the anomalies in schedule 15. That is all that it says.

Mr. Philip Dunne (Ludlow) (Con): I welcome the remarks that the Chief Secretary made in introducing the amendments, which attempt to establish some clarity for partnerships that would be caught incidentally. In other words, they would remove genuine partnership transactions that are not seeking to avoid stamp duty land tax, which is clearly the thrust of the schedule and clauses. However, I am not sure that he has done his job as well as the Committee would normally expect him to do. I am concerned that there are incidental consequences for members of existing partnerships that go beyond the special purpose vehicle type of partnerships that he seeks to catch.

I would appreciate it if he could give the Committee some clarity here and confirm that the Government amendments do not apply to those partnerships where property interests are held incidentally to the activity of the partnership rather than specifically, and interests in those partnerships change over time. My hon. Friend the Member for Chipping Barnet, in her thoughtful contribution, showed that by changing the definition of consideration in the Bill, a partnership gift interest from one individual to another, such as a gift from a partner to his spouse, his children or a family interest, could potentially trigger a stamp duty land tax charge if the partnership happens to hold property. That is quite clearly not the intent of the clause.

I am not sure that the Government amendment is sufficiently clear. We do not have a definition of a property investment partnership although it may exist in the Finance Act 2003. I apologise to the Chief Secretary for not having seen such a definition if it does exist. Perhaps he could put us straight on that. The second point on which I seek some clarity is whether it is intended to catch gifts in the manner that I have just

COLUMN 430

described if they arise in partnership interests. If a property is held outside a partnership, such a gift would not attract stamp duty land tax whereas if it is held within a partnership it would. Is that the Government's intention? If so, I think that it is quite inappropriate.

Mr. Timms: As I have indicated already, the clause aims to prevent tax avoidance schemes that were initially dealt with by regulations at the pre-Budget report. As with the previous clause, the regulations were time-limited and so now need to be replaced using the Finance Act. But the opportunity we have had to revise the legislation has been helpful. Not only has it allowed us to make changes to ensure that a variation on the schemes that we did not know about when we drafted the regulations can be dealt with, it has allowed us to consider whether there are any changes we can make to ensure that legitimate transactions are not affected by the legislation.

As far as the clause itself is concerned, I believe that we have been able to reassure most in the property sector that it will be clear, proportionate and effective. My hon. Friend the Member for Wolverhampton, South-West is right to draw attention to the views of the Chartered Institute of Taxation, which were communicated to all members of the Committee. It welcomed the amendments and the clause. The clause brings fairness to the property sector for taxation by ensuring that transactions using these complex avoidance schemes will be taxed in the same way as they would have been if they had been straightforward land transactions between two parties.

I should again point out that significant sums are at stake here. Until the PBR, when we made the regulations, only relatively few transactions had used these schemes, but the loss in stamp duty land tax yield is significant. These are major commercial transactions. The number would have certainly continued to rise. Closing this scheme alone will bring extra combined revenue for the years 2006-07 to 2009-10 respectively of £10 million, £25 million, £25 million and £25 million.

We believe that we have taken on all the suggestions we could that will facilitate those involved in innocent transactions without creating further opportunity for those seeking to avoid payment of the tax. As a result, we have certainly achieved a clearer and more effective clause, which hits our target of preventing avoidance without unduly affecting legitimate land transactions.

As I said during the debate on the previous clause, those developing avoidance schemes will, of course, keep on trying to find new ways to avoid paying stamp duty land tax and we must be ready to respond by closing avoidance schemes quickly, and we will. We have a duty to the majority of taxpayers, who are not using elaborate avoidance schemes, to ensure that there is a level playing field for everybody, so we will be keeping this area under review.

I would like to respond specifically to some of the points raised by Opposition Members. A concern was raised about charging when partnership interests are gifted between individuals, or by an individual to an unconnected company. I think that it was implicit in what the hon. Members asked, but I need to make it clear that charging applies only to cases where there are

Column 431

property transactions. However, in such cases, I do not think that there is any reason why such a transaction should be dealt with more favourably than other transactions where tax would be due.

Regarding the concern about gifts of partnership interests now being chargeable, again they will be chargeable only where the partnership is engaged in property dealing or property investment. Other forms of trading partnership, such as farming partnerships, are not affected. Indeed, partnerships where land ownership is incidental are also unaffected by the clause.

Mr. Dunne: I am grateful to the Minister for that clarification. Could he also clarify whether, in the case of an investment management partnership that manages property portfolios as part of its activity but not as its core activity, such a partnership would be caught?

Mr. Timms: I imagine that it would depend on the extent of the property interest, but I think that the answer is, quite rightly, yes. If the hon. Member wants to raise a more specific question with me, for example in a letter, I would be happy to provide him with an answer. Let me also make it clear that it is not the case that gifts of property from parents to children will be made liable to stamp duty land tax by the clause.

There are substantial sums at stake. The hon. Member for Chipping Barnet asked about the addition of a new partner who contributes cash. She is right that there will now be a charge, because the previous provisions were being used for avoidance purposes and it was necessary for us to ensure that that opportunity was blocked. She also asked about what happens when the profit share ratio between partners changes. Again, this applies only to property investment partnerships, but we think that it is right that there should be a charge where a partner acquires an increased right to income from the property.

This is a complex area, but the balance that we have struck in the clause, with the amendments that we tabled, is right. Certainly, the changes that we have made have been warmly welcomed. I hope that the Committee will support the clause, with these Government amendments.

Amendment agreed to.

Amendments made: No. 243, in clause 71, page 48, line 26, at end insert—

(13A) But the amendments made by subsections (6) and (10) do not have effect in respect of anything done in respect of a property-investment partnership established before the day on which this Act is passed if—

(a) the partnership does not acquire a chargeable interest on or after that day, and

(b) stamp duty land tax was paid in respect of each chargeable interest acquired before that day, by reference to chargeable consideration of not less than the market value.'.

No. 244, in clause 71, page 48, line 30, leave out "and" and insert "to".—*[Mr. Timms.]*

Clause 71, as amended, ordered to stand part ofthe Bill.

Clause 72 ordered to stand part of the Bill.

Appendix B

Statements of Practice

STATEMENT OF PRACTICE SP 10/87 (WITHDRAWN BY SP 8/93—SEE BELOW)
Stamp duty: conveyances and leases of building plots (22 December 1987)

INTRODUCTION

1. In 1957 the Inland Revenue published the attached statement summarising the law dealing with the stamp duty payable on conveyances and leases of building plots where, at the date of the contract, no house was built *or* a house was only partly built.

2. The Inland Revenue are advised that the 1957 statement still accurately reflects the law on this subject. That statement has, however, sometimes been misconstrued or misapplied. This Statement therefore restates the view the Inland Revenue takes and, subject to the proviso that ultimately each case depends on its own facts, clarifies the position in a number of respects.

GENERAL

3. The principle on which the statement is based is that the conveyance or lease is liable to *ad valorem* duty by reference to the amount of consideration fixed by and payable under the contract of sale to which that instrument gives effect. If there is a single bargain for the sale of a completed house, the aggregate consideration payable by the purchaser or lessee will provide the measure of the charge to stamp duty. If there is one contract for the sale of the land in its undeveloped state or with a partly erected house, and another (independent) contract for building work, the conveyance or lease is liable to duty by reference to the consideration payable under the former contract alone. In every case the question is whether there is one *contract* or two.

4. No single factor will be conclusive in answering this question, but whether one *document* or two is used is irrelevant. The Revenue's view is that, in general, arrangements for the sale of the land and for building work which are so interlocked that the purchaser or lessee cannot obtain vacant possession of the land until he has paid both the land price and the full building price, provide a strong indication that there is a single bargain for the sale of a completed house as a package deal.

SPECIFIC COMMENTS

5. The 1957 statement should be read as a whole, but the following points should be borne in mind in considering particular paragraphs.

Paragraph (i)

6. This paragraph covers the situation in which the parties intend to reach separate agreements for the sale of the land and the construction of the house. It applies only where:

(a) no building work has been started at the date of the contract for sale;
(b) independent contracts are made for the sale of the land and the building of the house; and

(c) the purchaser or lessee is entitled to a conveyance or lease in consideration *only* of the land price or the rent.

7. If the purchaser or lessee can only obtain a conveyance or lease for the land price or rent plus some other consideration, such as an undertaking or guarantee that he will pay the building price, condition (*c*) is not satisfied because the additional consideration is also part of the consideration for the sale.

Paragraph (ii)

8. This paragraph deals with the situation in which the parties intend to create a package deal. Since there is no entitlement to a conveyance or lease until after the building has been completed by the vendor or lessor, duty is chargeable on the total price for the land and the completed building.

Paragraph (iii)

9. This paragraph covers the rare situation in which a package deal has been varied, perhaps because one party or the other is unable to perform the original contract. Although there is no entitlement under the contract to a conveyance or lease until the building has been completed by the vendor or lessor (as in paragraph (*ii*)), the contract has been varied both as to the subject-matter of the sale and the consideration payable. As a result of the variation the house is sold in its incomplete state at the date of the conveyance or lease for a proportion of the original aggregate purchase price. Duty is payable on that proportion i.e. the revised consideration.

Paragraph (iv)

10. This paragraph was included to cover cases that would fall within (*i*) were it not that a house had been partly erected at the date of the contract for the sale of the land. It follows that the other conditions of paragraph *(i)* must be met: there must be independent contracts and an entitlement to a conveyance or lease giving the purchaser or lessee vacant possession in consideration *only* of the purchase price or rent of the site.

11. *Subparagraph (a)* applies in such a case if the partly erected building has been built by the vendor or lessor. The conveyance or lease is chargeable with *ad valorern* duty on the land price or rent plus the consideration for the building work at the date of the contract. If the purchaser or lessee is obliged to provide additional consideration for the completion of the building before he can obtain possession, that additional consideration forms part of the consideration for the conveyance or lease.

12. *Subparagraph (b)* applies where the partly erected building has been built by the purchaser or lessee. In this case the value of the work done at the date of the contract for sale does not normally form part of' the consideration for the conveyance or lease, and in consequence is not normally chargeable to duty.

Paragraph (v)

13. This paragraph emphasises the need to consider all the contractual arrangements between the parties. Any amendment of a printed form of contract and any other agreement oral or written, between the parties relevant to the arrangements between them forms part of those arrangements and therefore part of the contract.

PROCEDURES FOR SUBMITTING INSTRUMENTS

14. Where a person accepts that a conveyance or lease of a building plot is chargeable on the total price paid for the land and the completed building, it should be submitted for stamping in the usual way together with a covering letter giving the aggregate price and a remittance for the duty appropriate to that price.

15. Where the total price does not exceed the amount up to which the instrument is liable to nil duty (currently £30,000) and a certificate of value is included, a conveyance

may be sent direct to the Land Registry in England and Wales under the Stamp Duty (Exempt Instruments) Regulations 1985 (see Appendix I), where appropriate, or, in Scotland, to the Keeper of' the Registers of Scotland. A lease will need to be stamped in respect of the rent.

16. Where the total price for the land and the completed building exceeds the threshold *for* duty and the applicant takes the view that duty is payable on some lesser amount than the total price, the instrument should be submitted to the Stamp Office even if such lesser amount does not exceed the threshold and a certificate of value is included. The instrument should be accompanied by a copy of the agreement(s) for sale etc. and a letter stating the amount which the applicant regards as chargeable consideration, identifying separately any amount attributable to building work. Details of any contractual arrangements not covered by the agreement(s) should be given in the covering letter.

A statement from the Board of Inland Revenue was published in the *Law Society's Gazette* (1957), pp. *450–1* in these terms:

> The Board have taken legal advice concerning the stamp duty chargeable on conveyances or leases of building plots in cases where at the date of the contract for sale or lease no house has been erected or a house has been partly erected on the site which constitutes or is included in the subject-matter of the sale or lease, and at the date of the conveyance or lease a house has been wholly or partly erected on the site.
>
> The Board are advised that the law is as follows:
>
> (i) Subject to what is said under paragraph (iv), if under the contract for the sale or lease the purchaser or lessee is entitled to a conveyance or lease of the land in consideration only of the purchase price or rent of the site, the *ad valorem* duty on the conveyance or lease will be determined only by the amount of the purchase price or rent, although it may have been agreed that a house is to be built on the site at the expense of the purchaser or lessee.
> In such a case, the concurrent existence of a contract with the vendor or lessor or any other person for the building of a house on the site will not increase the stamp duty chargeable on the conveyance or lease.
>
> (ii) If under the contract the purchaser or lessee is not entitled to a conveyance or lease until a house has been built on the site at his expense and if the house is to be built by the vendor or lessor or by his agent or nominee, the payment of the building price by the purchaser or lessee will be part of the consideration or the conveyance or lease and the building price will be liable to *ad valorem* duty accordingly.
> (If the house is to be built by a person who is not the vendor or lessor or his agent or nominee, the payment of the building price will not form part of the consideration for the sale or lease except in so far as paragraph (iv) applies.)
>
> (iii) When the position is as in paragraph (ii), and a purchaser or lessee not entitled to a conveyance or lease until a house has been erected at his expense in fact obtains a conveyance or lease when the house has been only partly erected, *ad valorem* duty is payable on the conveyance or lease on the proportionate amount of the building price attributable to the partial erection of the house computed as at the date of the conveyance or lease.
>
> (iv)
>
> (a) If, at the date of the contract, a house has been wholly or partly erected by the vendor or lessor or by his agent or nominee or by a builder not employed by the purchaser or lessee, it normally forms part of the subject-matter of the sale or lease and the consideration or apportioned consideration for that building (as existing at the date of the contract) is accordingly liable to *ad valorem.duty.*

(b) If, at the date of the contract, a house has been wholly or partly erected by the purchaser or lessee or by any person on his behalf the consideration or apportioned consideration for the house wholly or partly erected will not normally form part of the consideration for the sale or lease and accordingly will not be liable to *ad valorem* duty.

(v) The contract referred to above may be contained in more than one instrument or it may be partly written and partly verbal. It includes any contractual arrangements between the parties.

These observations explain, so far as is possible in general terms, the view of the law at present adopted by the Board, but they have not, of course, the force of law, and are promulgated merely with the object of assisting the taxpayer. The Board are not bound by them, and in the circumstances of any particular case may call for special consideration.

STATEMENT OF PRACTICE SP 6/90

The Inland Revenue have published today a Statement of Practice (SP 6/90) concerning Stamp Duty on a conveyance or transfer where property is subject to a mortgage or other debt. A copy of the Statement is attached.

Scope of the Statement

The Statement relates to conveyances or transfers where:

— the transferee takes over liability for the whole or part of the debt; and
— there is no other consideration for the transfer (in particular, no monetary payment).

Situations where the Statement may apply include:

— transfers of mortgaged property between spouses, including into or out of joint names;
— transfers within a family of mortgaged business property, for example farmland.

Since the duty on gifts was abolished in 1985, there have been a number of enquiries and misunderstandings about the correct Stamp Duty treatment of such transfers. The Statement is being issued to clarify the Department's view of the law.

Effect

Broadly, the Statement records the Inland Revenue's view that certain transfers of mortgaged property where no money passes are nonetheless sales for Stamp Duty purposes. These are transfers where:

(i) the transferee makes an express covenant (in the form, for example, of a specific undertaking to the lender at the time of the transfer), either to pay part or all of the mortgage debt, or to indemnify the transferor against his personal liability to the lender; or

(ii) a covenant by the transferee in similar terms is (except in Scotland) implied by law and no contrary intention is established.

Such transfers of property are sales and subject to the Stamp Duty charge under the 'Conveyance or Transfer on sale' head. The duty payable is [3] per cent of the debt taken over by the transferee.

Notes for editors

1. Where property is conveyed or transferred subject to a debt (e.g. a house or flat on which there is a mortgage), the Stamp Duty payable on the sale reflects any part of the debt taken over by the transferee (section 57, Stamp Act 1891). If there is no cash element, the debt taken over will account for the whole of the chargeable consideration on which the duty is calculated.

Transfers between spouses

2. The Statement of Practice explains that, for example, where a mortgaged property held in the name of one spouse is transferred into the joint names of both spouses, the transferee acquiring a half share in the property may be regarded as taking over the obligation to discharge one-half of the out standing mortgage. Where that is so, the assumption of part of the debt will constitute consideration for the share acquired in the property and for Stamp Duty purposes the transaction is not a gift but a sale.

Separation and divorce

3. On the other hand, the Statement also explains that, in certain circumstances, where a share in the marital home, or the whole of it, is transferred subject to a mortgage from one partner of the marriage to the other as part of the arrangements for their separation or divorce, such a conveyance or transfer may be exempted from ad valorem duty (even if it would otherwise be chargeable for reasons explained above).

CONVEYANCES AND TRANSFERS OF PROPERTY SUBJECT TO A DEBT—*SA 1891, S 57*

Introduction

1. Since the abolition of the duty on voluntary dispositions in 1985, many enquiries have been received about the Stamp Duty chargeable on conveyances etc. subject to a debt where *no* chargeable consideration (e.g. money or stock) unrelated to the debt is given by the transferee. This Statement of Practice sets out the Board's view of the correct Stamp Duty treatment of such conveyances.

2. For the sake of completeness it should be noted that where chargeable consideration unrelated to debt *is* given by the transferee, section 57 renders the conveyance liable to ad valorem duty on the aggregate of that consideration and the debt whether the transferee assumes liability for the debt or not (*IRC v City of Glasgow Bank* 1881 8 R 389, 18 SLR 242).

Section 57, Stamp Act 1891

3. The most commonly misunderstood applications of section 57 arise where:

— a mortgaged property held in the name of the spouse is transfer red into the joint names of both spouses;
— a mortgaged property held in the name of one spouse or in their joint names is transferred into the sole name of the other;

— a mortgaged business property, frequently farmland, is conveyed from a sole proprietor to a family partnership or from a family partnership to a fresh partnership bringing in other members of the family.

4. The critical question is whether the transaction to which the conveyance gives effect is or is not a sale. If it is, section 57 will apply and the conveyance will be chargeable to ad valorem duty on the amount of the debt assumed. If it is not, then section 57 will not apply and ad valorem duty will not be payable.

Express covenants

5. Where property is transferred subject to a debt, the transferee may covenant, either in the instrument or by means of a separate written undertaking, to pay the debt or indemnify the transferor against his personal liability to the lender. Such a covenant or undertaking constitutes valuable consideration and, in view of section 57, establishes the transaction as a sale for Stamp Duty purposes.

6. Where the transferor covenants to pay the debt and the transferee does not assume any liability for it, no chargeable consideration has been given and there is no sale. The transfer would then be a voluntary disposition—i.e. an unencumbered gift capable of being certified as Category L under the Stamp Duty (Exempt Instruments) Regulations 1987 (SI 1987 No 516)—and so exempt from the 50p charge that would otherwise arise.

Implied covenants

7. Where no express covenant or undertaking is given by the transferee, the Board are advised that, except in Scotland, a covenant by the transferee may be implied. That makes the transaction a sale, as in paragraph 4 above.

8. Such an implied covenant may be negated if there is evidence that it was the intention of the parties at the time of the transfer that the transferor should continue to be liable for the whole of the mortgage debt. Where evidence of such a contrary intention exists, the transfer would again be treated for Stamp Duty purposes as a voluntary disposition.

9. Where property in joint names subject to a debt is transferred to one of the joint holders (though with no cash passing), a covenant by the transferee to indemnify the transferor may be implied even where both parties were jointly liable on the mortgage.

Amount chargeable

10. Where a conveyance of property subject to a debt is chargeable to ad valorem duty and the express or implied covenant by the transferee relates only to part of the debt, only the amount of that part is treated as chargeable consideration within section 57. A certificate of value under section 34(4) Finance Act 1958 may, where appropriate, be included in the conveyance where the relevant amount of the debt does not exceed the amount certified.

Other provisions

11. The foregoing does not affect any statutory exemption from duty that may apply, e.g. that for transfers to a charity (section 129 Finance Act 1982) and that available for certain transfers of property from one party to a marriage to the other in connection with their divorce or separation (section 83(1) Finance Act 1985 and Category H of the Stamp Duty (Exempt Instruments) Regulations 1987).

Procedure

12. Where the applicant is satisfied that the conveyance or transfer is made on sale, it may be sent or taken for stamping with a remittance for the duty payable. If the transfer contains an appropriate certificate of value—see paragraph 10 above—it may be sent direct to the Land Registry in the usual way if appropriate. In either case, if the amount of the debt outstanding is not given in the conveyance or transfer the amount should be stated in a covering letter.

13. Where the conveyance or transfer contains a covenant by the transferor to pay the debt (see paragraph 6) and is certified as within category L of the Stamp Duty (Exempt Instruments) Regulations 1987, it should also be sent direct to the Land Registry if appropriate.

14. In any other case where the applicant believes that the conveyance or transfer effects a voluntary disposition—see paragraph 8 above—it should be presented for adjudication accompanied by a statement of the facts and any supporting evidence.'

STATEMENT OF PRACTICE SP 3/93
Groups of Companies—Arrangements (13 January 1993)

INTRODUCTION

1. This statement supersedes Statement of Practice SP 5/80. Some features of the earlier statement have been omitted or revised but this does not indicate a more restrictive approach on the part of the Revenue.

2. This statement gives general guidance on how the Revenue interpret "arrangements" in the following provisions of TA 1988—

— s 240(11)(*a*)—surrender of ACT to a subsidiary company;
— s 247(1A)(*b*)—group income elections in certain consortium cases;
— s 410(1), (2)—group and consortium reliefs; and "option arrangements" in Sch 18 para 5B(1), group and consortium reliefs.

EXTRA-STATUTORY CONCESSION C10

3. Certain types of "arrangements" or "option arrangements "relating to groups and consortia which fall within the above legislation are in practice excluded from its scope by ESC C10, as revised January 1993.

GENERAL

4. This statement of practice gives general guidance in conjunction with ESC C10. Comprehensive guidance cannot be given about what constitutes "arrangements" or "option arrangements", nor about precisely when they come into existence. Particular cases depend on the particular relevant facts.

5. As regards "option arrangements "the Board's view is that if an agreement provides for the creation of specified option rights exercisable at some future time "option arrangements "come into existence when the agreement was entered into.

DISPOSAL OF SHARES OR SECURITIES IN A COMPANY

6. Where a holder of shares or securities in a company is preparing to dispose of them, straightforward negotiations for the disposal will not give rise to the existence of "arrangements" before the point at which an offer is accepted subject to contract or on a similar conditional basis. Equally, unless there are exceptional features, an offer made to the public at large of shares or a business will not at that stage bring "arrangements" into existence.

7. If a disposal requires the approval of shareholders, operations leading towards disposal will not give rise to the existence of "arrangements" before that approval is given or until the directors become aware that it will be given.

8. If following negotiations with potential purchasers a holder of shares or securities concentrates on a particular potential purchaser this will not of itself be regarded as bringing "arrangements" into existence. But "arrangements" might exist if there were an understanding between the parties in the character of an option. For example, an offer, whether formally made or not, might be allowed to remain open for an appreciable period so that the potential purchaser was allowed to choose the moment to create a bargain.

COMPANY RECONSTRUCTIONS

9. The approval of shareholders for a company reconstruction may be required under company law or to comply with the rules of a stock exchange. "Arrangements" will not come into existence before approval is given or until the directors become aware that it will be given.

ENFORCEABILITY

10. "Arrangements", though not "option arrangements", may exist between parties even though they are not enforceable.

STATEMENT OF PRACTICE SP 8/93
Stamp Duty—New buildings

This Statement sets out the practice the Board of Inland Revenue will apply in relation to the Stamp Duty chargeable in certain circumstances on the conveyance or lease of a new or partly constructed building. It affects transactions where, at the date of the contract for sale or lease of a building plot, building work has not commenced or has been only partially completed on that site but where that work has started or has been completed at the time the conveyance or lease is executed.

This Statement reflects the advice the Board have received on this subject in the light of the decision in the case of *Prudential Assurance Co Ltd v IRC* [1993] 1 WLR 211. This Statement does not apply to the common situation where the parties have entered into a contract for the sale of a new house and that contract is implemented by a conveyance of the whole property. This Statement replaces the Statements of Practice issued in 1957 and 1987 (SP 10/87) on this subject which are now withdrawn.

The Board are advised that, whilst each case will clearly depend on its own facts, the law is as follows:

1. TWO TRANSACTIONS/TWO CONTRACTS

Where the purchaser or lessee is entitled under the terms of a contract to a conveyance or lease of land alone in consideration of the purchase price or rent of the site and a second genuine contract for building works is entered into as a separate transaction, the ad valorem duty on the conveyance or lease will be determined by the amount of the purchase price or rent which the purchaser or lessee is obliged to pay under the terms of the first contract. In these circumstances it does not matter whether any building work has commenced at the date of the conveyance or lease. The consideration chargeable to ad valorem duty will still be only that passing for the land.

2. ONE TRANSACTION/TWO CONTRACTS

Where there is one transaction between the parties but this is implemented by two contracts, one for the sale or lease of the building plot and one for the building works themselves, the amount of ad valorem duty charged on the instrument will depend on the amount of the consideration, which in turn will depend on whether those contracts can be shown to be genuinely independent of each other.

(i) If the two contracts are so interlocked that they cannot be said to be genuinely capable of independent completion (and in particular where if default occurs on either contract, the other is then not enforceable) ad valorem duty will be charged on the total consideration for the land and buildings, whether completed or not, as if the parties had entered into only one contract.

(ii) If the two contracts are shown to be genuinely independent of each other, ad valorem duty will be charged by reference to the consideration paid or payable for the land and any building works on that land at the date of execution of the instrument. It follows that, where the instrument is executed after the building works are completed, ad valorem duty will be charged on the consideration for the land and the completed building(s).

3. SHAM OR ARTIFICIAL TRANSACTIONS

This Statement does not apply to cases where the transaction concerned, or any part of it, involves a sham or artificial transaction.

Contracts already entered into

Where unconditional contracts have been entered into before or within 28 days of the date of this Statement and the duty payable on the resulting conveyance or lease would have been less under the earlier Statements of Practice, the Stamp office will accept duty in the lesser amount. In such cases the instrument should be submitted together with all the evidence to support the claim that unconditional contracts were entered into within this transitional period.

Procedure for submitting documents

Where a person accepts that a conveyance or lease of a building plot is chargeable on the total price paid or payable for the land and the completed building, it should be submitted for stamping in the usual way together with a covering letter giving the aggregate price and a payment for the duty appropriate to that price.

Where the total price does not exceed the amount up to which the instrument is liable to nil duty (currently £60,000) and a certificate of value is included in the instrument, a conveyance may be sent direct to the Land Registry in England and Wales or, in Scotland, to the Keeper of the Registers of Scotland. A lease will need to be stamped in respect of the rent.

Where the total price exceeds the threshold at which duty becomes payable but the taxpayer takes the view that duty is payable on some smaller sum, the instrument should be submitted to the Stamp Office. This applies even where the taxpayer believes that the amount potentially chargeable to ad valorem duty is below the threshold and a certificate of value is included in the instrument. The instrument should be accompanied by a copy of the agreement(s) for sale etc. and a letter stating the amount which the taxpayer regards as chargeable consideration, identifying separately any amount attributable to building work. Details of any contractual arrangements not covered by the agreement(s) should also be given in the covering letter.

STATEMENT OF PRACTICE SP 3/98
Stamp Duty—Group relief

1. Section 42 Finance Act 1930 gives relief from Stamp Duty for transfers of property between members of the same group of companies. Section 151 Finance Act 1995 similarly gives relief from duty on the grant of a lease between members of the same group.

2. Section 27(3) Finance Act 1967 and section 151(3) Finance Act 1995 are designed to prevent the use of group relief to avoid Stamp Duty when property, or an economic interest in it, passes out of the group.

3. This statement sets out the Stamp Office's current general practice in order to assist practitioners in determining whether claims to relief might qualify. The treatment of a particular case will of course depend on the precise facts. This statement is for general guidance only; and the facts of a particular transaction may, exceptionally, place it outside the guidelines. It applies also to the equivalent Northern Ireland legislation.

GENERAL

4. Broadly, section 27(3) and the corresponding provisions in section 151, provide that relief is not to be given if the transfer was made in pursuance of, or in connection with, an arrangement under which:

(a) all or part of the consideration for the transfer was to be provided or received, directly or indirectly, by a person outside the group; or
(b) the interest being transferred was previously transferred by a person outside the group; or
(c) the transferor and transferee were no longer to be part of the same group.

5. The person claiming the relief when the relevant instrument is adjudicated has the onus of satisfying the Stamp Office that the intra-group transaction is not carried out in pursuance of, or in connection with, an arrangement of a kind which disqualifies the transaction from relief: *Escoigne Properties Ltd v IRC* [1958] AC 549, 564.

ARRANGEMENT

6. In this context, arrangement means the plan or scheme in pursuance of which the things identified in the subparagraphs of ss 27(3) and 151(3) have been or are to be done: *Shop and Store Developments Ltd v IRC* [1967] 1 AC 472, 493–494. The arrangement need not be based in contract. It is sufficient if the intra-group transaction is made in connection with that plan or scheme. The intra-group transaction may be the first bilateral step by which legal rights and obligations are created in pursuance of the arrangement. If there is an expectation that a disqualifying event will happen in accordance with the arrangement and no likelihood in practice that it will not, relief will be refused.

7. The words in connection with are very broad. In *Escoigne*, there was a gap of four years between the two steps in issue. Provision or receipt of consideration by a person outside the group: section 27(3)(*a*); section 151(3)(*a*) and (4).

8. Section 27(3)(*a*) denies relief where the instrument was executed in pursuance of or in connection with an arrangement under which any of the consideration is to be provided or received, directly or indirectly, by a person outside the group. It also denies relief if the arrangement is one under which the transferor or transferee (or a member of the same group as either of them) is to be enabled to provide any of the consideration, or is to part with it, in consequence of a transaction involving a payment or other disposition by a person outside the group. Section 151 lays down similar rules for leases.

9. In some cases, the question arises whether loan finance for the purchase or lease will disqualify an intra-group transaction from relief. It is necessary to look at all the facts of the individual case, but the Stamp Office will interpret the provisions in the light of their general purpose of denying relief where the intra-group transaction is a means of saving Stamp Duty when the property, or an interest in it, moves out of the group. Accordingly, the Stamp Office are likely to be satisfied that relief is due if the intra-group transaction is not to be followed by a sale of the property transferred, or an underlease, to a person outside the group. If the intra-group transaction is to be followed by a sale or underlease to a person outside the group, but the claimant can demonstrate that Stamp Duty will be paid in respect of that transaction in approximately the same amount as would have been payable if the intra-group transferor or

lessor had itself sold the property or granted the underlease, the Stamp Office are likely to be satisfied that the intra-group transaction and the transfer or lease out are independent for Stamp Duty purposes and grant the relief sought.

10. A transaction is not disqualified merely because the transferee within the group obtains a specific loan for the purchase of the asset; or the loan is secured on the asset; or arrangements are made to replace or novate an existing charge on the property transferred. It will be necessary to consider the facts as a whole, especially if the loan finance is not straightforward finance on ordinary commercial terms.

11. Intra-group transactions will be very carefully scrutinised, and relief may be refused, where, for example, the intra-group transaction involves or is to be followed by:

- the creation or transfer of loan stock or equity capital;
- a capital reorganisation of the transferee; a guarantee by a third party not associated with the group;
- the creation of a new charge or financial arrangement whereby title to the property is, or may be, vested in the lender otherwise than in satisfaction or all or part of the debt; or
- the assignment of the freehold reversion or the intra-group lease to a person outside the group.

12. Similarly transactions will be very carefully scrutinised where:

- all or part of the consideration for the transaction is to remain outstanding or is represented by intra-group debt, (as the aim and effect may be to reduce the value of the transferee company on a possible future sale outside the group); or
- the existing shareholders of the transferee include shareholders outside the group and the transaction is to be followed by the declaration of a dividend in specie, or by the liquidation of the transferee.

13. Further assurances by way of statutory declaration—the document in which the claim is made to the Stamp Office—will be required in any case in which the property transferred or vested intra-group is the only, or only substantial, asset of the transferee. Information to that effect should be provided in the statutory declaration submitted with the documents.

14. Where group member A has granted a lease to a person outside the group, and subsequently grants an underlease to its fellow group member B, so that the rent already payable by the lessee becomes payable to B rather than A, relief is likely to be given for the intra-group underlease, provided there are no other factors which suggest that relief should be denied.

PROPERTY PREVIOUSLY CONVEYED BY A PERSON OUTSIDE THE GROUP: SECTION 27(3)(*B*)

15. Section 27(3)(*b*) was intended to prevent the avoidance of duty on the transfer of property into a group by means of a sub-sale, so as to take advantage of section 58(4) of the Stamp Act 1891. For example, suppose the property is sold to a group member by a vendor outside the group, but the sale rests in contract without a transfer of the legal title. The group member then sells the property to another member of its own group, and directs the vendor to transfer the legal title to that other member. In accordance with section 58(4) the transfer completing the sale and the sub-sale is chargeable to duty only in relation to the sub-sale (thus relieving the effect of section 4 of the Stamp Act). However, section 27(3)(*b*) would deny group relief for that transfer.

16. The Stamp Office will continue to apply section 27(3)(*b*) to schemes of this type and to any other scheme where an attempt has been made to avoid the duty payable on the acquisition by the group. However, where an outside vendor sells a property to a member of the group, the sale is completed by a transfer and Stamp Duty is paid on that transfer, the Stamp Office will normally regard any subsequent intra-group transfer as independent, and grant relief for the transfer within the purchaser's group.

DISSOCIATION OR DEMERGER OF TRANSFEREE: SECTION 27(3)(*C*): SECTION 151(3)(*B*)

17. Before the introduction of section 27(3), almost all the avoidance devices encountered in this area involved the transfer of property to a subsidiary, often created solely as a vehicle for that property, followed by the transfer of the shares in the subsidiary out of the group. Compared with a transfer of the property out of the group, a substantial amount of duty could be avoided even where the subsidiary paid for the property from its own resources. If the consideration for the intra-group transaction remained outstanding or was represented by debt, duty could be reduced further by reducing the value of the shares—hence section 27(3)(*a*).

18. Section 27(3)(*c*) was introduced to counter this avoidance in relation to conveyances and transfers on sale. Section 151(3)(*b*) deals with leases on similar lines.

19. In cases of this kind, the Stamp Office will need to be satisfied that the intra-group transfer or lease is not a step in pursuance of an arrangement to demerge the transferee. The existence of such an arrangement may be apparent from company documents, correspondence and other dealings between members of the group and professional advisers, or from discussions or negotiations with the potential purchasers, underwriters or minority shareholders.

20. In practice, the Stamp Office will apply these provisions so as to preclude group relief if there is evidence of a plan or scheme to dispose of the subsidiary and there is no practical likelihood that the scheme will not be carried through. It will not be regarded as sufficient for the claimant to contend that such an arrangement which is less than contractual may possibly be frustrated by unforeseen events or unlikely occurrences. Even a contract may be frustrated.

21. As the liability of the relevant instrument must, as a matter of general principle, be determined as at the date of the instrument, the question whether an arrangement of the relevant kind exists must also be determined at that time, although the Stamp Office may have regard to what is said and done thereafter to establish the true position (*Wm Cory and Son Ltd v IRC* [1965] AC 1088). For the purposes of Stamp Duty, it is therefore the existence of the scheme or plans to which these provisions direct attention, not the ultimate outcome of steps which may be taken to implement that scheme. Accordingly, statements of practice in relation to other taxes have no application in this context.

STATEMENT OF PRACTICE SP 1/03
Disadvantaged areas relief (April 2003)

This Statement of Practice is intended as guidance for those claiming exemption from Stamp Duty in respect of transfers of property situated in designated areas ("Disadvantaged Areas Relief") and explains how Inland Revenue Stamp Taxes will interpret the extension to the relief introduced with effect from 10 April 2003.

The relief is one of a number of measures set out in the Government's Urban White Paper "*Our Towns and Cities—The Future—Delivering an Urban Renaissance*" published in November 2000. The measure is designed to stimulate the physical, economic and social regeneration of the UK's most disadvantaged areas by attracting development and by encouraging the purchase of residential and commercial property by individuals and businesses. The areas eligible for relief were designated "Enterprise Areas" by the Chancellor in his 2002 Pre-Budget Report. In addition to the relief, a range of other Government policies designed to support enterprise and economic regeneration, including the Community Investment Tax Relief, will benefit these areas, helping to support the development of new and existing businesses.

INTRODUCTION

1. Disadvantaged Areas Relief (provided for by section 92 of, and Schedule 30 to, the Finance Act 2001) was introduced on 30 November 2001 and was initially only available for conveyances or transfers on sale (of both residential and commercial property) for which the consideration did not exceed £150,000. Stamp Duty in respect of conveyances or transfers of commercial property in disadvantaged areas was abolished in consequence of the Stamp Duty (Disadvantaged Areas) (Application of Exemptions) Regulations 2003 ("the Regulations"), which have effect in relation to instruments executed on or after 10 April 2003. Thereafter the £150,000 limit applies only in relation to residential property.

2. Finance Act 2002 inserted the following provisions in Finance Act 2001 to distinguish residential from other property and to provide for differing Stamp Duty exemptions:

— Section 92A which enables Stamp Duty relief in designated disadvantaged areas in respect of all properties to be varied depending on whether or not the property is "residential";
— Section 92B which defines "residential property" for the purposes of the relief. Non-residential property, in respect of which unlimited relief is available, is therefore defined in the Act by exclusion. The section also sets out particular building uses that are specifically included within, or specifically excluded from, the definition.

3. In most cases there will be no difficulty in practice in establishing whether or not a property is "residential". This statement sets out in more detail the Stamp Office's approach to borderline cases and gives guidance on the practical application of the legislation. The annexed flowchart provides a quick guide for simpler cases as to whether property constitutes "residential property".

CERTIFICATION

4. Claims for unlimited relief must be accompanied by a certificate stating either that none of the land in question is residential property or, if part is residential, the proportion that is non-residential (together with the usual certificate of value for the remainder).

— Residential property—section 92A(4) of Finance Act 2001, together with the Regulations, provides that the exemption will only apply if the document is certified to the effect that the amount or value of the consideration does not exceed £150,000.
— Non-residential property—subsection (2) of section 92 of Finance Act 2001 provides that the exemption will only apply if the document is certified to the Commissioners as being an instrument on which Stamp Duty is not chargeable by virtue of subsection (1) of that section.

5. The following are suggested forms of words for particular certificates:

— Residential Property—"I/We hereby certify that the transaction effected by this instrument does not form part of a larger transaction or series of transactions in respect of which the amount or value of the consideration exceeds £150,000 and that Stamp Duty is not chargeable thereon by virtue of the provisions of sections 92 and 92A of the Finance Act 2001."
— Non-residential Property—"I/We hereby certify that this is an instrument in respect of non-residential property on which Stamp Duty is not chargeable by virtue of the provisions of section 92 of the Finance Act 2001."
— Mixed Use Property—"I/We hereby certify that the transaction effected by this instrument is in respect of property part of which is residential property, and which does not form part of a larger transaction or series of transactions in respect of which the amount or value of the consideration relating to the residential part exceeds £150,000 so that Stamp Duty is not chargeable by virtue of sections 92 and 92A of the Finance Act 2001, and part of which is non-residential property on which Stamp Duty is not chargeable by virtue of the

provisions of section 92 of the Finance Act 2001. The basis upon which the allocation between residential and non-residential parts has been made is as follows: . . . "

6. While the legislation does not specifically require the certificate to be included as part of the document, it is suggested that it should be so included. If the person submitting the document for stamping does not provide a certificate, either in the document or separately in writing, exemption will not be granted.

7. Appropriate contemporaneous evidence should be retained to support any certificate provided. Estate agents' specifications, site plans, planning applications or permissions, marketing material and photographs may all provide relevant information.

8. Anyone falsely certifying a document with a view to obtaining relief that is not due will be committing a Stamp Duty fraud.

THE MEANING OF RESIDENTIAL PROPERTY

9. Section 92B defines "residential property" as a building which:

- is used as a dwelling; or
- is suitable for use as a dwelling; or
- is in the process of being constructed or adapted for such use.

If a property meets any one of these separate tests it will be treated as residential property and be subject to the £150,000 limit for relief, as will any garden or grounds belonging to it or any interests or rights attaching to it. Each element of the definition is considered in turn below.

The question of whether and to what extent a building and grounds are defined as residential property for Stamp Duty purposes may also have implications for its treatment for capital gains tax and local authority rates.

Use as a dwelling

10. Where a building is in use at the date of execution of the relevant instrument, it will be a question of fact whether and to what extent it is used as a dwelling. Use at the date the instrument is executed overrides any past or intended future uses for this purpose.

11. Where the property in question is in use as a dwelling at the date of execution, it is residential property for the purposes of the relief unless it is part of a multiple transaction qualifying for relief under the Regulations (see paragraphs 35 to 39 below).

12. For the treatment of buildings put to both residential and non-residential use, see paragraphs 17 and 18 below.

Suitable for use as a dwelling

13. The suitability test applies to the state of the building at the time the instrument is executed, having regard to the facilities available and any history of use. For example, the Inland Revenue will not regard an office block as "suitable for use as a dwelling", but a house which has been used as an office without particular adaptation may well be so.

14. If a building is not in use at the date of execution but its last use was as a dwelling, it will be taken to be 'suitable for use as a dwelling' and treated as residential property for the purposes of the relief, unless evidence is produced to the contrary (see paragraph 15).

15. Whether a building is suitable for use as a dwelling will depend upon the precise facts and circumstances. The simple removal of, for example, a bathroom suite or

kitchen facilities will not be regarded as rendering a building unsuitable for use as a dwelling. Where it is claimed that a previously residential property is no longer suitable for use as a dwelling, perhaps because it is derelict or has been substantially altered, the claimant will need to provide evidence that this is the case. See also paragraph 29.

16. Where a building has been used partly for residential purposes and partly for another purpose, its overall suitability for use as a dwelling will be judged from the facilities available at the date of execution of the relevant document. For example, if two rooms of a house were in use as a dentist's surgery and waiting room at the date of execution, the Inland Revenue would nevertheless normally consider this property suitable for use as a dwelling unless the claimant provided evidence to the contrary. In other words, the interaction of the Regulations with section 92B(1) enables a building that is used only partly as a dwelling to be nevertheless suitable for use wholly as a dwelling, with the effect that the £150,000 limit applies to the whole of the consideration. Where only a distinct part of the building is used and suitable for use as a dwelling, that part will be residential property for the purposes of the relief and the mixed use provisions will apply (paragraphs 17 and 18 below).

Mixed use

17. Where only part of a building (and land or interest relating to it) is "residential property" within section 92B(1), the consideration "shall be apportioned on such basis as is just and reasonable" between the residential and non-residential elements. The £150,000 limit is then applied only to the residential portion, in accordance with the appropriate certification (regulation 5 of the Regulations). For example a property situated wholly within a disadvantaged area is bought for:

(a) £200,000
(b) £400,000

50% of the property is "residential property" on the basis of a just and reasonable apportionment. Relief is conferred by FA 2001 s 92, applied in conjunction with regulation 5 of the Regulations. Paragraph (3) of regulation 5 calls for an apportionment of the total consideration between residential and non-residential elements. Paragraph (4) confirms that relief applies to the residential property element only where the consideration attributed to it does not exceed £150,000. In these examples:

(a) £100,000 is attributed to the residential property element, so relief is due. The part of the land that is not residential property is also exempt under the normal operation of FA 2001 s 92. So no duty is payable.
(b) the £200,000 attributed to the residential property element is not exempt, because of regulation 5(4), but attracts duty at the rate of 1% (Stamp Duty payable £2,000). The non-residential property element is exempt as above.

18. The "just and reasonable" test is necessarily subjective, and each case will be considered on its merits. Apportionment might be on the basis of the percentage areas quoted in planning applications, where appropriate, or alternatively of floor space relating to the respective uses. Other methods of apportionment will be considered as part of a claim.

SPECIFIC CASES

19. Some types of communal or institutional building are used neither as dwellings nor for commercial purposes. The legislation therefore outlines how these are classified for the purposes of relief, specifically including some such buildings within the definition of "dwelling" (section 92B(2)) and specifically excluding others (section 92B(3)). If they do not fall within any of the specific categories of section 92B(3), most residential institutions will come within section 92B(2)(*d*) and will be treated as dwellings by default.

20. Categories of building use specifically included within the definition of "use as a dwelling" (so that transfers of such buildings only qualify for relief if the consideration does not exceed £150,000) (section 92B(2)) are:

(a) residential accommodation for school pupils, for example accommodation blocks in boarding schools;
(b) residential accommodation for students, other than that within section 92B(3)(*b*). Student accommodation provided by private landlords is 'a dwelling', as is accommodation leased to students by universities or colleges in flats or houses rather than in halls of residence (see section 92B(3)(*b*));
(c) residential accommodation for members of any of the armed forces, including accommodation for their families (section 92B(2)(*c*));
(d) an institution that is the sole or main residence of at least 90% of its residents and does not fall within any of the categories referred to in section 92B(3) (see section 92B(2)(*d*) and also paragraph 21 below). This would include, for example:
    — sheltered accommodation for the elderly where no nursing or personal care is provided;
    — accommodation for religious communities (subject to the rules regarding mixed use; see paragraphs 17 and 18).

21. Categories of building use specifically excluded from the definition of 'use as a dwelling' (so that transfers of such buildings in a disadvantaged area will qualify for unlimited relief) (section 92B(3)) are—

(a) a home or other institution providing residential accommodation for children;
(b) a hall of residence for students in further or higher education. This is not defined in the legislation but in practice property provided by a university or similar establishment will be judged on the facts (number of inhabitants, type of facilities, availability of communal areas);
(c) a home or other institution providing residential accommodation with personal care for persons in need of personal care by reason of old age, disablement, past or present dependence on alcohol or drugs or past or present mental disorder;
(d) a hospital or hospice;
(e) a prison or similar establishment, or
(f) a hotel or inn or similar establishment.

22. The specific inclusions and exclusions set out in paragraphs 20 and 21 above apply not only to a building's actual use at the date of the transfer, but to the uses for which it is suitable at that date. Where, however, a building is being put to one of the non-residential uses specified in section 92B(3), this overrides any suitability for another use (section 92B(4)). For example, a building used as a children's home may also be suitable for use as a school boarding house, but this will not preclude a claim to unlimited relief.

23. Where a vacant building is suitable for at least one of the uses specified in section 92B(2) and at least one specified in section 92B(3), the tiebreaker in section 92B(5) determines, for the purposes of the relief, the use for which it is "most suitable". Whether or not a vacant building has one or more uses for which it is most suitable is a question of fact. Evidence supporting such uses should be provided with the claim for relief.

24. Where there is a single use for which a building is most suitable, the fact that it is also suitable for another use will be discounted.

25. If there are a number of uses for which a building is most suitable and they all come within either of the two subsections, any other use for which the building is suitable will be discounted.

26. Where no most suitable use can be shown, the default will be to classify the building as residential property and apply the £150,000 limit.

27. Land and buildings that are not suitable for any use at the date of execution will be treated as residential property if they are "in the process of being constructed or adapted for such use"—see paragraphs 28 and 29 below.

PROCESS OF BEING CONSTRUCTED OR ADAPTED FOR USE AS A DWELLING

28. Undeveloped land is in essence non-residential, but land may be "residential property" for the purposes of disadvantaged areas relief if a residential building is being built on it at the date the instrument is executed. The process of construction is taken as commencing when the builders first start work. A development of six or more dwellings is deemed to be non-residential under regulation 6 of the Regulations, even if in the process of construction at the date of the instrument (see paragraph 35 below).

29. Where (at the date the relevant instrument is executed) an existing building is being adapted for, or restored to, domestic use, it is "residential property" for the purposes of the relief. This may apply, for example, where a derelict building is being made fit for habitation, or where a previously non-residential building is being converted to a dwelling. Again, the process is taken as commencing when the builders start work.

THE GARDEN OR GROUNDS OF A BUILDING USED ETC. AS A DWELLING

30. Section 92B(1)(*b*) includes within the definition of residential property "land that is or forms part of the garden or grounds of a building within paragraph (*a*) (including any building or structure on such land)". The test the Inland Revenue will apply is similar to that applied for the purposes of the capital gains tax relief for main residences (section 222(3) of the Taxation of Chargeable Gains Act 1992). The land will include that which is needed for the reasonable enjoyment of the dwelling having regard to the size and nature of the dwelling.

31. A caravan or houseboat is not a "building" for this purpose.

32. Commercial farmland is not within the definition of residential property. A farmhouse situated on agricultural land would be dealt with under the mixed use provisions (paragraphs 17 and 18 above).

33. Outhouses on land within the section 92B(1)(*b*) definition will also be "residential property" unless it can be demonstrated that they have a specific non-residential purpose. Where a distinct non-residential use can be demonstrated, the mixed use provisions will apply.

INTEREST IN OR RIGHTS OVER RESIDENTIAL PROPERTY

34. The treatment of interests in, or rights over, land or buildings for the purposes of disadvantaged areas relief will follow that of the land or buildings to which they relate.

SIX OR MORE SEPARATE DWELLINGS TRANSFERRED BY SINGLE CONTRACT

35. The Regulations provide that "where there is a single contract for the conveyance, transfer or lease of land comprising or including six or more separate dwellings, none of that land counts as residential property . . . "Accordingly the transaction will qualify for unlimited relief. This recognises that commercial developers and institutional landlords, for example, frequently deal in numerous properties at one time. The fact that those properties may individually be "residential property" does not detract from the inherently commercial nature of the transaction itself.

36. To qualify as "separate", the dwellings must be self-contained. So for example, flats within a block, sharing some common areas but each with their own amenities, will qualify as separate dwellings. Rooms let within a house will not constitute separate dwellings if tenants share amenities such as a kitchen and bathroom.

37. A transaction in respect of six or more such dwellings must be carried out by means of a single contract in order to qualify for relief. Several instruments may however be presented for stamping if the properties are held under separate title.

38. Qualifying multiple transactions will be treated as non-residential property for the purposes of relief, even where the proportionate consideration for individual dwellings

exceeds the £150,000 limit for residential property. It is not a condition of relief that multiple transactions comprise only dwellings.

39. The fact that some of the six or more dwellings within the single contract are outside a designated disadvantaged area will not prevent them from constituting a non-residential transaction. However relief will only be available for the portion of the land situated within the disadvantaged area.

PROPERTY ONLY PARTLY WITHIN A DISADVANTAGED AREA

40. Schedule 30 to Finance Act 2001, together with the Regulations, determines how property situated partly within and partly outside a designated disadvantaged area is to be treated for the purposes of the relief. Such cases are relatively rare in practice. Queries may be referred to Inland Revenue (Stamp Taxes) for guidance.

LEASE DUTY

41. Relief is also available from duty on the rental element of new leases executed on or after 10 April 2003. Rental leases of residential property shall be eligible for relief where the average annual rent is no more than £15,000 and/or where any premium does not exceed £150,000. For non- residential property, full relief is available for the rental element of leases as well as for any premium.

OTHER ISSUES

42. The extended relief applies to documents executed on or after 10 April 2003, irrespective of whether the contract was entered into before or after that date. There is no scope to reclaim Stamp Duty already paid in respect of transfers executed on or before 9 April 2003.

Flow chart to determine whether property is or is not 'residential property'

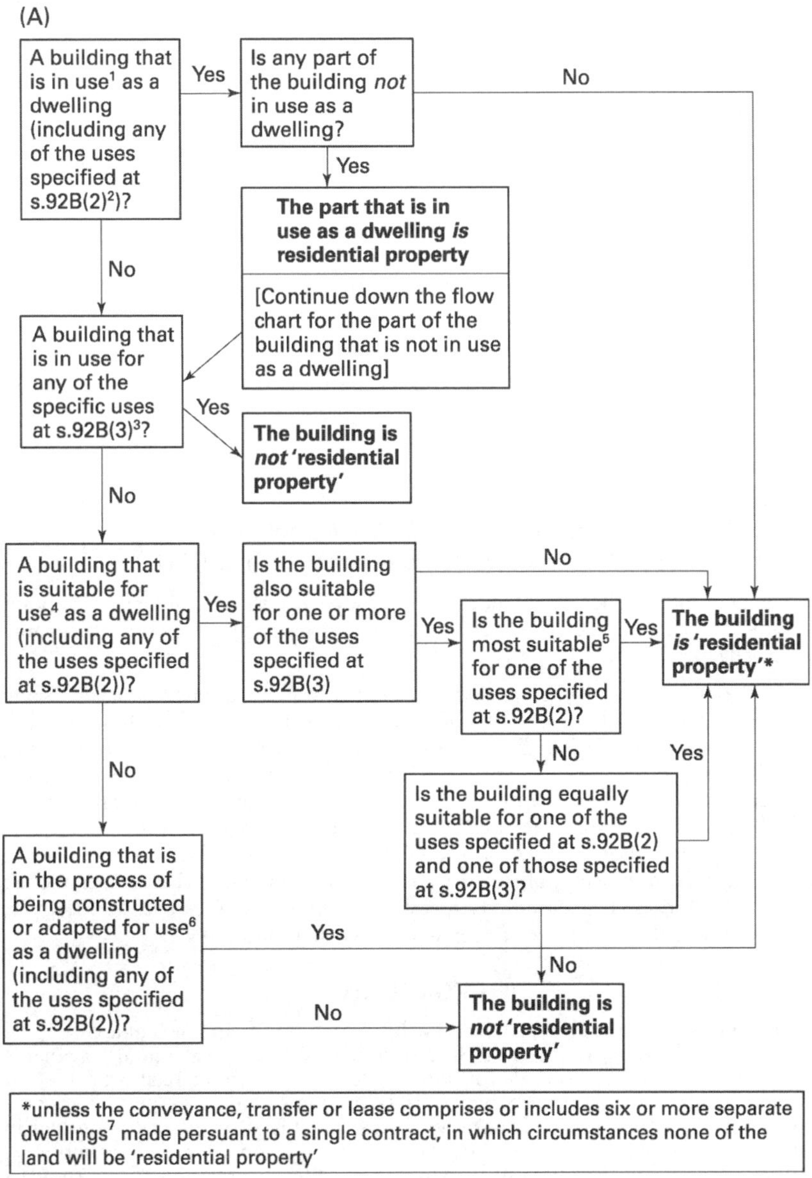

(B)

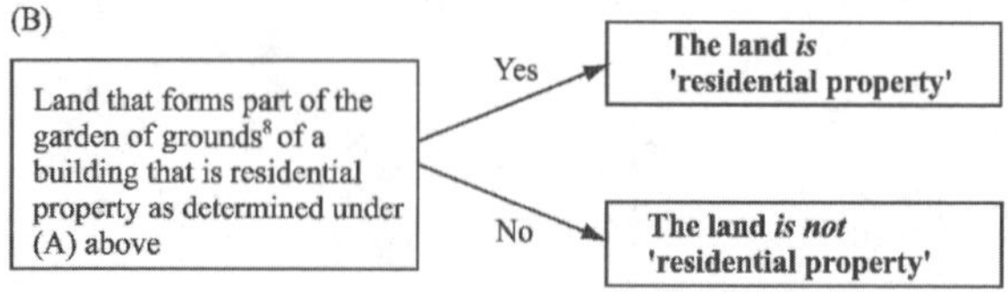

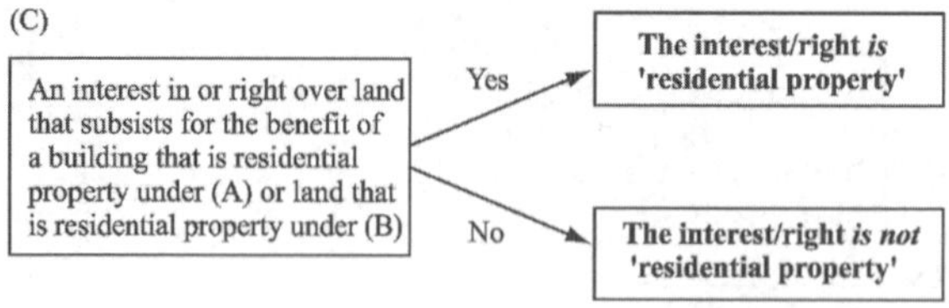

STATEMENT OF PRACTICE SP 1/04
Stamp Duty Land Tax: Disadvantaged area relief

This Statement of Practice is intended as guidance for those claiming exemption from Stamp Duty Land Tax in respect of transfers of property situated in designated areas ('Disadvantaged Area Relief).

The relief is one of a number of measures set out in the Government's Urban White Paper "Our Towns and Cities: The Future: Delivering an Urban Renaissance" published in November 2000. The measure is designed to stimulate the physical, economic and social regeneration of the UK's most disadvantaged areas by attracting development and by encouraging the purchase of residential and commercial property by individuals and businesses. The areas eligible for relief were designated "Enterprise Areas" by the Chancellor in his 2002 Pre-Budget Report. In addition to the relief, a range of other Government policies designed to support enterprise and economic regeneration, including the Community Investment Tax Relief, will benefit these areas, helping to support the development of new and existing businesses.

BACKGROUND

1. Disadvantaged Area Relief (provided for by section 92 of, and Schedule 30 to, the Finance Act 2001) was introduced on 30 November 2001 and was initially available for conveyances or transfers on sale (of both residential and commercial property) for which the consideration did not exceed £150,000. Stamp duty in respect of conveyances or transfers of commercial property in disadvantaged areas was abolished in consequence of the Stamp Duty (Disadvantaged Areas) (Application of Exemptions) Regulations 2003 ("the Regulations"), which have effect in relation to instruments executed on or after 10 April 2003. Thereafter the £150,000 limit applies only in relation to residential property.

2. Finance Act 2002 inserted the following provisions in Finance Act 2001 to distinguish residential from other property and to provide for differing Stamp Duty Land Tax exemptions:

- FA 2002 section 92A which enables stamp duty relief in designated disadvantaged areas in respect of all properties to be varied depending on whether or not the property is "residential";

DISADVANTAGED AREA RELIEF UNDER STAMP DUTY LAND TAX

3. Section 57 and Schedule 6 Finance Act 2003 provides for Disadvantaged Area Relief under Stamp Duty Land Tax.

4. The definition of residential property under Stamp Duty Land Tax is provided at section 116 FA 2003. Non-residential property is therefore defined in the Act by exclusion. Section 116 also sets out particular building uses that are specifically included within, or specifically excluded from, the definition.

5. In most cases there will be no difficulty in practice in establishing whether or not a property is "residential". This statement sets out in more detail the Stamp Office's approach to borderline cases and gives guidance on the practical application of the legislation. The annexed flowchart provides a quick guide for simpler cases as to whether property constitutes "residential property".

CLAIMING THE RELIEF

FA 2003 section 76 requires that most land transactions, including those that qualify for Disadvantaged Area Relief, must be notified to the Inland Revenue on a Land Transaction Return Form (SOLT 1).

7. Relief is claimed by simply completing a box within this form. Certificates of Value are no longer required and no supporting evidence or documentation is required at this point. Once the return has been submitted and we are satisfied with the information provided, the purchaser is issued with a certificate which they must present with documents when applying for registration of title at Land Registry, Registers of Scotland or Land Registry of Northern Ireland.

8. FA 2003 Schedule 10 Part 3 gives the Inland Revenue the power to enquire into a Land Transaction Return. These provisions permit the Inland Revenue to open an enquiry into any aspect of a Land Transaction Return, including claims to reliefs.

Appropriate contemporaneous evidence should be retained to support any claim to the relief. There is no need to create records that would otherwise not be available. Estate agents' specifications, site plans, planning applications or permissions, marketing material, photographs and print outs of an internet post code search may all provide relevant information should there be an enquiry into a land tax return.

9. As with all claims the onus is on the purchaser to check whether or not the relief is due.

THE MEANING OF RESIDENTIAL PROPERTY

10. FA 2003 section 116(1) defines "residential property" as a building which:

- is used as a dwelling;
- or is suitable for use as a dwelling;
- or is in the process of being constructed or adapted for such use.

If a property meets any one of these separate tests it will be treated as residential property and be subject to the £150,000 limit for relief, as will any garden or grounds belonging to it or any interests or rights attaching to it. Each element of the definition is considered in turn below. The question of whether and to what extent a building and grounds are defined as residential property for stamp duty purposes may also have implications for its treatment for capital gains tax and local authority rates.

USE AS A DWELLING

11. Where a building is in use at the effective date of the transaction it will be a question of fact whether and to what extent it is used as a dwelling.

Use at the effective date overrides any past or intended future uses for this purpose. For example, a purchaser is buying a house with the intention to refurbish it to create, in its place, an alternative therapy treatment centre. For the purposes of the relief the house is considered to be a dwelling because it was suitable for that use at the effective date of the transaction. (For another example see paragraph 34.)

12. Where the property in question is in use as a dwelling at the effective date of the transaction, it is residential property for the purposes of the relief unless it is part of a multiple transaction qualifying for relief under s 116(7) FA 2003 (see paragraphs 40 to 44 below).

13. There is no motive test applicable to the usage of land or buildings, so where a residential property is purchased with the owner intending to use it as a non-residential business the building is considered residential, under the suitability test, for the purposes of the relief.

14. For the treatment of buildings put to both residential and non-residential use, see paragraphs 19 and 20 below.

SUITABLE FOR USE AS A DWELLING

15. The suitability test applies to the state of the building at the effective date of the transaction, having regard to the facilities available and any history of use. For example, the Inland Revenue will not regard an office block as "suitable for use as a dwelling", but a house which has been used as an office without particular adaptation may well be so.

16. If a building is not in use at the effective date of the transaction but its last use was as a dwelling, it will be taken to be "suitable for use as a dwelling" and treated as residential property for the purposes of the relief, unless evidence is produced to the contrary (see paragraph 17).

17. Whether a building is suitable for use as a dwelling will depend upon the precise facts and circumstances. The simple removal of, for example, a bathroom suite or kitchen facilities will not be regarded as rendering a building unsuitable for use as a dwelling, Where it is claimed that a previously residential property is no longer suitable for use as a dwelling, perhaps because it is derelict or has been substantially altered, the claimant will need to provide evidence that this is the case. See also paragraph 34.

18. Where a building has been used partly for residential purposes and partly for another purpose, its overall suitability for use as a dwelling will be judged from the facilities available at the effective date of the transaction. For example, if two rooms of a house were in use as a dentist's surgery and waiting room at the effective date of the transaction, the Inland Revenue would nevertheless normally consider this property suitable for use as a dwelling unless the claimant provided evidence to the contrary. A building that is used only partly as a dwelling may nevertheless be suitable for use wholly as a dwelling, with the effect that the £150,000 limit applies to the whole of the consideration. Where only a distinct part of the building is used and suitable for use as a dwelling, that part will be residential property for the purposes of the relief and the mixed use provisions will apply (see paragraphs 19 and 20 below).

Mixed use

19. Where only part of a building (and land or interest relating to it) is "residential property" within section 116(1), the consideration "shall be apportioned on such basis as is just and reasonable" between the residential and non-residential elements. The £150,000 limit is then applied only to the residential portion (Schedule 6 FA 2003). For example:

A property situated wholly within a disadvantaged area is bought for

(a) £200,000
(b) £400,000

50% of the property is "residential property" on the basis of a just and reasonable apportionment.

In these examples:

(a) £100,000 is attributed to the residential property element, so relief is due. The part of the land that is not residential property is also exempt. So no duty is payable.
(b) the £200,000 attributed to the residential property element is not exempt, because of Schedule 6 paragraph 6, but attracts duty at the rate of 1% (Stamp Duty Land Tax payable £2,000). The non-residential property element is exempt as above.

Where a transaction involves six or more mixed use properties, under s 116(7) FA 2003, providing certain conditions are met, the residential element is exempt and no Stamp Duty Land Tax is payable. See paragraphs 40 to 44.

20. The "just and reasonable" test is necessarily subjective, and each case will be considered on its merits. Apportionment might be on the basis of the percentage areas quoted in planning applications, where appropriate, or alternatively of floor space relating to the respective uses. Other methods of apportionment will be considered as part of a claim.

Specific cases

21. Some types of communal or institutional building are used neither as dwellings nor for commercial purposes. The legislation therefore outlines how these are classified for the purposes of relief, specifically including some such buildings within the definition of "dwelling" (section 116(2)) and specifically excluding others (section 116(3)). If they do not fall within any of the specific categories of section 116(3), most residential institutions will come within section 116(2)(d) and will be treated as dwellings by default.

22. Categories of building use specifically included within the definition of "use as a dwelling" (so that transfers of such buildings only qualify for relief if the consideration does not exceed £150,000) (section 116(2)) are:

(a) residential accommodation for school pupils, for example accommodation blocks in boarding schools;
(b) residential accommodation for students, other than that within section 116(3)(b). Student accommodation provided by private landlords is "a dwelling", as is accommodation leased to students by universities or colleges in flats or houses rather than in halls of residence (see section 116(3)(b));
(c) residential accommodation for members of any of the armed forces, including accommodation for their families (section 116(2)(c));
(d) an institution that is the sole or main residence of at least 90% of its residents and does not fall within any of the categories referred to in section 116(3) (see section 116(2)(d) and also paragraph 23 below).
This would include, for example,
- sheltered accommodation for the elderly where no nursing or personal care is provided. An example of this would be where an elderly person purchases a home on a warden-assisted housing development.
- accommodation for religious communities (subject to the rules regarding mixed use; see paragraphs 19 and 20).

23. Categories of building use specifically excluded from the definition of "use as a dwelling" (so that transfers of such buildings in a disadvantaged area will qualify for unlimited relief) (section 116(3)) are:

(a) a home or other institution providing residential accommodation for children;
(b) a hall of residence for students in further or higher education. This is not defined in the legislation but in practice property provided by a university or similar establishment will be judged on the facts (number of inhabitants, type of facilities, availability of communal areas);
(c) a home or other institution providing residential accommodation with personal care for persons in need of personal care by reason of old age, disablement, past

or present dependence on alcohol or drugs or past or present mental disorder (for example, an institution that provides accommodation as part of a wider care service such as residential care homes or residential drug treatment centres);

(d) a hospital or hospice;
(e) a prison or similar establishment, or
(f) a hotel or inn or similar establishment.

Bed and Breakfasts/Guest Houses

24. Each case will be taken on its merits, however, paragraph 25 below provides general examples of the treatment of B&Bs/guest houses.

25. A property providing a Bed and Breakfast (B&B) service, which has amenities installed in each room such as bathing facilities, telephone lines etc and is available all year round as the rooms do not need any further adaptation, would be considered non residential for the purposes of the relief.

Example

Mr and Mrs Boyd run a bed and breakfast in a disadvantaged area of Blackpool. They live on the premises and it is open all year round but trade declines during the winter months.

Under section 116(3) FA 2003, the Boyd's B&B is a "hotel or inn or similar establishment" and is therefore not used as a dwelling.

Mrs Leaver lives in Southwest London and lets out two spare rooms on a B&B basis during the fortnight of the Wimbledon tennis tournament. She doesn't make any adaptations to the rooms other than the removal of some of her personal items.

For the purposes of the relief Mrs Leaver's property is, at all times, considered to be in use as and suitable for use as a dwelling.

---

26. Buy-to-let properties suitable for use as a dwelling are residential unless they are a development of six or more dwellings whereby they would be non-residential under s 116(7).

27. The specific inclusions and exclusions set out in paragraphs 22 and 23 above apply not only to a building's actual use at the effective date of the transaction, but to the uses for which it is suitable at that date. Where, however, a building is being put to one of the non-residential uses specified in section 116(3), this overrides any suitability for another use (section 116(4)). For example, a building used as a children's home may also be suitable for use as a school boarding house, but this will not preclude a claim to unlimited relief.

28. Where a vacant building is suitable for at least one of the uses specified in section 116(2) and at least one specified in section 116(3), section 116(5) determines, for the purposes of the relief, the use for which it is "most suitable". Whether or not a vacant building has one or more uses for which it is most suitable is a question of fact. Evidence supporting such uses should be retained.

29. Where there is a single use for which a building is most suitable, the fact that it is also suitable for another use will be discounted.

30. If there are a number of uses for which a building is most suitable and they all come within either of the two subsections, any other use for which the building is suitable will be discounted.

31. Where no most suitable use can be shown, the default will be to classify the building as residential property and apply the £150,000 limit.

32. Land and buildings that are not suitable for any use at the effective date of the transaction will be treated as residential property if they are "in the process of being constructed or adapted for such use" – see paragraphs 33 and 34 below.

Process of being constructed or adapted for use as a dwelling

33. Undeveloped land is in essence non-residential, but land may be "residential property" for the purposes of Disadvantaged Area Relief if a residential building is being built on it at the effective date of the transaction. A development of six or more dwellings is deemed to be non-residential under s 116(7), even if the process of construction or marketing has begun at the effective date of the transaction (see paragraph 40).

34. Where (at the effective date of the transaction) an existing building is being adapted for, marketed for, or restored to, domestic use, it is residential for the purposes of the relief. The process is taken as commencing when the developer begins marketing the properties for sale or starts physical work on the site which ever is earlier.

This may apply, for example, where a derelict building is being made fit for habitation, or where a previously non-residential building is being converted to a dwelling. For example:

(a) Kristian is buying an apartment, in what will be a converted church, off-plan. The sale is completed on 15 March 2004, the properties were marketed for sale on 3 January 2004 and work on converting the church commenced on 2 February 2004. For the purposes of this transaction the church is considered to be a dwelling, even though it has yet to be fully converted, from 3 January. If the consideration is greater than £150,000 Kristian will have to pay the appropriate rate of Stamp Duty Land Tax.

In the above example the developer that initially purchased the church will have bought it as a non-residential property regardless of the intention to turn the building into residential units.

The garden or grounds of a building used etc. as a dwelling

35. Section 116(1)(b) includes within the definition of residential property "land that is or forms part of the garden or grounds of a building within paragraph (a) (including any building or structure on such land)". The test the Inland Revenue will apply is similar to that applied for the purposes of the capital gains tax relief for main residences (section 222(3) of the Taxation of Chargeable Gains Act 1992). The land will include that which is needed for the reasonable enjoyment of the dwelling having regard to the size and nature of the dwelling.

36. A caravan or houseboat is not a "building" for this purpose.

37. Commercial farmland is not within the definition of residential property. A farmhouse situated on agricultural land would be dealt with under the mixed use provisions (paragraphs 19 and 20 above).

It may often be the case that farmhouses will occupy only a small fraction of the total land and will therefore, when apportioned, fall below the £150,000 consideration limit thus attracting the residential relief.

38. Outhouses on land within the section 116(1)(b) definition will also be "residential property" unless it can be demonstrated that they have a specific non-residential purpose. Where a distinct non-residential use can be demonstrated, the mixed use provisions will apply.

Interest in or rights over residential property

39. The treatment of interests in, or rights over, land or buildings for the purposes of Disadvantaged Area Relief will follow that of the land or buildings to which they relate.

40. Section 116(7) FA 2003 provides that "where six or more separate dwellings are the subject of a single transaction involving the transfer of a major interest in, or the grant of a lease over, them, then . . . those dwellings are treated as not being residential property". This recognises that commercial developers and institutional landlords, for example, frequently deal in numerous properties at one time. The fact that those properties may individually be "residential property" does not detract from the inherently commercial nature of the transaction itself.

41. To qualify as "separate", the dwellings must be self-contained, So for example, flats within a block, sharing some common areas but each with their own amenities will qualify as separate dwellings. Rooms let within a house will not constitute separate dwellings if tenants share amenities such as a kitchen and bathroom.

42. A transaction in respect of six or more such dwellings must be carried out by means of a single transaction in order to qualify for relief

43. Qualifying multiple transactions will be treated as non-residential property for the purposes of relief, even where the proportionate consideration for individual dwellings exceeds the £150,000 limit for residential property. It is not a condition of relief that multiple transactions comprise only dwellings. One example of this would be where a purchaser is buying eight houses and four shops. Mixed use properties, such as pubs with self-contained residential accommodation, are also treated as non-residential.

44. The fact that some of the six or more dwellings within the single transaction are outside a designated disadvantaged area will not prevent them from constituting a non-residential transaction. However relief will only be available for the portion of the land situated within the disadvantaged area.

PROPERTY ONLY PARTLY WITHIN A DISADVANTAGED AREA

45. Schedule 6, Part 3, FA 2003 determines how property situated partly within and partly outside a designated disadvantaged area is to be treated for the purposes of the relief. Such cases are relatively rare in practice. Queries may be referred to Inland Revenue (Stamp Taxes) for guidance.

GRANTS OF NEW LEASES

46. FA 2003 Schedule 6 Part 2 deals with the charge to Stamp Duty Land Tax on the grant of a new lease.

Land all non-residential

47. If all of the land is non-residential it is exempt from any charge to Stamp Duty Land Tax.

Land all residential

48. The general rule is that:

(a) if the premium (and any other consideration than rent) does not exceed £150,000 then this is exempt from Stamp Duty Land Tax, and
(b) if the "net present value" of the rental payments does not exceed £150,000 then this is exempt from Stamp Duty Land Tax.

"Net present value" is, broadly speaking, the total rental payments due under the lease, discounted to reflect the fact that future rental payments are of less value than current rental payments. There is a tool for calculating net present value on the Inland Revenue website.

There is a special rule where the average annual rent exceeds £600. In such a case there is no relief or exemption for any premium. Any premium, however small, will be charged at 1% (or at higher rates if it exceeds £250,000).

49. Where there is mixed use apportionment is applied. The non-residential portion is exempt from lease duty.

If the consideration includes rent and the relevant rental value does not exceed £150,000, the rent does not count as chargeable consideration.

50. If the consideration includes consideration other than rent then:

(a) If the annual rent does not exceed £600 and the relevant consideration does not exceed £150,000, the consideration other than rent does not count as chargeable consideration.
(b) If the annual rent exceeds £600, the consideration other than rent is counted as chargeable consideration

The "annual rent" is the average annual rent over the term of the lease.

Further Resources

Information can be found on our website, which also contains:

- A postcode search tool to help identify whether a property falls within a disadvantaged area, and
- an intelligent decision-maker to help you decide whether a property is residential or non-residential.
- a lease duty calculator which provides the amount of Stamp Duty Land Tax payable on a lease transaction.

STATEMENT OF PRACTICE SP 1/06
Self Assessment: Finality and Discovery

OVERVIEW

Self Assessment tax returns are usually issued to taxpayers in April, shortly after the end of the tax year. The Return has to be completed and sent in by the following 31 January. The Revenue can open an enquiry into that return within twelve months of 31 January to check that the self assessment returns the right amount of tax. If it is incorrect the self assessment can be corrected.

There are some circumstances in which the tax inspector can assess further tax after the twelve month enquiry period. This usually happens when tax was under-assessed because of fraud or negligence by the taxpayer but it can also happen if the taxpayer does not provide enough information for the inspector to realise, within the enquiry period, that the self assessment is insufficient.

The judgement of the Court of Appeal the case of *Langham v Veltema* was concerned with how much information the taxpayer needs to provide to remove the possibility of the inspector making a further assessment, known as a discovery assessment. This Statement of Practice clarifies the circumstances in which HMRC seeks to recover tax when a self assessment is found to be insufficient either:

- after the end of the period in which a notice of enquiry may be given, or

- after an enquiry into a return has been completed,

and it is considered that the information provided by the taxpayer was not sufficient to make the Inspector aware of the insufficiency. The following examples illustrate what information taxpayers must disclose to guard against the possibility of a subsequent discovery assessment:

- Most taxpayers who use a valuation in completing their tax return and state in the Additional Information space at the end of the Return that a valuation has been used, by whom it has been carried out, and that it was carried out by a named independent and suitably qualified valuer if that was the case, on the appropriate basis, will be able, for all practical purposes, to rely on protection from a later discovery assessment, provided those statements are true.
- Most taxpayers will be able to gain finality with exceptional items in accounts. An example might be a deduction in the accounts under Repairs. If an entry in the Additional Information space points out that a programme of work has been carried out that included repairs, improvements and new building work and that the total cost has been allocated to revenue and capital on a particular basis, the inspector should not enquire after the closure of the enquiry period unless he becomes aware that the statement was patently untrue or unreasonable.
- Taxpayers who adopt a different view of the law from that published as the Revenue's view can protect against a discovery assessment after the enquiry period. The Return would have to indicate that a different view had been adopted by entering in the Additional Information space comments to the effect that they have not followed Revenue guidance on the issue or that no adjustment has been made to take account of it.

This Statement does not cover cases where a self assessment is insufficient due to fraudulent or negligent conduct by or on behalf of the taxpayer.

This Statement applies to the two main areas of self assessment:

- Income Tax and Capital Gains Tax ("IT");
- Corporation Tax ("CT").

This statement of practice applies to the following for the years specified:

- Individuals – for returns from 1996/97;
- Partnerships – for returns from 1996/97;
- For bodies within the charge to Corporation Tax – accounting periods ending on or after 1 July 1999.

BACKGROUND

1. Prior to the introduction of self assessment, discovery assessments were subject to statute, case law and practice. Cases of particular relevance were *Cenlon Finance Co Ltd v Ellwood* (40 TC 176) and *Scorer v Olin Energy Systems Ltd* (58 TC 592). Statement of Practice 8/91 explained how the provisions were applied.

2. When IT self assessment ("ITSA") was introduced by *FA 1994*, new *TMA 1970 s 29* was intended to reproduce the mix of law and practice on discovery set out in SP 8/91. The Self Assessment Legal Framework issued in 1995 explained that the redrafting of *TMA 1970 s 29* was to ensure

> that a taxpayer who has made a full disclosure in the return has absolute finality twelve months after the filing date. This will be the case if the return is subsequently found to be incorrect, unless it was incorrect because of fraudulent or negligent

conduct. In any case where there was incomplete disclosure or fraudulent or negligent conduct the Revenue will still have the power to remedy any loss of tax.

The intention was to offer finality, but there was also a recognition that there would be circumstances, even without fraud or neglect, that could still result in a discovery assessment. The equivalent legislation for CT self assessment ("CTSA") is at *FA 1998 Sch 18, paras 41 to 49*.

3. The Court of Appeal in the case of *Langham v Veltema* [2004] STC 544, considered when disclosure was incomplete. It concluded that information made available, as defined in statute, must make an Inspector aware of an actual insufficiency in the assessment for that information to be complete enough to prevent the making of a discovery assessment. That conclusion gave rise to two concerns:

- the lack of finality for the taxpayer at the close of the enquiry window; and
- the inherent difficulty of complying with the law as expounded in the Court of Appeal.

4. Guidance was issued in December 2004 to help ITSA taxpayers achieve finality when completing their 2004 returns. This Statement of Practice confirms the position in respect of ITSA and extends it to CTSA. The circumstances in which HMRC will regard a taxpayer as having made a full disclosure are set out and assurance of finality is given in particular situations.

DISCOVERY POWERS

5. The authority to make a discovery assessment is given by *TMA 1970 s 29* (ITSA), *FA 1998 Sch 19, para 41* (CTSA). In all cases, the relevant requirement for the purposes of this Statement is a discovery "that an assessment to tax is or has become insufficient". Mere suspicion that an assessment may be insufficient is not adequate grounds for making a discovery assessment.

6. Where there has not been fraudulent or negligent conduct, discovery can only take place where HMRC "could not have been reasonably expected, on the basis of information made available before that time, to be aware of" the insufficiency in the assessment [*TMA 1970 s 29(5)*; *FA 1998 Sch 18 para 44(1)*].

7. "Information made available" is defined at *TMA 1970 s 29(6)* (ITSA), *FA 1998 Sch 18, para 44(2)* (CTSA). Relevant information includes that contained in documents accompanying the return.

8. The requirement that HMRC must discover that an assessment is insufficient restricts the opportunity for using discovery powers to make an assessment. If HMRC considers that an assessment may be insufficient, it may seek more information using *TMA 1970 s 20* to establish whether the assessment is insufficient. However, where there is no reason to suspect fraud, the taxpayer will be told about the use of *section 20* and will have the opportunity to make representations to an independent Commissioner. The ability of HMRC to "enquire" after the closure of the enquiry window is therefore subject to external oversight.

DISCOVERY IN PRACTICE

9. A taxpayer can further restrict the opportunity for discovery by providing enough information for an HMRC officer to realise within the enquiry period that the self assessment is insufficient. However taxpayers are encouraged to submit the minimum necessary to make disclosure of an insufficiency. The Veltema judgement does not require the provision of enough information to quantify the effect on the assessment. Information will not be treated as being made available where the total amount supplied is so extensive that an officer "could not have been reasonably expected to be aware" of the significance of particular information and the officer's attention has not been drawn to it by the taxpayer or taxpayer's representative.

10. HMRC recognises that a taxpayer, unless acting fraudulently or negligently, will consider his return to be correct and complete with no insufficiency. Most figures

entered on a return will be absolute, however some will be open to interpretation or uncertain. In these circumstances, the taxpayer will have made a judgement as to the correct figure to enter. HMRC may regard this figure as insufficient. Where the taxpayer has fully alerted HMRC to the full circumstances of such an entry on the return, then the HMRC officer is in a position to determine whether or not there is an insufficiency, the conditions set by the Court of Appeal in *Langham v Veltema* have been met and the assessment will not be open to discovery on that point.

The following examples illustrate common situations.

EXAMPLES OF COMMON SITUATIONS

Valuation cases

11. Some entries on tax returns depend on the valuation of an asset. For example, if a company transfers a property to a director at less than market value, both the company and the director will need to use the market value in calculating the capital gain and benefit respectively. There is no obligation on the director to do any more than enter the resulting benefit in the relevant box on his return. However, the Court of Appeal decided in*Langham v Veltema* that the figure on the return does not give HMRC the level of information that is necessary to prevent a later discovery assessment.

12. Most taxpayers who state that a valuation has been used, by whom it has been carried out, and that it was carried out by a named independent and suitably qualified valuer if that was the case, on the appropriate basis, will be able, for all practical purposes, to rely on protection from a later discovery assessment, provided those statements are true.

13. The main exception will be where, as in the example of a property transferred to a director, the same transaction is the subject of an agreed valuation in a related tax return, that of the company. It may then come to light that the director's return was insufficient and a discovery assessment raised. It is also likely that the insufficiency can be quantified without further enquiry. For this purpose, a related tax return is that of another party to the same transaction, rather than another transaction involving a similar or identical asset. The returns of several parties disposing of a jointly owned asset or shareholders disposing of all the shares in the same company in a single transaction, for example, may be related for this purpose. Where taxpayers' interests in an asset or assets are similar, but not the same, any valuations agreed would not necessarily bind other taxpayers.

14. Information about the valuation may be provided in the Additional Information space (ITSA) or in accompanying documents (ITSA and CTSA). The return of capital gains for ITSA purposes requires an entry to indicate that a valuation has been used and asks for a copy of any valuation received. If these provide the information mentioned above the taxpayer can rely on protection from a later discovery assessment.

OTHER JUDGEMENTAL ISSUES

15. There are many items such as reserves, provisions and stock valuation that are routinely included in accounts, as well as some exceptional items such as capital/revenue expenditure in repairs, which require an element of judgement on the part of the taxpayer or representative. Prior to the introduction of self assessment it was customary to provide details of such items in the accounts or computations and many taxpayers have continued to do so.

16. It is difficult to see how HMRC might come to the conclusion that an assessment is insufficient because of one of these items without making an enquiry. There will be instances in which it becomes clear from an in-year enquiry that previous years figures were incorrect. The decision in the *Veltema* case does not alter that situation.

17. It may be possible to gain finality with the more exceptional items. An example might be a deduction in the accounts under Repairs. If an entry in the Additional

Information space or accompanying documentation points out that a programme of work has been carried out that included repairs, improvements and new building work and that the total cost has been allocated to revenue and capital on a particular basis, the HMRC officer will not use discovery powers after the closure of the enquiry period unless he becomes aware that the statement was patently untrue or the basis of allocation was so unreasonable as to be negligent.

TAKING A DIFFERENT VIEW

18. It is open to a taxpayer properly informed or advised to adopt a different view of the law from that published as HMRC's view. To protect against a discovery assessment after the enquiry period, the return or accompanying documents would have to indicate that a different view had been adopted. This might be done by comments to the effect that the taxpayer has not followed HMRC guidance on the issue or that no adjustment has been made to take account of it. This would offer an opportunity to HMRC to take up the return for enquiry. It is not necessary to provide all the documentation that HMRC might need to quantify that insufficiency if an enquiry into the Return is made.

19. Provided the point at issue is clearly identified and the stance adopted is not wholly unreasonable, the existence of an under-assessment or insufficiency is demonstrated by the statement that a different view of the law has been followed. In these circumstances the taxpayer achieves finality if no enquiry is opened within the statutory time limit.

Appendix C

Extra Statutory Concessions

C10 GROUPS OF COMPANIES: ARRANGEMENTS

1. The following provisions of TA 1988 contain special rules which apply if there are "arrangements" in existence which may involve a future change in the ownership of the shares or securities in a company:

— s 240(11)(*a*)—surrender of ACT (in respect of accounting periods ended before 6 April 1999) to a subsidiary company;
— s 247(1A)(*b*)—group income elections in certain consortium cases;
— s 410(1), (2)—group and consortium relief.

In addition, Sch 18 para 5B(1) applies if there are "option arrangements".

JOINT VENTURE COMPANIES

2. But in practice these special rules are not applied in relation to certain types of agreement regulating the affairs of two or more member companies holding shares or securities in a joint venture company carrying on a commercial undertaking. The types of agreement to which the concession applies are ones which could involve the transfer of shares or securities in the joint venture company on, or as the result of, the happening of one or more triggering events. Until such a triggering event occurs, such agreements are not regarded as "arrangements" or "option arrangements".

3. Triggering events are:

(a) the voluntary departure of a member;
(b) the commencement of liquidation, administration or receivership of a member;
(c) a serious deterioration in the financial condition of a member;
(d) a change in the control or ownership of a member;
(e) a default by a member in performing its obligations under the terms of an agreement between the members or with the joint venture company, including its articles of association;
(f) an external change in the commercial circumstances in which the undertaking operates such that its viability is seriously threatened;
(g) unresolved disagreement among the members;
(h) any contingency of a similar kind provided against, but not intended to happen, when the agreement in question was entered into.

4. The details of such agreements will vary but they will be of a kind (*a*) allowing or requiring remaining members to acquire the holding of a departing company, or (*b*) allowing or requiring a departing company to transfer its holding to remaining members.

5. The transfer of the shares or securities will be on the basis of:

— an offer pro rata to the remaining members' holdings of shares or securities, with price fixed by agreement or independent valuation (which may allow for a penalty against a defaulting company); or
— a competitive tender among the remaining members; or
— a reciprocal process where one member offers to sell its holding to another at a certain price per share, when that other can either accept the offer or require the offeror to buy the offeree's holding at the same price (and the reverse, offer to purchase/call option arrangement); or

— other arrangements designed to ensure that a price appropriate to the commercial circumstances is struck.

6. The Articles of a joint venture company may provide for the suspension of a member's voting rights on the happening of a triggering event. Such a provision is not of itself regarded as "arrangements" before the triggering event occurs.

MORTGAGE OF SHARES OR SECURITIES

7. If shares or securities in a company are used as security under a mortgage (or legal or equitable charge) the mortgage will not by itself be regarded as constituting "arrangements" or "option arrangements" until the default or other triggering event occurs which allows the mortgagee to exercise his rights against the mortgagor. This only applies if prior to default the mortgagee possesses no more control over the shares or securities which are the subject of the mortgage than is required by the mortgagee to protect his interest.

8. If a default occurs but is remedied before the mortgagee exercises his rights, "arrangements" and "option arrangements" will be regarded as not having come into existence as a result of the default.

APPLICATION

9. The concession does not apply when the person or persons standing to acquire shares, securities or control could, alone or with connected persons within the meaning of TA 1988 s 839, dictate the terms or timing of the acquisition in advance of the triggering event having occurred. For this purpose members will not be regarded as connected by reason only of their membership of the joint venture company and a mortgage will not be regarded as connected with the company whose shares are the subject of the mortgage by reason only of the mortgage.

Appendix D

Inland Revenue Publications

INLAND REVENUE TAX BULLETIN: ISSUE 18—AUGUST 1995
Stamp Duty

FINANCE ACT 1994

1. We have received a number of enquiries about the Stamp Duty provisions in sections 240–243 of the Finance Act (FA) 1994. This article aims to give some general guidance on these points. The precise treatment of a particular document will, of course, depend on all the facts of the case and the legal effect of the document.

EXCHANGES ETC—SECTION 241 FA 1994

2. Section 241 introduced new rules of Stamp Duty on exchanges of interest in land or buildings. section 241 operates in a similar manner to section 6, 55 and 57 Stamp Act 1891. These provisions impose a charge on instruments which implement transactions which would not be characterised as a sale at common law because the consideration is something other than a price in money paid or promised. Pursuant to these provisions, certain kinds of consideration are to be treated for the purposes of the charge as equivalent to a money price, the charge being imposed by reference to the value of the consideration to be given. (In relation to section 57, Statement of Practice SP 6/90 remains effective).

3. For the purposes of the charge to duty under the 'conveyance or transfer on sale' heading in the Stamp Act 1891, section 241(1) attributes a value to the consideration and states that 'the instrument shall be charged with ad valorem duty under that heading' where a charge is not imposed in respect of that consideration by virtue of any other provision.

4. As Stamp Duty is charged on instruments, rather than transactions, section 241(1) falls to be applied to each instrument which satisfies the terms of the provision. Accordingly, if, for example, the consideration for the transfer of an interest in land is the transfer of an interest in land, each transfer is chargeable by reference to the market value of the interest transferred by the other.

THE £60,000 THRESHOLD

5. The £60,000 threshold is applied separately to each side of the exchange. For example, if there is a straightforward exchange of one house worth £50,000 for another worth £50,000, both transfers are within the threshold and no duty would be payable on either provided each is certified in accordance with section 34(4) Finance Act 1958.

6. Where there is a multiple exchange for example, properties A and B are exchanged for property C—the transfers of properties A and B would be regarded as parts of a larger transaction (under section 34(4) Finance Act 1958). The threshold would not apply to either of them if the total consideration for both was more than £60,000, but would be applied separately to the transfer of property C.

EQUALITY MONEY

7. Where the market values of two properties being exchanged are not equal, a payment of money (or some other consideration) is often given with the lower value

property, so as to equalise the bargain. In many cases the wording of the conveyance of the lower value property may not fully reflect the consideration expressed in the original contract or agreement. Where it is clear from the contract that the lower value property has been transferred for the higher value property less the equality money, the Stamp Office will limit the charge to duty accordingly. For example, if the initial contract provided for an £80,000 house to be exchanged for a £100,000 house, and for £20,000 to be paid as equality money, the amount charged to duty on the transfer of the £80,000 house would be limited to £80,000. In these cases the Stamp Office needs to see the relevant contract as well as the conveyance.

8. Where there is a multiple exchange of properties, an apportionment on similar lines may be made to determine how much of the consideration is attributable to each of the transfers. For example, two or more properties may be exchanged for one larger property, with or without a payment of equality money.

SALES

9. In many cases, transactions which in the past have been structured and documented as an exchange could equally well be carried out as a sale for a price which may be partly satisfied in kind. For example, when a person offers a property for sale, he may receive the price from the buyer in the form either of money, or partly of money and partly of the buyer's existing house. Such a transaction can be carried out and documented (commencing with the initial contract as a sale). Section 241 does not apply where duty is already imposed under the conveyance on sale head of charge. Accordingly, if the transaction is within the common law concept of 'sale', section 241 is excluded and duty is simply charged by reference to the price of the sale.

10. Although a sale ordinarily involves a price in money paid or promised (*IRC v Littlewoods Mail Order Stores Ltd* [1963] AC 135 at page 152), the Courts have held that the transaction is still a 'sale' if property is taken in satisfaction of part of the purchase price: *Simpson v Connolly* [1953] 2 All ER 474 p 477; *Connell Estate Agents v Begej* [1993] 2 EGLR 35. In the Connell case, the purchaser had agreed to purchase land for £109,000. In satisfaction of this price the vendor was 'to receive ownership of 10 Milner Road, Finedon, plus balance of £53,000'. The Court of Appeal held that the transaction was a sale of the more valuable property for the price of £109,000 and that the purchaser's property was part of that price. The Court confirmed however, that a transaction cannot be characterised as a sale unless some money is paid by the purchaser to the vendor and the cash element is more than merely nominal. So if, for example, the buyer is buying a house for £100,000, and pays for it with £30,000 in cash plus his existing house worth £70,000, duty of £1,000 (1% of £100,000) would be charged on the transfer of the £100,000 house.

11. The house which the vendor accepts as part payment for the sale would not be regarded as a separate sale for Stamp Duty purposes. The consideration for the purchaser's property is not the vendor's property but merely the discharge of a potential obligation to pay part of the purchase price on completion. Accordingly, section 241 does not apply to the transfer of the purchaser's property. Section 57 Stamp Act 1891 does not apply to the transfer of the purchaser's property because the purchaser's property is not conveyed to the vendor in consideration, wholly or in part, of any 'debt due' to the vendor. The word 'due' when used in relation to a debt means due and payable (*Re European Life Assurance* [1869] LR 9 Eq 122, and the other cases cited in Stroud's Judicial Dictionary 5th Ed Vol 2 pp 781–783). As the purchase price is not payable until completion, a transfer of property by the purchaser on or before completion cannot be said to be in consideration of a debt due. Ordinarily, on completion, the transfer of the purchaser's property will be handed to the vendor's solicitor, together with a cheque or other means of payment, at the same time as the vendor's solicitor hands over the transfer of the vendor's property. For there to be a debt due to the vendor, the purchaser would have to be put in the position of having taken a transfer of the vendor's property without having paid for it.

12. On the basis that there is a sale for cash to be satisfied in part by the transfer of another property, ad valorem Stamp Duty is charged on the consideration for the sale, but not on the transfer of the other property. That transfer would only be charged to the fixed duty of 50 pence. The threshold would not be relevant to this transfer as it is not a conveyance on sale.

SURRENDER AND REGRANT OF LEASES

13. Where a lease is granted in consideration only of the surrender or abandonment of an existing lease of the same property, section 77(1) Stamp Act 1891 provides exemption from duty. If the new lease is granted in consideration of a premium and/or rent as well as the surrender of the existing lease, there is a grant of a lease which is partly exempt (the surrender) and partly chargeable to duty (the premium and/or rent). The Stamp Office would not seek to refuse exemption under section 77(1) Stamp Act 1891 merely on the grounds that there were some minor changes in the property subject to the lease, provided that these could be regarded as de minimis. The same treatment would apply where a variation of a lease takes effect in law as a surrender and regrant.

14. Where the lease on one property is being replaced by a lease on another property, the Stamp Duty treatment will depend on the facts of the case and the effect of the document. But if, for example, the document granted a new lease on one property and the consideration was the surrender of a lease on another property, duty would be charged on the grant of the new lease, by reference to the market value of the lease surrendered (as premium/consideration) and any other payment by way of premium or rent.

15. The Stamp Duty treatment of the surrender of the old lease will similarly depend on the facts and the documents. In most cases where there is a surrender and regrant, the Stamp Office's experience is that no deed of surrender is submitted for stamping, either because the new lease simply supersedes the old one by operation of law and there is no surrender document, or possibly because any surrender document is not submitted for stamping.

SALE AND LEASEBACK

16. Where there is a sale and leaseback, the Stamp Office normally sees a contract of sale for a price, and an agreement for lease (followed by the grant of a lease), rather than an exchange of one for the other. In that case, the sale would be liable to duty in the normal way by reference to the price and the agreement for lease would be charged by reference to any premium and rent.

17. If, however, the property is transferred in consideration of a leaseback of the same property, alone or together with a sum of money, duty would be assessed on the transfer by reference to the value (if any) of the lease plus any cash element. Duty would also be assessed on the lease by reference to any amount by which the value of the property transferred exceeded the cash consideration.

UNASCERTAINABLE CONSIDERATION—SECTION 242, FINANCE ACT 1994

18. Section 242 deals with sales of land or buildings where the price is not ascertainable at the time the relevant document is executed. In these circumstances, the open market value of the property is to be taken as the consideration for Stamp Duty purposes. Similarly, where the rent under a new lease is not ascertainable the open market rent is to be taken.

19. That rule does not, however, apply where the amount of the consideration can already be determined by reference to the 'contingency principle' section 242(3)(*a*). Under this principle, if the consideration agreed between the parties and specified in the instrument is subject to possible future variation, the specified figure would be taken for Stamp Duty purposes (*Independent Television Authority v IRC* [1961] AC 427 p 443). Thus if the consideration is 25% of profits over 5 years, but not to be less than £100,000, the consideration for Stamp Duty purposes would be £100,000. The existence of additional but unascertainable consideration would bring the transaction within section 242.

20. The ascertainable figure produced by the contingency principle may be a maximum or minimum, or a basic sum which is subject to future variation. But a minimum figure which was merely a nominal figure inserted in a lease to avoid section 242, or which did not represent the agreed consideration or rent, would not satisfy section 242(3)(*a*) as it would not be a minimum rent for the purpose of the contingency principle as formulated by Lord Radcliffe in the Independent Television Authority case. We consider that for this purpose a minimum rent must be an amount genuinely agreed between the parties as such, i.e., as an amount which is contemplated by the parties and accepted by the landlord as compensation for the use and occupation of the premises by the tenant(s). It is therefore necessary to consider all the facts in order to ascertain the true nature and intended purpose of the instrument (*Oughtred v IRC* [1958] Ch 678 p 688; [1960] AC 206).

21. The market value rule applies where part of the consideration or rent is unascertainable. Duty would then be charged on the market value or rent (but not the market value or rent **plus** the ascertainable consideration). Where the rent under a lease is unascertainable for only part of the term, the market rent will be taken for the whole term in order to calculate the average annual rent. In establishing the market rent, all the terms and conditions of the actual lease will be taken into account under normal valuation principles; section 242(3)(*b*). It is the market rent for the particular **lease** and not merely the market rent for the land at a particular time which must be established for the purposes of section 242(2).

22. It has been suggested to us that section 242 is ineffective on the grounds that if there is a valid contract, the consideration will be ascertainable, even though it may not be immediately quantifiable. For a contract to be valid, it is sufficient that the consideration is ascertainable either at the time of the contract or subsequently. Section 242 by contrast applies where the consideration is not ascertainable at the time the document is executed. The section has to be read in conjunction with section 55 Finance Act 1963, which refers to the amount or value of the consideration, and the words 'cannot . . . be ascertained' clearly mean 'cannot be ascertained for the purpose of the charge', rather than 'cannot be ascertained as a matter of contract law'. Our view is that the wording of section 242(1) is apt to cover the case where the amount or value of the consideration cannot be ascertained at the relevant time for the purposes of Stamp Duty chargeable under the conveyance on sale head of charge.

23. It has also been suggested that some transactions could come within both section 241 and section 242, on the grounds that where the amount or value of the consideration is not ascertainable, the right to it might be 'property' within section 241(1). In general, the two sections deal with distinct types of cases. There may be some cases which could fall within both sections, but the precise treatment will depend on the facts of the case. In practice, where the transfer is for full value, it should make little or no difference to the amount of duty whether section 241 or section 242 applies. Where there is a difference, duty would be charged under the provision which produces the higher amount of duty (following the principle in *Speyer Bros v CIR* [1908] AC 92).

24. The treatment of split-term leases set out in our letter of 2 January 1963 to the Law Society's Gazette (where they are described as leases of type (*c*)) no longer applies. The annex on page 237 reproduces the relevant part of the 1963 letter.

SURRENDERS—SECTION 243, FINANCE ACT 1994

25. Section 243 provides that where, in pursuance of an agreement, a lease is surrendered or renounced without a deed of surrender, the agreement is liable to duty as if it were a deed.

26. We have been asked what particular types of document would be regarded as an 'agreement'. In an individual case, it would of course be necessary to consider the facts and the terms of the relevant document. The case of *Fleetwood—Hesketh v CIR* [1936] 1 KB 351 shows that a document recording or implementing an agreement may itself be treated as an agreement for Stamp Duty purposes whether there is a previous oral agreement or an oral agreement contemporaneous with the written agreement. Where such a document satisfies the requirements of section 2 of the Law of Property (Miscellaneous Provisions) Act 1989, it will be an agreement within section 243.

VALUATIONS

27. Although the Stamp Duty legislation does not provide for appeals on valuation to go to the Lands Tribunal, a reference by consent could be made to the Tribunal under section 1(5) of the Lands Tribunal Act 1949 on a question of land valuation. We would normally consent. However, where questions of both law and valuation arise in relation to an appeal relating to liability and quantum respectively, we would wish to resolve the legal issue in the High Court prior to any determination of value by the Lands Tribunal. In contrast, a valuation issue would after appeal go to the Lands Tribunal.

AGREEMENT FOR LEASE—SECTION 240, FINANCE ACT 1994

28. Section 240 provides that if an agreement for lease and the lease which gives effect to the agreement, are presented for stamping at the same time, and any duty chargeable on the agreement is paid, the agreement shall be treated as having been executed at the same time as the lease for the purposes of the provisions relating to penalties for late stamping. We have been asked whether section 28 FA 1931 means that the agreement must nevertheless be produced to the Stamp Office within 30 days of execution. Presentation of the agreement with the lease, within 30 days after the execution of the lease, will be accepted as satisfying the requirement under section 28 to produce the agreement.

GENERAL

29. This article supersedes the relevant parts of the Press Releases of 30 November 1993 and 18 April 1994 and the Stamp Office guidance notes issued in December 1993.

EXTRACT FROM THE CONTROLLER OF STAMPS' LETTER OF 2 JANUARY 1963 TO THE LAW SOCIETY'S GAZETTE

'The Board of Inland Revenue have recently given consideration to the basis of assessment of duty on leases which contain one or more of the following provisions:

(*c*) a rent or rents fixed for part only of the term, the rent for the remainder of the term to be agreed subsequently.

Leases of type (*c*) present great difficulty and the Board are advised that in the absence of authority, it cannot be said with certainty how the provisions of the lease head of charge should properly be applied. In the absence of such authority and with the object of securing a consistent practice, hitherto lacking, and to bring the assessment of duty as far as possible into line with the facts, the Board have decided that such leases shall be assessed by treating separately the part of the term in respect of which the rent is known from that in respect of which it is unknown; ad valorem duty under "Lease (3)" will be assessed in respect of the former part as if it were a lease at the known rate or average rate of rent for a term of that length, and fixed duty under "Lease (4)" will be assessed in respect of the latter part.

The practice explained above in relation to leases of type (*c*) will not affect the basis of assessment of leases where there is a rent of one description (eg a ground rent) of known amount for the whole of the term and a further rent of another description (eg a service rent) ascertainable for part only of the term. In such cases the basis of assessment will continue to be ad valorem duty under "Lease (3)" on the average ascertainable annual rent payable throughout the term and fixed duty under 'Lease (4)' on the further uncertain rent.'

INLAND REVENUE TAX BULLETIN: ISSUE 30—AUGUST 1997
Interpretations
Stamp Duty litigation

(1) UNSTAMPED DOCUMENTS, OVERSEAS OR ONSHORE;
(2) CONTINGENCY PRINCIPLE

Parinv (Hatfield) Ltd v IRC [1996] STC 933—OFF-SHORE DECLARATION OF TRUST INEFFECTIVE TO AVOID AD VALOREM DUTY ON SUBSEQUENT TRANSFERS

This case concerned the effectiveness of an off-shore declaration of trust in avoiding ad valorem Stamp Duty on subsequent transfers. The High Court held that the device was ineffective. The taxpayer has lodged an appeal. In the meantime, the Stamp Office will continue to apply the law on the basis of the High Court's decision.

In the *Parinv* case, the taxpayer sought to rely on a copy of an unstamped overseas document to argue that the Stamp Office should stamp a transfer of property to a purchasers at 50p rather than 1%, on the basis that the transfer transferred only bare legal title and that the equitable interest in the property was transferred by the unstamped document. This argument was rejected by the Court on the grounds that the unstamped document was not admissible as evidence, in view of section 14(4) of the Stamp Act 1891.

UNSTAMPED DOCUMENTS—INLAND REVENUE PRACTICE

Following enquiries from customers, the Inland Revenue has decided to publicise its current practice with regard to unstamped documents. Under the terms of section 14(4) Stamp Act 1891 . . . 'an instrument executed in any part of the United Kingdom, or relating wheresoever executed, to any property situate, or to any matter or thing done or to be done, in any part of the United Kingdom, shall not, except in criminal proceedings, be given in evidence, or be available for any purposes whatever, unless it is duly stamped in accordance with the law in force at the time when it was first executed'.

It has been the Inland Revenue's view that an unstamped document cannot be offered in evidence in any legal proceedings other than criminal proceedings, and that this includes hearings before the Special or General Commissioners. Following the case of *Parinv (Hatfield) Ltd v CIR*, the Inland Revenue's current practice will be as follows.

In the *Parinv* case, the Inland Revenue argued that an unstamped instrument was itself excluded from being used in civil proceedings, a view accepted by Lindsay J. Furthermore he took the view that a true copy, sometimes called a conformed copy, of an original unstamped document cannot be used to provide information or material or evidence of the original to the court.

The court then went on to consider the Inland Revenue's position in connection with copy documents. In his analysis of section 14(4) Stamp Act 1891 Lindsay J. considered the words 'shall not . . . be available for any purpose whatever'. He indicated that these words were not an absolute prohibition because this would prevent an unstamped document being examined even in order to determine what should be the appropriate stamp. The Court referred to a judgement in an earlier case and endorsed the view that the words mean that one person cannot compel another person to rely on and accept an unstamped document.

The Inland Revenue in addition, argued that it was able to look at the copy document with the purpose of establishing the liability to duty of another document. The Court held that because the taxpayer is obliged by section 5 of the Act to provide all facts and circumstances affecting the liability to duty of a document including all such evidence deemed necessary by the Board to form a view if adjudication or assessment is required, the Inland Revenue was not obliged by the Act to exclude from its consideration the contents of a copy of an unstamped document which had been supplied to it in order to meet that obligation. It was unlikely that Parliament would have imposed a fine for non-disclosure (i.e. a fraudulent act) and yet required the Revenue to ignore the disclosure. So the Inland Revenue can have regard to a document for the purpose of an assessment of duty. But that does not compel the Inland Revenue to go any further.

The Inland Revenue is aware that documents executive overseas are frequently retained there with a view to deferral or avoidance of payment of Stamp Duty. It will not be the Inland Revenue's practice to request sign of original documents in these or other circumstances, merely to check whether they have been duly stamped or not. However, if the documents are to be relied on by a person in support of any claim to relief, or otherwise used in evidence in relation to any liability to tax, or the amount thereof, that pension should be aware that the Revenue cannot be compelled to accept in support of such claim or as evidence unstamped original or conformed unstamped copies of documents.

PENALTY FOR FRAUD

Section 5 of the Stamp Act 1891 requires that all the facts and circumstances affecting the liability of an instrument to duty, or the amount of the duty chargeable, shall be fully and truly set forth in the instrument, and that any failure to do so by the parties or their advisers with intent to defraud the Crown, shall attract a fine. The Stamp Office takes the view that a failure to disclose the fact that the parties are attempting to rely on an unstamped instrument, contrary to section 14(4) of the Stamp Act, in executing a transfer which purports to convey the bare legal estate, will constitute a breach of section 5, and appropriate action will be taken.

The Stamp Office also takes the view that any attempt by the parties to an instrument containing a certificate under the exempt instruments' legislation which relied on another instrument executed overseas which was not duly stamped, would constitute a breach of section 5.

LM Tenancies 1 PLC V CIR [1996] STC 880—CONSIDERATION CALCULATED IN ACCORDANCE WITH A FORMULA ASCERTAINED BY APPLICATION OF CONTINGENCY PRINCIPLE

This case concerned the application of the contingency principle. The High Court held that where the calculation of duty relied on a future value, (the price of a gilt at some time after execution of the document) the Stamp Office could rely on the last published figure.

The taxpayer has lodged an appeal against this decision. In the meantime the Stamp Office will apply the law on the basis of the Court's decision, subject to the normal right of appeal in any individual case. On that basis, duty is payable on an ascertainable amount where the contingency principle can be applied in the way outlined above.

The Stamp Office is of the view that the contingency principle, as it was held to apply in this case, will apply to other reference values which are unknown at the date of execution. An example is the practice of making future rent increases subject to an increase in an index, typically the RPI. The Stamp Office will apply the published increase in RPI over the 12 months prior to execution of the lease or agreement for lease to calculate the average annual rent.

Where the contingency principle does not apply, section 242 Finance Act 1994 now provides that where the consideration for an interest in land is unascertainable ad valorem Stamp Duty is chargeable on the basis of the value of the property conveyed.

INLAND REVENUE TAX BULLETIN: ISSUE 37—OCTOBER 1998
Stamp Duty Reserve Tax (SDRT)—penalties for failure to notify liability

This article explains the Stamp Office's practice in relation to the penalties to which an accountable person may be liable in the event of a failure to notify SDRT liability before the accountable date.

BACKGROUND

Broadly speaking, SDRT is charged on agreements to transfer shares where no stock transfer form is used (and accordingly no Stamp Duty is paid).

Most SDRT arises on transfers of dematerialised shares held in CREST, where the SDRT concerned is accounted for centrally through CREST. However not all securities are able to be held in CREST and so SDRT also arises in a variety of other situations. One common example is where such 'residual' securities that have been purchased but not yet delivered are soon sold again and accordingly registered directly into the name of the second purchaser.

Where SDRT arises that is not accounted for in CREST, Regulation 4 of the SDRT Regulations SI 1986/1711 (as amended by SI 1997/2430) requires the accountable person to give written notice of each charge to SDRT, and to pay the SDRT due direct to the Inland Revenue, on or before the accountable date.

The written notice (which should set out the date of the agreement, and the parties, securities and consideration involved) should be sent together with the SDRT itself to the Shares Unit of the Stamp Office at the address below.

Where the shares are purchased on an exchange the accountable person, as defined by Regulation 2 of the SDRT Regulations 1986, will be one of the brokers (or qualified dealers) involved in the transaction. Otherwise the purchaser is accountable.

The accountable date is the seventh day of the month following the month in which the trade date of the transaction occurred. Interest is charged from that date on any SDRT paid late.

Penalties apply to late notices under section 93 Taxes Management Act (TMA) 1970, as applied to SDRT by SI 1986/1711 (as amended by SI 1997/2430). The level of penalties depends on how late the notice is provided as set out below.

NOTICE GIVEN LATE BUT WITHIN ONE YEAR OF THE ACCOUNTABLE DATE

Section 93(2) TMA 1970 states that each Regulation 4 failure will incur a liability to a penalty of £100; that is to say that each transaction which is accounted for to the Stamp Office after the accountable date will attract a potential penalty of £100. Composite monthly notifications are very welcome, but it should be noted that a late composite notice covering say 10 transactions would potentially be liable to 10 penalties of £100.

However, to prevent the size of the potential penalty being disproportionate to the amount of SDRT involved, the amount of the statutory penalty in relation to each individual transaction will normally be limited to the lesser of:

- the total SDRT due on the transaction reported; and

- £100.

So, for example, if a late composite notice for a particular month relates to just two transactions attracting SDRT of £10 and £1000 respectively, the mitigated penalty would normally be £110 rather than £200.

Whenever an agreement to transfer chargeable securities is not reported before the accountable date the accountable person can now expect to have to account for a maximum penalty of £100 along with interest on the SDRT from the accountable date to the date of payment.

NOTICE GIVEN MORE THAN ONE YEAR AFTER THE ACCOUNTABLE DATE

In addition to the penalty described above, if the failure continues for twelve months or more the accountable person becomes liable, under section 93(5) TMA 1970, to a tax geared penalty not exceeding the amount of SDRT which should have been paid. In the event of such a penalty becoming due, consideration will be given to mitigating the amount charged in line with the Board's established policy. Full details are given in Stamp Office leaflet SO14 (available from the address below) but, briefly, the three factors taken into consideration are; the readiness with which the disclosure is made, the amount of co-operation given and the overall gravity of the offence committed.

CASES WHERE TRANSFER DOCUMENT STAMPED AFTER ACCOUNTABLE DATE

SDRT arises wherever a stock transfer form relating to a transaction in securities is not stamped before the accountable date. However, in practice accountable persons handling residual securities sometimes find they cannot get stock transfer forms stamped by that time, but are nevertheless confident that such a form will be stamped shortly thereafter (which will then cancel the SDRT charge).

Where a stock transfer form relating to residual securities is stamped within 60 days of the date of the transaction the Stamp Office will not seek interest on the SDRT in the meantime and no notice need be given. This extends the practice set out at the end of paragraph 1.11 of the SDRT Notes for Guidance published in February 1998.

However, should a stock transfer form not in fact be duly stamped within this time then interest on the unpaid SDRT will still run from the accountable date. In addition, if a notice was not delivered by that date the penalties described above will apply.

It should also be noted that if the stock transfer form is presented for stamping more than 30 days after it is executed there may be a penalty for late stamping.

CONTACT POINT

SDRT Notices and payments, and requests for further information, should be sent to: Shares Unit, Ground Floor, East Block, Barrington Road, Worthing BN12 4SE. Telephone: 01903 509467/471.

INLAND REVENUE TAX BULLETIN: ISSUE 43—OCTOBER 1999

STAMP DUTY RESERVE TAX: CHANGES TO INTEREST RATES; PENALTIES FOR FAILURE TO NOTIFY LIABILITY; INTERACTION WITH STAMP DUTY

This article notes the changes to the arrangements for interest on late paid and overpaid SDRT from 1 October (announced in a Press Release of 10 September 1999), describes a modification to the practice about penalties for late notifications of SDRT (set out in an article in the October 1998 edition of Tax Bulletin, page 589) and highlights some points on the interaction of SDRT with Stamp Duty from 1 October.

Background

Broadly speaking, SDRT is charged on agreements to transfer shares where no stock transfer form is used (and accordingly no Stamp Duty is paid). Most SDRT arises on transfers of dematerialised shares held in CREST, where the SDRT concerned is accounted for centrally through CREST. But not all securities are able to be held in CREST and so SDRT also arises in a variety of other situations.

In such cases, the accountable person has to give written notice of each charge to SDRT, and to pay the SDRT due, on or before the accountable date. Where the shares are purchased on an exchange the accountable person will generally be one of the brokers involved in the transaction. Otherwise the purchaser is accountable.

The accountable date is the seventh day of the month following the month in which the trade date of the transaction occurred. Interest is charged from the accountable date on any SDRT paid late. Late notices may also attract penalties. The level of penalties depends on how late the notice is provided.

More detailed background information was contained in the earlier article.

Changes to SDRT interest rates from 1 October 1999

Before 1 October the rates of interest charged on late paid SDRT and paid on SDRT repayments were the same. But from 1 October, as with other taxes, the interest rates will differ. The rates for SDRT (and for Stamp Duty) will be the same as those for income tax. Details of these changes can be obtained from leaflets issued by the Stamp Office, obtainable from the Stamp Office helpline, 0845 6030135 or on the Inland Revenue website.

Penalties for failure to notify SDRT liability on time

As set out in the previous article, the rules depend on whether a late notice is provided within a year of the accountable date, or after a longer period. No changes are being made to the practice regarding notices given more than one year after the accountable date, which remains as set out in the previous article.

In the light of the changes to interest rates, and a review of the first year of operation of the practice on penalties in the previous article, the practice in the case of notices provided within a year of the accountable date is being modified in the case of multiple late notices made by an accountable person. This article sets out the revised position, which will apply in relation to notifications relating to transactions for which the accountable date was on or after 1 October 1999.

Section 93(2) TMA 1970 (as applied to SDRT by SI 1986/1711) states that each failure to give timely notification will incur a penalty of £100; that is to say that each transaction which is accounted for to the Stamp Office after the accountable date may attract a potential penalty of £100. While composite monthly notifications by an accountable person are administratively convenient, a late notice covering, say, 10 transactions is potentially liable to 10 penalties of £100. The amount of the penalty in relation to each individual transaction is in practice limited so that it does not exceed the SDRT due on the transaction concerned.

From 1 October, to coincide with the introduction of a fully up to date interest rate regime, where there is a composite notice relating to a number of transactions in a single month, the Stamp Office will normally only seek a single £100 penalty charge, provided that the accountable person takes steps to eliminate sources of recurrent error. So, if a composite notice relating to 3 transactions in one month and 4 transactions in the next month is sent in after the accountable date for the second month, the penalty would normally be £200 rather than £700.

If the total SDRT relating to the transactions in a single month is less than £100, then the lesser figure would be used, in keeping with the existing practice. So if in the example above the 3 transactions in the first month involved an aggregate amount of £50 SDRT, and the 4 transactions in the second month involved over £100 then the penalty would be £150 rather than £200.

Interaction with Stamp Duty

Where a stock transfer form relating to residual securities (securities that cannot be settled in CREST) is stamped within 60 days of the date of the transaction, it remains the case that the Stamp Office will not seek interest on the SDRT in the meantime and no notice need be given. However, should a stock transfer form not in fact be duly stamped within this time then interest on the unpaid SDRT will still run from the accountable date. In addition, if a notice was not delivered by that date the penalties described above will apply.

It should be noted here, and more generally, that if a stock transfer form is presented for stamping more than 30 days after it is executed, and the duty is paid late, then interest will run on the Stamp Duty and there may be a penalty for late stamping.

The introduction of interest on Stamp Duty from 1 October, in parallel to the changes to SDRT also means that the procedures described in paragraphs 1.13 of the (February 1998) SDRT Guidance Notes no longer apply either in 'wait and see' cases or where a document has been presented for an adjudicated relief. In future the question of SDRT will only be raised where difficulty is experienced in securing the stamping of the document.

PRIVATE FINANCE INITIATIVE PROJECTS: STAMP DUTY

Introduction

This article considers the correct Stamp Duty treatment of the documents likely to be encountered in a typical PFI scheme.

This article has been written following detailed consultation between Inland Revenue Head Office technical specialists and representatives from various parties advising public and private sector bodies. Background information about this working group is in the article on page 642 of the April 1999 edition of Tax Bulletin.

As indicated in that earlier article, PFI transactions are by their very nature complex. So it is important to emphasise that the Stamp Duty position in any particular case will depend on an analysis of the form of the particular documents to ascertain their true legal effect, and that what follows is based on straightforward situations and is necessarily only intended to give general advice. At the end of the day, the treatment of a particular transaction will always depend on its own particular facts.

Background—a typical transaction

In a typical PFI transaction, a public sector entity, e.g. an NHS trust, agrees to acquire services. Typically a specially formed private sector company agrees to carry out the project and supply the services. The public sector body is referred to as "Purchaser". The private sector supplier is referred to as "Operator".

The main documents will normally be:

(a) an outright transfer ("Project Land Transfer"), or head lease at a peppercorn rent ("Project Land Head Lease"), of the project site and buildings from the Purchaser to the Operator;
(b) a leaseback ("Project Land Lease") of the project site and buildings from the Operator to the Purchaser. Again, this lease is normally at a peppercorn rent;
(c) if the Purchaser has identified surplus land which it owns and can contribute to assist the economics of the project, a transfer of such surplus land by the Purchaser to the Operator ("Surplus Land Transfer");
(d) a master agreement ("Project Agreement"):
    - providing for the making of the above transfers or leases;
    - regulating the provision of all of the services which the Operator is to supply; and
    - providing for the Purchaser to make periodic payments, called the "Unitary Charge", to the Operator in return for the facilities and services under the project.

Transfer or lease of the project land

In these transactions, the consideration for the transfer of the project site under the Project Land Transfer, or for the grant of the Project Land Head Lease may well be, or include, the undertaking by the Operator to carry out building or refurbishment works on the Project Land.

If such an undertaking were the only consideration, no ad valorem duty would be chargeable, as (in particular) a contract to carry out works is not "consideration [which] consists of property" for the purpose of section 241 FA 1994. So the Project Land Transfer or Head Lease would only attract fixed duty.

Section 241 FA 1994 charges ad valorem duty on a transfer of land or the grant of a lease in exchange for any property (alone or with other consideration). So a charge under that section would arise if the Operator's grant of the leaseback to the Purchaser, the Project Land Lease, represented part or all of the consideration for the Project Land Transfer or Head Lease.

The article in the August 1995 edition of Tax Bulletin (paragraph 16, page 234) described the situation where, in the case of a sale and leaseback, there is a contract of sale for a price and a separate agreement for lease (rather than the leaseback forming part of the consideration given for the sale, in effect by way of exchange). In such situations the sale is liable to duty by reference to the price, and the leaseback is charged by reference to any premium and rent.

It is quite possible that transactions which this article considers may fall to be treated in this way. For example, if the various documents:

- clearly identify the only consideration as the Operator's undertaking to carry out the building works; and
- do not describe the grant of the Project Land Lease as the consideration for the Project Land Transfer or Head Lease

the Stamp Office would normally expect to charge the Project Land Transfer or Head Lease only to fixed duty.

The project land lease

Exemptions from ad valorem Stamp Duty exist for leases in favour of ministers of the Crown, the Treasury Solicitor, NHS Trusts and charities. However, where a PFI transaction involves other types of body, notably local authorities, the liability arising on such documents falls to be considered.

The Project Land Lease is likely to be expressed to be at a peppercorn rent. And so in normal circumstances, in accordance with long standing practice, only fixed duty would apply. But, as with leases generally, it is possible that in some cases another amount (here, potentially a part of the unitary charge) should also be properly regarded as forming part of the rent for Stamp Duty purposes, if that is the true legal effect of the transaction.

If, in a case where the position is doubtful, a Project Land Lease is presented for stamping on the basis of a rational apportionment of the expected unitary charge between the part to be regarded as rent and the part to be regarded as relating to services, the Stamp Office would normally expect to accept the taxpayer's approach.

It should be noted that the position for Schedule A purposes (set out in the next article) is not the same as that for Stamp Duty.

Surplus land transfers

A Surplus Land Transfer, by the Purchaser to the private sector Operator, will normally be made without immediate monetary consideration. The following points of interest arise:

(a) however, should there be some immediate monetary consideration, it would attract ad valorem duty. This may, for example, arise where the Purchaser has waived exemption from VAT in relation to the surplus land in question, and the Operator makes a payment of VAT on the transfer.

(b) a charge to ad valorem duty under section 241 FA 1994 will not normally arise on the basis that there is an exchange, unless the documentation describes the grant of the Project Land Lease as consideration for the Surplus Land Transfer, or describes the Surplus Land Transfer as consideration for the grant of the Project Land Lease.

(c) in general, the transfer of the surplus land will be described as made in one of three ways:
- by way of a contribution to the Operator's cost of carrying out the project works; or
- in satisfaction of a specific monetary amount of the future unitary charge; or
- in consideration of the Operator agreeing to accept a lower level of unitary charge than it would otherwise have done.

Various matters arise from the situations described in (*c*) above.

(1) Where the surplus land is transferred as a contribution towards expenses of the Operator on the building works, and there is no other consideration, the Surplus Land Transfer will only attract a fixed duty. This is because the Operator's agreement to execute the building works is not "property" for the purposes of section 241 FA 1994. Where there is other consideration, of course, it may, depending on the facts, attract duty.

(2) If the Surplus Land Transfer is made in satisfaction of an amount of the future unitary charge, or in consideration of the Operator agreeing to accept a lower level of unitary charge than it would otherwise have done, it will not normally attract ad valorem duty. Section 57, SA 1891 does charge duty on conveyances

made in satisfaction of a debt, but it only applies where the debt is due or accruing due at the date of execution. Normally that will not be the case in the type of transaction which the article considers.

(3) Where surplus land is transferred under the type of arrangements described above, the project documentation will normally contain rules about what is to happen if the Operator later re-sells the land at a profit. Sometimes, the Operator will be required to pass back a proportion of the profit to the public sector Purchaser by way of a contingent price for the surplus land. In that case, for Stamp Duty purposes, the contingency principle applies. If the documents provide that a minimum or maximum additional amount may become payable, that amount will attract ad valorem duty. If an amount cannot be determined under the contingency principle, then ad valorem Stamp Duty will be payable on the market value of the surplus land, applying section 242 FA 1994.

(4) Sometimes, any profit on a resale is to be retained by the Operator but part or all of it is to be brought into the economics of the project. The amount in question may be treated:
  (i) as itself a contribution to the Operator's cost of carrying out the project, or
  (ii) as satisfying a specific future amount on account of the unitary charge.

In either case the principles set out earlier in this article should normally mean that there will be no charge to ad valorem duty.

Project agreement

The Project Agreement normally provides for all of the intended land transfers or leases. As an agreement for one or more leases, it will be liable to the same ad valorem Stamp Duty in respect of each such lease as if it were that lease itself, and it will be entitled to the same exemptions as the actual leases would have qualified for.

In the same way as for other documents, the Stamp Duty on a Project Agreement, as an agreement for lease, will attract interest, and may attract a penalty, if it is presented for stamping out of time. The time allowed for stamping the Project Agreement is 30 days from the date of execution unless it is presented with the granted lease when the 30 days start to run on the execution of the lease.

If the parties intended to stamp the Project Agreement and the related leases together, but the leases were not granted because a dispute had arisen, this would be a factor we would take into account in considering the mitigation of any penalty arising on stamping the agreement late.

Credit for Stamp Duty paid on a Project Agreement is allowed against the duty payable on a lease granted pursuant to that agreement—provided that the lease is in conformity with the project agreement or relates to substantially the same property and term. Exceptionally, there may be a major change of plan during the course of a PFI scheme. Where difficulties occur, especially where as a result of matters beyond the parties control, we would expect to apply this rule in a common sense way.

PRIVATE FINANCE INITIATIVE

This article addresses the appropriate schedule of charge of income arising from a PFI deal involving a lease of fully serviced accommodation. It reflects the Revenue's view of how such income should be assessed, and the consequential effects on loss relief available.

Schedule A or Schedule D

CASE I

General principles

1. Many PFI schemes will be structured in the form of a lease granted by the body commissioning the work—"the purchaser"—to "the service provider"—"the operator"—followed by a lease back from the operator to the purchaser. Where this happens—or similar arrangements are entered into under which the operator acquires an interest in or rights over land in the UK and derives sums from exploiting that interest—it will be necessary to consider whether all or any part of the payments made to the operator are chargeable under Schedule A. A similar problem was addressed in the previous article in relation to Stamp Duty. As foreshadowed there, the application of the legislation in Part I ICTA 1988 will not necessarily give the same result as Stamp Duty law and practice.

2. If the operator itself has an interest in land, and grants rights of occupation to the purchaser (normally by way of a sublease or licence to occupy), some part of the unitary charge will necessarily be attributable to the right of occupation, and hence assessable under Schedule A. This will be so even where the lease prescribes in terms a rent of a peppercorn, and even though payment of the unitary charge is contingent on performance by the operator of other services to specified standards. The Revenue would expect the part of the unitary charge payable for the right to occupy land to be calculated on a just and reasonable basis.

3. It will be a question of fact whether the "other services" referred to in the previous paragraph are sufficient to constitute a trade on first principles. If the operator is carrying on a trade, the Revenue will accept that it is a "trading company" for the purposes of consortium relief (section 413(3)(*c*) ICTA 1988) provided that trade is its sole or main activity. The test is what the company does. The mere fact that the Schedule A element of a unitary charge constitutes a significant proportion—or even exceeds 50%—of the total gross income will not **of itself** mean the company is not a trading company for the purposes of section 413(3)(*c*). The test is whether, as a matter of fact, the **main** activity of the company is trading.

4. If the operator retains the right to grant leases or licences to third parties in respect of part of the land or property in question, any sums received under such agreements will ordinarily be within Schedule A.

5. References above to payments made to or sums received by the operator do not include payments of interest for late settlement, payments under normal commercial indemnities or other non-recurring commercial payments. The tax treatment of such amounts will depend on their commercial character.

Group relief

6. In many PFI schemes the operator will be a consortium company (that is (*a*) a directly held company owned by the consortium members or (*b*) a company owned 90% by a consortium holding company as defined by section 413(3)(*b*)). Where losses arise in a consortium company, group relief will be available where the consortium company is a "trading company"—that is "*a company the business of which consists wholly or mainly in the carrying on of a trade*".

7. If a consortium company is a "trading company," any Schedule A losses (as from 1 April 1998) will be capable of being surrendered as consortium relief assuming that all the other relevant conditions are met.

8. In determining whether a consortium company is a "trading company", it will be necessary to establish what the company mainly does. If its main activity is the provision of services—and the provision of accommodation (and the generation of rental income) is ancillary to that—then the company will ordinarily be a trading company as defined by section 413(3)(*c*).

9. As discussed in paragraph 3, it will be a question of fact what a company's main activity is. It will be necessary to look not merely at the level of income generated by

each activity but to consider, for example, how the company's resources (e.g. management time, capital employed etc.) have been used.

10. There are PFI cases where a Revenue view on the schedule of charge has already been sought in accordance with the terms of Code of Practice 10, and where agreement has been given that the whole of the unitary charge is assessable as trading income. The Revenue will not seek to revisit the treatment of any such case.

INLAND REVENUE TAX BULLETIN: ISSUE 50—DECEMBER 2000
Limited Liability Partnerships

This article sets out the Revenue's views on how the members of a Limited Liability Partnership ("LLP"), regulated by the Limited Liability Partnership Act 2000 ("the LLP Act"), which carries on a trade or profession, will be taxed.

In this article the following expressions are used:

- "Ordinary Partnership" means a partnership within the meaning of the Partnership Act 1890.
- "Limited Partnership" means a partnership regulated by the Limited Partnership Act 1907.
- "Old Partnership" includes both an "ordinary" and a "limited partnership".

During the passage of the LLP Act, Ministers announced that the tax treatment would be reviewed for those LLPs used for businesses for which the LLP structure was not originally intended. Legislation would be brought forward in the Finance Bill 2001 after appropriate consultation. This review was prompted by concerns that some businesses, particularly investment businesses, could be motivated to adopt LLP structure for tax reasons rather than to obtain limited liability. Further details of the tax treatment of LLPs were announced by the Chancellor in his pre-Budget Report (PBR) on 8 November 2000. Details and an invitation to comment were given in the PBR Press Release—Inland Revenue 5. An announcement will be made in due course of the further changes to the tax treatment of LLPs (if any) which are required because of points raised during this consultation.

GENERAL

LLPs are in law regarded as "bodies corporate" and will be subject to aspects of company law. But for tax they will generally be treated as "partnerships". As mentioned above this guidance covers LLPs carrying on a trade or profession. It does not cover the detailed tax treatment of investment businesses for which the LLP structure was not originally intended.

Section 10 of the LLP Act ensures that where an LLP carries on a "business with a view of profit" the members will be treated for the purposes of income tax, corporation tax and capital gains tax as if they were partners carrying on business in partnership.

That is to say the LLP will be regarded as transparent for tax purposes and each member will be assessed to tax on their share of the LLPs income or gains. For members liable to income tax their share of the partnership's profits to be charged to tax will be calculated in accordance with the rules set out in section 111 ICTA 1988 and for those members liable to corporation tax in accordance with the rules set out in section 114 ICTA 1988.

This article deals with the UK tax treatment of LLPs formed under the LLP Act (i.e. UK LLPs as opposed to overseas LLPs). It would be for the tax authorities of other countries to decide how to tax UK LLPs under their own tax codes.

COMPUTATION OF TAXABLE PROFITS OF PROFESSIONAL BUSINESSES

In *Tax Bulletin*, Issue 38 (December 1998, page 606) the Revenue set out guidance on what is meant by "true and fair view" for the purposes of calculating the taxable profits of a professional business.

It is confirmed that those rules will apply equally to the computation of the Case II Schedule D profit of a LLP which carries on a professional business for the purposes of calculating the Income Tax liability of the members of the LLP.

CAPITAL ALLOWANCES

Where a LLP succeeds to a business previously carried on by an old partnership this will not of itself give rise to a balancing event for the purposes of the Capital Allowance provisions.

INTEREST RELIEF

Members of a LLP, who are individuals, will be entitled to claim interest relief on the loans they obtain in order to defray money applied in the circumstances set out in section 362(1) ICTA 1988; provided that they otherwise meet the conditions of the relief.

ESC A43 covers interest for investments in partnerships. Where an ordinary partnership converts to a LLP, the existing terms of the extra-statutory concession are not appropriate, to preserve existing relief. To rectify this we are currently considering what changes should be made to the text. (A 1907 limited partner would not have been entitled to such relief in the first place, so it would be inappropriate to extend ESC A43 to those circumstances.)

LOSS RELIEF

(a) Unlike section 117 ICTA, the undrawn profits of a member of a LLP cannot normally be added to their subscribed capital in order to calculate the limit of their entitlement to sideways loss relief. This is because, subject to any agreement between them, a member's undrawn profits will normally be regarded as a debt of the LLP. This means that the member ranks, for that sum, alongside the other creditors in the event of liquidation. If however the terms of the agreement between the members specifically provide that the undrawn profit stands as part of a member's capital contribution and that agreement is unconditional then that amount can be taken into account in calculating the limit.

(b) The following is an example of how the provisions of section 118C–D will apply: Mr A becomes a member of a LLP on 6 April 2003. He introduces capital of £10,000 into ed 5 April 2006 he makes a further capital contribution of £6,000. His share of the LLP's Case I loss is as follows and he claims relief under section 380 ICTA for those losses against his other income.

- Year 5 April 2004 £6,000
- Year 5 April 2005 £6,000
- Year 5 April 2006 £3,000

Mr A is entitled to section 380 relief as follows:

- 2003/2004 £6,000 (unrelieved capital contribution £4,000)
- 2004/2005 £4,000(1) (unrelieved loss £2,000)
- 2005/2006 £5,000(2) (unrelieved capital contribution £1,000)

(1) sideways loss relief is restricted to the unrelieved capital contribution brought forward of £4,000. The balance of the loss of £2,000 (£ 6,000—£4,000) is carried forward.

(2) sideways loss relief of £5,000 available i. e. loss of year £3000 + unrelieved loss brought forward £2,000. Unrelieved capital contribution carried forward is £1,000 i.e. total contributions £16,000 less total sideways loss relief given £15,000)

Where a member of a LLP makes a capital contribution to a partnership in order to meet a liability for negligence for which they are personally responsible then that amount will be taken into account in determining the amount of their capital contribution to the partnership for the purposes of section 118ZC ICTA. Provided that the conditions for relief are otherwise met then that partner will be entitled to relief up to a maximum of the amount of that additional contribution either under the normal sideways loss relief provisions, or under section 109A ICTA if he/she has left the partnership, or the partnership has ceased business.

(c) The provisions in section 118C-D ICTA (restriction of sideways loss relief to members of a LLP) do not apply to a LLP which carries on a profession; only to one which carries on a trade. Provided that the conditions for relief are otherwise met; a member of a LLP, which carries on a profession rather than a trade, will be entitled to loss relief, either under the normal sideways loss relief provisions, or under section 109 ICTA, if he/she has left the partnership, or the partnership has ceased business.

OVERLAP RELIEF

Where a partnership carries on a trade or profession each partner is deemed to carry on a personal trade or profession. The basis period rules are applied to that deemed trade or profession and any overlap profit is personal to each partner.

If, on conversion, a LLP succeeds to the business previously carried by an old partnership then a partner's personal trade or profession will be regarded as continuing. He/she will be entitled to a deduction for overlap relief at the time they finally retire from the LLP (or perhaps earlier if the LLP changes its accounting date).

DEMERGERS

Where a LLP takes over only part of the old partnership's trade, such an event constitutes a "demerger" to which Statement of Practice 9/86 applies. Unless it can be shown that on the demerger the part of the business carried on by the LLP is recognisably "the business" previously carried on by the old partnership then the cessation provisions will apply. In that event each member of the old partnership will be entitled to their personal overlap relief. Equally the commencement provisions will apply to all the members of the LLP.

But if it can be shown that the LLP does carry on "the business" previously carried on by the old partnership then, as it will have succeeded to the old partnership's business, the cessation provisions will not be applied to the old partnership and any overlap relief will be carried forward. Equally the commencement provisions will not be applied to the members of the LLP. But the old partnership will be assumed to have commenced a new business in relation to the part of the trade it retains.

Whether or not the business carried on by the LLP is recognisably "the business" previously carried on by the old partnership is a question of fact.

CASH BASIS—CATCHING UP CHARGE

Again if on conversion the LLP succeeds to the business previously carried on by an old partnership then the spreading rules for the catching up charge will continue to apply as if the conversion had not occurred.

CESSATION

Where a LLP succeeds to a business previously carried on by an old partnership this will not of itself involve the cessation of the old partnership's trade or profession.

TAX RETURNS

Where an old partnership incorporates as a LLP during an accounting period then if the partners so wish a single partnership return need only be made for the one tax year. They may do this even if the partnership changes its accounting date. Single PAYE returns may also be made for the tax year in which an old partnership incorporates as a LLP.

UK BRANCHES OF OVERSEAS LLP'S

The tax treatment of a UK branch of an overseas Limited Liability Partnership, and the members of such an LLP, will depend on how the foreign entity is regarded for the purposes of the UK taxation provisions. Where the foreign LLP is regarded as a "body corporate" for the purposes of the UK Taxes Acts the profits of the UK branch will be chargeable to corporation tax. On the other hand if it is regarded as a partnership then members will be separately liable to tax on their share of the branch's profits under the existing legislation for partnerships rather than under the LLP Act. The latter act only applies to UK registered LLPs.

DOUBLE TAXATION RELIEF

Where an overseas tax authority regards a foreign branch of a UK LLP as a "body corporate" the UK members will be entitled to claim Tax Credit Relief in respect of their proportionate share of the foreign tax paid on the overseas branch's profits.

DIVIDENDS

A UK LLP is not itself "liable to tax" in the UK as the LLP tax provisions identify other persons (i.e. the members) as the persons who are to be taxed. Accordingly for the purposes of the Double Taxation Agreements (DTA) the LLP it is not regarded as being resident in the UK and cannot itself therefore claim relief from foreign taxes under such Agreements. As is now the case with ordinary and limited partnerships the members must make the claim.

Assuming they are UK residents in accordance with the provisions of the relevant DTA the members of an LLP will be entitled to relief for any withholding tax on overseas dividends. Normally a DTA provides for withholding tax of a maximum of 15% to be deducted and relief for that tax will be given. Where a partner is an individual then no relief will be due in respect of the taxes paid (the underlying taxes) on the profits out of which the dividend is paid.

In the very narrow circumstances where the LLP is not treated as transparent, but instead as a body corporate for tax purposes (such as when the LLP is in liquidation or being wound up in circumstances where transparency cannot be retained in the manner explained below under "Capital Gains—Liquidation/Winding Up"), we can confirm the LLP could itself claim relief for foreign taxes, including if appropriate underlying tax.

PARTNERSHIP ANNUITIES

Where an obligation to pay an annuity is transferred from the old partnership to the LLP then the members of the LLP will be entitled to higher rate income tax relief for their share of the ongoing payments; and incoming LLP members who assume part of that obligation will also be entitled to such relief for their share.

If an obligation to pay an annuity is not transferred to the LLP and the members of the old partnership continue to pay it they will be entitled to higher rate income tax relief for their share of those payments until such time as they cease to be a member of the LLP or until the business originally carried on by the old partnership ceases, whichever is the earlier.

CAPITAL GAINS

Partners capital interests

So long as the LLP carries on a trade or profession with a view to profit a partner's capital interest as a member of a LLP will not be regarded as a chargeable asset in its own right. In these circumstances the members of the LLP will be directly taxable on their share of the chargeable gains arising on the disposal of the LLP's assets and there will be no concurrent charge on a non-transparent basis.

Temporary cessation of trading

The transparency of a LLP, for capital gains purposes, is not disturbed by reason of temporary periods of time during which no trade or profession is carried on by it. For example, if the LLP ceases to carry on one business and disposes of its assets in order to realise funds to commence another business then those asset disposals, and any gains or losses arising in consequence, will be treated as those of the members.

Transfer of a business to a LLP

Where a business, previously carried on by an old partnership, is transferred to a LLP then, for the purposes of the Capital Gains legislation, this will not of itself constitute a disposal by the partners in their interests in the old partnership's assets. This applies equally to the members of partnerships in Scotland as it does to those in England and Wales.

Furthermore such a transfer will not affect:

- the availability of indexation allowance;
- the ownership period for retirement relief;
- the holding period for taper relief.

Application of Statement of Practice D12

The rules set out in Statement of Practice D12 apply equally to the members of a LLP as they do to members of an old partnership. When D12 is next updated it will be amended to incorporate this confirmation.

LIQUIDATION/WINDING UP

Liquidations

Where a LLP ceases to carry on a trade or profession then it will no longer be regarded as a "partnership" for the purposes of the taxation provisions and will instead be regarded as a "body corporate". The LLP will thus cease to be transparent (section 59A(2) TCGA).

Where a LLP goes into liquidation, chargeable gains on the disposal of the LLP's assets by the liquidator will be computed by reference to the date on which they were first acquired by the LLP and their cost at that date. In the liquidation period, the LLP's capital gains will be treated in precisely the same way for tax purposes as those for any other body corporate (section 8(6) TCGA).

LLP members will be taxed on any gain (or given relief for any loss) that arises on the disposal of their capital interests in the LLP. The base cost of a partner's capital interest is not equal to the market value of that interest at the time when transparency is lost. The allowable acquisition cost of each partner's interest will be determined according to the historical capital contributions made as if the LLP had never been transparent. This treatment does not affect preliquidation asset disposals, which remain undisturbed.

Informal winding up

Where the members of a LLP proceed to wind up its affairs in an orderly way, without the formal appointment of a liquidator, by settling outstanding liabilities and realising the assets following or in the course of a cessation of commercial activity, then it will be accepted that the transparency of the LLP will be preserved during the period in which the assets are being disposed of provided the conditions set out below are met.

Those conditions are:

- that the LLP is not being wound up for reasons connected in whole or in part with the avoidance of tax; and
- that, following the termination of the LLP's business, the period of winding up is not unduly protracted taking account of the LLP's assets and liabilities.

If these conditions are not met, then the transparency of the LLP may be regarded as coming to an end before the informal winding up process has been completed. It is also emphasised that, whatever the circumstances, transparency cannot continue beyond any date on which a liquidator is formally appointed (whether or not that liquidator is charged for a period with completing any outstanding business transactions).

CGT ROLL-OVER RELIEF

Where, as a result of claiming business asset roll-over relief (sections 152–154 TCGA 1992) a LLP member postpones a chargeable gain through their acquisition of a share in a LLP asset, there is the potential for that gain to fall out of charge in the future by reason of the LLP ceasing to be transparent. This could occur, for example, where the LLP asset remains unsold when the LLP goes into liquidation and vests in the liquidator (who will compute the gain arising on the disposal of the asset in the course of liquidation without regard to past roll-over relief claims by any LLP member). Accordingly, there is a tax liability on the member, at the point in time when the LLP ceases to be transparent, which is based on an amount equal to the postponed gain or gains which have not then come back into charge (section 156A TCGA 1992). Gains which accrue to a member in consequence of this special provision do not attract taper relief.

Annuities

Provided that the rights remain substantially the same then:

- the transfer of a partner's annuity rights and/or
- the transfer of annuity obligations to former members

- from an ordinary partnership to a LLP will not be regarded as a chargeable disposal.

Similarly where an annuitant agrees to the substitution of the LLP for the predecessor partnership as the payer of the annuity, and the terms otherwise remain substantially the same, then the annuitant will not be regarded as making a chargeable disposal.

INHERITANCE TAX

Business property relief and agricultural property relief

Where an old partnership incorporates as a LLP a partner's period of ownership for both reliefs will not be regarded as being interrupted.

Deemed transfers by close companies

Because section 267A(d) IHTA 1984, inserted by section 11 of the LLP Act, deems transfers of value to be made by the members of the LLP and not by the LLP itself, liability under section 94 IHTA 1984 cannot arise even if the LLP might otherwise be a close company.

Availability of reliefs

The normal reliefs and exemptions available to partners in an old partnership will equally be available to members of a LLP. In particular section 10 IHTA 1984, which provides an exemption for dispositions not intended to confer gratuitous benefit, will apply.

Stamp Duty

Transfer of property to a LLP

Section 12 of the LLP Act requires that for the Stamp Duty exemption to apply the proportions of property conveyed or transferred into a LLP must either be unchanged "before" and "after" the transfer, or the proportions must not have been changed for tax avoidance reasons. Strictly under property law the partners' interest in the LLP will replace their interests in the old partnership's assets. In determining whether the Stamp Duty exemption applies the Revenue will not, however take this point.

The Revenue will accept that any property transferred to the LLP within one year of its incorporation will qualify for relief from Stamp Duty under section 12 of the LLP Act, provided that the conditions for that relief are met.

Section 12(2) of the LLP Act prevents Stamp Duty exemption being available if property is transferred at the time of the LLP's incorporation and also there are retirements of former partners and/or admission of new partners to the LLP.

Provided that all the other conditions for the exemption are met the Revenue accepts that this charge can be averted by arranging matters so that the change of partners takes place the instant before or after incorporation. To confirm that matters were organised in this way the Stamp Office will need to see all associated documents effecting any change in the membership of the old partnership and of the LLP prior to and/or after incorporation, as well as evidence that any Stamp Duty appropriate to those documents has been paid. It may be necessary to call for further information once these documents have been reviewed.

Transfers of interests in a LLP

An interest in a LLP is not a chargeable security for Stamp Duty purposes. So if Stamp Duty is due on the transfer of such an interest it will be payable at the 1%, 3% or 4% rate, as appropriate, rather than the 0.5% rate applicable to shares. This is in line with the intention behind the LLP Act that the treatment of LLPs should be the same as for partnerships. Since the sale of an interest in any other type of partnership bears duty at the property rates, the sale of an interest in a LLP will be charged in the same way.

General

As with all transactions potentially liable to Stamp Duty, the Technical Services Unit Manager at any Stamp Office will be happy to assist customers in connection with any enquiries regarding the operation of the Stamp Duty relief in the Act.

National Insurance Contributions

The National Insurance Contributions (NICs) position of members of a LLP is the same as that of partners in an ordinary partnership. Thus the members of a LLP will be liable to Class 2, Class 3 and Class 4 NICs as appropriate.

INLAND REVENUE TAX BULLETIN: ISSUE 70—APRIL 2004
Stamp Duty Land Tax: Group Relief

1. This article gives practical and technical guidance on claims for group relief in Stamp Duty Land Tax under Schedule 7 to the Finance Act 2003. It deals with material which was previously covered by the Statement of Practice issued for stamp duty group relief, SP3/98 published on 13 October 1998. That Statement does not apply to Stamp Duty Land Tax but will continue to apply to stamp duty.

HOW TO CLAIM GROUP RELIEF IN STAMP DUTY LAND TAX

2. In contrast to stamp duty, documents must not be submitted with a claim. The claim should be made on form SDLT1 by putting a cross at box 9 and inserting code 12.

3. Following procedures for other returns within Stamp Duty Land Tax, the certificate that enables title to be registered will be issued provided that the return is complete. Certificates will not be delayed simply because the Inland Revenue may wish to enquire into particular aspects of the return including a claim to group relief.

4. The relief is self-assessed and will be dealt with on a process now/check later' basis along with all other Stamp Duty Land Tax matters. Under Stamp Duty Land Tax the Inland Revenue does not require the preparation and submission of the letter of claim covered in (see paragraph 6.641 of the Inland Revenue Stamp Taxes manual).

5. This means that companies must judge the admissibility of the claim themselves. Under Stamp Duty Land Tax the Inland Revenue has the power to assess and collect under-declared tax and seek penalties in cases where errors in returns (including errors in group relief claims) are the result of negligence or fraud.

ENQUIRIES INVOLVING GROUP RELIEF CLAIMS

6. If the decision is taken to enquire into a return where the transaction is subject to a group relief claim, the Inland Revenue will open an enquiry under paragraph 12 of Schedule 10 FA 2003. The enquiry must be made within 9 months of the filing date. Enquiries may cover all aspects of the return and will not necessarily be limited to the group relief claim itself.

7. The decision to enquire into a transaction will be made after the certificate (form SDLT5) is issued and will not therefore delay registration of title. But the issue of the

certificate should not be taken as an indication that the Inland Revenue either accepts the validity of a group relief claim or has chosen not to enquire into that return.

8. Enquiries will consider all aspects of the transaction, including the group relief claim. Documents may be called for and these may include the instruments of transfer and related documents. The Inland Revenue may also ask for more information about the claim. In particular, evidence may be sought to show that the tests in paragraphs 1 and 2 of Schedule 7 were met.

9. If the evidence presented does not support the claim the self assessment will be amended to remove the relief.

PARAGRAPH 1 OF SCHEDULE 7

10. Paragraph 1 of Schedule 7 to FA 2003 provides exemption from Stamp Duty Land Tax where, at the effective date of the transaction, the companies are members of the same group. Exemption extends to the grant of leases between group companies.

Meaning of company

11. Relief is extended to any "body corporate" through the definition of "company" in section 100(1) FA 2003. To determine whether an entity qualifies as a body corporate the Inland Revenue will follow the guidelines for stamp duty set out at paragraph 6.124 of the Stamp Taxes Manual.

Meaning of subsidiary

12. Paragraph 1(2)(b) requires that the companies claiming relief must be 75% subsidiaries of one another or 75% subsidiaries of a third company.

13. Paragraph 1(3) provides that for a company (A) to be a 75% subsidiary of another company (B) if:

- company B is the beneficial owner of at least 75% of the ordinary share capital of company A;
- it is beneficially entitled to not less than 75% of profits available for distribution to equity holders; and
- it would be entitled to not less than 75% of any assets of A available for distribution to equity holders on winding up.

14. Paragraph 1(4) provides that "ownership" for these purposes is either directly or indirectly through another company or group of companies. The rules in section 838(5) to (10) ICTA 1988 apply to determine the amount of ordinary share capital. Paragraph 1(5) defines "ordinary share capital".

15. Paragraph 1(6) applies Schedule 18 ICTA 1988 which defines "equity holder".

16. The meaning of subsidiary is also relevant to the arrangements test in paragraph 2(2)(b) of Schedule 7 (see 19 below).

17. The tests in paragraph 1 of Schedule 7 apply independently of the tests in paragraph 2 and claims are not allowable if these tests are not met.

PARAGRAPH 2 OF SCHEDULE 7

18. Paragraph 2 provides anti-avoidance rules which restrict the availability of group relief. It will prevent relief being allowable in circumstances where certain "arrangements" are in place.

Meaning of arrangements

19. "Arrangements is defined generally for the purposes of paragraph 2 in paragraph 2(5) to include any scheme, arrangement or understanding, whether or not legally enforceable". This definition is used in section 76(6A)(b) FA 1986 (inserted by section 112(6) FA 2002) but "arrangements" was not defined for the equivalent stamp duty provisions in section 42(2) FA 1930 or section 27(2) FA 1967. Under this new definition, "arrangements" will include schemes, arrangements or understandings not in writing and the existence of arrangements in a particular claim will depend on a consideration of all of the facts relating to the claim and the surrounding circumstances.

20. In considering whether arrangements exist that might disqualify the claim, the Inland Revenue will seek to establish whether there was any scheme arrangement or understanding.

Paragraph 2(1): Arrangements for change of control of purchaser

21. Paragraph 2(1) prevents a claim to group relief if arrangements are in existence at the time of the claim for a person (or persons together) to obtain control of the purchaser but not the vendor. Arrangements under paragraph 2(1) have to be in existence at the effective date of the transaction.

22. Where there is a change of control, paragraph 2(1) is intended to prevent avoidance of Stamp Duty Land Tax by passing property, or an economic interest in it, out of the group.

23. The statements of the Economic Secretary during debate in Parliament on the equivalent stamp duty provision in Finance Act 2000 are still relevant. The Economic Secretary said:

> I have received representations expressing concern about the blocking of relief for transfers from the company about to leave the group to another group member — in other words, when the company leaving the group is the transferor I am persuaded that there are commercial situations in which an asset is transferred to another group company after arrangements are in place for the transferor company to leave the group. In a sense, therefore, the asset never leaves the original group. I am willing to make a concession for such cases, which will be useful to businesses, as their legal advisers have suggested.
>
> I have some worry that it might be possible to construct avoidance devices from the concession, so I have asked the Stamp Office to monitor carefully the use of the relief. If the concession is abused, the Govemment will not hesitate to act swiftly.

(see Hansard 18 July 2000, column 253)

24. The Inland Revenue will not argue that paragraph 2(1) denies group relief in cases where the transferor is to leave the group having transferred the land to other group members.

25. Furthermore, paragraph 2(1) does not apply if the arrangements that are in place are those for the acquisition of shares by a company under a reconstruction as long as the conditions in paragraph 2(1)(a), (b) and (c) are met. These are:

- that section 75 FA 1986 will apply to the acquisition and the conditions for relief under that section will be met;
- that after the acquisition the purchaser will be a member of the same group as the acquiring company.

Paragraph 2(2) of Schedule 7

26. Paragraph 2(2)(a) denies relief where there are arrangements under which consideration is to be provided or received (directly or indirectly) by a person other than a group company.

27. Where group relief is claimed the Inland Revenue will consider all of the facts and interpret paragraph 2(2)(a) as not denying relief unless the loan finance is provided as part of a scheme to save Stamp Duty Land Tax when the property or an interest in it leaves the group.

28. For example, it is unlikely that there will be arrangements within paragraph 2(2)(a) if:

- the claim is not to be followed by a sale or underlease outside the group; or
- the claim is followed by a sale or underlease outside the group but Stamp Duty Land Tax is to be paid by the purchaser outside the group on consideration close to market value (or is deemed to be a grant of a lease under paragraph 11 of Schedule 17A FA 2003), then again it is unlikely that relief will be prevented by paragraph 2(2)(a).

29. Loans from commercial lenders on ordinary commercial terms to facilitate the transfer between group members will also not normally disqualify a claim for the purposes of the arrangements test in paragraph 2(2)(a). For example, a claim can be accepted if:

- a specific loan is taken for the purchase of the asset; or
- the loan is secured on the asset; or
- arrangements are made to replace or novate an existing charge on the property transferred.

30. Paragraphs 27 to 29 above are limited to paragraph 2(2)(a) of Schedule 7. They do not mean that if other tests in paragraphs 1 and 2 of Schedule 7 are not met the claim is acceptable.

31. When an enquiry is opened the case will be considered on their particular facts. Some examples of the type of circumstances which the Inland Revenue might want to examine in more detail during an enquiry are where the claim is part of (or is to be followed by):

- the creation or transfer of loan stock or equity capital;
- a capital reorganisation of the transferee;
- a guarantee by a third party not associated with the group;
- the creation of a new charge or financial arrangement whereby title to the property is, or may be, vested in the lender otherwise than in satisfaction of all or part of the debt; or
- the assignment of the freehold reversion or the intra-group lease to a person outside the group.

32. Other circumstances which can indicate that the claim is not admissible include where:

- all or part of the consideration for the transaction is to remain outstanding or is represented by intra-group debt, (as the aim and effect may be to reduce the value of the transferee company on a possible future sale outside the group); or
- the existing shareholders of the transferee include shareholders outside the group and the transaction is to be followed by the declaration of a dividend in specie, or by the liquidation of the transferee.

Subsales and group relief in Stamp Duty Land Tax

33. Paragraph 2(2) provides rules for Stamp Duty Land Tax based on those for stamp duty in section 27(3) FA 1967. Section 27(3)(b) FA 1967 (intended to prevent acquisitions of land from outside the group without stamp duty being paid) is not included in Schedule 7 and this is because the problem it seeks to address, resting on contracts, is not relevant to Stamp Duty Land Tax. It is not possible to "rest on contract" to avoid Stamp Duty Land Tax because of the "substantial" performance rule in section 44 FA 2003.

Paragraph 2(2)(b): arrangements for the purchaser to cease to be a member of the same group

34. A claim for relief is not appropriate if there are arrangements for the purchaser to cease to be a 75% subsidiary of the vendor or a third company. In deciding whether there are any such arrangements, the practical likelihood of the scheme being carried through is not in itself relevant.

35. But the Inland Revenue will not take the view that just because land is transferred to a group company which does nothing other than hold property it follows that there are arrangements for the purchaser to leave the group. We recognise that there are many commercial reasons why groups may transfer property internally. It is necessary to consider the full circumstances of the case to decide whether such arrangements are in place.

36. Whether such arrangements were or were not in place must be decided at the time of the return and Inland Revenue enquiries will seek to establish the facts at the effective date of the transaction.

RELEVANCE OF ARRANGEMENTS UNDER PARAGRAPH 2 TO A RECOVERY OF TAX UNDER PARAGRAPH 3 ("CLAWBACK")

37. Paragraph 3 of Schedule 7 is independent of paragraph 2. When an enquiry is made into a claim the question will be the admissibility of the claim itself in accordance with the statutory provisions. The fact that the arrangements, if carried out as planned, could lead to a recovery or will be exempt from a recovery will not mean that claim itself is allowable except as provided in paragraph 2.

Paragraph 3(1)(a)(ii): Arrangements during the three year recovery period

38. Paragraph 3 imposes a requirement to make a return (under section 81 FA 2003) for the withdrawal of relief when the purchaser ceases to be a member of the same group within three years of the effective date of the transaction.

39. Paragraph 3(1)(a) deals with the recovery period. Paragraph 3(1)(a)(ii) provides that group relief will be recovered if the transfer outside the group after the end of the period is under arrangements made before the end of the period.

40. "Arrangements" is defined in paragraph 3(4) with the same definition as in paragraph 2.

41. When there is a transfer outside the group, companies will need to decide whether to make a return under section 81. If the transfer outside the group is after the end of the three year period, companies will still need to consider whether there were arrangements in place for the transfer during the three year period. To make this decision a proper consideration of all of the circumstances will be required.

42. The Inland Revenue will not assume that just because a company is transferred outside the group shortly after the end of the three year period it will be in accordance with arrangements made within the three year period. We will only seek to argue that there should have been a recovery return if the facts of the case point to there having been such arrangements.

SECTION 54(4) FA 2003: EXCEPTION FROM THE CONNECTED COMPANY CHARGE ON A WINDING UP

43. Section 54(4) FA 2003 provides the third case of exception from the deemed market value rule in section 53 FA 2003. The exception applies to the distribution of assets on the winding up of a company, as long as the subject matter of the transaction or an interest from which that interest is derived, has been the subject of a transaction in respect of which a claim to group relief was made by the vendor. But it is not the Inland Revenue's intention that section 54(4) should apply where a group relief claim was made by the vendor but recovered under paragraph 3 of Schedule 7 either at the time of or before the effective date of the transaction.

HMRC TAX BULLETIN: ISSUE 83—JUNE 2006

CAPITAL GAINS TAX: TREATMENT OF GOODWILL IN FRANCHISED BUSINESSES

We have been asked by a number of professional advisers whether our views on the treatment of goodwill in a franchised business have changed following the Special Commissioner's decision in the case of Balloon Promotions Ltd and Others. The following commentary summarises the salient facts and sets out our views on the implications of the decision. As the Commissioner's conclusions were based on findings of fact we do not consider that the decision is of general application to other cases involving the sale of franchised businesses.

Decision of Special Commissioner (SpC524) 3 March 2006: Balloon Promotions Limited (Appellant 1) and Alonso Vela-Castro, Edward Kidney and Natale Lucibello (Appellant 2) v Wilson and Rodin

Roll-over relief and goodwill

Briefly, the facts were that the appellants were members of partnerships whose Pizza Express franchised restaurants were acquired by Pizza Express (Restaurants) Ltd for the purpose of operating them in-house. Pizza Express (Restaurants) Ltd entered into contracts with the partnerships for the purchase of the businesses and termination of the Franchise Agreements. The purchase price was allocated mainly to goodwill with only a nominal amount for the termination of the Franchise Agreements. In addition, the directors/shareholders of Balloon Promotions Ltd and Messrs Vela-Castro, Kidney and Lucibello received payments for entering into restrictive covenants that prevented them from operating pizza restaurants for certain periods of time and in certain locations.

The appellants claimed roll-over relief under s 152 TCGA 1992 in respect of the chargeable gains arising on the sale of goodwill. HMRC refused the claims on the grounds that the proceeds for the sale of goodwill were, in fact, payments of compensation for the termination of the Franchise Agreements.

The Special Commissioner accepted that HMRC had the legal authority to re-apportion the sale consideration on a just and reasonable basis pursuant to s 52(4) TCGA 1992 if the appellants had erred in law in their apportionment. Furthermore, he concluded that the contention of Messrs Vela-Castro, Kidney and Lucibello that HMRC had no lawful authority to re-apportion the sale consideration after the issue of a s 28 TMA 1970 Completion Notice was without foundation. HMRC's apportionment under s 52(4) TCGA 1992 did not affect the amended self-assessments and did not open new lines of enquiry.

The Special Commissioner held that the question of whether a franchisee owns goodwill is determined principally by an examination of facts and not solely by principles of law. He was satisfied on the evidence put before him that the appellants enjoyed considerable discretion in the operation of their restaurants and did not work to a prescribed business format. He found that Pizza Express was not a well-known brand until after 1994 and that each of its franchised restaurants was unique in design rather than part of a chain of outlets based on a set "get up". He concluded that Pizza Express was a "soft" brand and that it was the appellants who had established the reputation of their restaurants by the standards of customer service they provided. The Special Commissioner held that the consideration allocated to goodwill in the sale agreements was correctly described as goodwill within the context of TCGA 1992 and that the goodwill in question was attached to the appellants' businesses rather than to the Pizza Express brand.

The appellants' appeals were allowed in principle.

In reaching his decision the Special Commissioner took account of evidence that came to light during the hearing that the Franchise Agreements for the partnerships between Messrs Vela-Castro, Kidney and Lucibello were subject to termination on six months' notice by either party. In view of that evidence HMRC conceded that the rights associated with the Franchise Agreements were of minimal value.

We do not intend to lodge an appeal in the High Court.

We accept the finding of the Special Commissioner that the question of whether a franchisee owns goodwill is principally a question of fact. Where a franchised business is disposed of as a going concern the question of whether there has been a disposal of goodwill will be determined in the light of the relevant facts. These will include a detailed consideration of the terms of the franchise agreement, the extent of control exercised by the franchisor and the terms and conditions relating to the sale. Therefore, we do not consider that the decision in these appeals is of general application to other cases involving the sale of franchised businesses.

Our opinion that a franchisee's rights under a franchise agreement are an asset within the meaning of s 21(1) TCGA1992 and that they are not part of goodwill is unchanged. However, we do accept that a franchisee may be able to generate some goodwill in a franchised business. The values of franchise rights and goodwill will depend upon the precise facts of each individual case and, in particular, the level of control exercised by the franchisor.

HMRC agrees with the Special Commissioner's conclusion that, for the purposes of TCGA 1992, the term "goodwill" must be construed in accordance with the principles established by the legal authorities on goodwill and that the accountancy definition is deficient for the purposes of construing its meaning in that context.

In reaching his conclusion the Special Commissioner questioned the approach adopted by HMRC of restricting roll-over relief to specific categories of goodwill. He indicated that he considered that goodwill should be looked at as a whole to include whatever adds value to a business by reason of situation, name and reputation, connection, introduction to old customers and absence from competition. We do not accept that the term "goodwill" in TCGA 1992 embraces all of the various types of goodwill described in the CG Manual. We will continue to treat inherent and adherent goodwill as part of an asset in the form of a freehold or leasehold interest in land or buildings.

We are hoping to be in a position shortly to publish an updated version of the goodwill guidance in the CG Manual.

FOREIGN ENTITIES: CLASSIFICATION FOR UK TAX PURPOSES

This Tax Bulletin updates and supersedes Tax Bulletins 39 and 50.

When considering the classification of a foreign entity (i.e. whether it is either opaque or transparent) for UK tax purposes, due regard is given to the approach of the Court of Appeal in the case of Memec plc v CIR (70 TC 77) and the line of case law that precedes it. In particular, the following matters should be considered:

(a) Does the foreign entity have a legal existence separate from that of the persons who have an interest in it?
(b) Does the entity issue share capital or something else, which serves the same function as share capital?
(c) Is the business carried on by the entity itself or jointly by the persons who have an interest in it that is separate and distinct from the entity?
(d) Are the persons who have an interest in the entity entitled to share in its profits as they arise; or does the amount of profits to which they are entitled depend on a decision of the entity or its members, after the period in which the profits have arisen, to make a distribution of its profits?
(e) Who is responsible for debts incurred as a result of the carrying on of the business: the entity or the persons who have an interest in it?
(f) Do the assets used for carrying on the business belong beneficially to the entity or to the persons who have an interest in it?

Some of those factors may point in one direction; others may point in another. An overall conclusion is reached from looking at all the factors together, though some have more significance than others. Particular attention is paid to factors (*c*) and (*d*). In considering them we look at the foreign commercial law under which the entity is formed and at the internal constitution of the entity. How the entity is classified for tax purposes in any other country is not relevant. The conclusion that is reached is then used in considering the relevant piece of UK tax law.

A list of foreign entities where we have been asked our view on the question of transparency/opacity is set out below. A separate list of foreign entities, which have been considered for Stamp Duty purposes, appears in the Stamp Taxes Manual available on the HMRC website.

It should be noted that the list only gives our general view as to the treatment of the specified foreign entity. In a particular case regard may also need to be had to:

- The specific terms of the UK taxation provision under which the matter requires to be considered;
- The provisions of any legislation, articles of association, by-laws, agreement or other document governing the entity's creation, continued existence and management, and;
- The terms of any relevant Double Taxation Agreement.

It should also be borne in mind that in relation to the classifications set out on the list:

- In some instances HMRC's view was given many years ago, and there may have been significant changes in the relevant foreign law which may mean that a different conclusion as to the status of that entity might now be reached. Changes in foreign law after the publication of this article may be significant for the same reason.
- Entities are described as either fiscally "transparent" or "opaque" solely for the purposes of deciding how a member is to be taxed on the income they derive from their interest in the entity. In the case of a "transparent" entity the member is regarded as being entitled to a share in the underlying income of the entity as it arises and is charged to tax in the UK on their share of the profits on that basis. But, in the case of an "opaque" entity the member generally is taxed only on the distributions made by the entity.
- It should be noted that the expressions "transparent" and "opaque" are not interchangeable with "partnership" and "company" or "body corporate". For example, a fiscally transparent entity is not necessarily a partnership. Likewise

an UK company is a "body corporate" and is opaque for the purposes of UK tax on income, but a fiscally opaque entity is not necessarily a "body corporate" or a "company" for UK tax purposes.

Where clarification is sought in relation to a foreign entity we will attempt to give a view in particular cases in line with Code of Practice 10. The following are the contact points:

(1) In all cases (except in relation to whether an entity may be a collective investment scheme)

David Price
HM Revenue & Customs
CT & VAT Products & Processes
International CT
3rd Floor
100 Parliament Street
London SW1A 2BQ
Tele: 020 7147 2645
Fax: 020 7147 2649
e-mail: david.e.price@hmrc.gsi.gov.uk

(2) The list does not indicate whether the particular entities constitute collective investment schemes. Where clarification is needed on this point you should contact:

David Moran
HM Revenue & Customs
CT & VAT Products & Processes
Financial & Insurance Team
3rd Floor
100 Parliament Street
London SW1A 2BQ
Tele: 020 7147 2612
Fax: 020 7147 2640
e-mail: david.moran@hmrc.gsi.gov.uk

List of Foreign Entities

ANGUILLA		Partnership	Transparent	Oct 91
ARGENTINA		Sociedad de responsibilidad limitada	Opaque	Jun 58
AUSTRIA	KG	Kommanditgesellschaft	Transparent	Aug 71
	KEG	Kommand Erwerbsgesellschaft	Transparent	Nov 03
	GmbH & Co KG		Transparent	May 02
	GmbH	Gesellschaft mit Beschrankter Haftung	Opaque	Nov 05
	AG	Aktiengesellschaft	Opaque	Nov 05
BELGIUM	SPRL	Societe de privee a responsabilite limitee	Opaque	Aug 94
	SNC	Societe en nom collectif	Transparent	May 92

	SA	Societe Anonyme	Opaque	Nov 05
	NV	Naamloze Vennootschap	Opaque	Nov 05
	SCA	Societe en commanditaire par actions	Opaque	Nov 05
	CVA	Commanditaire venootschap op aandelen	Opaque	Nov 05
BRAZIL	Srl	Sociedad por quotas de responabilidade limitada	Opaque	Jan 77
CANADA		Partnership and limited partnership	Transparent	Nov 05
CAYMAN ISLANDS		Limited partnership	Transparent	Nov 93
CHILE	SRL	Sociedad de responsibilidad limitada	Transparent	Sep 03
CHINA	WFOE	Wholly Foreign Owned Entity	Opaque	Oct 05
CZECH REPUBLIC	as	Akciova spolecnost	Opaque	Nov 05
	sro	Spolecnost s rucenim omezenym	Opaque	Nov 05
EUROPEAN UNION	SE	Societas Europeas	Opaque	Jul 05
FINLAND	Ky	Kommandiittiyhtio	Transparent	May 91
	Oy	Osakeyhtio	Opaque	Nov 05
	Ab	Aktiebolag	Opaque	Nov 05
FRANCE	GIE	Groupement d'Interet economique	Transparent	May 88
	SNC	Societe en nom collectif	Transparent	Aug 00
	SCI	Societe civile immobiliere	Opaque	Nov 05
	SCA	Societe civile agricole	Opaque	Feb 98
	SCS	Societe en commandite simple	Transparent	Sep 97
	SP	Societe en participation	Transparent	Jun 92
	SARL	Societe a responsabilite limitee	Opaque	
	FCPR	Fonds Commun de Placement a risques	Transparent	Jan 97
	SAS	Societe par Actions Simplifee	Opaque	Apr 04
	SA	Societe Anonyme	Opaque	Apr 04
	GFA	Groupement Foncier d'Agricole	Opaque	May 01
	SC	Societe Civile	Opaque	Nov 05
GERMANY		Stille Gesellschaft	Opaque	Jun 98
	KG	Kommandit Gesellschaft	Transparent	Feb 97
	OHG	Offene Handelsgesellschaft	Transparent	Sep 96
	GmbH	Gesellschaft mit Beschrankter Haftung	Opaque	Feb 97
	GmbH & Co KG		Transparent	Feb 97
	GBR	Gesellschaft des Burgerlichen Rechts	Transparent	Apr 94
	AG	Aktiengesellschaft	Opaque	Nov 05

GUERNSEY	LP	Limited Partnership	Transparent	Jan 05
	PCC	Protected Cell Company	Opaque	Nov 04
		Open Ended Investment Company with Limited Liability	Opaque	Nov 04
HUNGARY	Kft	Koriatolt felelossegu tarsasag	Opaque	Nov 05
	Rt	Reszvenytarsasag	Opaque	Nov 05
ICELAND		Hlutafelag	Opaque	Nov 05
IRELAND		Limited Partnership	Transparent	
		Irish Investment Limited Partnership	Transparent	
	CCF	Common Contractual Fund	Transparent	Jan 04
ITALY	SpA	Societa per Azioni	Opaque	
JAPAN		Goshi-Kaisha	Transparent	Feb 97
		Gomei Kaisha	Transparent	
	TK	Tokumei Kumiai	Transparent	Nov 05
		Kabushikikaisha	Opaque	Nov 05
		Yugen-kaisha	Opaque	Nov 05
JERSEY	LLP	Limited Liability Partnership	Opaque	Feb 01
KAZAKHSTAN	LLC	Limited Liability Company	Opaque	Sep 05
LIECHTENSTEIN		Anstalt	Opaque	Mar 04
LUXEMBOURG	SCA	Societe en commandite par-actions	Opaque	Jul 92
	FCP	Fonds commun de placement	Transparent	May 05
	SA	Societe anonyme	Opaque	Nov 05
	SARL	Societe a responsabilite limitee	Opaque	Nov 05
	SJCAV	Societe d'investment a capitale variable	Opaque	Mar 06
NETHERLANDS	VOF	Vennootschap Onder Firma	Transparent	Feb 95
	CV	Commanditaire Vennootschap (both "open" and "closed")	Transparent	Aug 00
	NV	Naamloze Vennootschap	Opaque	Oct 81
	BV	Besloten Vennootschap Met Beperkte Aansprakelijheid	Opaque	Oct 81
		Maatschap	Transparent	Oct 93
		Stichting	Transparent	Jul 05
	Co-op	Cooperatie	Transparent	Jul 04
NEW CALEDONIA	SNC	Societe en nom collectif	Transparent	Jul 05
NORWAY	AS	Alkjeselskap	Opaque	
	KS	Kommandittselkap	Transparent	Jan 81
POLAND	SP.zo.o	Spolkaz ograniczonaodpowiedzialnoscia	Opaque	Mar 96

PORTUGAL	Lda	Sociedade por quotas	Opaque	Apr 93
	SA	Sociedade Anonima	Opaque	Apr 93
RUSSIA		Joint Venture under "Decree No 49"	Opaque	Jan 93
	LLC	Limited Liability Company	Opaque	Nov 03
SLOVAK REPUBLIC	sro	Spolocnost's rucenim obmedzenim	Opaque	Nov 05
SPAIN	SC	Sociedad Civila	Opaque	Dec 80
	SA	Sociedad Anonima	Opaque	Nov 05
		Comunidad de bienes	Transparent	Jun 01
	Srl	Sociedad de Responsabilidad Limitada	Opaque	Nov 05
SWEDEN	AB	Aktiebolag	Opaque	Nov 05
	KB	Kommanditbolag	Transparent	Oct 05
SWITZERLAND	SS	Societe Simple	Transparent	Dec 90
	GmbH	Gesellschaft mit beschrankter Haftung	Opaque	Nov 05
TURKEY	AP	Attorney Partnership	Transparent	Apr 04
	AS	Anonim Sirket	Opaque	Nov 05
	Ltd/S	Limited Sirket	Opaque	Nov 05
USA		Partnership set up under the Uniform Partnership Act	Transparent	Sep 83
		Limited Partnership set up under the Uniform Limited Partnership Act	Transparent	Aug 00
	LLC	Limited Liability Company	Opaque	Jun 97
	LLP	Limited Liability Partnership	Transparent	Dec 99
	MBT	Massachusetts Business Trust	Transparent	Feb 80
	S. Corp	S. Corporation	Opaque	Jul 05

Appendix E

Stamp Taxes Bulletins

STAMP TAXES BULLETIN ISSUE 1—AUGUST 2001
A welcome from the editor

Welcome to the first edition of the Stamp Taxes Bulletin, a new publication for customers to help you get the most out of our services and understand your obligations in paying the right amount of tax. It gives you up-dates on all the latest developments, reminds you about technical points and provides background to changes, which have taken place.

We have seen many changes over the past year. In October 2000 the Stamp Office became part of a new business—Stamp Taxes. This brings together the operational, technical and policy areas of our work to help us provide a more 'joined up' service to both customers and Ministers.

The organisation is headed by Craig Lester our new Business Director who took up post in May 2001, and Seb Beck our newly appointed Deputy Director of Operations who is responsible for the running of our local offices.

In this edition we also tell you about our achievements for 2000/01 and the stretching targets we have set ourselves for the year ahead, to improve our business still further.

I hope you will find the Bulletin both interesting and enjoyable to read. It does not however give you all the information you need to work out your Stamp Duty, and you should still contact us directly for more detailed guidance.

We want the publication to be relevant to our customers, so if you have any comments or suggestions about topics you would like to see covered in future issues please give me a call on 0117 927 3742.

We intend to publish the Bulletin at least twice a year and Issue No 2 is due in January 2002.

Pauline Hudd

Customer Service Manager

HELPING US TO HELP YOU

A reminder about adjudication procedures

For many years we have asked customers to provide a copy of the document when lodging an application for formal adjudication under the provisions of section 12 of the Stamp Act 1891, This copy is retained by Stamp Taxes after completion of the adjudication. There are recent instances where this has been overlooked by some customers.

Can we remind you, please, to send us a photocopy of all documents requiring adjudication. This will enable us to process adjudication applications swiftly.

Documents sent for straightforward stamping, without adjudication, need not be accompanied by a copy.

Remember you can send your adjudication documents to any of our local offices the addresses are listed below.

SETTING STANDARDS IN CUSTOMER SERVICE

Stamp Taxes sets itself demanding targets which reflect the high standards of service our customers expect. Last year we were proud to receive our third Charter Mark Award, which puts us among the top organisations in the country for service excellence and "going the extra mile" to help our customers.

We measure our performance in terms of the service the customers actually receive, including the length of time we take to deal with your documents. Provided that you send us the right amount of duty and we have all the information we need, we aim to process and return your documents within five working days.

We have continued to deliver responsive services to meet your needs. Last year we extended the availability of our telephone Helpline service which you can ring between 8.30am and 5pm on weekdays.

The number to remember for all general enquiries is **0845 6030135**.

We also gave our customers the opportunity to discuss current issues directly with us, by setting up User Groups at each of our locations. If you would like to get involved in these meetings please contact the local Customer Service manager at the address shown below.

Despite a fire at our Newcastle office and the relocation of our offices in Manchester and Edinburgh, we managed to return 96% of all documents in five working days. We aim to improve on this still further in the coming year.

We try to keep to a minimum our costs in administering the duty and your costs in complying with the legislation. In 200/01 the cost of collecting Stamp Duty was the lowest ever, at just 12p to collect every £100 of duty.

Overall the volume of documents processed is showing a decline and this is due to the growth in electronic trading as we move to the paperless dealing system for CREST transactions on the stock market.

Our Achievements

STAMP DUTY	*2000/01*		*2001/02*
	Forecast	*Result*	*Forecast*
Documents processed (millions)	2.70	2.12	1.98
Duty collected (millions)	3,951	4,375	4,271
Documents processed in 5 days	99.1%	96.5%	99.1%
Cost of collecting £100 of duty	13 pence	12 pence	15 pence

SDRT	*2000/01*		
	Forecast	*Result*	*Forecast*
Tax Collected (£ millions)	3255.40	3884.20	3750
Cost of collecting £100 of tax	2 pence	2 pence	2 pence

WHEN IS A FIXTURE NOT A FIXTURE?

Deductions for chattels (or moveables in Scotland)

Where the consideration for the conveyance or transfer on sale of a property includes an amount attributed by the parties to chattels (or moveables in Scotland), that amount will not normally be charged to Stamp Duty provided the chattels pass by delivery and are not conveyed in the document.

Case law provides that where assets of different character are agreed to be sold for one consideration for the whole, an apportionment between the chargeable and non-chargeable property must be a bona fide one. This is taken to mean that it must be based on the commercial value of the property concerned. A contract for sale based on a false apportionment may be unenforceable because of its improper intent and can therefore have more far-reaching consequences.

Over the last year or so, Stamp Taxes has seen a steady increase in the number of cases where the amount of consideration attributed to items claimed to be chattels is more than a small percentage of the total consideration. This is especially the case where this brings the chargeable amount just below the £250,000 or £500,000 thresholds.

Customers should note that in cases where it appears that an excessive amount of the consideration has been artificially attributed to non-chargeable items a full inventory and breakdown of the consideration will be requested by Stamp Taxes. This is to ensure that all the items claimed as chattels are properly within that description and that the allocation of the consideration is bona fide and not in breach of section 5 of the Stamp Act 1891.

Stamp Taxes does not provide a comprehensive list of items which are accepted as chattels or moveables since many cases need to be considered on their own merits and case law is evolving in this area all the time. However items which will generally be accepted as chattels or moveables include—carpets, curtains, light shades, pot plants, free-standing kitchen white goods and portable electric or gas fires.

Items which are generally unacceptable as chattels are—Fitted kitchen cabinets and cupboards, fitted kitchen white goods, fitted bathroom sanitary ware, central heating systems, plants growing in the soil, central heating systems and gas fires connected to a piped gas supply.

Loose plant and machinery

Plant and machinery may in certain circumstances be treated as "goods, wares and merchandise" and will then fall within the exception to the charge to Stamp Duty under Paragraph 7, Sch 13, Finance Act 1999.

The requirement for plant and machinery to be in an actual state of severance at the date of the agreement for sale for it to fall within the "goods, wares and merchandise" description is an historical one. It stems from case law based on circumstances involving mortgagees in possession. The two main tests as to whether plant and machinery constitutes goods, wares and merchandise are essentially the same as for chattels, namely (1) the degree of annexation to the building or land and (2) the purpose or object of annexation. Stamp Taxes has for many years required customers to certify that plant and machinery claimed as loose plant must be in an actual state of severance if it is to be considered as goods and therefore outside the charge to duty on an agreement for sale. We will no longer insist upon this certification being given.

Where it would be possible for plant and machinery to be relatively easily severed from the property to which it is fixed, say for example by the simple expedient of removing some bolts securing it to the floor or walls, we will no longer insist that this is actually done before it will be considered to be 'loose plant and machinery'.

The position in law has not changed nor does this mean that all plant and machinery suddenly falls within the exception. As in the past, the consideration attributed to fixed plant will be chargeable to Stamp Duty on the agreement for sale document. [Author's note: the underlined sentence is incorrect except in the case of tenant's fixtures or agreements for the sale of equitable interest only—true fixtures are stampable at the conveyance stage]. Heavy plant and machinery which is integral to a building and plant where its removal would damage the building or land will still be considered fixed plant. This will be particularly relevant in respect of plant such as, for example, escalators and elevators, boilers, furnaces, walk-in refrigerators and restaurant cooking stations, none of which would be likely to be classed as loose plant for Stamp Duty purposes. Each case will be considered on its own merits. The Stamp Taxes form Stamps 22 will be amended to reflect this new treatment. The equivalent forms used in Scotland and Northern Ireland do not require amendment since they did not previously include the certification requirement.

Archie Brown—Technical Adviser

STAMP DUTY ON GOODWILL AND INTELLECTUAL PROPERTY

With the rapidly changing face of today's business world and the growth of new technology, there are now many different types of assets relating to the trade of a company.

We are receiving an increasing number of enquiries about certain types of 'intellectual property' relating to computer applications.

This is a brief outline of what is and isn't chargeable.

Intellectual property including:

- Domain names
- Databases
- Software applications

All these are not chargeable.

- Goodwill—Traditionally this refers to the rights associated with carrying on the business, the "good name" and established reputation which brings with it the promise of trade.

Business goodwill is chargeable with Stamp Duty.

However, if the goodwill is derived from intellectual property, for instance, it is associated with a trademark, then it is exempt from duty under s.129 (2) Finance Act 2000.

- 'Know-how' is not chargeable with Stamp Duty

HOW TO MAKE THE MOST OF YOUR STAMP OFFICE

A guide to services

We have offices in 8 locations throughout the UK, in Belfast, Birmingham, Bristol, Edinburgh, London, Manchester, Newcastle and Worthing.

All of our offices offer a comprehensive range of services including the facility for dealing with adjudication matters, such as charity exemptions and inter-company relief.

You can send your documents, including those requiring formal adjudication to any of our local offices. The addresses are printed below.

Our London office provides a counter-only service for personal callers. Any postal applications should therefore be sent to one of our other offices.

Don't adjudication documents have to be sent to Worthing?

No. You can send adjudication applications to any office.

Although in the past, Worthing was our main adjudication centre, where claims for exemption and special relief had to be sent. For some time now this service has been available in local Stamp Offices throughout the country and you should send adjudication documents to the office that you normally use for all your general Stamp Duty applications.

What if I need help on a technical point?

We have technical advisers in each of our offices, who can provide you with information and guidance on more complex issues and explain the procedures for making an exemption claim.

On more general matters, our Helpline operators are available to assist you in answering your basic Stamp Duty enquiries from 8.30am to 5pm on weekdays.

The Helpline number is 0845 6030135

All calls are charged at local rate to keep your costs to a minimum.

Where do I find out more?

If you want to know more about a specific subject, we publish a range of leaflets covering different topics. These are available free of charge from any of our offices. They can also be found on the Internet.

To find out what's new and all the latest developments visit our web-site at www.inla ndrevenue.gov.uk/so.

IN YOUR INTEREST

News about recent interest rate changes

In line with other taxes, we charge interest on late payments of Stamp Duty. This is aimed at making sure the tax operates fairly for all our customers by encouraging everyone to pay us the right amount of duty on time.

We also pay you interest in certain circumstances. If you pay more duty than is due and your document is over-stamped we will add interest to the repayment amount. The interest charged on late paid tax is higher than that added to repayments.

The interest rates for Stamp Duty, like those for other taxes are set by reference to changes in the base rate.

New rates of interest came into effect from 6th May 2001.

This table gives you a quick guide to recent changes in the rates of interest.

	Late paid duty	*Repayments*
1/10/99	7.5%	3%
6/2/00	8.5%	4%
6/5/01	7.5%	3.5%

If the delay crosses over periods where different interest rates apply, we will charge interest at the old rate for any period prior to the rate change, and at the current rate for any subsequent period.

CASTING THE NET WIDER

Developments in e-business

More than 25% of our customers regularly access our web-site to find out all the latest information and news about Stamp Duty changes.

We receive a number of suggestions from customers about the things they would like to see on the web. In particular, our Northern Ireland users said they would like an electronic version of the form PD1 to be available on-line.

We responded by including this on our web-site.

We are also working hard to make sure that every contact with our customers counts, enabling them to understand and meet their obligations in paying the right amount of duty.

To help customers find their way around our forms, we have recently incorporated a "help" feature on our form Stamps 61 on the web-site. This guides the reader through the various sections, telling them what information to include. We are intending to extend this facility to all our forms in time, and we are currently working on a "help" index for our form LA451 to give guidance in completing the information. This will replace the printed information on completing our forms, which was available in the SO5 leaflet.

Noticeboard

This section tells you about the latest Stamp Taxes publications, and highlights recent information.

Did you see—

Stamp Taxes Customer Newsletter—Interest & Penalties—Interest Rate Charges May 2001

Stamp Taxes Customer Newsletter—Penalties & Interest—further guidance on calculating penalties in cases over one year late Feb 2001

Internet announcement

Stamp Duty Reserve Tax and Individual Pension Accounts (IPAs)

Unit Trusts and Open Ended Investment Companies (OEICs)

Stamp office addresses

Belfast Stamp Office
Third Floor
Dorchester House
52–58 Great Victoria Street
Belfast
BT2 7QE
028 90 505127
DX: 2003 Belfast 2
Manager: Martine MacLaughlin

Birmingham Stamp Office
5th Floor
Norfolk House
Smallbrook Queensway
Birmingham
B5 4LA
0121 633 3313
DX: 15001 Birmingham 1
Office Manager: Claire Fell

Bristol Stamp Office
The Pithay
All Saints Street
Bristol
BS1 2NY
0117 927 2022
DX: 7899 Bristol 1
Office Manager: Judith Baydoun

Edinburgh Stamp Office
Grayfield House
5 Bankhead Avenue
Edinburgh
EH11 4BF
0131 442 3161
DX: 543303 Edinburgh 33
Office Manager: David Hunter

London Stamp Office
South West Wing
Bush House
Strand
London
WC2B 4QN
020 7 438 7252/7452
Office Manager: Trevor England
DX: 146766 London (Somerset House)

Worthing Stamp Office
(Postal service only)
Room 35
East Block
Barrington Road
Worthing
BN12 4XJ
01903 508962
DX: 3799 Worthing 1
Office Manager: Paul Cox

Manchester Stamp Office
Upper Fifth Floor
Royal Exchange
Exchange Street
Manchester
M2 7EB
0161 834 8020
DX: 14430 Manchester 2
Office Manager: Les Shiell

Worthing Stamp Office
(Postal service only)
Room 3
East Block
Barington Road
Worthing
BN12 4XJ
01903 508962
DX: 3799 Worthing 1
Office Manager: Paul Cox

SDRT (Operations)
Customer Service Unit
Room 5
East Block
Barrington Road
Worthing
BN12 4XJ
Tel: 01903 509471
Office Manager: Penny Darburn

Newcastle Stamp Office
Cale Cross House
156 Pilgrim Street
Newcastle upon Tyne
NE1 6TF
0191 201 7402
DX: 61021 Newcastle upon Tyne 1
Office Manager: Tony Stoker

Stamp Taxes Contracts Unit
Manchester Stamp Office
Upper Fifth Floor
Royal Exchange
Exchange Street
Manchester
M2 7EB
Tel: 0161 839 6260
Fax: 0161 834 3350

Stamp Taxes Enquiry Line:
0845 603 0135

The content of Stamp Taxes Bulletin gives the views of our technical specialists on particular issues. The information published is reported because it may be of interest to tax practitioners. Publication will be twice a year.

- You can expect that interpretations of the law contained in the Bulletin will normally be applied in relevant cases, but this is subject to a number of qualifications.
- Particular cases may turn on their own facts, or context, and because every possible situation cannot be covered, there may be circumstances in which the interpretation given here will not apply.
- There may also be circumstances in which the Board would find it necessary to argue for a different interpretation in appeal proceedings.
- The Bulletin does not replace formal Statements of Practice.
- The Board's view of the law may change in the future. Readers will be notified of any changes in future editions.

Nothing in this Stamp Taxes bulletin affects a taxpayer's right of appeal on any point.

STAMP TAXES BULLETIN ISSUE 3—OCTOBER 2002
Options—a response to press articles

Stamp Offices have received a significant number of telephone enquiries following the publication of certain newspaper articles that promoted the use of options as a Stamp Duty saving scheme. Callers have been asking us to confirm that the scheme works in the manner described in the articles.

The Inland Revenue considers that these articles contain serious errors in Stamp Duty law. We are therefore publishing this item to clarify the issues.

The articles suggested that Stamp Duty on a purchase of a property at a price of £700,000 could be reduced by structuring the transaction so that the purchaser paid a price of £210,000 for an option to acquire the property at a price of £490,000. It was suggested that by doing so the duty of £28,000 that would apply to a purchase at £700,000 would be reduced to £14,700 (ie duty at 3 per cent on the consideration of £490,000 only).

Under Stamp Act 1891 s 5, all relevant facts and circumstances affecting the liability of an instrument to duty or the amount of that duty must be "fully and truly set forth in the instrument". To comply with section 5 it would therefore be necessary when presenting a transfer document reciting a purchase price of £490,000, to produce the Option Agreement for stamping. An Agreement granting an option to purchase property made for consideration, is a document liable to ad valorem conveyance on sale duty (*George Wimpey & Co Ltd v IRC* [1975] 2 All ER 45).

The transfer of the property at a price of £490,000 would not be stampable at the 3 per cent rate as suggested in the press articles. Since it stems from the Option Agreement, it forms part of a larger series of transactions at an aggregate value exceeding £500,000. A certificate of value for £500,000 could not be validly inserted in the transfer document and duty would, accordingly, be payable at 4 per cent.

The question also arises as to the rate of duty that should apply to the stamping of the option agreement. In any transaction structured in the manner set out in the articles the Stamp Office will require full disclosure of all correspondence surrounding the negotiations and the manner in which the purchase money or monies was paid. Each case will be treated on its merits, but it should be borne in mind that, in some cases, the Stamp Office are likely to contend that the Option Agreement is itself part of a series of transactions, so that any certificate of value to be included in it must take into account the price to be paid upon exercise of the option.

STAMP TAXES BULLETIN ISSUE 4—MARCH 2003
Introduction

Welcome to Issue 4 of the Inland Revenue Stamp Taxes Bulletin.

In the last edition we told you about our plans for modernising Stamp Duty. Since then we have introduced some changes to our current way of working as part of our preparation for the modernising regime. In this edition we tell you about the areas of work affected.

Now that the postcode search tool is available online more and more of our customers are carrying out postcode searches to check if the property they are purchasing, or thinking of purchasing, falls within a disadvantaged area to qualify for exemption from Stamp Duty. In this edition, we have tried to deal with questions that are asked of us most frequently by customers who have carried out these searches.

Finally, the Chancellor has announced by written Ministerial statement that the Budget Statement will be delivered on Wednesday 9 April 2003.

Judith Baydoun

Customer Relations Manager

MODERNISING STAMP DUTY

As part of our preparation for Modernising Stamp Duty we have decided to make some changes to the service that we currently offer you.

The purpose of this article is to explain the changes we have made in relation to two particular areas of our work and what we would like you to do in future.

The areas of work affected are:

- Share/Stock Transfer forms
- Telephone Enquiry Line—postcode checks
- Share/Stock Transfer Forms

At the end of this year as part of the modernisation programme we will no longer have the facilities to stamp documents at all our local offices. For this reason we have started to centralise some areas of our work and this includes stock transfer forms. All stock transfers currently stamped at local stamp offices, including those presented at the public counters are to be processed at a single location- London Stamp Office.

We have selected the London office as it already handles a high proportion of this kind of work and it is now able to receive postal applications.

With immediate effect we would ask you to send all stock transfer forms except those that require formal adjudication direct to the London Stamp Office for stamping.

Where stock transfers require formal adjudication please continue to use your local stamp office.

The postal address for London Stamp Office is:

London Stamp Office
Ground Floor
Bush House
The Strand
London WC2B 4QN

Or by DX to:

London Stamp Office
DX: 146766 London
(Somerset House)
Telephone Enquiry Line: 0845 6030135

From 17 March 2003 we will be centralising all postcode telephone enquiries.

If you do not have access to the Internet and you would like a postcode check to be carried out please will you contact our Enquiry Line where we have a team dedicated to handling these enquiries. All calls to this number are charged at a local rate to keep your costs to a minimum.

The Enquiry Line is open from Monday to Friday from 8:30am to 5:00pm to deal with your calls please ring: 0845 6030135.

We would like to remind customers that the postcode search tool is available for your use on our website at: www.inlandrevenue.gov.uk/so—click on Disadvantaged Areas: p ostcode search tool.

DISADVANTAGED AREAS—SECTION 92, FINANCE ACT 2001

Since the postcode search tool has been available on our website we have received a number of follow up telephone calls from customers seeking further advice about this exemption.

In response to this we have compiled a list of frequently asked questions (FAQs) and the answers to these questions that we hope you find helpful.

Q: Do I have to claim this relief from Stamp Duty?

A: Yes as an adjudicated relief the onus is on the customer to make a claim for exemption from Stamp Duty.

Once you are satisfied that you meet all the qualifying criteria you should submit all the relevant information and documentation to your local stamp office. You should not submit any payments.

Q: What happens if I make a claim for relief and it fails?

A: In the event that you fail to meet all the qualifying criteria your claim for exemption will fail and we will request payment of the Stamp Duty together with any interest that may be due.

Q: What happens if I have paid the Stamp Duty and later find out that the property qualifies for exemption from Stamp Duty?

Providing that you find this out within two years from the date of the document you will be able to claim back any Stamp Duty paid in error. If we agree with your claim we will add interest to any monies that we repay. You should in the first instance contact the office that dealt with the stamping of your document.

Q: What happens if the result of my postcode search is negative and the message says that the postcode has not been 'found'?

A: The result of your postcode search may be negative because your property/land:

- is part of a new development and/or has been allocated a postcode recently which does not appear on our postcode database yet;
- has yet to be allocated a postcode.

In cases such as this if you are claiming exemption from Stamp Duty you should tell us that the postcode has not been found or no postcode is available.

You should name the ward in which the property was located as at the qualifying date.

A map showing the location of the property and the ward boundaries should be supplied. If this is not possible we will accept a map showing the location of the property, in relation to established adjacent properties. The status of the surrounding properties will enable us to confirm that the property, on which relief is claimed, falls within a qualifying area.

A list of the qualifying wards (postcode areas in Scotland) as at the qualifying dates is available on our website)

Q: What are the current rates of interest?

A: The current rates of interest which came into effect from 6 November 2001 are 6.5% on duty that has been paid late and 2.5% on any monies that is due for repayment.

NOTICE BOARD

Budget statement: 9 April 2003

For more information about articles covered in this Bulletin and other Stamp Duty matters visit our website at: www.inlandrevenue.gov.uk/so.

The content of Stamp Taxes Bulletin gives the view of our technical specialists on particular issues. The information is published is reported as it may be of interest to tax practitioners. We aim to issue a publication twice a year.

You can expect that the interpretations of the law contained in the Bulletin will normally be applied in relevant cases, but this is subject to a number of qualifications.

Particular cases may turn on their own facts, or context, and because every possible situation cannot be covered, there may be circumstances in which the interpretation given here will not apply.

There may also be circumstances in which the Board would find it necessary to argue for a different interpretation in appeal proceedings.

The Bulletin does not replace formal Statement of Practice

The Board's view of the law may change in the future. Readers will be notified of any changes in future editions.

IR STAMP TAXES: NETWORK OFFICES

Belfast Stamp Office
Third Floor
Dorchester House
52–58 Great Victoria Street
Belfast
BT2 7QE
028 90 505127
DX: 2003 Belfast 2
Manager: Martine MacLaughlin

Birmingham Stamp Office
5th Floor
Norfolk House
Smallbrook Queensway
Birmingham
B5 4LA
0121 633 3313
DX: 15001 Birmingham 1
Office Manager: Claire Fell

Bristol Stamp Office
The Pithay
All Saints Street
Bristol
BS1 2NY
0117 927 2022
DX: 7899 Bristol 1
Office Manager: Judith Baydoun

Edinburgh Stamp Office
Grayfield House
5 Bankhead Avenue
Edinburgh
EH11 4BF
0131 442 3161
DX: 543303 Edinburgh 33
Office Manager: David Hunter

London Stamp Office
South West Wing
Bush House
Strand
London
WC2B 4QN
020 7 438 7252/7452
Office Manager: Trevor England
DX: 146766 London (Somerset House)

Worthing Stamp Office
(Postal service only)
Room 35
East Block
Barrington Road
Worthing
BN12 4XJ
01903 508962
DX: 3799 Worthing 1
Office Manager: Paul Cox

Manchester Stamp Office
Upper Fifth Floor
Royal Exchange
Exchange Street
Manchester
M2 7EB
0161 834 8020
DX: 14430 Manchester 2
Office Manager: Les Shiell

Worthing Stamp Office
(Postal service only)
Room 3
East Block
Barington Road
Worthing
BN12 4XJ
01903 508962
DX: 3799 Worthing 1
Office Manager: Paul Cox

SDRT (Operations)
Customer Service Unit
Room 5
East Block
Barrington Road
Worthing
BN12 4XJ
Tel: 01903 509471
Office Manager: Penny Darburn

Newcastle Stamp Office
Cale Cross House
156 Pilgrim Street
Newcastle upon Tyne
NE1 6TF
0191 201 7402
DX: 61021 Newcastle upon Tyne 1
Office Manager: Tony Stoker

Stamp Taxes Contracts Unit
Manchester Stamp Office
Upper Fifth Floor
Royal Exchange
Exchange Street
Manchester
M2 7EB
Tel: 0161 839 6260
Fax: 0161 834 3350

Stamp Taxes Enquiry Line:
0845 603 0135

Appendix F

IR Stamp Taxes Customer (sic) Newsletters

STAMP OFFICE CUSTOMER NEWSLETTER
Stamp Duty and VAT: transfer of business

The Stamp Office is publicising a change in practice on the sale of a business as a going concern on behalf of HM Customs and Excise.

Reproduced from the Stamp Office Customer Newsletter

BUSINESS SALES AND VAT

Sales of businesses often involve the payment of VAT, and we will charge Stamp Duty on the consideration including that VAT.

If the sale relates to a going concern this is exempt from VAT, which means Stamp Duty is payable only on the consideration without the addition of VAT.

When you present a business sale document to us, we need to find out whether VAT is payable or not, and whether Custom & Excise accepts that the business qualifies for VAT relief as a transfer of a going concern.

In the past this has often taken the form of advance clearance from Customs & Excise confirming the position.

NEW ARRANGEMENTS

Most Customs & Excise offices will no longer issue these letters, but will instead refer you to the guidance in Public Notice 700/9 (November 1996). Clearance will generally only now be given after the sale has taken place.

DOES THIS MEAN STAMP DUTY WILL BE CHARGED ON THE CONSIDERATION PLUS VAT?

No. Provided that the document does relate to a going concern and there is no clause which allows VAT to be charged at a later date, then duty is payable on the consideration exclusive of VAT.

WHAT IF VAT CAN BE CHARGED?

If the document allows for VAT to be charged later on, for instance if Customs & Excise refuse clearance, then we would stamp the document on the initial consideration stated and ask you for a written undertaking to return the document to us for payment of the additional duty if the position changes.

WHAT CERTIFICATE OF VALUE DO I INCLUDE?

Documents should be certified in respect of the initial consideration paid which is exclusive of VAT.

If a subsequent charge to VAT increases the total amount paid so that the threshold is exceeded, duty will be payable on the VAT-inclusive sum at the higher rate.

QUESTIONS OR COMMENTS ABOUT THESE NEW ARRANGEMENTS

If you have any questions or comments about these new arrangements contact your local Stamp Office.

Alternatively, you can write to, or telephone Pauline Hudd, communication officer at: The Stamp Office, First floor, The Pithay, All Saints Street, Bristol BS1 2NY; DX 7899 Bristol 1; tel: 0117 927 2022; fax: 0117 925 3599.

STAMP TAXES CUSTOMER NEWSLETTER

February 2001

PENALTIES & INTEREST

Background

The 1999 Finance Act introduced measures to make Stamp Duty fairer by encouraging everyone to pay the right amount of duty on time.

If you do not present your documents within the 30-day time limit you should expect to pay a penalty.

Interest will also be charged if you delay in paying us some or all of the money.

Full information about penalty and interest charges is contained in our leaflet SO10, available free of charge from any Stamp Office.

Latest information

When the new arrangements were introduced we explained that certain cases would be subject to individual review. We are now receiving enquiries about the basis for charging penalties where the delay is longer than a year. These further guidelines explain how penalties will be worked out in these cases to ensure fairness and consistency for all our customers.

Delays of more than a year

In cases over one year late, the legislation gives us authority to charge a maximum amount equivalent to the duty or £300—whichever is higher.

However, this maximum is only charged where there is a substantial delay and we would normally mitigate the penalty to a lower amount. If the duty payable on your document is £5000 or less then the penalty rates in our leaflet SO10 will apply.

For cases where the duty exceeds £5000 the following table shows how your penalty will be worked out [Author's note: see also Stamp Office Manual, Section 3.32]:

Duty over £5,000

Months late	*% of duty*
Under 15	20%
Under 18	40%
Under 21	60%
Under 24	80%

Duty over £5,000

Months late	*% of duty*
24 and over	100%

Documents over two years late, No mitigation is appropriate where a document is more than two years late, and we will charge an amount equivalent to the duty, subject to an overriding minimum of £300.

Fixed duty cases

You will not normally be charged a penalty on fixed duty cases which are less than one year late. If there is substantial delay the following rates will usually apply:

- £10 for cases over 12 months late but not over 24 months late
- £25 for cases over 24 months late

We will still charge a penalty of £300 if people try to avoid paying duty or repeatedly fail to get documents stamped.

Explaining the delay . . .

So that we can decide if the penalty can be mitigated, you need to tell us of any factors you consider relevant to the delay when sending your documents to us.

There is no mitigation of interest charges and the full amount will always be payable. The rate of interest we charge on late paid duty is currently 8.5%.

Further information & advice

These guidelines supplement the information contained in our leaflet SO10 which explains our penalty and interest charges more fully.

If you want advice you can telephone our Helpline on 0845 6030135.

Our operators are available to take your calls from 8.30am to 5pm. on weekdays.

Further information can also be found on our website — www.inlandrevenue.gov.uk/so.

STAMP TAXES CUSTOMER NEWSLETTER
Disadvantaged areas Stamp Duty exemption

In his Pre-Budget Report of 27 November the Chancellor of the Exchequer announced his Government's intention to implement the first phase of the Stamp Duty exemption relating to the purchase of property in certain designated disadvantaged areas of the UK, which will apply where the consideration, or premium for a lease, does not exceed £150,000. Relief will be available with effect from 30th November 2001.

This Newsletter has been designed to help you make an application for the exemption and sets out the information that we need from you in order to deal with your document promptly. If you have any questions about the exemption which are not answered in this Newsletter please telephone the Stamp Taxes Helpline on 0845 603 0135 (office hours only) where one of our staff will be pleased to assist you.

- The Stamp Duty (Disadvantaged Areas) Regulations 2001 [see www.inlandrevenue.gov.uk/si/2001-3747.pdf].
- Wards qualifying for the Stamp Duty relief for Disadvantaged Areas [see www.inlandrevenue.gov.uk/so/disadvantaged.htm#1].

- If you have your postcode you can use our Disadvantaged Areas Relief Search tool [see www.inlandrevenue.gov.uk/so/pcode_search.htm] to assist you in det ermining whether your property is in a designated area qualifying for Stamp Duty relief.

What documents are covered by the exemption?

The exemption applies to all conveyances and transfers of land or an interest in land, and to all leases of an interest in land, executed on or after 30 November 2001, where the land falls wholly or partly within one of the disadvantaged areas designated under The Variation of Stamp Duties Regulations 2001 and the consideration for the transfer or the premium for the lease is more than £60,000 but not more than £150,000.

If a lease has a premium of £150,000 or less but also has a rent, is it exempt from Stamp Duty under this relief in respect of the rent?

No. The rent will be liable to duty even though the premium may be exempt from duty under this relief.

If VAT has been paid by the purchaser, in addition to the consideration or premium for the transfer or lease, does the £150,000 limit apply to the gross or net figure?

Stamp Duty applies to the VAT-inclusive consideration or premium. If the VAT, when added to the consideration or premium, brings the total amount above the £150,000 limit the exemption will not apply.

Are conveyances, transfers and leases previously liable to £5 fixed Stamp Duty within the new exemption?

No. The exemption does not currently apply to documents liable to fixed duty which must continue to be stamped. The exception is for duplicate documents that do not attract Stamp Duty in excess of that paid on the original document. If the original is exempt from duty under the disadvantaged areas provisions the duplicate will not bear any duty either but must be sent to us to be denoted as a duplicate document.

Where can I find out whether the property I am buying, or dealing with on behalf of my client, is within one of the designated areas?

A list of the designated areas has been published on our website and can be viewed here. The list has been drawn up on the basis of electoral wards, except in Scotland where it is based on postcodes.

Will I need to know the postcode for the property?

Yes. We need everyone who claims this exemption to let us know the postcode for the property so that we can confirm that it is within a designated disadvantaged area. See Stop Press–Disadvantaged Areas Stamp Duty Exemption.

Where can I find the postcode for a property if I do not already know it?

Postcode information is readily available for any given postal address from the Postcode Enquiry Line on 08457 111 222 or via the internet at www.royalmail.co.uk/

quick_tools/postcodes/Please note that if you are reading this newsletter on our web site, clicking on this link will take you to the Royal Mail homepage where you can link to the postcode finder page. If you enter the above URL in an internet browser yourself, please note that there is an underscore '_' between the words 'quick' and 'tools' which must be shown or the URL will not work.

What happens if the property I am buying is a piece of land with no buildings and it has no postcode designated?

If you are claiming the exemption on the document relating to such a piece of land you should tell us in your application letter that no postcode is available. You should include a map of the property with sufficient detail to pinpoint the location of the property and tell us which ward on the list of designated areas it falls within. If you know where the ward boundary lies you should indicate it on the map. We will check this information. Cases such as these are likely to take longer to process than those where a postcode is known.

What happens if the postcode for the property covers a number of properties, some of which are inside one of the qualifying areas and some of which are outside the area?

The legislation provides that where a single postcode straddles the boundary of a ward all properties covered by that one postcode will be considered to fall within the ward and will qualify for the exemption. If all the properties covered by one postcode are outside the ward boundary the exemption will not apply to any of those properties.

Does any certificate have to be included in the document?

Section 92(2) of the Finance Act 2001 provides that the exemption will only apply if the document is certified to the Commissioners as being an instrument on which Stamp Duty is not chargeable by virtue of subsection (1). It is suggested that an appropriate wording for the certificate is as follows:

'I/We hereby certify that this is an instrument on which Stamp Duty is not chargeable by virtue of the provisions of section 92 of the Finance Act 2001.'

While the legislation does not specifically require the certificate to be included as part of the document we suggest that it should be included in it. If the position is not certified to us, either in the document or separately in writing by the person submitting the document for stamping, exemption will not be granted.

Anyone falsely certifying a document with a view to obtaining relief that is not due will be committing a Stamp Duty fraud.

Do I have to send the document for stamping even though it is exempt from duty under section 92?

Yes. Like most Stamp Duty exemptions the legislation requires the document to be lodged for formal adjudication if the exemption is to be granted.

Do I still need to supply a completed Particulars Delivered form with the document even though I am claiming exemption from duty?

Yes. If you would normally have had to provide a PD form with the document in the past you will still need to do so. Even though the document may be exempt from Stamp Duty there will still be valuable information which the Valuation Office Agency need which they glean from these forms.

When I claim exemption do I need to include a duplicate of the document?

Yes. As required by the legislation in all adjudication claims, you need to let us have a photocopy of the document on which the exemption is claimed. We will retain that copy for our records.

What is the position where the land concerned is on the boundary of a designated disadvantaged area and some of the property is within the area and some is outside it?

The legislation in paragraph 1 of Schedule 30 of the Finance Act 2001 provides that in this scenario the full consideration is to be apportioned between the part inside and the part outside the disadvantaged area on a just and reasonable basis. Only the consideration in respect of the part outside the disadvantaged area is to be charged to Stamp Duty.

You must draw this to our attention when claiming partial exemption from duty and you must explain the basis on which you consider the apportionment of the consideration, including any VAT paid in addition to the consideration, to be a just and reasonable one.

Does the document need to include a £250,000 Certificate of Value where the consideration is £150,000 or less and I am claiming the exemption?

Yes. The certificate proves that the document is not part of any larger or series of transactions which would mean the relief was not appropriate.

Does the document need to include a £150,000 Certificate of Value where the consideration is £150,000 or less and I am claiming the exemption?

No. The legislation does not require there to be a £150,000 certificate in the document. However, it is important to remember that the legislation does provide that if a £150,000 certificate could not properly be included in the document, if that were one of the levels of certificate mentioned in the Finance Act 1999, the exemption is not appropriate.

In other words, where the document shows a consideration of £150,000 or less it can only qualify for exemption if it does not form part of a larger transaction or a series of transactions in respect of which the amount or value, or the aggregate amount or value, of the consideration exceeds £150,000.

What about phase two?

Under phase two, which is expected to start in 2002, the Government intends to significantly raise the level of Stamp Duty exemption, or abolish it entirely, in the designated areas but only in respect of non-residential property.

SUMMARY CHECKLIST: DISADVANTAGED AREAS STAMP DUTY RELIEF—SECTION 92, FINANCE ACT 2001

All instruments in respect of which relief is claimed must be formally adjudicated. To prevent delay in processing claims it will greatly assist if all the following information is supplied at the time the instrument is presented for stamping.

(1) The document contains a certificate confirming it is within the provisions of section 92 Finance Act 2001.

(2) The full postcode for the property being transferred is supplied.
(3) The relevant PD form is enclosed, if appropriate.
(4) A full photocopy of the transfer document is provided.
(5) A copy of the contract or sale agreement is provided.
(6) The document contains a £250,000 certificate of value.
(7) If the document is a lease, a payment in respect of the rent element is enclosed.

Provision of all the information above when the document is presented for stamping should enable claims to be processed without further correspondence.

You are reminded that if examination of the claim results in a decision that relief under section 92 FA 2001 is not due, and, as a consequence, payment of Stamp Duty is made after the proper time, a charge to interest may be incurred.

Wards qualifying for the Stamp Duty relief for Disadvantaged Areas

- ENGLAND [www.inlandrevenue.gov.uk/so/england.pdf]
- NORTHERN IRELAND [www.inlandrevenue.gov.uk/so/nireland.pdf]
- SCOTLAND [www.inlandrevenue.gov.uk/so/scotland.pdf]
- WALES [www.inlandrevenue.gov.uk/so/wales.pdf]

To view these documents you need to use a PDF file viewer such as Acrobat Reader.

If you have trouble viewing, downloading or printing PDF files with Acrobat Reader then visit Adobe's online technical guides].

STAMP TAXES CUSTOMER NEWSLETTER
Contracts for the sale of an estate or interest in UK land—Section 115 and Schedule 36 Finance Act 2002

1 GENERAL

1.1 This Newsletter provides guidance on the general application of the legislation at section 115 and Schedule 36 FA 2002. That legislation brings within the charge to Stamp Duty contracts for the sale of interests in UK land where the purchase consideration in respect of that land exceeds £10 million. Duty is chargeable on such contracts as though they were conveyances.

1.2 The Newsletter also outlines

- the procedures for making applications to extend the 90-day time limit under section 115 (2) FA 2002 to the newly-established Stamp Taxes Contracts Unit located in Manchester; and
- the Inland Revenue's view of the application of the new legislation in a number of specific circumstances.

1.3 The administration of the legislation, including stamping of contracts within the scope of section 115, the processing of applications to extend the 90-day time limit, and the granting of the benefit of sub-sale relief are all matters that will be exclusively dealt with by the Stamp Taxes Contracts Unit in Manchester (see Appendix B). It follows that such matters should not be referred to other Stamp Offices.

2 BACKGROUND

2.1 In his Budget on 17 April 2002, the Chancellor announced a package of measures intended to counter avoidance of Stamp Duty on property transactions. These measures are intended to discourage a range of techniques currently used to avoid Stamp Duty on high-value property deals.

2.2 Under section 115 Finance Act 2002, certain contracts or agreements for the sale of land situated in the UK are brought within the charge to ad valorem Stamp Duty.

This addresses the avoidance of Stamp Duty on large deals where the parties stop short of executing a formal conveyance of the land, which is the instrument that normally attracts the Stamp Duty charge, and 'rest' on the contract instead.

2.3 The contracts within the scope of section 115 are those where the amount or value of the consideration given for an estate or interest in land in the UK exceeds £10 million, or where the instrument forms part of a larger transaction or series of transactions relating to UK land in respect of which the amount or value, or aggregate amount or value, of the consideration exceeds £10 million.

2.4 Such contracts will be stampable with ad valorem duty as if they were conveyances on sale, if, upon the expiry of a 90–day period from the date that the contract, including one that is conditional, is entered into, a conveyance or transfer has not been presented for stamping.

2.5 The legislation has effect in respect of contracts or agreements executed after 24 July 2002.

2.6 Where it is envisaged that completion of a transaction by the execution of a formal conveyance of the land will not happen within the 90 day period, the legislation provides for an application to be made to the Commissioners of Inland Revenue to extend this period. The procedure and conditions for such applications are set out at 4 below.

2.7 References in this Newsletter to contracts and conveyances include, for transactions in Scotland, the conclusion of missives and dispositions respectively.

3 THE STAMP TAXES CONTRACTS UNIT

3.1 A specially dedicated unit has been established in Manchester to deal with all aspects of the operation of the new legislation, including formal applications for extending the 90–day period. Communications should be addressed to:

Stamp Taxes Contracts Unit
Manchester Stamp Office
Upper Fifth Floor
Royal Exchange
Exchange Street
Manchester M2 7EB
Telephone: 0161 839 6260
Fax: 0161 834 3350

3.2 A contract that is chargeable under section 115 must be presented for stamping to the Contracts Unit in Manchester only. The Unit will also be solely responsible for processing applications for extending the 90-day time limit. It follows that the benefit of relief in respect of sub-sales, including, where appropriate, any repayment of duty paid on the original sale or an earlier sub-sale, (see Appendix A of this Newsletter), will also be dealt with by the Unit in Manchester and not by any other Stamp Office.

3.3 The Contracts Unit will be happy to deal with enquiries as to whether a particular contract is, or will be, within the scope of the section 115 charge.

4 APPLICATIONS TO EXTEND THE 90–DAY PERIOD

4.1 Section 115 (2)(*b*) FA 2002 provides that the Commissioners of Inland Revenue may grant an extension to the 90–day period allowed for presentation of a conveyance for stamping where completion of a transaction is not anticipated within that period.

4.2 Applications for an extension should be made in writing, to the Stamp Taxes Contracts Unit, by a responsible officer of the transferee company, which may include a solicitor or accountant acting on behalf of the company and who is aware of the full circumstances of the application, or, where the transferee is not a company, an authorised representative of the transferee, and must contain all of the following:

(a) the full postal address of the land contracted to be sold;
(b) the date of the contract;
(c) the full names and addresses of the vendor and purchaser (if a company, the registered office address and the name of the ultimate parent company are also required);
(d) the amount of the purchase consideration, specifying amounts already paid and any further amounts that will or may become payable by the purchaser;
(e) any apportionment of value between land and buildings, on the one hand, and other assets;
(f) a description of the nature of the transaction, including details of any sub-sales or part sub-sales already in contemplation;
(g) the anticipated completion date and a full explanation of the reason for requesting an extension;
(h) where the contract or agreement forms part of a larger transaction or series of transactions in respect of which the amount or value, or aggregate amount or value, of the consideration attributable to land in the UK exceeds £10 million, details of all relevant transactions;
(i) details of any Stamp Duty reliefs (e.g. group relief) to be claimed in respect of the transaction.

NOTE: it is not necessary to provide a copy of the contract with the application, although this may be requested later.

5 TREATMENT OF APPLICATIONS TO EXTEND THE 90–DAY PERIOD

5.1 The Stamp Taxes Contracts Unit will consider all applications to extend the 90-day period, and may seek additional information and documentation before granting an extension.

5.2 The length of the extension granted is a matter for the Unit's discretion having regard to all the facts and circumstances of the case under consideration, and compliance with any conditions that it sees fit to impose (section 115(3)(*b*)).

5.3 The Unit may, on behalf of the Commissioners of Inland Revenue, refuse to extend the period in any case unless full documentation, including, where requested, a copy of the contract, is provided (section 115(3)(*a*)). An extension will also be denied if 'the whole, or substantially the whole, of the intended consideration' has changed hands (section 115(3)(*c*)). 90% or more of the consideration will usually be regarded as 'substantially the whole' for this purpose.

5.4 Applications for an extension should be submitted to the Stamp Taxes Contracts Unit as soon as it is appears likely that a conveyance will not be produced within the 90–day time limit. The Unit will endeavour to process applications within thirty days of receipt. To be certain of knowing the outcome of an application by the 90 day point, an application for extension should be lodged with the Contracts Unit no later than 60 days after the contract is entered into. Where applications are made later than that, if an extension is not agreed by the 90 day point, there may be a short period where the contract is technically in charge because an extension has still to be approved. If, however, an extension is subsequently approved, the contract will again be protected from coming into charge until the extension expires (see section 115(2)(*b*)).

5.5 Where an extension has been granted, the Contracts Unit will be prepared to consider one or more further applications for extension of the period allowed under section 115(2)(*b*). When considering such applications, the Unit may request further information and documentation. If a further extension is not granted, the contract will become chargeable to ad valorem duty on the date upon which the existing extension expires.

5.6 When, in due course, legislation is introduced to modernise the Stamp Duty regime, further guidance will be provided as necessary concerning the transitional treatment of extensions granted under section 115(2)(*b*) that remain outstanding at the date of implementation of the new legislation.

6 CONSIDERATION ISSUES

6.1 The figure of £10 million that appears in section 115(1) relates to the amount or value of the consideration given for the sale of an estate or interest in UK land. So a contract for the sale of UK land and other assets for £12 million, only £8 million of which is attributable to the UK land, will be outside the scope of section 115.

6.2 The apportionment between UK land and other assets must be made on a just and reasonable basis.

6.3 Where the contract forms part of a larger transaction or series of transactions the aggregate value of which exceeds £10 million attributable to UK land, section 115 will apply. For example, four connected and inter-linked contracts for £3 million each will be within the scope of the provision.

6.4 The £10 million is a VAT inclusive figure. So where the consideration is £9 million plus VAT of £1.575 million, the contract is within section 115.

6.5 Where, when the contract is made, all or part of the consideration is unascertainable, but a maximum, minimum or basic amount can be ascertained, construction of the new legislation as one with the Stamp Act 1891 (para 10, Sch 36) means that the contingency principle applies. So a contract showing consideration of £8 million with a further £4 million contingent upon the happening of some event, will be treated as a contract for £12 million and within the scope of the provision. Where the consideration cannot be ascertained under the contingency principle, section 242 FA 1994 applies (see paragraphs 18–22 of the August 1995 Tax Bulletin article).

7 SUBSEQUENT CONVEYANCE

7.1 Where Stamp Duty is paid upon a contract under the provisions of section 115 and subsequently a conveyance is presented for stamping, the conveyance is only chargeable with duty if the duty chargeable on it exceeds the duty paid on the contract (para 5(1)(*a*), Schedule 36). In this circumstance only the excess duty is payable on the conveyance. The duty paid on the contract will be either denoted on, or transferred to, the conveyance (para 5(4), Schedule 36).

8 USE OF CONTRACT IN COURT PROCEEDINGS

8.1 Where a contract within section 115 remains unstamped, it will nevertheless be admissible as evidence in Court proceedings until the expiry of the 90–day or extended period granted by the Contracts Unit (section 115(5)(*a*)).

9 INTEREST & PENALTIES

9.1 A contract that is chargeable with duty under section 115 is treated, for the purposes of the late stamping interest and penalty provisions (sections 15A and 15B Stamp Act 1891) as if it had been executed at the end of the 90 day or extended period allowed by the Inland Revenue. Thereafter the normal 30 day limit for presenting a document which has been executed applies before interest and penalties become eligible.

10 SUB-SALES

10.1 Section 115 and Schedule 36 FA 2002 introduce a new form of sub-sale relief for contracts that are chargeable under section 115. The relief is similar to the existing relief in paragraph 7(2), Schedule 13 FA 1999 for property sold under an agreement which is sold on before the original purchaser takes a conveyance. The existing scheme of sub-sale relief under section 58(4) and (5) Stamp Act 1891 is preserved unaltered for contracts that are not chargeable under section 115 FA 2002.

10.2 The broad scheme of the new relief is that any duty paid on the original sale contract and any intervening sub-sale contracts is credited against duty payable upon the conveyance. Where the duty paid on the contract(s) exceeds that due in respect of the conveyance(s), repayment of the excess will be made.

10.3 Full details of how the relief operates in conjunction with section 115, together with a series of examples, is set out in Appendix A. The examples do not cover every possible situation that might arise in practice, but the Contracts Unit will be pleased to advise on the application of the law to particular circumstances that are not specifically covered in the Appendix.

APPENDIX A

Sub-sale relief

Section 115(2) provides for sub-sale relief where duty has not been paid on contracts under section 115 [**Author's Note: this statement is incorrect**]. Schedule 36 deals with sub-sale relief where duty has been paid on contracts within section 115. 'Sub-sale' is defined as the situation where a purchaser, or sub-purchaser, under a contract, without having obtained a conveyance of the property contracted to be sold, contracts to sell the whole or part of the property to another person, putting that person in the position to call for a conveyance from the original seller (para 2, Schedule 36). In these circumstances there will be more than one contract potentially chargeable under section 115. For example, suppose A contracts to sell UK land to B for £11 million, and, before completing the transaction, B contracts to sell the land to C for £12 million, with the land being conveyed by A directly to C. Both the A–B and B–C contracts are within the scope of section 115 (although duty would not, of course, be payable on the B–C contract if completion took place within 90 days). The examples below illustrate how section 115(2) and Schedule 36 deal with this situation.

Sub-sale relief will be administered only by the Stamp Taxes Contract Unit in Manchester, to which all sub-sale contracts and final conveyances should therefore be sent.

1 Sub-sale where no duty paid on the contracts followed by a subsequent conveyance

In the above example the conveyance from A to C is regarded as made in conformity with both the A–B and the B–C contracts and duty will be payable upon the conveyance for £12 million (section 115(2)). [**Author's Note: presumably this example assumes that the conveyance occurs within 90 days of the A–B contract**].

2 Sub-sale where duty paid on the contract followed by a subsequent conveyance

A contracts to sell UK land to B for £11 million, and B pays Stamp Duty on the contract of £440,000 (£11m × 4%). B then contracts to sell the land to C for £12 million and A conveys the land directly to C.

The conveyance to C for £12 million is only chargeable with duty if the duty chargeable on it (£480,000) exceeds the duty paid on the contract (£440,000)–para 5(1)(*a*) of Schedule 36. As £480,000 exceeds £440,000, duty of £40,000 must be paid on the A–C conveyance.

In the event that the consideration for the conveyance from A–C is less than the consideration on which B paid Stamp Duty on the A–B contract, para 6 of Schedule 36 provides for repayment. So if B paid duty on £11 million (£440,000) and the conveyance from A–C was for £9 million (£360,000), para 6(1) applies and B, as the person who paid the duty on the original sale, will be entitled to a repayment of £440,000—£360,000 = £80,000. This assumes that the £9 million is not less than the value of the property immediately prior to the sub-sale (see s112 FA 1984).

3 Sub-sale contract for part followed by conveyance where additional duty payable

A contracts to sell UK land to B for £30 million and B pays Stamp Duty on the contract. Before taking a conveyance, however, B contracts to sell one-third of the land to C for £12 million and A conveys one-third of the land directly to C.

The sub-sale to C is in respect of part only of the property that was the subject of the original sale. Duty on the A–C conveyance is chargeable in respect of the amount by which the ad valorem duty chargeable on it exceeds an 'appropriate proportion' of the ad valorem duty paid on the original sale (para 5(2) of Schedule 36).

The appropriate proportion is determined on a just and reasonable basis having regard to the ad valorem duty paid on the original sale together with any intervening subsale. In this example, B paid duty on the original sale of £1.2 million. B has sold ⅓ of the land to C. So the appropriate proportion of duty to be credited on the A–C conveyance might, depending upon the circumstances, be £1.2 million × ⅓ = £400,000. Duty on the A–C conveyance is therefore £12 million × 4% = £480,000–£400,000 = £80,000.

4 Sub-sale contract for part followed by conveyance where duty repayable

Once the whole of a property contracted to be sold in parts has been conveyed, and the aggregate duty chargeable on the conveyances is less than the duty paid on the original sale and the intervening sub-sales, then a repayment is due under para 6 Schedule 36.

For example—A contracts to sell UK land to B for £11 million. B pays duty of £440,000 on the contract. B then parcels the land into 60 parts and contracts to sell them for £200,000 each. Once the final part has been conveyed from A to the 60th purchaser, if the duty chargeable on the conveyances is less than £440,000, a repayment will be due.

The duty on each conveyance is £200,000 × 1% = £2,000. £2,000 × 60 conveyances = £120,000. Therefore a repayment of duty is due to B in the sum of £440,000 – £120,000 = £320,000.

5 Where whole property sold and duty previously paid on original sale (or an earlier sub-sale)

Suppose that A contracts to sell land to B for £11 million but, before taking a conveyance, B contracts to sell the land on to C for £12 million. B pays duty on £11 million, but the conveyance from A to C does not take place. Duty on the B-C contract is chargeable only in respect of the excess of the chargeable consideration on that contract over the chargeable consideration on the A–B contract. So C would pay duty on £1m (£12m – £11m.) @ 4% = £40,000 (paragraph 3(1), Sch 36).

If, in turn, C, having paid duty on the B–C contract, contracts to sell the whole property on to D for £15 million, D will be liable for duty calculated by reference to the excess of £15 million over the higher amount of chargeable consideration on which duty has been paid on an earlier transaction. The higher amount of chargeable consideration in this case is the £12 million on the B–C contract, and so D will pay duty on £3m (£15m – £12m) @ 4% = £120,000 (para 3(2), Sch 36).

6 Where part only of property sold and duty previously paid on original sale or earlier sub-sale

Suppose A contracts to sell UK land to B for £30 million. Before taking a conveyance B contracts to sell one-third of the land to C for £12 million, and subsequently contracts with D to sell the remaining two-thirds of the land for £25 million. B pays duty on the £30 million consideration for the A–B contract.

The sub-sale to C is in respect of part only of the property that was the subject of the original sale. Duty on the B-C contract is chargeable in respect of the amount by which the consideration of £12 million exceeds an 'appropriate proportion' of the consideration on the earlier transaction (paragraph 3(3), Sch 36). The appropriate proportion is determined on a just and reasonable basis having regard to the subject matter of the sub-sale and the earlier transaction (paragraph 3(4)). In this case C would pay duty on £12m less £10m (£30m × $^1/_3$) = £2m @ 4% = £80,000.

Similarly, D would pay duty on £25m less £20m (£30m × $^2/_3$) = £5m @ 4% = £200,000.

If D paid the duty but did not take a conveyance from A, but instead sold the whole of his two-thirds of the original property on to E for £27 million, E would be required to pay duty on the amount by which the chargeable consideration on the D-E contract exceeds the higher amount of chargeable consideration on an earlier sale or sub-sale of that property. In this example, the chargeable consideration on which duty was paid by D was £25 million, so E pays duty on £2m (£27m–£25m) = £2m @ 4% = £80,000.

If D only sold on to E half of the property he bought from B, for £15 million, then the calculation of duty payable by E would need to take into account the higher of the 'appropriate proportion' of the chargeable consideration on the original sale (A–B) and the 'appropriate proportion' of the chargeable consideration on the intervening sub-sale (B–D), as follows:

- B's chargeable consideration £30m
- Appropriate proportion thereof (£30m × $^2/_3$ × $^1/_2$) £10m (X)
- D's chargeable consideration £25m
- Appropriate proportion thereof (25m × $^1/_2$) £12.5m (Y)
- (Y) is greater than (X), so E pays duty on £15m–£12.5m = £2.5m @ 4% = £100,000 (paragraph 3(1)–(5), Sch 36)

7 Where part sub-sold and part retained by original purchaser, and duty paid on original contract

Suppose A contracts to sell UK land to B for £15 million. Before taking a conveyance, B agrees to sell one-third of the land to C for £7 million and a further third of the land to D, also for £7 million. B pays duty on the £15 million consideration for the A-B contract. Following the principle in 5. above, both C and D would pay duty on £7m less £5m (£15m × $^1/_3$) = £2m @ 4% = £80,000. The conveyance from A to B of the land not agreed to be sub-sold is liable to duty, not on a consideration of £1m, but following the decision in *Maples v IRC* [1914] 3 KB 303, on £5m, which represents the proportionate value of the land in relation to the original contract price. The conveyance is therefore liable to duty of £200,000 (£5m @ 4%). As the original contract was stamped with £600,000 duty, and £400,000 has been credited against the stamping of the conveyances to C and D, the balance is available to satisfy the liability on the conveyance from A–B.

8 Rate of duty

Where duty is chargeable on a contract within section 115 and, under paragraph 3 of Schedule 36, duty on a sub-sale is chargeable in respect of part only of the consideration for the sub-sale, the rate of duty chargeable on the sub-sale is the rate that would be applicable if the whole of the chargeable consideration on the sub-sale were taken into account.

A contracts to sell UK land to B for £30 million. B pays Stamp Duty at 4% on the contract. B then contracts to sell the land to C for £30.1 million. Duty is payable by C on the additional £100,000 consideration at 4% under paragraph 3(6) of Schedule 36.

APPENDIX B

Appendix B

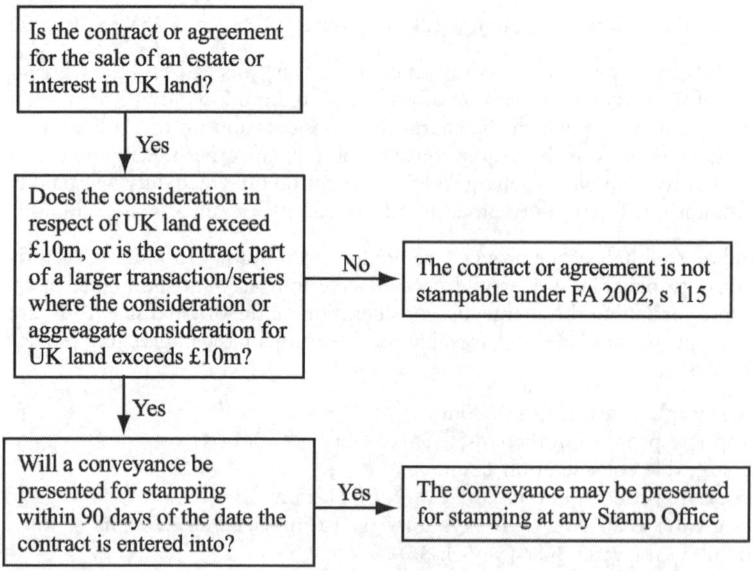

STAMP TAXES CUSTOMER NEWSLETTER
Split title schemes and section 90 FA 1965

In recent months Stamp Offices have received a significant number of documents and enquiries in connection with a perceived Stamp Duty avoidance scheme known as 'title splitting'. The purpose of this article is to publicise the Stamp Taxes' view of the Stamp Duty consequences of documents executed in connection with the implementation of the scheme, and is based on advice received from the Board's Solicitor.

The scheme typically involves the transfer of the legal title in a property by the beneficial owner to an associated company that holds the property on trust for the beneficial owner as its nominee. A number of such documents have been received on which duty of £5 has been offered, when it has been clear that discussions have been taking place at the same time for the sale of the beneficial interest in the property to a purchaser at full market value. Sometimes these further discussions may also include agreements to purchase the shares in the nominee company, or the purchase of the legal title.

It is Stamp Taxes' view that, where the transfer of the legal interest takes place at a time when there is a concurrent intention to sell the property, the transfer is made in contemplation of a sale and ad valorem duty on the full market value of the property (not simply on the nominal value of the legal interest) is payable under section 90 of the Finance Act 1965.

Section 90 charges transfers 'in contemplation of a sale'. Although no definition of that phrase is given in the section, practitioners may find the following helpful. Whilst individual cases fall to be treated according to their particular facts, the Stamp Office generally regard the presence of any of the following as indicating that a sale was in contemplation at the relevant time:

- the property is being marketed;
- negotiations for a sale have been commenced;
- an offer to purchase the property has been received;
- the property is owned by a company and the company's Board of Directors has resolved to sell it.

The above statement does not apply to any transfer made to a nominee where no sale is in contemplation and such transfers will continue to be liable to fixed duty of £5. But when such transfers are presented for stamping, the Stamp Office will require a letter confirming that no sale of the property is in contemplation. Where this clarification cannot be given we will seek to charge duty under section 90 FA 1965.

When presenting nominee transfer documents the full facts and circumstances should be disclosed to the Stamp Office. A failure to disclose the possibility of a future sale would be a breach of section 5 Stamp Act 1891.

This article reflects the view of Stamp Taxes and does not affect any person's rights to adjudication and appeal.

SDLT CUSTOMER NEWSLETTER ISSUE 1

The switch to Stamp Duty Land Tax planned to take place on 1 December 2003

Welcome to the first of a series of newsletters designed to provide guidance on the introduction of Stamp Duty land tax later this year.

BACKGROUND

In Budget 2002, the Government announced its intention to modernise the Stamp Duty charge on UK land and buildings. Current legislation was considered outdated, incompatible with modern commercial practice and the move to e-business. A modernised regime is needed to support the automated electronic systems that the land registries intend to introduce in the next 3–8 years. There has also been increasing evidence of widespread avoidance of duty in large commercial transactions. In April 2002 a consultative document was published outlining proposals of how the duty might be modernised. A number of consultative committees were established and met regularly through the summer and autumn of last year. The responses to the Consultative Document and the contributions of the various committees informed the next stage of the modernisation project. In November 2002 we published draft legislation to stimulate further debate. Following from this, the publication of the Finance Bill 2003, on 16 April sets out the statutory framework for the modernised tax, which the Chancellor has announced is planned for introduction from 1 December 2003. Not all aspects of the tax have been finalised and there is to be a further round of consultation about how it will apply in a number of complex commercial areas. But the basic fundamentals that will apply to the vast majority of transactions are set out in the primary legislation. This newsletter provides information about them and how the changes will affect our customers.

THE KEY CHANGES

Stamp Duty has always been a tax on documents. But Stamp Duty land tax will be a tax on transactions involving interests in land in the UK. The tax will not be triggered by the execution of a document. Instead, tax will become payable automatically on the due date, which will be 30 days after the effective date of the transaction. The effective date is generally the date that the purchaser acquires the subject matter of the transaction, which may be in advance of legal completion of the transfer. Another major change is that the tax will become mandatory. Stamp Duty has sometimes been regarded as a "voluntary tax" because it was not directly enforceable against any person and the Stamp Office could not compel payment of it. Payment of duty has traditionally been made as a result of the pressures that stem from having an unstamped document, the chief ones being the inadmissibility of such documents in court in civil proceedings and the fact that registrars, particularly the land registries, cannot register stampable documents that have not been stamped. The legislation introducing the tax will provide that the Purchaser, or person acquiring the subject-matter of the transaction must notify the Stamp Office of the transaction by making a land transaction return together with a self-assessment of the tax due. For this purpose "purchaser" includes a lessee where the transaction in question is the grant or assignment of a lease.

HOW WILL THE PROCESS WORK IN PRACTICE?

There are specific transitional rules that will apply to contracts entered into prior to the implementation date but which are completed after it. These will be covered in a separate newsletter. But generally from 1 December 2003, the purchaser will be required to deliver a land transaction return, giving particulars of the transaction and paying the tax that is due. The Land Transaction Return and payment should be sent to our Processing Centre at Netherton. It will not be necessary to send any supporting documentation such as the contract or the actual transfer. The return can also be submitted to local stamp offices, but this will result in a slower service, as the return has to be processed in the central location. The Processing Centre will process the return and issue a Stamp Duty land tax certificate. The certificate will be required by the land registries before they will accept documents as evidencing a change of ownership. In effect therefore, the certificate replaces the traditional duty stamps that are currently impressed on documents. The issuing of the Stamp Duty land tax certificate does not necessarily mean that the matter is finalised. We will be operating a "process now, check later system". We can open an enquiry into a transaction notified to us at any time within 9 months of the date that the return is due, or is actually notified to us, if later, (the "filing date.") As now, some transactions will not be liable to the tax either because they are below the threshold or because the transaction qualifies for a relief. These will still have to be notified to us on a land transaction return if chargeable consideration has been provided and the transaction is the transfer of a freehold, the assignment or transfer of an existing lease or the grant of a new lease for a term of seven years or more. By contrast, certain transactions will not require notification and documents can be self certified as being exempt from the tax and sent direct to the land registries. These will be subject to audits and the same enquiry process. Further guidance will be issued on this in a later newsletter. Eventually we plan to streamline the system further. The introduction of electronic conveyancing and land registration systems should allow the tax to be paid at the time of registration.

ARE THERE ANY CHANGES TO THE RATES OF DUTY?

For conveyances and transfers of land, tax will continue to be charged as a percentage of the "chargeable consideration". The definition of chargeable consideration has been widened so that it is now defined as "money or money's worth". The present rates of Stamp Duty will continue to apply to purchases of residential property and the threshold remains at £60,000. But for transactions in non-residential and mixed- use properties the threshold will be increased to £150,000 from the implementation of Stamp Duty land tax. For leases, tax on premiums will be calculated in exactly the same way as now, that is as a percentage of the amount paid. Again the threshold for non–residential and mixed-use properties will be increased to £150,000. But the Finance Bill includes legislation that provides for an entirely different method of calculating tax on new lease rents. The new charge will be levied at 1% of the net present value of rental payments payable under the terms of the lease. However, the Government has stated that it will consult further on this proposal and will not implement it if an acceptable alternative basis can be found.

LATE NOTIFICATION OF TRANSACTIONS AND LATE PAYMENT OF TAX

A land transaction return must be delivered and payment of the tax must be made within 30 days of the effective date of the transaction. Penalties are payable if the transaction is notified late and interest is payable on tax paid late.

FURTHER INFORMATION

More information will be provided in later customer newsletters. We recognise that the changes represent a major reform of part of the conveyancing system and that our customers need to be fully informed. For this reason we have developed a customer education programme that was launched in Somerset House on 16 May. We will follow this up with further customer newsletters, information bulletins and articles in Solicitors' and Conveyancers' journals and magazines. We will be enhancing our Internet site and publishing revised leaflets. In addition, we are planning a series of regional training events for the legal profession in partnership with the Law Societies of England & Wales, Scotland and Northern Ireland. In the meantime, you may like to consult our website at www.inlandrevenue.gov.uk/so/index.htm for the details published on Budget Day and when the Finance Bill was issued.

TRANSACTIONS IN SHARES

It is stressed that the information in this leaflet applies only to interests in UK land. Transactions in shares are not affected by the changes and they will continue to be liable to Stamp Duty or Stamp Duty Reserve Tax exactly as they are now.

SDLT CUSTOMER NEWSLETTER ISSUE 3
The switch to Stamp Duty Land Tax planned to take place on 1 December 2003.

COMMENCEMENT AND TRANSITIONAL PROVISIONS

This issue of the Newsletter is concerned with the introduction of Stamp Duty Land Tax on 1 December 2003. It provides guidance on whether transactions that may have been entered into prior to that date but which are completed at a later date are within the existing Stamp Duty regime, or come within the scope of Stamp Duty Land Tax.

In this article we focus on general principles and the main points that are likely to arise. It is not possible to cover every possible scenario. We have already published on our web site a flow chart that can be used to determine whether or not a transaction is a Stamp Duty or Stamp Duty Land Tax matter.

More detailed guidance will be available in the new Stamp Duty Land Tax manual that will be published in electronic form. A draft version of the manual will be published on the Internet in the beginning of October 2003. We would welcome comments on the content of the manual. Please send comments by post to; Vivienne Scrimshire, Room 116, New Wing, Somerset House, London WC2B 1LR; or alternatively these may be e-mailed to Vivienne.Scrimshire@ir.gsi.gov.uk.

The legislation dealing with the commencement and transitional provisions is contained in Schedule 19 Finance Act 2003. The Finance Act 2003 received Royal Assent on 10 July 2003 and this is an important date in considering whether or not a transaction is to be subject to Stamp Duty or Stamp Duty Land Tax.

THE BASIC CHARGE TO STAMP DUTY LAND TAX

As a general rule, a land transaction falls within the scope of Stamp Duty Land Tax if the "effective date" of the transaction is on or after "implementation date". The "effective date" of a transaction is the earlier of the transaction being completed by a conveyance, or the date that the contract is "substantially performed". Substantial performance of a contract occurs when:

- the purchaser (which includes a lessee under the terms of a lease) has paid any rent; or
- the purchaser has paid the whole or substantially the whole (not normally less than 90%) of any consideration other than rent; or
- the purchaser has taken possession, or become entitled to possession of the property. This includes receipt of, or entitlement to receipt of, rents and profits.

Implementation date means 1 December 2003.

EXAMPLE 1

A contracts to sell a property to B on 15 December 2003. The transaction is completed by the purchase price being paid in full on 15 January 2004 and a transfer is executed the same day. This is a Stamp Duty Land Tax transaction as the effective date of the transaction is after "implementation date," 1 December 2003.

Accordingly the transaction will be notifiable as a Stamp Duty Land Tax transaction on a Land Transaction Return. (For guidance on this please refer to Customer Newsletter 1, which is available on our web site).

In example 1 both the contract and the effective date of the transaction were after implementation date. It is not necessary however for the contract to have been entered into after 1 December 2003 for a transaction to be subject to Stamp Duty Land Tax. Contracts entered into prior to 1 December 2003 may give rise to a Stamp Duty Land Tax charge. (see example 2).

EXAMPLE 2

A contracts to sell a property to B on 18 September 2003. The transaction is completed by the purchase price being paid on 7 December 2003 and a transfer is executed the same day. As the effective date of the transaction is after "implementation date", the transaction is a Stamp Duty Land Tax transaction.

CONTRACTS ENTERED INTO ON OR BEFORE 10 JULY 2003

There are however, special rules that apply for land transactions that implement contracts entered into on or before 10 July 2003. The key points are as follows—

- Contracts that are substantially performed on or before 10 July 2003 are not Stamp Duty Land Tax transactions. (see example 3)

- Contracts that are not substantially performed on or before 10 July 2003 are not Stamp Duty Land Tax transactions (see example 4) unless—
  (a) there is any variation of the contract or assignment of rights under the contract after 10 July 2003; or
  (b) the transaction is effected in consequence of the exercise after 10 July 2003 of any option, right of pre-emption or similar right; or
  (c) the purchaser under the transaction is a person other than the purchaser under the contract because of a further contract (for example a sub-sale contract) made after 10 July 2003.

A variation of a contract under (*a*) does not include minor matters peripheral to the contract such as changes to colour schemes or pets being permitted on premises. It does however, include any changes to the following; the parties to the transaction, the subject matter of the sale, the contractual consideration or in an agreement for lease, the length of the term.

EXAMPLE 3

On 1 May 2003, A contracted to sell a property to B. On 1 June 2003, B paid the purchase price in full (an act of substantial performance). The contract is completed by a conveyance dated 1 March 2004. This is not a Stamp Duty Land Tax transaction because it was substantially performed on or before 10 July 2003. The conveyance is liable to Stamp Duty.

EXAMPLE 4

A contracts to sell a property to B on 1 July 2003. The contract is not substantially performed in advance of completion and none of the exceptions listed at (*a*) to (*c*) above apply. A conveyance of the property is made to the contracting purchaser, B, on 7 March 2004. This is not a Stamp Duty Land Tax transaction but the conveyance is liable to Stamp Duty.

VARIATIONS AND CONTRACTS ENTERED INTO ON OR AFTER 10 JULY 2003

Paragraph 4(3) Schedule 19 Finance Act 2003 makes special provisions for contracts entered into prior to implementation date. These include a contract made on or before 10 July 2003 which has not been substantially performed before 10 July 2003, a similar contract that has been varied after that date, or where the contracting purchaser has sub-sold or transferred his rights after that date. It also makes provision for contracts entered into in the period between 10 July 2003 and 1 December 2003.

The substantial performance of such contracts before implementation is disregarded. Consequently a charge to Stamp Duty Land Tax can only arise on completion. The following examples illustrate this.

EXAMPLE 5

A contracts to sell a property to B on 1 October 2003. Substantial performance of the contract takes place on 20 November 2003 when B pays the purchase price in full. The contract is completed by the conveyance of the property to B on 1 July 2006. A charge to Stamp Duty Land Tax arises on 1 July 2006.

EXAMPLE 6

A contracts to sell a property to B on 1 September 2003 and substantial performance occurs on 15 October 2003 when B pays the purchase price in full. On 1 November

2003 B contracts to sell the property to C. The contract is completed on 1 February 2004, when A transfers the property direct to C. There is no charge to Stamp Duty Land tax on B because the conveyance to the ultimate purchaser does not trigger a Stamp Duty Land Tax charge. C incurs a Stamp Duty Land Tax liability on 1 February 2004.

In the example above, B has been able to benefit from the availability of a modified form of sub-sale relief. But it should be borne in mind that this relief was available only because substantial performance of the A–B contract occurred before 1 December 2003. Sub-sale relief will only be available in respect of contracts entered into after 10 July 2003 in very limited circumstances. More guidance on sub-sales will be provided in a later Newsletter.

EXAMPLE 7

A contracts to sell a property to B on 1 November 2003, which is substantially performed (for the first time) on 1 March 2004 in advance of completion when B pays the purchase price. As substantial performance occurred after 1 December 2003 a Stamp Duty Land Tax charge arises on B, on 1 March 2004.

STAMP DUTY CREDIT AVAILABLE TO OFFSET AGAINST STAMP DUTY LAND TAX CHARGE

Where a Stamp Duty Land Tax transaction is effected pursuant to a contract entered into before 1 December 2003 any ad valorem Stamp Duty paid on the contract is available for crediting against the Stamp Duty Land Tax liability that arises when the transaction is substantially performed or completed. There is however, no entitlement to a refund if it transpires that the Stamp Duty liability exceeds the Stamp Duty Land tax charge.

Examples of contracts liable to ad valorem Stamp Duty are pre implementation date—

- Agreements for Lease, and
- Contracts for sale chargeable under s 115 FA 2002 (consideration exceeding £10 million).

STAMP DUTY PROVISIONS AFFECTING LAND TRANSACTIONS

- An instrument effecting a land transaction is not subject to Stamp Duty if the transaction is a Stamp Duty Land Tax transaction (s 125(5)(*a*) FA 2003)—See example 2 above.
- If a conveyance is within the charge to Stamp Duty there is no charge to Stamp Duty Land Tax—See example 4 above.
- Paragraph 8 Schedule 19 makes special provisions that broadly replicate the provisions of s 240 FA 1994 as amended, relating to Agreements for Lease and leases. The following is an example of this.

EXAMPLE 8

An agreement for lease is entered into on 1 October 2003,which is completed when the lease is executed on 1 March 2004. The Agreement for Lease is a Stamp Duty transaction because at the time that it was executed it did not effect a Stamp Duty Land Tax transaction. It is liable to Stamp Duty under paragraph 14 Schedule 13 FA 1999. Under the provisions of s 240 FA 1994 as amended, stamping of the Agreement can be deferred until 30 days after the execution of the lease without the penalty or interest provisions applying.

In these circumstances the delivery of a Stamp Duty Land Tax Return, the Agreement for Lease and payment within 30 days of 1 March 2004 will not give rise to the

Agreement incurring a Stamp Duty penalty or interest charge. Procedural guidance will be issued at a later date regarding the manner that the Return and the Agreement should be presented to Stamp Taxes.

If the Agreement for Lease had been stamped prior to the lease being granted, the duty paid on the Agreement would be credited against the Stamp Duty Land Tax charge. Again further guidance will be provided at a later date regarding the procedural arrangements.

An important point to note is that the timing differences of the Agreement for Lease and lease, which straddle the "implementation date," means that an entirely different basis of calculation is used to determine the amount of Stamp Duty payable on the Agreement, and the amount of Stamp Duty Land Tax payable when the lease is granted. This is because lease rents are charged to Stamp Duty on the average annual rent, whereas Stamp Duty Land Tax calculates tax on the net present value of the lease rents over the term. Additional information will be provided on how Stamp Duty Land Tax on lease rents is calculated in a later Newsletter.

ADDITIONAL MISCELLANEOUS PROVISIONS

In this Newsletter we have attempted to concentrate on the main issues that are likely to arise on the more routine transactions. It is not proposed to comment in greater detail on the following, which are, nevertheless, listed for information.

- Contracts liable to Stamp Duty under paragraph 7 Schedule 13 FA 1999 (equitable interests) are deemed to have been duly stamped if they are completed by a Stamp Duty Land Tax transaction. (Paragraph 6(1) Schedule 19 FA 2003.
- Transitional provisions that apply in relation to group relief and acquisition relief are provided at paragraphs 6(2) and 6(3) Schedule 19 FA 2003.
- Paragraph 7 Schedule 19 FA 2003 makes provisions for transactions which are not themselves Stamp Duty Land tax transactions but are "linked" to Stamp Duty Land Tax transactions.
- Paragraph 9 Schedule 19 FA 2003 makes provisions for options and rights of pre-emption acquired before implementation date but exercised on or after implementation date.

In addition to the further Newsletters that will be published in the run up to implementation further guidance will be given at a number of regional training events. For further information on these please refer to Newsletter issue 2, which is available on our website.

SDLT CUSTOMER NEWSLETTER ISSUE 7

Stamp Duty Reserve Tax and Stamp Duty: amalgamations and mergers of Unit Trusts and open-ended investment companies: effect of Save & Prosper Securities Ltd v CIR (SpC 251), [2000] STC (SCD) 408

BACKGROUND

Since August 2000, the Inland Revenue has, on a number of occasions, been asked to consider whether the scope of the Special Commissioners' decision in *Save & Prosper Ltd v CIR* extends to situations other than that with which that case was immediately concerned (namely, the amalgamation of two authorised unit trusts with a common trustee and manager).

This newsletter sets out the Revenue's view, following the Special Commissioners' decision, of the stamp duty and stamp duty reserve tax (SDRT) implications of various other mergers and reconstructions involving UK authorised unit trusts and open-ended investment companies.

THE *Save & Prosper* CASE

Save & Prosper Income Units and Save & Prosper UK Equity Income Fund (both authorised unit trusts with a common trustee and manager) amalgamated on 13 December 1996.

The Inland Revenue argued that a Stamp Duty Reserve Tax (SDRT) charge had arisen under section 87 Finance Act 1986. This section applies where one person agrees with another to transfer chargeable securities for money or money's worth. In this case the Revenue argued that an agreement had been made between the unit holders of the discontinuing scheme and the Appellant (the trustee and fund manager of the continuing scheme) to transfer chargeable securities (the discontinuing scheme investments) in consideration of the issue of units in the amalgamated scheme.

The Special Commissioner (Dr A N Brice) held that:

- no "agreement" was made between the unit holders of the discontinuing scheme and the Appellant. The amalgamation was a scheme of arrangement which took effect by operation of law, under the terms of the trust deed of the discontinuing scheme, the Financial Services Act 1986 and the Financial Services (Regulated Schemes) Regulations 1991. Accordingly, the amalgamation did not take effect as an agreement between the parties.
- there was no "transfer" of units in the discontinuing scheme to the unit holders of the enlarged scheme. The units in the discontinuing scheme were surrendered in return for new units in the (enlarged) continuing scheme.

WIDER IMPLICATIONS

The Inland Revenue accepts, following the Special Commissioner's decision in *Save & Prosper*, that in the following circumstances section 87 Finance Act 1986 will not normally impose a charge to SDRT, provided that the transaction in question takes place under a scheme of arrangement which has effect by virtue of section 251 of the Financial Services and Markets Act 2000, or regulation 21 of the Open-ended Investment Companies Regulations 2001 (SI 2001/1228), and the appropriate section of the Financial Services Authority Handbook (which for this purpose has replaced the Financial Services (Regulated Schemes) Regulations 1991).

Authorised Unit Trusts (AUTs)

- Where an AUT amalgamates with another AUT. This is the case whether the two AUTs share the same manager or trustee, or they have separate managers or trustees.

Sub-funds of AUTs

- Where two sub-funds of a common AUT merge.
- Where one or more sub-funds of one unit trust merge with a sub-fund of a different unit trust with the same manager or trustee.
- Where one or more sub-funds of one unit trust merge with a sub-fund of a different unit trust with a different manager or trustee.

Partitions

- Where part of the investments of an AUT or a sub-fund of an AUT are merged with the investments of another AUT or a sub-fund of that AUT.

Open-ended investment companies (OEICs)

- Where an OEIC merges with another OEIC. This is the case whether they have the same manager or depository, or different managers or depositories.

Sub-funds of OEICs

- Where two or more sub-funds of a common OEIC merge.
- Where one or more sub-funds of one OEIC merge with a sub-fund of a different OEIC with the same manager or depository.
- Where one or more sub-funds of one OEIC merge with a sub-fund of a different OEIC with a different manager or depository.

Partitions

- Where part of the investments of an OEIC or a sub-fund of an OEIC are merged with the investments of another OEIC or a sub-fund of that OEIC.

Reconstructions

- Where a sub-fund of an AUT or OEIC is reconstructed as a separate AUT or OEIC with the same manager, trustee or depository or different managers, trustees or depositories.
- Where a sub-fund of an AUT or OEIC is reconstructed as a sub-fund of a separate AUT or OEIC with the same manager, trustee or depository or different managers, trustees or depositories.
- Where the investments of an AUT or OEIC, or a sub-fund of an AUT or OEIC, are split between separate AUTs or OEICs, or separate sub-funds of an AUT or OEIC, with the same manager, trustee or depository or different managers, trustees or depositories.

Any transactions other than those listed above will continue to be dealt with on a case-by-case basis.

SDRT: SCHEDULE 19 FINANCE ACT 1999

Paragraph 2 of Schedule 19 Finance Act 1999 imposes an SDRT charge where a person surrenders units in a unit trust scheme to the manager of that scheme or requires the manager to treat him as no longer interested in units. Paragraph 18 of Schedule 19 treats each part of an umbrella scheme as a unit trust scheme. Regulations 4 and 4A of The Stamp Duty and Stamp Duty Reserve Tax (Open-ended Investment Companies) Regulations 1997 (SI 1997/1156), as amended, apply these provisions to shares in OEICs in the same way as to units in a unit trust scheme.

We accept that a charge to SDRT under para 2 of Schedule 19 does not arise in the case of conversions, amalgamations, partitions, or reconstructions of AUTs or OEICs where units or shares in the discontinuing scheme are cancelled and extinguished by the manager to allow the scheme assets to be transferred to the continuing scheme in accordance with the terms of a scheme of arrangement. In this case the unit or shareholders in the discontinuing scheme do not authorise or require the trustee or manager of that scheme to treat them as no longer interested in the units or shares.

Similarly, the issue of units or OEIC shares by the continuing scheme in accordance with the terms of a scheme of arrangement is not regarded as being an issue for the purposes of Schedule 19 Finance Act 1999.

STAMP DUTY

Paragraph 1 of Schedule 19 Finance Act 1999 disapplies a stamp duty charge on a transfer or other instrument relating to a unit under a unit trust scheme. However, units in a unit trust are "stock" for stamp duty purposes and, by virtue of para 1(2), where they form the whole or part of the consideration for a transfer on sale of property other than units under a unit trust scheme, an ad valorem stamp duty charge may still apply. Regulation 4 of SI 1997/1156 applies these provisions to shares in an OEIC.

Following the principles established in *Save & Prosper*, we accept that an amalgamation, partition or reconstruction of AUTs or OEICs under a scheme of arrangement in the situations set out above will not normally give rise to a transfer on sale and so will not normally attract ad valorem stamp duty. Nor, by virtue of para 1(1) of Schedule 19, will a fixed £5 stamp duty charge apply to any instrument of title.

STATUTORY RELIEFS: SI 1997/1156

Regulations 7–10 of SI 1997/1156 provide statutory reliefs from stamp duty and SDRT on a transfer of fund investments where an authorised unit trust converts to an OEIC, or merges with an existing OEIC.

We accept that units or OEIC shares held as an investment by an AUT or OEIC are "property" or "securities" for this purpose and that the reliefs apply where the transferring fund's investments include such units or OEIC shares.

CREST TRANSACTION STAMP STATUS

Where a transfer of securities is undertaken in CREST in consequence of any of the specific transactions referred to above, in accordance with the terms of a scheme of arrangement, CREST TSS value 6 can be used when reporting the transaction. Use of this value will be subject to periodic compliance checks and reviews.

FURTHER ENQUIRIES

Requests for advice about cases other than those identified above may be addressed in writing to Inland Revenue Stamp Taxes, Room 131 New Wing, Somerset House, London WC2R 1LB. Please include full details of the transaction concerned.

NOTE

The appropriate section means section 11.5 of the Collective Investment Schemes Sourcebook (CIS) or section 7.6 of the New Collective Investment Schemes Sourcebook (COLL) introduced by the New Collective Investment Schemes Sourcebook Instrument 2004 (FSA 2004/33).

Appendix G

Miscellaneous Stamp Office Publications

RELIEF FROM STAMP DUTY IN RESPECT OF DOCUMENTS EFFECTING INTRA-GROUP TRANSFERS OF STOCK OR MARKETABLE SECURITIES

SECTION 42, FINANCE ACT 1930, AS AMENDED

This note is a short guide on how to make a claim to relief from Stamp Duty in respect of instruments effecting certain transactions between companies in the same group. It does not cover all the points that can arise, so if further information is required please contact the Stamp Office. Alternatively, more detailed information is in the Stamp Taxes Manual which is available on the HMRC internet site: www.hmrc.gov.uk/so

INTRA-GROUP TRANSFERS

An instrument which has the effect of passing a beneficial interest in property between bodies corporate in the same group, which would otherwise be chargeable with ad valorem Stamp Duty as a transfer on sale, will not be chargeable with duty provided that a valid claim for relief is made under the provisions of Section 42 Finance Act 1930, as amended by Section 27 Finance Act 1967 and Section 123 Finance Act 2000.

BODY CORPORATE

A "body corporate" is one which has perpetual succession and a legal personality distinct from that of its members. In the United Kingdom a body corporate includes companies with limited or unlimited liability, companies limited by guarantee, charter companies and bodies created by statute. The relief is not restricted to a body corporate situated in the United Kingdom and is available to non-UK companies which the applicant can show are bodies corporate within the meaning of the legislation.

ASSOCIATED BODIES CORPORATE

One body corporate is associated with another if the following conditions are met:-

(a) the first is the beneficial owner of not less than 75% of the ordinary share capital of the second, or a third body corporate is the beneficial owner of not less than 75% of the ordinary share capital of each;

(b) the first is beneficially entitled to not less than 75% of any profits available for distribution to equity holders of the second body; and

(c) the first would be beneficially entitled to not less than 75% of any assets of the second available for distribution to its equity holders on a winding up.

Ordinary share capital means all the issued share capital of whatever description except capital the holders of which are entitled to a fixed dividend but have no other right to a share in the profits of the body corporate.

The association can be direct or through intermediate companies. A claim can, for example, be made for transactions between A and B if there is a direct relationship or between B and C which are both associated with A provided that the relationship with A meets the required test.

In cases of doubt applicants are encouraged to read the section "Bars to Relief" in the Stamp Duty Manual 6.169

HOW TO CLAIM STAMP DUTY RELIEF

Write to the Stamp Office. The letter of claim needs to be signed either by a named board member of the company through which the associated company relationship is being established, or a named solicitor or accountant acting on behalf of the parent company who is aware of the full facts and circumstances of the transaction as set out in the letter from personal knowledge. Phrases such as "I am advised" or "To the best of my knowledge and belief" are not acceptable.

With your letter include

- the instrument or instruments in respect of which relief is being claimed.
- the supporting evidence See the section below on what you need to provide

All instruments on which a claim to relief under Section 42 is made need to be lodged with the Stamp Office for formal adjudication under Section 12 of the Stamp Act 1891, together with all relevant supporting documentation. One consequence of the provisions of Section 12 is that the Stamp Office may require the evidence in support of a claim to relief to be provided in the form of a Statutory Declaration, rather than in plain letter form. In general the Stamp Office will not insist that a Statutory Declaration is sworn in support of a group relief claim although we do reserve the right to require this where we deem it to be necessary.

INFORMATION TO INCLUDE IN THE CLAIM

The letter of claim needs to include **all** of the following:-

(1) It should state that a claim for relief from Transfer on Sale duty is made under Section 42 Finance Act 1930, as amended, in respect of specified instruments.
(2) Details of the dates of all instruments on which relief is claimed.
(3) Details of the authorised and issued share capital of the parent and subsidiary companies and of any intermediate companies through which the relationship required under the legislation is traced. In the case of non-UK companies, include sufficient information to show that they qualify as bodies corporate for the purposes of the relief. A list of non-UK entities previously accepted as bodies corporate can be found in section 6.124 of the Stamp taxes manual. If the parties to the document(s) on which relief is claimed are indirectly associated a family tree diagram should also be supplied, showing percentage of ownership for each branch.
(4) State whether any class of share detailed at 3 above carries a right to only a fixed dividend and no other share in the profits.
(5) If there is more than one class of share in issue, set out the profit rights attached to each class of share and set out the asset distribution rights attached to each class of share in any winding up of the company.
(6) State whether any of the bodies corporate is in liquidation.
(7) Show details of the shareholders of all the issued shares in each subsidiary company and any intermediate company through which the relationship

required under the legislation is traced. If the relationship between companies is dependant upon shares held by nominees, documentary evidence of the beneficial ownership of the shares should be provided.

(8) Confirm that at the date of execution of the instrument on which relief is being claimed no arrangement was in existence by virtue of which at that or some later time any person had or could obtain, or any persons together had or could obtain, control of the transferee but not the transferor.

(9) Say whether it is intended that:

- the relationship required by the legislation is to be maintained
- the transferee body corporate will retain the beneficial ownership of the transferred property

(10) Give the amount of the consideration and say whether it was satisfied from cash resources (see note 4 below), through an inter-company loan account or by way of a third party loan (see note 5 below).

(11) Give an assurance that none of the documents were executed in pursuance of or in connection with an arrangement described in Section 27(3) Finance Act 1967.

SUPPORTING EVIDENCE NEEDED FOR THE CLAIM

The completed and signed letter of claim should be accompanied by:-

(1) The original of all documents and instruments referred to in the letter.

(2) Certified copies all the documents and instruments.

(3) A certified extract from the Register of Members of all subsidiary and intermediate companies as at the date of the instrument(s) on which relief is being claimed, so that the relationship between the transferor and the transferee can be easily established.

(4) A copy of the latest accounts of the transferee company if the consideration was provided from cash resources.

(5) Copies of any agreement with a third party relating to the provision of consideration.

(6) Copies of correspondence, agreements, board minutes or any other writings, etc., if the relationship between the parties or the ownership of the transferred property is not intended to continue or there was any possibility that it might not continue.

WHERE TO SEND THE CLAIM

Send your claim marked "Stamp duty – Group relief claim" to

Birmingham Stamp Office
9th Floor
City Centre House
30 Union Street
Birmingham B2 4AR
or DX 15001 Birmingham 1

Note. The publication reproduced below is the previous Stamp Office guide to intra-group relief and it pre-dated the major changes to *FA 1930, s 42* made by *FA 2000, s 123* and the announcement in Press Release REV5 on 21 March 2000 that the Stamp Office would no longer routinely require formal statutory declarations. It is reproduced for reference purposes.

STAMP OFFICE INFORMATION SHEET
Inter (sic) Group Relief from Stamp Duty (Finance Act 1930, Section 42)

This leaflet is a short guide on how you can claim relief from paying Stamp Duty in respect of documents executed between companies in the same group. It does not cover all the points that can arise, so if any further information is required please contact Worthing Stamp Office Telephone 01903 288835 or the Stamp Office (Scotland) Telephone 0131 556 8511.

The purpose of this guide is to tell you what information we need so that your claim can be processed quickly.

STAMP DUTY RELIEF IN RESPECT OF INTER GROUP TRANSACTIONS

A document which has the effect of passing a beneficial interest in property between 'bodies corporate' which would normally be liable to ad valorem duty as a conveyance or transfer on sale will be exempt from this duty provided a claim for relief is made successfully under the provisions of section 42 Finance Act 1930 as amended by section 27 Finance Act 1967 and section 149 Finance Act 1995. Section 151 Finance Act 1995 also extends the relief to Agreements for Leases and Leases which are executed inter group on or after 1 May 1995.

TRANSFER OF BENEFICIAL INTEREST

If relief from conveyance or transfer on sale duty or lease duty is being sought, a chargeable consideration must be provided and in the former case there must also have been the transfer of a beneficial interest.

Relief would not be available on documents which transferred to or from a 'body corporate' which acted in a trustee capacity, e.g. for a group pension scheme. Equally relief would not be available if a mortgagee under power of sale were to transfer property to an associated company

WHAT IS A 'BODY CORPORATE'?

A 'body corporate' is one which has perpetual succession and a legal personality distinct from that of its members. In the United Kingdom a body corporate would include companies with limited or unlimited liability, companies limited by guarantee, charter companies and bodies created by statute The relief is not restricted to a body corporate situated in the United Kingdom and is available to any non UK 'body corporate'.

ASSOCIATED BODIES CORPORATE

Bodies corporate have to be associated as follows:

(a) Prior to 1 May 1995, a body corporate had to be the beneficial owner of not less than 90% of the **issued** share capital of the other party to the transaction or a third body corporate had to be the beneficial owner of not less than 90% of the issued share capital of both the transferor and transferee companies.

(b) **For documents executed on or after 1 May 1995 bodies corporate will be associated if one is the beneficial owner of not less than 75% of the issued**

ordinary share capital of the other, or a third body corporate is the beneficial owner of not less than **75% of the issued ordinary share capital** of each body corporate. **Ordinary share capital are shares of whatever description except those which are entitled to a Fixed Dividend but have no other right to a share in the profits of the body corporate.**

In either case the relationship can be direct or through intermediate companies. So a claim can be made for transactions between A and B if there is a direct relationship or between A and C which are both associated with A provided that the relationship with A meets the required test.

DOES STAMP DUTY RELIEF UNDER SECTION 42 FINANCE ACT 1930 APPLY IN RESPECT OF AGREEMENTS FOR LEASES AND LEASES?

Yes, in respect of documents executed on or after 1 May 1995.

WHAT IS THE POSITION IF AN AGREEMENT FOR LEASE WAS EXECUTED BEFORE AND THE LEASE WAS EXECUTED ON OR AFTER 1 MAY 1995

A Lease executed on or after 1 May 1995 would not bring an Agreement for Lease executed prior to 1 May 1995 within the relieving provisions offered by section 151 Finance Act 1995. The Agreement would be chargeable to duty under section 75(1) Stamp Act 1891.

WHAT IS THE POSITION IF A BUSINESS SALE AGREEMENT AND THE TRANSFER WERE EXECUTED BEFORE AND AFTER 1 MAY 1995?

A Business Sale Agreement executed prior to 1 May 1995 might have been granted exemption from Stamp Duty under section 42 Finance Act 1930, by reason of the association of 90% of the issued share capital. An exemption for supplementary documents executed on or after 1 May 1995 would not however be available if the relationship test of 75% of the issued ordinary share capital did not exist at the date of the transfer document.

If however a Business Sale Agreement was executed prior to 1 May 1995 and did not qualify for relief, transfer documents executed on or after 1 May 1995 may qualify for relief if the relationship test of **75% of the issued ordinary share capital** did exist at the date of the supplementary document (subject of course to the other conditions being satisfied).

HOW CAN I CLAIM STAMP DUTY RELIEF?

A Statutory Declaration has to be completed which can be sworn both, within or outside the United Kingdom, before an Official authorised to administer oaths. The person swearing the Statutory Declaration should be a board member of the immediate parent company or a solicitor acting on its behalf.

WHERE SHOULD STATUTORY DECLARATIONS BE SENT?

When completed your original Statutory Declaration together with your original documents (and exhibits) should be sent to:

Worthing Stamp Office
Postal applications only
Room 35
East Block
Barrington Road
WORTHING
West Sussex BN12 4XJ
Tel: 01903 508962
DX 3799 WORTHING 1

or for companies registered in Scotland or Northern Ireland

The Stamp Office (Scotland)
Grayfield House,
5 Bankhead Avenue
EDINBURGH EH11 4BF
Tel: 0131 442 3161
DX: 54303 EDINBURGH 33

COMPLETION OF THE STATUTORY DECLARATION

To enable claims for relief from Stamp Duty under section 42 Finance Act 1930 or section 151 Finance Act 1995 to be dealt with, the following information should be provided in the Statutory Declaration:

(1) it should state that a claim under section 42 Finance Act 1930 as amended by section 27 Finance Act 1967 and section 149 Finance Act 1995 is made in respect of specified documents for Conveyance on Sale duty and/or section 151 Finance Act 1995 if in respect of Lease duty. Copies of the relevant documents should be attached to the Statutory Declaration;
(2) give details at the dates of all documents of the authorised and issued share capital of the subsidiary companies and of any intermediate companies and whether any class of share carries a right only to a Fixed Dividend and no other share in the profits. (If the parties to the transaction are indirectly associated a family tree should also be supplied);
(3) state whether any of the bodies corporate is in liquidation;
(4) show details of shares held by each shareholder in each subsidiary company and any intermediate company. If the relationship between companies is dependant upon shares held by nominees, documentary evidence evidencing the beneficial ownership of the shares should also be provided;
(5) say whether it is intended that:
  (a) the relationship required by the legislation is to be maintained;
  (b) the Transferee body corporate will retain the beneficial ownership of the transferred property.
(6) give the amount of the consideration and whether it was satisfied from cash resources, through an Inter Company Loan Account or by way of a Third Party Loan. If the latter, details of any conditions imposed on the loan should be given;
(7) give an assurance that none of the documents were executed in pursuance of or in connection with an arrangement described in section 27(3) Finance Act 1967.

The Statutory Declaration should be sent with:

- the original of all documents referred to in the Declaration;
- certified copies of all the documents;
- a certified extract from the Register of Members of all subsidiary and intermediate companies;

and where appropriate:

- a copy of the latest accounts of the Transferee company if the consideration was provided from cash resources;
- copies of any agreement with a third party relating to the provision of consideration;
- copies of correspondence, agreements, board minutes etc if the relationship between the parties or the ownership of the transferred property were not to continue.

THE STAMP OFFICE

MAY 1995

STAMP OFFICE NEWSLETTER—15 MAY 2001
Stamp Duty Reserve Tax and Individual Pension Accounts (IPAs)

UNIT TRUSTS AND OPEN-ENDED INVESTMENT COMPANIES (OEICS)

The Finance Act together with regulations published on 14 March contain the new SDRT exemption for units in unit trusts and shares in OEICs held within IPAs. The exemption came into effect from 6th April 2001. A Budget Press Release dated 7th March 2001 (REV BN8) explains the three methods (a, b or c) Investment Fund Managers have in order to operate the new exemption.

Investment Fund Managers wishing to undertake this type of business and claim the new exemption will need to ensure their systems enable them to identify units held within IPAs and provide the Stamp Office SDRT Operations Unit with relevant details.

Method (*a*) applies if a unit trust instrument requires that all units be held in IPAs, (or in the case of an OEIC the instrument of incorporation requires that all the shares must be held within IPAs). In such a unit trust or OEIC all transfers of units or shares will be exempt and no monthly return to the SDRT Operations Unit will be necessary.

Method (*b*) applies to oeics that have one or more share classes that the company's instrument of incorporation restricts to holding in IPAs, and the oeic also has at least one other class of shares which is not restricted in this way. Surrenders of shares in IPA share classes are exempt from SDRT and are left out of account for the purpose of calculating tax payable under Schedule 19 Finance Act 1999.

We suggest that an additional "exempt" category be added to the monthly SDRT Return in which you state the number of shares in the IPA class (or classes) that have been surrendered. No return will be necessary where there is no charge to SDRT for a particular month (for example, if all surrenders were of shares in the IPA classes).

Method (*c*) is only available to a unit trust that has in place systems that enable the person making the return to provide a certificate in or with the return in the following terms:

(a) that at all times in the period to which the Return relates, the trustees or managers were able to identify which of the units under the scheme were held within individual pension accounts; and
(b) that at no time in that period have the trustees or managers imposed any charge on, or recovered any amount from, an IPA unit holder which included an amount directly or indirectly attributable to tax payable by the trustees under Part II of Schedule 19 FA 1999.

In a qualifying unit trust, surrenders of units held in IPAs are exempt from SDRT and are left out of account for the purpose of calculating tax payable under Schedule 19 Finance Act 1999.

If exemption is claimed, we suggest that an additional 'exempt' category be added to the monthly SDRT return in which you state the number of exempt units that have been surrendered. No return will be necessary where there is no charge to SDRT for a particular month (for example, if all surrenders were of units held within IPAs).

Any enquiries relating to the above can be made to SDRT Operations staff, David Why 01903 509752 or Ian Timms 01903 508793.

STAMP TAXES HEADLINE ANNOUNCEMENT
Disadvantaged areas Stamp Duty exemption

The first phase of the Disadvantaged Areas relief came into force on 30 November 2001 and applies where the consideration, or premium for a lease, does not exceed £150,000. At that time the Chancellor announced his intention for the second phase to raise significantly or abolish the cap for non-residential property in disadvantaged areas.

The Chancellor has now announced that the second phase will also:

- provide for the higher cap to apply to any contract to purchase together 6 or more separate dwellings situated in a disadvantaged area; and
- ensure that the relief will extend to the grant of new leases where the average annual rent does not exceed 10% of relevant cap (depending on whether the leased property is residential or non-residential).

These changes are in response to consultation on the definition of residential for the purposes of this relief carried out earlier this year.

An announcement about the implementation date for these proposals will be made in due course.

Q&A

What is the level of the cap going to be for commercial property?

- An announcement will be made in due course, once discussions with the European Commission have been concluded.

Why classify bundles of residential property as 'non-residential' property?
Why not extend the more generous relief to any residential property?

- The landlords we are trying to encourage usually wish to acquire large numbers of properties in the same location in order to achieve economies of scale in the management of those properties.
- The purpose of this more generous relief is to encourage institutional landlords to invest in disadvantaged areas.

Are there any other changes in response to consultation?

- More minor changes to the definition may be announced when the Finance Bill is published.

How is residential property defined?

- Our consultation document published on 21 December set out a proposal for the definition of residential property;
- It is available on our website;

The legislation to be introduced in the Finance Bill will be broadly similar (but amended as explained above).

Why insist on purchases of at least six dwellings?

— This is a clear and simple rule which aims to distinguish between institutional landlords who buy in bulk in order to achieve economies of scale on management costs and individuals who may only rent out one or two properties.

— Institutional landlords are more likely to ensure the rented properties meet minimum standards

How does the relief for new leases work?

— Lease duty is a charge on the average annual rent of newly granted leases. The rate of charge depends on the length of the lease.

— The relief for disadvantaged areas will apply where the average annual rent does not exceed 10% of the relevant cap.

So for residential properties where the cap is £150,000, the relief on new leases will apply to those where the average annual rent does not exceed £15,000.

STAMP OFFICE MANUAL
Section 3.32

3.32 Customers are advised in leaflet SO10 that it is important for them to tell us about any factors which they consider relevant to the delay, when sending a document to us. They are also told that if they do not agree with the amount of penalty we are asking for they should let us know why they disagree. They should provide us with any additional information relating to the delay which might help us in reconsidering their case. See the note headed "General" in the following table.

TABLE OF MITIGATED PENALTIES ON LATE STAMPING

Ad valorem duty cases under one year late

Months Late	*Up to £300*	*£305– £700*	*£705– £1,350*	*£1,355– £2,500*	*£2,505– £5,000*	*Over £5,000*
Under 3	Nil	£20	£40	£60	£80	£100
Under 6	*£20	£40	£60	£80	£100	£150
Under 9	*£40	£60	£80	£100	£150	£200
Under 12	*£60	£80	£100	£150	£200	£300

* or duty if less

Ad valorem duty cases over one year late

Months Late	*Under £5,000*
Under 15	15% or £100 if greater
Under 18	25% or £150 if greater
Under 21	35% or £200 if greater
Under 24	45% or £250 if greater

Percentage amounts are to be rounded **down** to the nearest multiple of £5.

Cases that are over one year late **and** over £5,000 duty and any cases two years late or more are to be submitted to your Technical Service Unit Manager and will be subject to individual review.

FIXED DUTY CASES

The statutory rule is that the penalty due on late presentation of a document liable to duty of £5 is a maximum of £5 if it is up to one year late and a maximum of £300 if it is over one year late.

However in practice we will mitigate the statutory penalty due to Nil if the document is presented up to 1 year late. No penalty will therefore be charged. Cases where a fixed duty document is presented over 1 year late should be submitted to your Technical Service Unit Manager and will be subject to individual review.

GENERAL

Deviations from the amounts prescribed in this table, say for example down if there is a reasonable excuse for lateness, or up depending on the circumstances, and all fixed duty cases over one year late must be agreed by your TSU Manager who will seek advice from the Assistant Director (Policy, Technical & Legislation). It is expected that cases which warrant any deviation from this table will be very rare.

SDLT—CONSTRUCTION CONTRACTS
Sale of land with associated construction, etc, contract
2 April 2005

We have been asked how to determine the chargeable consideration for Stamp Duty Land Tax purposes where V agrees to sell land to P and V also agrees to carry out work (commonly works of construction, improvement or repair) on the land sold. Our view is that the decision in *Prudential Assurance Co Ltd v IRC* [1992] STC 863 applies for the purposes of Stamp Duty Land Tax as it does for stamp duty. This is because the basis of the decision was the identification of the subject matter of the transaction and this is as relevant for Stamp Duty Land Tax as it is for stamp duty.

It follows that SP8/93 will be applied for Stamp Duty Land Tax as it was for stamp duty. The paragraphs on 'contracts already entered into' and 'procedure for submitting documents' are, however, not relevant to Stamp Duty Land Tax.

Where, however, the sale of land and the construction, etc, contract are in substance one bargain (as they were in the *Prudential* case) there must be a just and reasonable apportionment of the total consideration given for all elements of the bargain in order to arrive at the chargeable consideration for Stamp Duty Land Tax purposes.

SDLTM31800—APPLICATION
Transactions involving Pension Funds

Any transaction, where a pension fund is the purchaser, is subject to SDLT in the same way as any other transaction. There are no special rules for pension funds. SDLT will only be due where there is chargeable consideration (paragraph 1, Schedule 4, Finance Act 2003) for the transaction.

Where there is a transfer of assets and obligations from one pension fund to another, e.g. on the payment of a statutory cash equivalent transfer value for an individual, or on a merger of funds, the transfer of land from the trustees of one pension fund to the trustees of another is the acquisition of a chargeable interest under FA03/S48. This means it is within the scope of SDLT.

The normal charge to tax under SDLT arises on the consideration given for the land transaction.

In our view the assumption by the transferee fund or by the trustees of the transferee fund, of obligations to provide benefits is not chargeable consideration.

If other consideration is given by the transferee fund, or trustees of the transferee fund, in the form of money or money's worth then that will be chargeable consideration.

There would also be chargeable consideration if the transfer of obligations were in consideration of a defined monetary sum to be satisfied by the release of obligations by the former trustees.

SDLTM31810—APPLICATION
Transactions involving Pension Funds—Borrowing and Mortgages

A pension fund may borrow money and may grant a mortgage or other charge over land as security.

For SDLT purposes, it is necessary to consider the borrowing and the mortgage separately in the context of a transfer described above.

BORROWING

If the transferee fund, or trustees of transferee fund:

- assume an existing liability of the transferor fund or trustees of the transferor fund to repay borrowing or
- otherwise bring about the release of the transferor fund or trustees of the transferor fund from the debt and
- they do so as part and parcel of such a transfer

then we will not treat FA03/SCH4/PARA8 as meaning that there is chargeable consideration given for the land transaction.

MORTGAGES

Mortgages and other legal charges are security interests and dealings with them, including their creation and release, are specifically exempt from SDLT.

NOTIFICATION

A land transaction for no consideration is exempt from notification under FA03/S77, so notification is only required where chargeable consideration over £40,000 is given for the transaction.

See examples at SDLTM31811 and SDLTM31812.

SDLTM31811—APPLICATION—TRANSACTIONS INVOLVING PENSION FUNDS—EXAMPLE

Example 1

Pension fund A purchases a dwelling house from individual A for £275,000. SDLT is due on that consideration at the appropriate rate.

An SDLT1 should be lodged showing the £275,000 as consideration.

SDLTM31812—APPLICATION—TRANSACTIONS INVOLVING PENSION FUNDS—EXAMPLE

Example 2

Pension fund A transfers all its assets to Pension fund B, these assets include UK land and property. There is a £500,000 mortgage secured on these properties and the transfer is subject to this charge plus a sum of £2.3m. The transfer of this land is a land transaction: the chargeable consideration will be a just and reasonable apportionment of the £2.3m (i.e. the amount that relates to the UK land and property) plus the £500,000 debt. The obligation to provide benefits to A's pension holders is not chargeable consideration.

An SDLT1 should be lodged showing the total of the apportioned consideration plus the £500,000 debt assumed.

[**Author's note:** This example appears to contradict the statement in SDLTM31810 above that the assumption of borrowings or release of the transferor fund by the transferee fund as part and parcel of the transfer will not be treated as chargeable consideration.]

SDLTM31820—APPLICATION

Pension Funds and linked transactions

Purchases by pension funds are subject to the provisions of section 108 Finance Act 2003. Where a fund purchases more than one property, the question of linkage should be addressed. If the transactions are part of a single scheme or arrangement or a part of a series of transactions between the same vendor and purchaser or, in either case, persons connected with them, then they will be regarded as linked. Tax is due on each transaction at the rate applicable to the total of the chargeable considerations passing for all those transactions involved.

Example

Fund A agrees with individual B to purchase 3 parcels of land for £150,000 each. These purchases are regarded as linked. SDLT is due on each parcel at the rate applicable to the total consideration passing, £450,000.

One SDLT1 covering the three properties, or three separate SDLT1's, each showing the transaction to be linked and the total consideration for all three shown, should be lodged.

Note: the previous announcement concerning pension schemes is reproduce below for reference.

PENSION SCHEMES—STAMP DUTY, SDRT AND SDLT

8 June 2005

Q: Do SDRT, stamp duty or SDLT arise on the transfer of assets and liabilities between pension schemes where the only consideration is the assumption by the receiving scheme of the obligation to pay pension benefits?

A: Where, on the merger of pension schemes or on other transfers of assets between such schemes, the only consideration for the transfer of assets from the transferring scheme to the receiving scheme is the assumption by the receiving scheme of the obligation to pay pension benefits (and any other benefits permitted to be provided by Inland Revenue approved pension schemes) to the former members of the transferring scheme:

(1) No charge to SDRT will arise. This will be the case whether or not the assets of the transferring scheme consist of or include units or shares in a UK unit trust or open-ended investment company. There is no consideration in money or money's worth for SDRT purposes and therefore no charge arises under section 87 FA 1986 or Schedule 19 FA 1999.
Notwithstanding the absence of a Schedule 19 charge to SDRT, where units or shares in a UK unit trust or open-ended investment company are transferred in such a way that a change of ownership needs to be recorded in the unit or share register, the fund manager will need to report as a third party exemption the number of units or shares surrendered on his monthly SDRT Notice. The fund manager will also need to retain sufficient evidence to support the third party exemption in the event of an inspection by the Inland Revenue.

(2) No ad valorem stamp duty will arise in respect of the agreement for the transfer of assets from the transferring scheme to the receiving scheme because the assumption of the liability by the trustee of the receiving scheme to provide pension benefits to members of the transferring scheme is not chargeable consideration for stamp duty purposes. However, all transfer documents or other instruments that give effect to the transfer of stock or marketable securities from the transferring scheme to the receiving scheme are liable to a fixed stamp of £5.

(3) No charge to SDLT will arise on any transfers of land from the transferring scheme to the receiving scheme because there is no agreement to transfer land for consideration in money or money's worth.

STAMP DUTY LAND TAX (VARIATION OF THE FINANCE ACT 2003) REGULATIONS 2006
Interim guidance on section 75A Finance Act 2003

This note gives guidance on new *section 75A Finance Act 2003*, inserted by *paragraph 1* of the *Schedule* to the *Stamp Duty Land Tax (Variation of the Finance Act 2003) Regulations 2006 (2006 SI No 3237)*. It supplements the Technical Note issued by HM Revenue & Customs on 6 December 2006.

The guidance in this note has been produced in response to enquiries and representations, as an interim measure to assist taxpayers and their advisers. It should not be taken as representing HM Revenue & Customs' settled view, nor as being of general application. The guidance has effect only for transactions to which the Regulations apply and not for transactions to which any provisions of *Finance Act 2007* will apply. Revised guidance will be published for transactions to which any similar provisions of *Finance Act 2007* might apply.

HM Revenue & Customs will accept that the *2006 Regulations* may be applied subject to the following guidance:

- A construction contract is not a scheme transaction in relation to a land transaction where the circumstances are such that, by virtue of the decision in *Prudential Assurance Co Ltd v IRC* [1992] STC 863 (see SDLTM04015), the consideration properly attributable to the construction contract is not part of the chargeable consideration for the land transaction.
- The carrying out of works of construction, improvement or repair of a building or other works to enhance the value of land is not a scheme transaction in relation to the purchase of the land provided that the works are not carried out by the vendor or a person connected with the vendor.
- The purchase of assets other than land is not a scheme transaction in relation to a land transaction where the provisions of *paragraph 4 of Schedule 4 Finance Act 2003* apply to the apportionment of consideration between the purchase of assets and the land transaction.
- A transfer of shares in a company or units in a unit trust which is not preceded by any land transaction in relation to which it might be a scheme transaction is not a scheme transaction in relation to any subsequent land transaction.
- A loan from a person who is not a party to, or connected with a party to, any other scheme transaction to fund the purchase of property is not a scheme transaction in relation to the purchase of the property.
- Where a land transaction qualifies for reconstruction relief or acquisition relief the issue of shares under *paragraph 7(2) or 8(2) of Schedule 7 Finance Act 2003* is not a scheme transaction in relation to that land transaction.
- Where the only transactions are the transfer of a number of properties into a partnership by partners none of the transfers is a scheme transaction in relation to any of the other transfers.
- Where the only transactions are the purchase of land and a lease (or leases) of all or part of the land to a person not connected with the purchaser of the land the purchase is not a scheme transaction in relation to the lease(s) and vice versa.
- Land transactions involving separate parcels of land are not scheme transactions in relation to each other.

STAMP DUTY LAND TAX (SDLT) TECHNICAL NEWS
Issue 5 – August 2007

SDLT FINANCE ACT CHANGES 2007

The main SDLT changes contained in the Finance Act 2007, which received Royal Assent on 19 July 2007 are:

- SDLT rates and thresholds remain unchanged by Budget 2007.

For transactions with an effective date on or after 22 March 2007:

- Reliefs for alternative property finance will be extended, to allow dealings in the interest held by the financial institution to take place free of SDLT. Further details about this measure are published in Technical Note [http://www.hmrc.gov.uk/so/further-provisions.htm].

Apart from the extension of reliefs for 'alternative property finance' there were no changes which took effect before Royal Assent to the Finance Bill.

From Royal Assent to the Finance Bill:

- The relief from SDLT offered to shared-ownership leases will be replicated for shared ownership trusts (a new way of providing affordable housing).
- The exchange of property between connected persons will no longer be treated as a linked transaction for the purposes of SDLT.
- Existing stamp duty and SDLT reliefs for certain transfers of surplus school land under provisions in the School Standards and Framework Act 1998 will be repealed. These provisions are amended by the Education and Inspections Act 2006 and Regulations will be introduced to bring transactions under the amended provisions within the general SDLT relief for statutory transfers involving public bodies.
- The Government will make two minor changes to SDLT legislation which will facilitate development of electronic conveyancing and registration systems.
- There will be permanent provision to counter SDLT avoidance schemes, replacing the Regulations made on 6 December 2006. These provisions, in particular, increase the number of circumstances in which a charge on a partner in property investment partnership can arise, for example, where there are new properties added into the investment portfolio on or after Royal Assent and where there are changes to profit sharing ratios.
- For those of you who read documents placed on the HMRC website following Budget 2007, we regret that there was a slight discrepancy between what paragraph 3 of Budget Note 22 says about the effective date of the anti-avoidance measures and what was in the Finance Bill. **The Budget Note stated "This change will have effect for any transaction the effective date of which is on or after the date on which Finance Bill 2007 receives Royal Assent."** At the time of the Budget this was what we were planning to do but following further discussion of our draft legislation our intentions changed.

  We would therefore like to clarify that as Clause 71 was enacted in its current form by the Finance Act 2007, the version of section 75A contained in the Act (and not that in the Regulations) will apply to any transaction on or after 6 December 2006, subject to the transitional provisions.
- Changes will be made to the stamp duty and stamp duty land tax acquisition reliefs. A company that has purchased its own shares will no longer be regarded as a shareholder of itself for the purpose of the reliefs.

From 1 October 2007:

A time limited relief from SDLT for most zero-carbon homes on first acquisition will be introduced to help kick start the market for new technologies and techniques that will be needed to support the Government's ambition that all new homes be zero carbon by 2016. The relief will be available on the first sale of new zero-carbon homes from 1 October 2007. More details [at http://www.hmrc.gov.uk/budget2007/bn26.pdf].

More detail on specific measures can be found on the Budget 2007 page [http://www.hmrc.gov.uk/budget2007/index.htm].

FINANCE ACT 2007 MEASURE IN RELATION TO FORM SDLT 60

Section 81 of the Finance Act 2007 which inserts a new paragraph 2A into Schedule 11 FA 2003 only allows agents to sign an SDLT 60 self-certificate where this is in a form specified by HMRC for this purpose. This measure is intended to allow electronic submission of self-certificates to Registers of Scotland via the ARTL (Automated Registration of Title to Land) system and in due course to the Land Registry via the forthcoming e-Conveyancing system.

Although we had not intended to extend this facility to the paper SDLT 60 we will consider whether there is any merit to doing such. Meanwhile agents should not amend the form in order to sign it on their clients' behalf; it will not be accepted by the land registries.

SECTION 75A FINANCE ACT 2003

1. Section 75A FA 2003 is intended to counter certain schemes which have the effect of reducing stamp duty land tax (SDLT) liability. Section 75A exists in two versions. The first was introduced by The Stamp Duty Land Tax (Variation of the Finance Act 2003) Regulations 2006 (2006 SI No 3237) ('the Regulations'). The Regulations were made on 6 December 2006. The second was introduced by section 71 FA 2007 (which also introduces supplementary provision in sections 75B and 75C).

Commencement

2. The FA provisions have effect (replacing the provisions in Regulations) in respect of disposals and acquisitions if

   - the disposal (see below) takes place after 2 p.m. on 6 December 2006, and
   - all the scheme transactions (see below) take place after that time.

3. However section 75C does not have effect where a disposal takes place before 19 July 2007 (the date of Royal Assent to FA 2007) and the effect of section 75C would be to impose a higher tax charge than that provided for in the Regulations.
4. The transitional provisions are set out in paragraphs 35–37 below.

General application of section 75A

5. Section 75A applies where

   - one person ('V') disposes of a chargeable interest,
   - another person ('P') acquires that interest, or a chargeable interest derived from it, and
   - a number of transactions ('scheme transactions'), including the disposal and acquisition, are involved in connection with the disposal and acquisition, and
   - the total SDLT payable in respect of all the scheme transactions is less than the amount that would be payable on a notional land transaction effecting the acquisition (the 'tax saving' test).

6. 'Chargeable interest' is as defined in section 48. 'Disposal' and 'acquisition' have the extended meanings set out in section 43.

Scheme transactions

7. The term 'transaction' includes in particular:

   - a transaction which is not a land transaction;
   - an agreement, offer or undertaking not to take specified action;
   - any kind of arrangement whether or not it could otherwise be described as a transaction;

- a transaction which takes place after the acquisition by P of the chargeable interest.

8. Section 75A(3) gives examples of what may be scheme transactions:

- the acquisition by P of a lease deriving from a freehold owned or formerly owned by V;
- a sub-sale to a third person;
- the grant of a lease to a third person subject to a right to terminate;
- the exercise of a right to terminate a lease or to take some other action;
- an agreement not to exercise a right to terminate a lease or to take some other action;
- the variation of a right to terminate a lease or to take some other action.

Scheme transactions 'involved in connection with' a disposal and acquisition

9. The first three bullet points in paragraph 5 above must be read together. Thus the first step is to identify a disposal and the relevant V, the second step is to identify an acquisition and the relevant P and the third step is to consider whether a number of transactions are 'involved in connection with' the disposal and acquisition. In a complex scenario this process may need to be repeated with different identifications of V and P, possibly with different results.

10. The phrase 'involved in connection with' implies that there must be some connection between the disposal and acquisition on the one hand and the transactions on the other which goes beyond the fact that a number of transactions happen in chronological order, and that they affect the same property.

11. In particular it is unlikely that (except on a transfer of rights, see below) section 75A can apply to a disposal by V and an acquisition by P where

- neither P nor his associates nor his advisers have had any involvement in or any connection with transactions other than the one by which P acquired the property, *and*
- neither P nor his associates obtains any SDLT benefit from the way in which the acquisition is effected

12. However section 75A will apply where the acquisition by P is effected by a 'transfer of rights' within the meaning of section 45, for example a sub-sale. So if V agrees to sell to X and X agrees to sell on to P section 75A applies to the disposal by V and the acquisition by P whether or not P or his associates or his advisers had any involvement in or connection with the V–X contract.

13. Section 75A(1)(b) refers to the scheme transactions as being 'involved in connection with' *the disposal and acquisition*. Thus scheme transactions need not necessarily be connected with each other. For example, if V agrees to sell to X and X agrees to sell to P the two transactions are 'involved in connection with' the disposal by V and the acquisition by P even if V is unaware of the sale on by X.

14. There follow some examples where section 75A does not apply to a disposal by V and an acquisition by P because there are not a number of transactions involved in connection with the disposal and acquisition.

Examples

(1) V sells two properties at arm's length to third party purchasers N1 and N2. At some later stage, and in transactions which are not connected in any way with the purchases by N1 and N2, P buys both properties at arm's length. Section 75A does not apply as regards the disposal by V and the acquisition by P.

(2) V grants a long lease to X. At a later stage, and in a transaction which is not connected in any way with the grant of the lease, X assigns the lease to an unconnected third party P. P exercises a statutory right of enfranchisement. Section 75A does not apply as regards the disposal by V and the acquisition by P.

(3) V grants an option to purchase land to X. At a later stage, and in a transaction which is not connected in any way with the grant of the option, X assigns the benefit of the option to an unconnected third party P. P exercises the option. Section 75A does not apply as regards the disposal by V and the acquisition by P.

(4) V agrees to sell land to H. H agrees to sell on to his spouse W. These transactions are completed at the same time. At a later stage W sells on to an unconnected third party P. Section 75A does not apply as regards the disposal by V and the acquisition by P (although section 75A will apply as regards the disposal by V and the acquisition by W).

(5) V agrees to sell land to P. P agrees to sell on to C. The transactions are completed at the same time. Section 75A does not apply as regards the disposal by V and the acquisition by P (although section 75A will apply as regards the disposal by V and the acquisition by C). The sale on to C is not 'involved in connection with' the disposal by V and the acquisition by P because it does not in any way affect the nature of the interest acquired by P.

15. There follow some examples where a number of transactions *are* involved in connection with a disposal by V and an acquisition by P.

Examples

(1) V grants a 999-year lease to N for no premium and a peppercorn rent. V assigns the freehold reversion to P for a nominal sum. P pays N £X in consideration of N's agreement to vary the lease by the insertion of a provision giving the landlord the right to terminate the lease for no payment. P exercises the right to terminate.

(2) V grants a 999-year lease to N for no premium and a peppercorn rent. The lease includes a right for the landlord to terminate the lease on payment of £X to the tenant. V assigns the freehold reversion to P for a nominal sum. P exercises the right to terminate and pays N £X.

(3) V grants a 999-year lease to P for no premium and a peppercorn rent. The lease gives the landlord a right to terminate it within 14 days of the date of grant. P offers to pay V £X if V allows the 14 days to elapse without exercising the right to terminate. V does so (an example of a scheme transaction which occurs after the acquisition of the chargeable interest by P).

(4) V agrees to sell property to N for £10 million. N agrees to sub-sell the property to P. Both transactions are completed at the same time. (See the note above on the application of section 75A where an acquisition is effected by means of a 'transfer of rights').

(5) V agrees to sell property to N Ltd for £10 million. N Ltd declares a dividend in favour of P, its sole shareholder, the dividend to consist of the property and to be paid at the same time as completion of the V–N Ltd contract. The contract is completed and the property transferred to P.

The tax-saving test and notional consideration

16. If there is a disposal and acquisition, and a number of transactions are involved in connection with the disposal and acquisition, the final step is to consider the tax saving test. For this purpose it is necessary to identify the 'amount that would

be payable on a notional land transaction' and compare the SDLT payable on that amount with the sum of the amounts of SDLT payable in respect of the scheme transactions.

17. The amount that would be payable on a notional land transaction (referred to in this guidance as the 'notional consideration') is specified in section 75A(5). It is the largest amount (or aggregate amount):

- given by or on behalf of any one person by way of consideration for the scheme transactions, or
- received by or on behalf of V (or a person connected with V) by way of consideration for the scheme transactions.

18. 'Connected with' has the same meaning as in section 839 ICTA 1988.

19. The following show how the notional consideration is calculated.

Examples

HM Revenue & Customs does not accept that the tax saving test is necessarily satisfied in any of these examples.

(1) V grants a 999-year lease to N for no premium and a peppercorn rent. V assigns the freehold reversion to P for a nominal sum. P pays N £X in consideration of N's agreement to vary the lease by the insertion of a provision giving the landlord the right to terminate the lease for no payment. P exercises the right to terminate.
The notional consideration is £X, the amount given by P and received by N.

(2) V grants a 999-year lease to N for no premium and a peppercorn rent. The lease includes a right for the landlord to terminate the lease on payment of £X to the tenant. V assigns the freehold reversion to P for a nominal sum. P exercises the right to terminate and pays N £X.
The notional consideration is £X, the amount paid by P and received by N.

(3) V grants a 999-year lease to P for no premium and a peppercorn rent. The lease gives the landlord a right to terminate it within 14 days of the date of grant. P offers to pay V £X if V allows the 14 days to elapse without exercising the right to terminate. V does so (an example of a scheme transaction which occurs after the acquisition of the chargeable interest by P).
The notional consideration is £X, the amount paid by P and received by V.

(4) V agrees to sell property to N for £10 million. N agrees to sub-sell the property to P for £5. Both transactions are completed at the same time.
The notional consideration is £10 million, the amount received by V.

(5) V agrees to sell property to N Ltd for £10 million. N Ltd declares a dividend in favour of P, its sole shareholder, the dividend to consist of the property and to be paid at the same time as completion of the V–N Ltd contract. The contract is completed and the property transferred to P.
The notional consideration is £10 million, the amount received by V.

Incidental transactions

20. In calculating the notional consideration the consideration properly attributable to 'incidental' transactions (on a just and reasonable apportionment) is disregarded. Incidental transactions are those that are *merely incidental* to the disposal by V and the acquisition by P.

21. Examples of incidental transactions are:

- the sale or supply of anything other than land (for example, the sale of chattels or moveables);
- the construction of a building on the subject matter of the disposal and acquisition;
- a loan to P secured by a mortgage, to enable P to pay for all or part of the chargeable interest he acquires.

22. However a transaction is not incidental if:
    - it forms part of a process, or series of transactions, by which the disposal and acquisition are effected, or
    - it is one of the examples of scheme transactions in section 75A(3) (paragraph 8 above), or
    - (except in the case of the sale or supply of anything other than land) the disposal and acquisition is conditional on the completion of the transaction.

The effect of section 75A

23. Where section 75A applies:
    - the individual scheme transactions are disregarded for SDLT purposes
    - there is instead a notional transaction effecting the acquisition of V's chargeable interest (that is the chargeable interest which was the subject matter of the disposal by V) by P
    - the chargeable consideration for the notional transaction is the notional consideration (see above).
24. Thus in the Examples in paragraph 19 above the notional transaction is as follows (assuming again that the tax saving test is satisfied) and the chargeable consideration is the notional consideration as stated above:
    (1) The acquisition of the freehold by P.
    (2) The acquisition of the freehold by P.
    (3) The grant by V of a 999-year lease to P.
    (4) The acquisition of the property by P.
    (5) The acquisition of the property by P.
25. The effective date of the notional transaction is the last date of completion of the scheme transactions or, if earlier, the last date on which a contract in respect of the scheme transactions is substantially performed.
26. Stamp duty land tax paid in respect of a land transaction which is disregarded because of the application of section 75A is treated as having been paid in respect of the notional transaction.

Other provisions

27. A transfer of shares or securities (or units in a unit trust scheme) is ignored for the purposes of section 75A if it would otherwise be the first of a series of scheme transactions (and several such transfers are likewise ignored if they all precede any other scheme transaction).
28. The notional transaction attracts any relief which it would attract if it were an actual land transaction. In addition the consideration attributable to any scheme transaction which would qualify for relief under section 60, 61, 63, 64, 65, 66, 67, 69, 71, 74 or 75, or Schedules 6A or 8, is disregarded in calculating the notional consideration.
29. Some reliefs involve a number of transactions where the tax saving test will almost certainly be satisfied. Accordingly, section 75A does not apply where the tax saving test is satisfied by reason only of sections 71A to 73 (alternative

property finance) or a provision in Schedule 9 (right to buy, shared ownership leases, &c).

30. If any of the scheme transactions is entered into for the purposes of or in connection with the transfer of an undertaking or part of an undertaking for the purposes of paragraphs 7 or 8 of Schedule 7 (reconstruction and acquisition relief) then the notional transaction is also deemed to be entered into for such purposes or in such connection. This enables the notional transaction to qualify for reconstruction or acquisition relief if the other conditions for relief are satisfied.
31. The notional transaction will be subject to the market value rule in section 53 if P is a company connected with V.
32. If part of the consideration for the notional transaction is a land transaction entered into by V as purchaser, or by P as vendor, then the market value rules in paragraph 5 of Schedule 4 will apply.
33. An interest in a property investment partnership is treated as a chargeable interest for the purposes of section 75A.
34. Where V or P is a partnership the provisions in Part 3 of Schedule 15 apply as they would to the transfer of a chargeable interest into or out of a partnership.

Transitional provisions

35. Section 75A, and the Regulations, do not have effect in relation to:

- any scheme transaction which is effected in pursuance of a contract entered into and substantially performed before 2 p.m. on 6 December 2006 (the 'relevant time');
- any other scheme transaction which is effected in pursuance of a contract entered into before the relevant time and which is not an 'excluded transaction'.

36. For this purpose, a scheme transaction effected in pursuance of a contract is an excluded transaction if:

- at or after the relevant time the contract is varied in a way that significantly affects the scheme transaction,
- the subject-matter of the scheme transaction is not identified in the contract in a way that would have enabled its acquisition before the relevant time,
- rights under the contract are assigned at or after the relevant time,
- the scheme transaction is effected in consequence of the exercise, at or after the relevant time, of any option, right of pre-emption or similar right, or
- at or after the relevant time there is an assignment, sub-sale or other transaction (relating to the whole or part of the contract's subject-matter) as a result of which a person other than the purchaser under the contract becomes entitled to call for a conveyance to him.

37. A contract is varied in a way that significantly affects the scheme transaction if (and only if):

- it is varied so as to substitute a different purchaser in relation to the scheme transaction,
- it is varied so as to alter the subject-matter of the scheme transaction, or
- it is varied so as to alter the consideration for the scheme transaction.

PARTNERSHIP PROPERTY

A chargeable interest is partnership property for SDLT purposes if:

- it is held by or on behalf of the partnership, or by all the members of the partnership, and
- it is held for the purposes of the partnership business (paragraph 34 of Schedule 15 FA 2003).

These two tests must both be satisfied in order for a chargeable interest to be partnership property. Each is a question of fact. Often there will be an agreement between the partners which will be determinative as to the facts in the particular case.

In practice whether a chargeable interest is or is not partnership property for SDLT purposes will be decided in similar manner as whether or not it is partnership property by virtue of section 20 of the Partnership Act 1890. So a chargeable interest acquired, whether by purchase or otherwise, on account of the firm, or for the purposes and in the course of the partnership business, will be partnership property for SDLT purposes.

The mere fact that a business is carried on in property belonging to one or more partners does not make that partner's chargeable interest partnership property. Where a chargeable interest is owned by all the partners then whether it is partnership property will depend upon the basis on which it is held by the co-owners.

It is unlikely (in England & Wales and Northern Ireland) that a chargeable interest in which the equitable interests were subject to an express declaration of joint tenancy on acquisition is partnership property unless there is clear evidence of a change of intention to bring the chargeable interest in as an asset of the partnership business.

There is further guidance on the definition of partnership property at BIM72058 [http ://www.hmrc.gov.uk/manuals/bimmanual/BIM72058.htm]. This article supersedes the guidance in draft SDLTM35100 [http://www.hmrc.gov.uk/so/pftmanual.htm#20].

SDLT CODE OF PRACTICE 10 EXTENSION

At Budget 2007, HM Revenue & Customs (HMRC) announced that it would take forward the proposals in the Review of Links with Large Business [http://www.hmrc.gov.uk/large-business/review-report.pdf] (published in November 2006). The second proposal was:

> "The extension of existing clearances so that as normal business practice, HMRC will provide businesses with their view of the tax consequences of significant commercial issues whenever there is uncertainty."

Code of Practice 10 (COP 10) (Information and Advice), the guidance on clearances, says that where there is genuine uncertainty about the meaning of the law HMRC will advise upon their interpretation of legislation passed in the last four Finance Acts. The proposal from the Review of Links with Large Business means that, by Budget 2008, regardless of when legislation was enacted, HMRC will provide advice on the tax consequences of genuine significant commercial issues.

Also announced at Budget 2007, was that during 2007/08, there would be an early extension of clearance work where there is genuine uncertainty regarding the interpretation of tax legislation (without time limit) in two particular areas of tax law:

- Stamp duty land tax from Royal Assent of Finance Act 2007; and
- Substantial Shareholding Exemption (SSE) from 01 June 2007

The Code of Practice 10 facility for the purpose of the Substantial Shareholding Exemption was reinstated on 1 June 2007. Following the Royal Assent of Finance Act

2007 on 19 July 2007 HMRC will now, in line with the commitment made at Budget 2007, be extending the application of the Code of Practice 10 for all businesses to areas of genuine uncertainty regarding stamp duty land tax without a time limit. This means that the Code of Practice facility will cover all stamp duty land tax legislation going back to its introduction in Finance Act 2003.

Clearance requests under Code of Practice 10 on stamp duty land tax matters should be submitted to

HM Revenue & Customs
Birmingham Stamp Office (COP 10)
9th Floor
City Centre House
30 Union Street
Birmingham B2 4AR

SDLT 1 QUESTION 9 (ARE YOU CLAIMING RELIEF?) – THE CHARITIES REGISTRATION NUMBER THAT SHOULD BE ENTERED

It is not uncommon for a corporate trustee – for example a charity in its own right – to be trustee of charitable trusts that are not separate persons but have their own charity numbers.

The charities registration number entered at question 9 on the SDLT 1 Return should be that of the person which is the purchaser for SDLT purposes, as this is also the claimant of the relief. Where the legal purchaser purchases as a bare trustee, the purchaser for SDLT purposes will be the beneficial owner.

SDLT 6 GUIDANCE NOTES – GUIDANCE ON COMPLETING SDLT 1 QUESTION 12

What form does the consideration take? – Code 34 or 37

For transactions where SDLT is chargeable on the **market value** of the property acquired rather than the actual consideration paid (for example, an exchange of properties where at least one of the interests is a major interest), **code 34** should be used at question 12 unless it is an exchange in which case code 37 applies. See the guidance below contained within the SDLT 6 Guidance Notes for using codes 34 and 37.

'Other (such as an annuity)' – Code 34

[See SDLTM06010 http://www.hmrc.gov.uk/manuals/sdltmanual/SDLTM06010.htm.]

> *'Any other consideration, in money's worth, not otherwise listed here, or, as noted above, the market value of the interest in land acquired should be notified using code 34 except for exchanges where code 37 should be used'.*

Within this section of the guidance, the reference to the market value of land under Code 34 is intended to refer back to the note about market value and Code 34 on the preceding page. However we agree that the reference in the guidance notes could be made clearer and will consider dividing the Code 34 guidance into two bullets; one for annuities, and one for market value cases.

The completion of question 12 is non-mandatory when the answer to question 2 is L

The guidance within the SDLT 6 Guidance Notes was changed in March 2007. Previously the guidance stated that SDLT 1 question 12 was mandatory. However, following representations from users of the online service, we agreed to a change to the current version of the notes.

Customers may now ignore question 12 if they have entered L at question 2.

STAMP TAXES ONLINE SERVICE – LINKED FREEHOLD TRANSFER AND GRANT OF NEW LEASE

Users can notify online a deal involving purchase of a freehold plus the grant of a lease (same parties). However as these are two different interests, the transactions have to be completed and submitted as separate transactions, as would be the case if completing on paper.

Each transaction should be marked as linked at 13.1 and the total consideration entered in 13.2. In question 10 the' total consideration' should be apportioned to each interest.

We have now taken steps to make our guidance [http://www.hmrc.gov.uk/so/online/completion.htm] on this clearer.

CONSIDERATION AND EXCHANGES

Paragraph 5 of Schedule 4 FA 2003 charges SDLT by reference to the market value of the chargeable interest acquired when

- one or more land transactions is entered into by a person (alone or jointly) as purchaser
- wholly or partly in consideration of
- one or more other land transactions being entered into by him (alone or jointly) as vendor
- and the subject matter of any of the relevant transactions is a major interest (for example, the transaction is the transfer of a freehold, the grant of a lease or the assignment of a lease).

Put simply the provision imposes a market value charge where one land transaction takes place wholly or partly in consideration of another land transaction.

We have been asked about the meaning of 'in consideration of' in this provision. This article replaces paragraphs 2 and 3 of the article in Technical Newsletter 2 [http://www.hmrc.gov.uk/so/tech-newsletter2.pdf]. The contents of this article will be incorporated in the Manual in due course.

In many cases a contract will provide expressly that land transaction 1 is wholly or partly in consideration of land transaction 2 and vice versa. If so paragraph 5 of Schedule 4 clearly applies.

If there is no such express reference then it is in our view a question of fact whether land transaction 1 is in consideration of land transaction 2.

In our view it is the element of 'reciprocity and mutuality', or 'quid pro quo', or 'give and take' that is crucial. Although land transactions are often preceded by a formal contract we do not consider that the existence of a prior contract is necessary in order for one land transaction to be in consideration of another. A contract that refers to both transactions will often be evidence that each is in consideration of the other but even in the absence of such a contract it might be clear from the circumstances that as far as the parties were concerned each transaction was in return for the other.

So if land transaction 1 is as a matter of fact in whole or part a quid pro quo for land transaction 2 then each is in consideration of the other.

Often an A to B land transaction takes place at the same time as one from B to A or to a person connected with A. In the absence of proof to the contrary, it would be inferred that land transaction 2 was a benefit in return for land transaction 1, and so each is in consideration of the other.

On the other hand, if land transaction 1 from A to B takes place at the same time as one from B to C (not connected to A), perhaps a lease of the land acquired by B, then in the absence of some linked benefit for A or a person connected with A, or some linked benefit from land transaction 1 for C or a person connected to C, then land transaction 1 would not be in consideration of land transaction 2. Such benefit might arise from an associated land transaction 3 from C to A.

Mere incidental benefit to A or a person connected with A which happens to arise from land transaction 2 would not be sufficient to make it be in consideration of land transaction 1.

Completion of the land transactions need not be at the same time. Land transaction 1 from A to B may be in consideration of an agreement by B to make land transaction 2 to A at a later date. Whether there is such an agreement would be a matter of fact and inference from fact. If land transaction 2 is soon after land transaction 1 then it is likely to have been agreed at the time of land transaction 1, but it would be possible to show that it arose because of some unexpected change of circumstance in the intervening period.

Nature of consideration

As regards the test for what is consideration we will be guided by we will be guided by the comments of the Court of Session in *Glenrothes Development Corporation v IRC* [1994] STC 74 (although this case concerned stamp duty the meaning of consideration is in our view the same for SDLT as it was for stamp duty, subject to any express provision to the contrary).

The Court indicated that 'consideration' must be construed according to its ordinary meaning and not by reference to any technicalities peculiar either to English or to Scottish law. Thus for SDLT purposes 'consideration' does not in our view have the technical meaning peculiar to the law of contract.

The judges made a number of comments about the nature of consideration for stamp duty purposes:

- 'closely linked in its ordinary meaning to the principle of mutuality of contractual obligations' (the Lord President at page 80)
- 'what the purchaser had to do in order to compel implementation by the seller of his obligations' (same page)
- 'the ordinary meaning of the word involves the element of reciprocity or mutuality between the obligation to provide it and that or those in respect of which it is given' (Lord Morison at page 82)
- 'something given or promised in return for something else' (Lord Mayfield at page 83)
- 'the element of reciprocity or mutuality' (Lord Mayfield at page 84)
- 'what the purchasers paid in exchange for implement of the seller's obligations to provide title' (Lord Mayfield at page 85).

SECTION 77

We are conscious that section 77 presents us with opportunities for simplification and deregulation and it is an area we shall continue to keep under review. For example, certain practitioners have suggested to us that it seems odd that they do not need to complete an SDLT 1 Return for assignment (whole or part) of a short lease for small consideration but they do need to complete it for a surrender.

'Major interests'

In particular, we have recently received queries concerning "major interests" as described in section 77. For example, section 117 refers to fee simple or term of years, however there has been a difference in whether or not practitioners consider that granting a freehold right of way for say £100k is "major", and therefore use form SDLT 60 to notify the transaction instead of an SDLT 1 Return.

Our view is that the definition is, as the wording suggests, intended to mirror the wording of section 1(1) LPA 1925. The words 'in equity' are intended to extend the scope of 'major interest' to equitable interests which are equivalent to an estate capable of subsisting at law. So interests which are within section 1(2), such as those mentioned in section 1(2)(a), and their equitable equivalents, are not major interests.

In addition, we would not wish to argue that an undivided share was a major interest.

Freehold easements and easements for a term of years are not major interests.

A minor can be the purchaser of a chargeable interest

There is no reason why a minor should not be the purchaser of a chargeable interest for SDLT purposes. This would normally be by operation of paragraph 3 of Schedule 16.

TRANSFER OF PROPERTY ON WINDING UP – LOAN FROM SHAREOWNERS

We would not seek to argue that the dividend in specie should bear SDLT in a situation for example where A owns the shares of B Ltd. A lends money to the company to buy property, the loan being secured by mortgage on the property.

Later B Ltd is wound up and there is a transfer to A as beneficial owner of the equity. That is the reason for the Transfer. The loan is not released etc. but obviously the mortgage will be taken off as the lender also owns the property because of the liquidation.

Clearly in this scenario A has not assumed any liability or given any other form of consideration.

PREVIOUS ISSUES OF THE SDLT TECHNICAL NEWS

Issues of Technical News are current at the time of publication but may become outdated or incorrect with the passage of time. Such material should not be relied on as a permanent source of guidance.

We do not retain hard copies of previous issues, but they are all available from our website at http://www.hmrc.gov.uk/so/bull_news_flyers_sdlt.htm#technical.

To ensure only current information is held on our website, we will be removing previous issues over 12 months old from 3 September 2007. In the unlikely event old Newsletters are required, they can be requested via Des Newman.

QUICK LINKS

Stamp Taxes welcome page (http://www.hmrc.gov.uk/so/index.htm).

STAMP DUTY & STAMP DUTY RESERVE TAX
Intermediary and Stock Lending Reliefs — FA 2007 Changes

Section 73 and Schedule 21 Finance Act 2007 made significant changes to the Stamp Duty and Stamp Duty Reserve Tax ('SDRT') intermediary and stock lending relief legislation to reflect the implementation in the United Kingdom of the Markets in Financial Instruments Directive 2004/39/EC ('MiFID'). This note describes the changes to the legislation, which take effect on 1 November 2007, and explains how the relief will operate in practice. All statutory references are to the provisions of *Finance Act 1986*, as amended by *Finance Act 2007*.

INTERMEDIARY RELIEF

1. Definitions of 'intermediary' and 'options intermediary'

1.1 These remain unchanged. An intermediary is a person who carries on a bona fide business of dealing in chargeable securities (or, in the case of an options intermediary, in quoted or listed options to buy or sell chargeable securities) and who does not carry on an excluded business (see sections 80A/88A(4) & (5). There are no changes to the definition of excluded business.

2. Recognition as an intermediary

2.1 Up to 31 October 2007, an intermediary must be recognised as such, in accordance with arrangements approved by HMRC, by the EEA exchange, prescribed multilateral trading facility (MTF), or recognised foreign exchange of which he is a member and on which securities of the kind that are the subject of the transfer are regularly traded.

2.2 From 1 November 2007, intermediary relief will be available to members of a regulated market, MTF or recognised foreign exchange, who are recognised by that market, facility or exchange in accordance with arrangements approved by HMRC (see sections 80A/88A(1) & (1A)). The requirement that the stock be regularly traded on the market, MTF or exchange remains. A stock is regularly traded for these purposes where it is admitted to trading on that market, MTF or exchange.

2.3 Firms that have already been recognised as intermediaries, under the pre-1 November arrangements, by the exchanges etc. of which they are members will not need to re-apply. Firms newly applying for recognised intermediary status should approach the relevant market, MTF or exchange of which they are, or are intending to become, a member.

2.4 In addition, from 1 November 2007, it will also be possible for persons to apply direct to HMRC for approval as intermediaries. Applicants must be authorised under the law of an EEA state to execute orders on behalf of clients or deal on own account. The authorisation need not be directly under MiFID so that it will be possible, for example, for a bank or credit institution authorised under the Banking Consolidation Directive to apply. Applications for approval may also be made by credit institutions and investment firms operating through a branch in an EEA Member State who, although not authorised directly under MiFID, are authorised by the regulator in an EEA Member State under the arrangements envisaged by Recital 28 of MiFID.

2.5 An application for approval by HMRC as an intermediary for the purposes of intermediary relief should be made to
Birmingham Stamp Office,
SDRT Operations,
9th Floor,
City Centre House,
30 Union Street,
Birmingham B2 4SA
and should contain a full and clear description of the applicant's business sufficient to demonstrate that it falls within the terms of sections 80A/88A(4)(a), together with a declaration that the applicant does not carry on an excluded business as defined in sections 80A/88A(5). The application must provide evidence of the applicant's authorisation by its home state regulator. HMRC may require applicants not based in the UK to supply a UK address where records of transactions may be inspected for audit purposes.

3. Recognition as an options intermediary

3.1 Up to 31 October 2007, an options intermediary must be recognised as such, in accordance with arrangements approved by HMRC, by the EEA exchange, prescribed MTF, or recognised foreign options exchange of which it is a member and on which options to buy or sell securities of the kind that is the subject of the transfer are regularly traded, and are listed by or quoted on that exchange.

3.2 From 1 November 2007, the relief will be available to members of a regulated market, MTF or recognised foreign options exchange who are recognised by that market, facility or options exchange in accordance with arrangements approved by HMRC (see sections 80A/88A(2) & (2A)). The requirement that options and stock be regularly traded on, and are listed by or quoted on, the market, facility or exchange remains.

3.3 Firms that have already been recognised as options intermediaries, under the pre-1 November arrangements, by the exchanges etc. of which they are members will not need to re-apply. Firms newly applying for recognised options intermediary status should approach the relevant market, MTF or exchange of which they are, or are intending to become, a member.

3.4 In addition, from 1 November 2007, it will also be possible for persons to apply direct to HMRC for approval as an options intermediary. Applicants must be authorised under the law of an EEA state to execute orders on behalf of clients or deal on own account. The authorisation need not be directly under MiFID so that it will be possible, for example, for a bank or credit institution authorised under the Banking Consolidation Directive to apply. Applications for approval may also be made by credit institutions and investment firms operating through a branch in an EEA Member State who, although not authorised directly under MiFID, are authorised by the regulator in an EEA Member State under the arrangements envisaged by Recital 28 of MiFID.

3.5 An application for approval by HMRC as an options intermediary for the purposes of intermediary relief should be made to
Birmingham Stamp Office,
SDRT Operations,
9th Floor,
City Centre House,
30 Union Street,
Birmingham B2 4SA
and should contain a full and clear description of the applicant's business sufficient to demonstrate that it falls within the terms of sections 80A/88A(4)(b), together with a declaration that the applicant does not carry on an excluded business as defined in sections 80A/88A(5). The application must evidence of the

applicant's authorisation by its home state regulator. HMRC may require applicants not based in the UK to supply details of where records of transactions may be inspected in the UK for audit purposes.

3.6 Lists of market-recognised intermediaries and regularly traded shares will be held in the CREST system and maintained by the appropriate market. A separate list of HMRC-approved intermediaries will be maintained by Euroclear UK & Ireland. For information on CREST processing from 1 November 2007 please see the Euroclear UK & Ireland booklet "UK SDRT: reliefs for principal traders". This is available for download from www.euroclear.co.uk.

4. Execution venue and transaction reporting

4.1 Up to 31 October 2007, relief is only available if the sale or agreement to transfer the securities is 'effected on' the exchange/MTF by which the intermediary is recognised, i.e. it is subject to the rules of the exchange/MTF and is reported to the exchange/MTF in accordance with those rules. For options intermediaries, the sale or agreement must be effected on any exchange/MTF on which securities of that kind are regularly traded or, if the agreement is pursuant to the exercise of a relevant option, where options to buy and sell securities of the kind concerned are regularly traded and are listed or quoted by that exchange/MTF.

4.2 From 1 November 2007

- an intermediary that is a member of a regulated market on which the shares in question are regularly traded and recognised as such by that market will qualify for relief wherever the transaction takes place, i.e. on any regulated market, MTF or 'over the counter' (sections 80A/88A(1)). Transactions in shares that are regularly traded (admitted to trading on a regulated market) will no longer need to be reported to an exchange in order to qualify for relief. See examples 1-4 in Appendix 1;
- an intermediary that is not a member of a regulated market but is a member of an MTF or recognised foreign exchange, and that is recognised by that MTF/exchange as an intermediary, will qualify for relief if the transaction is in respect of shares regularly traded (admitted to trading) on the MTF/exchange and is subject to the rules of, and reported to, the MTF/exchange (see sections 80A/88A(1A) and examples 5–11 in Appendix 1);
- an HMRC-approved intermediary will qualify for relief in respect of a transfer of shares that are regularly traded on any regulated market wherever the trade is executed and there is no requirement to report the transaction to an exchange (see sections 80A/88A(1B) and example 12);
- an HMRC-approved intermediary will qualify for relief in respect of a transfer of shares that are regularly traded on an MTF or recognised foreign exchange provided that the transaction is executed on and reported to the MTF/exchange (see sections 80A/88A(1C) and example 13);
- an options intermediary, recognised as such by the regulated market, MTF or recognised foreign options exchange of which it is a member (being a market etc. on which options to buy or sell the particular stock are regularly traded and are listed by or quoted on that market etc.), will qualify for relief in respect of a transfer of stock that is regularly traded on a regulated market wherever that transaction takes place. There is no requirement to report the transaction to an exchange (see sections 80A/88A(2) and examples 14–17);
- where an options intermediary, recognised on the same basis as in the previous bullet, acquires shares that are regularly traded only on an MTF, recognised foreign exchange or recognised foreign options exchange,

relief will be available if the transaction is effected on and reported to such a MTF/exchange (see sections 80A/88A(2A) and example 18);

- an HMRC-approved options intermediary who acquires regulated market shares, and options to buy and sell shares of that kind are regularly traded on, and are listed by , or quoted on, a regulated market, MTF or recognised foreign options exchange, will qualify for relief wherever the transaction is carried out. There is no requirement to report the transaction to an exchange (see sections 80A/88A(2B) and example 19);
- where an HMRC-approved options intermediary acquires shares that are not regularly traded on a regulated market, but are instead regularly traded on an MTF, recognised foreign options exchange or recognised foreign exchange, relief will not be available unless the transaction is reported to the MTF/exchange (see sections 80A/88A(2C) and examples 21–22);
- the requirement that a transaction be reported to the exchange, MTF or market in accordance with the rules of that exchange, MTF or market will be regarded as satisfied if the transaction is reported in accordance with MiFID.

REPURCHASES AND STOCK LENDING RELIEF

5.1 Up to 31 October 2007, relief from stamp duty and SDRT in respect of repurchases and stock lending agreements is available where there is an arrangement for one party to the agreement to transfer stock to the other and for the other to return stock of the same kind and amount to the original transferor at the end of the arrangement. The essential conditions are that the arrangement/agreement is effected on (i.e. subject to the rules of and reported to) an EEA exchange, prescribed MTF or recognised foreign exchange, and that stock of that particular kind is regularly traded on that exchange/MTF.

5.2 From 1 November 2007 there are two alternative sets of conditions for relief. As far as exchange members are concerned, the conditions for relief set out at sections 80C/89AA(3) are essentially unchanged. But from 1 November 2007, the rules on where an arrangement or agreement is effected are brought into line with MiFID, so as to include any regulated market, MTF (which no longer needs to be prescribed by regulations) or recognised foreign exchange. The requirement for the stock to be regularly traded on the market/MTF/exchange is retained. See examples 23–24.

5.3 In addition, from 1 November 2007, relief will be available under new sections 80C/89AA(2A) where either party to the arrangement/agreement, whether or not an exchange etc. member, is authorised under the law of an EEA state to execute orders on behalf of clients and deal on own account in relation to securities of the type concerned. Here again specific authorisation under MiFID itself is not necessary. Relief under this sub-section is only available in respect of arrangements relating to stocks that are regularly traded on a regulated market, and applies irrespective of where the arrangement or agreement is effected. Under new sections 80C/89AA(2A), there is no requirement that the arrangement be effected on (i.e. subject to the rules of and reported to) any exchange etc. and may therefore be an over the counter transaction. See examples 25–26.

5.4 For stamp duty, the changes to stock lending relief apply to instruments executed on or after 1 November 2007. For Stamp Duty Reserve Tax, they are effective for conditional agreements to transfer chargeable securities made prior to 1 November 2007 where the condition is only satisfied on or after that date, and to all agreements made on or after I November 2007.

5.5 Lists of market members will be held in the CREST system and maintained by the appropriate market. A separate list of members authorised under the law of an EEA state will be maintained by Euroclear UK & Ireland.

NEW STAMP DUTY CERTIFICATES

6.1 New wording for certificates to be included in instruments of transfer where intermediary relief and stock lending relief are claimed is set out in Appendix 2.

APPENDIX 1

Examples

A. Intermediary Relief – 1 November 2007 onwards

Members of a Regulated Market

1. LSE member, recognised by LSE as an intermediary.
   Shares admitted to trading on LSE.
   Trade executed on LSE.
   Relief available – sections 80A/88A(1)
2. Member of both LSE and virt-x, recognised as intermediary by LSE only.
   Shares admitted to trading on LSE and virt-x.
   Trade executed on virt-x.
   Relief available – sections 80A/88A(1)
3. LSE member, recognised by LSE as an intermediary.
   Shares admitted to trading on LSE.
   Trade executed over the counter.
   Relief available – sections 80A/88A(1)
4. Member of both LSE and virt-x, recognised as intermediary by LSE only.
   Shares admitted to trading only on virt-x.
   Trade executed on virt-x.
   Relief not available under sections 80A/88A(1), but if intermediary has received HMRC approval, relief will be available under sections 80A/88A(1B).

Members of a Multilateral Trading Facility

5. Member of AIM, recognised by AIM as an intermediary.
   Shares regularly traded on AIM.
   Trade executed on, and reported to, AIM.
   Relief available – sections 80A/88A(1A)
6. Member of AIM, recognised by AIM as an intermediary.
   Shares regularly traded on AIM.
   Trade executed over the counter, but not reported to AIM.
   Relief not available because the sale/agreement is not 'effected on the MTF'.
7. Member of AIM and Chi-X, recognised as intermediary by AIM only.
   Shares regularly traded only on AIM and Chi-X.
   Trade executed on, and reported to, Chi-X.
   Relief not available under sections 80A/88A(1A), but if intermediary has received HMRC approval, relief will be available under sections 80A/88A(1C).
8. Member of Chi-X, approved by HMRC as (equity) intermediary.
   Shares regularly traded on LSE.
   Trade executed on LSE.
   Relief available – sections 80A/88A(1B)

9. Member of both virt-x and Chi-x, recognised as intermediary by Chi-X only.
Shares regularly traded on both virt-x and Chi-x.
Trade executed on virt-x.
Relief not available under sections 80A/88A(1) because not recognised as an intermediary by virt-x. No relief either under sub-sections (1A) because the sale/agreement is not effected on an MTF. Relief will, however, be available if HMRC has approved the applicant as an intermediary under sub-sections (1B)

Members of a Recognised Foreign Exchange

10. Member of a recognised foreign exchange and recognised as an intermediary by that exchange.
Shares regularly traded on LSE and the recognised foreign exchange.
Trade executed on the recognised foreign exchange.
Relief available – sections 80A/88A(1A)
11. Member of a recognised foreign exchange and recognised as an intermediary by that exchange.
Shares regularly traded on LSE only.
Trade executed on LSE.
Relief not available under sections 80A/88A(1A) because the shares are not regularly traded on the recognised foreign exchange. Relief may be available under sub-sections (1B) provided that the intermediary can meet the test set out in subsections (6A) i.e. authorisation under the law of an EEA State.

Non-members

12. Not a member of a regulated market, MTF or recognised foreign exchange.
Approved by HMRC for the purposes of sections 80A/88A.
Shares regularly traded on LSE.
Trade executed on LSE.
Relief available under sections 80A/88A(1B)
13. Not a member of a regulated market, MTF or recognised foreign exchange.
Approved by HMRC for the purposes of sections 80A/88A.
Shares regularly traded on Chi-X.
Trade executed on and reported to Chi-X.
Relief available under sections 80A/88A(1C)

Options Intermediary Relief

Members of a regulated market, MTF, recognised foreign options exchange

14. Member of LIFFE, recognised as options intermediary by LIFFE.
Option listed on LIFFE.
Underlying shares regularly traded on LSE.
Trade executed on LIFFE.
Relief available under sections 80A/88A(2)
15. Member of LIFFE, recognised as options intermediary by LIFFE.
Option listed on LIFFE.
Underlying shares not regularly traded on a regulated market, MTF or recognised foreign exchange.
Trade executed on LIFFE.
Relief not available because underlying securities are not regularly traded on a regulated market (sub-sections (2)(d)), MTF, recognised foreign exchange or recognised foreign options exchange (sub-sections (2A)(d))
16. Member of LIFFE, recognised as options intermediary by LIFFE.
Option not listed on LIFFE.
Underlying shares regularly traded on a regulated market/MTF, recognised foreign exchange, recognised foreign options exchange.

Trade executed over the counter.
Relief not available as option is not regularly traded on, and listed by or quoted on, the regulated market of which the options intermediary is a member (sub-sections 2(b) and 2A(b))

Hedge of an option with purchase of underlying equity

17. Member of LIFFE and LSE, recognised as an options intermediary by LIFFE.
Option listed on LIFFE.
Underlying shares regularly traded on LSE.
Trade executed on LSE.
Relief available under sections 80A/88A(2)

Exercise of Option

18. Member of LIFFE, LSE and Chi-X, recognised as options intermediary by LIFFE.
Option listed on LIFFE.
Underlying shares regularly traded on Chi-X.
Trade executed on Chi-X.
Relief available under sections 80A/88A(2A)
19. Member of LIFFE, approved by HMRC as options intermediary.
Option listed on LIFFE.
Underlying shares regularly traded on LSE and virt-x.
Trade executed on virt-x.
Relief available under sections 80A/88A(2B)
20. Not a member of a regulated market, MTF or recognised foreign options exchange, but approved by HMRC as an options intermediary.
Option not listed on regulated market, MTF or recognised foreign options exchange.
Underlying shares regularly traded on AIM.
Trade executed on and reported to AIM.
No relief unless further application made to HMRC seeking approval as an (equities) intermediary under sections 80A/88A(1B)
21. Not a member of a regulated market, MTF or recognised foreign options exchange, but approved by HMRC as an options intermediary.
Option listed on LIFFE.
Underlying shares regularly traded on POSIT.
Trade executed on and reported to POSIT.
Relief available under sections 80A/88A(2C)
22. Not a member of a regulated market, MTF or recognised foreign options exchange, but approved by HMRC as an options intermediary.
Option listed on EDX London Ltd.
Underlying shares listed only on POSIT.
Trade executed over the counter, but not reported to POSIT.
No relief due, because the sale/agreement is not in respect of shares that are regularly traded on a regulated market (sections 80A/88A(2B)(c)) or effected on a relevant qualifying exchange (sections 80A/88A(2C)(c))

B. Stock Lending Relief

23. Arrangement between two LSE members.
Stock regularly traded on LSE.
Arrangement/agreement effected on LSE.
Relief available under section 80C/89AA(3)
24. Arrangement between a French authorised firm and a member of Chi-X.
Stock regularly traded on Chi-X.
Arrangement/agreement effected on Chi-X.

Relief available under section 80C/89AA(3)

25. Arrangement between two LSE members.
Stock regularly traded on LSE.
Arrangement/agreement effected over the counter.
Relief available under section 80C/89AA(2A)
26. Arrangement between firm authorised under Spanish law to execute orders and deal on own account and a US broker.
Stock regularly traded on virt-x.
Arrangement/agreement effected over the counter.
Relief available under section 80C/89AA(2A)

APPENDIX 2

Form of certificate required when claiming relief from Stamp Duty under section 80A or 80C Finance Act 1986

Section 80A Finance Act 1986

'I/We [*insert name of individual or organisation & CREST Participant Code Id*] hereby certify in accordance with section 80A Finance Act 1986 (as amended by section 73 and Schedule 21 Finance Act 2007) , that this instrument dated [*insert date*] transfers stock of a kind that is regularly traded on the [*insert name of the regulated market, multilateral trading facility or recognised foreign exchange*] to an intermediary (or his nominee) recognised by a regulated market, multilateral trading facility, recognised foreign exchange, or approved by the Commissioners for Her Majesty's Revenue and Customs.

Authorised signatory: ....

Name in block letters: ....'

Section 80C Finance Act 1986

'I/We [*insert name of individual or organisation & CREST Participant Code Id*] hereby certify that this transfer dated [*insert date*] is made under an arrangement within the meaning of section 80C Finance Act 1986 (as amended by section 73 and Schedule 21 Finance Act 2007) and that either:

the stock is regularly traded on the [*insert name of the regulated market, multilateral trading facility or recognised foreign exchange*] and has been reported to that [*delete those not applicable: regulated market, multilateral trading facility or exchange*] in accordance with the rules of that [*Delete those not applicable: regulated market, multilateral trading facility or exchange*],

or

the conditions for relief contained within section 80C(2A) FA 1986 have been satisfied,

and the transfer has been reported under CREST Transaction Id [*insert CREST Transaction Id reference*]'

Authorised signatory: ....

Name in block letters: ....

STAMP DUTY LAND TAX: GROUP RELIEF — PARAGRAPH 4ZA OF SCHEDULE 7 FA 2003

INTRODUCTION

1. This article gives practical and technical guidance following the introduction of paragraph 4ZA of Schedule 7 to the FA 2003 in Budget 2008. HM Revenue & Customs (HMRC) will be monitoring this legislation and if necessary, further guidance will be published to assist customers.
2. This article also sets out how HMRC will interpret paragraph 4(4) of schedule 7 to the Finance Act 2003.
3. The guidance provided in this note will apply in normal commercial situations. But where it appears that the guidance is being used for avoidance purposes the circumstances may warrant strict application of the group relief legislation.

BACKGROUND

4. Paragraph 1 of schedule 7 to FA 2003 provides for relief from stamp duty land tax where land and buildings are transferred between companies, (or other bodies corporate), and, at the effective date of the transaction, the companies are members of the same group. The exemption extends to the grant of leases between group companies.
5. Paragraph 2 of schedule 7 to FA 2003 restricts the availability of group relief if certain events occur. See SDLTM 23030+.
6. Paragraph 3 of schedule 7 provides that relief may be withdrawn if certain events occur within 3 years of the effective date of the transaction. See SDLTM 23070+.
7. Paragraph 4 of schedule 7 provides that certain events will not result in group relief being withdrawn.
8. The first case is where the purchaser ceases to be a member of the same group as the vendor because the vendor leaves the group. This was previously dealt with in the now repealed sub-paragraphs 4(2) and 4(3).
9. The vendor is regarded as leaving the group where the purchaser and vendor cease to be members of the same group by reason of a transaction relating to shares in the vendor or another company that, as a result of the transaction, ceases to be a member of the same group as the purchaser.
10. It was acknowledged by the Economic Secretary to the Treasury when the legislation was introduced that there was scope for avoidance schemes to be constructed using this legislation.
11. HMRC Stamp Taxes was asked to monitor carefully the use of this relief. We have done so and found an increasing number of schemes which are structured so that the vendor leaves the group first, meaning that the subsequent sale of the purchaser will not trigger the withdrawal of the original relief.
12. Paragraph 4ZA has been introduced to counter such schemes, replacing paragraph 4(2) and 4(3) of schedule 7 to FA 2003. This legislation will also apply to those situations where, although no avoidance motive is present, the same sequence of events has occurred.
13. Further information concerning the other circumstances in which group relief will not be withdrawn is available at SDLTM 23080.

PARAGRAPH 4ZA OF SCHEDULE 7 FA 2003

14. This provision applies to all group relief claims for transactions where the effective date is on or after 13 March 2008.
15. Sub-paragraph 4ZA(1) of schedule 7 ensures that a vendor can still leave a group without triggering withdrawal of group relief, thus preserving the intention of the original legislation.
16. Sub-paragraph 4ZA(4) however, provides that it will no longer be possible to avoid the withdrawal of group relief where there is a subsequent change in control of the purchaser within three years of the effective date of the group-relieved intra group transfer, or at any time in the pursuance of or in connection with arrangements made before the end of that period.
17. For example, in the group of H (parent), P (purchaser) and V (vendor), V transfers a property intra group to P and group relief is claimed (the qualifying conditions are met). V then leaves the group. Although P is no longer part of the same group as V, group relief is not withdrawn at this stage. This maintains the position pre FA 2008.
18. Two years after the purchase by P, H sells its shares in P to an unconnected third party. This change in control of P will now trigger withdrawal of the original group relief.
19. Withdrawal of group relief will similarly be triggered if there is a change in the control of H as this effectively changes the control of P.

CHANGE IN CONTROL

20. This section considers certain situations involving a change in control which may lead to a withdrawal of group relief. The guidance sets out HMRC's general approach to these, but should be read in conjunction with the comments at paragraph 3.

    Sub-paragraph 4ZA(5) of schedule 7 states that there is a change in control of the purchaser if:

    a. a person who controls the purchaser (alone or with others) ceases to do so,
    b. a person obtains control of the purchaser (alone or with others) or,
    c. the purchaser is wound up.
21. Sub-paragraph 4ZA(8) of schedule 7 provides that any references to control are to be interpreted in accordance with section 416 of the Taxes Act 1988. This defines control as:
    - control over the affairs of the company
    - control through voting power
    - control through share capital or through issued share capital
    - control over income of the company
    - control over the assets of the company.
22. Further information concerning control is available at CTM60200+.

CIRCUMSTANCES WHERE HMRC CONSIDERS THERE HAS NOT BEEN A CHANGE IN CONTROL

Liquidation

23. The appointment of a liquidator and any subsequent liquidation results in a company losing its beneficial interest in its assets, including any shares it owns in other companies (Ayerst v C&K Construction) Ltd 50 TC651.

24. Without special provision, the commencement of a winding up of a holding company within a group would result in the breaking up of a group. This may present difficulties for groups undertaking genuine reorganisations.

25. To address these concerns HMRC will no longer view the appointment of a liquidator as resulting in a change of control of a company for the purposes of sub-paragraph 4ZA(5)(b), provided that the liquidation can be shown to be part of a scheme of reconstruction which involves a successful claim to reconstruction or group relief or where the economic ownership of the relevant assets remains within the group. Similarly the eventual liquidation of that company will not be regarded as giving rise to a change in control of its subsidiaries (if any) where the transfer of those shares on the liquidation involves a successful claim to relief from stamp duty or where the economic ownership of those shares remains within the group.

New intermediate holding company

26. Sub-paragraph 4ZA(6) provides that a change in control does not arise where a new holding company is inserted either between the original ultimate parent company and its shareholders, or between the purchaser and the parent company with no change in overall economic ownership of the group. This is because HMRC will look at the ultimate shareholding in order to establish whether there has been a change of control.

Loan creditors

27. Sub-paragraph 4ZA(7) provides that, where there is change in control of the purchaser because of a loan creditor, group relief will not be withdrawn if the persons (other than loan creditors) who controlled the purchaser before that change continue to do so. This ensures that difficulties will not arise in relation to the introduction of loan creditors, which may otherwise have impacted on the ability of a group to organise its financing in a commercial manner.

Share transactions in quoted companies

28. The Economic Secretary to the Treasury made the following comments during a debate in Parliament in response to concerns that HMRC might construe the meaning of change in control so widely that the change in one shareholder in a quoted company might be seen as a change in control.

> 'Similar concerns were raised in relation to reconstruction relief. I can confirm that we intend to take the same approach that- if control of a publicly owned company changes as a result of an ordinary market transfer of its shares there will be no recovery, because we do not intend to interpret change of control so widely that simple day to day transactions between unconnected minority shareholders in the stock exchange could trigger a claw back' (see Hansard 6 June 2008, column 521).

Partnerships

29. Where the purchaser group's majority shareholder is a partnership a withdrawal of group relief would arise if a partner leaves the partnership or a new partner joins, however small the relevant partnership interest involved. This is due to the wording in section 416(6) which, coupled with the provisions of s 417(3)(a) ICTA 88, means that each individual partner controls the group in its own right for 416 purposes, since the rights of all partners are attributed to each other.

30. For the purposes of this legislation, however, the rights or powers held by partners will not be attributed. In addition any changes in the general partner will also be disregarded for the purposes of establishing whether there has been a change in control.

CIRCUMSTANCES WHERE HMRC CONSIDERS THERE HAS BEEN A CHANGE IN CONTROL BUT MAY NOT SEEK TO WITHDRAW RELIEF

31. It is recognised that in certain situations strict application of the legislation will result in changes of control which do not reflect an actual change in the economic ownership of the asset. In order to ensure that group relief is not withdrawn in such circumstances a minimum controlling combinations test will be applied in order to establish whether there has been 'actual' change in ownership of the asset.

Example of minimum controlling combination test

32. If three persons, A, B and C, each hold one third of the shares in a company, and are not connected in any way which would allow the rights and powers of one to be attributed to another, then control is held by A and B, B and C, or A and C but not A, B and C together. This is because for the purposes of the 'minimum' controlling combinations, you disregard combinations containing superfluous members.
33. If A leaves then the 'minimum controlling combination' test ensures that a change in control will not be triggered. This reflects the fact that B and C 'control' the company before and after A's departure.
34. If, however, both A and B leave and are replaced by new shareholders D and E then the 'minimum' controlling combination test is no longer satisfied. In this situation a change in control has occurred.
35. Further information regarding minimum controlling combinations is available at CTM60250. The minimum controlling combination test will be applied for SDLT purposes in this matter.

Application of minimum controlling combinations

Share Options

36. It is possible for an option over shares to result in two unrelated parties both being treated as having control of a company. This is because, under section 416(2) ICTA 88, a person is taken to have control of a company if he exercises or is entitled to acquire direct or indirect control over the company's affairs.
37. An option over shares will not be taken into account in determining whether there has been a change in control of the purchaser. HMRC regards the grant or entitlement date to the shares to be the point at which an 'inalienable' right to the shares is triggered. This is the point at which any conditions attaching to share options are considered to be satisfied and it is at this point that a change in control of the purchaser may occur.
38. If the application of a minimum controlling combinations test at this point does not result in a change in control, then group relief will not be withdrawn.
39. However, if a change in control does occur as a result of the granting of the shares then group relief will be withdrawn.

Control established through different tests

40. It is possible for more than one person or one group of persons to 'control' a company. For example, one person may have a greater part of the voting power, while two people hold the greater part of the assets on winding up. All three combinations of people can be taken to have control of the company at the same time.

41. If there was a change in one of these three combinations, then a change in control would be triggered, which could result in relief being withdrawn.

42. In this situation there will not be a withdrawal of relief if one of the minimum controlling combinations established under the tests for control is present following the sale or transfer of shares.

CIRCUMSTANCES IN WHICH HMRC CONSIDERS THERE HAS BEEN A CHANGE IN CONTROL

Group takeover

43. Where this is a sale of an entire group and this has occurred within three years of the transaction, a withdrawal of group relief will be triggered as there has been a change in control of the purchasing company.

PARAGRAPH 4(4) OF SCHEDULE 7 FA 2003

44. Paragraph 4(4) of schedule 7 of Finance Act 2003 provides that group relief is not withdrawn where the purchaser ceases to be a member of the same group as the vendor because of anything done for the purposes of, or in the course of, winding up the vendor or another company that is above the vendor in the group structure.

45. A company is above the vendor in the group structure if the vendor (or another company above the vendor in the group structure) is a 75 per cent subsidiary of the company.

46. This provision has not altered following the introduction of paragraph 4ZA. However, our approach has. A company above the vendor in the group structure can be the purchaser.

47. If paragraph 4(4) applies the provisions of paragraph 4ZA will not normally apply.

Contacts

Customers seeking further guidance on the application of this legislation can apply for a non-statutory business clearance.

A non-statutory clearance is a written confirmation of our view of the application of tax law to a specific transaction or event that you can rely on in most circumstances, as our view of the tax consequences of your transaction.

We will aim to send you our view within 28 calendar days, though in complex cases this may take longer.

Clearances will be provided where you have demonstrated that:

- there is a material uncertainty; and/or
- that the issue is commercially significant.

We will provide non-statutory clearances both

- pre transaction where evidence is supplied that the transaction is genuinely contemplated
- post transaction.

Please see 'clearance service for businesses - how to get certainty on significant business tax issues'.

Clearance application requests should be made to:

Birmingham Stamp Taxes

Any queries about this article should be addressed to:

Yasmin Ali
Policy Adviser
Stamp Taxes
1/38
100 Parliament Street
London SW1A 2BQ

BRIEFING ON NEW TAX PENALTIES – FAQ'S ISSUED BY HMRC ON 14 DECEMBER 2010

QUESTIONS AND ANSWERS ABOUT INACCURACY PENALTIES

Q20. What happens if an agent, acting on behalf of their client, makes a mistake?

A return may be inaccurate because someone acting on behalf of a taxpayer, like a tax advisor, has failed to take reasonable care.

It is however, the taxpayer who is responsible for the accuracy of the return, and they may still be charged a penalty.

No penalty would be due if the person can show that they took reasonable care to ensure that the return was accurate.

Reasonable care in this context would include:

- appointing an agent competent to deal with their affairs
- giving the agent all the relevant information
- checking the return as far as they could, before it was submitted

SPOTLIGHT 10: STAMP DUTY LAND TAX AVOIDANCE (7 JUNE 2010)

Commercial and residential property sales are being carried out in ways intended to avoid Stamp Duty Land Tax (SDLT) by reducing the purchase price below the SDLT band or threshold. In some cases an intermediate sale, often on the same day, is introduced into the arrangements with the sole intention of removing the true purchase price from tax. These arrangements seek to exploit 'sub-sale relief'. This relief is intended to ensure that, where a property transaction happens in stages, SDLT is paid once on the full amount paid for the property by the person who ultimately acquires it and no double charge arises.

HM Revenue & Customs (HMRC) view is that these contrived transactions, including those involving sub-sales, produce a charge to SDLT on the full amount paid for the property. In some cases there is doubt about whether transactions actually meet the conditions for the sub-sale relief. Even if they do, anti-avoidance legislation effective from December 2006 counters any arrangements seeking to depress or avoid the tax on the full amount paid for the property, including those seeking to exploit sub-sale relief.

Where HMRC find property sale arrangements that have been artificially structured to avoid paying the correct amount of SDLT these will be actively challenged, through the courts where appropriate.

SECTION 75A FINANCE ACT 2003 (OFFICIAL GUIDANCE ISSUED ON 28 FEBRUARY 2011)

S.75A Finance Act (FA) 2003 is an anti-avoidance provision that is intended to counter certain schemes which have the effect of reducing Stamp Duty Land Tax liability.

COMMENCEMENT

S.75A has effect in respect of disposals and acquisitions, and all related scheme transactions, which take place after 2.00 pm. on 6 December 2006. S.75A has effect in respect of disposals and acquisitions, and all related scheme transactions, which take place after 2.00 pm. on 6 December 2006.

OVERALL APPROACH

Section 75A is an anti-avoidance provision. HM Revenue & Customs (HMRC) therefore takes the view that it applies only where there is avoidance of tax. On that basis, HMRC will not seek to apply s.75A where it considers transactions have already been taxed appropriately.

SECTION 75A APPLIES WHERE:

- One person ('V') disposes of a chargeable interest, and another person ('P') acquires, that interest, or a chargeable interest derived from it (s.75A (1) (a)).
- A number of transactions ('scheme transactions'), including the disposal and acquisition, are involved in connection with the disposal and acquisition (s.75A (1) (b)).
- The total Stamp Duty Land Tax payable in respect of all the scheme transactions is less than the amount that would be payable on a notional land transaction effecting the acquisition (s.75A (1) (c)).

All of the above must be read together.

WHERE IT APPLIES, THE EFFECT OF S.75A IS AS FOLLOWS:

- The individual scheme transactions are disregarded for Stamp Duty Land Tax purposes.

- There is instead a notional transaction effecting the acquisition of V's chargeable interest (that is the chargeable interest which was the subject matter of the disposal by V) by P.
- The chargeable consideration on the notional transaction is referred to as the 'notional consideration'.
- The effective date of the notional transaction is the last date of completion of the scheme transactions or, if earlier, the last date on which a contract in respect of the scheme transactions is substantially performed.

SCHEME TRANSACTIONS

The term 'transaction' includes:

- a transaction which is not a land transaction
- an agreement, offer or undertaking not to take specified action
- any kind of arrangement whether or not it could otherwise be described as a transaction
- a transaction which takes place after the acquisition by P of the chargeable interest

S.75A (3) gives some examples of what may be considered a scheme transaction:

- the acquisition by P of a lease deriving from a freehold owned or formerly owned by V
- a sub-sale to a third person
- the grant of a lease to a third person subject to a right to terminate
- the exercise of a right to terminate a lease or to take some other action
- an agreement not to exercise a right to terminate a lease or to take some other action
- the variation of a right to terminate a lease or to take some other action

This is not an exhaustive list of transactions to which s.75A applies.

APPLICATION OF S.75A

There are three steps to consider when contemplating the application of s.75A:

- firstly identify a disposal and the relevant person who is V
- secondly identify an acquisition and the relevant person who is P
- thirdly consider whether a number of transactions are 'involved in connection with' the disposal and acquisition

In a complex scenario this process may need to be repeated with different parties being identified as V and P, possibly with different results.

The meaning of the phrase 'involved in connection with' has not yet been tested in the courts and, therefore, the dictionary definition of 'connection' should be applied. In HMRC's view to be 'involved in connection with' each other the disposal, acquisition and other related transactions would normally involve more than one transaction in sequence relating to the same property. For example, related transactions would be considered to be 'in connection with' a disposal and acquisition ('the composite transaction') if the intended outcome of the composite transaction cannot be achieved in the form envisaged without those transactions taking place.S.75A will apply whether or not V, P or their associates or advisers have had any involvement with, or knowledge of, each other.

SITUATIONS WHERE HMRC ACCEPT THAT S.75A IS UNLIKELY TO APPLY

In deciding whether s75A applies to a set of transactions, it is necessary to look at the arrangements as a whole rather than simply at each individual step in isolation. Even the transactions below could be part of a scheme that purports to mitigate Stamp Duty Land Tax. But in general HMRC accepts that, to the extent that the situations below genuinely stand alone, the transactions will be taxed appropriately under the normal Stamp Duty Land Tax rules and so s.75A will not be triggered.

(1) X, Y and Z are individuals who decide to establish a partnership to manage their investment portfolio. They transfer investment property and cash into that partnership at value. HMRC considers this to be a straightforward establishment of and transfer of property into a partnership.

(2) X, Y and Z are the partners of a partnership. The purpose of the partnership is to acquire and develop a large residential property into 6 flats. When the development is complete they disagree as to how to manage the completed development so the partnership is dissolved and the partnership property (the flats and any partnership monies) is divided among the partners. It is assumed here that the agreements and documents relating to creation of the partnership demonstrate that the intention was for the partnership to manage the property after development and that the dissolution of the partnership arises from an unforeseen disagreement. HMRC would not seek to apply s.75A to this situation as long as the general Stamp Duty Land Tax legislation has been applied to the creation and dissolution of the partnership.

(3) A property investment business is carried on by a company owned in equal shares by four family members. The company is to be sold to an unconnected third party. The four individuals establish a partnership to hold the properties that were held by the company but that aren't included in the sale. There is a clear commercial reason for the properties to be transferred out of the company that is to be sold to the unconnected third party.

(4) A property lettings business is carried on by three individuals X, Y and Z through a partnership. X, Y and Z consider that, commercially, the best way to continue to carry on their business is through a company. They therefore decide to incorporate the business. X, Y and Z subscribe for shares in a new company in the same proportion as their respective partnership holdings. The properties are transferred to the company.

(5) X and Y are corporate partners in a joint property-letting venture. They are unconnected except through their shares in the partnership. The partnership owns one property. Y's shareholders have accepted an offer from a third party, Z, to acquire all of its share capital. Z does not wish to continue to operate the business with X so the decision is taken to distribute the property to Y. There is a clear commercial reason for the transactions. The normal Stamp Duty Land Tax rules applied to the original acquisition of the property by the company.

(6) V sells land to X and at the same time X sells the land to P. P pays Stamp Duty Land Tax based on the full amount of consideration received by V.

(7) V sells land to X and at the same time X sells the land to P. P pays Stamp Duty Land Tax based on the full amount of consideration received by V. At a later date P sells the land to Y and Y pays the full amount of Stamp Duty Land Tax that arises from the consideration that P received.

(8) V sells two properties at arm's length to third party purchasers N1 and N2. Subsequently, and in transactions which are not connected in any way with the purchases by N1 and N2, P buys both properties at arm's length. It is assumed that there is no connection between the sale by V and the purchase by P.

(9) V grants a long lease to X. At a later stage, and in a transaction which is not connected in any way with the grant of the long lease, X assigns the lease to an unconnected third party P. P exercises a statutory right of enfranchisement.

S.75A does not apply as regards to disposal by V and the acquisition by P because it is taxed appropriately under the normal Stamp Duty Land Tax rules.

(10) V grants an option to X to purchase land. Subsequently, and in a transaction which is not connected in any way with the grant of the option, X assigns the benefit of the option to an unconnected third party P. P exercises the option. There is no connection between the transactions.

SITUATIONS WHERE HMRC CONSIDERS THAT S75A APPLIES

(1) V agrees to sell land to X, and X agrees to sell the same land to P which is a partnership where the partners are X and persons connected to him. At the same time as the completion of the V-X contract, the X–P contract completes, this acquisition is effected by means of a 'transfer of rights'. X argues that no Stamp Duty Land Tax is due as his contract is disregarded by s.45, whilst P argues that no Stamp Duty Land Tax is due per Schedule 15 of FA 2003 given its connection with X. Section 75A applies because HMRC considers that the conditions of s75A 1(a) – (c) are met and that the notional transaction V-P could have been achieved in a more straight forward manner that would not have satisfied s75A(1)(c); Stamp Duty Land Tax is due on the notional consideration which is the full amount of consideration received by V.

(2) V grants a 999-year lease to Nominee for no premium and a peppercorn rent. V assigns the freehold reversion to P for a nominal sum. P pays Nominee £x in consideration of Nominee's agreement to vary the lease by the insertion of a provision giving the landlord the right to terminate the lease for no payment. P exercises the right to terminate. Under s.75A, the notional transaction is the acquisition of the unencumbered freehold by P and the notional consideration chargeable is £x given by P to Nominee.

(3) V grants a 999-year lease to Nominee for no premium and a peppercorn rent. The lease includes a right for the landlord to terminate the lease on payment of £x to the tenant. V assigns the freehold reversion to P for a nominal sum. P exercises the right to terminate and pays Nominee £x. Under s.75A, the notional transaction is the acquisition of the unencumbered freehold by P from V, and the notional consideration chargeable is £x given by P to Nominee.

(4) V grants a 999-year lease to P for no premium and a peppercorn rent. The lease gives the landlord a right to terminate it within 14 days of the date of grant. P offers to pay V £x if V allows the 14 days to elapse without exercising the right to terminate. V does so. Under s.75A, the notional transaction is the grant by V of a 999-year lease to P and the notional consideration, which is the chargeable consideration, is £x, the amount paid by P and received by V.

(5) V agrees to sell property to X Ltd for £10 million. X Ltd declares a dividend in favour of P, the dividend to consist of the property and to be paid at the same time as completion of the V–X Ltd contract. The contract is completed and the property transferred to P. X argues that the £10 million is not chargeable to Stamp Duty Land Tax as his contract is disregarded under s.45. P argues that there is no Stamp Duty Land Tax charge on the transfer of the property to him because a dividend in specie is a transaction that does not constitute consideration for the purposes of the Stamp Duty Land Tax legislation. Under s.75A, the notional transaction is the acquisition of the property by P, and the notional consideration, which is the chargeable consideration, is £10 million, the amount received by V.

(6) V agrees to sell land to X, and X agrees to sell the same land to P which is a partnership where the partners are X, X1 Ltd. and X2 Ltd. companies connected to X which manage a trust for which X is the beneficiary. V and X enter an arrangement where V settles a nominal amount into X's trust, thereby creating

a connection between V and X as per s.839 of ICTA 1988. The V-X contract completes and at the same time and simultaneously the X–P contract completes. X claims that no Stamp Duty Land Tax is due as his contract is disregarded by s.45 of FA 2003, whilst P claims that no Stamp Duty Land Tax is due per Schedule 15 of FA 2003 given its connection with X. Section 75A applies and the notional transaction involved is V-P Stamp Duty Land Tax is due on the notional consideration which is the full amount of consideration received by V.

OTHER PROVISIONS

- A transfer of shares or securities - or units in a unit trust scheme - is ignored for the purposes of s.75A if it would otherwise be the first of a series of scheme transactions (and several such transfers are likewise ignored if they all precede any other scheme transaction).
- The notional transaction attracts any relief which it would attract if it were an actual land transaction.

Examples:

(1) V sells land to X and at the same time and simultaneously X sells to P. V, X and P are all companies within the same group. The notional transaction involved is V-P but, provided the conditions for group relief at Schedule 7 of FA 2003 are met, Group Relief will apply to the notional transaction.

(2) V sells land to X and at the same time and simultaneously X sells to P, which is a registered charity. The notional transaction involved is V-P; but, provided the conditions for Charities relief at Schedule 8 of FA 2003 are met, P can claim Charities relief which will apply to the notional transaction and no Stamp Duty Land Tax will be due.

(3) Section 75A does not apply where the relief is available only by reason of sections 71A to 73 (alternative property finance) or a provision in Schedule 9 (right to buy, shared ownership leases, etc.)

(4) If any of the scheme transactions is entered into for the purposes of, or in connection with, the transfer of an undertaking or part of an undertaking for the purposes of paragraphs 7 or 8 of Schedule 7 (reconstruction and acquisition relief) then the notional transaction is also deemed to be entered into for such purposes or in such connection. This enables the notional transaction to qualify for reconstruction or acquisition relief if the other conditions for relief are satisfied.

(5) The notional transaction will be subject to the market value rule in s53 if P is a company connected with V.

(6) Where applicable s.75A will charge consideration to tax regardless of the s45 position including any amount paid as a deposit.

(7) If part of the consideration for the notional transaction is a land transaction entered into by V as purchaser, or by P as vendor, then the market value rules in paragraph 5 of Schedule 4 will apply.

(8) An interest in a property investment partnership is treated as a chargeable interest for the purposes of s.75A.

(9) Where V or P is a partnership the provisions in Part 3 of Schedule 15 apply as they would to the transfer of a chargeable interest into or out of a partnership for all transactions with an effective date before 24 March 2010.

(10) But for transactions where the effective date is 24 March 2010 or later, S.75C(8)(b) no longer applies to treat the notional transaction between V and P as a transaction involving a partnership under Schedule 15. The normal rules under s75A will apply to ascertain the chargeable consideration on such transactions.

RELIEF FOR TRANSFERS INVOLVING MULTIPLE DWELLINGS (19 JULY 2011) FA03/S83/SCH6B

OVERVIEW

This is a relief for transactions which include the acquisition of interests in more than one dwelling. The relief must be claimed in a land transaction return.

Where the relief is claimed, the rate of SDLT which applies to the consideration attributable to interests in dwellings is determined by reference to the amount of this consideration, divided by the number of dwellings, i.e. the mean consideration attributable to the dwellings. This is subject to a minimum rate of 1 per cent.

The rate of SDLT which applies to the consideration attributable to interests in land other than dwellings, if any, is the rate which would apply in the absence of the relief.

Superior freehold or leasehold interests in dwellings subject to leases granted for an initial period of 21 years or more are not eligible for relief.

The relief includes provision for 'off-plan' purchases where construction or adaptation of the property for residential use may not have commenced by the effective date of the transaction. It also provides for the tax calculation to be adjusted if the number of dwellings involved is reduced within three years of the effective date of the transaction.

THE RELIEF

(1) The relief is available for transactions the effective date of which is on or after 19 July 2011 and which is not linked with any transaction with an effective date before that date except for either of the following:

- an option binding the grantor to enter into the later transaction
- a right of pre-emption restricting the right of the grantor to enter into the later transaction.

(3) The relief must be claimed in a land transaction return or an amendment to a return, using relief code 28 - other relief - initially. We expect that a dedicated code will be available from October 2011. We will publicise the new code, and the date from which it is to be used, nearer the time.

RELEVANT TRANSACTIONS FA03/SCH6B/PARA2

(4) The relief may be claimed in respect of a transaction which is a 'relevant transaction'. A relevant transaction is either of the following:

- a transaction, the main subject-matter of which includes interests in more than one dwelling
- a transaction which is one of a number of linked transactions, the main subject-matter of which includes interests in at least one dwelling and where one or more transactions linked to it includes interests in at least one other dwelling.

(3) In either case, the main subject-matter of the transaction may include interests in land other than dwellings.

APPLICATION TO PARTNERSHIP TRANSACTIONS

(4) An ordinary partnership transaction to which FA03/SCH15/PART2 applies, or a transfer of a chargeable interest to which FA03/SCH15/PARA10/18/23 applies, can be a relevant transaction.

(5) A transfer of a partnership interest which is deemed to be a land transaction by FA03/SCH15/PARAS14/17, an acquisition of a partnership interest which is treated by FA03/SCH15/PARA16 as a major interest in land or a withdrawal of money, etc., from a partnership which is deemed to be a land transaction by FA03/SCH15/PARA17A, cannot be a relevant transaction for the purposes of this relief.

EXCLUSIONS FA03/SCH6B/PARA2(4)

(6) A transaction cannot be a relevant transaction if relief under FA03/S74 (Exercise of collective rights by tenants of flats) or FA03/S75 (Crofting community right to buy) applies to it.

(7) A transaction cannot be a relevant transaction if relief under FA03/SCH7 (Group relief, reconstruction relief and acquisition relief) or FA03/SCH8 (Charities relief) is available for it, would be available on the making of a claim or has been withdrawn from it.

SUPERIOR INTERESTS FA03/SCH6B/PARA2(6)

(8) For the purpose of determining whether a transaction is a relevant transaction, a superior interest (freehold or headlease) over property which includes dwellings is treated as if it were an interest in those dwellings.
Example: a purchaser acquires the freehold of a new block of four flats which are untentanted. The transaction is a relevant transaction.

(9) However, such a superior interest cannot be taken into account for this purpose to the extent that it is a superior interest in relation to a lease over a dwelling which was granted for an initial term of 21 years or more.
Example: a purchaser acquires the freehold of a block of four flats. The transaction is not linked with any other transaction.

- Where two of the four flats are tenanted under long leases, the transaction is a relevant transaction, the main subject-matter of which includes two dwellings, i.e. the two flats not tenanted under long leases.
- If three of the four flats are tenanted under long leases, the transaction is not a relevant transaction, because only one flat can be taken into account, i.e. that which is not tenanted.

THE TAX CALCULATION FA03/SCH6B/PARA4

(3) The chargeable consideration for a relevant transaction is apportioned between the following:

- the consideration attributable to interests in dwellings
- the remaining consideration, if any.

The consideration must be so apportioned on a 'just and reasonable' basis.

(3) The percentage rates of tax which apply, firstly to the consideration attributable to interests in dwellings and secondly to the remaining consideration, are then calculated separately.

(4) For this purpose the chargeable consideration can include the market value of the subject-matter of the transaction where this is substituted by FA03/S53 or FA03/SCH4/PARA5, or an election is made under FA03/SCH15/PARA12A.

CONSIDERATION ATTRIBUTABLE TO INTERESTS IN DWELLINGS FA03/SCH6B/PARA5(1)-(6)

(5) The relevant consideration for the purposes of FA03/S55 is the aggregate consideration:

- for this transaction and any transactions linked to it - whether relevant transactions or not,
- which is attributable to dwellings, interests in which are included in this and any relevant transactions linked to it,

divided by the number of such dwellings.

(3) The rate of tax that applies is set by Table A of FA03/S55, except that the minimum rate is 1 per cent (FA03/SCH22/PARA5(2)).

(4) FA03/S116(7) (six or more dwellings treated as non-residential property) does not apply.

Consideration attributable to interests in dwellings FA03/SCH6B/PARA5(1)-(6)

(5) The relevant consideration for the purposes of FA03/S55 is the aggregate consideration for the transaction and all transactions which are linked to it (whether relevant transactions or not).

(6) In most cases Table B of FA03/S55 will apply, but Table A may apply in some circumstances where the transaction or transactions consist wholly of property comprising five or fewer dwellings (some of which are excluded from relief by FA03/SCH6B/PARA2(6)).

(7) The rate of tax that applies is the rate that would apply by virtue of FA03/S55 in the absence of the relief.

Tax due on consideration in the form of rent FA03/SCH6B/PARA4(5)

(8) Where the chargeable consideration for a relevant transaction includes rent, the normal provisions of FA03/SCH5 apply to determine the amount of tax chargeable on the rent.

Meaning of 'dwelling' FA03/SCH6B/PARA7

(9) For the purposes of the relief a 'dwelling' means a building or part of a building which is suitable for use as a single dwelling or is in the process of being constructed or adapted for such use.

(10) Land that is, or is to be, occupied or enjoyed with the dwelling such as a garden or grounds, including any building or structure on such land, is taken to be part of the dwelling. This will usually be a question of fact depending on the individual circumstances of each case.

(11) Land that subsists, or is to subsist, for the benefit of the dwelling is taken to be part of the dwelling. This applies to an interest in land which is not contiguous with the dwelling and its garden or grounds: for example, a separate lease of a garage in a block.

(12) FA03/S116(2)-(5) apply to determine whether certain types of property are or are not dwellings.

'Off plan' transactions FA03/SCH6B/PARA7(5)-(6)

(13) For the purposes of the relief, the main subject-matter of the transaction will be taken to consist of or include an interest in a dwelling where the following applies

- there is a contract to purchase a building, or part of a building, which is to be constructed or adapted under the contract for use as a dwelling or dwellings
- the contract is substantially performed before construction of the building, or part of the building, concerned has commenced and the effective date of the transaction is deemed to be the date of substantial performance by virtue of FA03/S44/44A/45/45A or FA03/SCH17A/PARA12A or 19(3)

(3) For this purpose a contract includes any agreement including, in Scotland, missives of let not constituting a lease.

FURTHER RETURN WHERE NUMBER OF DWELLINGS IS REDUCED FA03/SCH6B/PARA6

(4) Further tax may be due where:

- relief is claimed under FA03/SCH6B for a relevant transaction,
- during a period following the effective date of the transaction(s) (the 'relevant period') an event occurs and if that event had occurred, immediately before the effective date, either the transaction would not have been a relevant transaction or the rate of tax charged on dwellings would have been higher
  Tax is chargeable in these circumstances on the transaction as if the event took place immediately prior to the effective date of the transaction.

(3) For this purpose, 'event' includes any change of circumstance or change of plan but does not include an onward sale of individual dwellings.

(4) This provision may be triggered where either of the following apply:

- the subject-matter of the transaction ceases to include dwellings (so that the transaction ceases to be a relevant transaction)
- the number of dwellings included in the subject-matter of the transaction is reduced - for example by combining smaller dwellings into larger ones.

(3) The relevant period is:

- the period ending three years after the effective date of the transaction or, in respect of a dwelling,
- the date on which the purchaser disposes of that dwelling to a person who is not connected with him.

(3) In the case of a transaction substantially performed before completion, the relevant period runs from the date of substantial performance.

(4) The recalculation of the tax due is based on the whole of the consideration given for the subject-matter of the transaction and the number of dwellings following the event, including any dwellings sold on prior to the event.

(5) Where the result of a recalculation following an event is that more tax is due, the purchaser must make a further return and pay the additional tax within 30 days of the event.

(6) Further returns should be made by letter to the Birmingham Stamp Office.

(7) References in FA03/SCH10 to the effective date of the transaction are to be read as references to the date of the event. The tax chargeable is calculated by reference to the rates in force at the effective date of the transaction.

RELIEF FOR TRANSFERS INVOLVING MULTIPLE DWELLINGS FA03/S83/SCH6B

EXAMPLES

1. The freehold of a new block of 20 flats is purchased for £2.5 million. There is no headlease and none of the flats is subject to a long lease.

The transaction is a relevant transaction for the purposes of the relief as it involves the acquisition of more than one dwelling – i.e. the 20 flats. The freehold is treated as if it were interests in the individual dwellings. The chargeable consideration divided by the number of dwellings is £125,000. This is below the normal 0 per cent SDLT threshold but the minimum rate of tax under the relief is 1 per cent.

The tax due is therefore 1% of £2.5 million = £25,000.

2. The freehold of a block of 10 flats is purchased for £1.4 million. There is no headlease but five flats are let on 99-year leases.

The transaction is a relevant transaction for the purposes of the relief as it involves the acquisition of more than one dwelling – i.e. the five untenanted flats. The freehold is treated as if it were interests in the individual dwellings. The chargeable consideration is apportioned between the five untenanted flats (£1,250,000) and the five tenanted flats (£150,000).

The rate of tax on the consideration attributed to the untenanted flats is set by the amount of that consideration divided by the number of dwellings concerned. This is £250,000 so the rate of tax is 1 per cent. The tax due in respect of these flats is therefore 1% of £1,250,000 = £12,500.

The rate of tax on the consideration attributed to the tenanted flats is set by the chargeable consideration for the transaction (£1.4 million). As the transaction involves six or more dwellings, it is treated as involving non-residential property so the rate of tax is 4 per cent. The tax due in respect of these flats is therefore 4% of £150,000 = £6,000.

The total tax due on the transaction is therefore £12,500+£6,000 = £18,500.

3. The freehold reversion of a block of 20 flats is purchased. A 999-year headlease over the whole block has been granted to a company controlled by the tenants, with ten flats let on 99-year leases and the rest on leases of less than 21 years

The transfer of the reversion is not a relevant transaction for the purposes of the relief as all the dwellings are subject to the 999 year headlease - a lease of more than 21 years. No relief is due. If the transfer had been of the headlease this would be a relevant transaction in respect of the ten flats subject to leases of less than 21 years.

4. A 999 year headlease over five flats and four lock-up shops in a block is purchased for a premium of £1.25 million and annual rent of £6,000. Two of the flats are subject to 99 year underleases.

The transaction is a relevant transaction for the purposes of the relief as it involves the acquisition of more than one dwelling – i.e. the three untenanted flats. The lease premium is apportioned between the three untenanted flats (£750,000), the two tenanted flats (£100,000) and the four shops (£400,000).

The rate of tax on the premium attributed to the untenanted flats is set by the amount of that premium divided by the number of dwellings. This is £250,000 so the rate of tax is 1 per cent. The tax due in respect of these flats is therefore 1% of £750,000 = £7,500.

The rate of tax on the premium attributed to the tenanted flats and the shops (£500,000) is set by the total premium (£1.25 million). As the transaction involves both residential and non-residential property, the rate of tax is 4 per cent. The tax due in respect of these flats and shops is therefore 4% of £500,000 = £20,000.

Tax due on the net present value of the rent payable under the lease is calculated in the usual way. In this case the net present value is £165,739 and the tax due is 1% of £15,739 = £157 (rounded to the nearest pound).

The total tax due on the transaction is therefore £7,500+£20,000+£157 = £27,657.

5. The freeholds of four houses and two lock-up shops are purchased in separate linked transactions. Two of the houses cost £250,000 each and the other two cost £350,000 each. The lock-up shops cost £150,000 each.

The transactions involving the houses are relevant transactions for the purposes of the relief. The rate of tax on these transactions is set by the total consideration given in these transactions (£1,200,000) divided by the number of dwellings. This is £300,000 so the rate of tax is 3 per cent. The tax due is therefore 3% of £1,200,000 = £36,000.

The transactions involving the shops are not relevant transactions for the purposes of the relief. The rate of tax on these transactions is set by the total consideration given in all the linked transactions (£1,500,000). As the linked transactions include both residential and non-residential property, the rate of tax is 4 per cent. The tax due is therefore 4% of £300,000 = £12,000.

The total tax due on the transactions is therefore £36,000+£12,000 = £48,000.

6. The freehold of a building divided into six flats is purchased for £1.2 million and relief is claimed. The flats are let on Assured Shorthold tenancies but, two years later, the tenancies cease and the purchaser begins work to convert the building into a hotel.

At the time of purchase, the transaction is a relevant transaction as it involves the acquisition of more than one dwelling – i.e. the superior interest in six flats where the term of the lease is less than 21 years. The rate of tax is set by the total consideration given, divided by the number of dwellings. This is £200,000 so the rate of tax is 1 per cent. The tax due is therefore 1% of £1.2 million = £12,000.

When conversion work starts, within three years of the effective date of the transaction, the flats cease to be suitable for use as dwellings. The change is deemed to have taken place immediately before the purchase so the transaction ceases to be a relevant transaction. The rate of tax is now set solely by the consideration given. The subject-matter of the 110715 examples v3 Page 2 transaction is now non-residential so the rate of tax is 4 per cent. The tax due is therefore 4% of £1.2 million = £48,000.

The purchaser is required to make a further return within 30 days of conversion work starting and pays the additional tax due of £36,000.

7. A purchaser agrees to purchase the freehold of an uncompleted block of six flats for £1.2 million. The consideration is paid prior to completion. Six months later, the contract is varied to provide for construction of four larger flats. The consideration is unchanged.

The purchase was a relevant transaction as it involved the acquisition of more than one dwelling – i.e. the six flats. The contract was substantially performed when the full consideration was paid. The rate of tax was set by the total consideration given, divided by the number of dwellings. This was £200,000 so the rate of tax was set at 1 per cent. The tax due at the time the contract was substantially performed was therefore 1% of £1.2 million = £12,000.

The variation of the contract is deemed to have taken place immediately prior to substantial performance. The rate of tax is now set by the consideration divided by the revised number of dwellings. This is £300,000 so the rate of tax is now 3 per cent. The tax due is therefore 3% of £1.2 million = £36,000.

As the rate of tax has increased, the purchaser is required to make a further return within 30 days of the contract variation and pay the additional tax due of £24,000.

If however the number of flats had been increased, this change would be ignored for the purposes of SDLT.

8. A purchaser acquires the freehold of a block of eight flats for £1 million. Six months later he grants 99-year leases of two flats to unconnected third parties. After a further six months, the remaining six flats are knocked together to make three flats.

The purchase is a relevant transaction as it involves the acquisition of more than one dwelling – i.e. the eight flats. The rate of tax is set by the total consideration given, divided by the number of dwellings. This is £125,000. As the 0% band does not apply under the relief, the rate of tax is 1 per cent.

The grant of the leases is not an event which requires recalculation of the tax due, even though it occurs within the 'relevant period' following the original purchase. Neither does it bring that period to an end as the whole of the interest acquired in that purchase has not been disposed of.

The combination of the six remaining flats to make three also takes place within the relevant period. This is a relevant event for the purposes of para. 6 so a recalculation is required. The event is deemed to have occurred immediately before the original purchase.

The rate of tax is now set by the original consideration of £1 million, divided by five – that is, the three combined flats and the two in respect of which leases were granted. The result is £200,000 so the rate of tax is still 1 per cent and the amount of tax due is unchanged. No further return is required.

9. A wealthy individual purchases a freehold estate consisting of a mansion, stable block and four acres of gardens, together with twelve flats and houses for domestic and estate workers, farm buildings and fifty acres of farmland for £12 million.

The transaction is a relevant transaction as it involves the acquisition of a total of 13 dwellings – the mansion, the flats and the houses.

The mansion, stable block and gardens are treated as part of a single dwelling. The consideration attributed to dwellings is £8 million and the remaining consideration attributed to the farm buildings and farmland is £4 million.

The rate of tax on the dwellings consideration is set by the amount of that consideration, divided by the number of dwellings. £8 million divided by 13 is £615,385 so the rate of tax is 4 per cent. The rate of tax on the remaining consideration of £4 million is also 4 per cent as the farm buildings and farmland are non-residential property and the transaction as a whole is a 'mixed' transaction, so the non-residential scale of rates applies.

The whole transaction is therefore taxed at 4 per cent. This is no different from the rate which would apply in the absence of the relief, so relief is not claimed.

10. An individual acquires the freeholds of six semi-detached houses. Six months later, he sells two houses to an unconnected third party, who combines them into one. After another six months he sells another two houses to his wife, who combines them into one. After a further six months he combines the two remaining houses into one and sells it to an unconnected third party.

The first sale is not an event for the purposes of FA03/SCH22/PARA6. It brings the relevant period to a close in respect of those houses, because the sale is to an unconnected third party, so the subsequent combination of the two houses into one does not affect the original purchaser's relief.

The second sale is not an event for this purpose. However the relevant period is not affected, because the sale is to a connected person, and the subsequent combination of the two houses into one is an event in respect of the original purchase. The amount of tax due is recalculated on the basis of five dwellings – that is, the combined houses, the two which were previously sold on and the two remaining in the original purchaser's hands.

The combination of the remaining two houses into one is an event for this purpose. The amount of tax due is recalculated on the basis of four dwellings – that is, the two combined houses and the two sold to the unconnected third party.

The sale of the last remaining house brings the relevant period completely to a close, eighteen months after the transaction.

Appendix H

HMRC Stamp Taxes Forms

COMPANY RECONSTRUCTIONS
Specimen letters issued by the Stamp Office

HM Revenue & Customs

The attached draft letter should be used when relief is claimed under S75 FA 1986. Completed claims should be sent to Birmingham Stamp Office, **9th Floor City Centre House 30 Union Street Birmingham B2 4AR. DX 15001 Birmingham 1**

Dear Sir

…… Limited/plc

Section 75 Finance Act 1986

1. We act for ……………………………………………………………………………… Limited/plc ("the Acquiring Company").

2. In connection with the transactions referred to below we hereby apply on behalf of the Acquiring Company for exemption from transfer duty under Section 75 Finance Act 1986.

3. The Acquiring Company, whose registered office is at ……………………………………………………………………………, was incorporated in [England] on ……………………… ……… [under the Companies Act[s] ……… [to ………] with No ……………………]. A copy of the Certificate of Incorporation [and the Certificate of Incorporation on Change of Name] [is/are] enclosed marked "A".

4. …………………………………………………………………………………………… Limited/plc ("the Target Company"), whose registered office is at ……………………………………………………………………………………, was incorporated in [England] on ……………………………………………… [under the Companies Act[s] ……… [to ………] with No ……………………]. A copy of the Certificate of Incorporation [and the Certificate of Incorporation on Change of Name] [is/are] enclosed marked "B". A list of all members of the Target Company immediately prior to ……………………………………, certified by the Registrars of the Target Company, is enclosed marked "C".

[NOTE – A computerised print-out, which need not be certified, is acceptable (if available) instead of the list of members.]

5. The Acquiring Company has acquired [the whole] [part of] the undertaking of the Target Company in pursuance of a scheme for the reconstruction of the Target Company in order that … [set out briefly the reasons for the transactions].

ADJ 475 (Substitute)(LexisNexis) W57-1-00(1)u:word/stamps

6. By an Agreement dated .... and made between the Target Company (i) and the Acquiring Company (ii) ("the Agreement"), it was provided (inter alia) that the Target Company should sell and the Acquiring Company should purchase the [whole of] [part of] the undertaking of the Target Company as described in Schedule .... to the Agreement ("the Business") in pursuance of a scheme for the reconstruction of the Target Company and that as consideration for such sale the Acquiring Company should allot credited as fully paid to all the shareholders of the Target Company [....................../the [respective] number[s] of] [...................... per cent .... Preference Shares of .... each and] .... Ordinary Shares of .... each of the Acquiring Company set out in [Clause .... of/column (................) of] such Schedule] ("the Consideration Shares"). [In addition the Acquiring Company [assumed] [discharged] certain liabilities of the Acquired Company as specified in Schedule .... to the Agreement]. A copy of the Agreement is enclosed marked "D".

7. The said sale was duly completed on .... when the Target Company transferred the Business to the Acquiring Company.

8. At a Meeting of [a Committee of] the Directors of the Acquiring Company held on .... the Consideration Shares (which had been created by Resolution No .... passed at the Extraordinary General Meeting held on ....) were duly allotted to the shareholders of the Target Company pursuant to the provisions of the Agreement. We enclose marked ["E"] [and ["F"] respectively] [a] certified [copy/copies] of the Resolution of the Directors of the Acquiring Company passed on .... [appointing the said Committee and of the Resolution of the said Committee of the Directors] making such allotment. We also enclosed marked ["G"] a certificate under the hand of ...., [the senior official of the Registration Department of .... Limited/plc, the Registrars] [the Company Secretary] of the Acquiring Company, confirming that the names of the respective allotees of the Consideration Shares have been entered in the Register of [Members of] the Acquiring Company in respect of the Consideration Shares together with a list of all members of the Acquiring Company immediately following the allotment, certified by [the Registrars] [the Company Secretary] of the Acquiring Company, marked ["H"].

[NOTE – A computerised print-out, which does not have to be certified, is acceptable instead of the list of members.]

9. It is confirmed that no part of the consideration for the acquisition consisted of the issue of redeemable shares in the Acquiring Company.

10. It is confirmed that, immediately after the acquisition:

   a. each shareholder of the Target Company was also a shareholder of the Acquiring Company;

   b. each shareholder of the Acquiring Company was also a shareholder of the Target Company; and

W57-1-00(3)u:word/stamps

c. each shareholder held the same proportion of shares in the Target Company as that shareholder held in the Acquiring Company.

11. [An] [No] application(s) for clearance under [Section 138 or 139 TCGA 1992] [Section 707 ICTA 1988] [has/have] been made by the [Acquiring] [Target] Company. A copy of the application(s) [together with copies of the correspondence with the Board of Inland Revenue] [are/is] enclosed marked ["I"].
[Note: if advance clearance was not obtained then please provide the information detailed below.]

12. It is submitted that the acquisition was/is effected for bona fide commercial reasons and did not form part of a scheme or arrangement of which the main purpose, or one of the main purposes, is avoidance of liability to stamp duty, income tax, corporation tax or capital gains tax, and all the appropriate conditions of Section 75 of the Finance Act 1986 have been complied with, and accordingly exemption from ad valorem stamp duty under the head "Conveyance or Transfer on Sale" is claimed in respect of the Agreement and the transfers executed pursuant thereto.

13. We enclose for adjudication [describe document] together with [a] certified [copy/copies].

Yours faithfully

Information to be supplied if advance clearance was not obtained (see paragraph 11 above):

1. a copy of the latest accounts of the Target Company;

2. full details of any scheme or arrangement of which the acquisition of the Target Company forms a part;

3. confirmation, if appropriate, that the shares in the Target Company are still held by the Acquiring Company and that there is no intention to dispose of them; and

4. a detailed note of the bona fide commercial reasons for the acquisition.

Please write to the Technical Service Manager at any Stamp Office if you require any further information.

W57-1-00(3)u:word/stamps

Birmingham Stamp Office
9th Floor
City Centre House
30 Union Street
Birmingham B2 4AR

DX 15001 Birmingham 1
Tel: 0121 616 4513

W57-1-00(4)u:word/stamps

HM Revenue & Customs

The attached draft letter should be used when relief is claimed under S77 FA 1986. Completed claims should be sent to Birmingham Stamp Office, **9th Floor City Centre House 30 Union Street Birmingham B2 4AR DX 15001 Birmingham 1.**

Dear Sir

.... Limited/plc

Section 77 Finance Act 1986

1. We act for .... Limited/plc ("the Acquiring Company").

2. In connection with the transactions referred to below we hereby apply on behalf of the Acquiring Company for exemption from transfer duty under Section 77 Finance Act 1986.

3. The Acquiring Company, whose registered office is at ...., was incorporated in [England] on .... [under the Companies Act[s] .... [to ....] with No ....] and immediately prior to .... the authorised share capital of the Acquiring Company was £ .... divided into [................... per cent .... Preference Shares of .... each and] .... Ordinary Shares of .... each, of which [.......................... such Preference Shares and] .... such Ordinary Shares had been issued and were fully paid up]. A copy of the Certificate of Incorporation [and the Certificate of Incorporation on Change of Name] [is/are] enclosed marked "A".

4. .... Limited/plc ("the Target Company"), whose registered office is at ...., was incorporated in [England] on .... [under the Companies Act[s] .... [to ....] with No ....] and immediately prior to .... the authorised share capital of the Target Company was £ .... divided into [................... per cent .... Preference Shares of .... each and] .... Ordinary Shares of .... each, of which [.......................... such Preference Shares and] .... such Ordinary Shares had been issued and were fully paid up]. A copy of the Certificate of Incorporation [and the Certificate of Incorporation on Change of Name] [is/are] enclosed marked "B". A list of all members of the Target Company immediately prior to ...., certified by the Registrars of the Target Company, is enclosed marked "C".

ADJ 473 (Substitute)(LexisNexis) W55-1-00(1)u:word/stamps

[NOTE – A computerised print-out, which need not be certified, is acceptable (if available) instead of the list of members.]

5. The transactions referred to below were carried out in order that … [set out briefly the reasons for the transactions]. [Note: if advance clearance was not obtained (see paragraph 12) then please give a detailed explanation of the bona fide commercial reasons for the transaction.]

6. By an Agreement dated ……………………… ……… and made between …………………………………………… and ………………………………… (the "Shareholder[s]") (i) the Target Company (ii) and the Acquiring Company (iii) ("the Agreement"), it was provided (inter alia) that the Shareholder[s] should sell and the Acquiring Company should purchase the [respective] number[s] of [……….. per cent ………. Preference Shares of …………….. each and] ……………… Ordinary Shares of ……………… each of the Target Company set out in [Clause …………….. of/columns[s] (…………..) [and (…………..) respectively] of Schedule ……………. to the Agreement (such Shares amounting in the aggregate to the whole of the issued share capital of the Target Company) and that as consideration for such sale the Acquiring Company should allot credited as fully paid to the Shareholders (being all the shareholders of the Target Company) [………………/the [respective] number[s] of] [……….. per cent ………. Preference Shares of …………….. each and] ……………… Ordinary Shares of ………………….. each of the Acquiring Company set out in [Clause …………… of/column (………………) of] such Schedule] ("the Consideration Shares"). A copy of the Agreement is enclosed marked "D".

7. The said sale was duly completed on ……………………… ……… when the Shareholders delivered to and in favour of the Acquiring Company duly executed transfers of the whole of the issued Shares of the Target Company. Immediately following such delivery one Ordinary Share of ………………………………… of …………………………… was transferred to …………………………………… [jointly] as nominee[s] of the Acquiring Company in order that there could be the necessary minimum number of Members of the Target Company and a quorum of Members could be present at General Meetings of the Target Company. There was also delivered to the Acquiring Company the relevant Share Certificates.

8. At a Meeting of [a Committee of] the Directors of the Acquiring Company held on …………………… ……… the Consideration Shares (which had been created by Resolution No …………….. passed at the Extraordinary General Meeting held on …………………… ………) were duly allotted to the Shareholders pursuant to the provisions of the Agreement. We enclose marked ["E"] [and ["F"] respectively] [a] certified [copy/copies] of the Resolution of the Directors of the Acquiring Company passed on ………………………… ……… [appointing the said Committee and of the Resolution of the said Committee of the Directors] making such allotment. We also enclose marked ["G"] a certificate under the hand of Mr ………………………………………, [the senior official of the Registration Department of ………………………………………………… Limited/plc, the Registrars] [the

W55-1-00(2)u:word/stamps

Company Secretary] of the Acquiring Company, confirming that the names of the respective allottees of the Consideration Shares have been entered in the Register of [Members of] the Acquiring Company in respect of the Consideration Shares together with a list of all members of the Acquiring Company immediately following the allotment, certified by [the Registrars] [the Company Secretary] of the Acquiring Company, marked "H".

[NOTE – A computerised print-out, which need not be certified, is acceptable (if available) instead of the list of members.]

9. Immediately after the acquisition the authorised share capital of the Acquiring Company was £ .... divided into [................ per cent .... Preference Shares of .... each and] .... Ordinary Shares of .... each, of which [................... such Preference Shares and] .... such Ordinary Shares had been issued and were fully paid up.

10. It is confirmed that immediately after the acquisition the classes of shares in the Acquiring Company were in the same proportions as they had been in the Target Company immediately before the acquisition was made.

11. It is confirmed that immediately after the acquisition the proportion of shares of any particular class in the Acquiring Company held by each shareholder was the same as the proportion of shares of that class in the Target Company held by him immediately before the acquisition was made.

12. [An] [No] application(s) for clearance under [Section 138 or 139 TCGA 1992] [Section 707 ICTA 1988] [has/have] been made by the [Acquiring] [Target] Company. A copy of the application(s) [together with copies of correspondence with the Board of Inland Revenue] [are/is] enclosed marked ["I"].
[Note: if advance clearance was not obtained then please provide the information detailed below.]

13. It is submitted that the acquisition was effected for bona fide commercial reasons and does not form part of a scheme or arrangement of which the main purpose, or one of the main purposes, is avoidance of liability to stamp duty, stamp duty reserve tax, income tax, corporation tax or capital gains tax and the appropriate conditions of Section 77 Finance Act 1986 have been complied with, and accordingly exemption from ad valorem stamp duty under the head "Conveyance or Transfer on Sale" is claimed in respect of the agreement and the transfers executed pursuant thereto.

14. We enclose for adjudication [describe document] together with [a] certified [copy/copies].

Yours faithfully

W55-1-00(3)u:word/stamps

Information to be supplied if advance clearance was not obtained (see paragraphs 5 and 12 above):

1. a copy of the latest accounts of the Target Company;

2. full details of any scheme or arrangement of which the acquisition of the Target Company forms a part;

3. confirmation, if appropriate, that the shares in the Target Company are still held by the Acquiring Company and that there is no intention to dispose of them; and

4. a detailed note of the bona fide commercial reasons for the acquisition.

Please write to the Technical Service Manager at Birmingham Stamp Office if you require any further information.

Birmingham Stamp Office
9th Floor
City Centre House
30 Union Street
Birmingham B2 4AR

DX 15001 Birmingham 1
Tel: 0121 616 4513

W55-1-00(5)u:word/stamps

PARTICULARS OF INSTRUMENTS TRANSFERRING OR LEASING LAND

Specimen form issued by the Stamp Office

Inland Revenue

PARTICULARS OF INSTRUMENTS TRANSFERRING OR LEASING LAND

SECTION 28 FINANCE ACT 1931
as amended by the Land Commission Act 1967
and Section 89 Finance Act 1985

FOR OFFICIAL USE

VO No. ....
PD No. ....
ANALYSIS CODE ....
DESC ....
GV/NAV ....
DW CODE ....
....
RETURN ....
O.S. No. ....
OTHER ....

1. Description of Instrument

2. Date of Instrument

3. Name and address of Transferor or Lessor *(Block Letters)*

4. Name and address of Transferee or Lessee *(Block Letters)*

5. Situation of the land. Sufficient information must be given to enable the land to be identified accurately, e.g., by including any dimensions stated in the instrument and by attaching a plan to this form or by describing the boundaries in full. For premises the full postal address including the post code is required. Please indicate whether a plan is provided in the appropriate box.

Plan Attached Yes ☐
Plan Attached No ☐

COUNTY .... RATING AUTHORITY ....

6. Estate or Interest Transferred. Where the transaction is the assignment or grant of a lease, or the transfer of a fee simple subject to a lease, the terms of the lease, the date of commencement of the term and the rent reserved must be stated.

7. Consideration — State separately:

(a) any capital payment, with the date when due if otherwise than the execution of instrument:

(b) does the consideration stated include a charge to VAT

Yes/No

If Yes please state the amount paid:

(c) any debt released, covenanted to be paid or to which the transaction is made subject:

(d) any periodical payment (including any charge) covenanted to be paid:

(e) any terms surrendered:

(f) any land exchanged:

(g) any other thing representing money or money's worth:

8. Any Minerals, Mineral Rights, Sporting Rights, Timber or Easements reserved: (on separate sheet if necessary)

9. Any Restrictions, Covenants or Conditions affecting the value of the estate or interest transferred or granted: (on a separate sheet if necessary)

10. Signature of Transferee or Lessees or person on his behalf:

.... Date ....

11. Name and Address of the Transferor's or Lessor's Solicitor: *(Block Letters)*

12. Name, Address and Telephone Number of Signatory if other than Transferee or Lessee: *(Block Letters)*

STAMPS L(A) 451 (3/95) **(Substitute)(LexisNexis)**

NOTES

FINANCE ACT, 1931

1. The Commissioners of Inland Revenue direct attention to the provisions of Section 28 of the Finance Act, 1931, as amended by the Land Commission Act, 1967 and Section 89. Finance Act 1985 which require that as from 1st September 1931, on the occasion of:

   i. any transfer on sale of the fee simple of land;
   ii. the grant of any lease of land for a term of seven or more years;*
   iii. any transfer on sale of any such lease,

   it shall be the duty of the transferee, lessee, or proposed lessee to produce them within thirty days of its execution the instrument by means of which the transfer is effected, or the lease is granted or agreed to be granted. Where, however, the instrument is first executed at a place out of Great Britain, the period of thirty days runs from the date when it is first received in Great Britain.
   (N.B. Any part of the term of the lease prior to the date of execution is ignored for the purpose of determining the length of the term).

2. The person producing any such instrument is required by the Act (as amended) to furnish to the Commissioners with the instrument a statement of certain particulars regarding the instrument.

3. The provisions of the Act as to production of instruments do not apply to an instrument which related solely to incorporeal hereditaments or to a grave or right of burial.

4. Where an agreement for a lease has been produced, the lease itself need not be produced, unless inconsistent with the agreement. If however, the lease is produced, it will be stamped with the appropriate stamp (see paragraph 5).

5. An instrument produced in accordance with the provisions of the Act will be stamped with a stamp denoting that it has been so produced. Without such a stamp, no instrument of which production is required shall be deemed to be duly stamped for the purpose of Section 14 of the Stamp Act, 1891.

6. By virtue of amendments made to Section 28 and Schedule 2, Finance Act, 1931, by the Land Commission Act, 1967:

   (a) the provisions of the 1931 Act as to production of instruments shall also apply to any instrument which is a mining lease only or by means of which the transfer of a mining lease only is effected, and
   (b) if a transferee, lessee or proposed lessee fails to comply with the provisions either of Section 28 (as set out in paragraph 1 above) or of Schedule 2 to the 1931 Act, he shall be liable on summary conviction to a fine not exceeding four hundred pounds.

7. Attention is also drawn to Section 89 Finance Act 1985.

STAMP DUTY LAND TAX FORMS
Sample forms issued by HMRC

HM Revenue & Customs — **Land Transaction Return**

For official use only

Your transaction return

How to fill in this return

The guidance notes that come with this return will help you answer the questions.

- Write inside the boxes. Use black ink and CAPITAL letters.
- If you make a mistake, please cross it out and write the correct information underneath.
- **Leave blank any boxes that don't apply to you** – please don't strike through anything irrelevant.
- Show amounts in whole pounds only, rounded down to the nearest pound. Ignore the pence.
- Fill out the payslip on page 7.
- Do not fold the return. Send it back to us unfolded in the envelope provided.
- **Photocopies are not acceptable.**

If you need help with any part of this return or with anything in the guidance notes, please phone the Stamp Taxes enquiry line on **0845 603 0135**, open 8:30am to 5:00pm Monday to Friday, except Bank Holidays. You can get further copies of this return and any supplementary returns from the Orderline on **0845 302 1472**.

Starting your return

ABOUT THE TRANSACTION

1 **Type of property**

Enter code from the guidance notes

2 **Description of transaction**

Enter code from the guidance notes

3 **Interest transferred or created**

Enter code from the guidance notes

4 **Effective date of transaction**

D D M M Y Y Y Y

5 **Any restrictions, covenants or conditions affecting the value of the interest transferred or granted?** Put 'X' in one box

Yes No

If 'yes' please provide details

6 **Date of contract or conclusion of missives**

D D M M Y Y Y Y

7 **Is any land exchanged or part-exchanged?** Put 'X' in one box

Yes No

If 'yes' please complete address of location

Postcode

House or building number

Rest of address, including house name, building name or flat number

8 **Is the transaction pursuant to a previous option agreement?** Put 'X' in one box

Yes No

SDLT 1 (Substitute)(LexisNexis) PG 1 IMS6/05

+

ABOUT THE TAX CALCULATION

9 Are you claiming relief? Put 'X' in one box

Yes No

If 'yes' please show the reason

Enter code from the guidance notes

Enter the charity's registered number, if available, or the company's CIS number

For relief claimed on part of the property only, please enter the amount remaining chargeable

£ . 0 0

10 What is the total consideration in money or money's worth, including any VAT actually payable for the transaction notified?

£ . 0 0

11 If the total consideration for the transaction includes VAT, please state the amount

£ . 0 0

12 What form does the consideration take?
Enter the relevant codes from the guidance notes

13 Is this transaction linked to any other(s)?
Put 'X' in one box

Yes No

Total consideration or value in money or money's worth, including VAT paid for all of the linked transactions

£ . 0 0

14 Total amount of tax due for this transaction

£ . 0 0

15 Total amount paid or enclosed with this notification

£ . 0 0

Does the amount paid include payment of any penalties and any interest due? Put 'X' in one box

Yes No

ABOUT LEASES

+

If this doesn't apply, go straight to box 26 on page 3.

16 Type of lease

Enter code from the guidance notes

17 Start date as specified in lease

D D M M Y Y Y Y

18 End date as specified in lease

D D M M Y Y Y Y

19 Rent-free period
Number of months

20 Annual starting rent inclusive of VAT (actually) payable

£ . 0 0

End date for starting rent

D D M M Y Y Y Y

Later rent known? Put 'X' in one box

Yes No

21 What is the amount of VAT, if any?

£ . 0 0

22 Total premium payable

£ . 0 0

23 Net present value upon which tax is calculated

£ . 0 0

24 Total amount of tax due – premium

£ . 0 0

25 Total amount of tax due – NPV

£ . 0 0

Check the guidance notes to see if you will need to complete supplementary return 'Additional details about the transaction, including leases', SDLT4.

SDLT 1 PG 2

+

ABOUT THE LAND including buildings

Where more than one piece of land is being sold or you cannot complete the address field in the space provided, please complete the supplementary return 'Additional details about the land', SDLT3.

26 **Number of properties included**

27 **Where more than one property is involved, do you want a certificate for each property?** Put 'X' in one box

Yes No

28 **Address or situation of land**

Postcode

House or building number

Rest of address, including house name, building name or flat number

Is the rest of the address on the supplementary return 'Additional details about the land', SDLT3?
Put 'X' in one box

Yes No

29 **Local authority number**

30 **Title number, if any**

31 **NLPG UPRN**

32 **If agricultural or development land, what is the area (if known)?** Put 'X' in one box

Hectares Square metres

Area

33 **Is a plan attached?** Please note that the form reference number should be written/displayed on map. Put 'X' in one box

Yes No

+

ABOUT THE VENDOR including transferor, lessor

34 **Number of vendors included** (Note: if more than one vendor, complete boxes 45 to 48)

35 **Title** Enter MR, MRS, MISS, MS or other title
Note: only complete for an individual

36 **Vendor (1) surname or company name**

37 **Vendor (1) first name(s)** Note: only complete for an individual

38 **Vendor (1) address**

Postcode

House or building number

Rest of address, including house name, building name or flat number

SDLT 1 PG 3

ABOUT THE VENDOR CONTINUED

39 **Agent's name**

40 **Agent's address**
Postcode

Building number

Rest of address, including building name

41 **Agent's DX number and exchange**

42 **Agent's e-mail address**

43 **Agent's reference**

44 **Agent's telephone number**

ADDITIONAL VENDOR

Details of other people involved (including transferor, lessor), other than vendor (1). If more than one additional vendor please complete supplementary return 'Land Transaction Return – Additional vendor/purchaser details', SDLT2.

45 **Title** Enter MR, MRS, MISS, MS or other title
Note: only complete for an individual

46 **Vendor (2) surname or company name**

47 **Vendor (2) first name(s)**
Note: only complete for an individual

48 **Vendor (2) address**

Put 'X' in this box if the same as box 38.

If not, please give address below
Postcode

House or building number

Rest of address, including house name, building name or flat number

SDLT 1 PG 4

ABOUT THE PURCHASER including transferee, lessee

49 **Number of purchasers included** (Note: if more than one purchaser is involved, complete boxes 65 to 69)

50 **National Insurance number (purchaser 1), if you have one.** Note: only complete for an individual

51 **Title** Enter MR, MRS, MISS, MS or other title
Note: only complete for an individual

52 **Purchaser (1) surname or company name**

53 **Purchaser (1) first name(s)**
Note: only complete for an individual

54 **Purchaser (1) address**

Put 'X' in this box if the same address as box 28.
If not, please give address below
Postcode

House or building number

Rest of address, including house name, building name or flat number

55 **Is the purchaser acting as a trustee?** Put 'X' in one box

Yes No

56 **Please give a daytime telephone number** – this will help us if we need to contact you about your return

57 **Are the purchaser and vendor connected?**
Put 'X' in one box

Yes No

58 **To which address shall we send the certificate?**
Put 'X' in one box

Property (box 28) Purchaser's (box 54)
Agent's (box 61)

59 **I authorise my agent to handle correspondence on my behalf.** Put 'X' in one box

Yes No

60 **Agent's name**

61 **Agent's address**
Postcode

Building number

Rest of address, including building name

62 **Agent's DX number and exchange**

63 **Agent's reference**

64 **Agent's telephone number**

SDLT 1 PG 5

+

ADDITIONAL PURCHASER

Details of other people involved (including transferee, lessee), other than purchaser (1). If more than one additional purchaser, please complete supplementary return 'Land Transaction Return – Additional vendor/purchaser details', SDLT2.

65 **Title** Enter MR, MRS, MISS, MS or other title
Note: only complete for an individual

66 **Purchaser (2) surname or company name**

67 **Purchaser (2) first name(s)**
Note: only complete for an individual

68 **Purchaser (2) address**

Put 'X' in this box if the same as purchaser (1) (box 54).

If not, please give address below
Postcode

House or building number

Rest of address, including house name, building name or flat number

69 **Is purchaser (2) acting as a trustee?** Put 'X' in one box

Yes No

+

ADDITIONAL SUPPLEMENTARY RETURNS

70 **How many supplementary returns have you enclosed with this return?** Write the number in each box. If none, please put '0'.

Additional vendor/purchaser details, SDLT2

Additional details about the land, SDLT3

Additional details about the transaction, including leases, SDLT4

DECLARATION

71 **The purchaser(s) must sign this return.** Read the guidance notes in booklet SDLT6, in particular the section headed *'Who should complete and sign the Land Transaction Return?'*.

If you give false information, you may face financial penalties and prosecution.
The information I have given on this return is correct and complete to the best of my knowledge and belief.

Signature of purchaser 1

Signature of purchaser 2

Please keep a copy of this return and a note of the unique transaction reference number, which is in the 'Reference' box on the payslip.

Finally, please send your completed return to:
HM Revenue & Customs, Stamp Taxes/SDLT, Comben House, Farriers Way, NETHERTON, Merseyside, Great Britain, L30 4RN, or the DX address is: Rapid Data Capture Centre, DX725593, Bootle 9

Please don't fold it – keep it flat and use the envelope provided. Fill out the payslip on the next page and pay in accordance with the 'How to pay' instructions.

SDLT 1 PG 6

Inland Revenue

Land Transaction Return

Additional vendor/purchaser details

When to fill in this return

You must fill in this return for each additional vendor and/or purchaser. The guidance notes will help you answer the questions.

If you need help with any part of this return or with anything in the guidance notes, please phone the Stamp Taxes enquiry line on **0845 603 0135**, open 8:30am to 5:00pm Monday to Friday, except Bank Holidays. Calls are charged at local rates. You can get further copies of this return from the Orderline on **0845 302 1472.**

For official use only

VENDOR OR PURCHASER

1 **Please indicate if this return is for an additional vendor or an additional purchaser.** Put 'X' in one box

Vendor Complete section below only

Purchaser Complete section below and the section over the page

COMPLETE IN ALL CASES

2 **Title** Enter MR, MRS, MISS, MS or other title
Note: only complete for an individual

3 **Surname or company name**

4 **First name(s)**
Note: only complete for an individual

5 **Address**
Postcode

House or building number

Rest of address, including house name, building name or flat number

Please turn over for additional purchaser details.

ADDITIONAL PURCHASER DETAILS

Only complete this section if this return is for an additional purchaser.

6 **Are the purchaser and vendor connected?**
Put 'X' in one box

☐ Yes ☐ No

7 **Is the purchaser acting as a trustee?** Put 'X' in one Box

☐ Yes ☐ No

8 **Declaration**

The purchaser(s) must sign this return

Read the notes in Section 1 of the guidance notes, SDLT6 'Who should complete the Land Transction Return?'

If you give false information, you may face financial penalties and prosecution.

The information I have given on this form is correct and complete to the best of my knowledge and belief.

Signature of purchaser.

SDLT 2 PG 2

Inland Revenue

Land Transaction Return

Additional details about the land

When to fill in this return

Fill in this return when you cannot fit all the details on the main Land Transaction Return, SDLT1. The guidance notes will help you answer the questions.

If you need help with any part of this return or with anything in the guidance notes, please phone the Stamp Taxes enquiry line on **0845 603 0135**, open 8:30am to 5:00pm Monday to Friday, except Bank Holidays. Calls are charged at local rates. You can get further copies of this return from the Orderline on **0845 302 1472**.

REFERENCE

Insert the reference number from the payslip on page 7 of the Land Transaction Return, SDLT1, here.

For official use only

ABOUT THE LAND

1 **Type of property**

Enter code from the guidance notes

2 **Local authority number**

3 **Title number, if any**

4 **NLPG UPRN**

5 **Address or situation of land**

Postcode

House or building number

Rest of address, including house name, building name, flat number or continuation from the SDLT1

Please turn over

SDLT 3(Substitute)(LexisNexis) PG 1

ABOUT THE LAND CONTINUED

6 **If agricultural or development land, what is the area (if known)?**

☐ Hectares ☐ Square metres

Area

☐☐☐☐☐☐☐☐☐☐ . ☐☐☐

7 **If there are any minerals or mineral rights reserved enter the code below**

☐☐ Enter code from the guidance notes

8 **Is a plan attached?** Please note that the form reference number should be written/displayed on map. Put 'X' in one box

☐ Yes ☐ No

9 **Interest transferred or created**

☐☐ Enter code from the guidance notes

SDLT 3 PG 2

Inland Revenue

Land Transaction Return

Additional details about the transaction, including leases

When to fill in this return

You must fill in this return where additional information about the transaction and/or lease can be provided.
The guidance notes will help you answer the questions.

If you need help with any part of this return or with anything in the guidance notes, please phone the Stamp Taxes enquiry line on **0845 603 0135**, open 8:30am to 5:00pm Monday to Friday, except Bank Holidays. Calls are charged at local rates. You can get further copies of this return from the Orderline on **0845 302 1472**.

REFERENCE

Insert the reference number from the payslip on page 7 of the Land Transaction Return, SDLT1, here.

For official use only

ABOUT THE TRANSACTION

1 If this transaction is part of the sale of business, please say if the sale includes Put 'X' in relevant boxes

Stock

Goodwill

Other

Chattels and moveables

What is the total amount of the consideration for the sale of the business apportioned to these items?

£ . 0 0

2 If the property is for commercial use, what is it?
Put 'X' in the appropriate box(es)

Office

Hotel

Shop

Warehouse

Factory

Other

Other industrial unit

3 Have you applied for and received a post transaction ruling in accordance with Code of Practice 10, or asked us for advice on the application of the law to this transaction? Put 'X' in one box

Yes

No

If 'yes' have you followed it when completing this return?
Put 'X' in one box

Yes

No

Ruling not received

4 Is any part of the consideration contingent or dependent on uncertain future events?

Yes

No

5 Have you agreed with the Inland Revenue that you will pay on a deferred basis?

Yes

No

6 If there are any minerals or mineral rights reserved enter the code below

Enter code from the guidance notes

7 If the purchaser is VAT registered, give their VAT reference number

8 If the purchaser is a company please give the following details

Tax reference number

Company registration number

If registered abroad, give its place of registration

Please turn over

ABOUT THE TRANSACTION CONTINUED

9 Give a description of the purchaser
Enter code from the guidance notes

ABOUT LEASES

Complete if the transaction notified on SDLT1 is for the grant of more than one lease

10 Type of property
Enter code from the guidance notes

11 Address or situation of land
Put 'X' in this box if the same as box 28 on SDLT1
If not, please give address below
Postcode

House or building number

Rest of address, including house name, building name, flat number or continuation from the SDLT1

continued at the top of the next column

12 Local authority number

13 Title number, if any

14 NLPG UPRN

15 If the transaction is for land, what is the unit and area of measurement? Put 'X' in one box

Hectares Square metres
Area

16 Is a plan attached? Please note that the form reference number should be written/displayed on the map.
Put X in one box

Yes No

17 Interest transferred or created
Enter code from the guidance notes

18 Type of lease
Enter code from the guidance notes

SDLT 4 V2 PG 2

+

ABOUT LEASES CONTINUED

19 Start date as specified in lease

D D M M Y Y Y Y

20 End date as specified in lease

D D M M Y Y Y Y

21 Rent free period
Number of months

22 Annual starting rent inclusive of VAT (actually) payable

£ . 0 0

End date for starting rent

D D M M Y Y Y Y

Later rent known? Put 'X' in one box

Yes No

23 What is the amount of VAT, if any?

£ . 0 0

24 Total premium payable

£ . 0 0

25 Net present value upon which tax is calculated

£ . 0 0

26 Total amount of tax due - premium

£ . 0 0

27 Total amount of tax due - NPV

£ . 0 0

28 Any terms surrendered

29 Break clause type Put 'X' in one box

Landlord Tenant only

Either

30 What is the date of the break clause?

D D M M Y Y Y Y

31 Which of the following relate to this lease?
Put 'X' in relevant boxes. If none, leave blank

Option to renew

Market rent

Turnover rent

Unascertainable rent

Contingent reserved rent

32 Rent review frequency

33 Date of first review

D D M M Y Y Y Y

+

34 Rent review clause (type) Put 'X' in one box

Open market RPI

Other

35 If Schedule 17A para 7FA 2003 has been used in calculating the NPV, what is the date of the rent change?

D D M M Y Y Y Y

Please turn over

SDLT 4 V2 PG 3

ABOUT LEASES CONTINUED

36 Service charge amount if known

£ . 0 0

37 Service charge frequency Put 'X' in one box

Monthly

Annually

Quarterly

Other

38 Other consideration – tenant to landlord
(for example, services, building works)
Enter the relevant codes from the guidance notes

39 Other consideration – landlord to tenant
(for example, services, building works)
Enter the relevant codes from the guidance notes

SDLT 4 V2 PG 4

HM Revenue
& Customs

Notice of Appeal
Stamp Duty Land Tax

Appeal against a penalty determination

We should receive your land transaction return within 30 days of the effective date of the transaction. The effective date is normally the completion date of the transaction.

If your return is received late we will charge you a penalty. You may appeal against the penalty if you do not think it is payable or you think you have a reasonable excuse for not sending the return in on time.

For examples of what we may consider is reasonable, please refer to our leaflet SD7 *Penalties for land transaction returns* which is available from our website at www.hmrc.gov.uk/leaflets/stof.htm

Agent's details (if used)

Name

Address

Postcode

Your reference

About the purchaser(1)

Surname or company name

First name(s) *only complete for an individual*

Address

Postcode

About the purchase

Address or situation of land

Postcode

Unique reference *shown on SDLT1 Land Transaction Return*

SDLT46 **(Substitute)(LexisNexis)** 1

Appeal

I appeal against the penalty determination dated

D D M M Y Y Y Y

Stamp Office reference *shown on penalty determination*

Reason for the appeal

Tick one box only and give details as requested

☐ I wish to appeal against the penalty charged because the return was not delivered late as

the effective date of the transaction was

D D M M Y Y Y Y

the land transaction return was sent to HMRC on

D D M M Y Y Y Y

☐ I wish to appeal against the penalty charged for another reason *give details aside, including dates of events*

If we accept your reason, we will write to you and cancel the penalty. Otherwise, we will ask the Appeal Commissioners to decide.

Appeal Commissioners hearing

The General Commissioners will usually consider your appeal. However, if the matter is unusually complicated or technical the Special Commissioners may be asked to consider your appeal. Please tick the appropriate box(es).

I want my hearing to be heard by

General Commissioners ☐

Special Commissioners ☐
These hearings are normally public and are held in London, Manchester, Belfast or Edinburgh.

If the General Commissioners consider this appeal, I want it to be heard in the area where

I live ☐ I have my business premises ☐

I work ☐

Signature

Date

D D M M Y Y Y Y

Reason for the appeal *give details, including dates of events*

Please send this form to

HMRC Stamp Taxes
Newcastle Stamp Office
15th Floor Cale Cross House
156 Pilgrim Street
Newcastle upon Tyne
NE1 6TF

or DX 61021
Newcastle upon Tyne 1

2

STAMP TAXES FORM 22
Stamp Duty

APPORTIONMENT OF CONSIDERATION UNDER AGREEMENT FOR SALE

(see next page)

Re And	Ref No		Charge duty on the Agreement for Sale	Take into account for Certificate of Value purposes
	£		£	
Amount of Consideration payable in Cash, or Bills		Legal Estates in Freehold Property and Fixed Plant and Machinery and other Fixtures thereon		
Amount of Consideration payable in Shares, Debentures, etc		Legal Estates in Leasehold Property		
Liabilities assumed by Purchaser:		Fixed Plant and Machinery on Leasehold Property (including Tenant's trade and other Fixtures)		
Amounts due on mortgages of freeholds and/or Leaseholds, including interest to date of sale		Equitable Interests in Freehold or Leasehold Property		
Hire Purchase Debts in respect of Goods acquired		Loose Plant and Machinery, Stock-in-Trade and other Chattels		
Other Liabilities of the Vendor				
Any other consideration		Goods, wares and Merchandise subject to Hire Purchase* Agreements (Written Down Value)		
		Goodwill and Benefit of Contracts		
Certificate to be signed by the Vendor or Purchaser (the Secretary in the case of a company) or by an Accountant or Solicitor acting in the sale.		Patents, Designs, Trade Marks, Licences, etc		
		Book Debts		
I hereby certify that the particulars shown in this form are in every respect fully and truly stated according to the best of my judgement and belief		Cash in Hand and at Bank on Current Account, Bills, Notes, etc		
Signed		Cash on Deposit		
Address		Shares, Debentures and other investments		
Date		Other Property, viz		
		**Benefit of Contract i.e. Value of Goods subject to HP less the HP Debt*		
£		£		

Appendix I

Precedents

Dear Sir

Application for adjudication under Finance Act 1930, Section 42 (As amended by Finance Act 2000, Section 123)

[NAMES OF VENDOR AND PURCHASER]

1 Definitions

In this letter:

'equity holders' has the same meaning as in paragraph 1 of Schedule 18 to the Income and Corporation Taxes Act 1988

'ordinary share capital' means all the issued share capital of the body corporate concerned other than capital the holders of which have a right to a dividend at a fixed rate but have no other right to share in the profits of the body corporate

'Section 42' means Finance Act 1930, Section 42 as amended by Finance Act 1967, Section 27, Finance Act 1995, Section 149 and Finance Act 2000, Section 123

'the transferor' means [name of transferor]

'the transferee' means [name of transferee]

'the transferred assets' means [the assets] described in and transferred by the transfer instrument

'the transfer instrument' means the [description of instrument] dated [ ] and made between [the transferor] and [the transferee], enclosed with this letter

[*'the parent'* means [name of parent if relevant]]

[*'relevant intermediate company'* means a company through which it is necessary to trace ownership in order to establish that the transferor and the transferee are associated for the purpose of Section 42]

2 Position of signatory

I am [a director] [a solicitor acting on behalf] of [the immediate parent] [the transferor] [the transferee].

3 Claim for exemption

A claim for exemption under Section 42 is made hereby in respect of the transfer instrument the original of which is submitted for adjudication with this letter.

4 Details of companies

Relevant details of the transferor and the transferee [and of the parent] [and of any relevant intermediate companies] at the date of the transfer instrument are as follows:

A. TRANSFEROR

1	Registered number	:	[ ]
2	Date of incorporation	:	[ ]
3	Place of incorporation	:	[ ]
4	Authorised share capital	:	[ ]
5	Issued ordinary share capital	:	[ ]
6	Issued non-ordinary share capital	:	[ ]
7	Shareholders		

No of shares	*Ordinary/ non-ordinary shares*	*Registered holder*	*Beneficial owner if different*
[ ]	[Ordinary/ non-ordinary]	[ ]	[ ]

B. TRANSFEREE

1	Registered number	:	[ ]
2	Date of incorporation	:	[ ]
3	Place of incorporation	:	[ ]
4	Authorised share capital	:	[ ]
5	Issued ordinary share capital	:	[ ]
6	Issued non-ordinary share capital	:	[ ]
7	Shareholders		

No of shares	*Ordinary/ non-ordinary shares*	*Registered holder*	*Beneficial owner if different*
[ ]	[Ordinary/ non-ordinary]	[ ]	[ ]

[C. PARENT

1	Registered number	:	[ ]
2	Date of incorporation	:	[ ]
3	Place of incorporation	:	[ ]
4	Authorised share capital	:	[ ]
5	Issued ordinary share capital	:	[ ]]

[D. [ ] LIMITED (‘[ ]’5)

1	Registered number	:	[ ]
2	Date of incorporation	:	[ ]
3	Place of incorporation	:	[ ]
4	Authorised share capital	:	[ ]
5	Issued ordinary share capital	:	[ ]
6	Issued non-ordinary share capital	:	[ ]]
7	Shareholders		

No of shares	*Ordinary/ non-ordinary shares*	*Registered holder*	*Beneficial owner if different*
[ ]	[Ordinary/ non-ordinary]	[ ]	[ ]

[E.REPEAT AS NECESSARY]

A chart illustrating the relationship between the companies concerned is attached to this letter as Appendix [ ].

5 Liquidation

Neither the transferor nor the transferee [nor the parent] [nor any relevant intermediate company] was at the date of the transfer instrument or is now in liquidation.

6 Relationship between companies

For the purposes of section 42, at the date of the transfer instrument and of this letter:

6.1 [the [transferee] [transferor] was the beneficial owner of not less than seventy five per cent of the ordinary share capital of the [transferor] [transferee].]

– *OR* –

[the parent was the beneficial owner of not less than seventy five per cent of the ordinary share capital of the transferor and of the transferee.]

6.2 [the [transferee] [transferor] was beneficially entitled to not less than seventy five per cent of any profits available for distribution to equity holders of the [transferor] [transferee].]

– *OR* –

[the parent was beneficially entitled to not less than seventy five per cent of any profits available for distribution to equity holders of the transferor and of the transferee.]

6.3 [the [transferee] [transferor] would be beneficially entitled to not less than seventy five per cent of any assets of the [transferor] [transferee] available for distribution to its equity holders on a winding-up.]

– *OR* –

[the parent would be beneficially entitled to not less than seventy five per cent of any assets of the transferor and of the transferee available for distribution to their equity holders on a winding-up.]

[A certified copy of an extract from the register of members of the [transferor] [transferee] [each relevant intermediate company] is attached to this letter as Appendix [ ].]

[A copy of a declaration of trust evidencing the beneficial ownership of [ ] in the shares in [ ] is attached to this letter as Appendix [ ].]

7 Continuance of relationship

The [parent] [transferor] [transferee] has no present intention to undertake any transaction which would cause the transferor and the transferee to cease to be associated for the purpose of section 42.

8 Continuance of ownership

The transferee has no present intention to dispose of its beneficial ownership of the transferred assets.

9 Consideration

The consideration for the transfer of the transferred assets [was [ ]] [is set out in the transfer instrument] [is set out in an agreement dated [ ]] and made between [amongst others] the transferor and the transferee a copy of which is attached to this letter as Appendix [ ].

[The consideration was provided by the transferee in money out of its own resources].

[The consideration was left outstanding on an inter-company loan which is repayable to the transferor by the transferee on [date] OR [demand] is unsecured and bears interest at the rate of [ ] and is otherwise on the terms set out in resolutions of the board of directors of the transferor and the transferee respectively. Certified extracts from the minutes of a board meeting of the transferor, held on [ ] and from the minutes of a board meeting of the transferee held on [ ] are attached to this letter as Appendix [ ] respectively.]

[A copy of the transferee;'s last available balance sheet dated [ ] is attached to this letter as Appendix [ ].]

[The consideration was paid out of a borrowing by the transferee from [ ] Bank plc under overdraft facilities provided to the transferee. Copies of the correspondence under which this facility was requested and granted [and the loan agreement] are attached to this letter as Appendix [ ].

10 Section 27(3) Finance Act 1967

The transfer instrument was not executed in pursuance of or in connection with such an arrangement as is mentioned in Finance Act 1967, section 27(3).

We look forward to hearing from you in due course and please contact [the writer] on [telephone no.] if you have any queries or require further information.

Yours faithfully

Appendix J

Miscellaneous

PRACTICE NOTE
Apportioning the Price Paid for a Business Transferred as a Going Concern

1. Background

1.1 An apportionment of the price paid for a business as a going concern between the underlying assets may be required for tax purposes in a number of instances, for example:

- a. For the purpose of calculating the capital gains arising on the disposal of the separate assets in accordance with the TCGA 1992.
- b. On an acquisition for the purpose of calculating the SDLT due on the interest in the land and buildings only.
- c. On an acquisition for the purpose of calculating the allowances available against Corporation Tax for Capital Allowances, such as Machinery and Plant Allowances (see Section 3), or for purchased goodwill (Schedule 29, FA 2002).

1.2 The price paid for a business sold as a going concern may include any or all of the following assets:

- a. The land and buildings including landlord's fixtures ('the property').
- b. The trade fixtures, fittings, furniture, furnishings and equipment ('the chattels').
- c. Any transferable licences.
- d. Goodwill.
- e. Other separately identifiable intangible assets (eg. registered trade marks).

The purchaser may also separately acquire consumables and stock but these are usually valued separately and will not normally be included in the sale price to be apportioned.

1.3 Some of the principles set out in this Practice Note are applicable to apportionments for all types of businesses but the note deals mainly with the particular issues that have arisen where the property is a 'trade related property' valued using a profits approach (eg. public houses, hotels, petrol filling stations, cinemas, restaurants, care homes etc). In these cases there can be particular difficulties in identifying the sum attributable to 'goodwill' and this is fundamental to the apportionment.

2. The Statutory Provisions

2.1 For the purposes of calculating a capital gain s.52 of the TCGA 1992 provides that any apportionment shall be on a 'just and reasonable' basis.

2.2 For the purposes of calculating any SDLT due paragraph 4, Schedule 4, FA 2003 similarly provides that any apportionment shall be on a 'just and reasonable' basis.

2.3 For the purposes of calculating any Capital Allowances claimed s.562 CAA 2001 similarly provides that any apportionment should be on a just and reasonable basis.

2.4 For the purpose of calculating the cost of purchased goodwill paragraph.4, Schedule 29 FA 2002 provides that 'goodwill' has the meaning it has for accounting purposes. Accounting guidance (FRS10) provides that 'goodwill' should be taken to be the "difference between the cost of an acquired entity and the aggregate of the fair values of that entity's identifiable assets and liabilities" (see paragraph 11 below).

2.5 The various statutory provisions do not define the method of arriving at a 'just and reasonable' apportionment but any apportionment should generally seek to apportion the price paid between the underlying assets included in the sale on the basis of their relative values and the contribution they make to the price that is being apportioned.

3. Legal Definitions of Goodwill

3.1 Halsbury's Laws of England, 4th edition, Vol. 35 at page 1206 states that:

> "The goodwill of a business is the whole advantage of the reputation and connection with customers together with the circumstances whether of habit or otherwise, which tend to make that connection permanent. It represents in connection with any business or business product the value of the attraction to the customers which the name and reputation possesses."

3.2 The definition contained in the Shorter Oxford Dictionary is:

> "Goodwill is the privilege granted by the seller of a business to a purchaser of trading as his recognised successor; the possession of a ready-formed connection with customers considered as a separate element in the saleable value of a business."

3.3 The leading legal authority on the meaning of goodwill is found in IRC v Muller & Co Margarine Limited [1901] AC 217. In answer to the question "what is goodwill?" Lord Macnaghten said:

> "It is a thing very easy to describe, very difficult to define. It is the benefit and advantage of the good name, reputation and connection of a business. It is the attractive force which brings in custom. It is the one thing which distinguishes an old-established business from a new business at its first stage."

Lord Macnaghten went on to say that:

> "Goodwill is composed of a variety of elements. It differs in its composition in different trades and in different businesses in the same trade. One element may preponderate here; and another there."

3.4 In the decision of the Special Commissioners in Balloon Promotions Ltd v Wilson, SpC 524 [2006] STC (SCD) 167, goodwill for CG purposes was construed in accordance with legal rather than accountancy principles.

3.5 Traditionally goodwill has been subdivided into different types such as 'inherent goodwill', 'adherent goodwill' and 'free goodwill'. These subdivisions are no longer considered helpful as they tend to cause confusion. 'Inherent' and 'adherent' goodwill are not really goodwill at all as they form part of the value of the property asset.

4. Accountancy and International Valuation Standards Council Definitions

4.1 International Financial Reporting Standards (IFRS 3, 2008 revised version, Appendix A) defines goodwill as;

"An asset representing the future economic benefits arising from assets acquired in a business combination that are not individually identified and separately recognised".

Intangible Assets are defined by IVSC as;

"Assets that manifest themselves by their economic properties. They do not have physical substance; they grant rights and privileges to their owner and usually generate income for their owner".

4.2 IVG Note 4 defines a subset of Intangible Assets as Grouped Intangibles;

"The residual intangible asset value left after all identifiable Intangible Assets have been valued and deducted from total Intangible Asset value. Alternative concepts include patronage, excess earnings and residual value. Grouped Intangibles are often called Goodwill. Goodwill has, at various times, been said to be the tendency for customers to return to a place of business, the extra income generated by a business over and above a fair return to the identified assets, and/or the extra value of the entity as a whole over and above the aggregate value of its constituent identifiable assets".

5. Goodwill in Trade Related Properties

5.1 It has in the past been argued that because the business in trade related properties is usually largely or wholly incapable of being sold separately from the property there is little or no goodwill (see the Lands Tribunal decision in Coles Executors v IRC (1973) concerning the valuation of a public house for Estate Duty). On the sale of a business operated from such properties, unless there were other separately identifiable intangible assets included in the sale, the whole of the purchase price would normally be apportioned to the property and chattels, it being argued that there was no goodwill.

5.2 The above view was often put forward by taxpayers seeking to claim Capital Allowances on fixtures which formed part of the property. However, since the introduction of SDLT and the provisions in Schedule 29 FA 2002 this view has been challenged by taxpayers seeking to maximise the amount apportioned to goodwill in order to maximise their claim under Schedule 29 FA 2002 and minimise the amount of SDLT payable.

5.3 The view now is that if a business is sold as a going concern then the sale must include some element of goodwill. The question to be answered is not whether goodwill exists but what is the value of that goodwill? That question has to be decided on the facts of each individual case. In some cases the value of the goodwill may be nominal but in some it may be substantial.

6. Valuing Goodwill and Other Intangible Assets

6.1 There is a broad consensus across the valuation, accountancy and legal professions that the value of goodwill and any other separately identifiable intangible assets (eg. registered trade marks) is represented by the difference between the value of a business as a going concern and the value of the tangible assets included in the sale.

6.2 The value of a business as a going concern will usually be represented by the actual sale price achieved in the open market. However, if it is necessary to value a business as a going concern, because the sale price was not at arm's length, then this is the responsibility of HMRC (SAV).

6.3 Similarly, if it is necessary to apportion the excess value between the goodwill and any other intangible assets this is the responsibility of HMRC (SAV).

6.4 However, the difficulties in arriving at the value of the goodwill usually relate to the assumptions and approach to be adopted when arriving at a valuation of the tangible assets. This is addressed in the paragraphs below.

7. Valuing the Tangible Assets – Assumptions

7.1 Difficulties relating to the assumptions to be adopted when valuing the tangible assets often arise in cases involving trade related properties. Some of the reasons for this relate to the fact that:

a. The established approach to valuation of this type of property typically relies on the profits method and in determining the income and trading potential there can be confusion with valuation of the operator's business. The profits approach remains an appropriate property valuation basis where it is based on expected fair maintainable levels of income that are expected to be achieved from use of the property and other tangible assets by a reasonably competent operator. This is distinct from any valuation of the actual operators own business.

b. The value of such properties is often significantly reduced if the property ceases to be occupied for any length of time because customers go elsewhere and the level of trade has to be built up again by the purchaser. (The enhanced value that arises as a result of the property being occupied by the vendor and any predecessors for the particular use is part of what in the past has been described as 'adherent' goodwill but is properly part of the property value).

c. The value is often significantly reduced if the property is stripped of chattels because the purchaser has to re-fit the premises and cannot re-open until the property has been fully fitted out and is ready to trade.

d. If licences are lost there may sometimes be difficulties in obtaining new licences.

If it were to be assumed for the purposes of valuation that the property has lost any licences, been stripped of chattels and left vacant for a period of time then the value will be significantly reduced and the value of goodwill in the final apportionment, arrived at by deduction, would be inflated.

7.2 When valuing goodwill using the approach outlined in paragraph 6 above it will usually be appropriate to value all the tangible assets together for sale as an operational entity so that a purchaser can if they wish trade from the day of purchase. It is critical that this availability is reflected to ensure a fair apportionment of the sale price (and any premium arising from a sale of combined assets) between the tangible and intangible elements and avoid any over or understatement.

7.3 Another area of difficulty regarding the assumptions to be made relates to the benefit of contracts entered into by the vendor with customers, staff and suppliers. In reality, if the business is sold as a going concern, any benefit attached to these contracts will normally pass to the purchaser and will be reflected in the price paid for the business as a going concern. However, these contracts do not form part of the tangible assets so, if they add any value, the added value should not be reflected in the valuation of the tangible assets.

7.4 When valuing goodwill using the approach outlined in paragraph 6 above it is considered appropriate to assume that the benefit of any contracts with customers, staff and suppliers would either have to be acquired separately from the vendor or the purchaser would have to make their own arrangements.

7.5 Applying the assumptions in paragraph 7.4 will have different effects depending on the facts of the particular case in question. For example:

a. A small public house to be run by the purchaser with help from part-time bar staff. The purchaser has acquired the business as a going concern but there are no contracts with customers and the purchaser wishes to enter their own contracts with suppliers and employ their own staff. In such a case there may be no identifiable difference between the price paid for the business as a going concern and the price that a purchaser would pay to acquire all the tangible assets. In such a case the value of the goodwill may be nominal.

b. A nursing home, offering an element of specialist care, that is fully occupied by residents and to be run by the purchaser with the help of full-time medically qualified staff. In such a case (depending on the degree of difficulty the purchaser may face in finding any new residents and staff) there may be a significant difference between the price paid for the business as a going concern and the price a purchaser would pay to acquire all the tangible assets. In such a case the value of the goodwill may be more substantial.

7.6 When purchasing such a business as a going concern the purchaser will often have obtained a valuation of the tangible assets as an 'operational entity' in accordance with the RICS Red Book GN1. An alternative valuation of the property based on special assumptions (eg. vacant following a failure of the business, no accounts providing evidence of trade, stripped of chattels and licences lost) may also be obtained for bank lending purposes. For the purposes of valuing goodwill it would not be appropriate to deduct a valuation based on such special assumptions that do not reflect the actual circumstances prevailing at the valuation date. The question of the assumptions underlying a valuation of the 'operational entity' and how they may differ from a valuation in accordance with paragraphs 7.2 and 7.4 above is considered in paragraph 10 below.

8. Valuing the Tangible Assets – Valuation Approach

8.1 Having decided on the appropriate assumptions (paragraphs 7.2 and 7.4 above) it is then necessary to consider the most appropriate method of valuation. For trade related properties that are valued on a profits basis two alternatives need to be considered, these are a capitalised EBITDA/fair maintainable trade (FMT) approach and a rental value/investment based approach. The aim should be to arrive at a capital value that fairly represents the price that an owner-occupier purchaser would be prepared to pay to acquire all the tangible assets, having regard to the circumstances existing at the valuation date.

8.2 The advantages of a capitalised EBITDA/FMT approach are as follows:

a. This is the method that is used in the market to arrive at both going concern values and valuations of the tangible assets as an operational entity under the RICS Red Book GN1.
b. The valuation represents the value to an owner-occupier purchaser.
c. The purchase price paid for the going concern and any GN1 valuation of the tangible assets as an operational entity can be analysed to provide evidence of the FMT and a multiplier for the actual subject property at the valuation date.
d. It produces a value for all the tangible assets to be valued together as a single operational entity.

The difficulty with this approach is that in cases where the contracts with customers, staff and suppliers are of some value it is necessary to reflect this in the valuation. However, it is considered that in most cases this approach will nevertheless give a reliable valuation in most cases.

Example

A simple example may be a nursing home like the one described in paragraph 7.5(b) above:

Say the business had been sold as a going concern for £2m and an analysis of this sale price was say FMT £250k pa x 8YP.
If it was estimated that it would take a purchaser of the tangible assets 1 year to get the property staffed, fully occupied and trading at FMT level again a valuation using this approach may be:

£250k x 8YP	=	£2,000,000
Defer for 1 year @ 10%	=	0.909
		£1,818,000

The value of the goodwill (and any other intangible assets) would be £2m – £1.818m = £182k.

8.3 A rental value/investment based approach may be useful in some cases but as a primary method of valuation the difficulties and flaws of this approach are as follows:

a. In order to arrive at a capital value the method involves making difficult judgements not only about the FMT but the percentage of profits to adopt as the rental value and the appropriate investment yield, both of which can only be derived from comparison with lettings and sales of other properties at different dates, which significantly increase the scope for disputes over the analysis and comparability of the evidence.

b. Much of the available comparable rental evidence will relate to new lettings of properties that are either new or have previously been vacant or rent reviews/renewals that disregard the occupation of the property by the tenant and predecessors in title in accordance with s.34 LTA 1954.

c. Much of the comparable rental evidence will relate to lettings where the tenant has had to provide the chattels and the return on this capital and risk is reflected in the rents paid.

d. The valuation using this approach represents the value of the property to an investor not an owner-occupier.

e. The valuation produces a valuation of the property only to which it is then necessary to add a valuation of the chattels. It will not include the premium value to an occupier of acquiring the tangible assets together as a package with the enhanced trading potential due to the established trading history and the ability to continue trading from day1. Isolating the bare property asset may unfairly apportion any premium or share of marriage value away and overstate the intangible elements.

However, in cases where there are particular difficulties in arriving at a valuation using the capitalised EBITDA/FMT approach the rental value/investment approach may provide a guide as to the minimum value of the property to an incoming purchaser.

Example
A simple example of the problems with the rental approach may be illustrated by considering a small public house like the one described in paragraph 7.5(a) above:
Say the property was trading at FMT level, it had been sold as a going concern for £1m and an analysis of this sale price was say FMT £125k pa x 8YP.

9. RICS Red Book GN1 – Valuations of the 'Operational Entity'

9.1 The question of the assumptions underlying a valuation of an 'operational entity' in accordance with the Red Book GN1 and how those assumptions may differ from the valuation required to arrive at the value of goodwill in accordance with paragraphs 7.2 and 7.4 above is a matter of some debate amongst valuers. The RICS issued some helpful guidance on this in July 2006 and a copy of this is attached as Appendix A.

9.2 The following reasons are put forward by some valuers as the justification for not adopting a GN1 valuation of the operational entity as representing the value of the tangible assets:

a. *A valuation of the operational entity will include 'transferable goodwill' and this includes all goodwill which is capable of being transferred.*

Comment

'Transferable goodwill' is defined in GN1 as "That intangible asset that arises as a result of **property-specific name and reputation, customer patronage, location and similar factors**, which generate economic benefits. **It is inherent to the specialized trading property** and will transfer to a new owner on sale". GN1 goes on to say "In previous RICS guidance **transferable goodwill has also been referred to as inherent goodwill. In the valuation context these terms are identical**". The use of the word 'intangible' in the definition causes some confusion but from the description of the trading potential included (in bold above) it seems clear that the only goodwill that should be included in a GN1 valuation is inherent goodwill which forms part of the value of the property. As advised at paragraph 3.5 above, inherent and adherent 'goodwill' are not strictly goodwill but form part of the property asset value.

b. *A GN1 valuation of the operational entity is a notional value because in practice it is always based on an assumption that the property is trading at FMT level even when in reality it is not.*

Comment

The GN1 valuation is supposed to represent the '**market value**' of the property and other tangible assets (ie. what a willing purchaser would actually pay in the open market). GN1 does not require valuers to assume FMT is achievable from day 1 but they may choose to do so because in reality the period to build up the trade is negligible. Alternatively valuers may choose to reflect some element of deferment in the YP adopted when capitalising the FMT.

c. *A GN1 valuation is a valuation of the actual business and usually the same as the going concern value.*

Comment

GN1 makes it clear that the valuation "should only reflect the transferable goodwill that relates to the **trading potential of the property**" (GN1, para. 4.4), not the trading potential of the particular business. GN1 paragraph 6 also makes it clear that a GN1 valuation of the operational entity is not the same as the going concern value of the business.

d. *A GN1 valuation is based on a capitalisation of the EBITDA/FMT and this includes the occupier's share of the profit. This element of occupier's or tenant's profit needs to be excluded and the way to do this is to adopt the rental/investment value approach described above.*

Comment

Valuers may well capitalise the total EBITDA/FMT but the fact that this is a 'gross' figure is reflected in the YP. If the element of occupier's profit were deducted from the EBITDA/FMT figure then the yield would have to be increased to reflect this (ie. valuers would have to analyse sales on a similar basis and then value on the same basis as they devalue). The tenant's share of the profit on taking a new lease is supposed to represent a fair reward for running the business and the risks involved but this potential share of the income on its own would not be expected to have a capital value (ie. one would not expect a tenant to pay a premium for the right to receive this income alone.) This is illustrated by the fact this income of course exists from day 1 when a new business takes a new lease but tenants do not generally pay landlords a premium to receive it. If they did then it would simply represent a premium for the property, it could not possibly represent goodwill because a new business does not have any goodwill, goodwill is something that grows over time.

e. *A GN1 valuation assumes that the purchaser receives the benefit of any contracts with customers, staff and suppliers (as they do in reality when they acquire the business as a going concern) so the valuation includes or reflects an element of value that is not automatically available to a purchaser of just the tangible assets.*

Comment

The assumptions that should be made by valuers regarding such contracts is not set out in GN1 and actual practice seems to vary. In some cases the valuer may have taken the view that the contracts in the particular case in question add little or no value but in others they may have assumed that any benefits automatically pass to the purchaser of the tangible assets. Some argue that a GN1 valuation should assume that such contracts are available but that they are not cost free (ie. if they are of value to the purchaser the purchaser would have to pay the vendor an additional sum to acquire the benefits). If in a particular case the contracts do add value then one would expect a GN1 valuation on this basis to be less than the sale price of the business as a going concern. Until such time as this area of confusion is clarified, caseworkers should value on the basis set out in paragraph 7.4 above – and in some cases there may therefore be a difference with a GN1 valuation of the operational entity.

10. Apportionment Approach – CGT and SDLT cases

10.1 In CGT and SDLT cases the apportionment of the sale price paid for a business as a going concern should be approached by first identifying the value of any goodwill (and other separately identifiable intangibles assets) along the lines described above. After deducting this from the total sale price, the in-situ value of the chattels may then be deducted to leave the value of the property.

10.2 In practice, for trade related properties, the approach outlined in paragraph 10.1 above will involve the following steps:

Step 1Estimate the market value of all the tangible assets together as an operational entity having regard to the special assumptions in paragraphs 7.2 and 7.4 above. (See paragraphs 10.3 and 10.4 below.)

Step 2Identify the sum attributable to goodwill and any other intangible assets included in the sale by deducting the value of the property, licences and chattels (Step 1 value) from the sale price (or market value) of the business as a going concern. (See paragraph 10.5 below.)

Step 3Identify the sum attributable to the chattels by estimating their 'in-situ' value (ie. the value to an incoming purchaser. (See paragraph 10.6 below).

Step 4Identify the sum attributable to the property by deducting the value of the chattels (Step 3 value) from the Step 1 value. (See paragraph 10.7 below).

Step 5Stand back and consider whether the answer produced is reasonable in the particular circumstances of the case (see paragraphs 2.11 – 2.12 below).

Step 1

10.3 The market value of the tangible assets should be assessed as at the date of disposal/sale on the basis defined in UKGN3 (Valuations for CGT, IHT and SDLT), subject to the special assumptions in paragraphs 7.2 and 7.4 above and the following:

a. The valuation should reflect the market's perception of the trading potential of the property excluding Goodwill.
b. The valuation should reflect the benefit of any transferable licences, consents and certificates. (If any of the licences[1] etc have been lost or are in jeopardy at the valuation date that fact should be reflected in the valuation).
c. The valuation should have regard to all the facts pertaining at the valuation date.
d. The valuation should assume that any accounts available to the purchaser are available at the valuation date to inform judgments as to reasonable future trading potential.
e. The valuation should assume that the purchaser may either bring in their own staff or seek to re-employ some of the existing staff.
f. The valuation should assume that the purchaser will take into account the likelihood of any future bookings sticking with the property if they choose to run the business in the same manner as the vendor.
g. The valuation should assume that the purchaser will take into account the likelihood of any existing care home residents opting to stay with the property if they choose to run the business in the same manner as the vendor.

10.4 The market value should reflect only that trade that can reasonably be expected to be maintained by a reasonably efficient operator purchasing the property and chattels. 'Reasonably efficient operator' has the same meaning as that used in the RICS Red Book GN1, paragraph 2.4:

> A market-based concept whereby a potential purchaser, and thus the valuer, estimates the maintainable level of trade and future profitability that can be achieved by a competent operator of a business conducted on the premises, acting in an efficient manner. The concept involves the trading potential rather than the actual level of trade under the existing ownership so it excludes *personal goodwill.*
>
> © IVSC GN 12, para 3.4.

The market value of the property interest should capture the true value of the property asset reflecting any enhancement from the established generic use at the valuation date but ignoring any additional value of the actual business carried on in the premises at that date. The aim is to establish the value that an incoming purchaser would bid for the property based on their views as to what might reasonably be achieved in terms of trading potential as distinct from the actual trade achieved by the current business.

Step 2

10.5 The sum attributable to goodwill and any other intangible assets included in the sale should be arrived at by deducting the value of the tangible assets (from Step 1 above) from the sale price (or market value) of the business.

Step 3

10.6 The sum attributable to any chattels included in the sale should be arrived at by estimating the value of the chattels to an incoming purchaser. The value of the chattels to an incoming purchaser will normally be based on their depreciated replacement cost but in some cases they may be of no value, for example, if the purchaser intends to refit the premises.

1 Licences are a separate asset for CGT purposes.

Step 4

10.7 The sum attributable to the property should be arrived at by deducting the value of the chattels (the Step 3 value) from the value of the tangible assets (the Step 1 value).

Step 5

10.8 Caseworkers should always stand back and consider whether the answer produced by the above approach is reasonable in the particular circumstances of the case. For instance, if a business is sold in an arms length transaction at a price that is significantly in excess of the market value of the business as a going concern it may be appropriate to firstly value the business and then apportion the excess sale price on a pro-rata basis.

Example:

Sale price	=	£600,000
Market value of business	=	£500,000
Property	=	£450,000
Chattels	=	£20,000
Goodwill	=	£30,000 (ie. £500,000 – (£450,000 + £20,000))

Pro-rata apportionment:

Property	=	450/500 x £600,000	=	£540,000
Chattels	=	20/500 x £600,000	=	£24,000
Goodwill	=	30/500 x £600,000	=	£36,000

10.9 A criticism of the above approach may be that it adopts a deduction approach and such an approach was criticised by the High Court in the case of Bostock v Totham (HMIT). However, the above approach does not just consider the value of one element, as was the taxpayer's approach which was criticised in the Bostock case, it considers the value of all elements on a basis that reflects the contribution of the various elements to the price being apportioned. If one were to value all of the elements in strict isolation then the apportionment may become artificially distorted to the extent that the answer may not be just and reasonable. For instance, the property value in isolation may be less than when it is lotted with the other tangible assets, the value of the chattels if not sold in-situ with the property may be little more than scrap value and any goodwill may be of nominal value if the business is not sold with the property as a going concern.

10.10 Taxpayers may also challenge the above approach based on the Special Commissioner's decision in the case of Balloon Promotions Limited v Wilson (Insp of Taxes) in which it was suggested that goodwill should be looked at as a whole and that the value of adherent goodwill was not automatically subsumed in the property value. The decision of the Special Commissioner in the Balloon case concerned appeals against a refusal to grant rollover relief under S152 of the Taxation of Chargeable Gains Act 1992 in respect of chargeable gains following the sale of the Company's franchised Pizza Express restaurants to the franchisor. Whilst the decision includes discussion of existing legal authorities dealing with goodwill the conclusions reflect the individual circumstances of the case. It is worth noting that in this case the values of the property interests submitted by the taxpayers were not challenged and there was no evidence to demonstrate whether or not those values included adherent goodwill. As mentioned above, the subdivisions of goodwill that were previously used are no longer considered helpful as they tend to cause confusion. The view now is that what used to be referred to as 'inherent' and 'adherent' goodwill are, in reality, attributes which add value to the property in which a business is carried on and that they do not represent goodwill at all.

11. Apportionment Approach – Schedule 29 FA 2002 cases

11.1 As noted above, for the purpose of calculating the cost of purchased goodwill paragraph 4, Schedule 29 FA 2002 provides that 'goodwill' has the meaning it has for accounting purposes. Accounting guidance (FRS10) provides that 'goodwill' should be taken to be the "difference between the cost of an acquired entity and the aggregate of the fair values of that entity's identifiable assets and liabilities".

11.2 FRS 15 sets out the principles for calculating the 'fair value' of tangible fixed assets and provides that non-specialised properties should be valued on the basis of existing use value (EUV) (FRS15, para.53).
FRS15, para. 56 states:

> "Certain types of non-specialised properties are bought and sold "and therefore valued" as businesses. The EUV of a property valued as an operational entity is determined by having regard to trading potential, but excludes personal goodwill that has been created in the business by the present owner or management and is not expected to remain with the business in the event of the property being sold"

FRS 15, para. 85 states:

> "It would not be appropriate, however, to treat the trading potential associated with a property that is valued as an operational entity, such as a public house or hotel, as a separate component where the value and life of its trading potential is inherently inseparable from that of the property".

The above guidance on the value to be deducted appears to accord with a valuation of the operational entity in accordance with GN1. Accordingly it would not be acceptable in a Schedule 29 case for a taxpayer to put forward a value different from their valuation in accordance with GN1.

12. Leasehold Interests

12.1 In some cases it will be necessary to apportion the price paid for a leasehold interest but the same principles apply. The valuations and apportionment should be approached using the same assumptions and approach described above.

12.2 It should be borne in mind that for trade related properties it is quite common for leasehold interests to be sold for substantial premiums even when the rent has recently been reviewed. The premium in such cases may be attributable to any or all of the following:

a. The reviewed rent may not reflect the full rental value because it may disregard the enhanced trading potential attributable to the occupation of the property by the tenant and predecessors (in accordance with s.34 LTA 1954).

b. The reviewed rent may not reflect the value of improvements carried out by the tenant or predecessors when fitting out the property (in some cases the rent may only represent a shell rent).

c. The value of the chattels and fittings belonging to the tenant.

d. The premium value to an occupier of offering the tangible assets together as a package with the enhanced trading potential due to the established trading history and the ability to continue trading from day1.

e. There may be some element of goodwill, particularly if the business is trading at above FMT level and contracts of some value are included in the sale.

f. There may be other separately identifiable intangible assets included in the sale (eg. registered trade marks).

g. Market perception and prevailing conditions whereby it is expected there will be some 'key money' or premium to acquire the interest in order to move in to this market sector.

12.3 The value of any goodwill and other intangible assets included in the sale should be determined by adopting the same valuation assumptions and approach outlined in paragraphs 7 and 8 above.

APPENDIX A – RICS GUIDANCE TO MEMBERS – 17 JULY 2006

Valuation for tax purposes of Specialised Trading Property - goodwill

This note provides the context within which goodwill is to be considered by RICS members when valuing trade related properties; and in particular the issues arising in the UK when valuing goodwill for tax purposes.

The usual basis of valuation for a property valuation is Market Value. This is defined in the Red Book, PS 3.2. The commentary to PS 3.2 recognises that certain categories of property change hands in the open market as fully operational business units for specific uses at prices based upon their trading potential.

Such properties are known as 'Specialised Trading Properties'. Guidance on the valuation of Specialised Trading Properties is contained within GN 1. Further information on the approach is contained in Valuation Information Paper No 2.

Some RICS members may also be asked to value the goodwill of a going concern business. The Red Book guidance relates to the valuation of tangible assets only; being the real property and other fixed assets.

Confusion may arise between the valuation of a going concern and the valuation of fixed assets because the profits method of valuing the property includes a requirement for the valuer to assess the fair maintainable level of trade and future profitability that could be achieved by a Reasonably Efficient Operator, usually including consideration of the occupier's actual accounts.

Care has to be taken not to include in the assessment any element of value that includes any personal goodwill to the present owner or operator which might pass to a purchaser of the going concern business but which is not inherent in the property by virtue of the fair maintainable level of trade.

The revision of VIP2 issued in early 2006 includes new guidance on this distinction.

The Red Book does not contain any guidance on the assessment of goodwill separate from the value of the property asset or the valuation of going concern businesses as a whole.

For these purposes the valuer is directed to the International Valuation Standard GN 6 which specifically relates to Business Valuation, usually as a going concern.

Both the RICS and IVS identify just two forms of goodwill; either inherent to the property and transferable as such, or else personal to the individual, partnership, company or other entity running the business, which may or may not be transferable as part of a going concern, but which does not attach to the property.

Whenever possible, RICS guidance follows the international IVS Guidance in relation to the valuation of real property assets, avoiding the creation of specific standards applying only to the UK.

UK tax legislation provides that the basis of value for tax computations shall be an open market price; whether for tangible property assets or for intangibles such as personal goodwill.

Although the statutory definitions and interpretation by the courts generally follow the Red Book definition of Market Value for tangible property, there are differences.

UKGN 3 provides a commentary on the basis of value for tax purposes in the UK. Where the property being considered is a specialised trading property GN1 will be relevant, but subject to UKGN3.

For some tax purposes, where a transaction relates to the transfer of a going concern business, it may be necessary to apportion the consideration into its various elements and it will be seen that the extent to which the transaction included either or both types of goodwill may affect the tax burden.

It is this apportionment issue which is to be discussed in the context of UK tax assessments.

Index

E

F

Property of DLA Piper UK LLP
Knowledge Centre
Victoria Square House
Victoria Square
Birmingham B2 4DL
Telephone: 08700 111 111
Fax: 0121 262 5942